P9-CEK-962

Architectural Graphics

ARCHITECTURAL

Rendering by Helmut Jacoby
Philip Johnson, Architect

GRAPHICS

SECOND EDITION

C. Leslie Martin

PROFESSOR EMERITUS OF ARCHITECTURE
University of Cincinnati

MACMILLAN PUBLISHING CO., INC.
New York

COLLIER MACMILLAN PUBLISHERS
London

Library of Congress catalog card number: 72–89929

MACMILLAN PUBLISHING CO., INC.
866 Third Avenue, New York, New York 10022

COLLIER-MACMILLAN CANADA, LTD.

Printed in The United States of America

Printing 9 YEAR 23456

Dedicated to Mildred
and our three sons
Philip, Richard, Donald

PREFACE
to the Second Edition

During the seventeen years that *Architectural Graphics* has been published continuously, changes have been made in graphics and in its use by architects and architectural students. The second edition has incorporated some of these changes in graphics. It has also been revised to make the book more easily understood and more useful. Some of the changes made in the second edition are mentioned in the following paragraphs.

New introductory material and terminology have been used for paraline drawings. A more complete treatment of interior perspective drawing and of shadows on interior perspectives has been provided. Simpler methods have been presented for some of the more difficult perspective constructions.

New material dealing with variations of light and shadow has two main objectives: first, to form a transition between shadow construction and rendering; second, to emphasize some of the simple basic considerations which provide the foundation for excellent renderings. The addition of new illustrations of rendering provides more numerous examples of that subject and shows a greater variety of rendering techniques.

Architectural models have always been used in the practice of architecture and in architectural education. Their use has increased a great deal in recent years. They are an important part of the study and presentation of architectural designs. The material on architectural models provides illustrations from a variety of sources of some of the basic types of architectural models.

Throughout the book many minor changes have been made in lettering, shading, drawings, and text. These changes give a better coordination between text and drawings and make both text and drawings clearer and more easily understood.

C. L. M.

ACKNOWLEDGMENTS for the Second Edition

The creative work provided by others and the assistance of others in many ways have been important factors in the revision of *Architectural Graphics.* I wish to express my very sincere thanks for their cooperation and help in obtaining and preparing manuscript material for the second edition of *Architectural Graphics* to several persons.

To the architects, delineators, and professional model builders who provided illustrations of their artistic creations.

To the students of the Departments of Architecture and Community Planning of the University of Cincinnati for the use of illustrations of their creative design and other projects.

To the faculty of the Departments of Architecture and Community Planning for their cheerful cooperation in providing material for photographic illustrations of their students' work. Professors Karl H. Merkel, Samuel V. Noe, Clay F. Hickerson, Robert L. Williams, Bruce E. Goetzman, and Harris N. Forusz were personally helpful in providing this material.

To Roland T. Docter for his skillful and timely work in inking and finishing drawings.

To Mildred C. Martin for expert typing, preparation of finished manuscript material, and many other types of work. She cheerfully and frequently put aside other work of her own to give her help promptly when it would speed up the preparation of this manuscript.

C. L. M.

PREFACE to the First Edition

Drawing is the universal language of the architect and designer. It is difficult or impossible to explain design and construction satisfactorily in written or spoken words alone. Shapes, sizes, and design relations require drawings for their clear explanation. In order to translate creations of the mind into terms which can be most clearly understood by clients, and into instructions which can be most easily followed by builders, it is necessary that architects and designers be thoroughly familiar with all methods of representing objects by drawings.

Some instruction in different phases of graphical representation has always been given in architectural schools. Often, formal courses are required in shades and shadows and perspective drawing; and engineering courses in descriptive geometry are required in some curricula for architectural students. In a number of schools various phases of drafting have been treated merely as stepchildren of design or other courses.

During recent years there has been a definite trend toward the segregation of all materials relating to architectural drafting methods into a single course under various names which usually include the term "graphics" in the title. It is the purpose of this book to provide information for teaching of such courses and also to furnish sufficient material for the subjects of shades and shadows and perspective where these are given as separate units. It is hoped that the information here provided will be found usable for students in courses other than architecture and will be of interest to designers and draftsmen also.

Multi-view orthographic drawing, the backbone of drafting work, is usually pretty well understood by anyone who has ever used the T-square and triangle. Here the subject has been treated briefly for those having no experience in this type of drawing.

Each of the parallel line types of pictorial drawing—isometric, dimetric, and oblique—has its own peculiar advantages. All three are useful for explanatory construction and design illustrations, and are sometimes considered satisfactory for presentation purposes. These types of drawings and their shadows are an important part of this work.

Perspective drawing and shades and shadows, generally recognized as an essential part of the training in every architectural school, constitute the major portion of this book.

Although the text is intended for classroom use, it is written so that it can be understood by persons who do not have the personal help of a teacher. The procedure followed in presenting the various subjects is, first, to explain the characteristics of the type of drawing and the principles used; then to give explanations and simple examples. In several cases explanations have been divided into a number of steps to simplify drawings and make the subject more easily understood.

The part on perspective drawing has been written to enable the reader to study only the essentials of constructing a perspective drawing or to continue to more advanced phases of the subject. This material is presented in order of usefulness to the greatest number of people.

No book was ever written without help from others either directly or indirectly. The author is particularly indebted to four people without whose help this book would never have been begun, written, rewritten, and carried to completion. I am especially grateful to Dean Ernest Pickering of the College of Applied Arts, University of Cincinnati, for practical help; to Dr. Earl C. Case, Professor of Geography of the University of Cincinnati, for advice and detailed help in writing; to Richard Martin for the precise inking of drawings; and to my wife Mildred Martin for unfailing encouragement and cheerful typing and retyping of manuscript.

To the architects who furnished photographs of rendered presentation drawings made in their offices I wish to express my sincere thanks.

I wish also to express grateful acknowledgment to preceding writers on the subjects treated here. Without the help of their efforts this book could not have been compiled. I have a special feeling of gratitude and admiration for the work of William Ware and am indebted to him for the help obtained from his thorough and scholarly treatise on perspective.

C. L. M.

CONTENTS

PART FOUR
Shades and Shadows

PART FIVE
Study and Presentation Graphics

Architectural Graphics

CHAPTER 1
Types of Projection Drawings

A thorough knowledge of projection drawing is an essential part of the equipment of the draftsman and designer. Drawings are a medium through which he conveys his ideas and instructions to others. An understanding of all types of drawing is necessary in order that he may use the best types to present his information in the clearest and most effective manner. It is the purpose of this introductory chapter to give a brief survey of the field of projection drawing to assist the reader to orient himself before taking up detailed discussions of specific types of drawing.

The theory of any type of projection drawing assumes that the drawing can be made by locating the intersections of lines, which are called projectors, from points on the object with a plane of projection called the picture plane, Fig. 1B. The lines connecting the points thus located on the picture plane make the projected drawing of the object. The three factors which determine the type of projection drawing are (1) The relation of the object to the picture plane, (2) the relation of the projectors to the picture plane, and (3) the relation of the projectors to each other. Relations of the picture plane and projectors for the three general divisions of projection drawing are illustrated in Fig. 1A, B, and C. Various types of orthographic and perspective projection are obtained by changing the relation between the object and picture plane. In oblique projection the different types are obtained by changing the relative positions of the object and picture plane and by changing the scale of the receding lines. Variations in pictorial effect of any type of oblique drawing can also be secured by using different directions for the projectors.

In actual drawing the paper is the picture plane on which the drawing is constructed by drafting methods to conform to the assumed relations of the object, projectors, and picture plane. Projection drawing is the science of constructing drawings of different types by the most efficient and direct drafting methods.

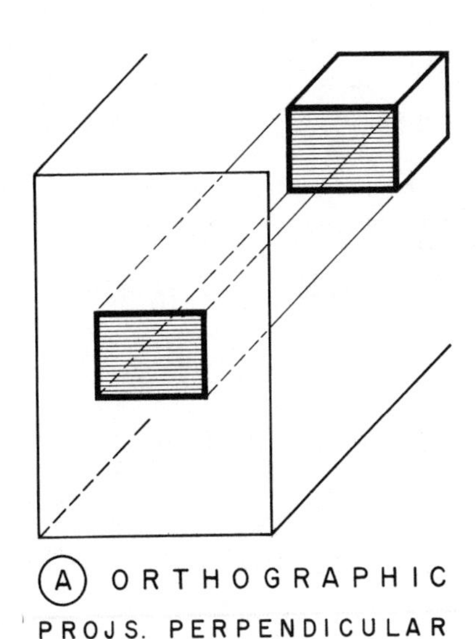

(A) ORTHOGRAPHIC
PROJS. PERPENDICULAR TO THE PICTURE PLANE

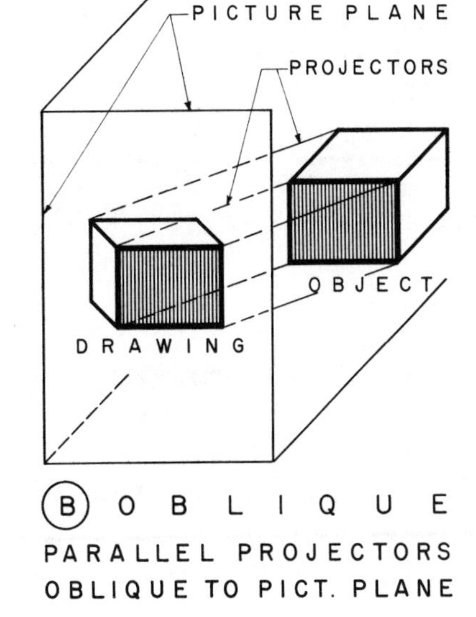

(B) OBLIQUE
PARALLEL PROJECTORS OBLIQUE TO PICT. PLANE

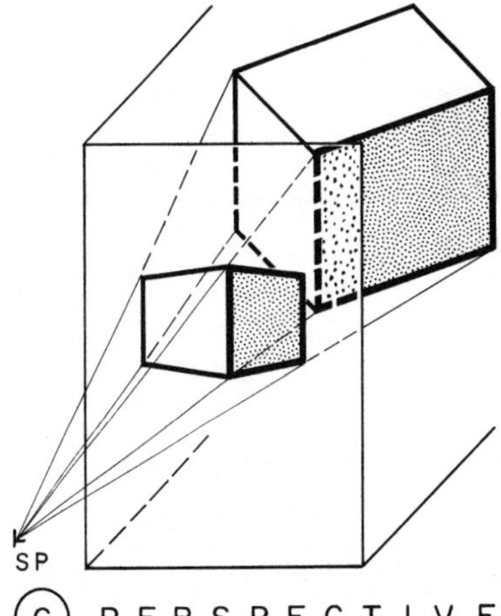

(C) PERSPECTIVE
PROJECTORS CONVERGE TO AN SP=STATION POINT

FIG-1 THE MAJOR DIVISIONS OF PROJECTION DRAWING

TYPE OF DRAWING				RELATION OF		
GENERAL TYPES		GRAPHIC DIAGRAM	SPECIFIC CLASSIFICATION	OBJECT TO PICTURE PL.	PROJECTORS TO EACH OTHER	PROJECTORS TO PICTURE PL.
MULTI-VIEW	ORTHOGRAPHIC	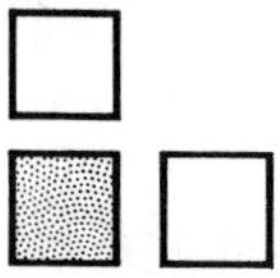	MULTI-VIEW	PARALLEL ON EACH FACE	PARALLEL FOR EACH FACE	PERPENDICULAR
PARALINE	ORTHOGRAPHIC	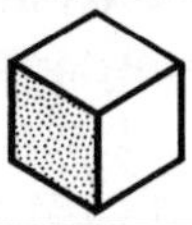	ISOMETRIC	OBLIQUE ALL THREE AXES EQUAL ANGLES TO PICTURE PLANE	PARALLEL	PERPENDICULAR
PARALINE	ORTHOGRAPHIC	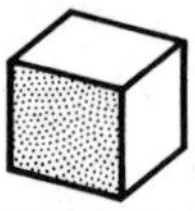	DIMETRIC	OBLIQUE TWO AXES AT EQUAL ANGLES TO PICTURE PLANE	PARALLEL	PERPENDICULAR
PARALINE	ORTHOGRAPHIC	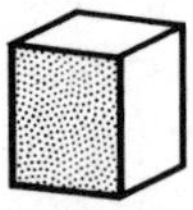	TRIMETRIC	OBLIQUE ALL AXES DIFFERENT. ANGLES TO PICTURE PLANE	PARALLEL	PERPENDICULAR
PARALINE	OBLIQUE	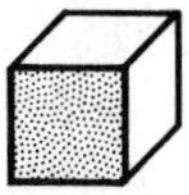	ELEVATION OBLIQUE	PARALLEL TO A FACE THAT IS VERTICAL	PARALLEL	OBLIQUE
PARALINE	OBLIQUE		PLAN OBLIQUE	PARALLEL TO A FACE THAT IS HORIZONTAL	PARALLEL	OBLIQUE
PERSPECTIVE			ONE POINT PERSPECTIVE	PARALLEL ON ONE FACE	CONVERGE TO A POINT	VARIOUS ANGLES
PERSPECTIVE		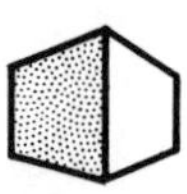	TWO-POINT PERSPECTIVE	OBLIQUE VERTICAL LINES PARALLEL TO PICTURE PLANE	CONVERGE TO A POINT	VARIOUS ANGLES
PERSPECTIVE		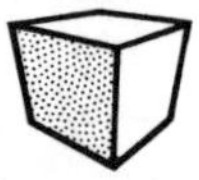	THREE-POINT PERSPECTIVE	OBLIQUE ALL THREE AXES OBLIQUE TO PICTURE PLANE	CONVERGE TO A POINT	VARIOUS ANGLES

FIG-2 CLASSIFICATION OF TYPES OF PROJECTION DRAWINGS

The most widely used general types of projection drawings are classified in the chart of Fig. 2. Multi-view, Paraline, and Perspective are given as the three major divisions of projection drawing here and throughout this book. This classification of major divisions is based on similarities of appearance, use, and construction of the types within each division. These considerations are very important to the architect, designer, and draftsman.

A second classification of general types of drawings as orthographic, oblique, and perspective is given with the first two terms in smaller letters. This classification is based on projection theory. It groups together drawings which vary widely in appearance and separates into different groups drawings which are similar in appearance, construction, and use.

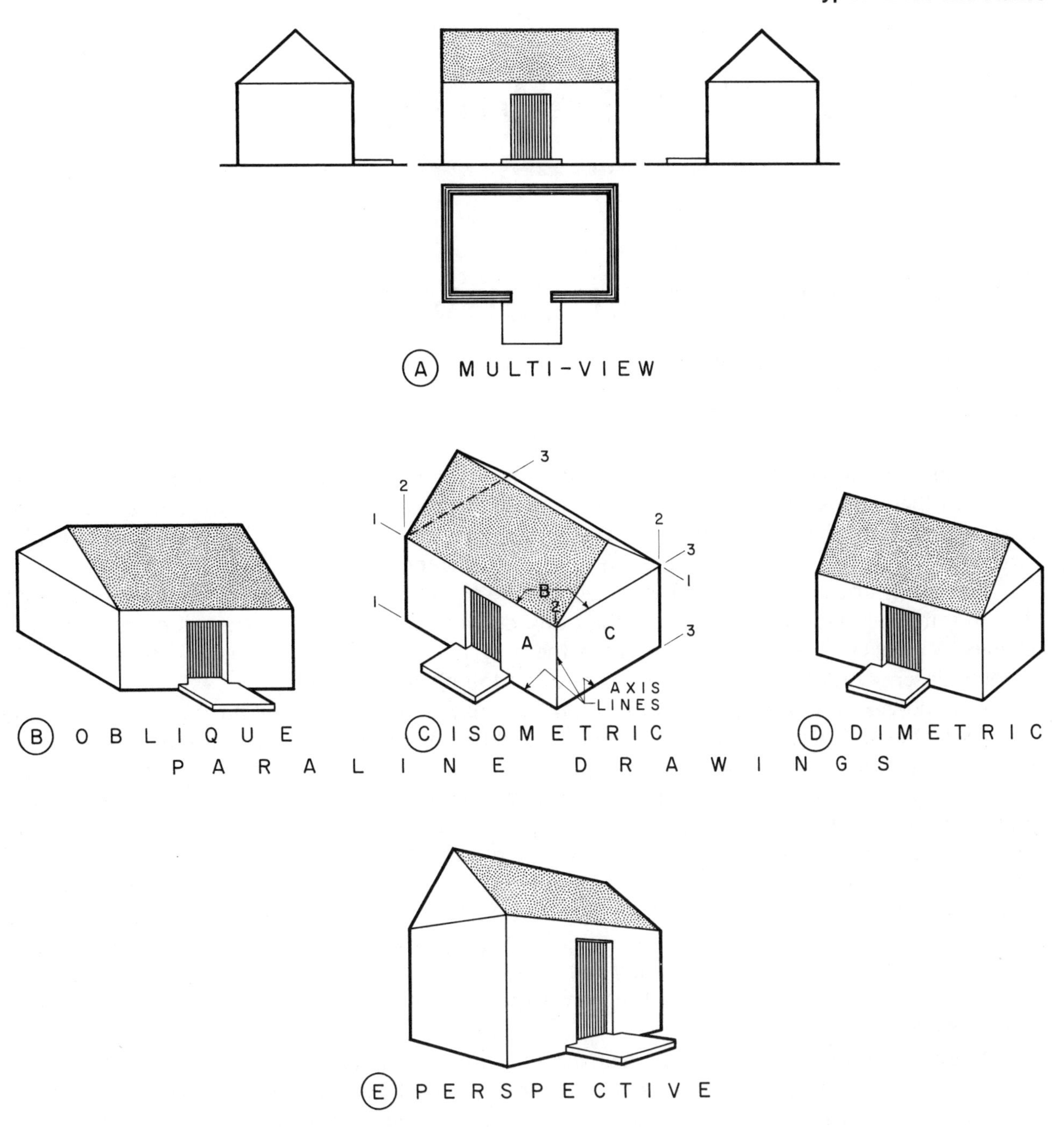

FIG—3 A COMPARISON OF FIVE DRAWING METHODS

Most of the objects drawn in architecture have three sets of planes and lines which are mutually perpendicular to each other. The following explanations of the various types of drawing are based to a great extent on the appearance of these three sets of lines and planes, which are illustrated in the large block shape at the bottom of Fig. 3C. The three lines of the edges of the block which meet at any corner are perpendicular to each other and may be called the axis lines of the object. All the lines of the object which are parallel to an axis line form a set of lines. In the following discussions of various types of drawing these three sets of lines, numbered 1, 2, and 3 here, will be called the typical lines of the object. The three sets of planes, lettered A, B, and C here, which are each parallel to two of the axis lines will be called the typical planes of the object.

PART ONE
Multi-view Drawing

CHAPTER 2
Multi-view Arrangements and Nomenclature

In any type of drawing those parts of the object which are parallel to the picture plane are shown in their true shapes. In orthographic and oblique drawing, where the projectors are parallel lines, all parts of the object which parallel the picture plane are shown in their correct relative sizes, that is, at the same scale, regardless of their distances from the picture plane.

Since only one set of planes of an object can be shown parallel to the picture plane in a single drawing, it is necessary to have more than one drawing of an object to give all of its sizes and shapes. Multi-view orthographic drawing is the only type of drawing which provides a complete graphic description of the shapes and sizes of all the planes of an object.

In multi-view orthographic drawing the object may be considered as having a picture plane parallel to the typical planes of each face of the object. When these picture planes are extended to meet, they form a transparent box-shape around the object. A view of the object is projected onto each picture plane with projectors perpendicular to that picture plane. Figure 4A shows projections onto three planes of the box. It should be observed that any line which is parallel to the projectors is represented in that view as a point and, furthermore, that any plane parallel to the projectors is represented as a line. Thus, parts of the object which are on the same horizontal plane, such as the edge of the roof and ground line of the building, are drawn as continuous horizontal lines on all vertical picture planes. Since they are at the same height, they are so represented on the drawing. The end planes of the building in Fig. 4A are drawn as vertical lines in the front view, since they are vertical planes perpendicular to the picture plane of that view and the projectors are parallel to them.

Theory of multi-view projection assumes that after the views of the object have been made by projecting onto the planes of the enclosing transparent box, they are all moved into a single plane which is represented by the plane of the paper. A widely used arrangement of the views is obtained by assuming that all the picture planes intersecting with the front view plane are hinged to the front and rotated into its plane. The rear view, which is on a plane not intersecting with the front, is attached to the left side view. Figure 4B shows the planes in the process of being revolved into one plane, and Fig. 4C shows the arrangement of drawings resulting from the complete revolution.

The number of views necessary to describe an object varies with different objects. In Fig. 4D three views, the front, top, and one side, are adequate. For a simple object two views are often sufficient, while for more complex objects all six of the standard views may be required and one or more other drawings also.

It should be observed that the side views face toward the front view and that the front of the top view is at the bottom of that drawing. Plans, whether made looking down or up, are turned with the front of the building down in architectural drawings. Thus the arrangements shown in Fig. 4D and E are both correct in architecture, although the plan in Fig. 4E is wrong for engineering.

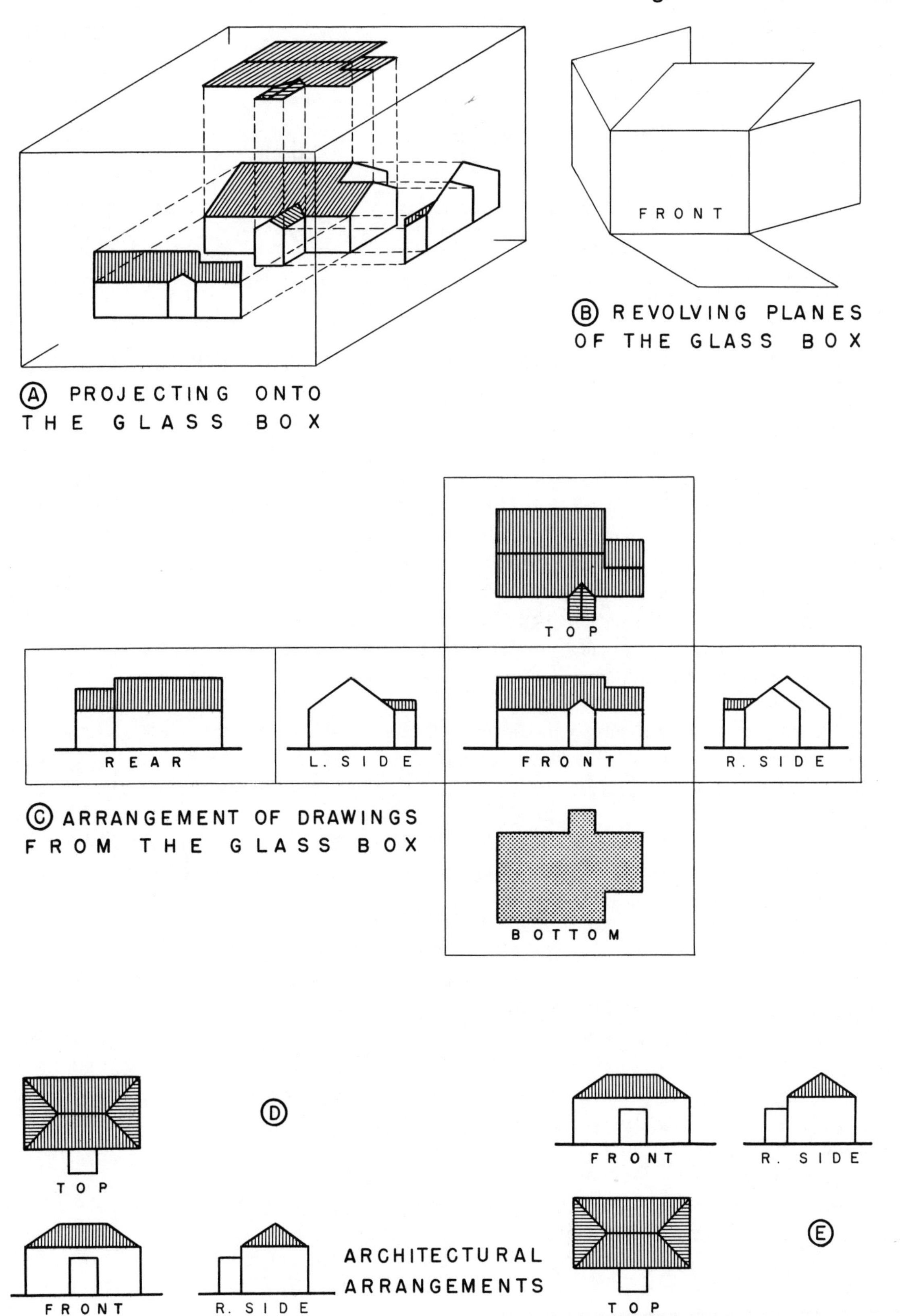

FIG-4 MULTI-VIEW ORTHOGRAPHIC PROJECTION DRAWING

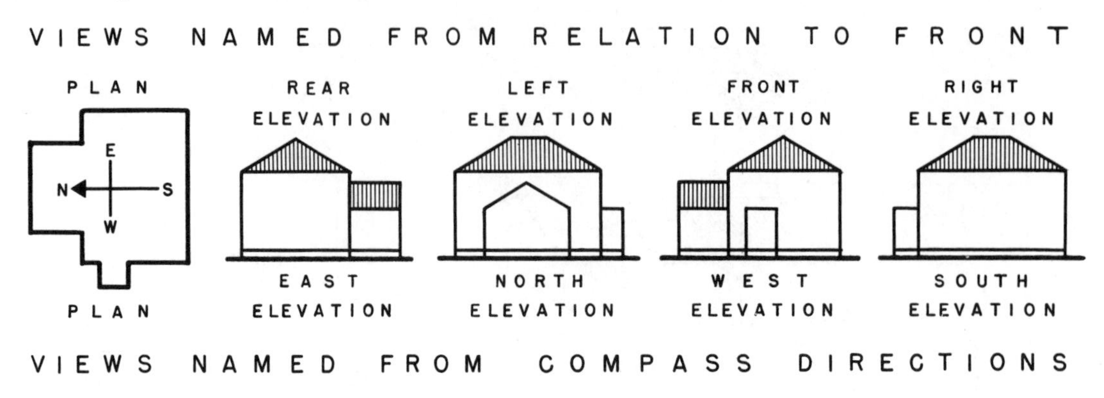

FIG-5 ARCHITECTURAL NOMENCLATURE OF VIEWS

In architecture all views of the exterior of a building on vertical planes are called elevations, and all views both exterior and interior on horizontal planes are called plans. The different elevations may be designated by the terms front elevation, side elevation, and rear elevation. The terms right elevation and left elevation are sometimes used to distinguish between the two side views, the right elevation being the drawing to the right of the front view in Fig. 5 and the left elevation the one which appears on the left of the front elevation. The compass directions are frequently used to differentiate between the elevations. In this system each elevation is named for the direction in which it will face on the building site. The north elevation is then the view of the side of the building which faces north.

The planes provided by the transparent box-shape of Fig. 4A are not always adequate to give true shape views of all sides of a building. When a wall of the building does not parallel one of the typical planes and consequently one of the faces of the transparent box, its true shape will not be shown by any of the conventional elevations. Picture planes which are added to the transparent box-shape in order to obtain true-shape views (auxiliary views) of planes of the object not parallel to the original planes of the box are called auxiliary planes, Fig. 6A and D.

The true shape of any oblique surface, such as a slanting roof or wall, can then be obtained by projecting onto an auxiliary plane parallel to the oblique surface.

The most common auxiliary views in architecture are elevations. The drafting process by which an auxiliary elevation is made may vary in details of its construction. However, in all cases the heights may be taken from any other elevation of the building and the horizontal dimensions from plan. Figure 6B and C show two methods of making the auxiliary elevation from a front elevation and plan. In B the auxiliary drawing is made to show the entire building, as would usually be done in architectural drawing. In some drawings of the type shown in C it may be advisable to show a small amount of the adjoining oblique parts of the elevation to suggest that the entire structure is not shown. When a separate plan is available, it can be turned in the most convenient direction to project the auxiliary view as shown by dotted lines in C.

The front roof plane of Fig. 6E is shown by the front elevation to be a rectangle. The length of this roof area is shown in the front view, and its true slant-height is shown in the side view. The rectangle made by using these two dimensions is the correct auxiliary view of the front roof plane. In E both the front and rear roof surfaces are drawn in the auxiliary view. In F all four planes of the simple hip roof are drawn in the auxiliary view. Such drawings are useful to show the true shapes and areas of the roof planes and the true lengths of lines in those planes. The slanting lines in the auxiliary view of F show the true length of the hips. Auxiliary drawings of roof areas would be used in constructing roofs for models. The length of any straight line can be determined graphically by making an auxiliary view on any picture plane parallel to the line.

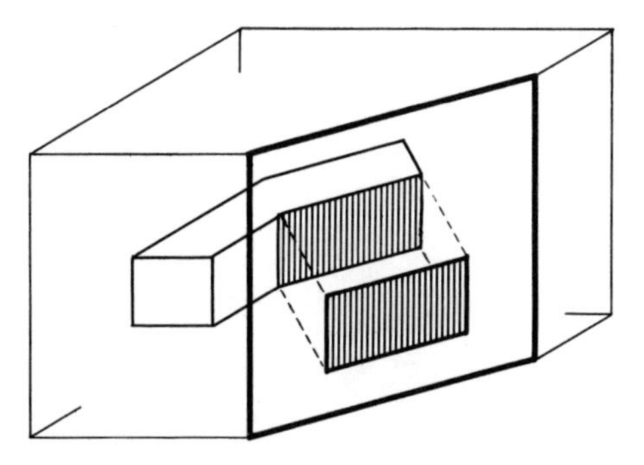

Ⓐ VERTICAL AUXILIARY PLANE

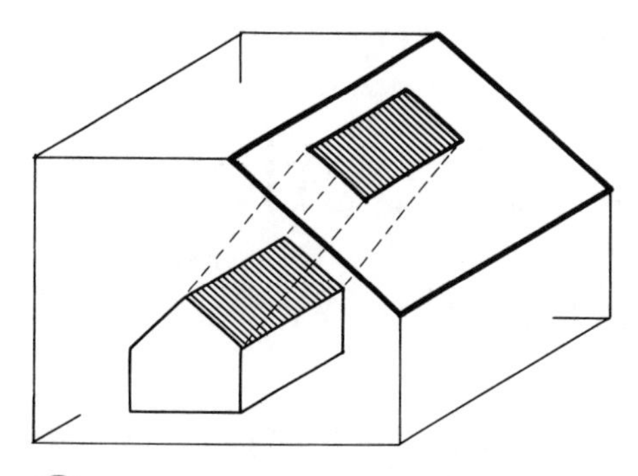

Ⓓ OBLIQUE AUXILIARY PLANE

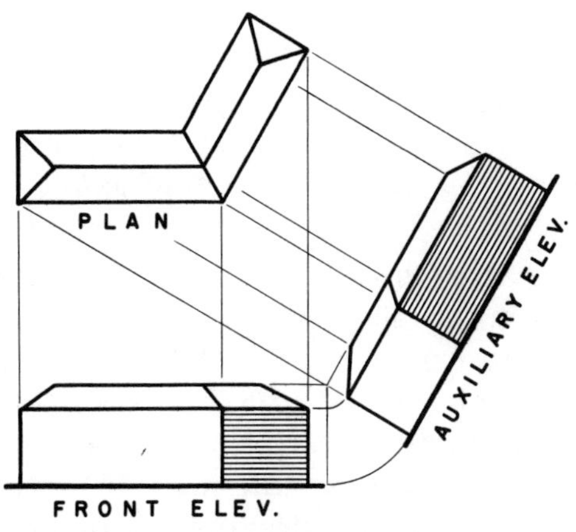

Ⓑ COMPLETE AUXILIARY VIEW

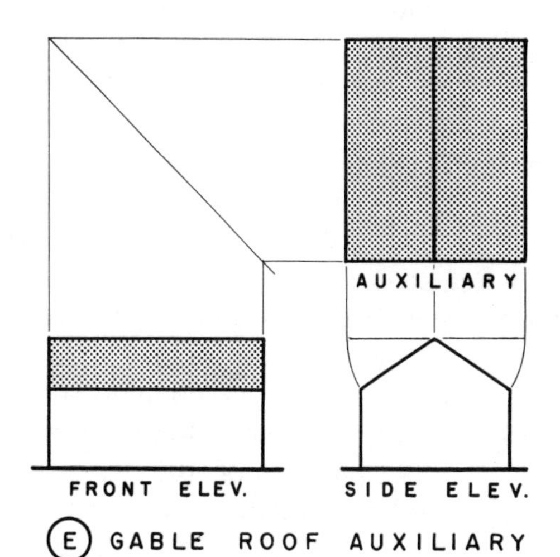

Ⓔ GABLE ROOF AUXILIARY

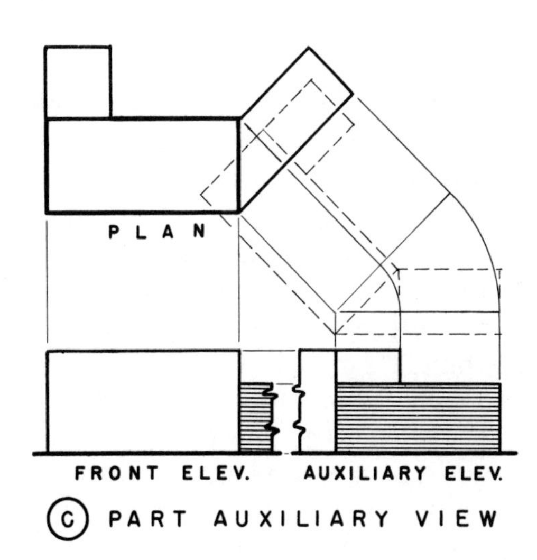

Ⓒ PART AUXILIARY VIEW

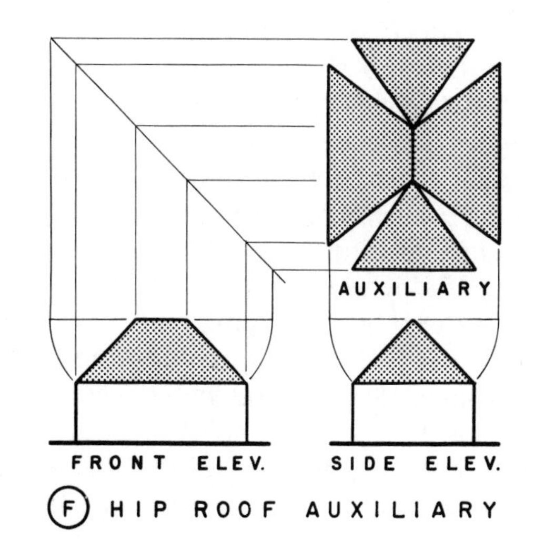

Ⓕ HIP ROOF AUXILIARY

ELEVATION AUXILIARIES

OBLIQUE PLANE AUXILIARIES

FIG-6 AUXILIARY VIEWS

CHAPTER 3
Construction of Multi-view Drawings

In the construction of multi-view drawings, it should be kept in mind that all the different views must check. As an example, all views showing the heights of a building must agree on all the heights shown, and all drawings showing a detail, such as the cornice, must be in accord.

Multi-view drawings should be drawn in alignment whenever it is possible to do so because they are easier to construct and understand. The sizes laid out in one view are transferred to other views by drawing. In Fig. 7A either the plan or front elevation can be drawn first; then the lengths of the other view can be obtained by drawing vertical lines between the two views. If it is more convenient, the two drawings can be developed together.

After the plan and front elevation are drawn, the side elevation is constructed by using the heights from the front elevation and the widths from the plan. The heights should be carried across with the T-square. The widths can very conveniently be transferred from the plan to the side elevation by one of the drafting methods shown in Fig. 7A or B.

The tick-strip, which is a narrow straight band of paper, is very convenient for transferring sizes from one view to another when the drawings are not in alignment so the dimensions can be transferred by direct drafting. It is laid on the drawing from which the dimensions are to be taken, in a position perpendicular to the lines to be transferred, and the locations of the lines are marked neatly and accurately on the edge of the paper with a sharp pencil. The strip is then moved to correct position on the drawing to be made, the measurements marked lightly on the paper, and the lines drawn through their marked positions. The tick-strip method of transferring sizes is more speedy than using a scale, and errors in drawings are less likely to occur.

The representation of curving or oblique wall surfaces in the elevations of multi-view drawings is often puzzling to the inexperienced draftsman. In drawing such surfaces it is necessary to draw first the plan view, which shows the true distances in a horizontal plane. The plan of the octagonal prism in Fig. 7C shows the sides to be equal. The elevation is made by projecting vertically from the plan to establish the elevation widths of the visible walls of the prism. Although the three walls shown in the elevation are actually identical, the two on the sides appear to be narrower than the center one because they are turned at an angle to the picture plane.

Equal spaces around the surface of a vertical cylinder are spaced off in the plan view then projected vertically to obtain the correct spacing for elevation, Fig. 7E. This construction procedure is followed for openings, columns, material units, fluting, and other details of architecture. A drawing of a curved surface should be constructed with precise accuracy so that the elevation view will be as expressive as possible. Some of the details of representing an oblique wall surface in elevation are illustrated in the drawing of the octagonal building in Fig. 7F. It should be observed that the lines of the roofing material which are drawn vertically in the center area are drawn parallel to the line from the top point of the roof to the center of the eaves line in the area over each oblique wall. The thickness of the wall is represented by a space on one side of each window on an oblique wall. Part of the window sash on the near side is hidden by the corner of the wall.

A circular stairway, such as shown in Fig. 7G, is first laid out in plan, then the height in elevation is divided into the correct number of equal spaces to agree with the number of riser lines shown in plan. The ends of the steps are then plotted by drawing from their ends in plan to the correct spaces in elevation, and the connecting lines are drawn. The spaces in elevation are numbered to correspond with their numbered lines in plan. The height of the railing for the balustrade is the same on the vertical line above the front edge of each step.

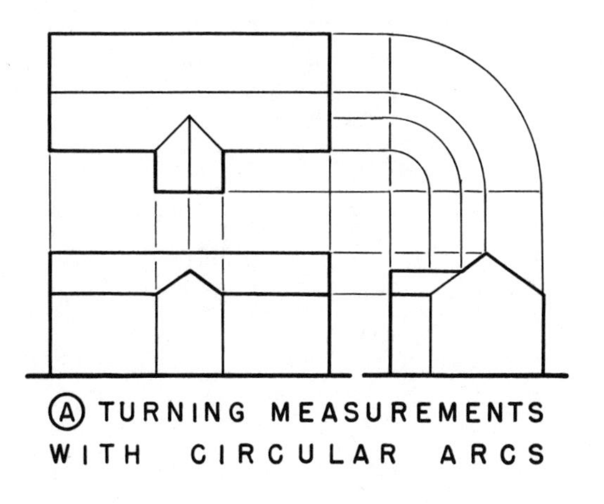

Ⓐ TURNING MEASUREMENTS WITH CIRCULAR ARCS

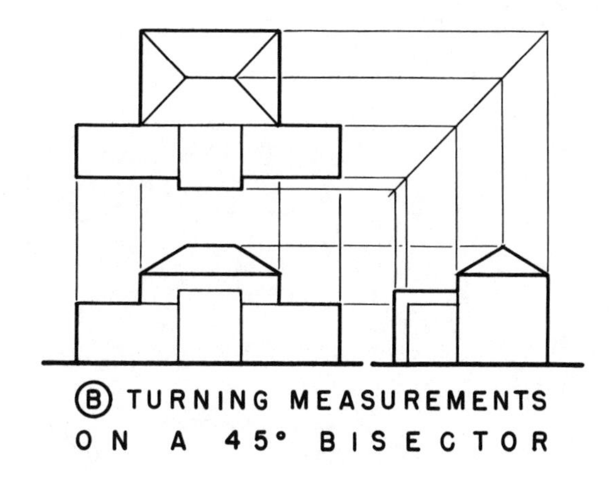

Ⓑ TURNING MEASUREMENTS ON A 45° BISECTOR

Ⓒ OCTAGON

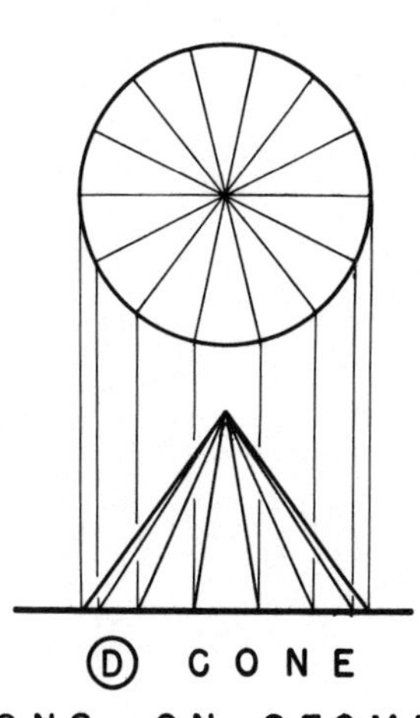

Ⓓ CONE

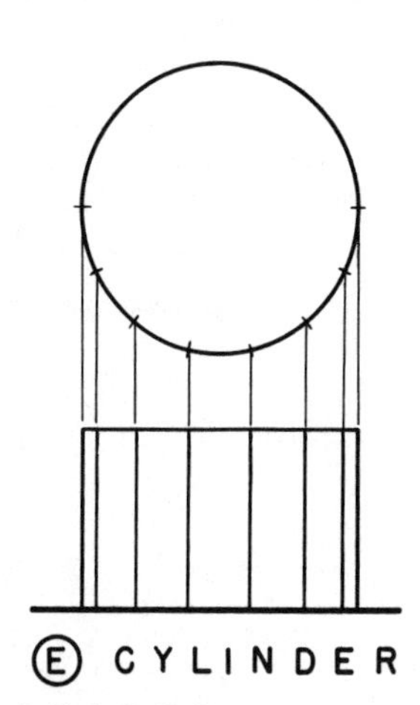

Ⓔ CYLINDER

EQUAL DIVISIONS ON GEOMETRIC SHAPES

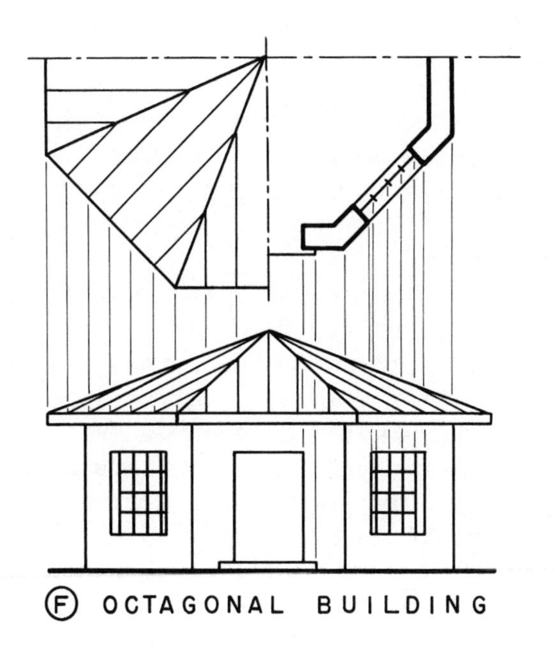

Ⓕ OCTAGONAL BUILDING

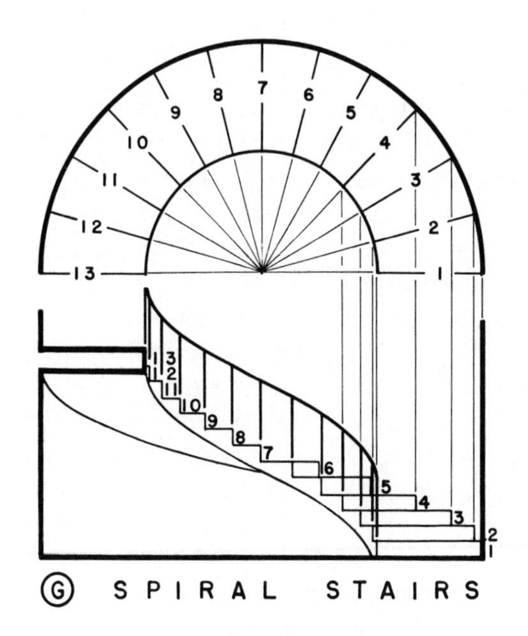

Ⓖ SPIRAL STAIRS

FIG-7 CONSTRUCTION OF MULTI-VIEW DRAWINGS

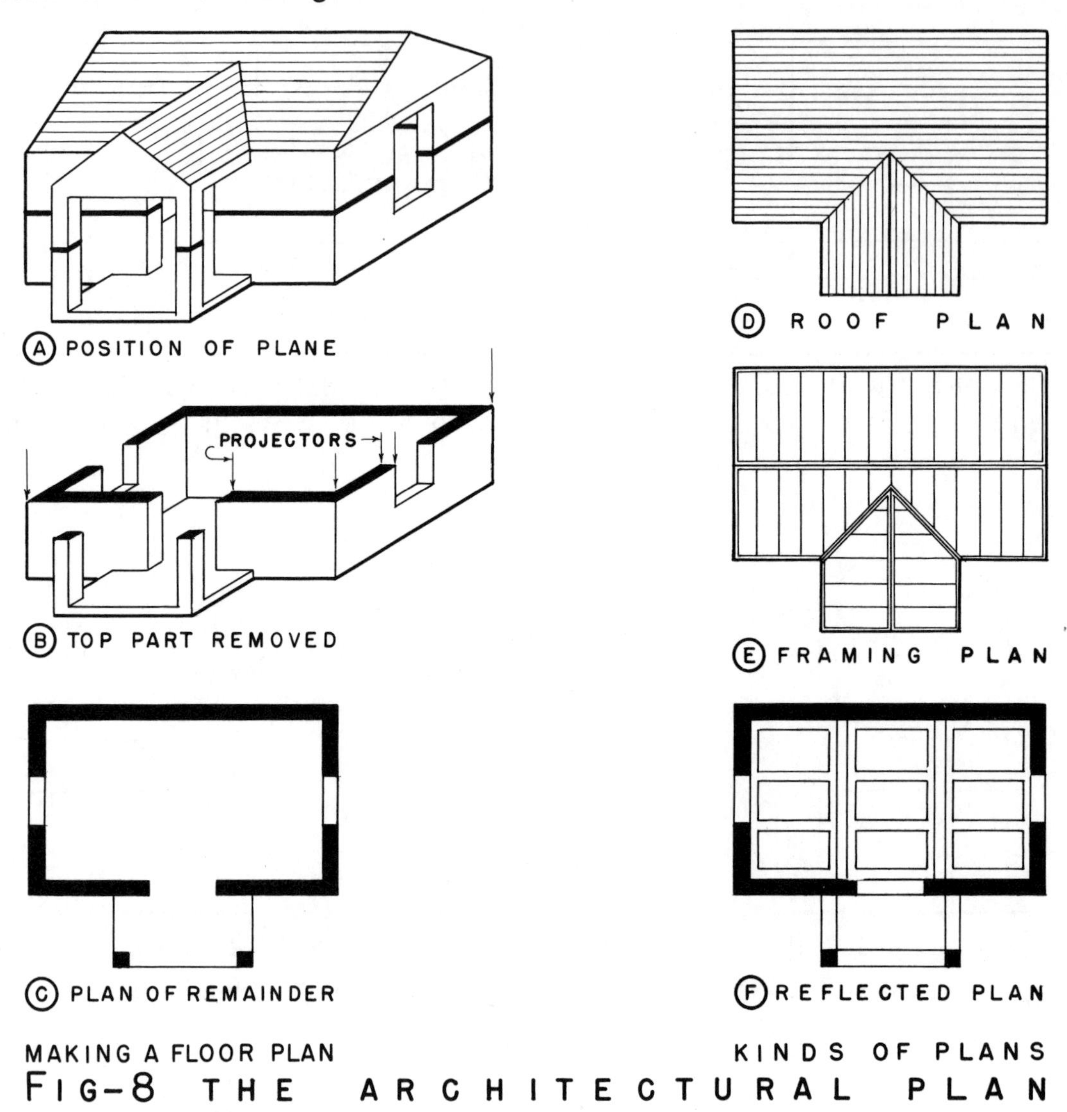

MAKING A FLOOR PLAN KINDS OF PLANS
FIG-8 THE ARCHITECTURAL PLAN

PLANS AND SECTIONS. In addition to the exterior views of buildings it is usually necessary to have one or more views made which cut through the structure and show the interior. These views are known by two general names: (1) plan, which is the term applied to any view on a horizontal picture plane either from the exterior or cut through, and (2) section, which is the name given to any view cutting through the building on a vertical plane.

The floor plan, which is the most commonly used of all plan views, is shown in the drawing of Fig. 8C. The building is assumed to be cut in two by a horizontal plane at a height above the floor which will pass through windows and doors, Fig. 8A. The part of the building above the cutting plane is then considered to be removed, and the drawing is made as though looking down on the remaining part of the building in a vertical direction. Any part of the structure above the cutting plane can be shown in the drawing with dotted lines if necessary. High windows are usually noted on design drawings, but not drawn. A plan showing the arrangement of walls, windows, doors, and other features of the design is usually made for each floor of a building except in cases where floors are exact duplicates. Additional plans are often made to show the entire plot, the foundation, roof, roof framing, floor framing, electrical layout, heating layout, or for other specific purposes.

The reflected plan or view looking up to show the ceiling treatment or other features of the building above the cutting plane, is made as though the observer looks down and sees the ceiling reflected in a mirror placed on the floor, Fig. 8F. This drawing differs in its theory from the other

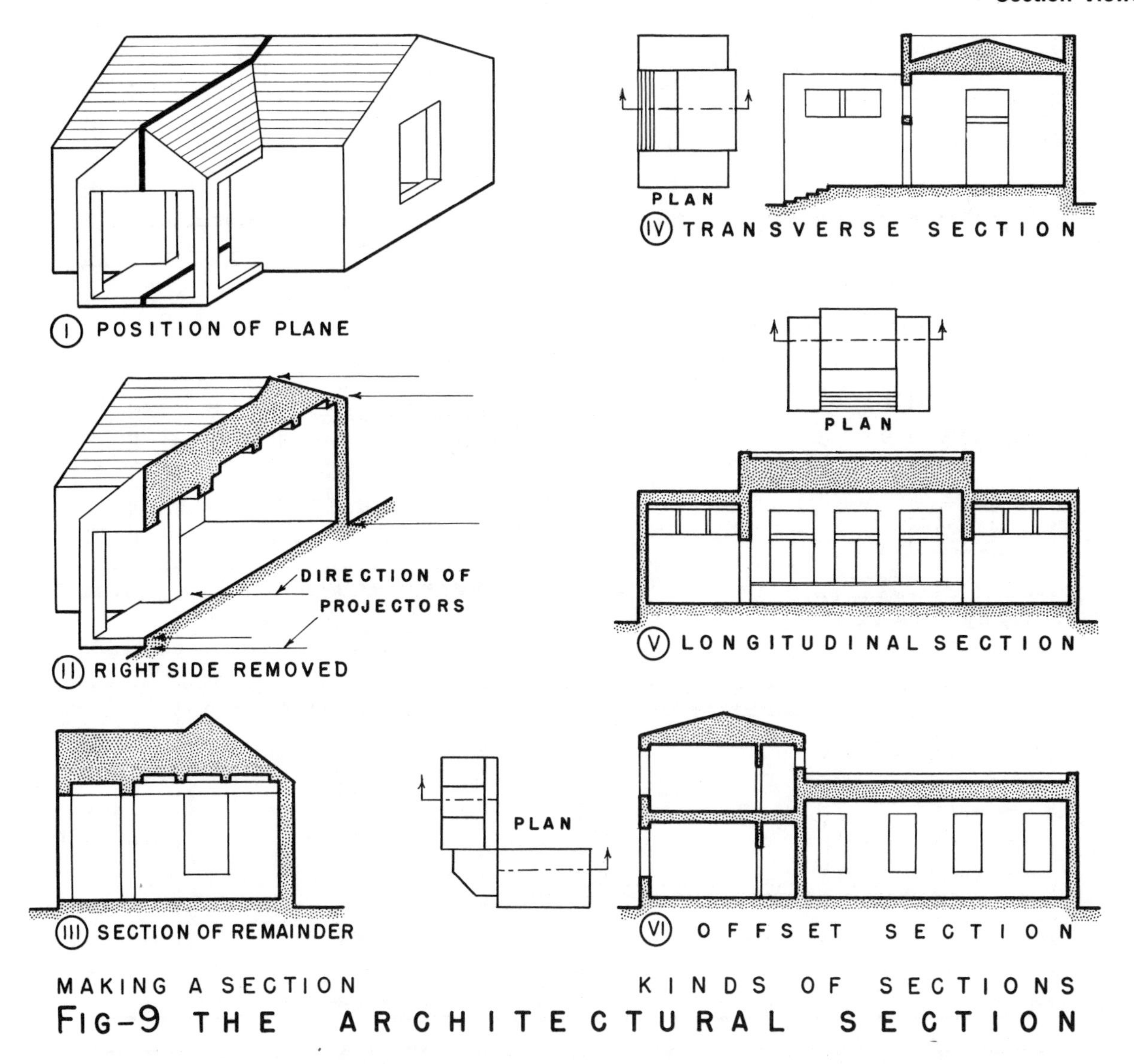

FIG-9 THE ARCHITECTURAL SECTION

multi-view drawings. However, it has these decided advantages: (1) the reflected plan can be traced over the floor plan; (2) the architectural convention of turning the front of a plan to the bottom of the sheet is retained; (3) on symmetrical designs one half of the plan can be made looking down, the other half looking up—without the confusion of having the drawings of the two parts turned in different directions.

The section is similar in theory of projection to the floor plan. The building is assumed to be cut by a vertical plane parallel to one of the sets of walls, and the part on one side of the cutting plane is removed, Fig. 9 I and II. The projection drawing of the remaining part of the building is made on a plane parallel to the cutting plane. A simple section drawing is shown in Fig. 9 III. Where the projectors are parallel to the walls, ceilings, and floor these surfaces are shown as lines.

The position of the section plane is often shown by a dot-dash line in plan, and the direction in which the observer looks to see the object as represented in the section is indicated by arrows at the ends of the line. The plans of the cutting planes are shown in the small-scale plans of Fig. 9 IV, V, and VI. A transverse section shows the width of the building. A longitudinal section shows the length of the building. Sections which are not taken on a continuous plane are called offset sections. On a symmetrical building the section planes usually pass through the center of the building. However, the section can be made at any desired location. A position is usually chosen to provide useful information which can be easily understood.

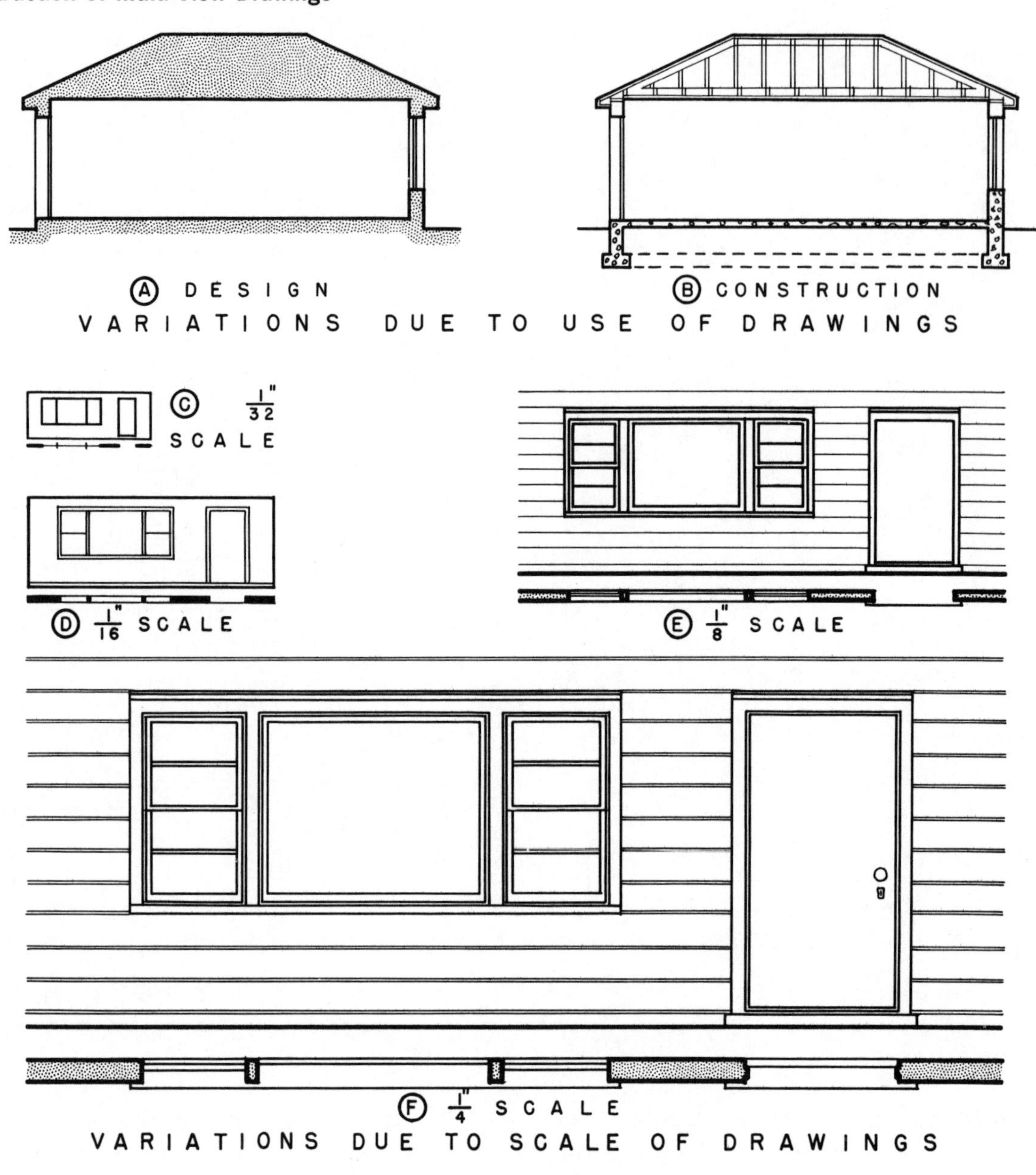

FIG—10 VARIATIONS OF DETAIL

Variations of detail may occur in multi-view drawings. In the preceding discussions it was stated that all the different views should agree in shapes and sizes. However, there are legitimate and desirable variations in drawings because of (1) difference in use of the drawings and (2) difference in scale. Architectural drawings are divided into the two general use types of design drawings and working drawings. It is primarily the purpose of the design drawings to show how the proposed building will appear to the observer, and details which will not ordinarily be seen in the finished structure can very appropriately be omitted from these drawings. These omissions make it easier to understand the design of the structure, Fig. 10A. Working drawings are explanations of the construction of the building. It is necessary that they give all instructions necessary for the builder. The parts between ceiling and roof, in the thickness of the walls, and below the finished floors are as important in these drawings as the visible parts of the finished building, Fig. 10B.

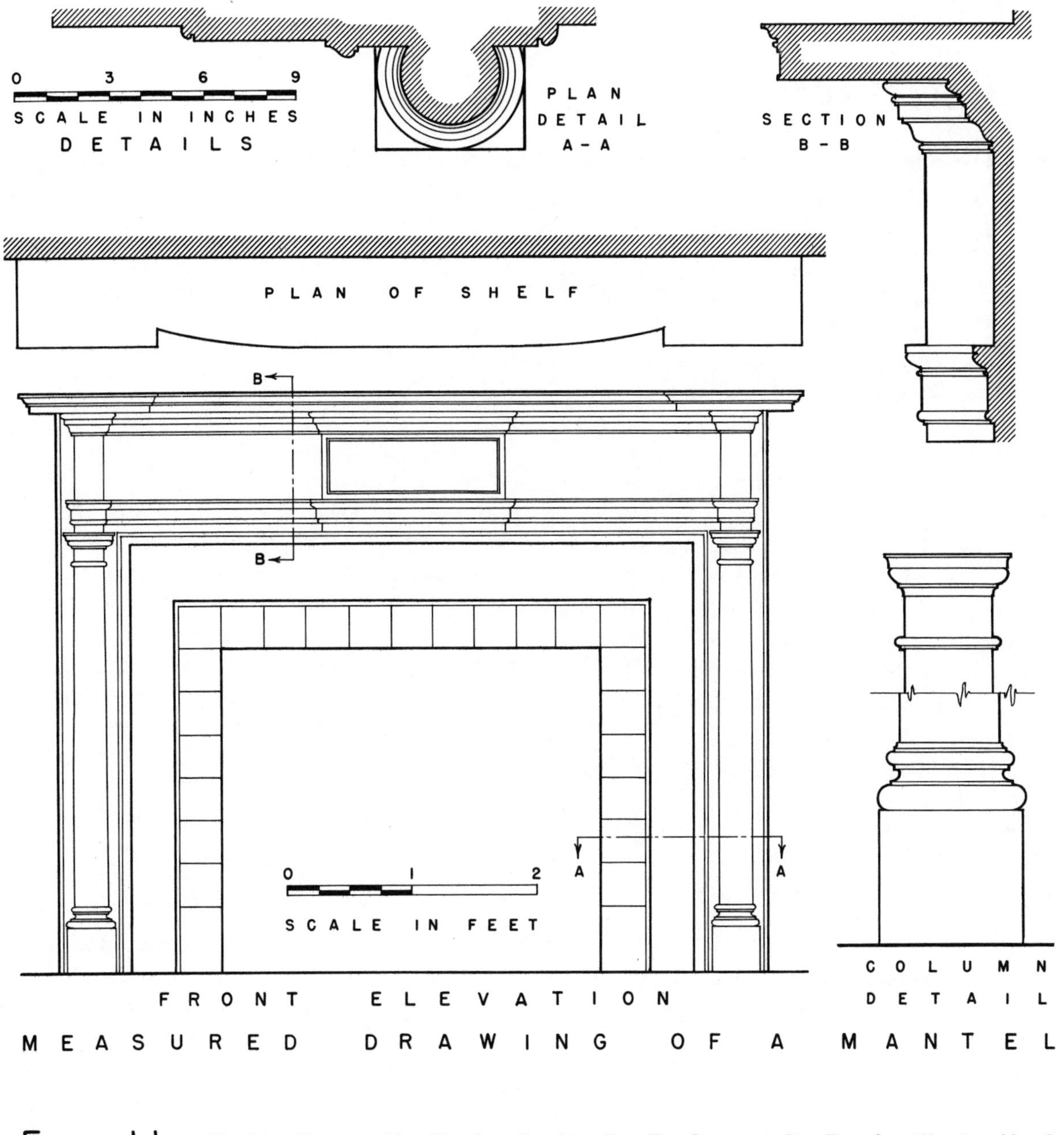

FIG-11 THE MEASURED DRAWING

In either working drawings or design drawings views of the structure at different scales are expected to vary in the amount of detail shown. It would be impractical if not physically impossible to show in a small-scale drawing all the details which would be represented in a large-scale or full-size drawing. However, the drawings representing the same thing at different scales should agree in the things that are shown. They should represent the same type of design, the same proportions, and the same details as far as size limitations permit them to do so. Figure 10C, D, E, and F show some of the variations which may occur in the plans and elevations of a window and door when they are drawn at different scales.

The measured drawing gives a description of some existing detail, element of architecture, or building. The example in Fig. 11 gives a contrast of details of moldings at different scales and also shows the method of indicating where details are located on small-scale drawings.

PART TWO
Paraline Drawings

CHAPTER 4
Characteristics of Paraline Drawings

Paraline drawings are those pictorial drawings in which all parallel lines of the object remain parallel in the drawings. Three major divisions of paraline drawings are described and illustrated on this and the following pages. These three divisions are (1) isometric drawing, (2) dimetric drawing, and (3) oblique drawing. Dimetric drawing is further divided into two divisions of symmetrical dimetric and unsymmetrical dimetric. Oblique drawing is also divided into two divisions called elevation oblique and plan oblique, Fig. 12.

In all paraline drawings parallel lines in any direction are drawn parallel. This simplifies construction but causes the more distant parts of the object to appear to be too large. The receding parallel lines appear to diverge because the eye is accustomed to seeing them converge as they do in perspective drawings, in photographs, and in nature. This pictorial defect is the principal criticism of these types of drawings.

The three typical sets of lines of the object are all measured to scale in paraline drawings. Therefore, most of the measuring and dimensioning can usually be done directly on the lines of the drawing itself. Simplicity and speed of construction are the chief advantages of these drawings over perspective drawing.

Because of the ease with which they can be drawn and understood, paraline drawings are widely used. They are used in architecture for exteriors of complete buildings, for plan drawings which show parts of the walls, for interiors of buildings and rooms, and for details of both interiors and exteriors such as fireplaces, cornices, entrances, stairways, and structural details. They are less often used than perspective for presentation drawings and design studies. However, in some cases they explain a design better than a perspective drawing. They are frequently used for explanatory drawings where exact pictorial effect is not as important as the advantages of ease of construction, of dimensioning, and of measuring directly on the drawing. There is little to choose between a good paraline or perspective drawing as far as ease of understanding is concerned. However, the draftsman should become familiar with all these pictorial methods so that he can choose the one best adapted to the needs of a given problem.

Isometric drawing is the easiest type of paraline drawing to construct because the angles of axes are drawn with a standard triangle and only one scale is required. It gives only one view of the three typical planes of an object, emphasizes all three planes equally, and is inflexible.

Dimetric drawing requires the use of two scales on all drawings and requires the use of odd angles for the typical lines. One adjustable triangle helps with the odd angles of dimetric drawing. Two adjustable triangles solve them completely. Symmetrical dimetric allows subordination of roof areas and emphasis on both walls equally. Unsymmetrical dimetric allows emphasis on one wall.

Oblique drawing has one great advantage. It allows true shapes to be shown in one set of typical planes. This is especially advantageous for circles and odd angular shapes in the true-shape planes. The three shapes can be drawn more easily and sometimes explain the forms more clearly.

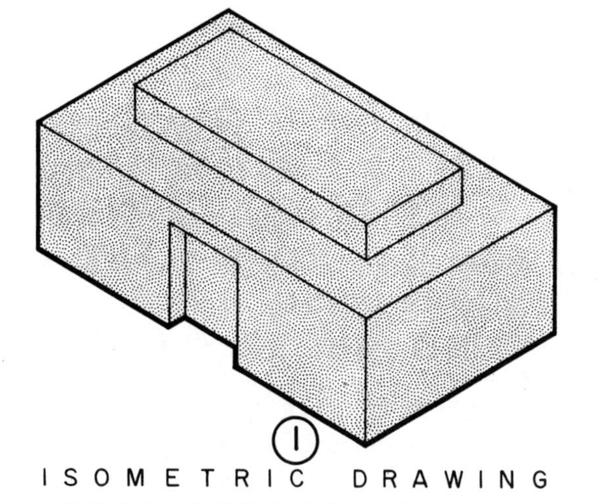

① ISOMETRIC DRAWING
ALL AREAS EMPHASISED EQUALLY

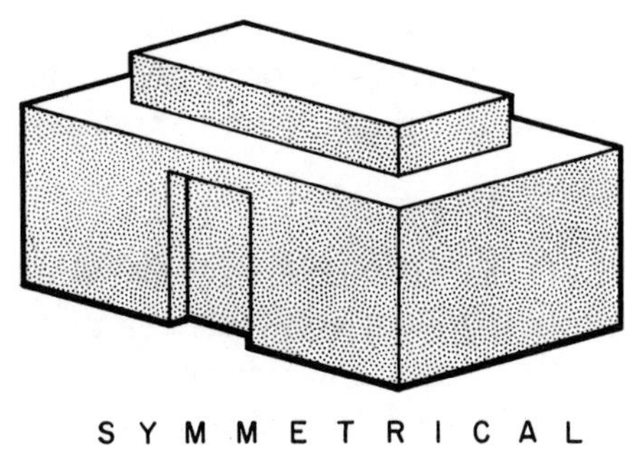

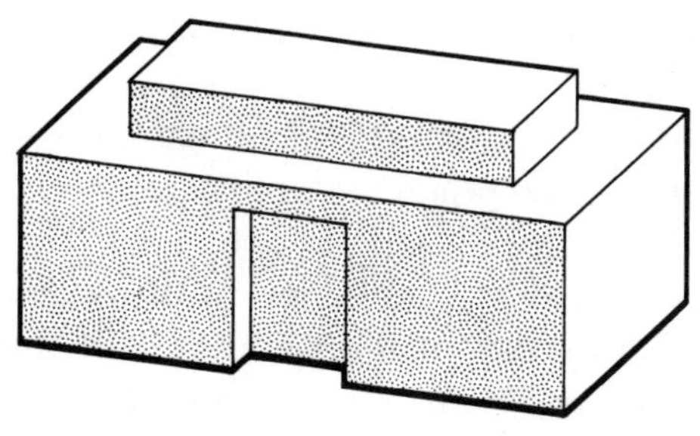

SYMMETRICAL ② UNSYMMETRICAL
DIMETRIC DRAWING
EMPHASISED AREAS ARE SHADED

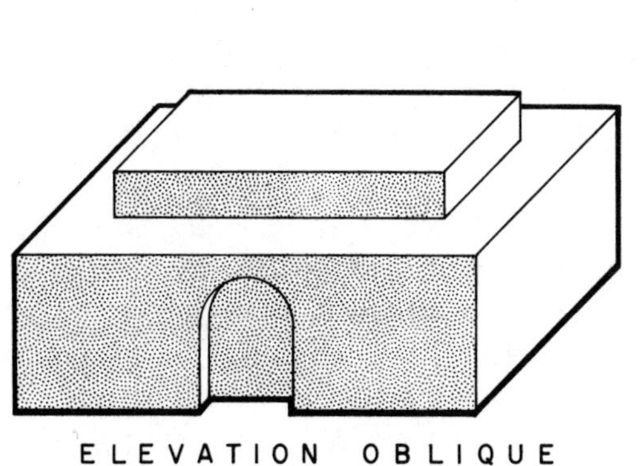

ELEVATION OBLIQUE ③ PLAN OBLIQUE
OBLIQUE DRAWING
TRUE SHAPE AREAS EMPHASISED AND SHADED

FIG—12 MAJOR TYPES OF PARALINE DRAWINGS

CHAPTER 5
Isometric Drawing

A paraline drawing in which the object is turned so that all three axes make the same angle with the picture plane is called an isometric drawing. Since the axes all make the same angle with the picture plane, they are foreshortened the same amount and are drawn at the same scale. Thus in the isometric drawing in Fig. 13A the axis lines on the three edges of the cube are of equal length. Furthermore, since the axis lines on the edges of the cube make equal angles with each other, their projections make equal angles also. The angles between the axis lines are all 120°.

ISOMETRIC PROJECTION. A scale is assumed for the object and the projected or foreshortened size drawing for that scale is shown in an isometric projection. The projected size of the axis lines is .816 of the actual length of the lines. Thus, when the object is assumed to be at a scale of $\frac{1}{8}''$ = 1′–0″ the isometric projection is at a scale of .816 × $\frac{1}{8}''$. An isometric drawing of an object is measured at any desired scale without considering the scale size of the object represented. Figure 13B and C show the difference in size between the isometric projection (B) made with the isometric scale and the isometric drawing (C) measured with the ordinary scale. Although isometric drawings are satisfactory for most purposes, isometric projections sometimes have advantages.

In a full-size drawing where the actual size should be expressed, it may be necessary to use the isometric projection of the object which shows the true projected size. Furthermore, in a series of drawings at the same scale it may sometimes be desirable to have the correct scale relations between the isometric and other drawings. An isometric drawing at a given scale will appear too large for plans and elevations made at that scale, but an isometric projection with its reduced size will be at correct relative scale. An isometric scale can be made by either of the methods shown in Fig. 13B. The scale can be transferred to a straight-edged strip of paper for use, or dimensions can be transferred to the drawing with the dividers.

MAKING AN ISOMETRIC DRAWING. The angle between any two adjacent axes of an isometric drawing is 120°. When one axis is vertical, the other two are at 30° with the horizontal and may be drawn with the 30° triangle on the T-square, as shown in Fig. 13D. A special triangle with a 30° slope in each direction and vertical edges is convenient because it can be kept in one position on the T-square, thus avoiding the loss of time in reversing the triangle. To make an isometric drawing of a simple rectangular object proceed as follows: From a point selected for one of the front corners of the object draw the three axis lines and lay out on these lines their scale sizes, Fig. 13F. From the ends of the lines draw lines parallel to the axes to complete the drawing, Fig. 13G.

POSITIONS OF THE AXES. One axis is usually vertical in isometric drawing. Most drawings for architectural use are made looking down on the object, as shown in Fig. 13H. However, the view looking up, Fig. 13 I, with one axis vertical is sometimes useful for cornices, ceiling treatments, structural details, or other subjects which can best be explained from that position. One axis can be turned horizontally as shown in Fig. 13J and K, or the axes can be turned so that none of them is either horizontal or vertical, if desired. However, it should be kept in mind that the axes must be spaced at 120° intervals regardless of the direction in which the object is turned. All the illustrations of Fig. 13H, I, J, K, L are intended to represent the outsides of cubes. However, they would be drawn in exactly the same way to represent three planes of the inside of a hollow object. In Fig. 13 I the drawing may represent the floor and walls of a room for an interior. This possibility of the drawing appearing inverted is usually eliminated in architectural isometrics by doors, windows, furniture, roofs, etc.

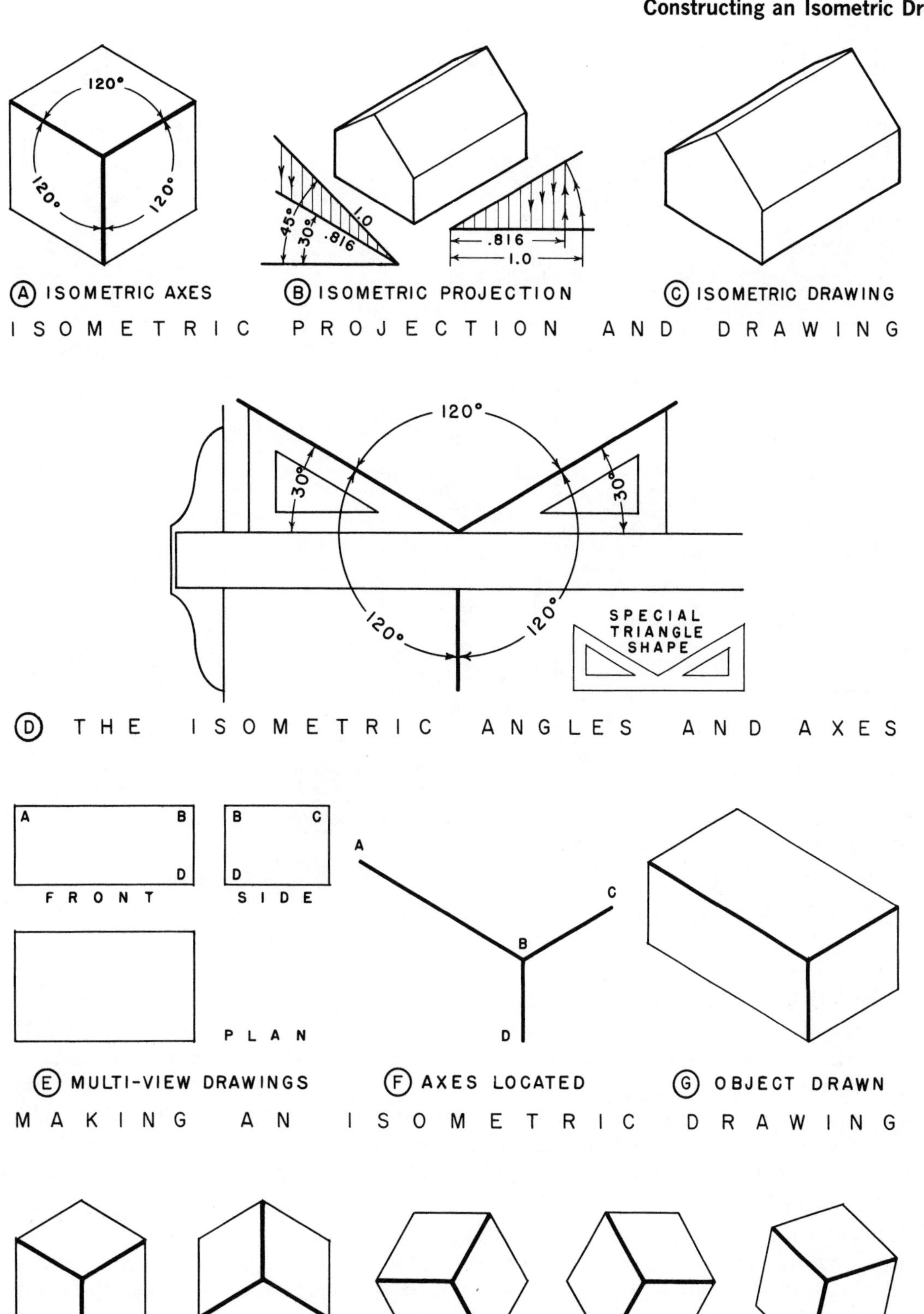

FIG—13 CONSTRUCTION OF AN ISOMETRIC DRAWING

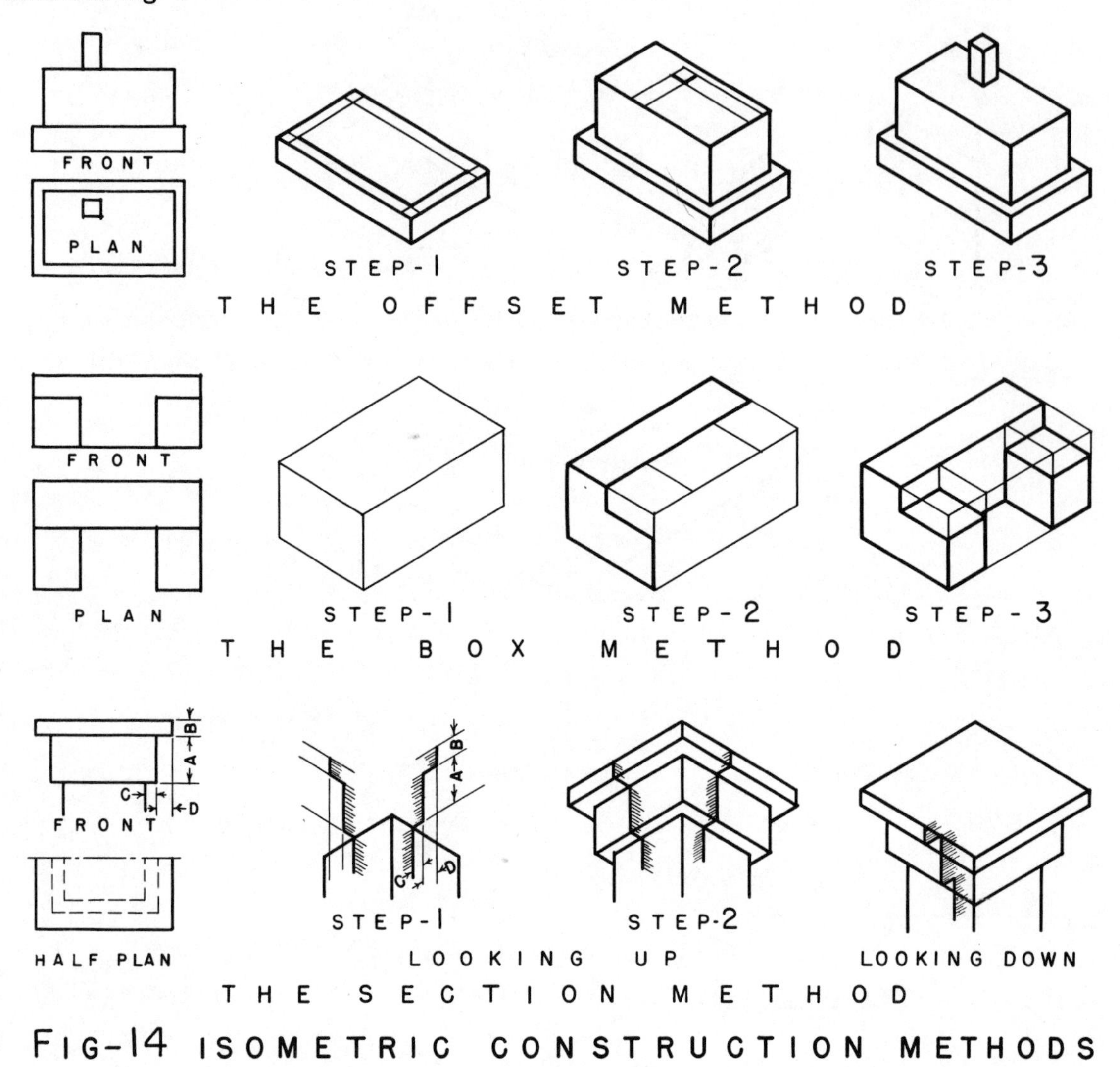

FIG-14 ISOMETRIC CONSTRUCTION METHODS

ISOMETRIC CONSTRUCTION METHODS. All measurements in an isometric drawing must be made parallel to one of the three axis lines. However, there are different ways in which these measurements can be applied to the construction of an isometric drawing. *The offset method* is illustrated in the three steps at the top of Fig. 14. This method is a building-up process which starts with one mass of the object and adds other masses in succession. Positions of features of the object are located by measuring the distances from corners along the edges of the object which are parallel to the axis lines. Lines are drawn from these measurements parallel to the axes to locate the positions of forms. *The box method* starts with the enclosing tangent box shape around the object and subtracts from this simple mass to secure the isometric form of the object. The box method reverses the procedure of the offset method. *The section method* is often the simplest means of working out details and irregular shapes in isometric drawing. These sections are always made parallel to one of the typical planes of the object so that all measuring can be done as directly as possible. The application of this method to simple projecting bands is shown in the illustrations in the bottom row of Fig. 14. An application of this method to a curved solid is given on page 22, Fig. 18C.

THE DRAWING OF DETAILS. Isometric presentations sometimes produce unexpected relations of lines and sizes. This is particularly true of projecting bands. In Fig. 15A the measurements for the projecting band, which is the same width, P, on all sides of the box shape, were laid off at the right and left corners on the extensions of the top edges to locate points A, B, C, D. The

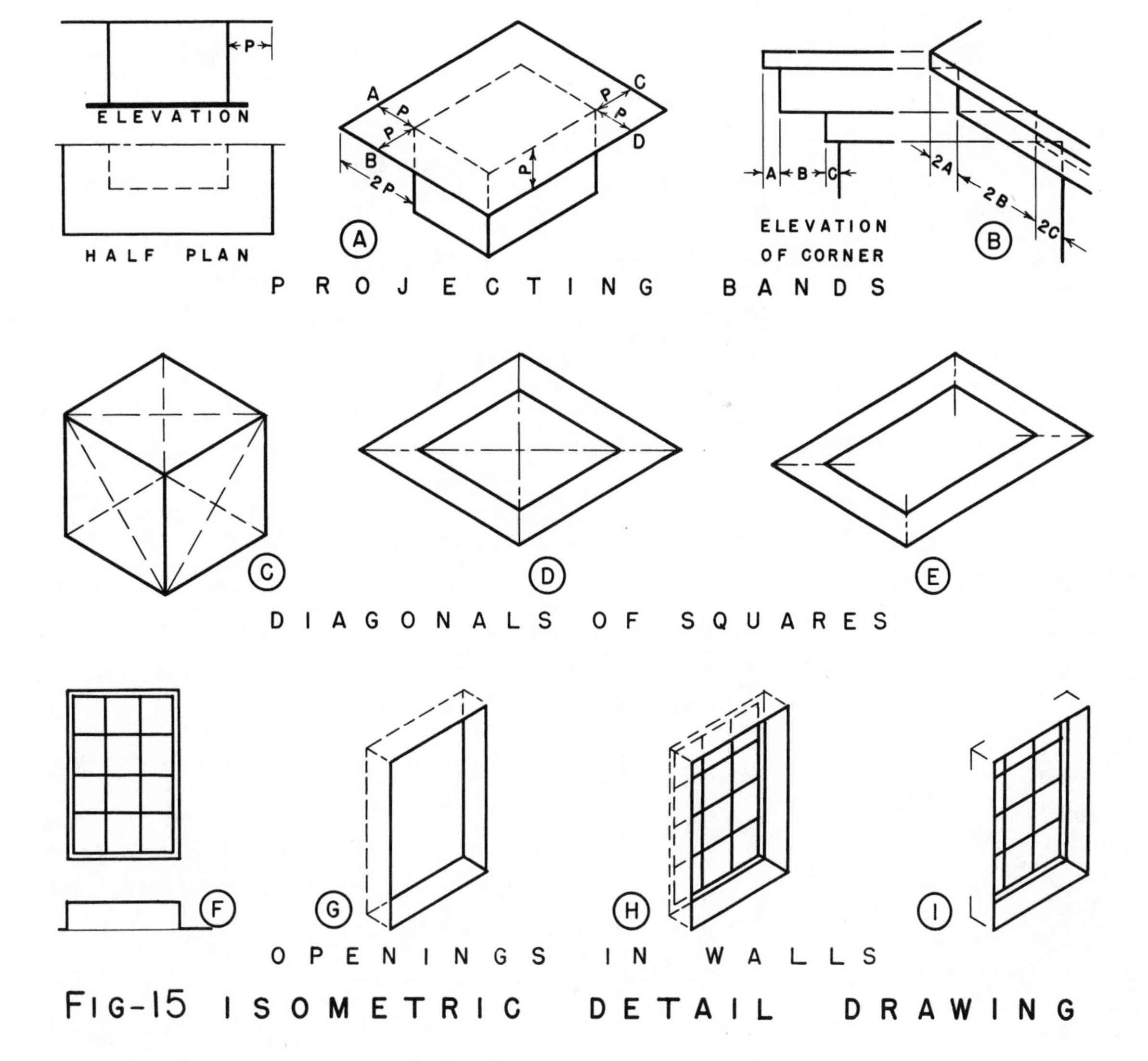

FIG-15 ISOMETRIC DETAIL DRAWING

lines of the edges of the projection were then drawn through these measured points. Three important facts are brought out by this drawing. (1) The nearest corner of the projecting edge lines exactly with the corner of the wall below it. (2) The amount of wall height concealed by the projecting horizontal plane is exactly equal to the amount of projection P. (3) The distance of the extension of the projecting edge beyond the walls at the right and left edges of the drawing is exactly twice the projection.

The diagonals of squares of which the sides are parallel to the axis lines are useful in reducing the amount of measuring for isometric construction. The directions of the diagonals are shown on all three of the visible sides of the isometric drawing of a cube in Fig. 15C. One diagonal of the horizontal square is vertical and the other is horizontal. One diagonal of each of the vertical squares is at 30° with the horizontal and the other is at 60°. The diagonals of the horizontal or plan square are more often used than those of the vertical squares. Figure 15D shows the use of the diagonals of the square and one measurement to construct an equal space around the four sides of the square. Figure 15E shows a similar construction for a rectangle. In this case the lines at the corners are not diagonals of the rectangle, but are the 45° lines bisecting the corners (lines parallel to the diagonals of the square).

Figure 15F, G, H, I shows how part of the area of the sunken plane of the window sash is concealed by the thickness of the wall at the top and one side of the opening when the drawing is made looking down on the window.

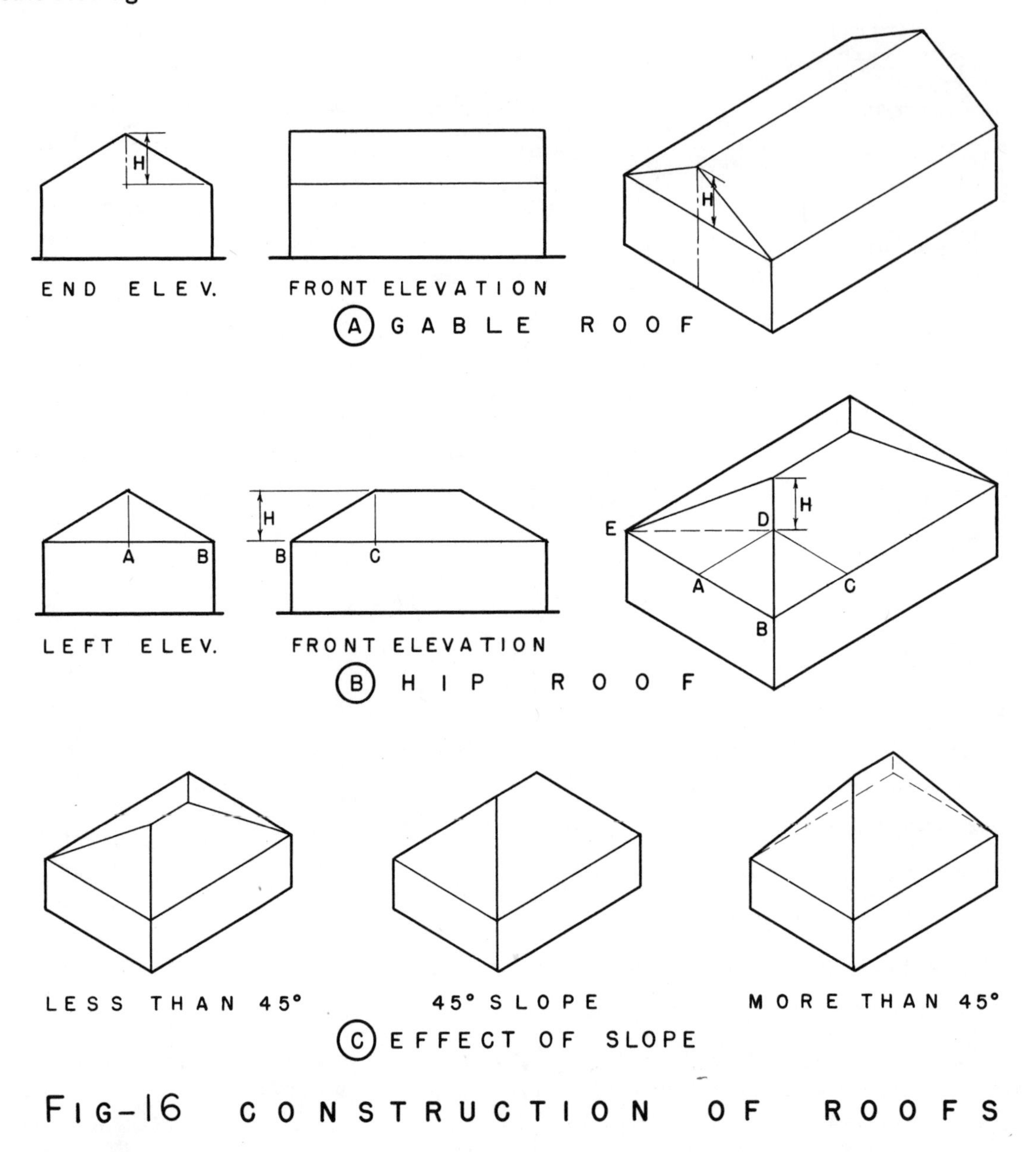

FIG-16 CONSTRUCTION OF ROOFS

Non-isometric lines is the term applied to lines which are not parallel to one of the axes of an isometric drawing. The positions of non-isometric lines can be found by locating the ends of the lines by the offset or box method of construction, as shown in Fig. 16A and B for gabled and hipped roofs, and in Fig. 17 II for a bay window. The height of the gabled roof is laid out on the vertical center line of the end of the building. The gable lines are then drawn to the top corners of the end wall. The ridge and eaves are isometric lines and the lines of the gable at the far end of the building are parallel to the nearer gable.

In constructing the hipped roof of Fig. 16B the distances A–B and B–C, which are one half of E–B, are laid off on the eaves line of the end and front of the roof. From A and C isometric lines are drawn to intersect at D. The height of the roof, H, is laid out above D. The length of the ridge is then drawn and also lines connecting the ends of the ridge to the corners of the eaves.

The hip lines connecting to the nearest and most distant corners are always vertical lines when the slope of the roof is the same on all sides. Furthermore, point D can be located by drawing

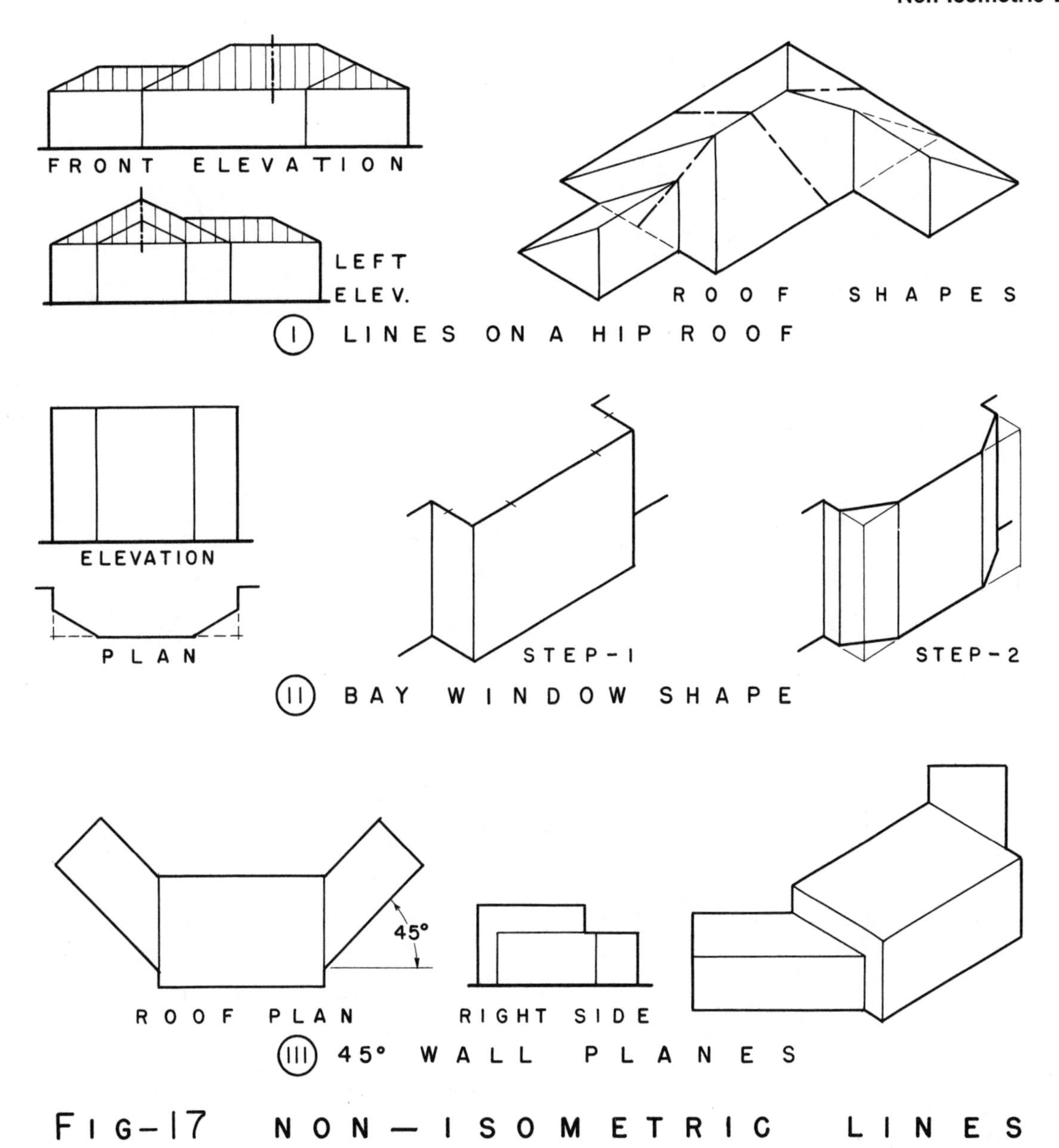

FIG-17 NON-ISOMETRIC LINES

a vertical line from point B to meet a horizontal line from E to simplify the construction of the roof. When the slope of a roof is at 45°, the far sides of the roof will be perpendicular to the picture plane and will not be visible. In a hipped roof at this angle the hip line and ridge will be one continuous line which coincides with the eaves line of the far side, Fig. 16C. This gives the worst possible picture effect in isometric drawing.

In constructing a more complex roof, as in Fig. 17 I, the minor parts of the roof can often be worked out by drawing parallel to the main roof. The lines of the roofing material which appear to be vertical lines in the elevations are drawn parallel to the center lines of symmetrical roof areas. All of these lines on parallel roof planes should be parallel.

In wall planes which are turned at 45°, Fig. 17 III, horizontal lines appear as either horizontal or vertical lines and give an unpleasant effect in isometric drawing. The bay window of Fig. 17 II gives a better effect because its oblique planes are turned at a smaller angle than 45° with the front and both are therefore visible in the drawing.

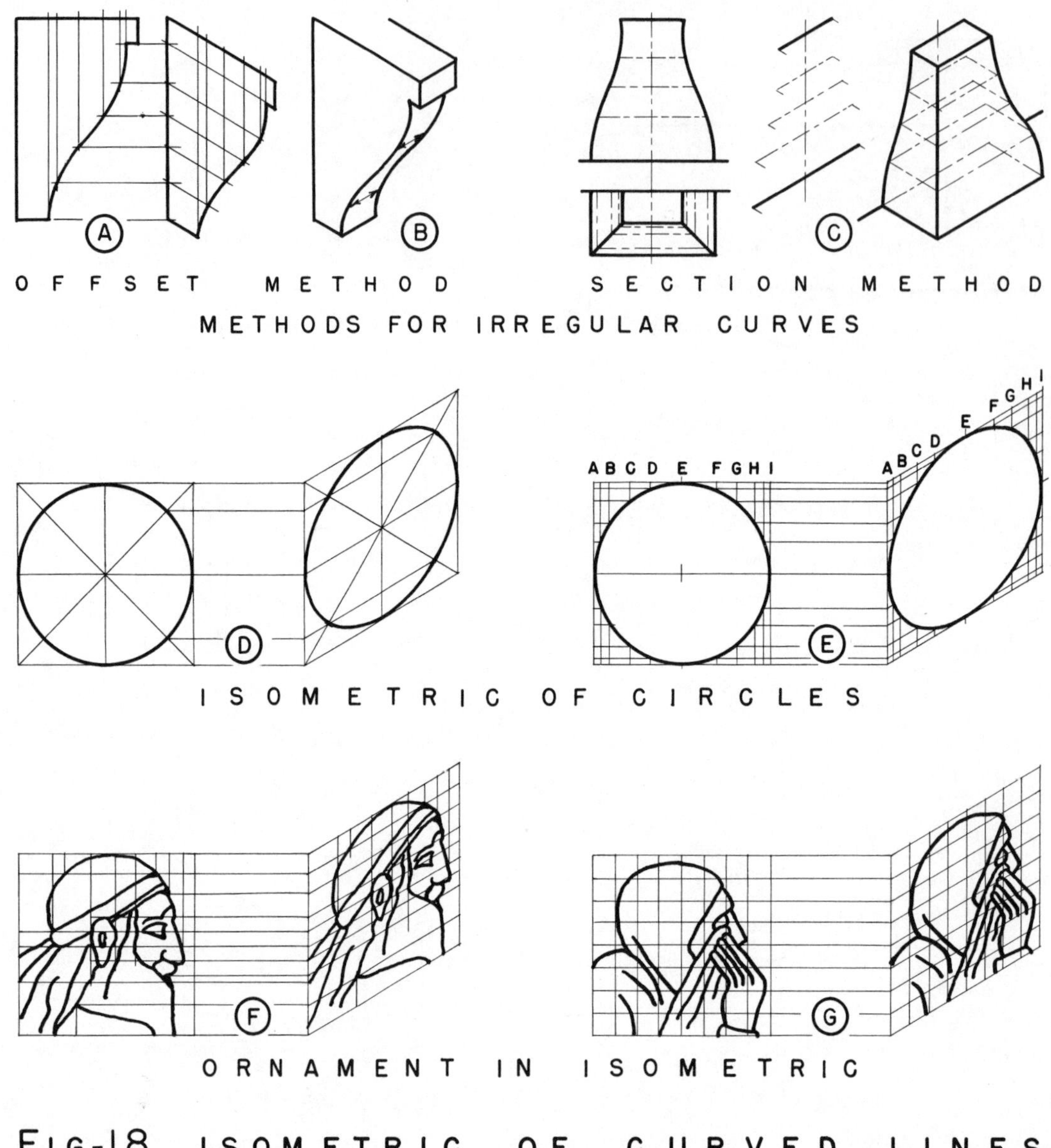

FIG-18 ISOMETRIC OF CURVED LINES

CURVES IN ISOMETRIC DRAWING. A curved line can be worked out in an isometric drawing by using the offset method to locate the isometric positions of a number of points on the curve as shown in Fig. 18A. When elements of a curved surface are parallel to one of the axes, a second curved line can be laid out from the first by use of equal measurements in the direction of the correct axis as shown in Fig. 18B, or the shape can be traced and transferred. Horizontal sections are used in Fig. 18C to locate points on the lines of an irregularly curved object.

The circle in isometric drawing appears as an ellipse. By using a tangent square and its diagonals, eight points can be located on the isometric of a circle as shown in Fig. 18D. Any number of points can be found on the isometric of a circle by using the offset method of measuring as illustrated in Fig. 18E.

Freehand ornament can be drawn in isometric by locating important points with the offset method, as shown in Fig. 18F, or by making uniform cross section pattern over the elevation drawing regardless of where the lines fall, and then duplicating the cross section pattern in isometric and fitting the drawing to it, Fig. 18G. This second method, in which a uniform grid spacing is used, is not as accurate as the first method, but is preferred by some draftsmen.

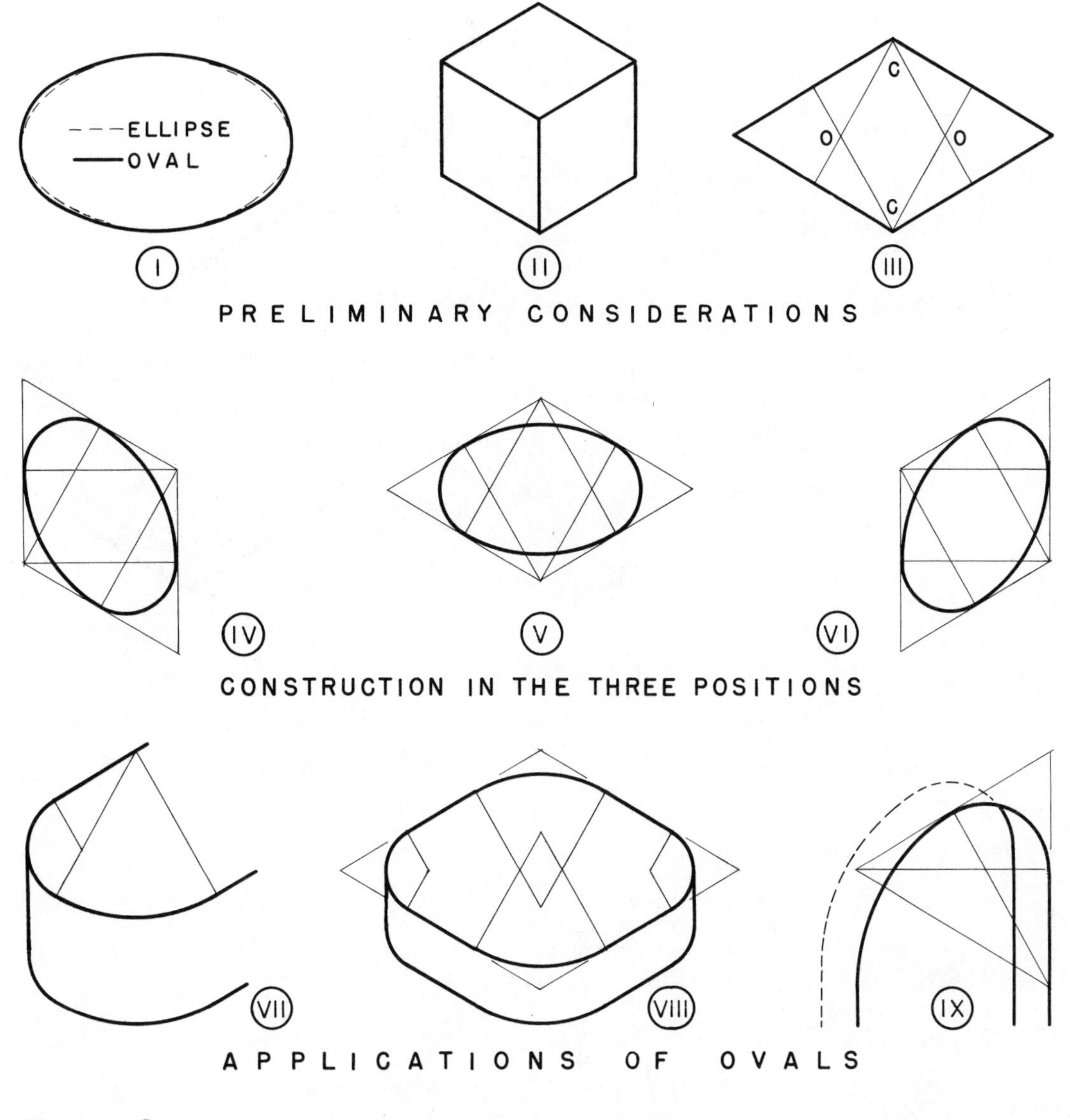

FIG-19 FOUR-CENTER OVALS IN ISOMETRIC

The four-center oval is an approximation of the shape of an ellipse. A comparison of the two shapes is given in Fig. 19 I. Since the four-center oval is drawn with the compass, it is much easier to draw than the ellipse, which has to be drawn freehand or in small parts with a french curve. To draw a four-center oval, first draw the tangent square, which will be a rhombus in isometric, Fig. 19 II; then draw a perpendicular from the midpoint of each side of the rhombus. These perpendiculars intersect in four points, which are the centers C, C and O, O for the arcs of the oval, Fig. 19 III. Two of these centers are always located at the corners of the rhombus. The arc drawn from each of the four centers stops at the midpoints of the sides of the enclosing rhombus. The completed oval and the construction lines for the isometric of a circle on each of the three typical planes is shown in Fig. 19 IV, V, VI. Extreme accuracy in drafting is essential in constructing four-center ovals. The draftsman should use a sharp pencil, draw fine lines, and be careful to draw exactly parallel to his triangle.

Uses of the four-center oval construction in drawing an arch on a wall, Fig. 19 IX, and of horizontal half ovals for a hemicylinder are shown in Fig. 19 VII. Figure 19 VIII shows the construction of quarter ovals, which are the isometric shapes of quarter circles at the corners of a square.

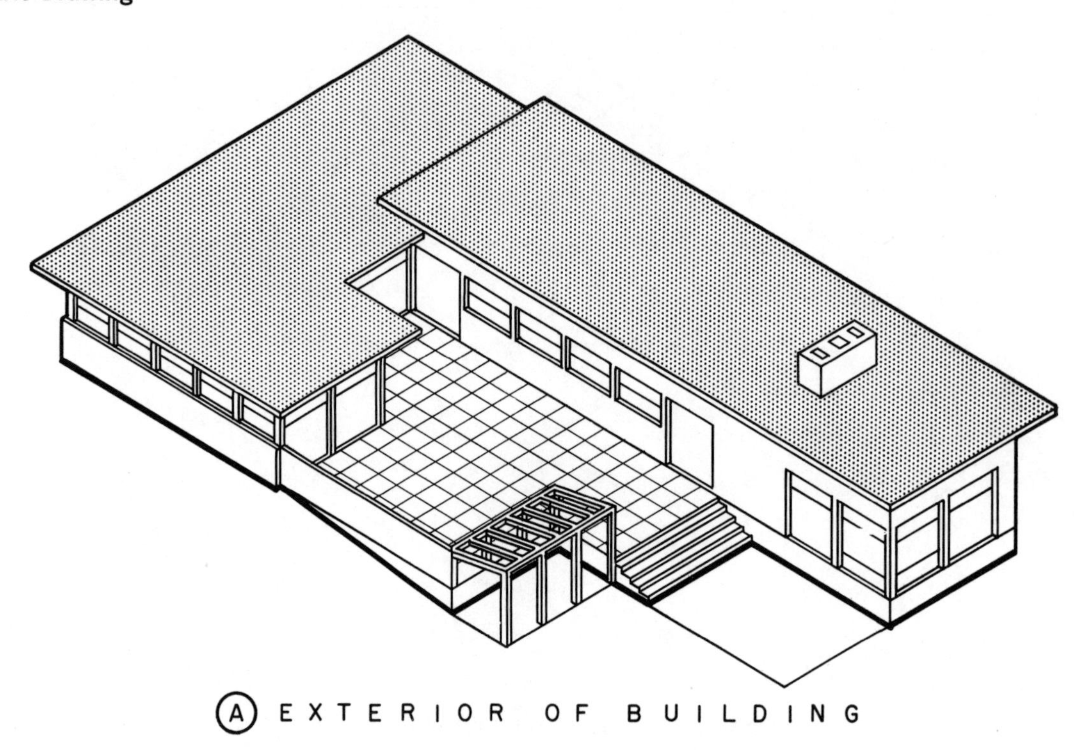

Ⓐ EXTERIOR OF BUILDING

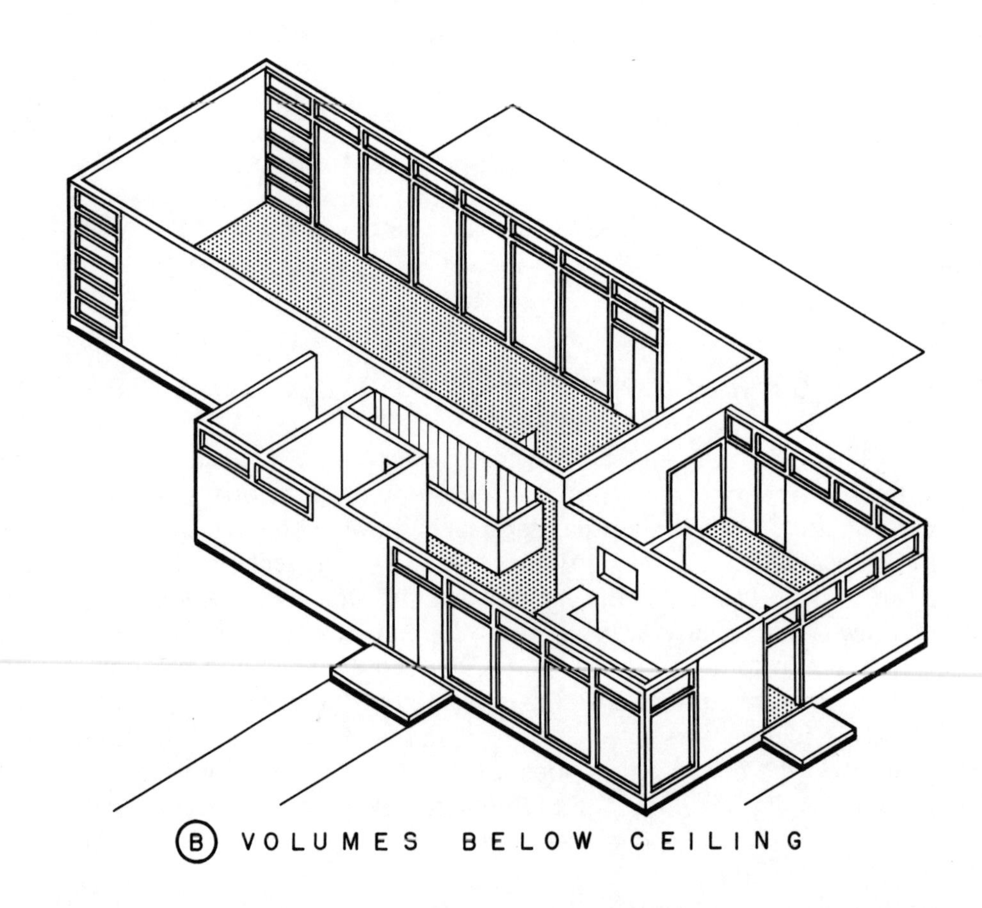

Ⓑ VOLUMES BELOW CEILING

FIG-20 EXAMPLES OF ISOMETRIC DRAWING

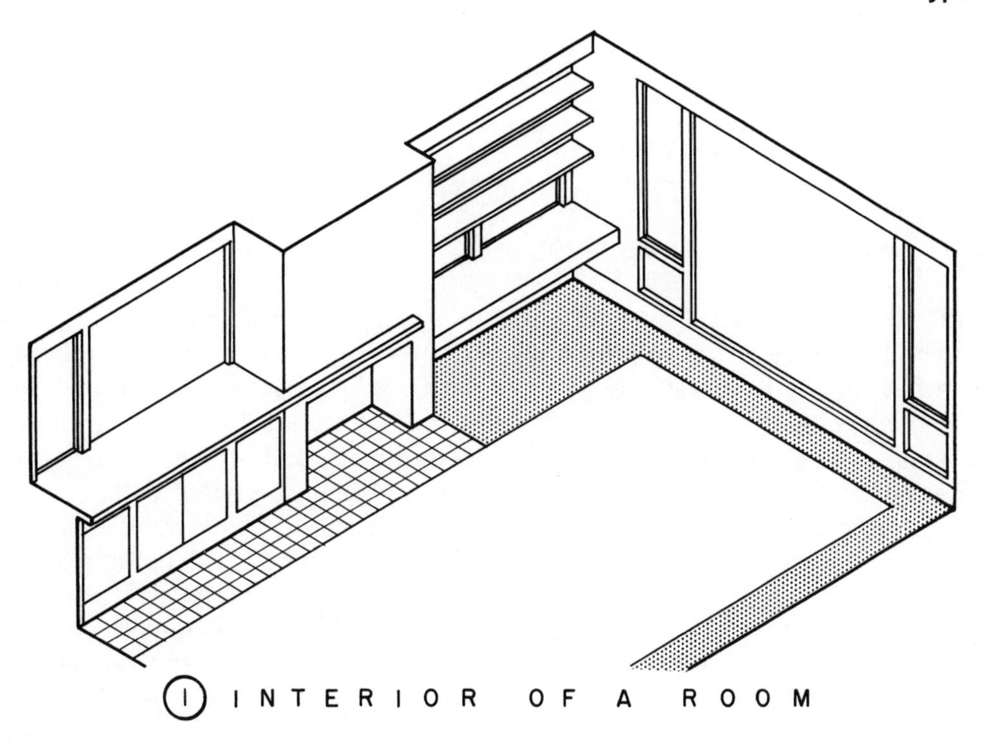

(I) INTERIOR OF A ROOM

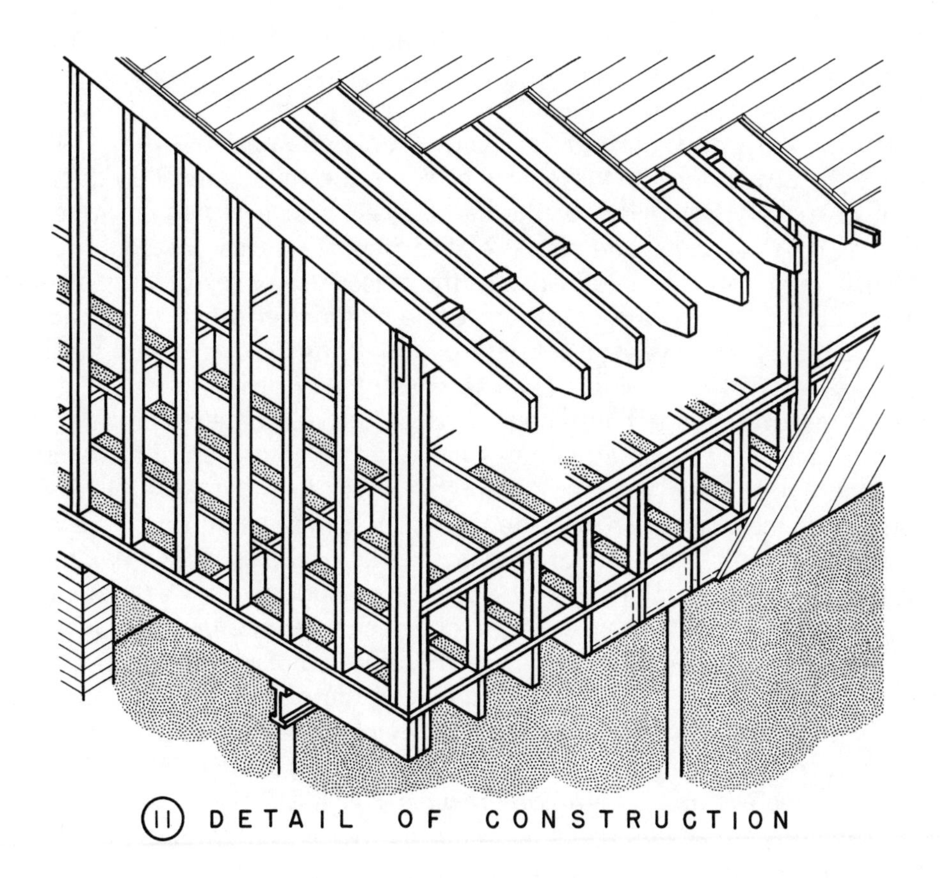

(II) DETAIL OF CONSTRUCTION

FIG-21 EXAMPLES OF ISOMETRIC DRAWING

CHAPTER 6
Dimetric Drawing

DIMETRIC DRAWING. That division of paraline drawing in which two of the three axes make equal angles with the picture plane and the third a different angle is dimetric drawing. Any position of the object which fulfills these requirements may be used in making a dimetric drawing.

Figure 22 1 shows a cube placed so that the top and bottom are horizontal and the two visible sides make equal angles with the picture plane. Imagine the cube to be rotated forward on a horizontal line which is parallel to the picture plane, thus keeping the sides always at equal angles to the picture plane, until the top is in a vertical position, Fig. 22 6. As the cube is rotated between these two positions the projections of its axes pass through all possible dimetric relations to each other. A few of the infinite number of possible dimetric positions obtained in this manner are illustrated in the left column of Fig. 22. The reader should visualize from these drawings the sequence of an unlimited number of views between the positions shown. In these illustrations the two equal axes are turned to make equal angles with a horizontal line. If one of these equal axes is turned vertically, then the axes to either side will be at different scales and at different angles with a horizontal line. Thus it is possible to use the same spacings of the axes that are shown in the left column and twist them to new positions with one of the two equal axes in a vertical position and get a new set of pictorial effects, such as are illustrated in the right column of Fig. 22. Dimetric drawings can then be made with the angles and scales giving either a symmetrical or an unsymmetrical arrangement.

Isometric drawing is rigid and inflexible. There is only one possible view of the three typical planes which meet in any corner of the object because the axes must be equally spaced. This view shows each of these visible sides at the same angle and gives equal importance to each, so that blank areas must be given the same relative importance as areas of greater interest. If the one possible isometric view of three planes of the object should give an unsatisfactory relation of lines or areas, nothing can be done to improve the pictorial effect of the given design.

Dimetric drawing's great variety of possible pictorial effects overcomes the following faults and shortcomings of isometric drawings. (1) The lines of a hip roof and of equal projections of the near corner form parts of one continuous vertical line in isometric drawing, Fig. 23A. This pictorial defect can be avoided in dimetric drawing by using the position of the axes, which causes the two sides of the object to be turned at different angles to the picture plane. (2) One of the three typical planes of the object can be emphasized in dimetric drawing by turning the object so that this plane is seen more directly and consequently occupies a greater proportionate area in the drawing, Fig. 23B. The emphasis on one plane and subordination of the other two can be in any desired ratio. (3) Two of the planes of the object can be emphasized equally and the third subordinated. Thus, it is possible to subordinate the roof or floor area and emphasize the walls or to subordinate one wall. Figure 23C gives an example of subordination of roof areas and relatively increased importance of wall areas. By showing less of the roof it is also possible to see more of the wall under an extending roof. (4) The unpleasantly rigid effect of wall planes at 45° in isometric drawing can be avoided in dimetric drawing, Fig. 23D.

Dimetric drawing has the advantage of allowing the choice of a symmetrical or unsymmetrical view of the object and emphasis on one or two of the three planes. It permits variation in the pictorial effect obtained, while isometric drawing is rigid and inflexible with no variation possible. A carefully chosen dimetric drawing usually gives the most pleasing results of any of the usable types of parallel-line pictorial drawing. It ranks next to perspective in desirability for presentation.

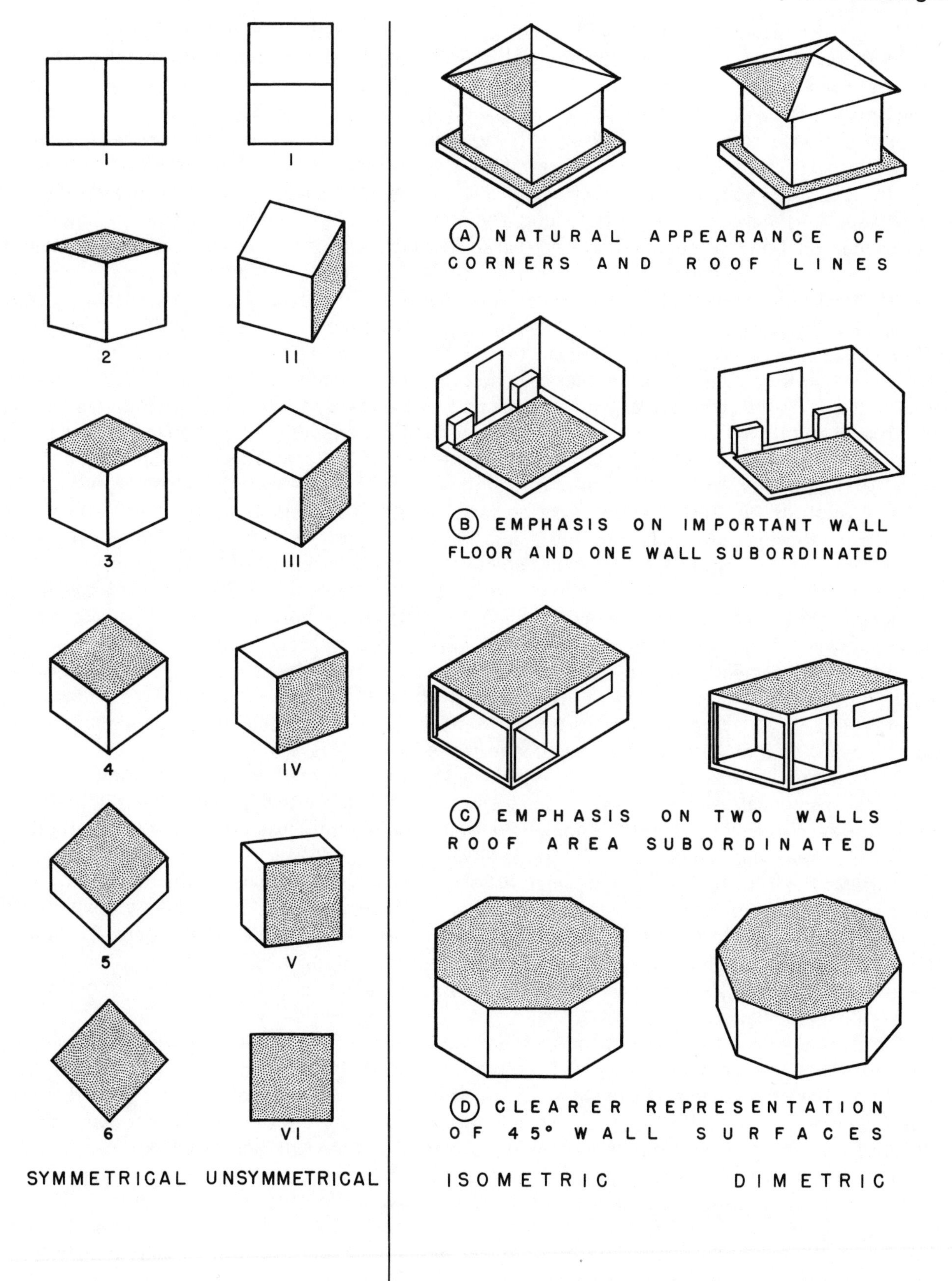

FIG-22 SCOPE OF DIMETRIC DRAWING

FIG-23 ADVANTAGES OF DIMETRIC DRAWING

DIMETRIC SCALES AND ANGLES. The two axes making equal angles with the picture plane in a dimetric drawing are foreshortened equally, while the third axis is foreshortened a different amount. Therefore two of the three axis lines of a dimetric drawing will be drawn at the same scale and the third at a different scale, Fig. 24A. The projections of the axes are so related that the angles a on each side of the axis V with the odd scale are equal, while the angle b between the two axes H having the same scale is a different size from the other two. Stated in a different way: the odd angle is between the two equal angles. There is a fixed relation of the angles and scales used in dimetric drawing. Thus, for a given scale relation there is only one spacing of the axes in their relation to each other, and vice versa. Throughout this discussion of dimetric drawing, the larger scale is assumed to be one and the smaller is expressed as a fraction.

POSITIONS OF THE AXES. One axis of a dimetric drawing is usually kept in a vertical position as shown in Fig. 24B, groups I and II. These figures give the possible basic variations of positions of the object with a vertical axis. However, they show only one of the infinite number of possible relations of area between the three planes. The block forms used can represent either exteriors or interiors. The effect with one axis horizontal can be obtained by turning the illustration sideways for groups I and II. The object can be turned with none of the axis lines either horizontal or vertical, group III, if the angles between the axes are made to suit the scales used. Such positions are rarely used, since they are difficult to understand.

The graph of Fig. 24C gives information for all possible combinations of angles and scales in dimetric drawing. The data for this graph were obtained by using the formula $\cos a = (-\sqrt{2H^2 - V^2})/2H$ in which a = one of two equal angles between projections of axes, H = one of two equal scales, and V = third scale. The angle A of the graph is a − 90°. It is the angle made by each of the two equal axes in a symmetrical dimetric with a horizontal line, Fig. 24A, and is the angle which would be most easily used in laying out a dimetric drawing.

It may be observed from inspection of the graph that when the two equal angles A are between 0° and 30°, the scale on the vertical axis is 1 and the scale on the other two axes varies from .71 at 0° to 1 at 30°. When the angles A vary from 30° to 45°, the scale on the single axis varies from 1 at 30° to 0 at 45° and the scale of the two equal axes is 1.

The graph gives the size of the two equal angles A for symmetrical dimetric drawing. When one of the two equal axes is vertical in unsymmetrical dimetric drawing, the other will make an angle A with the horizontal, and the angle B between the unequal axis and the horizontal will be 90° − 2A. Thus, when angle A is 12°, angle B will be $90° - 2 \times 12° = 90° - 24° = 66°$.

COMMON FRACTIONAL SCALES. Figure 24D gives drawings of cubes which show the proportions obtained with common fractional scale ratios. It repeats in a more directly usable form some of the information for scales and angles, which is also given in the graph of Fig. 24C. Since these scale relations often allow the standard architects' scale to be used for both scales, they are especially useful. The cubes which are shaded on all surfaces give three of the most useful angle and scale relations.

Dimetric drawing has some of the pictorial advantages of perspective drawing and some of the advantages of ease of construction of isometric drawing. However, dimetric drawings are not as easy to construct as isometric drawings. Throughout the entire range of angles used in dimetric drawing there is only one position of the axes which will allow the use of angles obtained with standard triangles to draw both sets of slanting lines. It is therefore necessary in most dimetric drawings to draw lines at angles which cannot be obtained directly with standard triangles.

Because of the use of odd angles and the use of two scales on the same drawing, dimetric drawings are somewhat more difficult to construct than isometric drawings. However, when efficient drafting methods are used, the work of making a dimetric drawing is not much greater than for an isometric drawing and considerably less than the work of making a perspective drawing. When special triangles are used in dimetric drawing, the work of making the drawing is decreased. Two adjustable triangles work very well for this purpose. They can be set to suit any drawing. Triangles made from sheet plastic for the correct angles can also be used.

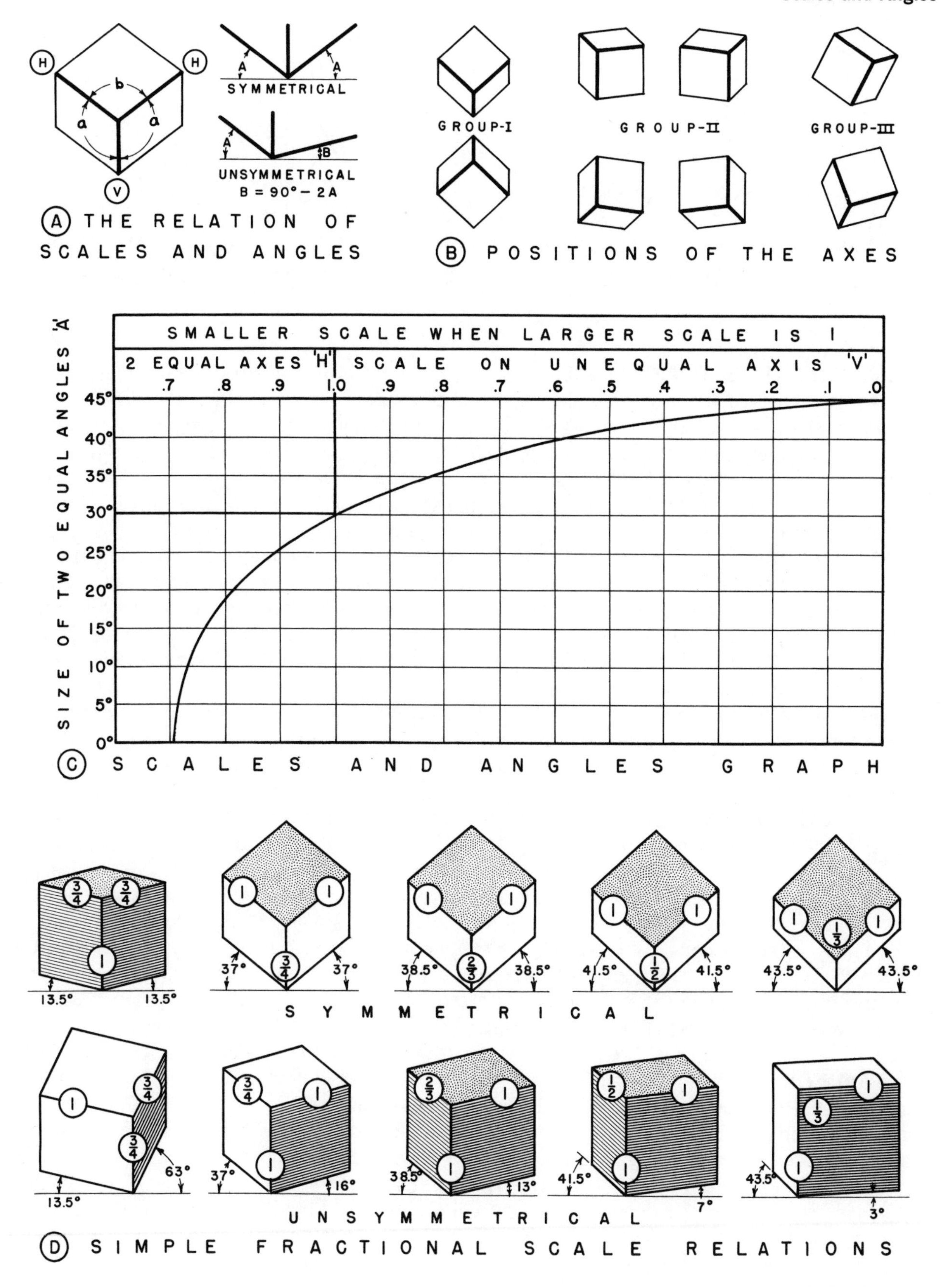

FIG-24 DIMETRIC SCALES AND ANGLES

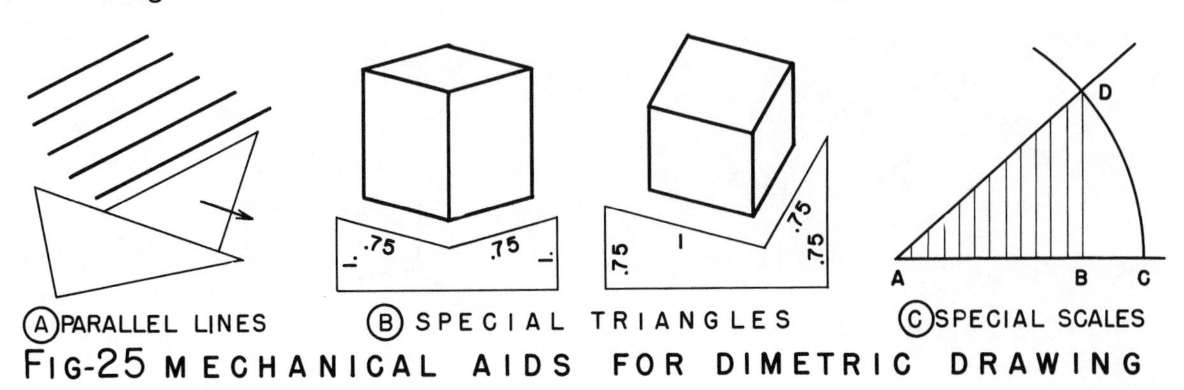

Ⓐ PARALLEL LINES Ⓑ SPECIAL TRIANGLES Ⓒ SPECIAL SCALES

FIG-25 MECHANICAL AIDS FOR DIMETRIC DRAWING

PARALLEL LINES AT ANY ANGLE. After the directions of the dimetric axes are laid out with a protractor, lines can be drawn parallel to the axes by the method of drawing parallel lines at any angle. This method, with which most draftsmen are familiar, is illustrated in Fig. 25A. The two triangles (or triangle and T-square) are held together at the edges and moved into position with one of the free edges of the triangle in line with the axis. When the triangle which has been aligned with the axis is moved along the stationary triangle (or T-square), its edge will always be parallel to the axis with which it was lined up. An adjustable triangle is easy to use for this purpose.

SPECIAL TRIANGLES. Two triangles can be combined for convenience so that it is not necessary to turn the triangle over on a given drawing. They can be made from standard triangles, thick cardboard, "pressedwood," transparent plastic, or other suitable materials. In the special triangles of Fig. 25B the relative scales are marked on the edges to be used for making the dimetric drawing. The first illustration of Fig. 25B shows a triangle to be used for a symmetrical dimetric drawing, and the second shows a triangle which is used for an unsymmetrical drawing.

SPECIAL SCALES. Whenever the scale relations for the proposed dimetric drawing cannot be obtained directly on the drafting scales at the desired size, a special scale can be made for one of the two scales to be used. Special scales can be made by the method of reducing and enlarging shown in Fig. 25C. To use this method, lay off horizontally from any point A the relative sizes A–B and A–C of the two scales in any unit of measure. Thus if the larger scale is 1 and the smaller $\frac{3}{4}$, then A–B is laid out as $\frac{3}{4}$ of A–C. From B draw a vertical line to meet at D an arc of radius A–C drawn from C with A as a center. Units of the larger scale laid off on A–D can be reduced to the correct size for the smaller scale by drawing vertical lines from points on A–D to meet line A–B. If the drafting scale is to be used for the smaller of the two scales, then lay off on line A–B the divisions of the smaller scale and enlarge them by drawing vertical lines to A–D to form the divisions of the larger scale. A special scale made in this manner can be transferred to a strip of paper to be used on the drawing as the drafting scale is used, or measurements can be transferred with dividers. When special scales are made in this way, one scale relation is as easy to use as another. Thus it is as convenient to use a ratio of 1 to $\frac{6}{10}$ as 1 to $\frac{1}{2}$.

MAKING A DIMETRIC DRAWING. Figure 26E, F, G, and H shows the procedure in making a simple dimetric drawing with the positions of the axes and scales as given in Fig. 26E. The methods of construction of curves and lines not parallel to the axes are the same in dimetric drawing as in isometric drawing. The four-center oval can be constructed only when the dimetric drawing of the square around the circle is an equal-sided quadrilateral (rhombus). The positions of the centers for the oval vary with the proportions of the rhombus as shown in Fig. 34C. If the acute angles of the rhombus are less than 60°, two centers are outside the rhombus; if more than 60° they are inside the rhombus. The centers are always found at the intersections of the perpendiculars drawn from the center points of the sides of the rhombus.

TRIMETRIC DRAWING. Since isometric and dimetric drawings are simpler and are satisfactory for most purposes, trimetric drawings are seldom used. Therefore, no explanation of them is given.

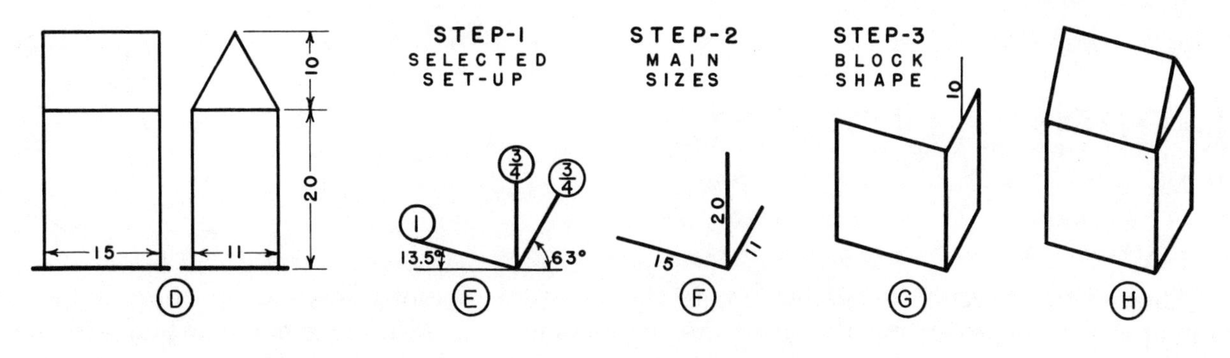

FIG-26 MAKING A DIMETRIC DRAWING

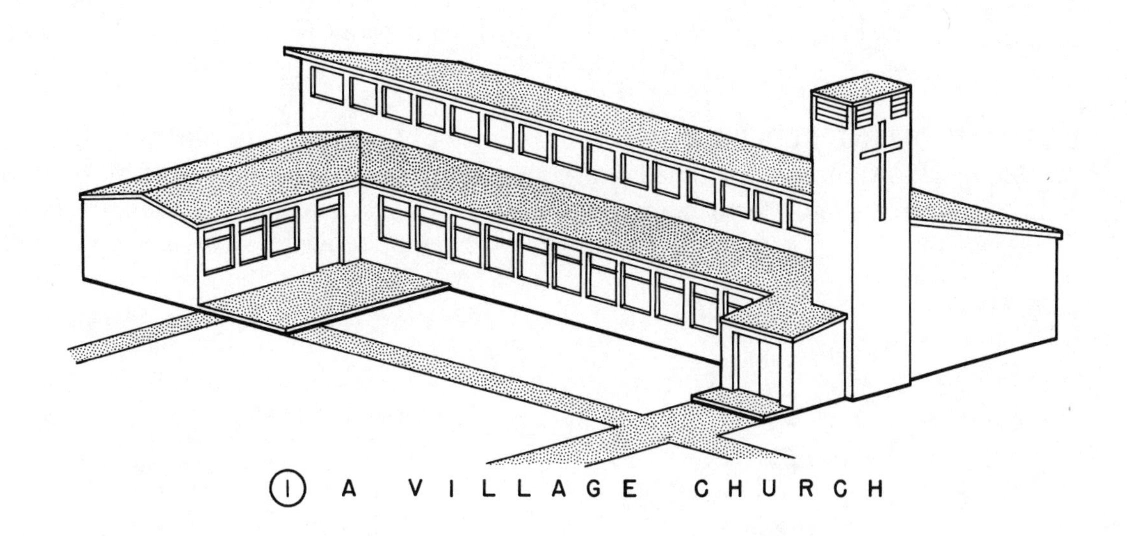

(I) A VILLAGE CHURCH

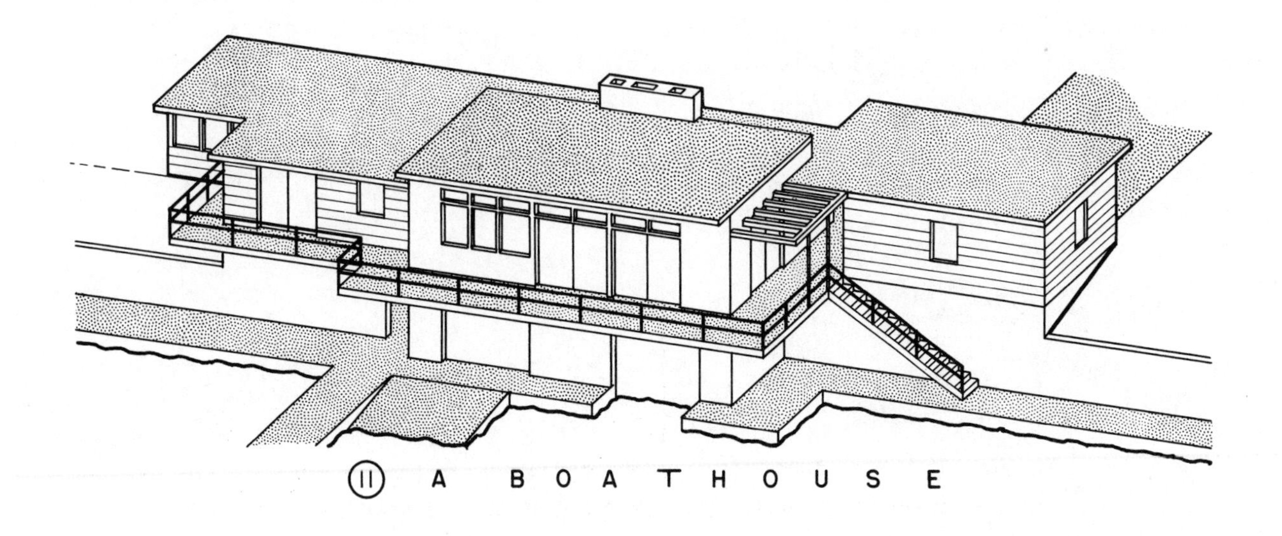

(II) A BOATHOUSE

FIG-27 EXAMPLES OF DIMETRIC DRAWING

CHAPTER 7
Oblique Drawing

In oblique projection the projectors are oblique to the picture plane and the object is turned with one of the typical planes parallel to the picture plane, Fig. 28A. In isometric and dimetric projection the projectors are perpendicular to the picture plane and the object has all three typical planes oblique to the picture plane. Thus, both the relation of the object to the picture plane and the direction of the projectors in oblique drawing differ from those of other paraline drawings. Although the drawings M and O of Fig. 28A may be considered oblique drawings, they are made with the projectors in planes parallel to one of the typical planes of the object and are neither good pictorial drawings nor characteristic oblique drawings. Drawing N shows the characteristic oblique drawing in which the projectors are oblique to the three typical planes of the object. Figure 28B shows these drawings as they would appear from in front of the picture plane or drawing.

THE LENGTH OF THE RECEDING LINES. The angle of the projectors with the picture plane determines the length of the receding lines of an oblique drawing. If the projectors make an angle of 45° with the picture plane, the receding lines will be projected in their true length. From the end b of a given receding line a–b, Fig. 28C, any number of projectors can be drawn making

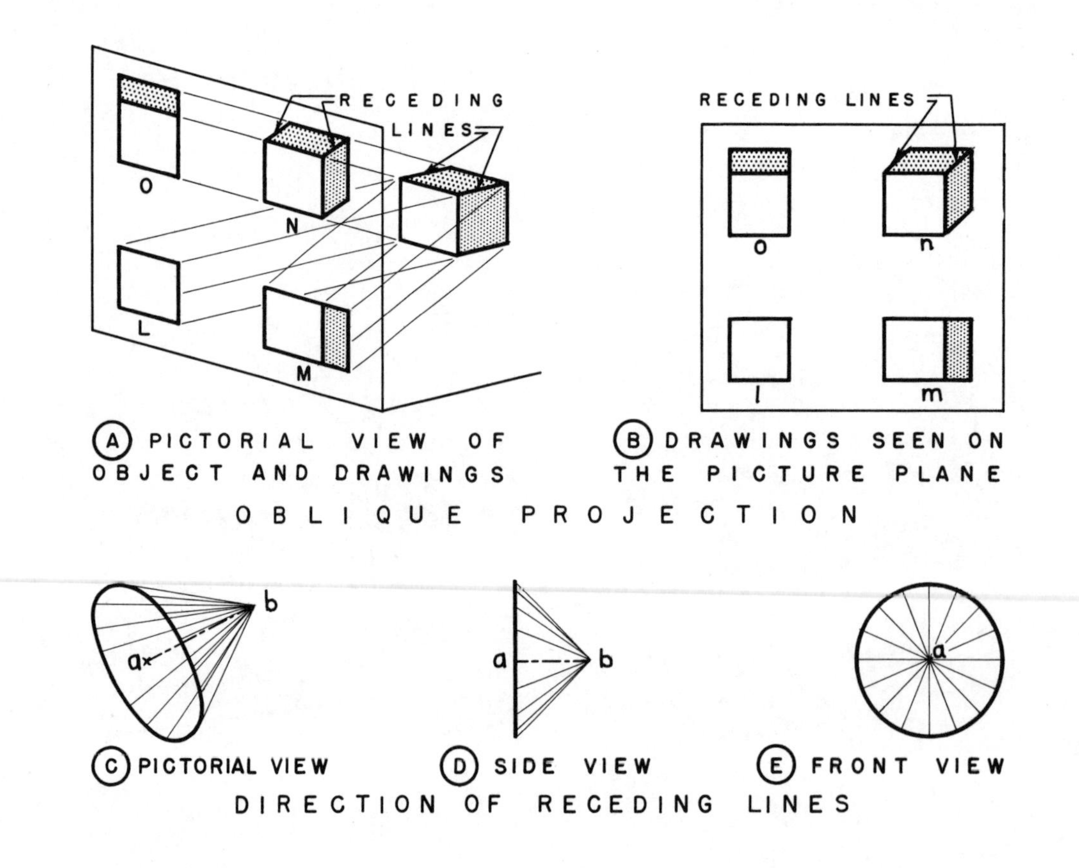

FIG-28 THEORY OF OBLIQUE DRAWING

an angle of 45° with the picture plane. The intersections of these projectors with the picture plane will form a circle with the end a of the line a–b as a center, and the projectors will form a right cone with b at the apex and a at the center of the base. The possible projections of the receding line a–b radiate in all directions from the end a of the line. Therefore a line can be drawn at any angle from a, Fig. 28E, to represent the receding line a–b in an oblique drawing, and the projection of the line a–b will be equal to the length of the line itself if the projectors make an angle of 45° with the picture plane. By varying the angle of the projectors with the picture plane the receding lines can be made larger or smaller than scale size.

TO MAKE AN OBLIQUE DRAWING. The block shown in the multi-view drawings of Fig. 29A is constructed in oblique drawing as follows: Step 1: Draw the horizontal and vertical axes and from their intersection lay out the receding axis at any desired angle. Step 2: Lay out the dimensions of the object on the axis lines. Step 3: Draw lines from the measurements to complete the drawing.

THE OFFSET METHOD. Measuring with the offset method is illustrated in the various steps in the construction of Fig. 29B. Usually most measurements on an oblique drawing can be made on lines parallel to the axes. However, the planes of the object which are parallel to the picture plane appear in their true shapes, and measurements can be made on them at any angle. Furthermore, any slanting lines which are parallel to the picture plane are drawn in their true directions and lengths.

TWO RULES OF OBLIQUE DRAWING. There are two rules of oblique drawing which should be followed when it is practical to do so, Fig. 29C. The rules are: (I) Turn the length of the object parallel to the picture plane. (II) Turn the most complex or characteristic face of the object parallel to the picture plane. The purpose of the first rule is to decrease the appearance of distortion by making the receding lines represent the short dimension of the object. The purpose of the second rule is to show the true shapes of characteristic forms of the object and simplify construction.

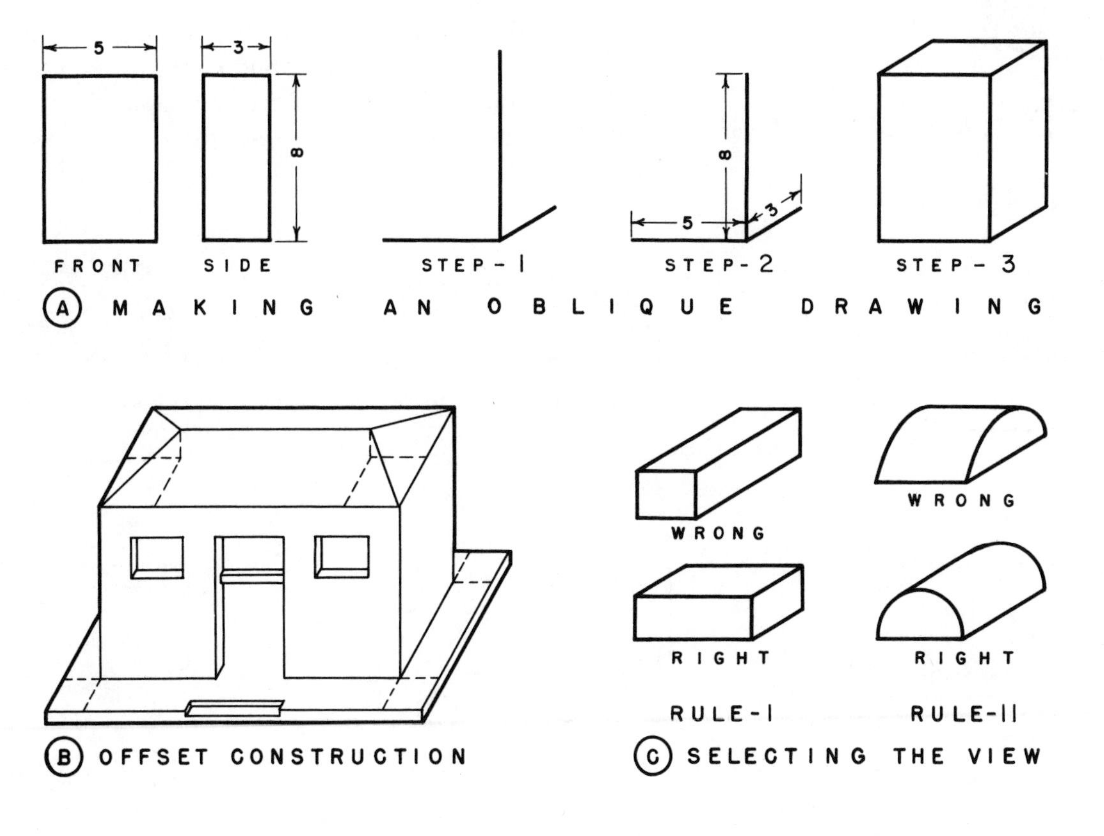

FIG-29 CONSTRUCTION OF OBLIQUE DRAWINGS

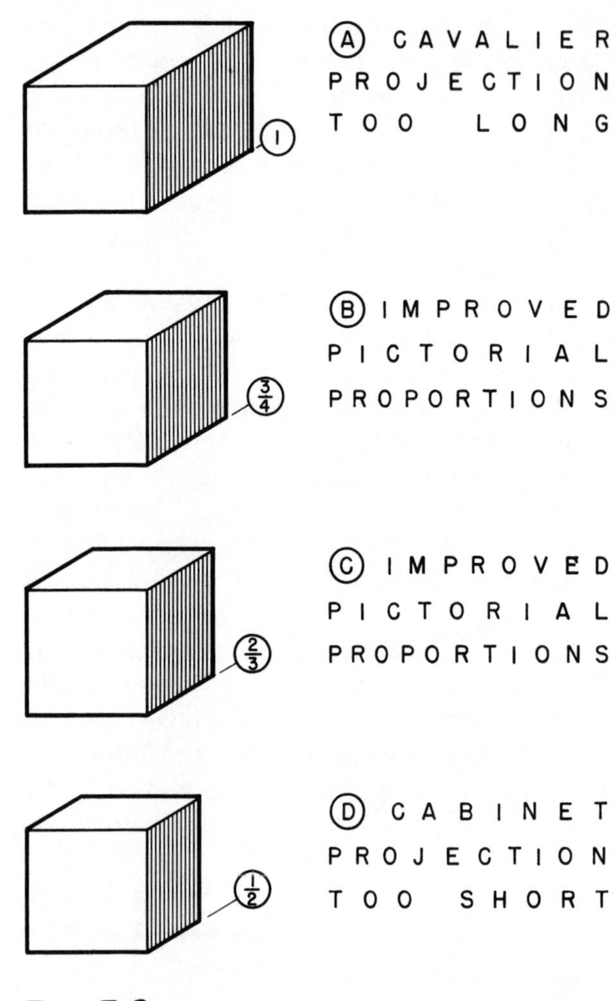

FIG-30 SCALE OF RECEDING LINES

THE SCALE OF THE RECEDING LINES. Since the projectors can be at any angle with the picture plane, the receding lines of an oblique drawing can be drawn at any scale. The four drawings of the cube in Fig. 30 show the effect of different scales for the receding lines on the proportions of the drawings. The receding lines of the cavalier projection, in which the same scale is used on all lines, appear to be too long. See also Fig. 29C. The cabinet projection, with half-scale on the receding lines, has gone too far in the other direction, making the receding lines appear too short and the object appear thin. When the scale of the receding axis is made $\frac{3}{4}$ or $\frac{2}{3}$ of the scale of the other two axes, the proportions of the drawings are better. Cavalier projection has the advantage of simplicity of construction. The use of $\frac{3}{4}$ or $\frac{2}{3}$ scale on the receding lines gives a better picture.

THE DIRECTION OF THE RECEDING LINES. Since the receding axis of an elevation oblique drawing can be drawn in any direction, it is possible to secure a great variety of pictorial effects. Figure 31 shows three variations of direction of the receding lines for an exterior and an interior, and suggests some of the possible pictorial variations in oblique drawing. Either one of the oblique planes can be subordinated and the other emphasized, or both can be made of equal importance.

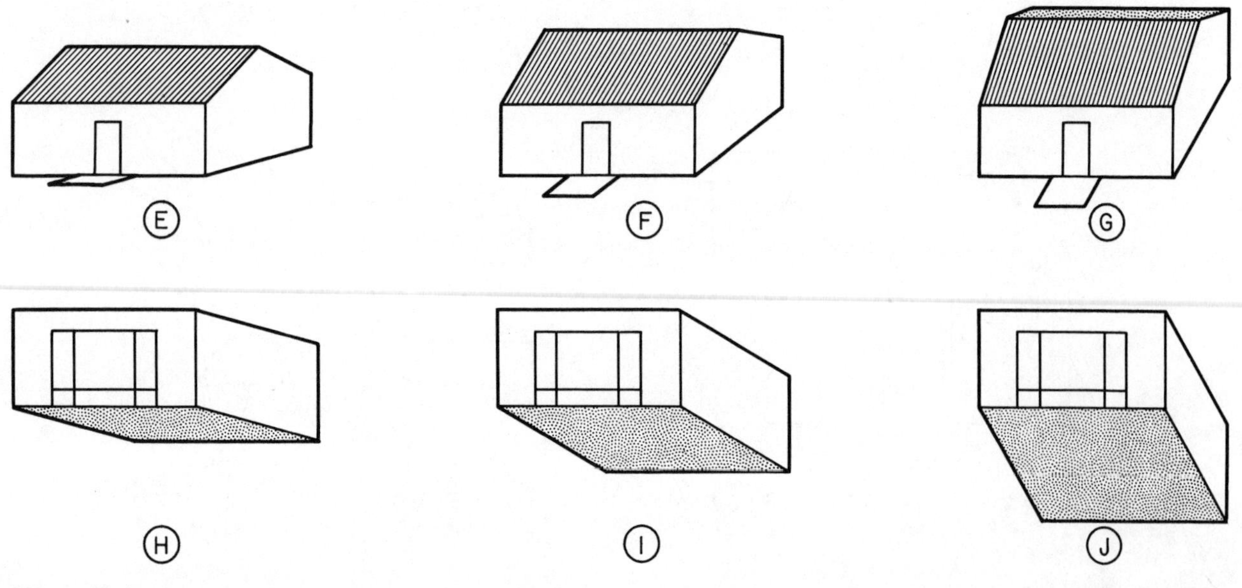

FIG-31 EFFECT OF DIRECTION OF RECEDING LINES

POSITIONS OF THE AXES. In all the preceding illustrations of oblique drawing one axis has been horizontal and another vertical. However, the axes may be turned in any position if two of the three are kept at 90° with each other. In Fig. 32 I one axis is vertical and another horizontal. In II the receding axis is horizontal. In III none of the axes is vertical or horizontal. In IV the receding axis is vertical. Drawings in which one set of elevation planes are true shape may be called *elevation oblique drawings,* and those in which horizontal areas are true shape *plan oblique drawings.*

The plan oblique axis position shown in Fig. 32 IV is often used in drawing pictorial views in which it is advantageous to have the picture plane horizontal and parallel to the floor plane. This position of the axis allows all horizontal areas to appear in their true forms. The floor areas of Fig. 33 are true shape and the horizontal semicircles of Fig. 33 VI are drawn with the compass. For either interior or exterior designs having horizontal, circular, or other complex forms this arrangement of the axes is to be recommended for simplicity of construction and for clearest representation of the shapes. With the oblique axis vertical, the other axes must be at 90° with each other but may be turned in any desired position. The receding lines (vertical) should be drawn at $\frac{2}{3}$ or $\frac{3}{4}$ scale.

(I) ELEVATION PLANE TRUE SHAPE ELEVATION OBLIQUE

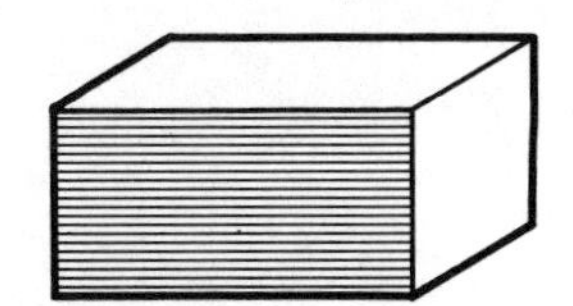

(II) END TRUE SHAPE RECEDING LINES HORIZONTAL

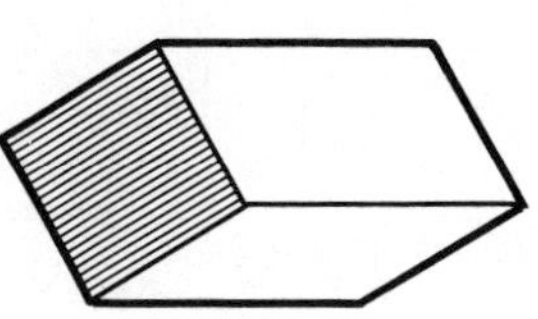

(III) INCLINED OBJECT ALL OF AXES OBLIQUE LINES

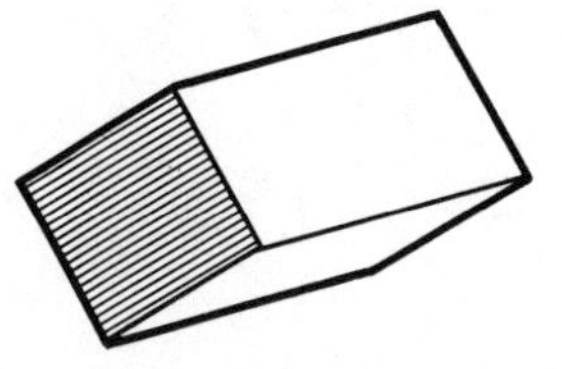

(IV) PLAN PLANE TRUE SHAPE PLAN OBLIQUE

FIG-32 POSITIONS OF THE AXES

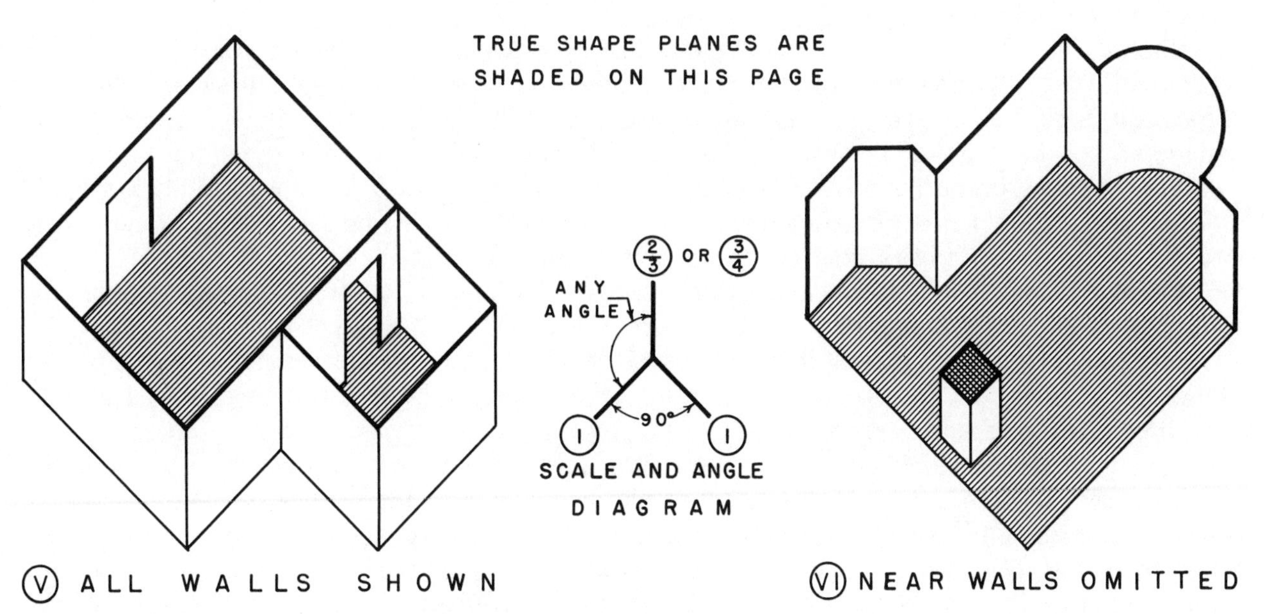

FIG-33 INTERIOR SHAPES IN PLAN OBLIQUE DRAWING

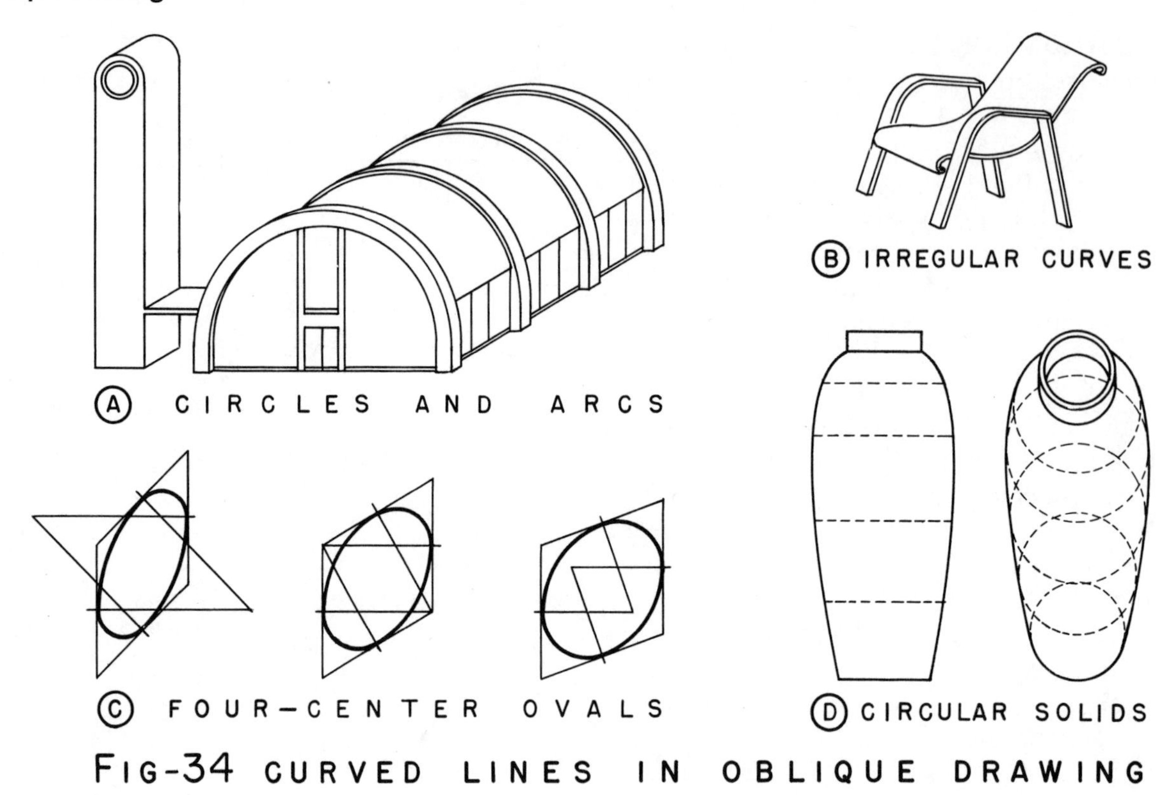

FIG-34 CURVED LINES IN OBLIQUE DRAWING

CURVED LINES. In oblique drawing curves are drawn in their true shapes when they are in planes parallel to the picture plane. Therefore the circular forms of Fig. 34A appear circular. They are constructed by locating their centers by the offset method and drawing with the compass. Irregular curves, such as those of Fig. 34B, can be drawn from multi-view drawings by tracing and transfer methods, if desired, when they are in planes parallel to the picture plane and appear in their true shapes. When irregular curved lines are not in planes parallel to the picture plane, their positions may be located by the offset method or the cross section paper method as illustrated for isometric drawing on page 22.

Circles which are not parallel to the picture plane are ellipses in oblique drawing. They may be worked out by plotting points by the offset method as shown in isometric drawing. When the same scale is used on all axes, the tangent square around the circle is an equilateral parallelogram (rhombus) and the four-center oval may be used. The positions of the centers for the four-center oval vary with the proportions of the rhombus as shown in Fig. 34C, but they are always found at the intersections of the perpendiculars to the midpoints of the sides. When a different scale is used on the receding lines, the four-center oval cannot be used.

Circular solids, such as vases and balusters, can be worked out in oblique drawing by finding a number of circular sections through the object. The outline of the object surrounds all of these sections and is tangent to each of them. When the axis of the object is perpendicular to the picture plane, the circular sections are parallel to the picture plane and are drawn as circles, Fig. 34D.

Oblique drawing is the most artificial of all types of pictorial drawing in its theory of projection. The observer is supposed to be looking in the direction of the projectors which are oblique to the picture plane; yet, the planes of the object which are parallel to the picture plane are drawn as they would be in multi-view drawing, in which the projectors are perpendicular to the picture planes. When the same scale is used on all axes, the distortion in oblique drawing is greater than in any other type of drawing. In spite of all of its faults, the advantages of showing true shapes in one set of planes makes oblique drawings very convenient and useful.

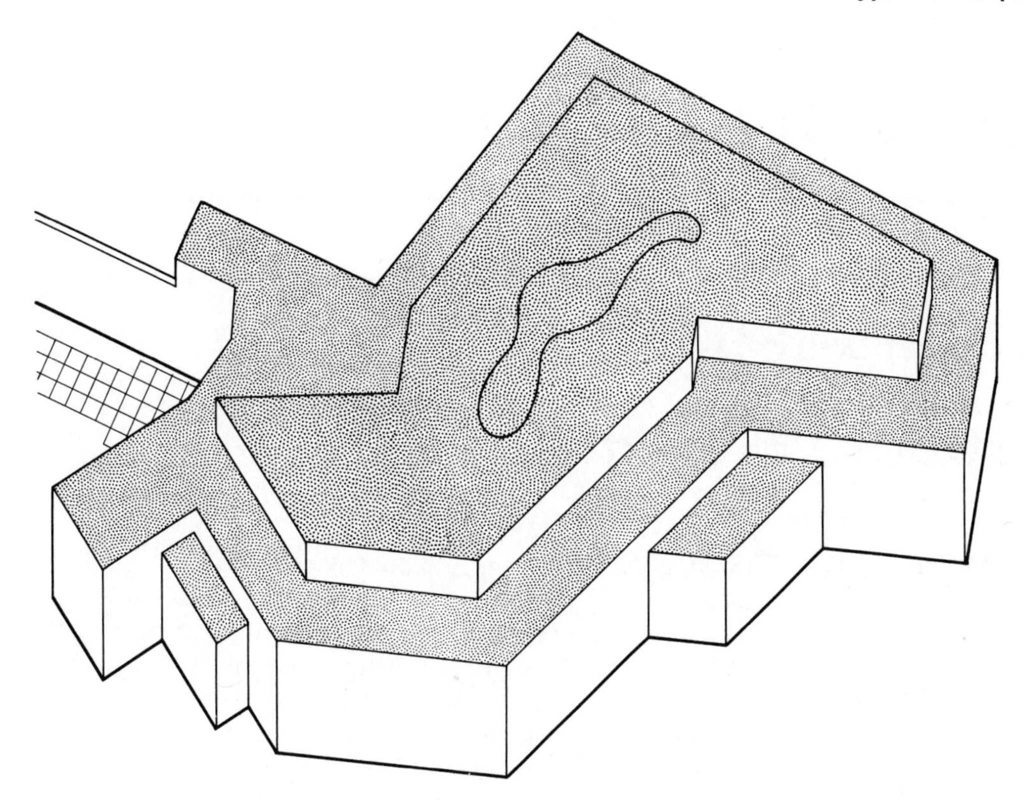

(I) PLAN OBLIQUE OF AN AQUARIUM

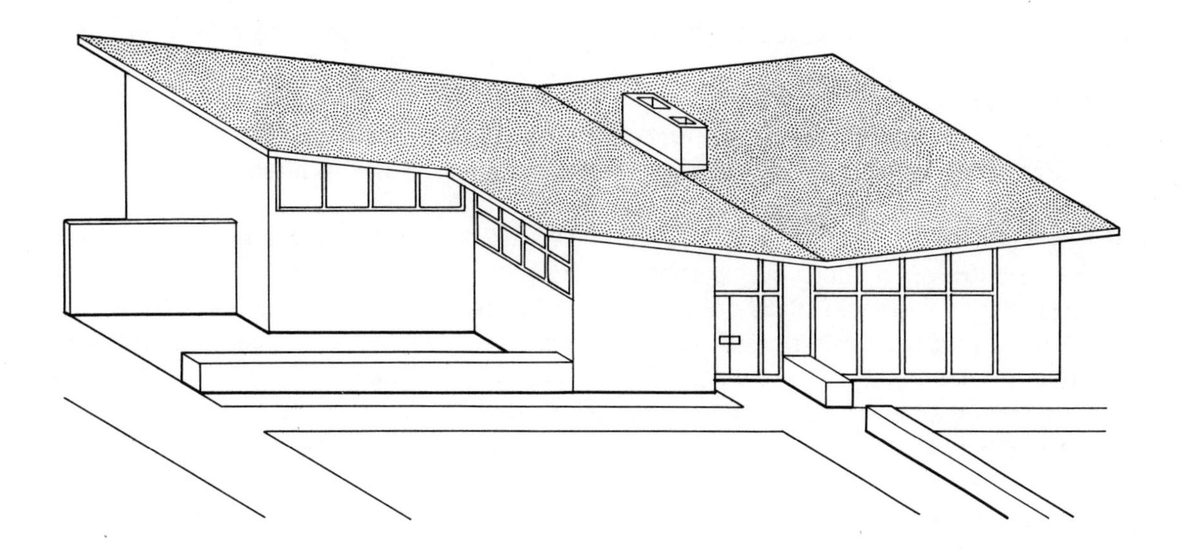

(II) ELEVATION OBLIQUE OF A RESTAURANT

FIG-35 EXAMPLES OF OBLIQUE DRAWING

PART THREE
Perspective Drawing

CHAPTER 8
Characteristics of Perspective Drawings

USE AND VALUE OF PERSPECTIVE DRAWING. Perspective drawing is essential in the work of the architect, interior decorator, industrial designer, and illustrators of all kinds because it is the only type of drawing which represents an object in the natural and pleasing way that it would actually appear to the eye. In all other types of pictorial drawing all parallel lines are drawn parallel and produce the illusion of becoming farther apart on the more distant parts of the object.

It is difficult for the average person to visualize a design from the plans, elevations, and sections of multi-view drawings, Fig. 36. Anyone can more readily understand a photograph or perspective drawing. Perspective drawing is therefore of great importance to the architect, since it presents his designs in a way which can be easily understood by his clients and avoids the distortions and unreal effects of other types of pictorial drawing.

Even the person who is trained in reading plans and elevations understands a design better in perspective. The architect often makes a number of perspective studies so that he may more clearly understand how his design would actually appear from different viewpoints and be able, consequently, to make a better design. Some architects design in perspective, others make perspective studies and renderings as a check after the design has been carefully worked out in elevations, plans, and sections. Practically every architect uses perspective drawings as an important part of his work.

In brief, perspective is of value to the architect for (1) drawings which can be easily understood, (2) an accurate method of studying and perfecting designs, (3) explanatory sketches and for rendered presentations.

THOROUGH TRAINING IN PERSPECTIVE DRAWING. Training in making perspective drawings should be sufficiently thorough so that the draftsman is able to make a good perspective. A perspective is a true picture of the object when it is made correctly. However, there are good and bad pictures, and good and bad perspectives. Not every person with a camera and film takes good pictures, nor does every person who is equipped with a knowledge of the elementary mechanics of making a perspective drawing make good perspectives. In both cases the well-trained person has a much better proportion of successes. The expert photographer seldom takes a bad picture and the expert draftsman with a comprehensive knowledge of perspective seldom makes a poor drawing, because he knows how to adjust the variables in a perspective setup to get the view he wishes to get.

CHARACTERISTICS OF PERSPECTIVE DRAWINGS. A perspective drawing represents the object as it would appear to the eye from a certain position. Often lines and areas of the object do not appear in their true shapes, sizes, or directions. A familiarity with some of the more common phenomena of perspective will help the draftsman understand how the lines and areas of an object should appear in perspective. The following paragraphs discuss some of the more common characteristics of perspective drawings and their variations from drawings of other types.

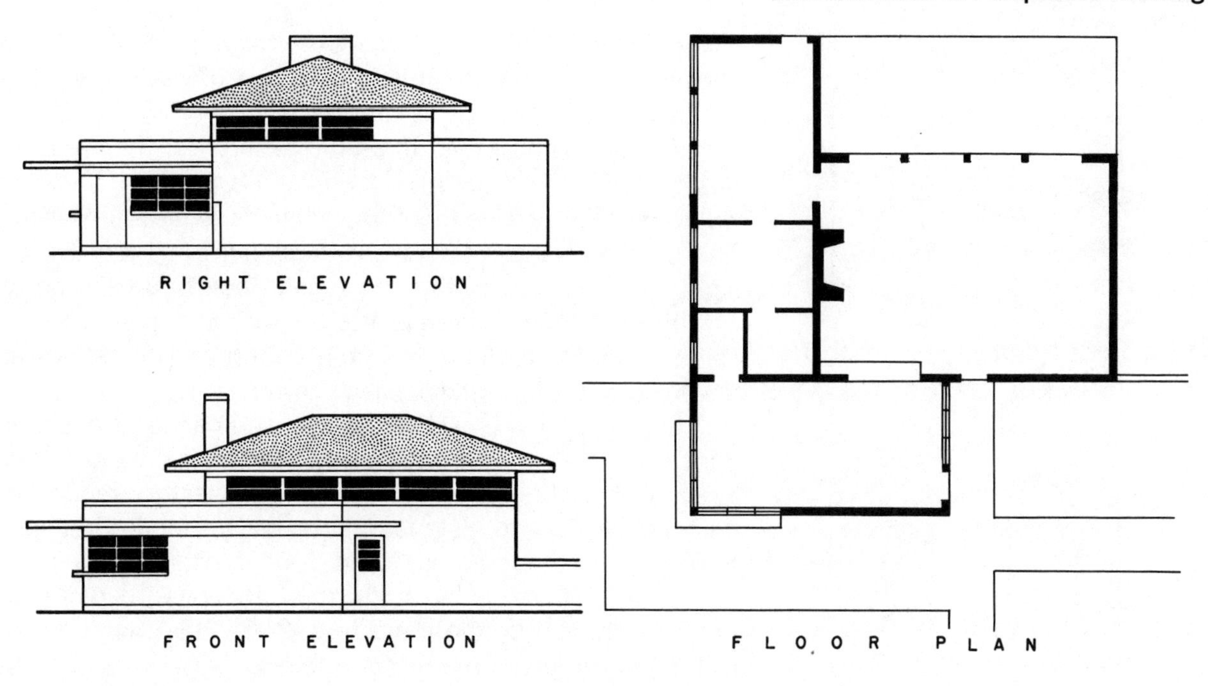

(A) MULTI-VIEW DRAWINGS

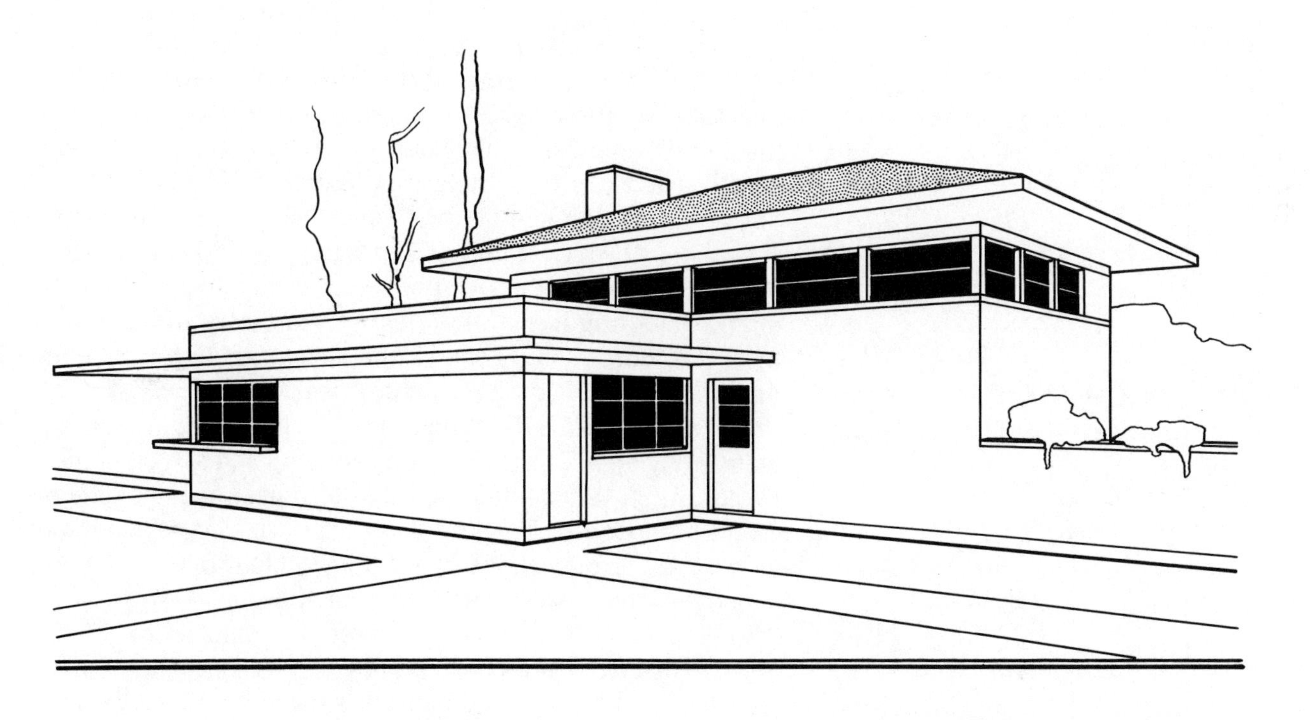

(B) PERSPECTIVE DRAWING

FIG–36 MULTI-VIEW AND PERSPECTIVE DRAWING

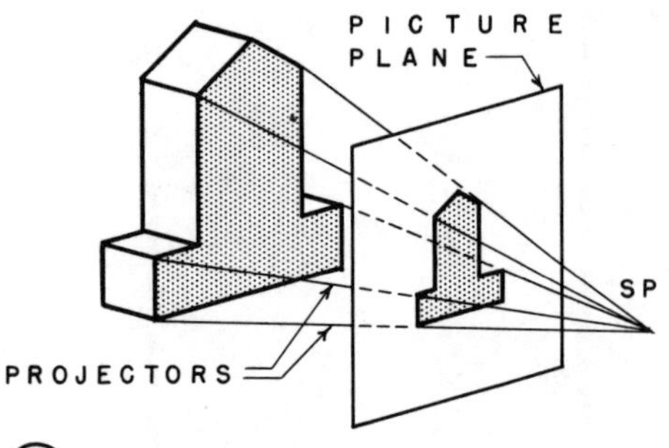

Ⓐ CONVERGING PROJECTORS IN PERSPECTIVE

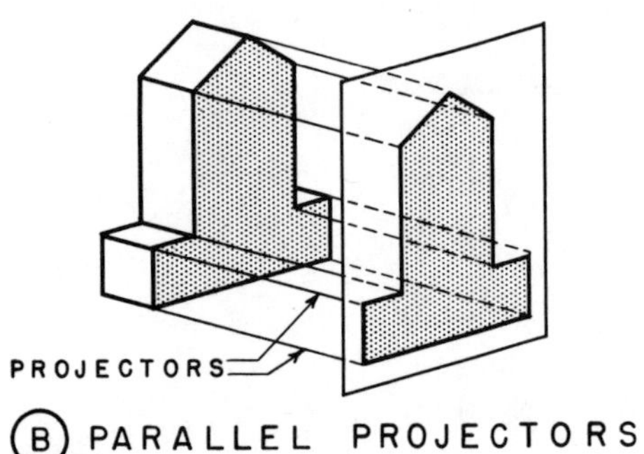

Ⓑ PARALLEL PROJECTORS IN ALL OTHER DRAWING

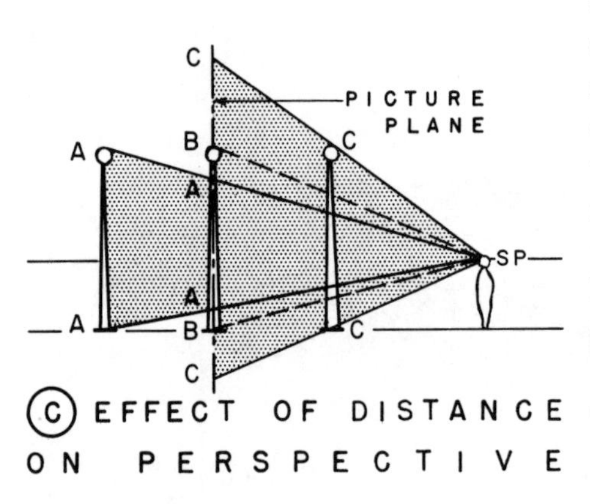

Ⓒ EFFECT OF DISTANCE ON PERSPECTIVE

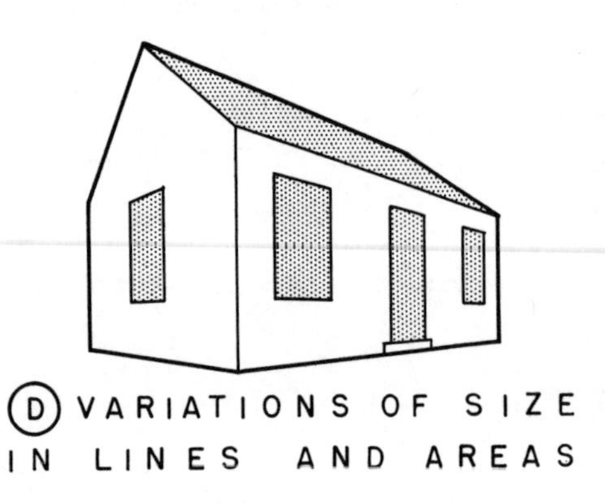

Ⓓ VARIATIONS OF SIZE IN LINES AND AREAS

FIG--37 PHENOMENA OF PERSPECTIVE DRAWING

PROJECTORS. In perspective drawing the projectors converge to a station point (SP) instead of being parallel as they are in all other types of drawing, Fig. 37A and B. This station point is assumed to be the position of the eye of the observer and consequently the position from which the object would be seen just as the perspective drawing represents it. The perspective projectors are then the imaginary lines of sight from the eye of the observer to points on the object. The intersections of these projectors with an imaginary plane called the picture plane give points through which lines are drawn to make the perspective drawing.

SIZES. In a perspective drawing sizes are shown as they appear to the eye from the position of the station point, not as they actually are. The converging projectors reduce the perspective sizes of distant objects, causing them to appear to be smaller than identical objects nearer the picture plane, A–A, Fig. 37C. Objects in front of the picture plane are enlarged in size by the projectors, C–C. Only the lines B–B in the picture plane *are drawn to their scale sizes.* Therefore, parallel lines representing the same actual size are often of varying lengths in a perspective drawing. The heights and widths of all the windows in the perspective drawing of Fig. 37D are actually the same. Yet they are represented by different sizes because that is the way they would appear to the eye from the chosen station point. The windows appear smaller in size and area as the distance from the SP increases. The three visible corners of the walls all represent the same height, but they vary greatly in actual size in perspective because their distances from the SP vary. They do not appear to be equal when seen from the station point. The angle at which a line or surface is seen also influences the size shown in the perspective drawing. In Fig. 37D the nearest slanting line of the main roof appears to be shorter than the more distant one in the visible gable because the line of sight from the SP is more nearly parallel to it.

MEASUREMENTS. Since lines of equal length on the object may appear in an infinite variety of sizes in a perspective drawing, it is seldom possible to measure sizes directly on the perspective. The determination of sizes, and especially of heights, is one of the most difficult features of making a perspective drawing. Any lines of the object which lie in the picture plane can be measured to scale. Parts of the object in front of the picture plane will be larger than scale size. Parts in back of the picture plane will be smaller than scale size, Fig. 37C. The various methods of perspective drawing obtain this correction of sizes in different ways.

SHAPES. In multi-view drawing the object is represented as it is. In perspective drawing the object is represented as it appears to the eye. Areas and angles usually do not appear in perspective as they really are. Rectangles and squares are often drawn as irregular quadrilaterals with four unequal sides and four unequal angles. A right angle seldom appears as such in a perspective, but is drawn as an acute or obtuse angle. A circle usually appears as an ellipse in perspective. Figure 38 I shows three cubes in perspective. All of the sides of the cubes are actually squares, yet none of them is drawn as a square. The largest cube has the tangent circles drawn in each of the three visible sides. These circles appear as ellipses of various proportions.

HORIZONTAL SURFACES. The horizon is at the level of the station point in a perspective drawing. The eye looks up at things above the horizon and down on things below the horizon. Horizontal surfaces above the horizon (eye level) are visible from below and horizontal surfaces below the horizon, such as steps and walks, are visible from above. Thus, both the ceiling and floor of a porch or room may be seen in the same perspective drawing, if the horizon line is located at some position between the floor and ceiling, Fig. 38 II. Contrast this with multi-view drawing, in which all horizontal surfaces appear as straight lines in elevations and sections, and with paraline drawing in which either top or bottom surfaces may be shown, but not both.

The size of a horizontal area in a perspective drawing depends on the distance and angle from which it is seen. With the area at a constant horizontal distance from the station point; a given horizontal area appears as a line when the area is at the level of the horizon and increases in visible size with its distance above or below the horizon, Fig. 38 III. When the height of a horizontal or vertical area is constant, its visible size increases as it approaches the station point and diminishes as it recedes farther from the station point, Fig. 38 IV; except that whenever the line of vision passes through the plane of a surface, the surface is always seen as a line. As an example; any horizontal plane at the level of the horizon would always appear as a straight line.

LINES PARALLEL TO THE PICTURE PLANE. These lines retain their true direction in perspective. Thus, horizontal and vertical lines parallel to the picture plane remain respectively horizontal and vertical in perspective. Sets of parallel lines which are parallel to the picture plane remain parallel in perspective just as they do in multi-view drawings: Fig. 38 II, vertical lines; Fig. 38 IV, horizontal and vertical lines. However, the length of the parallel lines in perspective varies with the distance from the picture plane.

LINES NOT PARALLEL TO THE PICTURE PLANE. In perspective each set of parallel lines which is not parallel to the picture plane converges to its vanishing point, Fig. 38 III and IV. In all other types of drawing, parallel lines are always drawn parallel regardless of their direction. The vanishing points of all sets of horizontal lines are located on the horizon, which is always on a level with the eye of the observer, the station point.

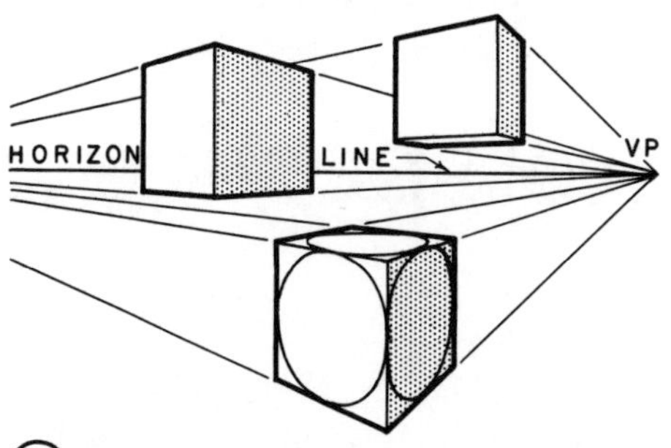

(I) APPEARANCE OF SHAPES OF AREAS AND MASSES

(II) HORIZONTAL AREAS IN PERSPECTIVE

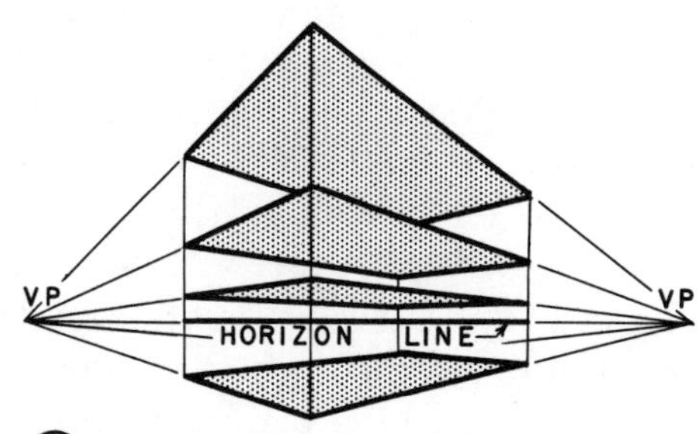

(III) EFFECT OF HEIGHT ON HORIZONTAL AREAS

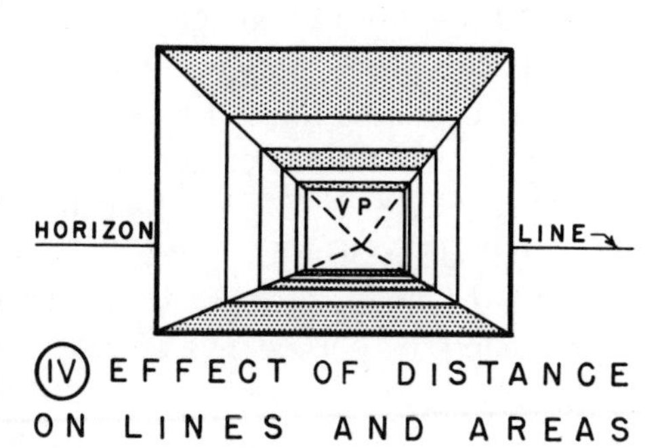

(IV) EFFECT OF DISTANCE ON LINES AND AREAS

FIG-38 PHENOMENA OF PERSPECTIVE DRAWING

CHAPTER 9
Perspective Systems and Methods

SYSTEMS OF PERSPECTIVE DRAWING. There are three systems of perspective drawing, which are classified according to the relation between the object and the picture plane and the resulting number of vanishing points for the three sets of typical lines. Most buildings have three sets of planes which are illustrated by a box. One of these sets of planes is horizontal (top and bottom). The other two are vertical and at right angles to each other. These planes meet in the three sets of typical lines, of which one set is vertical and the other two horizontal and at right angles to each other.

In the parallel or one-point perspective system one set of planes and two sets of lines of the object are parallel to the picture plane. In most cases the vertical lines and one set of the horizontal lines are parallel to the picture plane, Fig. 39A. Lines of these two sets remain respectively vertical and horizontal in perspective, Fig. 39B. The remaining set of horizontal lines is perpendicular to the picture plane and converges to a vanishing point.

In the angular or two-point perspective system the object is turned with both sets of horizontal lines at an angle to the picture plane, as shown in the plan of Fig. 39C. There are therefore two vanishing points, one for each of these sets of horizontal lines, Fig. 39D. Since the vertical lines are parallel to the picture plane, they remain vertical and parallel in the perspective.

In the oblique or three-point perspective system the object is turned, or the picture plane is tilted, so that none of the three sets of typical planes and lines of the object is parallel to the picture plane, as shown in the plan of Fig. 39E. Since all three sets of lines are at an angle to the picture plane, there are three sets of converging lines and three VPs, Fig. 39F.

The three vanishing points of the typical sets of lines are the only ones mentioned in this discussion of systems of perspective drawings. However, vanishing points of other sets of parallel lines are sometimes useful. Their location and use will be explained later.

IMPORTANCE OF ACTUAL DRAFTING IN LEARNING PERSPECTIVE DRAWING. The making of actual drawings is an important part of the study of perspective. Reading and study alone will not make the draftsman an expert in perspective drawing. Therefore, in addition to studying the various perspective methods described in the following pages, it is essential that the student make several perspective drawings to help him understand the subject.

Even greater accuracy is required in perspective than in any other type of drawing. The long construction lines and indirect construction methods demand accurate work. There are often very small spaces in a perspective drawing. If these small spaces are made too large, the design may appear to be heavy and coarse. If they are omitted, the effect of pictorial accuracy may be lost.

Some people have the faculty of knowing as each line is drawn on the perspective whether it is in the right place or not. This ability to visualize the appearance of the developing object and to detect errors is of great help to the draftsman.

THE USE OF MULTI-VIEW DRAWING IN MAKING A PERSPECTIVE DRAWING. In all methods it is common practice to use multi-view drawings to provide the design and size information from which the perspective of the object is to be made. It is therefore necessary to have a sufficient number of plans, elevations, and sections of the object to describe the parts which are to be shown in the perspective. A thorough understanding of multi-view drawings and the ability to visualize the object from such drawings are essential prerequisites to the study of perspective drawing. It is impossible to learn perspective drawing without understanding the drawings from which perspectives are made. In some perspective methods multi-view drawings are used for the actual construction of the perspective.

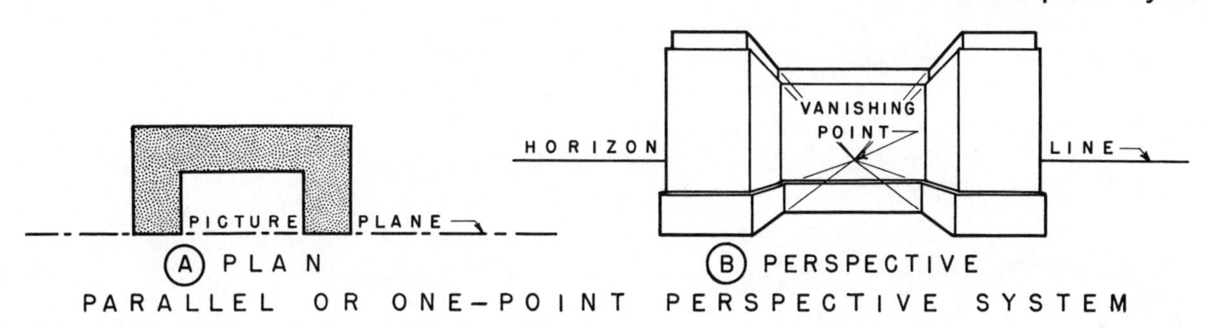

PARALLEL OR ONE-POINT PERSPECTIVE SYSTEM

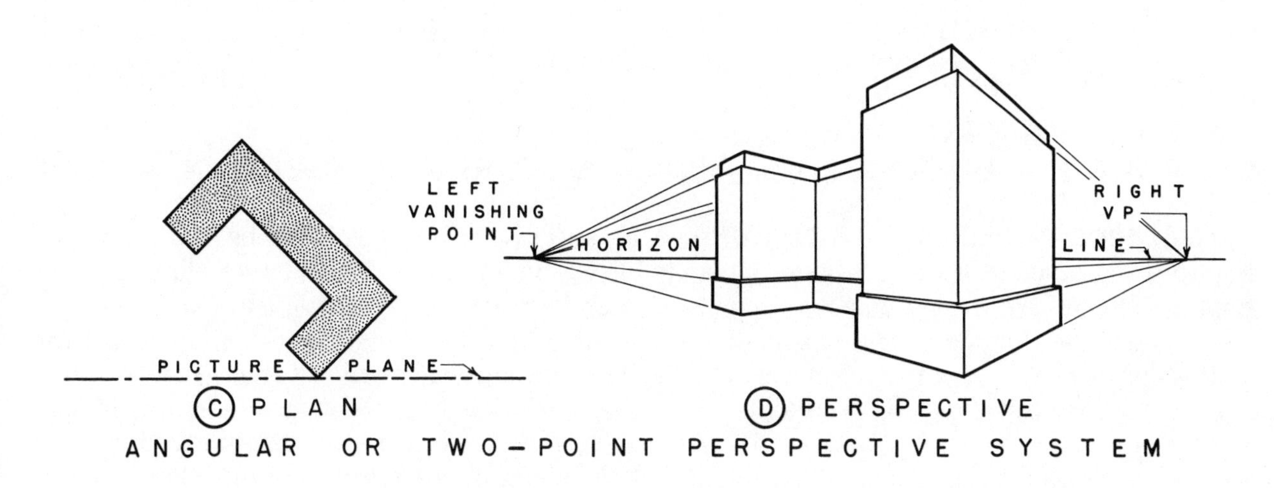

ANGULAR OR TWO-POINT PERSPECTIVE SYSTEM

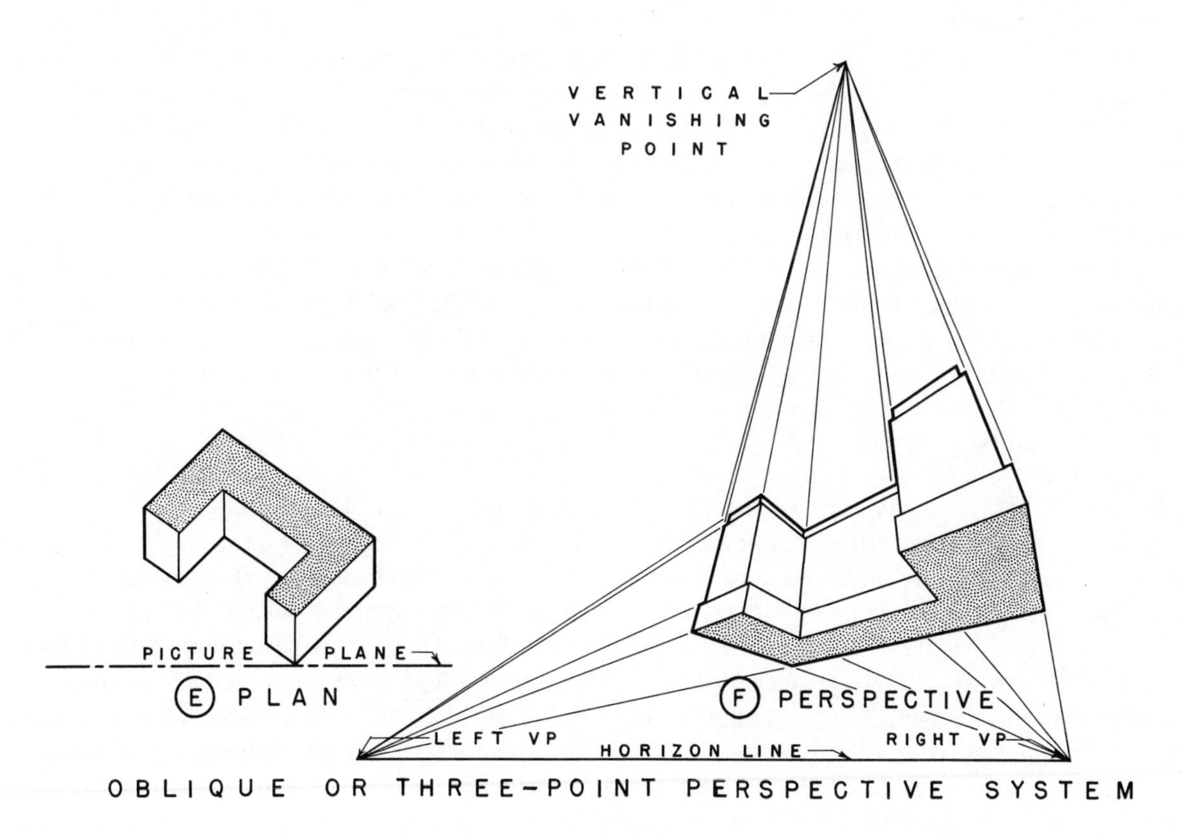

OBLIQUE OR THREE-POINT PERSPECTIVE SYSTEM

FIG-39 THE THREE PERSPECTIVE SYSTEMS

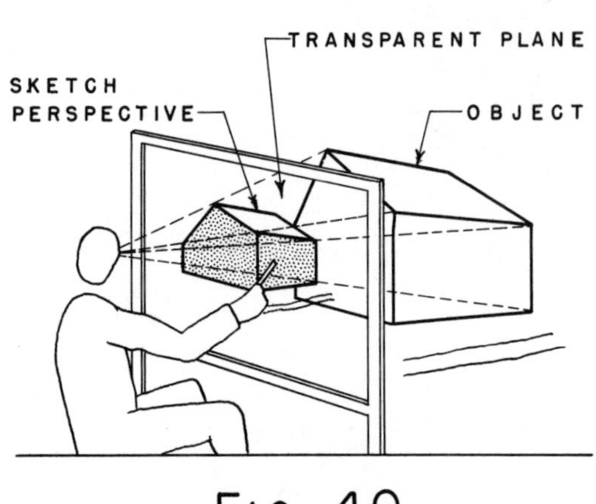

FIG-40
SKETCHING A PERSPECTIVE

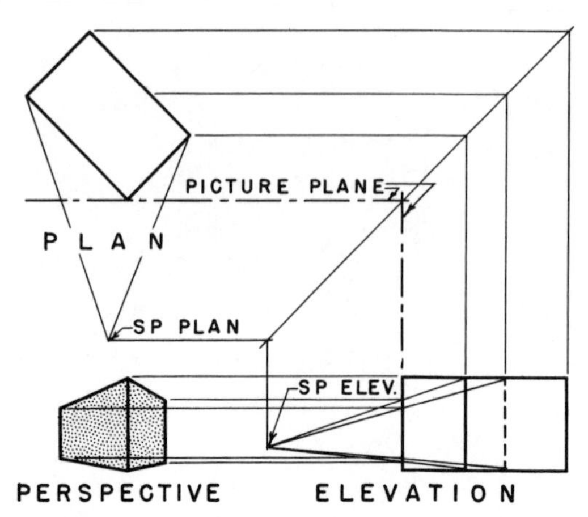

FIG-41
DIRECT PROJECTION METHOD

METHODS OF PERSPECTIVE DRAWING. A perspective of an object can be sketched on a picture plane made of a sheet of glass in the following manner: Place the picture plane at arms length, keep the eye in one position, and draw lines to exactly cover the lines of the object as seen through the stationary picture plane, Fig. 40. A window glass makes an excellent picture plane for this purpose. Whenever the object is not conveniently located, when greater accuracy is required, or when there is no existing object but only the drawings of some proposed structure, it is necessary to use some other method of making the perspective. The various drafting methods of making perspective drawings are based on this method of sketching the perspective of an existing object on a transparent plane.

A perspective drawing is made by working out by one of the drafting methods the positions of the lines of the object as they would appear on a given picture plane from a given station point. Three of these mechanical methods of constructing perspective drawings, (1) the direct projection method, (2) the perspective plan method, and (3) the common method, are widely used. These methods are described in a general way in the following paragraphs and are explained in detail in the chapters on one- and two-point perspective.

The direct projection method has the simplest theory of any method of perspective drawing. Plan and elevation views parallel to the picture plane showing the object, picture plane, and station point are first drawn, Fig. 41. The converging projectors are then traced to the picture plane in plan and elevation. Points on the perspective drawing are located from their heights, which are determined from the projectors in elevation, and widths, which are determined from the projectors in plan. The drawings are so arranged that the heights can be carried across horizontally with the T-square and the widths brought down vertically with the triangle to their positions in the perspective from the intersections of the projectors with the picture plane.

The direct projection method is a good method for one-point perspective because the auxiliary drawings used are the plan and elevations, or sections. These drawings are easily understood by the draftsman and are often available at the correct scale. In two-point perspective one or two special drawings are required for the direct projection method. These drawings are auxiliary elevations or sections from a corner (parallel to the picture plane) and are more difficult to construct and understand than the ordinary elevations and sections. If this method is used without vanishing points, very slight inaccuracies will change the directions of short lines and produce a warped effect. This method requires a great deal of space on the drafting board and many construction lines. Vanishing points will simplify the construction and increase accuracy.

The perspective plan method, Fig. 42, allows the entire perspective to be constructed from measurements made in the picture plane and brought into correct perspective sizes and positions by tracing lines to their vanishing points. The plan is first drawn in perspective. The vertical lines

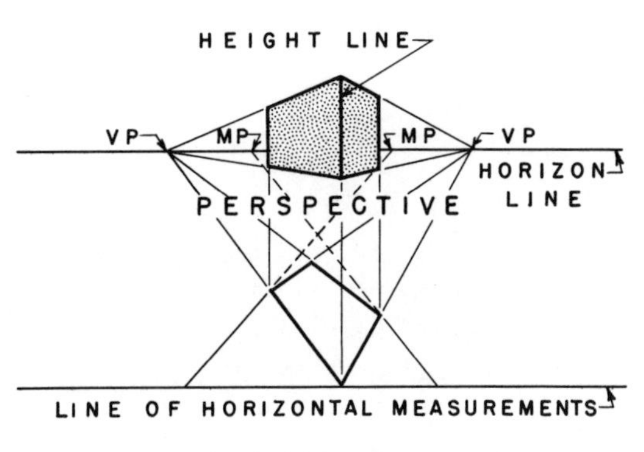

FIG-42
PERSPECTIVE PLAN METHOD

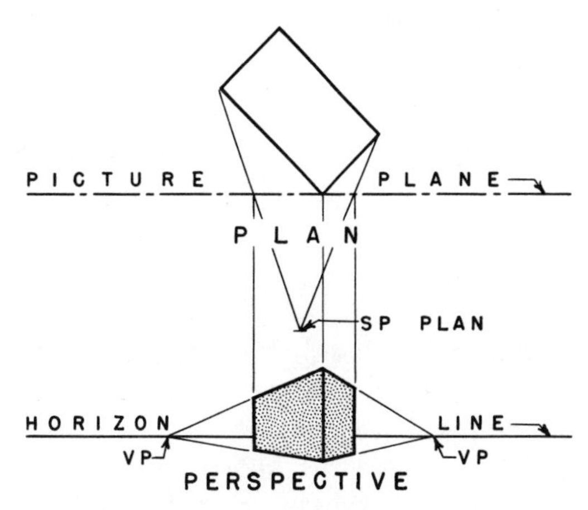

FIG-43
COMMON OR OFFICE METHOD

of the perspective drawing are then obtained by drawing vertically from the perspective plan. The scale heights are laid out on any convenient vertical line in the picture plane, from which they can be traced by lines toward the vanishing points into their correct perspective positions.

Since this method divides the construction into two steps, the construction lines are easier to trace to the perspective. In addition to the vanishing points of the sets of typical lines not parallel to the picture plane, the perspective plan method requires one or more measuring points to be used in drawing the perspective plan. A measuring point is the vanishing point for the set of parallel lines, which transfers scale measurements of horizontal dimensions from the horizontal measuring line to a base line of the perspective plan. The location and use of measuring points is explained under one- and two-point perspective.

The perspective plan can be drawn at any convenient height either above or below the perspective drawing. It can be placed on a plane of the perspective, such as the floor of an interior or ground plane of an exterior. It is practical and sometimes convenient to use more than one perspective plan for tall buildings. The perspective plan method requires less space on the drawing board than any other widely used method and is considered the best method by some expert draftsmen.

The common method is also called the office method and the mixed method. It combines the plan construction for horizontal spacing of vertical lines of the direct projection method and the height construction of the perspective plan method, Fig. 43. It is widely used in offices and schools. One reason for its popularity is that plans and elevations which are available at the correct scale may be attached to the drawing board and used as auxiliary drawings for the perspective.

CHOOSING A METHOD. Each of these methods of making perspective drawings has advantages and disadvantages. Some problems are more easily solved by one method, some by another. This is partly due to the varying nature of designs, and partly because of the information furnished by available drawings of the object of which the perspective is to be made. All accomplish the same result—a true picture of the object from some chosen position. The draftsman will find perspective drawing more easily understood if he learns thoroughly one of the methods explained in the following pages before studying other methods. It is possible to make any perspective drawing by any one of the methods described. The student may therefore learn only one of the three methods given for one- or two-point perspective.

It is the writer's opinion that the "common method" of one- and two-point perspective and the "direct projection method" of one-point perspective are most easily understood by the beginner. The perspective plan method is preferred by some expert draftmen, but is not so easily understood by the novice. In the following discussions of two-point and one-point perspective the methods are explained in the order of greatest usefulness to beginners.

CHAPTER 10
Two-Point Perspective

Two-point perspective is the most widely used of the three perspective systems. It is typical of the way in which buildings are usually seen and of photographs of buildings. It is therefore of greatest importance to the architect and draftsman. When only one kind of perspective is to be learned, two-point perspective is in most cases the one.

THE COMMON METHOD. The most popular and most widely used method of two-point perspective is called the common method. In this method, Fig. 44C, the plan of the object, picture plane, and station point is used to work out the horizontal spacing of points and vertical lines for the perspective. The plan is turned with the line of the picture plane horizontal. It is convenient to have an elevation at one side of and below the plan. From this elevation the heights can be carried across with the T-square to the construction for the correct heights for the perspective. Any elevation, or section, or part of either drawing which gives all of the heights necessary to construct the perspective drawing will serve for this purpose. Although it is not necessary to have an elevation or section included in the construction, its use makes the construction more easily understood, decreases the chance of error in working out heights, and makes the checking of construction easier.

THE CONSTRUCTION OF A SIMPLE TWO-POINT PERSPECTIVE. The construction by the common method has been divided into a series of steps in the explanation of the following paragraphs and illustrated in Fig. 44A, B, and C. These steps are typical of the procedure followed in this method of two-point perspective.

The auxiliary drawings are a plan and elevation. The plan of the object, picture plane, and station point is drawn with the picture plane line horizontal, Fig. 44A. The elevation is drawn and the horizon line and ground line placed to suit it. The horizon line is at the height of the eye of the observer. The ground line is drawn at the bottom of the elevation. The station point should be on a line perpendicular to the picture plane which is approximately through the center of the plan.

The vanishing points are located on the horizon line in the following manner, Fig. 44B. From the station point SP lines are drawn parallel to the two typical sets of horizontal lines of the plan to meet the picture plane. From these intersections, A and B, vertical lines are drawn to the horizon to locate the two vanishing points, VL and VR. All of the horizontal lines of the object which are parallel to the line SP—A in plan vanish in VL in the perspective drawing. Likewise, all of the horizontal lines of the object which are parallel to the line SP—B in plan vanish in VR in the perspective drawing.

Making the perspective requires the use of a plan and elevation. The horizontal spacing of all points and vertical lines of the perspective drawing is obtained from the plan. This is done by drawing lines from the necessary points on the plan toward the station point to meet the picture plane, then drawing vertical lines from these intersections to the perspective, Fig. 44C.

Since the nearest corner C—D of the wall is in the picture plane, its height is laid out to scale by drawing horizontal lines from the top and bottom of the wall in elevation to the line of the corner in the perspective. From these height measurements lines are drawn to VR to locate the top and bottom of the right side. Likewise, lines are drawn to VL to locate the lines of the left side.

The illustrations of Fig. 44A, B, and C show the elementary principles of two-point perspective by the common method. Additional information is necessary to enable the draftsman to make perspectives of more complex shapes under varying conditions. The remaining pages of this chapter and other succeeding chapters on perspective drawing give information which will provide material for a working knowledge of the mechanics and theory of perspective drawing.

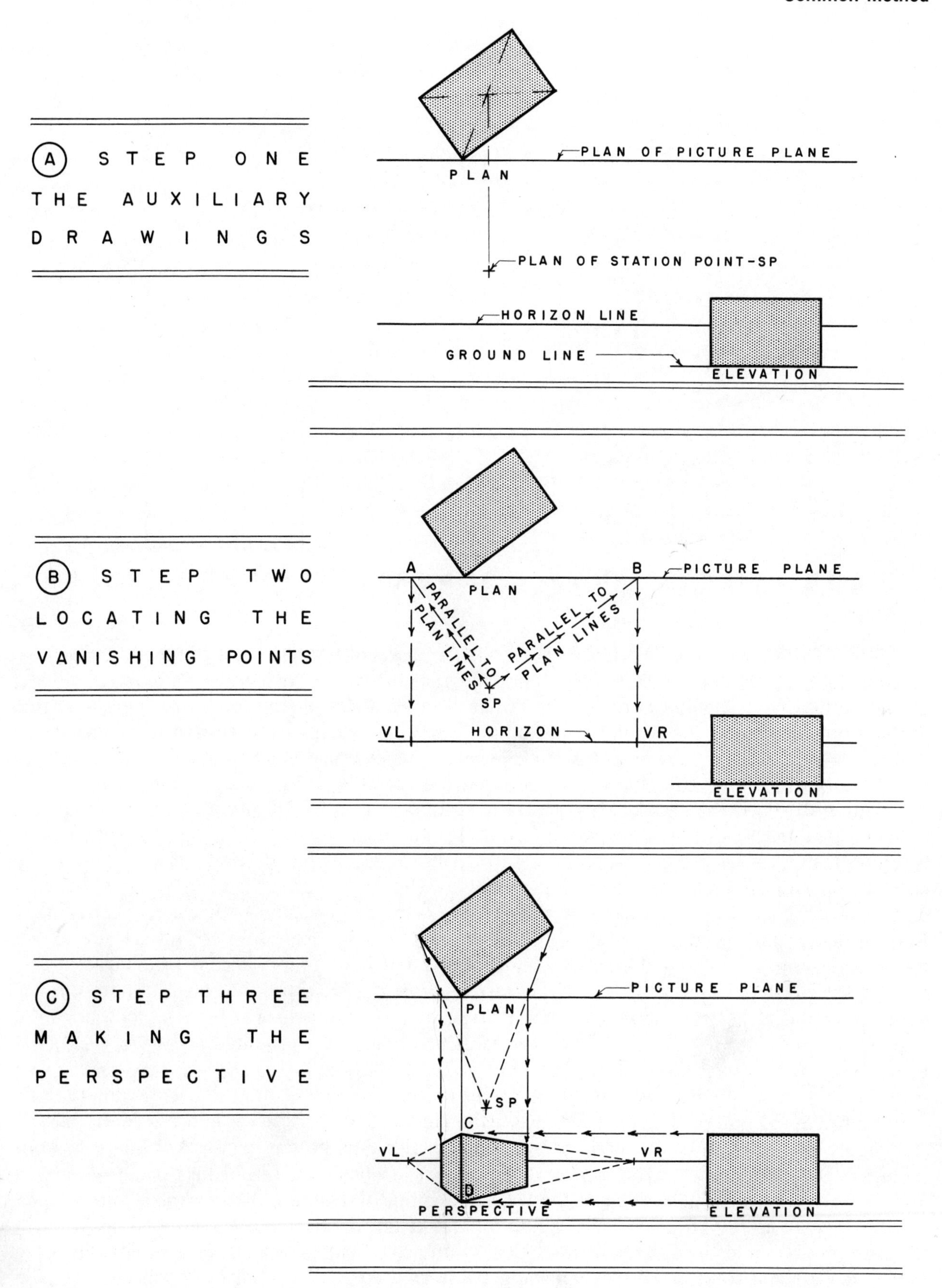

FIG-44 THE COMMON METHOD OF TWO-POINT PERSPECTIVE

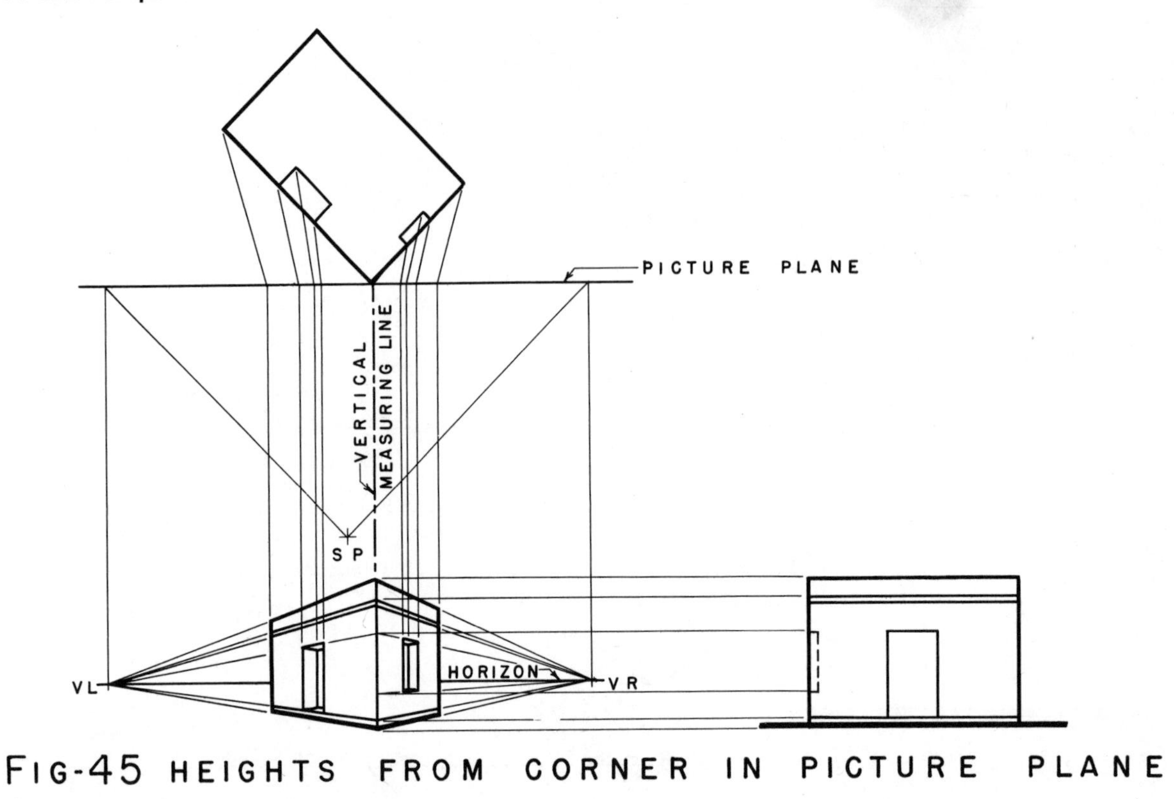

FIG-45 HEIGHTS FROM CORNER IN PICTURE PLANE

THE DETERMINATION OF HEIGHTS. The illustrations of Figs. 45 through 50 and the accompanying text explain the methods of determining perspective heights under various conditions. Two important facts should be kept in mind while studying these illustrations: *First* that all heights are laid out to scale in the picture plane only; *Second* that heights are carried from their scale sizes in the picture plane into correct perspective positions by tracing them along lines which vanish in the vanishing points and lead to the points on the object where the heights are used.

Figure 45 shows the simplest method of determining heights. The front corner of the object is in the picture plane (shown in plan). Therefore, any heights which lie in the two wall planes meeting in this corner are laid out on the corner and traced along the wall surfaces toward the correct vanishing points and into perspective position. The heights can be laid out by measurements on the corner itself from the ground line as a starting point, or they can be carried over horizontally from an elevation or section. The horizontal corners of the window and door reveals are drawn to the vanishing points after the outline shapes have first been drawn on the wall surfaces.

Figure 46 shows how heights can be carried around visible or concealed corners on any surfaces of the two typical sets of vertical planes; that is, on any surfaces in which horizontal lines vanish in either of the two established vanishing points. This method of tracing heights is useful on surfaces of the object itself, but *its use may be extended to imaginary surfaces and corners* to trace heights for points, lines, or areas of the object. This application is used in the indirect method of Fig. 50 and in the construction for the perspective of the stick and box in Fig. 48.

Figure 47 shows an object made of two block shapes. The bottom block or wall has its front corner in the picture plane. The top block or cornice extends over the picture plane. A vertical line dropped from the intersection of the cornice line and the picture plane in plan into the perspective serves as a vertical measuring line for the height of the cornice. This line lies in both the picture plane and the surface of the block. From scale heights laid out on this line, lines are drawn toward and away from the vanishing point to represent the edges of the cornice. The horizontal line for the height of the lower edge of the cornice also determines the height of the top of the wall.

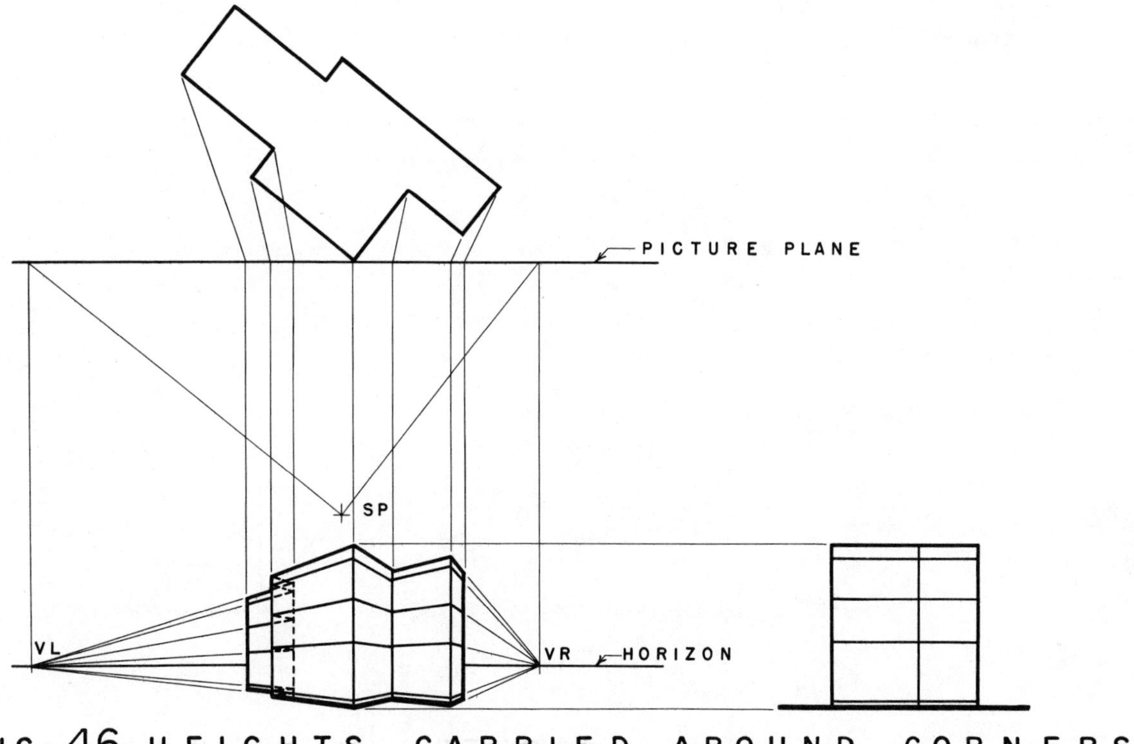

FIG-46 HEIGHTS CARRIED AROUND CORNERS

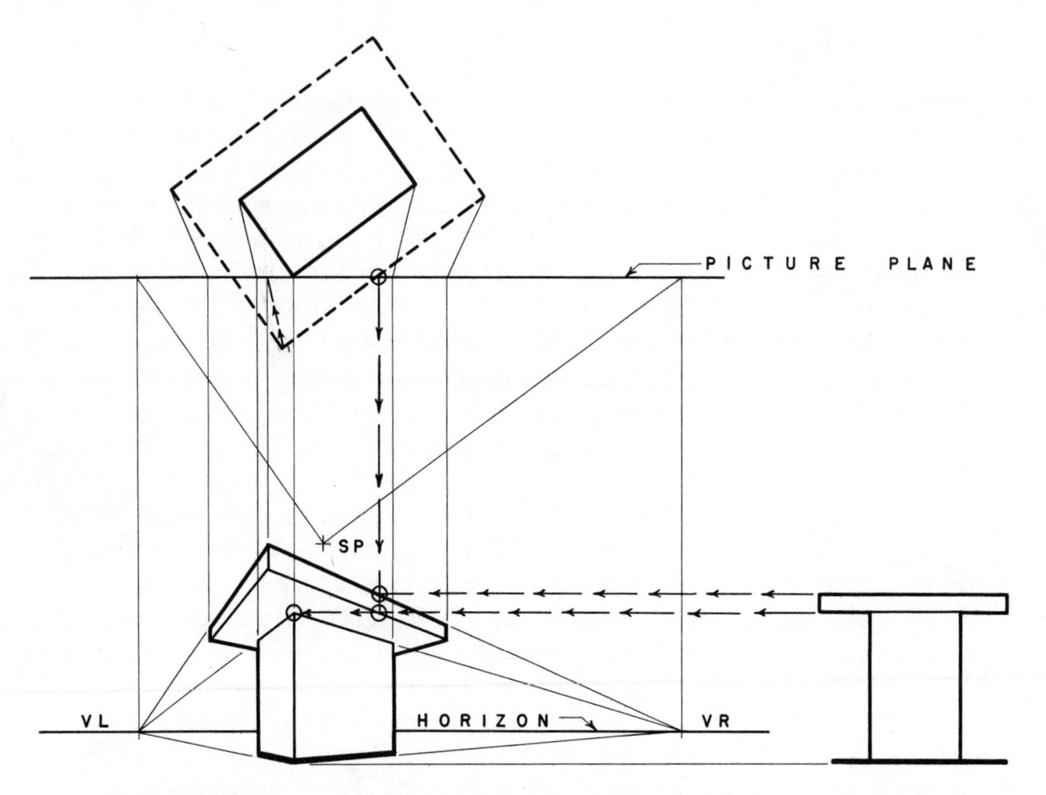

FIG-47 OBJECT EXTENDING THROUGH PICTURE PLANE

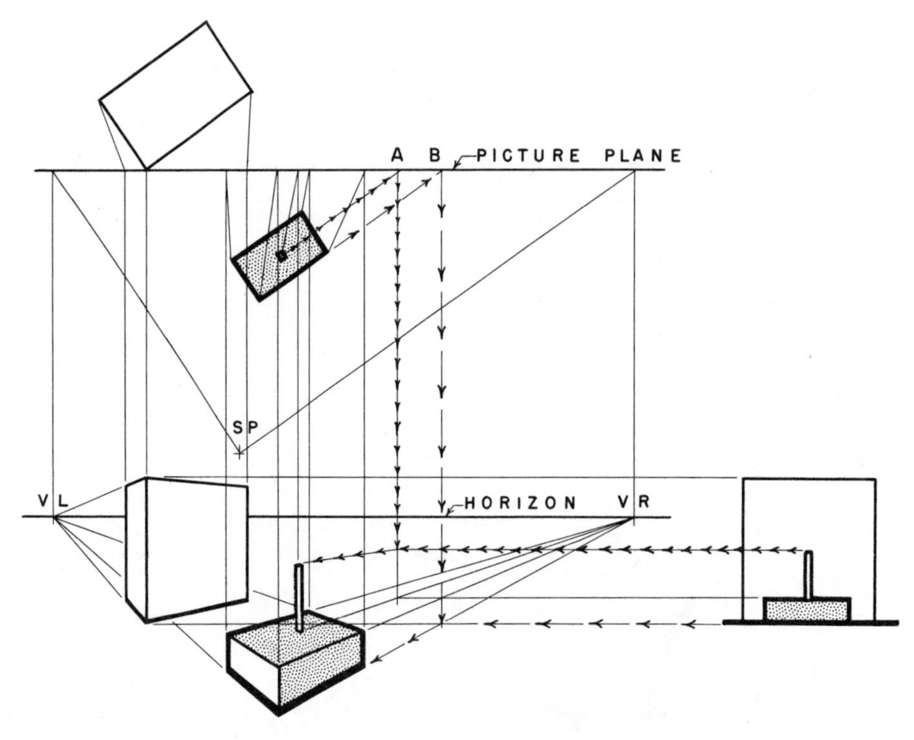

FIG-48 OBJECT IN FRONT OF PICTURE PLANE

Figure 48 shows an object which is entirely in front of the picture plane. The line of one of the visible sides is extended in plan to meet the picture plane at point B. The vertical line drawn from this point represents the imaginary intersection between the surface from which the line was drawn in plan and the picture plane, and is the vertical measuring line. The right front surface of the object has been used for this construction. Construction from the left side using the left vanishing point would give the same result. It is better to extend a visible front surface, not a concealed back one.

To find the height of the vertical stick on top of the box shape: Draw a line from the plan of the stick parallel to the plan lines to meet the picture plane at A. From this intersection the vertical measuring line is drawn, and the construction completed as shown. In this case an imaginary plane was extended from the stick parallel to vertical planes of the object to picture plane.

Figure 49 is drawn with one block shape having its front corner in the picture plane and a second block completely behind the picture plane. The line in plan representing one of the vertical surfaces of the block which is behind the picture plane is extended to intersect the picture plane at B. The vertical line drawn through this intersection is a vertical measuring line for the face of the object from which the construction originated in plan. The height of the top point of the stick is found by drawing in plan a line through the plan of the stick parallel to the sides of the object to intersect the picture plane at D. The height of the top of the stick is laid out on the vertical measuring line through this intersection. The height is carried from this line into correct position by drawing to the vanishing point of the line drawn in plan.

Figure 50 illustrates the method of laying out all the heights on a single vertical measuring line and tracing them around imaginary surfaces and corners by an indirect route to their correct perspective positions. It cannot be emphasized too strongly that there are often several ways of determining the same height and that the draftsman should learn to choose the best construction in each case. The heights must in all cases be laid out in the picture plane, then traced into their correct perspective positions by lines to the vanishing points which lead to the points to be located.

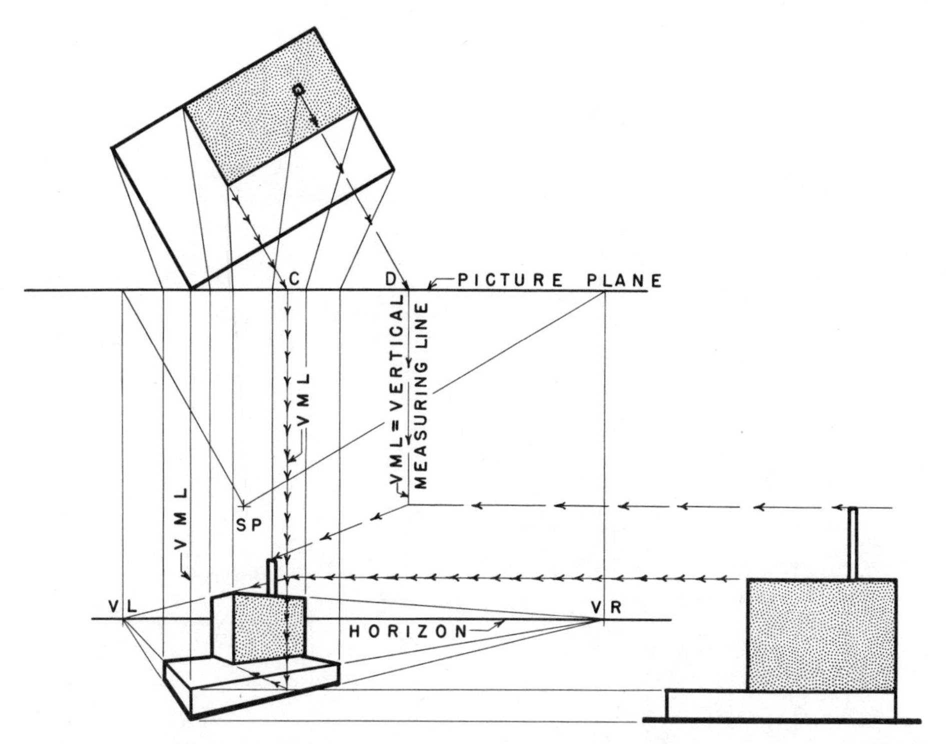

FIG-49 POINTS AND LINES BEHIND PICTURE PLANE

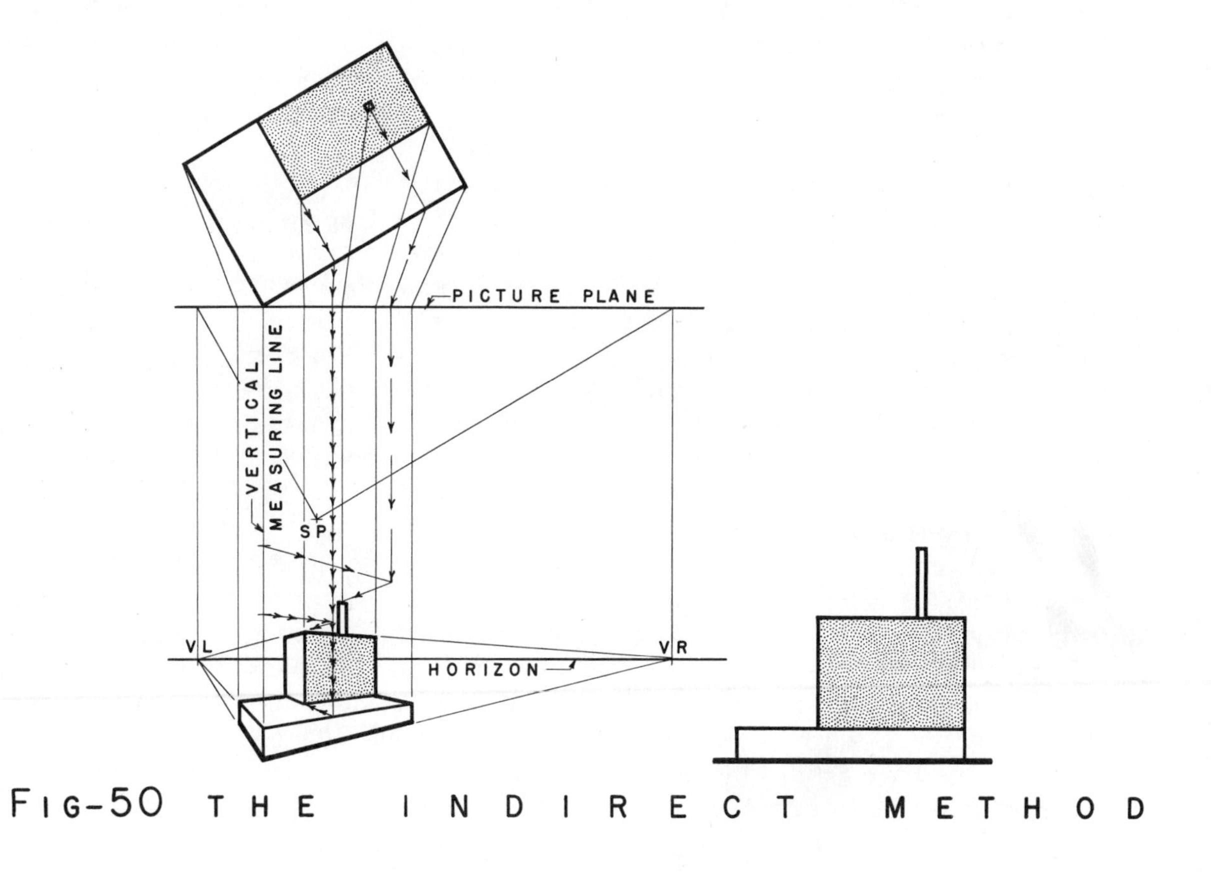

FIG-50 THE INDIRECT METHOD

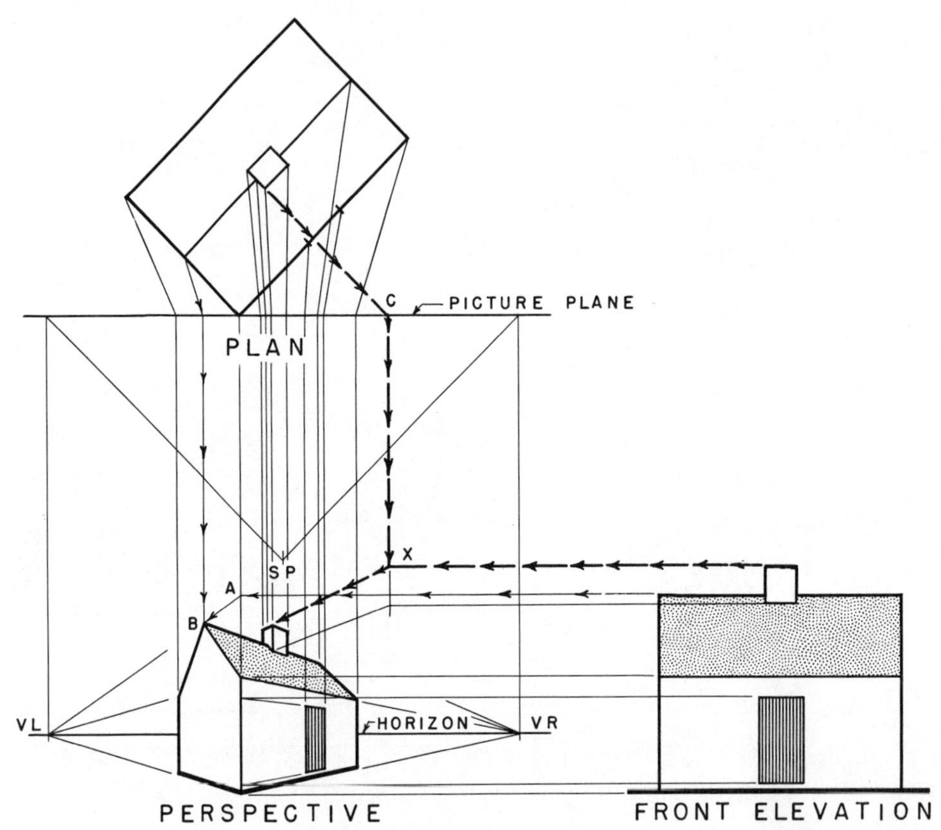

FIG-51 TWO-POINT PERSPECTIVE BY THE COMMON METHOD

THE COMMON METHOD OF TWO-POINT PERSPECTIVE. The essential principles of two-point perspective by the common method have been explained in the preceding pages. The application of these principles to the making of two-point perspectives is further illustrated and explained in this and the following three pages. In Figs. 51 and 53 the drawings have been spread out to prevent their overlapping and to make them more easily understood. In Figs. 52 and 54 they have been crowded together to save space and to keep them as large as possible.

Figure 51 has the heights of different parts of the perspective worked out in different ways by the methods explained on pages 48 to 51. Since the nearest corner of the wall in Fig. 51 is in the picture plane, its height is laid out to scale by drawing horizontal lines from the top and bottom of the wall in elevation to the line of the corner in the perspective. From these height measurements lines are drawn to VR to locate the top and bottom of the front wall. Likewise, lines are drawn to VL to locate the bottom line of the end wall and its top rear corner. Because the door lies in the plane of the front wall, its heights are carried across horizontally from the elevation to the corner in the picture plane (nearest corner of the wall) and then along the wall toward VR.

The height of the gable is obtained by carrying its height across horizontally from elevation to intersect at a point A, an extension upward of the wall corner in the picture plane, then to VL along an extension of the plane of the end wall to meet the line from plan at B.

The heavy dotted lines with arrowheads show the construction lines for the top of the chimney. The surface of the end of the chimney (which is parallel to the end of the building) is extended in plan to an imaginary corner in the picture plane at C. From this point a vertical line is drawn to meet the horizontal line from elevation in a point X, from which the construction line is drawn toward VL to locate the height of the end of the chimney, from which the construction line was drawn in plan. It should be observed that point X is the point of intersection of the extension of the top left corner of the chimney and the picture plane in perspective.

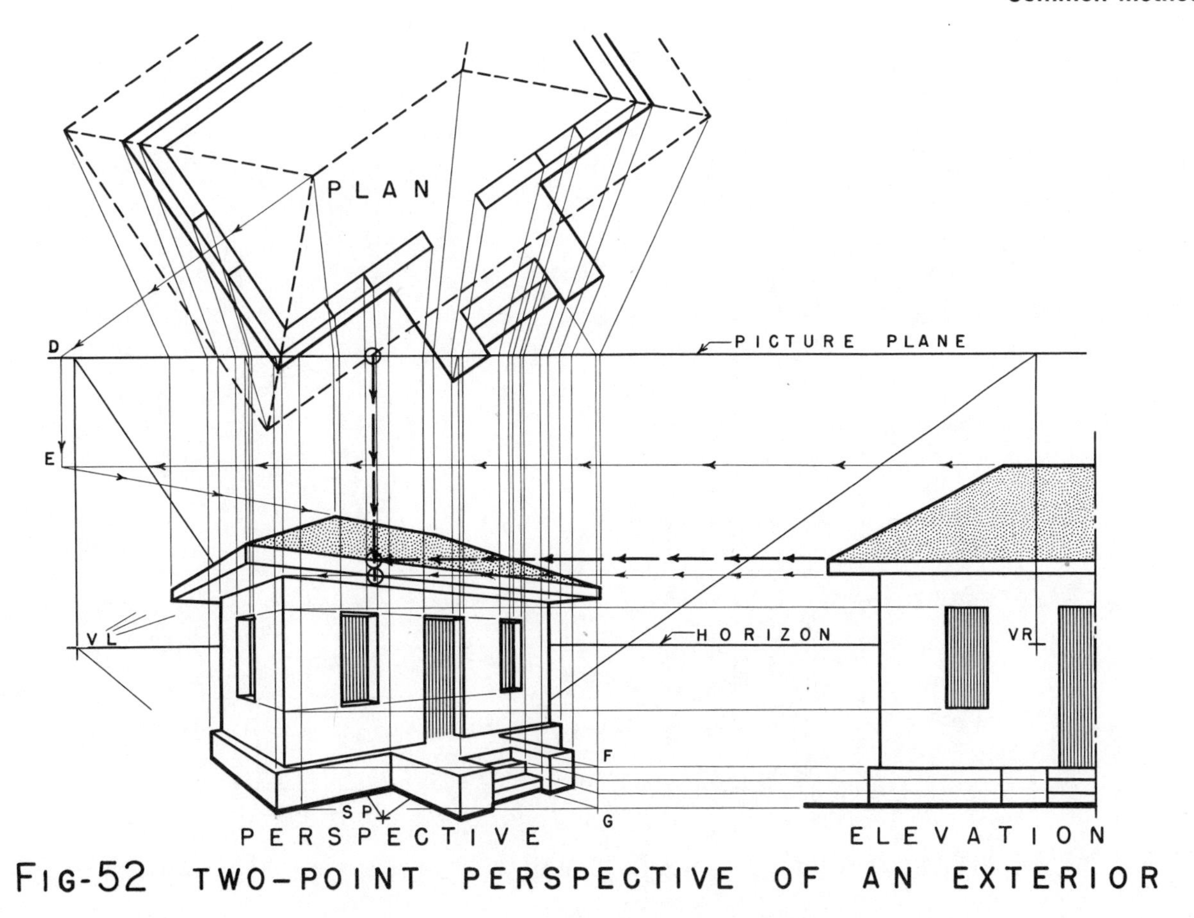

FIG-52 TWO-POINT PERSPECTIVE OF AN EXTERIOR

Figure 52 has the heights of the windows carried horizontally from the elevation to the nearest corner of the wall. From these points lines are drawn to VL and VR to obtain the lines of the bottoms and tops of the windows which lie in the wall surfaces. Note that the line of the corner must be in the picture plane to use this construction.

The scale-height of any part of the object which crosses the picture plane can be laid out on the vertical line brought down from the point of intersection of that part and the picture plane in plan. The heavy dotted line with arrowheads illustrates this construction. From the point of intersection of the front cornice line and picture plane in plan, a vertical line is drawn to meet the two heights of the cornice brought over from elevation and to locate one point on each of the two cornice lines in perspective. The cornice lines are then drawn toward and from VR through these points. The intersection of the end line of the cornice and picture plane in plan could have been used instead of the front intersection. This same method is used for the base course.

The height of the ridge in Fig. 52 is obtained, as shown, by the light construction lines with arrowheads. The line of the ridge in plan is extended to an imaginary intersection with the picture plane at D. From this intersection a vertical line is drawn to meet at E the height line brought over from elevation. The line from this point E to VR locates the height of the ridge. In other words, we have imagined that the ridge extends to the picture plane and then determined its height in just the same way that the heights of the tops and bottoms of the windows were determined. The step heights are constructed in a similar way by extending the surface of the block at the right side of the steps to an imaginary intersection with the picture plane on line F–G. The height lines are then carried along this imaginary surface toward the vanishing point VL as shown. The right side of the steps was chosen for the construction because the surfaces used are visible and the construction lines locate the visible lines of the ends of the steps. Working with hidden lines and surfaces of an object should be avoided in the construction of a perspective whenever possible. It causes confusion and additional work.

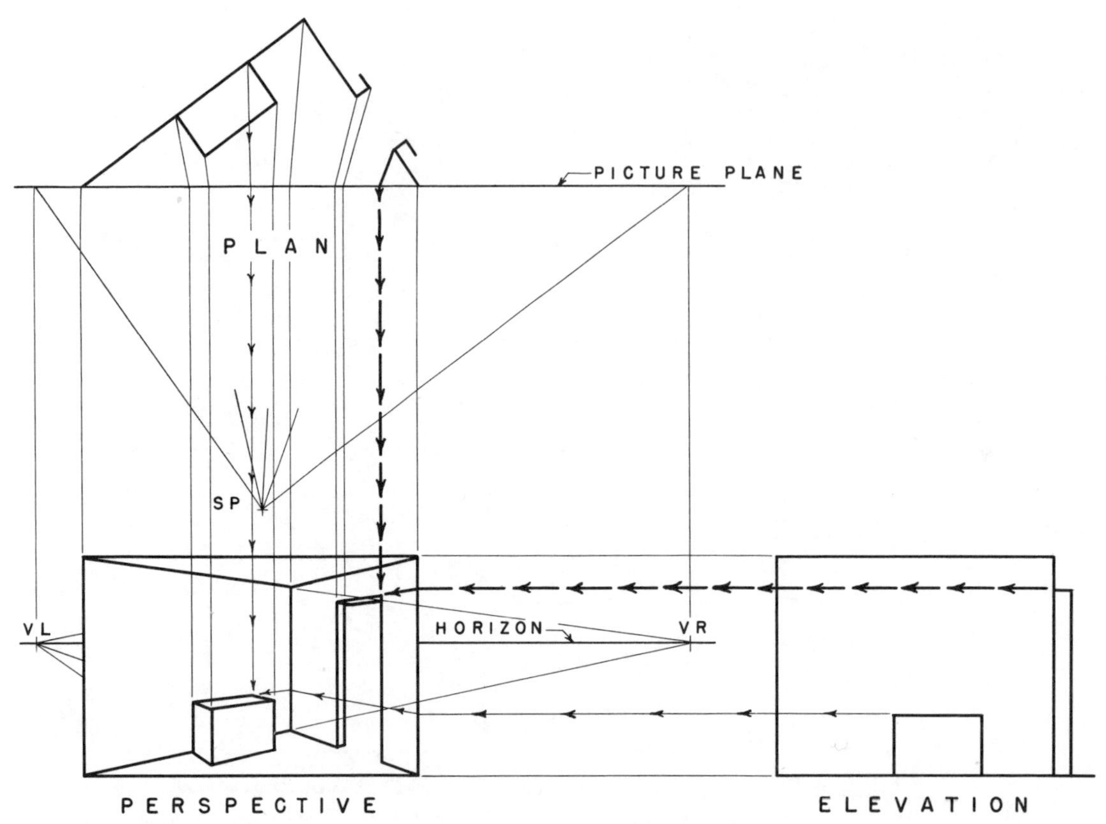

FIG-53 TWO-POINT PERSPECTIVE BY THE COMMON METHOD

INTERIOR TWO-POINT PERSPECTIVE. The preceding illustrations of the common method of two-point perspective show exteriors. The theory for location and relations of drawings, location of vanishing points, and determination of widths and heights as previously explained applies to interior as well as exterior perspective.

The construction of an interior two-point perspective of a simple room is shown in Fig. 53. Since the picture plane cuts through the room, its line of intersection with the walls, floor, and ceiling is at scale size. This intersection line is located in the perspective by drawing horizontal lines from the ceiling and floor of the elevation to meet vertical lines drawn from the intersections of the walls and picture plane in plan. From the corners of this rectangle, lines are drawn to the vanishing points to meet the rear corner of the room and outline the wall, floor, and ceiling areas. If there is any doubt regarding which vanishing point to use, it should be observed that the vanishing point located by drawing from the station point parallel to a set of lines in plan is the vanishing point of those lines. Any heights can be laid out on the vertical intersections of walls and picture plane and carried around the wall surface. The height of the door has been determined in this way and the construction is shown by the heavy dotted lines with large arrowheads. The construction of the height of the box is shown by the thin solid lines with small arrowheads. This height could also have been determined by the method shown in Fig. 51 for the chimney height, by extending one of the ends of the box in plan to meet the picture plane and form a vertical measuring line.

There are two convenient and commonly used positions of the picture plane for two-point perspectives of interiors. One is illustrated in Fig. 53, the other in Fig. 54. In the first example the object is behind the picture plane. The perspective ends at the intersection of object and picture plane. The size of the perspective is apparent from the auxiliary drawings. The height is the same as the height of the elevation, and the width is the plan distance between walls at picture plane.

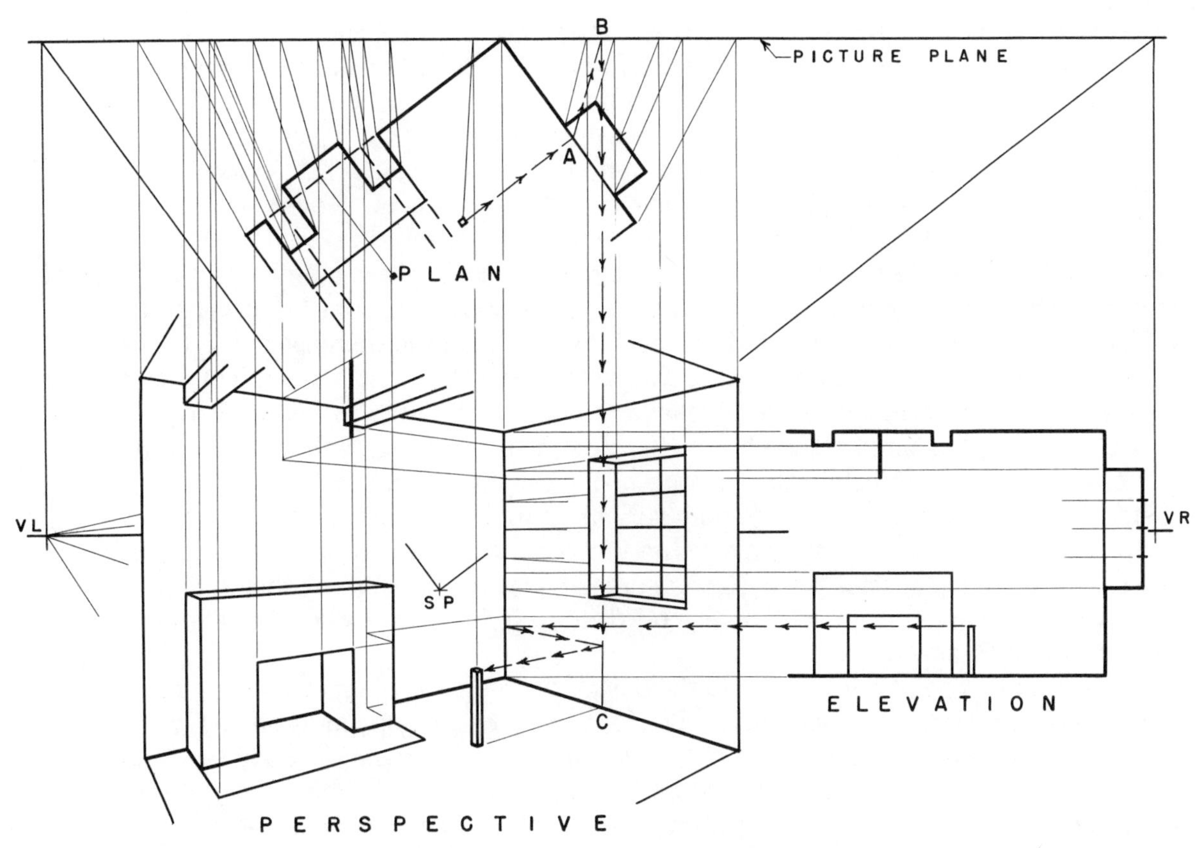

FIG-54 TWO-POINT PERSPECTIVE OF AN INTERIOR

Figure 54 has the corner of the interior surfaces of the walls touching the picture plane. The object is entirely in front of the picture plane. This corner of the two wall surfaces serves as a vertical measuring line from which heights can be traced along either wall and into perspective positions. In Fig. 54 it is necessary to block out the main shapes in the perspective to determine the size of the perspective drawing. This second position of the picture plane, Fig. 54, produces a larger perspective drawing with a given scale for the auxiliary drawings. The objects have terminated at the picture planes in the examples. However, parts of the objects can extend in front of the picture plane in Fig. 53 and behind it in Fig. 54. The parts of the object shown in a perspective drawing should never extend beyond the volume of the interior and exaggerate its size.

Height construction away from walls is illustrated for the vertical stick which is out in the clear floor area of Fig. 54. This method is used in locating lines on furniture or other objects which are not in contact with the walls. In this construction a line is drawn in plan through the plan of the stick parallel to one wall of the room to intersect the other wall at A. The vertical line B–C drawn from B, the projection of point A, to the picture plane is the position for change of direction of height lines traced along the wall surface from the corner in the picture plane. The height measurements are carried from this line B–C by lines from VR to establish the height of the stick. This height could be obtained in several different ways.

Objects turned obliquely and set out from the walls can most easily be constructed by enclosing the object in an imaginary box which has its sides parallel to the walls of the room. The tangent box is first drawn in perspective; then points and lines on its surfaces, which are also parts of the object, are located and the perspective of the object is drawn by connecting these with as little additional construction as possible. This procedure works very well for simple objects. When the oblique object is more complex, vanishing points for the oblique lines will be useful. See page 96 for location of VP of any horizontal line.

THE LOCATION OF THE STATION POINT. The pictorial effect obtained in a perspective drawing is determined by the position of the station point SP. Since it would be possible to have the eye of the observer in any one of an infinite number of positions in viewing an object, it is possible to have an infinite number of different perspective drawings of the object.

The location of the station point can be varied in three ways: (1) distance from the object; (2) height; (3) angle of view. These three variables and their effects on the perspective are discussed in the following paragraphs. The general theory applies to interiors as well as exteriors.

The distance from the station point to the object influences the pictoral effect and size of the perspective. When the station point is near the object the horizontal lines not parallel to the picture plane slant sharply, Fig. 55A. As the distance from the object is increased, the horizontal lines flatten out and the perspective approaches the form of an elevation perpendicular to the picture plane in which all horizontal lines are parallel and horizontal, Fig. 55B and C. Parts of the object which are in front of the picture plane become smaller as the distance from the object to the station point increases, and parts behind the picture plane become larger. Both approach scale size as the distance increases, and conversely, both vary more from scale size as the distance diminishes. When the station point is near the object, the bottoms of horizontal surfaces above the horizon are large, as are the top surfaces of horizontal areas below the horizon. As the station point moves farther away, these areas become smaller and disappear from view when the station point is at infinity, Fig. 55A, B, and C.

When the station point is very close to the object, the resulting perspective may appear unnatural. There are two different explanations for this. *First:* the station point should be a sufficient distance from the object, so that everything shown in the drawing can actually be included in the angle of vision of a person located at the station point. When the station point is too close, the observer will not be able to see the entire object clearly at one time and consequently the perspective will appear to be distorted. *Second:* the angle of vision is not the deciding factor, for a perspective is a true picture of the object only when the eye is located at the station point of the perspective when viewing it. If the eye has to be very close to the drawing, in an unnatural position, to see it correctly, it will then present a more distorted effect when seen from a normal distance.

The maximum angle of vision of the eye is usually assumed to be 45° to 60°. This angle should include everything shown in the perspective. When the height of the object is greater than its width, the height will determine the angle of vision. In one-point perspective the limit of vision is considered to be a cone of rays from the eye, thus avoiding the distorted effect sometimes found in the corners of one-point perspectives. To avoid excessive distortion in perspectives of spheres and circles, these shapes should be kept in a 30° cone of vision in any type of perspective.

As a practical consideration, the farther the station point is located from the object, the greater the distance from the drawings to the various centers of converging lines. When good results are obtained these centers should be in reach of the T-square and on the board.

The height of the station point SP determines whether the object is seen from above, below, or from within its own height in the perspective drawing. The perspective relation of the SP, vanishing points, and horizon is constant for varying heights of the SP if the distance from the picture plane to the SP and the angle between the object and picture plane are constant. The perspective position of the SP is on the horizon when the picture plane is vertical. The picture plane is almost always vertical in one-point and two-point perspective. The vanishing points of horizontal lines are always found on the horizon. When the eye of the observer (SP) moves up or down, the horizon and VP's of the horizontal lines move with it. The distance from the horizon to the ground line is the height of the eye of the observer above or below the base of the building. Figure 56D, E, and F uses the same position of the horizon, SP, and VP's; but uses three different distances to the ground line, so that the view in the center has the SP opposite the center of the object, while the other two have the SP above or below the object. The relation of the horizon and ground line then determines whether the perspective is a view from below (D), normal perspective (E), or an aerial view (F).

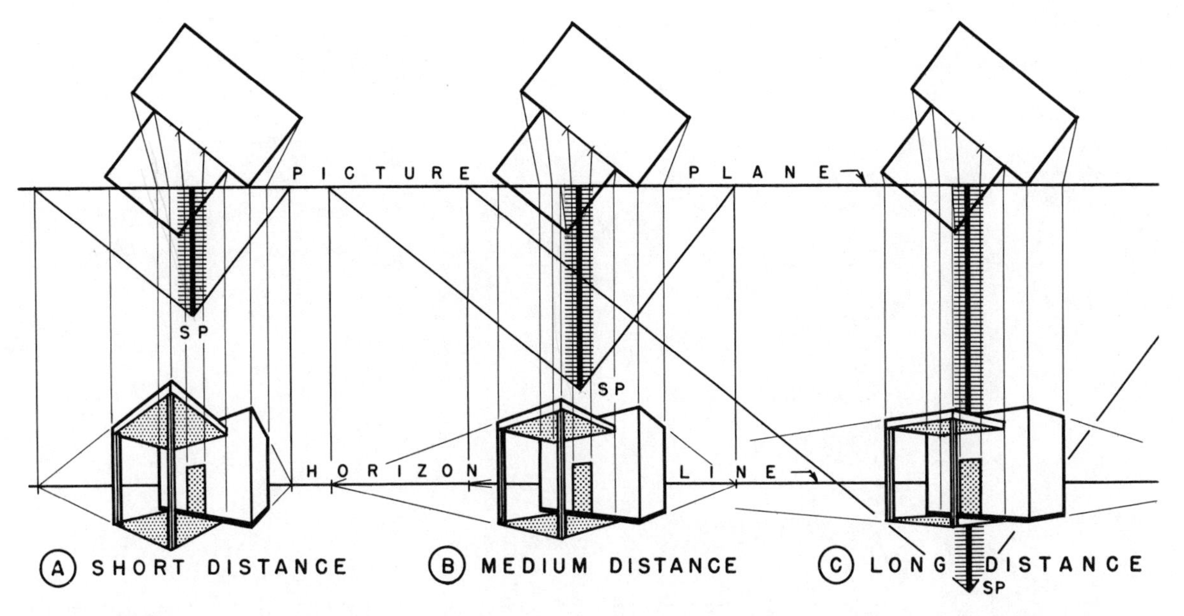

FIG-55 DISTANCE FROM STATION POINT TO OBJECT

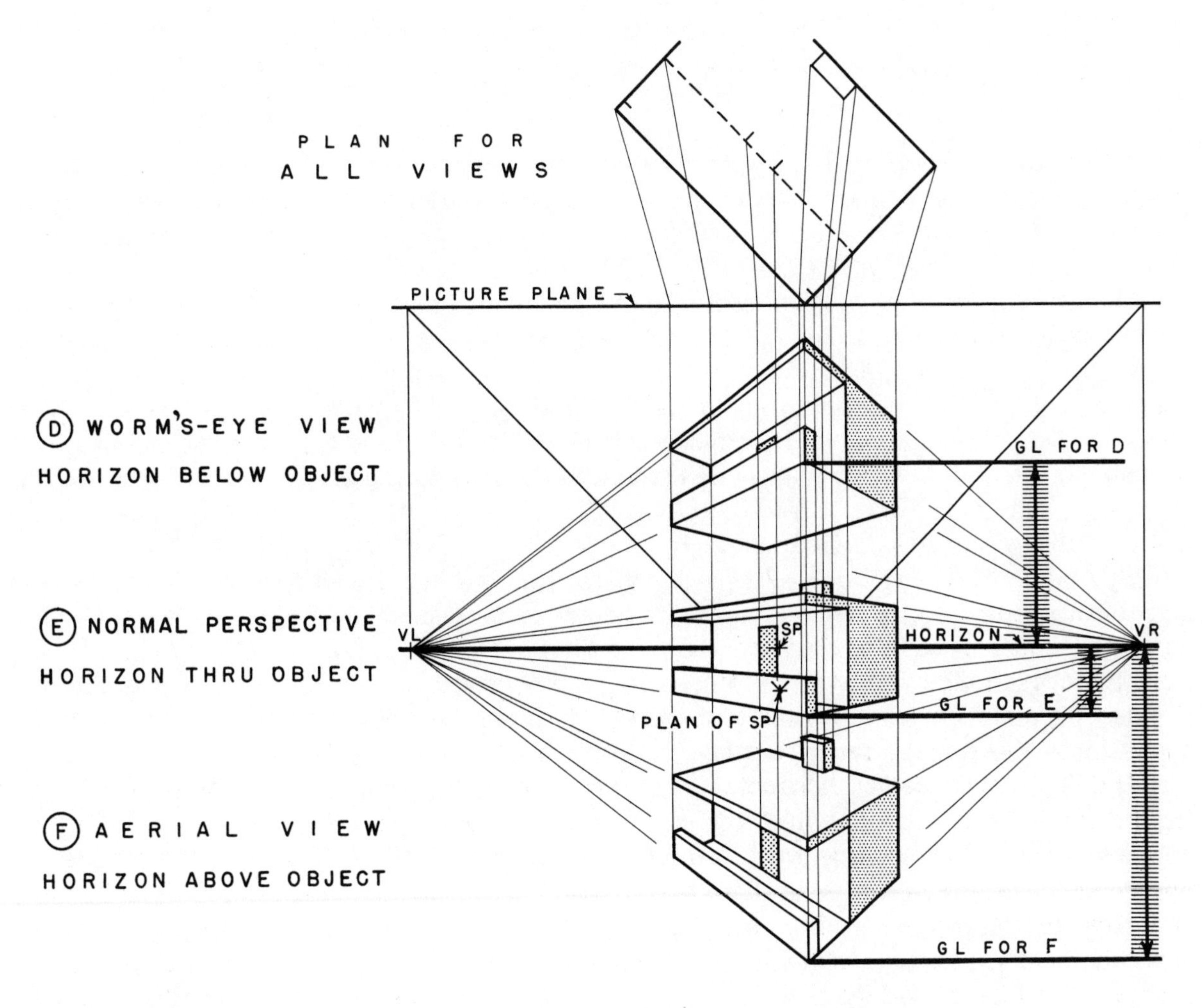

FIG-56 HEIGHT OF STATION POINT

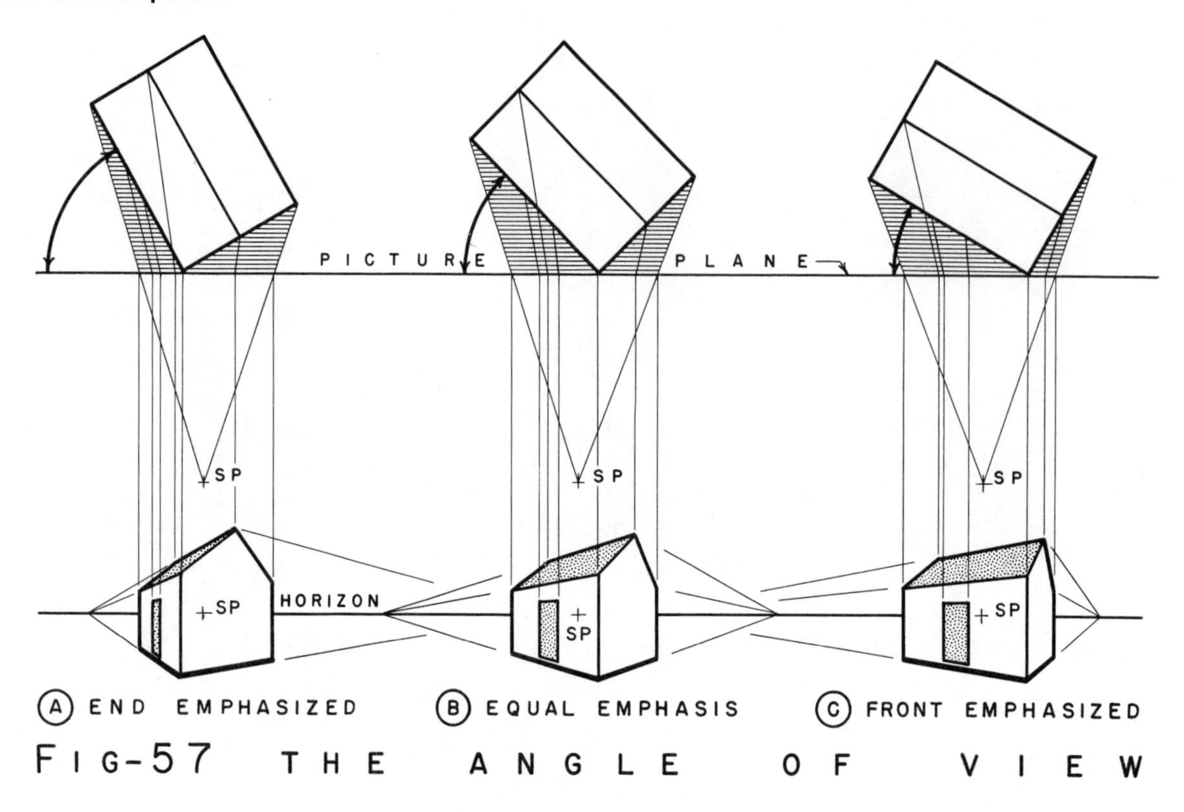

FIG-57 THE ANGLE OF VIEW

The angle of view determines which sides of the object are seen and their relative widths in the perspective. When a photographer takes a picture of a freestanding building, he walks around it to find the best position for his camera. The draftsman can get similar information in two dimensions from a plan of the building of which the perspective is to be made. He can choose a trial station point and, by turning a straight-edge on this point as a pivot, he can determine which wall areas will be visible in a perspective made from this point. Furthermore, he can determine the relative perspective widths and importance of these areas and whether there is any unfortunate alignment of the corners in an irregular plan. From these observations he may be able to select a more satisfactory station point. The experienced draftsman develops the ability to visualize the perspective effect from different positions around the plan of the object and thus choose the station point best suited to his purpose. The relative importance of the sides shown in the perspective has probably the greatest influence on the angle of view. Ordinarily it is desirable to look more directly at the important side and less directly at the unimportant one. In most perspectives of exteriors the entrance to the building is considered as an essential. A reasonable amount of the entrance should be visible when the shape of the building does not allow all of it to be shown from the chosen direction. When a model of the proposed building is available, it is very useful in selecting a station point. All three of the variables can be considered with a model. Figure 57 shows three views of the same object from different angles.

The SP should center horizontally on the perspective drawing for best pictorial results. Regardless of the angle from which the object is seen, the station point should always be located approximately on a line through the center of the plan and perpendicular to the picture plane. The perspective is distorted when the station point is located very far to one side of this line. It is a great temptation, where the plan is set up and the correctly located station point does not give satisfactory results, to take the easy way out and push the station point to one side. However, such a procedure causes the perpendicular to the picture plane to be off center on the plan and perspective. It will therefore cause the perspective to be out of proportion.

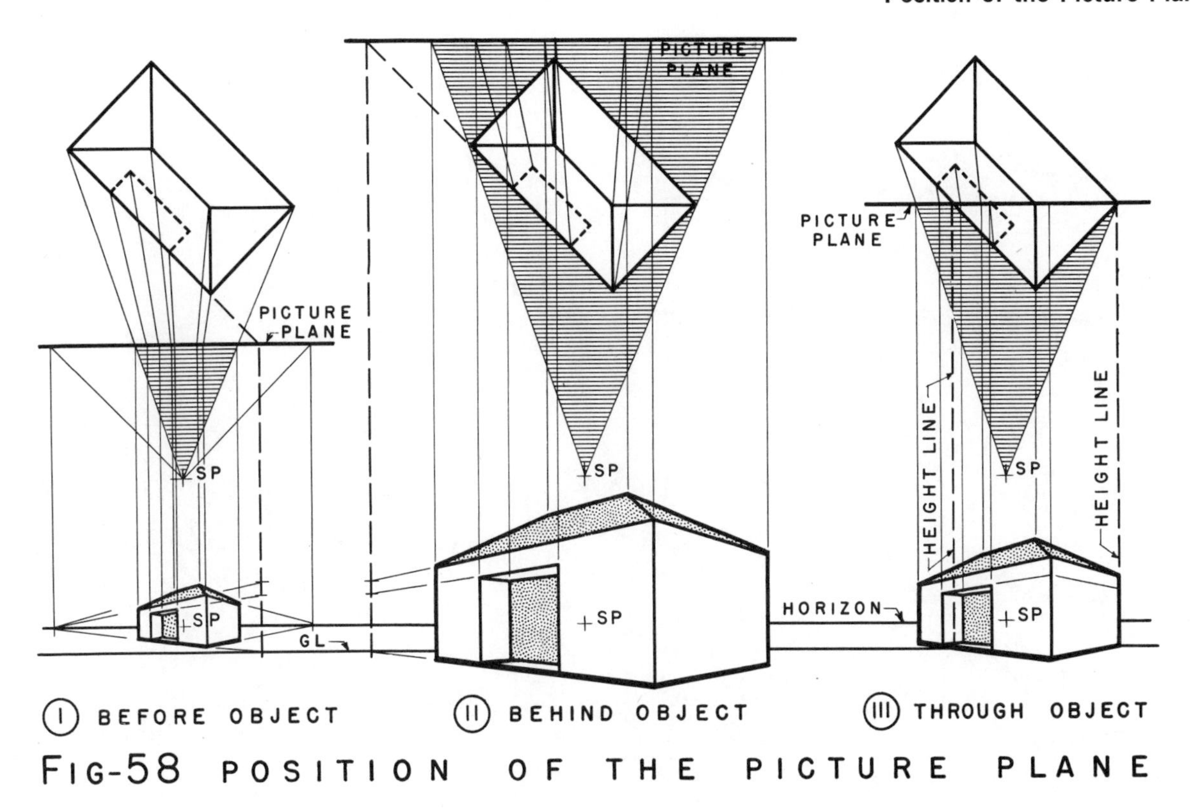

FIG-58 POSITION OF THE PICTURE PLANE

The position of the picture plane determines the size of the perspective drawing obtained with a given object, given scale, and given relation between station point and object, Fig. 58 I, II, and III. The nearer the picture plane to the station point, the smaller the perspective; the farther the picture plane from the station point, the larger the perspective. If all positions of the picture plane are parallel, the resulting perspective drawings will be identical in all respects except size.

The shifting of the position of the picture plane is a very helpful device for obtaining any size perspective desired. However, there are limits to its use. Extreme enlargements may be lacking in accuracy. Extreme reductions in size require too much space for construction, Fig. 58 I.

The most common position of the picture plane is through the nearest main corner of the object. Simplicity and directness of construction are the principal advantages of this location of the picture plane. However, similar advantages are secured by having the picture plane pass through any visible corner of the object. Corners which are hidden behind the perspective require use of hidden lines and complicate the construction. Constructions for points in front of and behind the picture plane have been given in the preceding pages.

Variations of the pictorial effect in perspective are obtained by changing the height, distance, and angle of view through manipulation of the station point. Variations in size of the perspective drawing can be obtained by change of scale of the auxiliary drawings, and by varying the position of the picture plane. An active imagination and the ability to visualize final results are as important to the draftsman as to the photographer in obtaining interesting pictures. The draftsman who understands the effects of the variables in perspective should be able to get the exact view that he wishes and make it the size best suited to his purpose.

When several perspective studies are made from a design and none of them looks well, the designer may conclude that he has not designed a beautiful building. It is even more difficult for the draftsman to make a beautiful perspective from a mediocre design than for the photographer to make a glamorous photograph of a homely person. Furthermore, the architect must prove the design in the actual building, and there is a question of professional integrity involved.

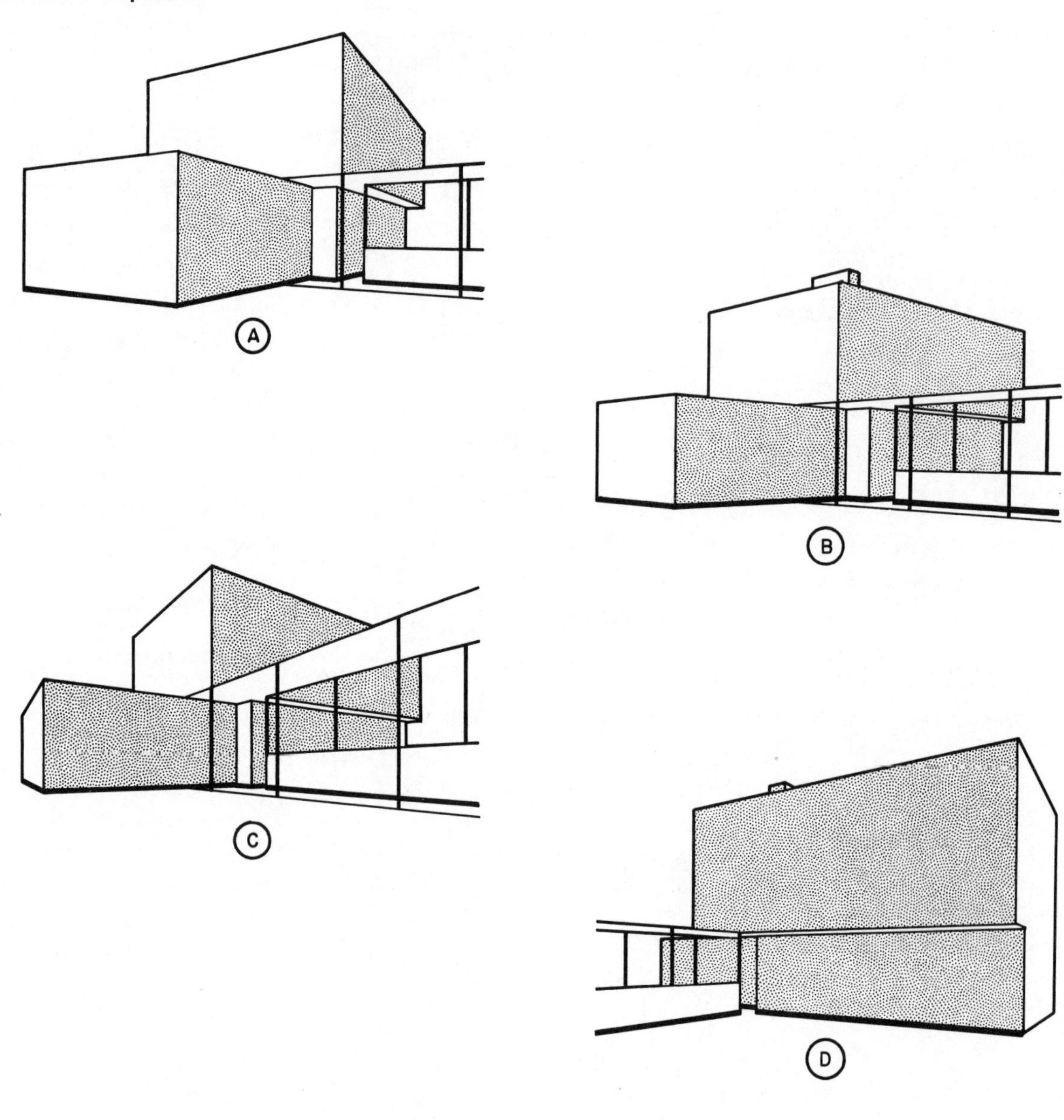

FIG-59 EXTERIOR BLOCK STUDIES

Block studies at small scale, which show only the masses and principal features of the object, can be made very quickly. They are of great value in choosing a station point for a larger and more detailed perspective drawing. They often save time because the large perspective can be made correctly the first time. With several possible variations considered in block form, a better pictorial effect can be secured. These simple preliminary studies may be compared to the proofs furnished by a photographer. One of the proofs is selected for the final pictures or perspective.

In Fig. 59 the emphasis on different parts of the design varies in each of the four studies. In A the left end walls are emphasized. By turning the plan to a different angle with the picture plane in B the front (shaded) walls are dominant. The plan is turned still farther in C; this brings the sheltered walk closer to SP and gives it a great deal more importance. In D the plan is turned to show the right end wall and emphasize the main area of the front wall.

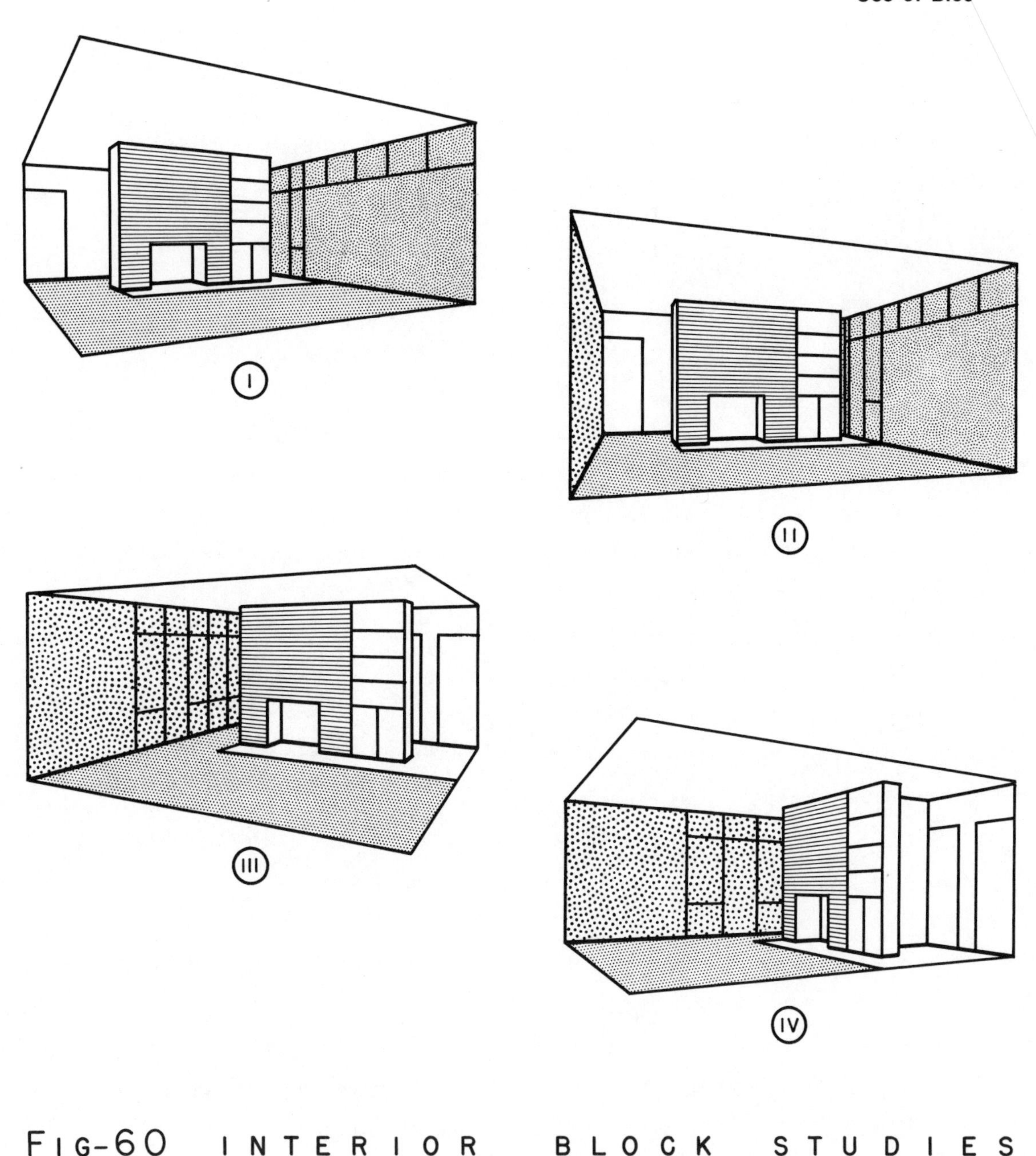

FIG-60 INTERIOR BLOCK STUDIES

While the beginner in perspective drawing needs the information from a number of block studies, he is usually not as willing to make them as the expert draftsman who appreciates their value from experience. On these speedy drawings the designer feels free to try arrangements which he would be very unlikely to try for a single large perspective. There is therefore a psychological advantage in a number of block studies which leads to greater imaginative freedom, and often to more dramatic results. Freehand studies are used by some designers for ideas for perspectives. They are valuable when they correctly express the proportions of the design but worthless when they vary appreciably from the correct proportions.

In Fig. 60 the four block studies of the interior have the plan turned at different angles with the picture plane. This allows different combinations of walls to be visible in the first three, and varies the amount of ceiling and floor and proportions of the walls in the last two.

Ⓐ UNIMPORTANT SIDE SUBORDINATED

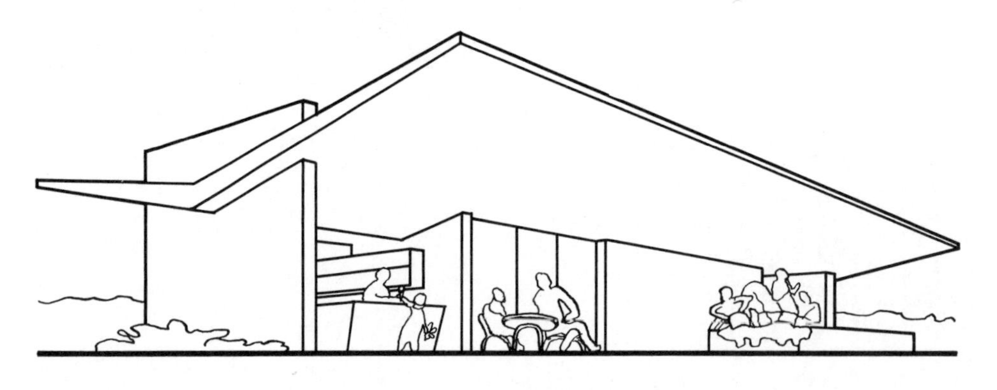

Ⓑ SP CLOSE AND LOW-ROOF SHAPE EMPHASIZED

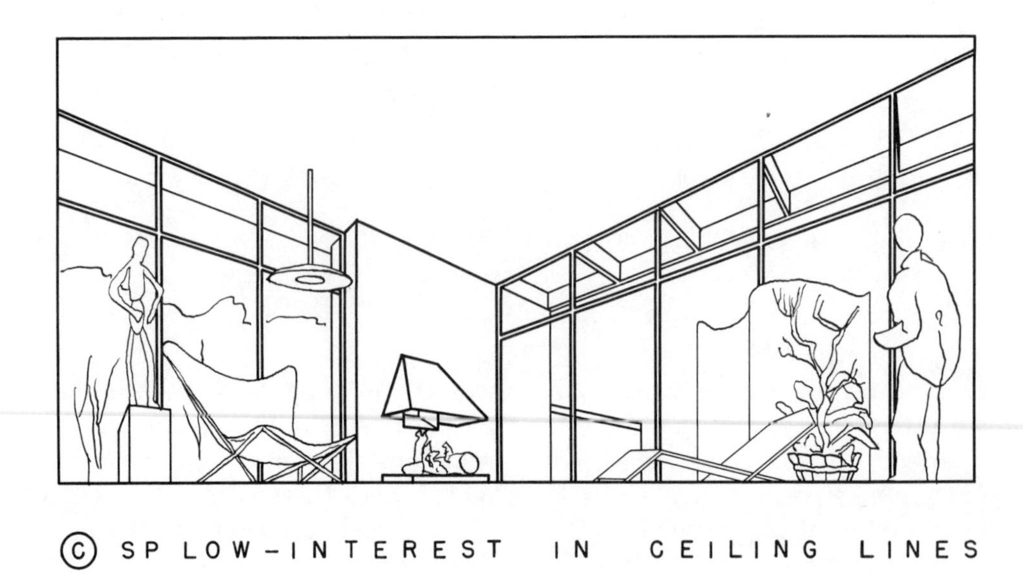

Ⓒ SP LOW-INTEREST IN CEILING LINES

FIG-61 EXAMPLES OF TWO-POINT PERSPECTIVE

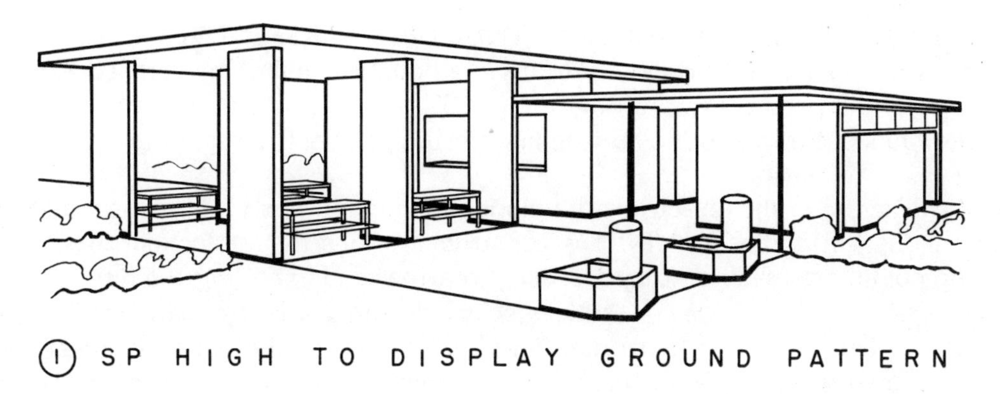

(I) SP HIGH TO DISPLAY GROUND PATTERN

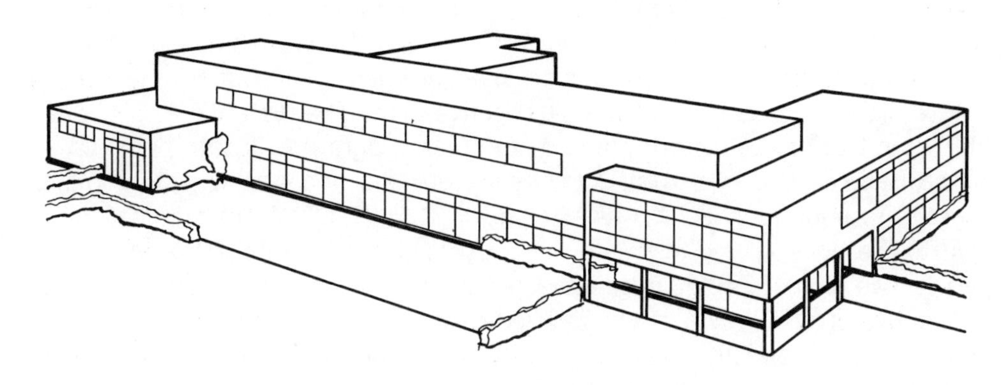

(II) AERIAL VIEW TO EXPLAIN PLAN OF MASSES

(III) SP CLOSE FOR INTERESTING LINES AND FORMS

FIG-62 EXAMPLES OF TWO-POINT PERSPECTIVE

THE PERSPECTIVE PLAN METHOD OF TWO-POINT PERSPECTIVE. The four examples shown in Figs. 63, 64, 65, and 66 illustrate this method. The following detailed explanation of the construction of the perspective drawing in Fig. 63 is divided into five numbered steps.

1–The elevation is drawn and the **horizon line** for the perspective placed at the height chosen for the eye level in the elevation.

2–The plan diagram of the object, picture plane, and station point is drawn with the plan line of the picture plane turned horizontally. The construction lines for the location of the vanishing and measuring points are made of long dashes with arrowheads showing the directions in which the lines were drawn. *Vanishing points* are located by drawing lines from the station point, SP, parallel to the two typical sets of horizontal lines of the plan of the object to meet the picture plane line of the plan diagram. From these two intersections, A and B, vertical lines are drawn to the horizon line to locate the two vanishing points of the sets of horizontal lines of the object. VL is the vanishing point of all horizontal lines of the perspective which are parallel in plan to line A–SP. Likewise, VR is the vanishing point of all horizontal lines of the perspective which are parallel in plan to line SP–B. *The measuring points* are the vanishing points of two sets of parallel lines, which transfer the horizontal scale measurements laid out on the perspective plan line of the picture plane to base lines of the perspective plan. The distance A–SP is laid out from A to the right on the line of the picture plane of the plan diagram to locate point D. In the same way the distance B–SP is laid out from B to the left on the line of the picture plane to locate Point C. Expressed in equations, A–D = A–SP and B–C = B–SP. From points C and D vertical lines are drawn to the horizon line to locate the two measuring points, ML and MR.

3–The perspective plan of Fig. 63 is constructed by the following procedure. The picture plane line of the perspective plan is drawn at any desired distance below the horizon. In these drawings it is located so that the perspective plan is entirely below the perspective drawing and there will not be any confusion caused by overlapping. The position of the corner which is in the picture plane is brought down vertically from the plan diagram to its correct position on the picture plane in the perspective plan. This point X is used as a base point from which the right side measurements of the plan are laid out to the right on the picture plane and the left side measurements are laid out to the left. From base point X, base lines are drawn to VL and VR. *The left side measurements* of the perspective plan are traced from their positions on the picture plane toward MR to meet the base line X–VL and then to VR. *The right side measurements* are traced from the picture plane toward ML to meet base line X–VR and then VL to complete the perspective plan.

4–The horizontal spacing of the points and vertical lines in the perspective drawing is obtained by drawing vertical lines from the perspective plan.

5–Heights of vertical lines in the picture plane are laid out to scale in the perspective. Heights of those parts not in the picture plane are laid out on lines in the picture plane, from which they can be traced into perspective position by drawing to the vanishing points. These constructions are shown in Figs. 63 and 64 and were explained in previous pages on the determination of heights.

The interior perspective of Fig. 64 follows Steps 1, 2, and 4 of the preceding explanation. The general theory of Steps 3 and 5 applies to Fig. 64. In applying Step 3 to Fig. 64 it should be noted that there are two base points in this perspective plan. These base points, E and G, are the points of intersection of the walls of the room with the picture plane. The measurements for the two sides of the room overlap. Those for the left side are marked on the picture plane with short vertical lines above the picture plane. They are carried toward ML to meet the base line E–VR, then drawn from VL to locate the lines of the perspective plan. Those for the right side are marked with short vertical lines below the picture plane. They are carried toward MR to meet base line G–VL, then projected from VR to complete the perspective plan. In this example the end measurement of each group is for the corner of the walls, and their lines to the measuring points should intersect at the intersection of base lines E–VR and G–VL. All the heights in Fig. 64 are carried across horizontally to the lines of intersection of the walls and picture plane, then traced around the walls to their perspective positions with lines to their correct VP's.

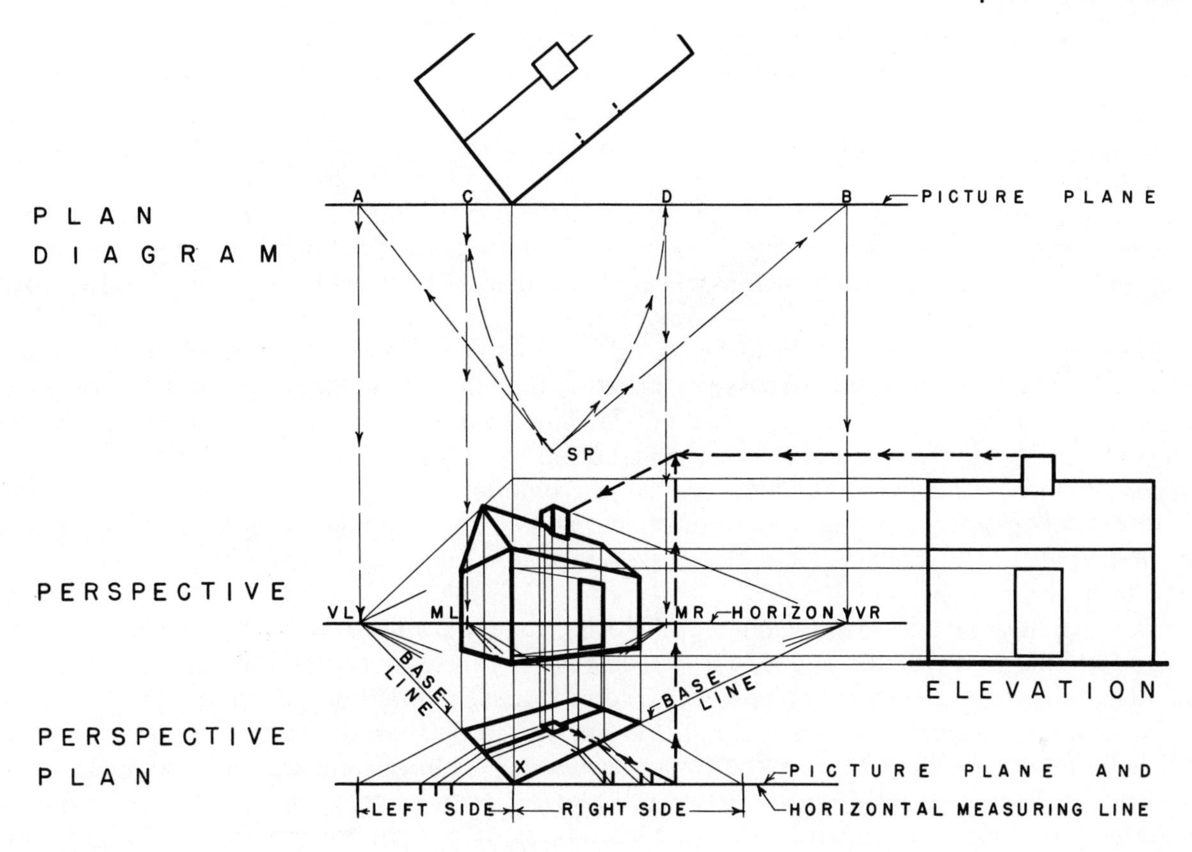

FIG-63 TWO-POINT EXTERIOR PERSPECTIVE PLAN METHOD

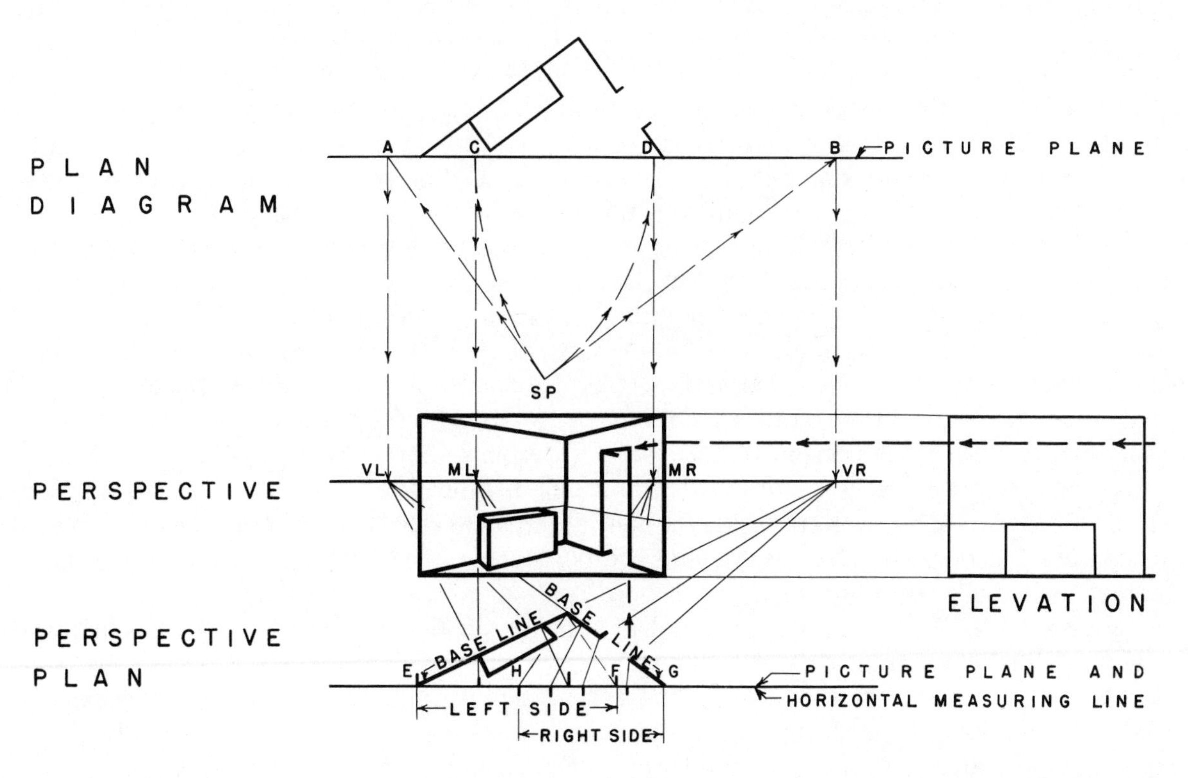

FIG-64 TWO-POINT INTERIOR PERSPECTIVE PLAN METHOD

In Fig. 65 the corner of the wall surface is in the picture plane. The heights on this line are therefore at scale size and are transferred horizontally from the elevation to the line. From the points thus located on the corner, lines are drawn to the vanishing points for the top and bottom of the main wall surfaces and for the lines of the tops and bottoms of openings in the wall surfaces.

The line of the ridge in the perspective plan is extended from VR to an imaginary intersection with the picture plane at A. From this point a vertical line is drawn to meet the horizontal line from elevation, and from their intersection X a line is drawn to VR to locate the perspective position of the ridge. Then X is the point where the extended ridge pierces the picture plane and the only point where the height of the ridge is at scale size.

The step wall at the right of the steps is extended to an imaginary intersection with the picture plane at B. The heights of the steps are carried around this intersection to correct perspective position. The height of the cornice is laid out on its line of intersection with the picture plane. This construction for the top line of the cornice is shown with the heavy dotted lines with arrows. The height of the base course is found in a similar manner.

In Fig. 66 the heavy dotted construction line shows the method of laying out the height of the window seat at its intersection with the picture plane. The height of the fireplace opening is obtained in a similar manner.

The plan diagram has been included in the construction drawings for the perspectives in Figs. 63 and 64. This plan diagram is used for the location of vanishing points, measuring points, and wall intersections with the picture plane, which serve as base points from which the scale measurements of the perspective plan are laid out. (In Fig. 63 the position of the corner, and in Fig. 64 the positions of the intersections of the two walls with the picture plane are the base points.) The plan of the object itself need not be drawn completely, since its only uses are to center the SP on the plan, to locate base points, and give the directions of lines for the location of vanishing points. In order to save space the plan diagram can be constructed on a separate sheet of paper and the points located from it transferred to the horizon of the perspective drawing. In Figs. 65 and 66 the plan diagrams were worked out with the horizon line of the perspective serving as the picture plane of the plan diagram. The construction lines of the diagrams are not shown.

An elevation has been drawn to make the construction of heights more easily understood in each of the four examples of this method. Any part of any elevation which gives all the required heights can be used for this purpose. The experienced draftsman often omits the elevation from the drawing. When the elevation is not used directly, all of the heights are usually laid out on one vertical measuring line, which is usually an important intersection of wall and picture plane. The height construction is then carried from this line into the perspective as it would be carried from an elevation. If this vertical measuring line is a line from which several of the heights are used directly, the construction is simplified. In Fig. 63 the corner in the picture plane would be used as the vertical measuring line, thus eliminating the horizontal construction lines to this corner. In Figs. 63 and 64, A, B, C, and D are the plan positions of VL, VR, ML, and MR respectively. These plan points are not given the vanishing and measuring point lettering because they are not used as vanishing and measuring points here. To letter them as such would be confusing.

The distance from the horizon line to the picture plane line of the perspective plan has no effect on the resulting perspective drawing because all distances give the same horizontal spacing. However, when the distance is made very small, the plan will become thin and be less accurate. As in one-point perspective, by this method the perspective plan may be placed either above or below the perspective drawing, or it can be on the floor or some other horizontal plane of the building. See Fig. 87B of one-point perspective and Fig. 38 III for a two-point perspective where the horizontal areas can represent various perspective plan positions. The position of the picture plane can be changed to vary the size of the perspective in this method, as has been explained for the common method. When the most distant corner of an interior touches the picture plane, a larger perspective is obtained and overlapping of measurements is eliminated or reduced, but there are not so many convenient scale height lines on furniture and wall features.

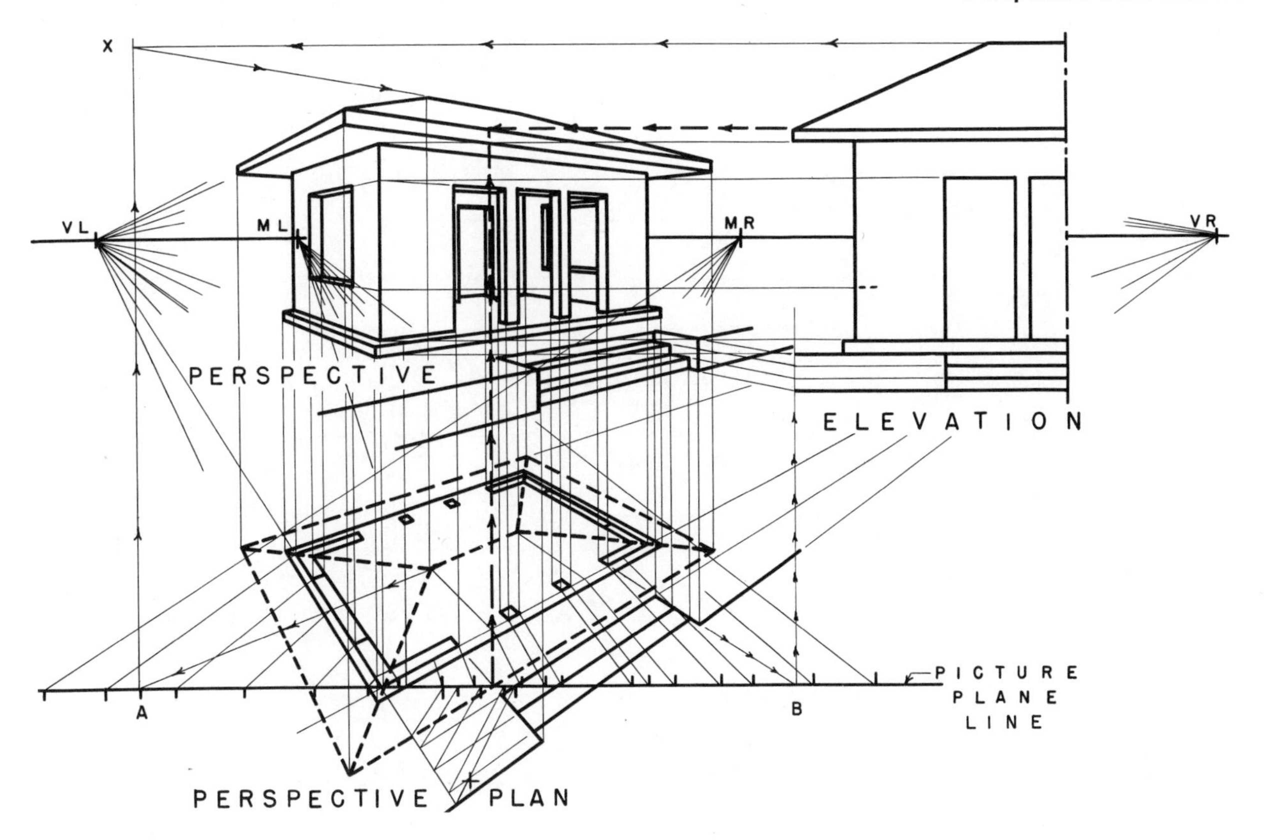

FIG-65 EXTERIOR BY PERSPECTIVE PLAN METHOD

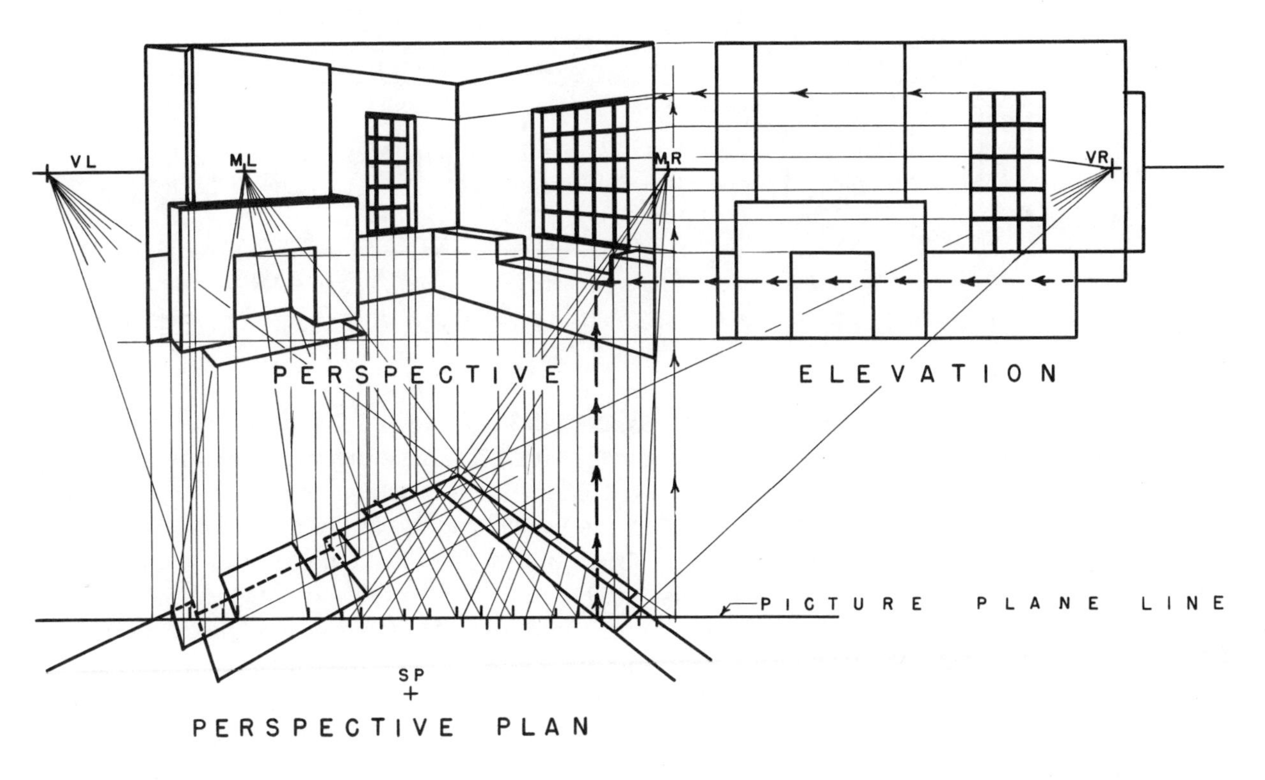

FIG-66 INTERIOR BY PERSPECTIVE PLAN METHOD

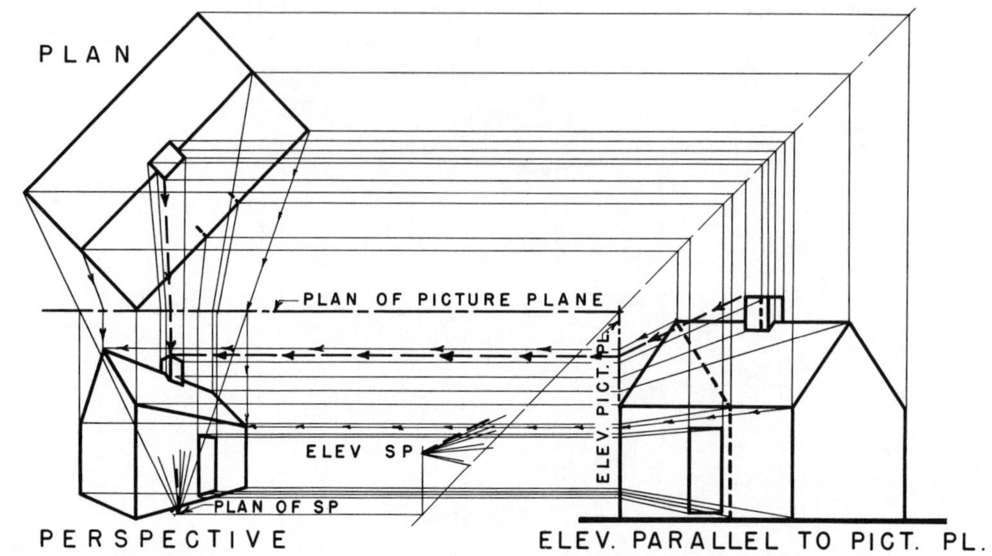

FIG-67 SIMPLE TWO-POINT EXTERIOR PERSPECTIVE

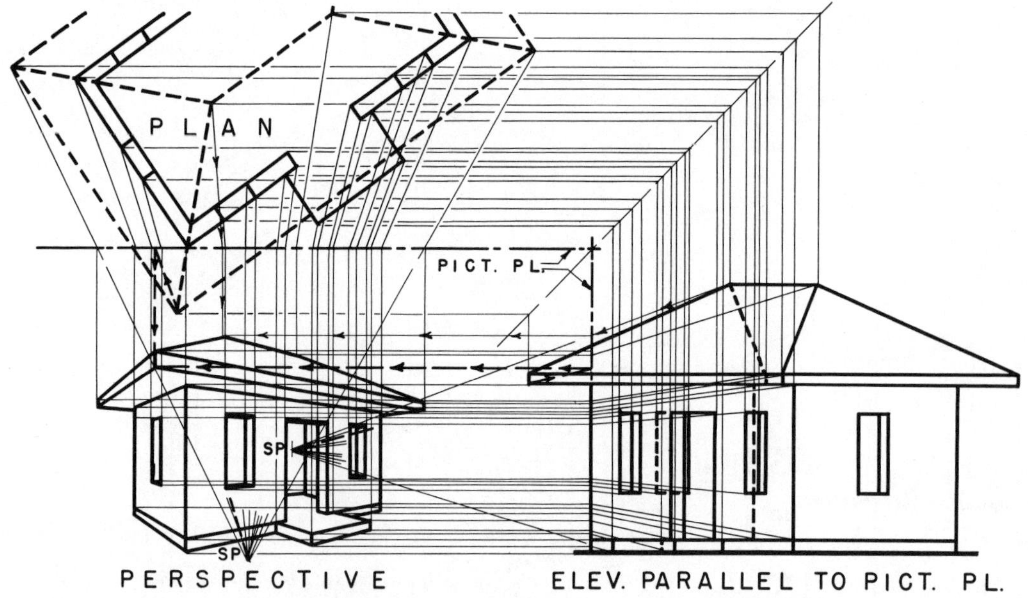

FIG-68 TWO-POINT DIRECT PROJECTION METHOD

THE DIRECT PROJECTION METHOD OF TWO-POINT PERSPECTIVE. This method requires the use of at least two auxiliary drawings for the construction. These drawings are (1) a plan and (2) an elevation parallel to the picture plane, Fig. 67. Each of the drawings shows the object, picture plane, and station point. The elevation parallel to the picture plane can be constructed by tracing the measurements horizontally from plan to a 45° line and then vertically to give the horizontal distances for the elevation. The heights of this special elevation are obtained from the multi-view drawings. When the design is sufficiently simple, the hidden parts of the design which are needed can be shown in the elevation by dotted lines, as has been done in the illustrations of Figs. 67 and 68. However, it is sometimes advisable or necessary to draw two elevations parallel to the picture plane, one from each direction as shown in Fig. 70.

Any point is found in perspective in the following manner. Locate the intersection with the picture plane of the projector through the point in each view. The vertical dropped from the plan

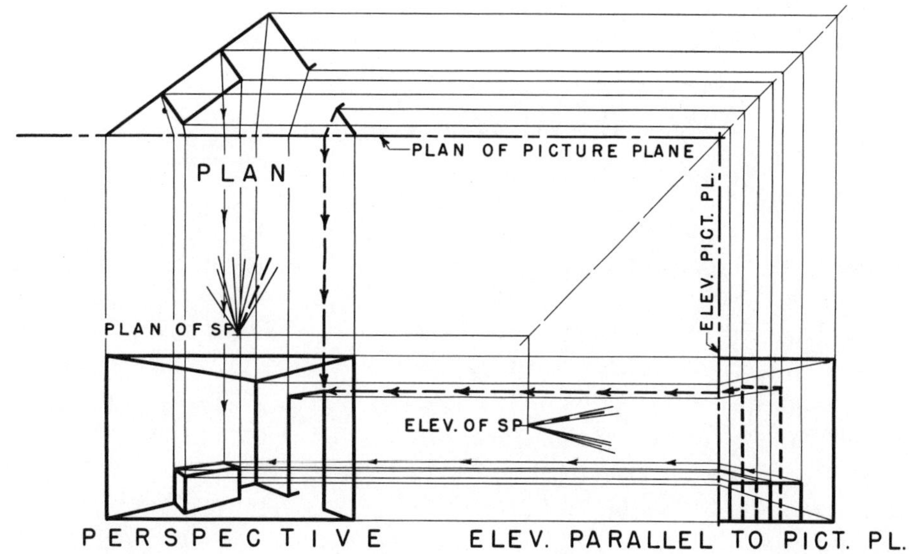

FIG-69 SIMPLE TWO-POINT INTERIOR PERSPECTIVE

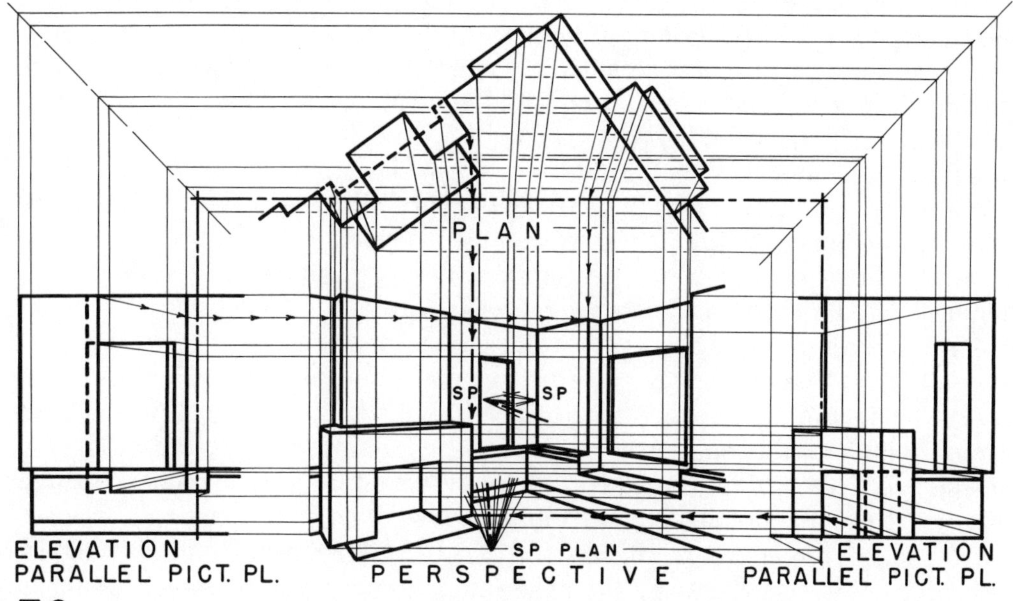

FIG-70 INTERIOR DIRECT PROJECTION METHOD

intersection meets the horizontal from the elevation intersection in the perspective of the point. Each perspective line is drawn through the perspective positions of the ends of the line. Construction lines are accented for two points in each example.

Vanishing points have not been used in the four examples of the direct projection method of two-point perspective given on pages 68 and 69. Vanishing points can be used if desired. They are located in the manner described for the common method of two-point perspective. When vanishing points are used, it is necessary to locate only one end of any line of the two typical sets of horizontal lines. The line can then be drawn from this point toward (or away from) its correct vanishing point. The directions of short lines can be determined much more accurately by drawing to a vanishing point than by finding both ends of the line and connecting the points. Exact direction of lines is of great importance for true pictorial effect. Where the lines are not accurate surfaces may seem warped or tilted.

CHAPTER 11
One-Point Perspective

One-point perspective is important to the architect and draftsman because it is frequently more suitable for the subject to be drawn or gives a more characteristic view than could be obtained with two-point perspective. The most striking and characteristic views of streets, landscape garden scenes, groups of buildings, single buildings, and parts of buildings both exterior and interior often show them as they would appear in one-point perspective.

One-point perspective is so named because only one of the three typical sets of lines converges to a vanishing point, Fig. 71. The remaining two sets of lines are parallel to the picture plane. Since lines which are parallel to the picture plane retain their true directions, the lines of each of these two sets remain parallel in perspective. In most one-point perspectives the picture plane is vertical. The vertical lines and one set of horizontal lines of the object are parallel to the picture plane, and remain respectively vertical and horizontal in the perspective drawing. The remaining set of horizontal lines is perpendicular to the picture plane and converges to a vanishing point.

One-point perspective can be used appropriately and effectively whenever the object presents a good appearance with the line of the center of vision of the observer perpendicular to one set of planes of the object, and consequently parallel to one set of lines; that is, when the conditions under which the object is naturally seen are those of one-point perspective.

Typical subjects for one-point perspectives are shown in the six illustrations of Fig. 71.

Figure 71A shows a group of buildings about a court with the observer looking toward one end of the court. This type of group or single U-shaped buildings seen from the open end of the U can be shown effectively in one-point perspective. One-point perspectives similar to that of Fig. 79A are often used for landscape designs showing walks, gardens, hedges, shrubs, trees, and walls.

Figure 71B presents a formal arrangement of objects balanced about a central motive in an appropriately formal and balanced way by using one-point perspective.

Figure 71C shows the interior of a room, with the observer between the two sides looking toward one end of the room. Long rooms, corridors, and hallways are especially striking subjects for one-point perspectives of this type when the line of vision is in the direction of the length of the room. Many such rooms are seldom seen in any other way.

Figure 71D shows a street scene, which is one of the most frequently observed and impressive one-point perspective effects. Whenever the observer is riding down the street, or walking along the sidewalk and looking parallel to the direction of the street, he sees the scene as a one-point perspective. The parallel lines of rows of lamp posts, curbs, and buildings converge to a single point in a most striking manner, since they are the long, continuous, and dominant lines of the scene.

Figure 71E, a single building, is often seen from an approach directly toward the center of the facade of the building. The perspective effect is more striking when there are definite projections of porches, wings, dormers, and other features of the design.

Figure 71F shows an entrance detail. One-point perspective is often very satisfactory for detail subjects, such as loggias, entrances, or other parts of buildings, as well as for complete buildings.

One-point perspective is extremely useful for both exterior and interior subjects and deserves the careful study and consideration of the person who wishes to become proficient in perspective drawing. Some of the most striking photographs used in illustrations of architectural magazines are one-point perspective views. Since the photographer usually has a wide-range of choice of views, the one-point perspective position is chosen in most cases because of its pictorial merits and not from necessity.

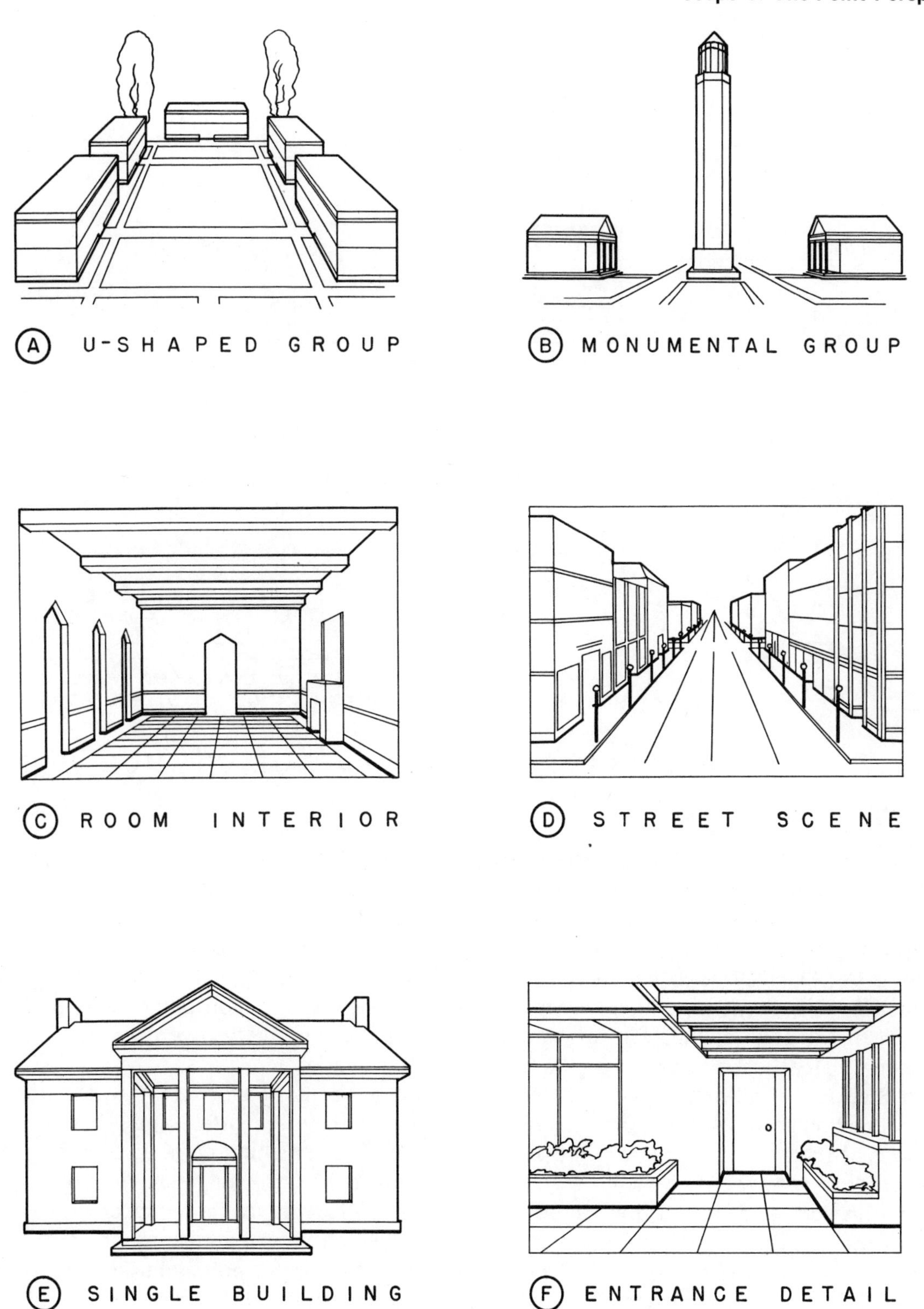

FIG-71 TYPICAL SUBJECTS FOR ONE-POINT PERSPECTIVES

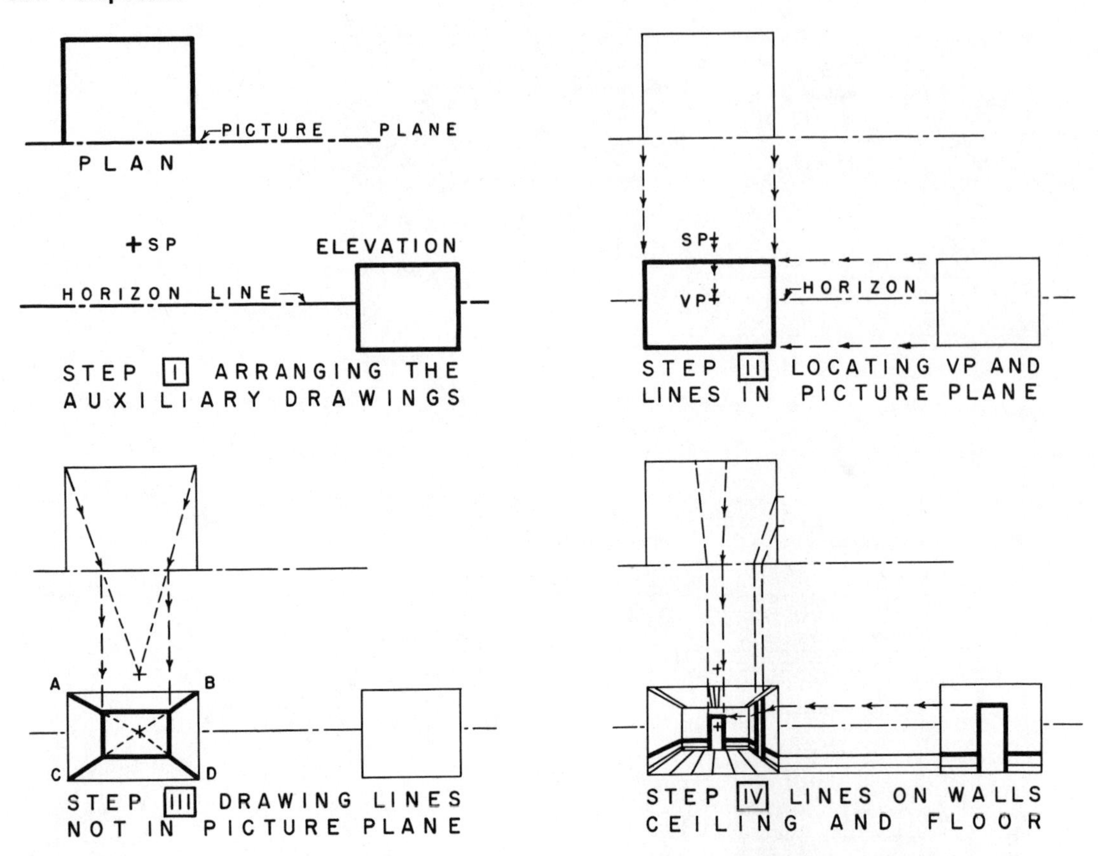

FIG-72 ONE-POINT PEPSPECTIVE BY THE COMMON METHOD

THE COMMON METHOD OF ONE-POINT PERSPECTIVE. The use of a plan showing the object, picture plane, and station point is required for the construction of the perspective drawing. This plan is used to work out the widths of the perspective drawing. An elevation is very useful in working out the heights of the perspective. It makes the heights used visually clear.

Step I of Fig. 72 shows the location of the plan and elevation as the first step in making a perspective. The elevation in this example is located below the station point of the plan and to the right of the edge of the plan to leave a clear area for the perspective drawing. The horizon has been located near the center of the height of the elevation.

In Step II vertical lines are drawn from plan and horizontal lines from the elevation to give the intersection of walls, floor, and ceiling of the room with the picture plane. This line of intersection is at scale size, since it lies in the picture plane. The vanishing point is located by drawing a vertical line from the plan of the station point to meet the horizon. When the position of one end of a line perpendicular to the picture plane has been located in the perspective drawing, the line can then be drawn through this point toward or away from the vanishing point.

Step III shows how the plan is used to determine the correct horizontal spacing of vertical lines for the perspective drawing. The projectors are drawn from the two rear corners of the plan toward the station point to meet the picture plane. From these intersections with the picture plane, vertical lines are drawn to the perspective locating the two vertical corners at the rear of the room. The lines of the intersections of walls with floor and ceiling are drawn from the corners A, B, C, D toward the vanishing point to meet the rear corners of the room. Horizontal lines from the two rear corners complete the simple perspective.

Step IV shows how lines can be traced around the walls and along the floor and ceiling from their correct scale positions on the lines in the picture plane.

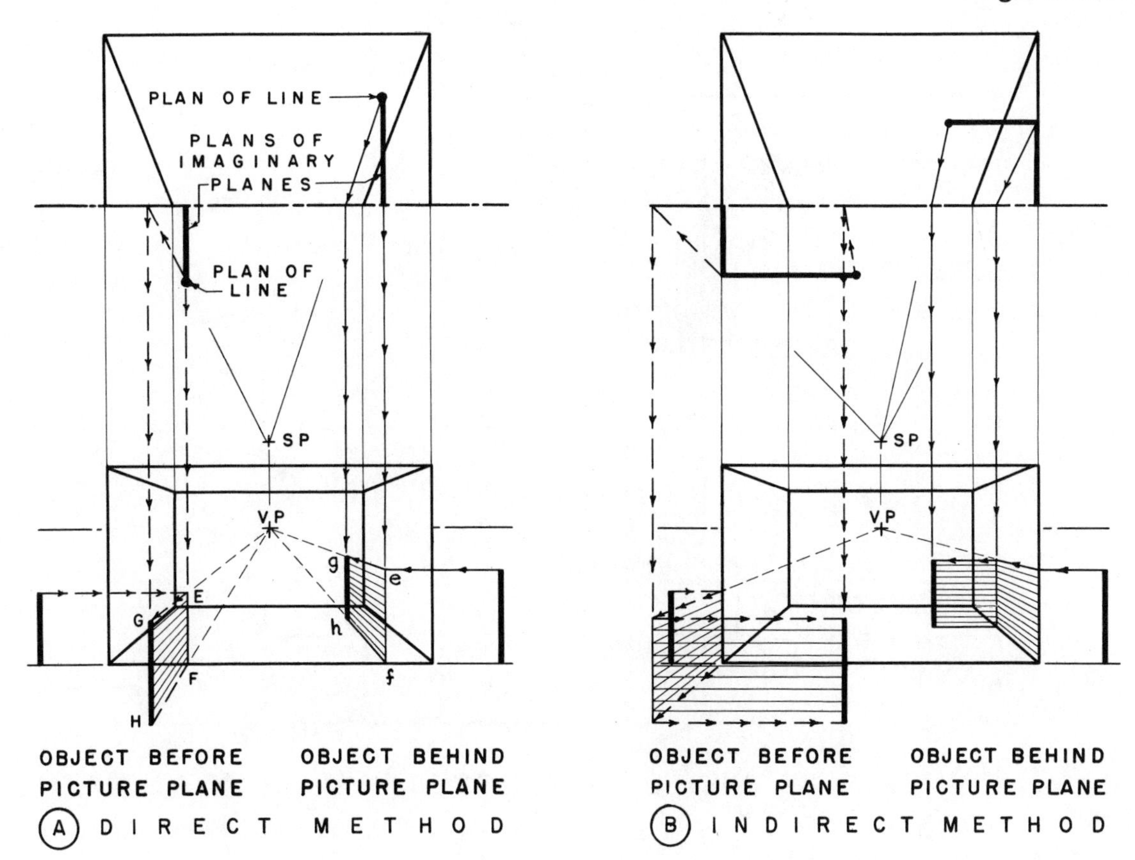

FIG-73 HEIGHTS OF FREE OBJECTS IN ONE-POINT PERSPECTIVE

Figure 73A and B shows two methods of determining heights of objects which do not lie in or touch the wall surfaces or picture plane of a one-point perspective drawing. In these examples the freestanding objects are vertical lines which rest on the floor. In each example there are two freestanding lines. The line object on the right of each example is behind the picture plane, and the one on the left is in front of the picture plane. The method shown can be repeated as many times as necessary for different parts of a solid object to obtain points to make the drawing.

In the direct method, Fig. 73A, an imaginary vertical plane which is parallel to the side walls of the perspective drawing and perpendicular to the picture plane is extended through the point plan of the freestanding line to meet the picture plane in plan. The height of the line is laid out to scale on the line E–F of intersection of the imaginary plane and picture plane. The height is then traced directly along the imaginary plane by lines through the vanishing point and brought to correct perspective position at G–H as shown. This is the most convenient and simple method of determining most heights of freestanding objects. However, in the special case when the freestanding line is on a vertical through the vanishing point, this method cannot be used, because the line from the vanishing point is a vertical line and will not intersect vertical lines brought down from plan to establish heights. Furthermore, the lines from the vanishing point must be at a sufficient angle so that their intersections with vertical lines can be accurately located. Objects which are very near a vertical line through the vanishing point cannot be accurately located by this method.

The indirect method carries the heights along the walls or other vertical planes perpendicular to the picture plane to the required distance, then along imaginary planes parallel to the picture plane to the correct perspective position. In the two examples of Fig. 73B the wall serves as the plane perpendicular to the picture plane for the object behind the picture plane. An extension of the wall has been used for the object in front of the picture plane.

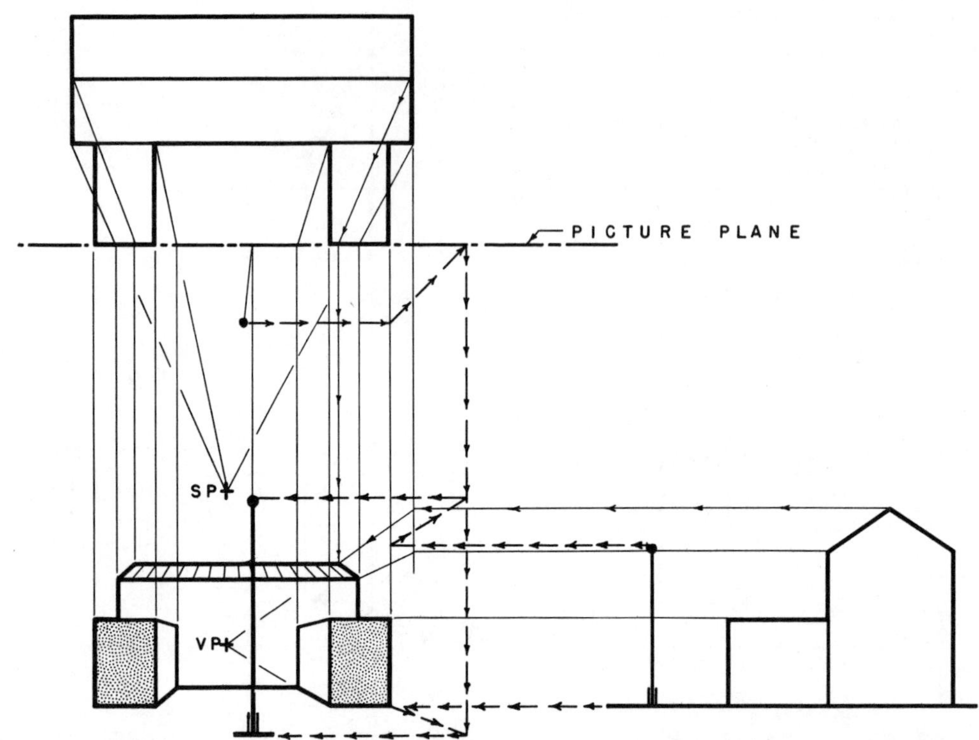

FIG-74 ELEMENTS OF ONE-POINT PERSPECTIVE - COMMON METHOD

The three examples of one-point perspective by the common method, Figs. 74, 75, and 76, show the application of principles previously explained to more detailed subjects. An elevation or section has been drawn in each example in order to make the methods of determining heights as clear as possible. It is not necessary to draw the elevation or section as a part of the construction of a perspective by the common method.

The heights and widths of the parts of the object in the picture plane are drawn to scale size. Heights of parts behind and in front of the picture plane are worked out by methods explained on pages 72 and 73.

In Fig. 74 the ends of the projecting wings of the building lie in the picture plane and are drawn to scale size by dropping verticals from plan to meet horizontals from elevation. The top and bottom lines of the wings, which are perpendicular to the picture plane, are drawn to the vanishing point to meet the construction lines brought down from the junction of the wings and main building in plan. The indirect method is used to determine the height of the flagpole, since it is too nearly on a vertical line through the vanishing point to use the direct method accurately. These construction lines are heavy dotted lines. The height of the roof is traced back into position by the direct method, using an extension of the end wall to the picture plane for the height construction.

In Fig. 75 the lines made of short dots on the right side of the perspective show the construction of heights by tracing around hidden surfaces. The lines with longer dots and arrows in this example show the construction of a height, by the direct method, around one imaginary corner. The indirect method is used to determine the height of the highest point of the building.

Figure 76 illustrates the tracing of heights around visible wall surfaces for the wainscoting, windows, and ceiling line. The height of the rectangular box is found by the indirect method, using an imaginary extension of a plane of the box to meet the wall. The sofa lines are projected directly from the scale profile (drawn in dotted lines in the picture plane) to perspective position.

There are often many different ways in which a height can be worked out. Choose the construction which is easy to use and which gives accurate results.

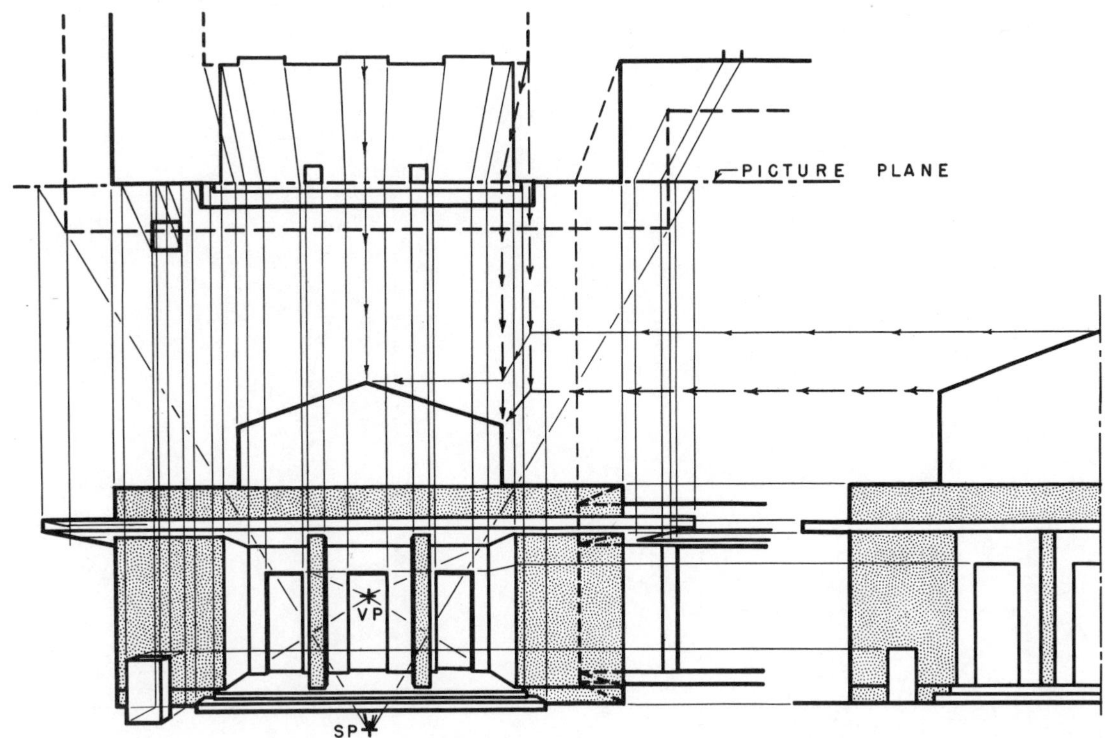

FIG-75 COMMON METHOD OF ONE-POINT PERSPECTIVE

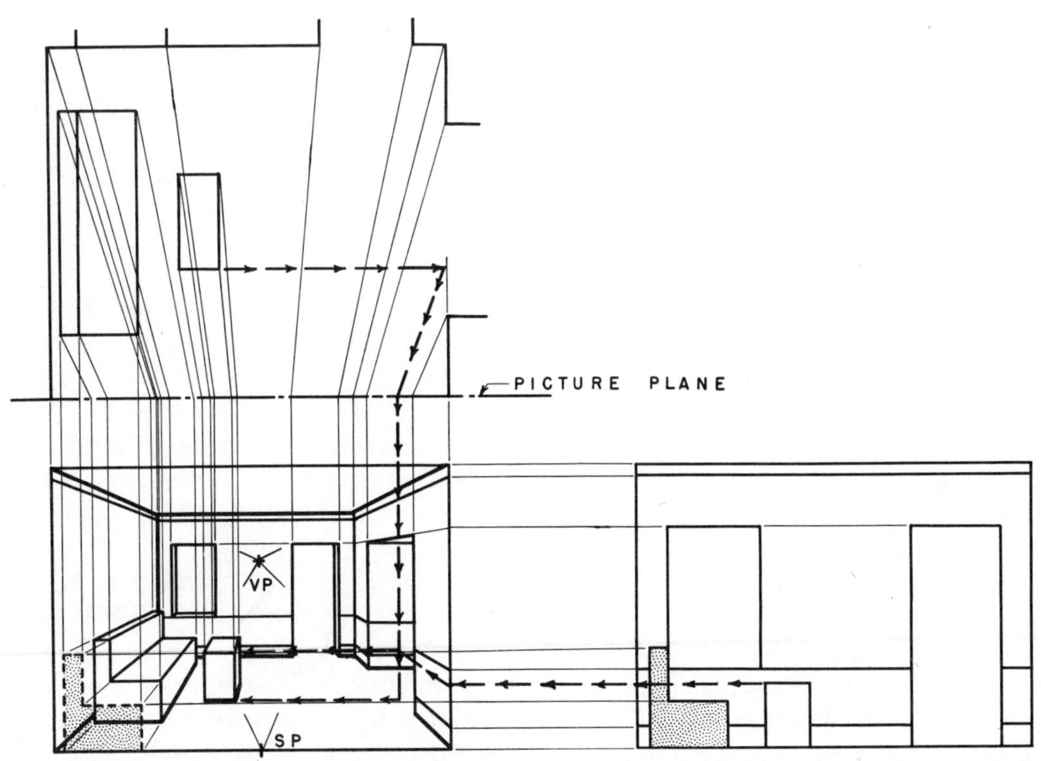

FIG-76 COMMON METHOD OF ONE-POINT PERSPECTIVE

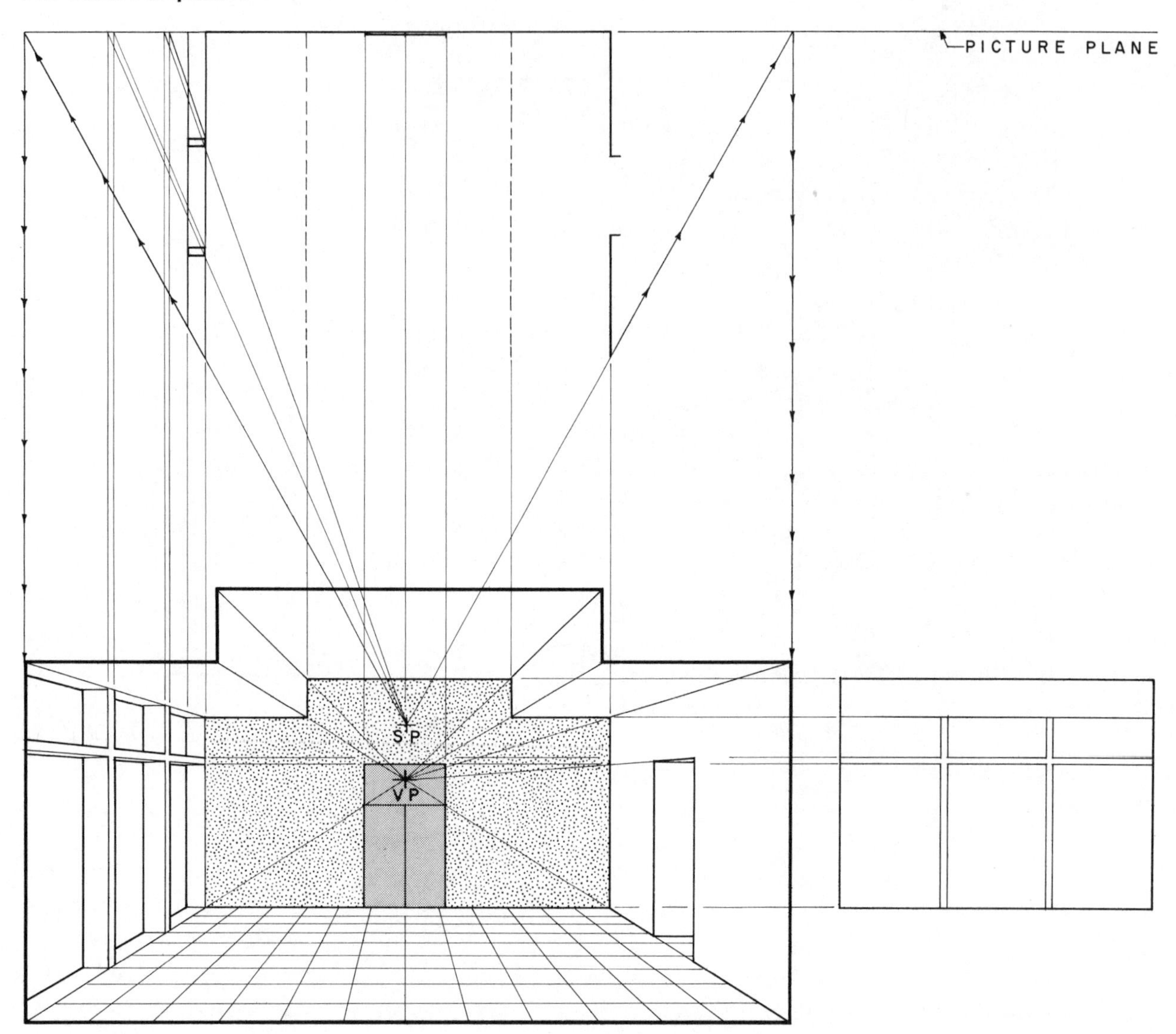

FIG-77 PICTURE PLANE AT FARTHEST VISIBLE WALL PLANE

POSITIONS OF THE PICTURE PLANE. In the preceding examples of one-point perspective the picture plane has been located on the nearest important wall plane which parallels the picture plane for exteriors. The important major areas of all interiors have ended at the picture plane. The objects have therefore been behind the picture planes, except for small details for both exteriors and interiors. This position of the picture plane has two advantages: (1) the heights are easily constructed and (2) the size of the perspective is predetermined. It will be almost exactly the same as the elevation looking in the same direction. The principal disadvantage is that relatively large elevations and plans are used to make small perspectives.

The picture plane at the farthest visible wall surface gives a relatively large perspective from a small plan and elevation, Figs. 77 and 78. All of the wall surface in the picture plane is at scale size and is true shape. Heights can be projected from any point in the picture plane with a line to or from VP to its correct perspective position as shown in Fig. 73A. This procedure is satisfactory when the VP line is sufficiently inclined to give an accurate intersection with the vertical line from the plan of the picture plane. When the VP line of the perspective is too nearly vertical to give an accurate intersection with a vertical line, the indirect method of Fig. 73B should be used.

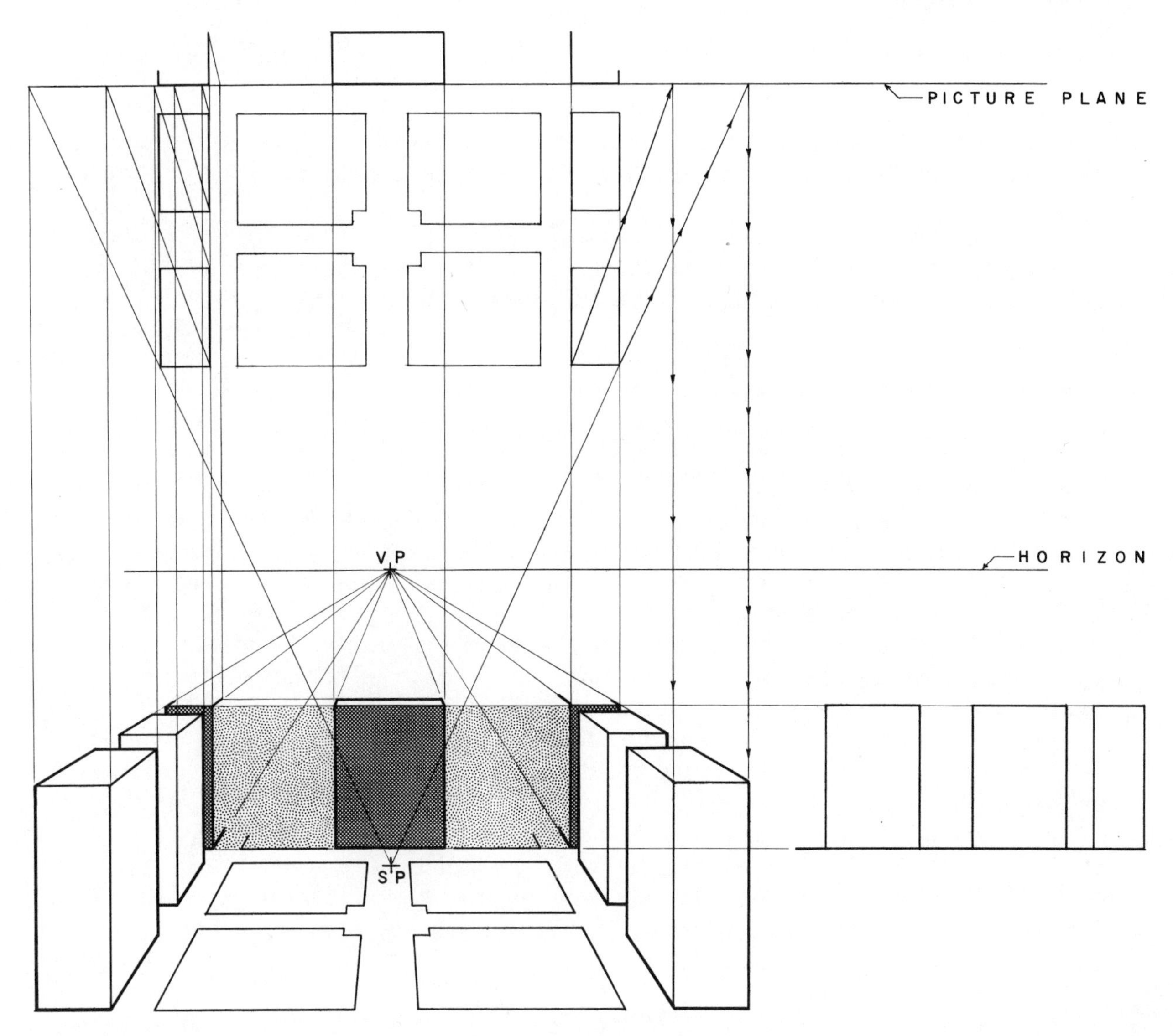

FIG-78 PICTURE PLANE AT FARTHEST VISIBLE WALL PLANE

The interior perspective of Fig. 77 has the interior surface of the end wall in the picture plane. Projectors from the vanishing point through the corners of the room shape in the picture plane give the lines of intersection of ceiling and floor with the side walls. The projector is drawn in plan from the SP through the nearest visible vertical line of each side wall to meet the picture plane. The vertical lines from these two points give the extreme right and left edges of the perspective. The intersections of these lines with the projectors from VP give points where horizontal lines are drawn to terminate the floor and ceiling. There is much less chance of confusion and errors in the perspective construction if the plan shows only the lines which will be visible in the perspective.

The perspective area should not exceed the actual size of the room being shown. Side walls, ceiling, and floor should not be extended indefinitely beyond their size and exaggerate the size of an interior space.

The exterior perspective of Fig. 78 has the picture plane at the visible wall surface of the most distant block. The perspective can begin with the elevation looking perpendicular to the picture plane drawn to scale on the picture plane. Lines from VP through corners of this elevation give the lines of the object which are perpendicular to the picture plane.

THE LOCATION OF THE PICTURE PLANE. With a fixed relation of object and station point and a given scale, the size of the perspective drawing obtained can be varied by changing the position of the picture plane, Fig. 79. The perspective drawings obtained with these parallel positions of the picture plane will be identical in all respects except size. The closer the picture plane to the station point, the smaller the perspective, and the farther the picture plane from the station point, the larger the perspective.

In a one-point perspective of a simple rectangular room there are two positions of the picture plane that are more convenient than others. These positions are (1) through the room where it is proposed to terminate the nearest part of the perspective; (2) to coincide with the visible plane of the rear wall of the room. In the first case, Fig. 79B, the perspective lines perpendicular to the picture plane are projected toward the vanishing point from the scale-size section cut through the room by the picture plane. In the second case, Fig. 79D, all parts of the rear wall which lie in the picture plane are drawn to scale, and lines perpendicular to the picture plane are projected away from the vanishing point through points on this true-scale part of the drawing.

An intermediate position can be used for the picture plane so that lines are extended both in front of and behind the picture plane from the scale-size intersection, Fig. 79C. The picture plane can be located in front of or behind the object to secure more extreme changes in size of the perspective drawing. In either of these cases the object is assumed to extend to an imaginary intersection with the picture plane for scale measurments, Fig. 79A and E. However, extreme increases in size obtained by pushing the picture plane behind the object lose in accuracy, while extreme reductions in size take an unreasonable amount of space for auxiliary plans and elevations in comparison with the size perspective obtained.

In exteriors the picture plane is usually located to coincide with some important visible plane of the object for convenience in measuring, but may be located at other positions through, behind, or in front of the object.

The position of the station point in one-point perspective can be varied in *distance* from the object, *height*, and *horizontal position* to obtain variations in the pictorial effect of the perspective drawing. These variations are limited by conditions imposed by the form of the object itself and by the requirements of one-point perspective. A familiarity with the possible variations, their limits, and their effects on the resulting perspective drawing will enable the draftsman to get the best possible results from his work.

The distance from the station point to the object determines the relative sizes of near and distant parts of the object and the amount of visible area of planes perpendicular to the picture plane (where height, and horizontal position of SP remain constant), and under certain conditions influences the size of the perspective drawing, Fig. 80.

Parts of the object which lie in the picture plane remain constantly at scale-size regardless of the distance to the station point, Fig. 80A, B, C far wall; D, E, F near walls.

Parts of the object which are behind the picture plane decrease in size as the station point gets nearer and increase in size as the station point becomes farther away, Fig. 80D, E, and F.

Parts of the object which are in front of the picture plane increase in size as the station point approaches the object and decrease in size as the SP moves away, Fig. 80A, B, and C.

When the station point is very near the object, the parts of the object at the outside edges of a one-point perspective drawing will appear distorted. To avoid excessive distortion the minimum distance from the station point should be great enough to include every part of the object shown in the perspective in a 45° (30° is better) cone from the station point.

The perspective position of the station point coincides with the position of the vanishing point in a one-point perspective drawing. The station point may be located above, below, or to one side of center for variations in pictorial effect, Figs. 81 and 82. When the station point is far from the center of the drawing, the perspective becomes distorted when viewed from a natural position. This distortion is not usually objectionable in views above buildings or from low viewpoints in street scenes. It is likely to produce a bad effect when the station point is moved far to one side.

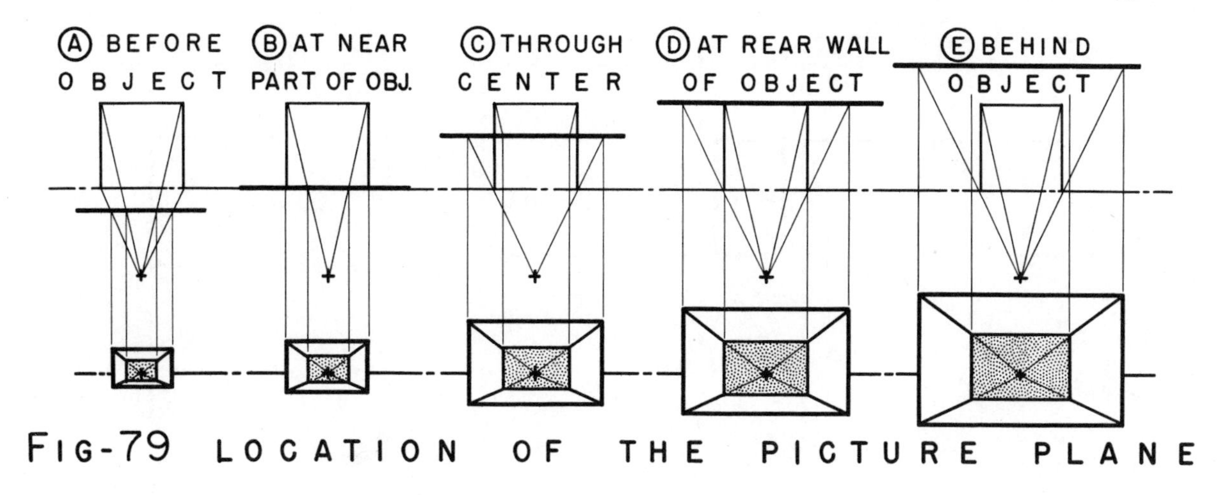

FIG-79 LOCATION OF THE PICTURE PLANE

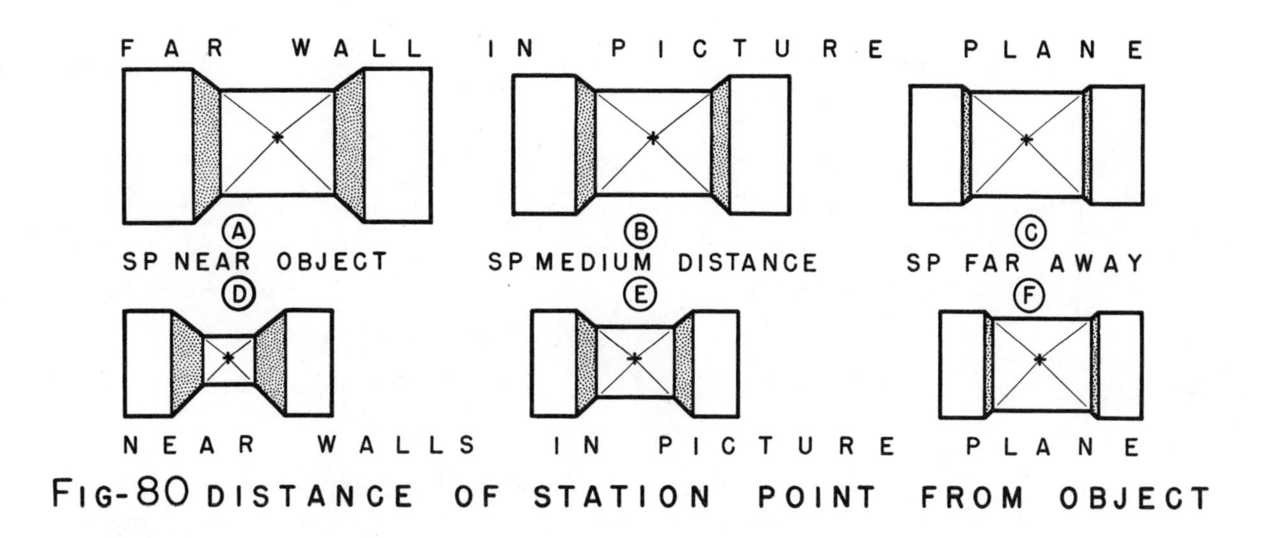

FIG-80 DISTANCE OF STATION POINT FROM OBJECT

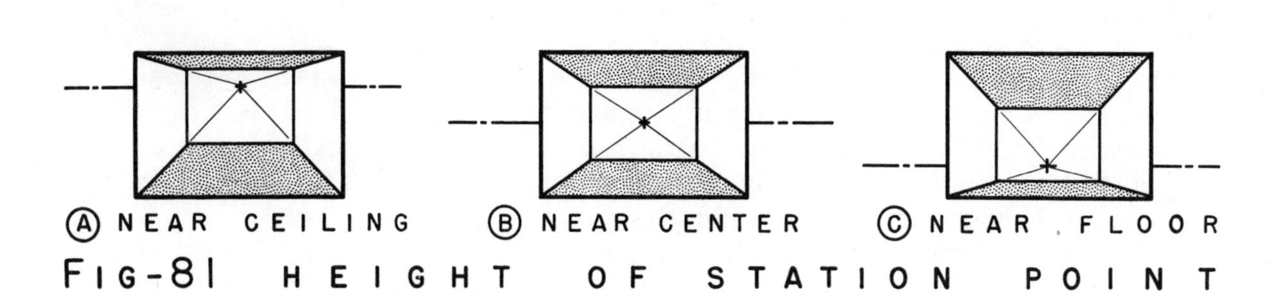

FIG-81 HEIGHT OF STATION POINT

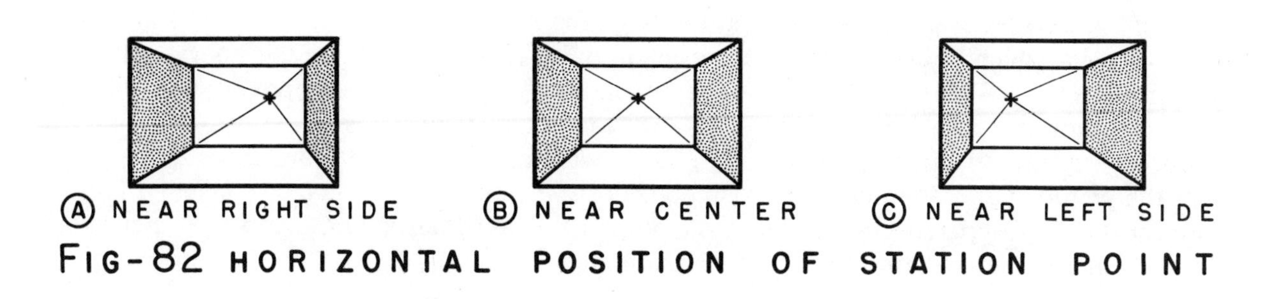

FIG-82 HORIZONTAL POSITION OF STATION POINT

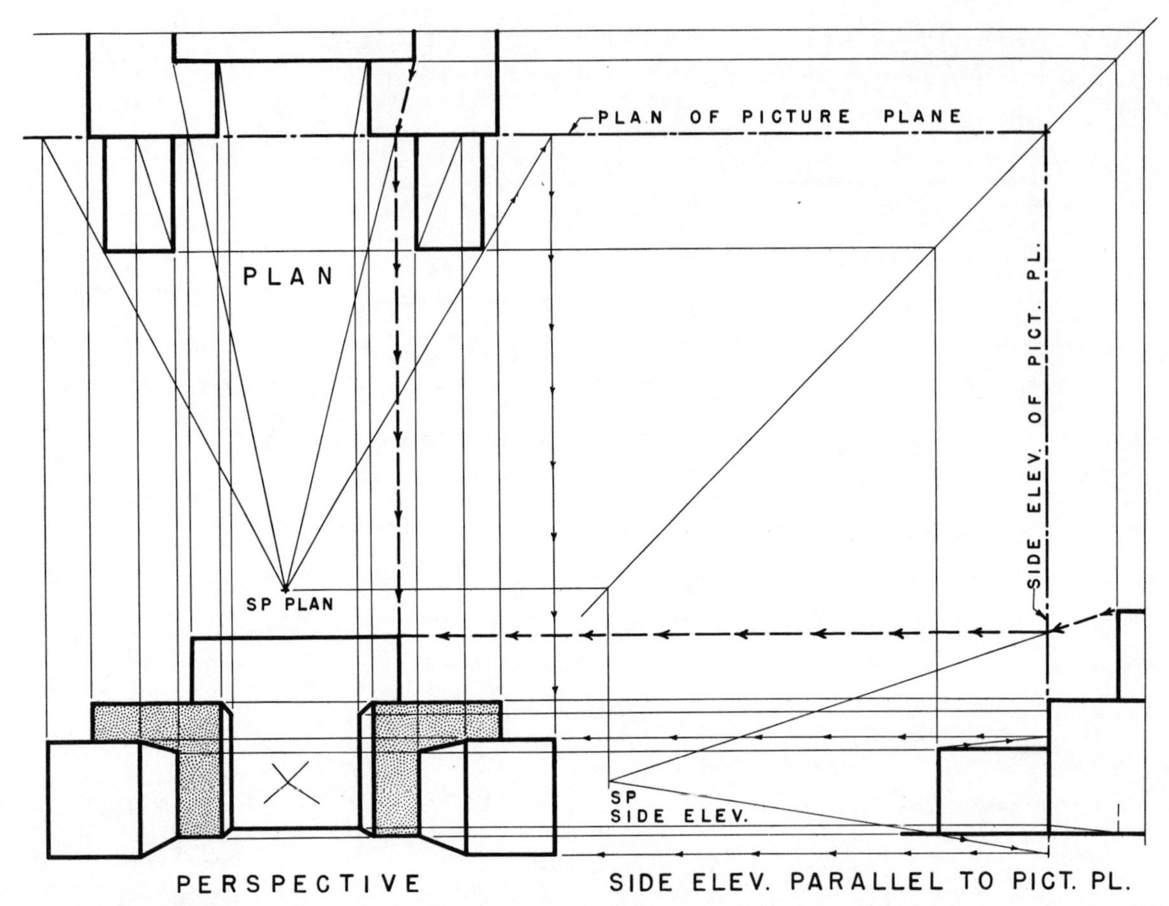

FIG-83 ONE-POINT PERSPECTIVE, DIRECT PROJECTION METHOD

The direct projection method of one-point perspective requires at least two preliminary drawings: (1) a plan, (2) a side view parallel to the picture plane. *The object, picture plane, and station point are shown in each of these views.* When the object is symmetrical, so that both side views are identical as in Fig. 83, or when the design is so simple that the features of one side which differ from the other may be shown in dotted lines, only one side view is necessary. When an unsymmetrical design is too complicated to have both sides shown in the same drawing, it is necessary to have two side views in order to construct the perspective. The use of two side views is illustrated in Fig. 84. Great accuracy is required for this type of perspective construction.

Widths for the perspective drawing are obtained from the plan, and *heights* from the side view, as shown by the construction lines in the examples.

The construction varies from different relations between the point on the object, the picture plane, and the station point. There are three possible relations: (1) the point may be back of the picture plane; (2) the point may be in front of the picture plane; (3) the point may lie in the picture plane. Typical construction lines for all three of these conditions are shown in Fig. 83. The shaded areas of the perspectives of Figs. 83 and 84 lie in the picture plane.

1–A point which is back of the picture plane is located as shown by the heavy dotted lines with arrows in Fig. 83. The arrows show the directions in which the lines were drawn. In the plan drawing, a line is drawn from the point toward the station point to meet the picture plane, then dropped vertically. In the side view the line is drawn from the point toward the station point to meet the picture plane, then drawn across horizontally to meet the vertical construction line from plan and locate the perspective position of the point. The construction lines for all points back of the picture plane are drawn in a similar manner.

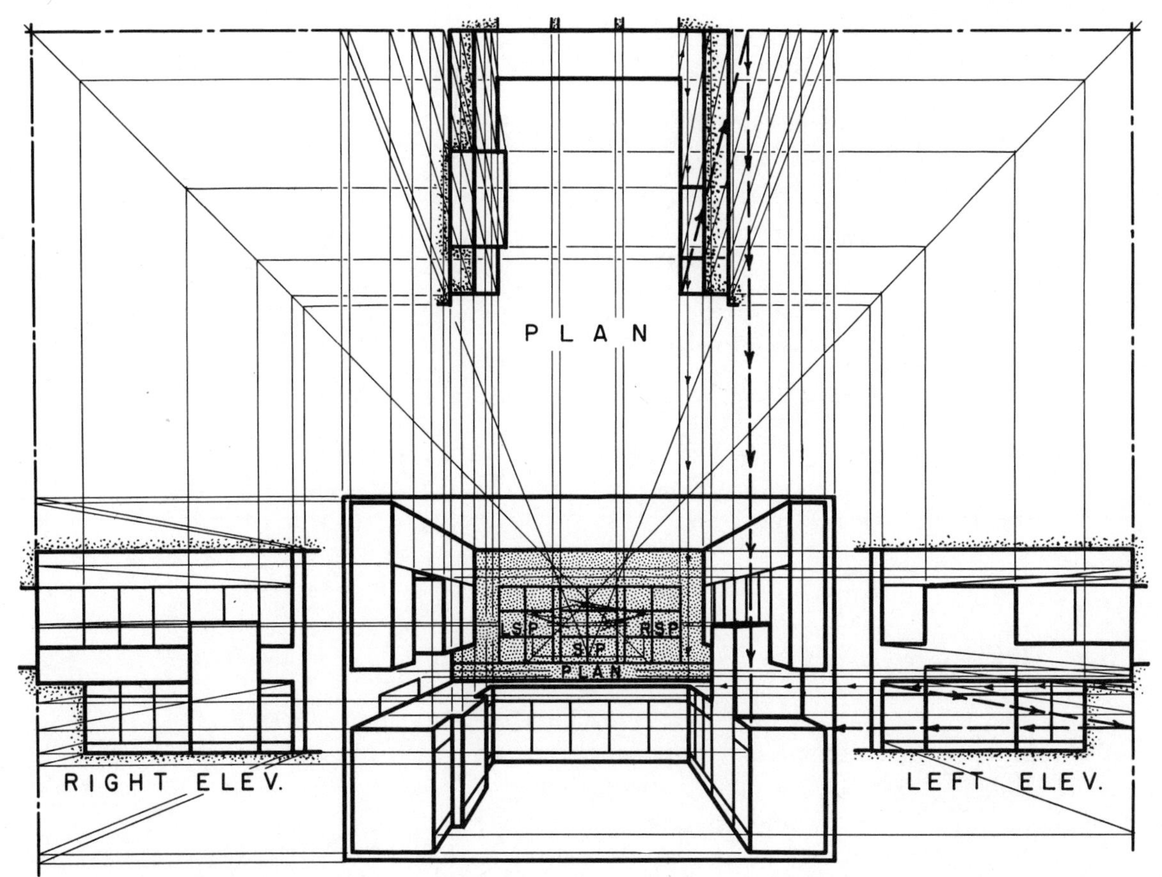

FIG-84 ONE-POINT INTERIOR-DIRECT PROJECTION METHOD

2–To find the perspective position of a point which is in front of the picture plane the procedure is similar to that for a point back of the picture plane, except that the projectors in plan and side view have to be drawn away from the station point to intersect the picture plane instead of toward it. The ends of the projecting wings of the building in Fig. 83 are located in perspective in this way. The construction lines for one corner of the projecting wing are marked with small arrowheads. In plan the construction line is drawn from the station point through the corner to meet the picture plane, and then dropped vertically. In the side view, lines which start at the top and bottom of the corner are drawn away from the station point to meet the picture plane, then projected horizontally to determine the height of the corner of the wall.

3–The perspective position of a point in the picture plane is found by drawing a vertical line from the plan position of the point to meet a horizontal line from the side view of the point. The two wall surfaces of the building in Fig. 83, which are in the picture plane, are scale-size and are located in the manner described above. In Fig. 84 the picture plane cuts through walls, floor, and ceiling, and this section is drawn at scale-size by the method of finding points in the picture plane. In this figure the drawings have been crowded together in order to keep them as large as possible. The plan and two side views of the station point lie within the area of the perspective drawing.

A vanishing point has not been used for the sets of lines perpendicular to the picture plane in either of the examples of the direct projection method shown in Figs. 83 and 84, since this method does not require the use of a VP for the set of lines perpendicular to the picture plane. By using the vanishing point the construction is simplified and greater accuracy is secured. The vanishing point may also be used as a check on construction. The vanishing point is located at the intersection of a vertical line from the plan position and a horizontal line from the side view of the station point.

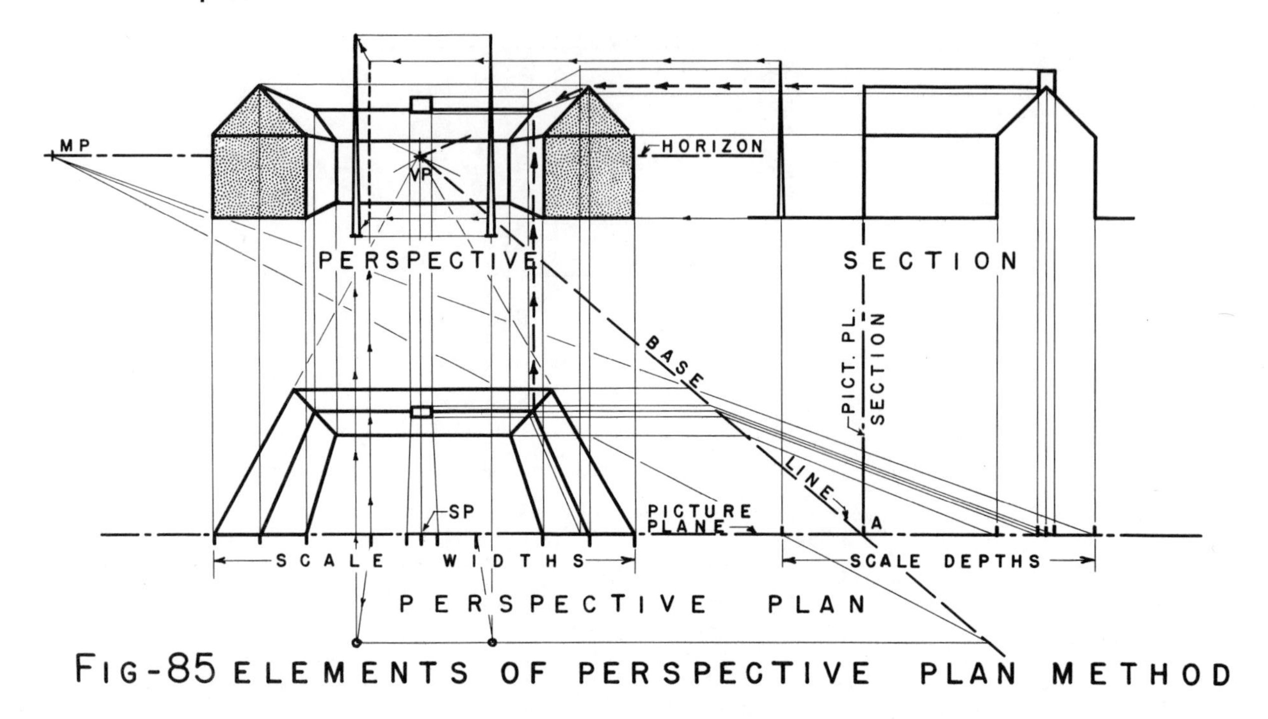

FIG-85 ELEMENTS OF PERSPECTIVE PLAN METHOD

The perspective plan method of one-point perspective requires that the plan be drawn in perspective. From this perspective plan vertical lines are drawn to the perspective to locate the correct positions of vertical lines and the correct horizontal spacing of points. The heights of parts of the object in the picture plane are drawn at scale size. Heights of parts of the object back of, or in front of, the picture plane must be laid out on vertical measuring lines in the picture plane. The heights are then traced to their correct positions by drawing lines around actual corners of the object or around imaginary corners made by drawing construction lines parallel to the typical sets of horizontal lines of the object. The construction of the example in Fig. 85 has been divided into a number of steps in the following explanation.

1–The section is drawn and the horizon line for the perspective placed at the correct height for the section.

2–The perspective plan position of the line representing the picture plane is drawn at any convenient distance from the horizon (far enough away so the perspective plan will not run into the perspective).

3–Scale widths for the perspective plan are laid out on the picture plane line where they will not overlap vertical lines brought down from the section. They are marked by short vertical lines below the picture plane line.

4–A vertical line is drawn from the perspective plan width measurement of the station point on the picture plane to locate the vanishing point of the perspective on the horizon.

5–From the vanishing point VP, a distance is laid out on the horizon equal to the multi-view plan distance from the picture plane to the station point. This locates the position of the measuring point MP, which is used to determine depths in the perspective plan.

6–Scale distances of depths are laid out on the picture plane by drawing vertical construction lines from the section. These points are marked with short vertical lines above the picture plane.

7–From the depth measurement for the picture plane at A, a base line is drawn to the vanishing point and extended below the picture plane.

8–Lines are drawn from the depth measurements toward the measuring point for points back of the picture plane, and away from the measuring points for points in front of the picture plane, to intersect with the base line. Horizontal lines are drawn from these intersections with the base line to locate the depths in the perspective plan.

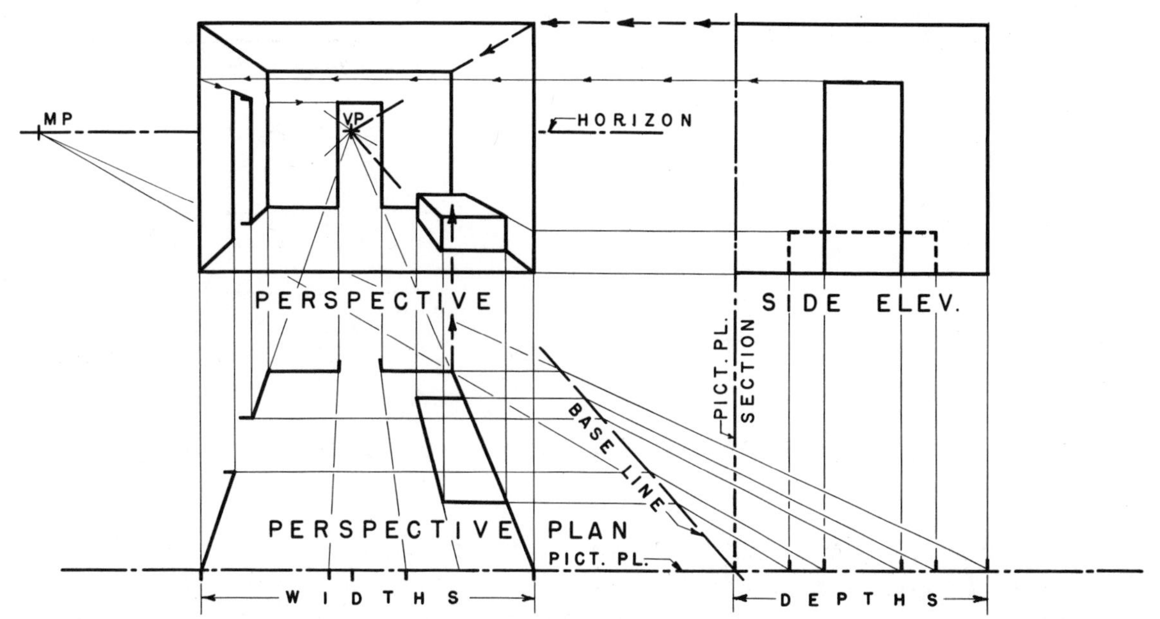

FIG-86 PERSPECTIVE PLAN METHOD, ONE-POINT PERSPECTIVE

9–Widths of the perspective plan are located by drawing lines from the width measurements to the vanishing point for points behind the picture plane, and away from the vanishing point for points in front of the picture plane.

10–Since the projecting end walls lie entirely in the picture plane, they can be located in the perspective by drawing vertical lines from perspective plan to meet horizontal lines from section.

11–The ridge, eaves, and base lines of the perspective are drawn from the end walls toward the vanishing point to meet the correct vertical lines brought up from the perspective plan. The horizontal connecting lines are then drawn from the ends of these lines.

The heavy dotted construction lines show the method of finding the height of the point of intersection of the ridges. In this case the construction line is carried along a line of the object.

The height of the chimney is carried around two imaginary corners. This height could not be carried directly back from the picture plane as was done in the case of the point of intersection of the ridges, because the line to the vanishing point would be practically vertical and its intersection with a vertical line could not be accurately determined.

If we imagine the flagpole on the left as extending back in a plane perpendicular to the picture plane and intersecting it, the line of intersection will be the dotted vertical line shown in perspective. From the ends of this line, construction lines can be drawn from the vanishing point to meet the vertical line brought up from the perspective plan position of the flagpole to determine its height.

The numbered steps above, from 1 to 9 inclusive, refer to Fig. 86 as well as Fig. 85. In Fig. 86 the line of intersection of the picture plane, walls, ceiling, and floor is drawn at scale-size. The height of the rear wall is found as shown by the heavy dotted construction lines with arrows. The heights of the doors and box are traced around the wall surfaces.

The position of the picture plane can be varied in the perspective plan method as in other methods of perspective drawing. However, this device for varying the size of the perspective drawing does not have as great advantages in this method. Since all measurements can be laid out to scale in the perspective plan method, size variations can be pretty well controlled by use of the scale. In other methods this would require construction of auxiliary drawings at the scale used. In the perspective plan method the perspective plan is the only auxiliary drawing used in the actual construction. It must always be drawn as a special drawing. Since plans and elevations are not used directly as auxiliary drawings, their size has no bearing on the amount of space required.

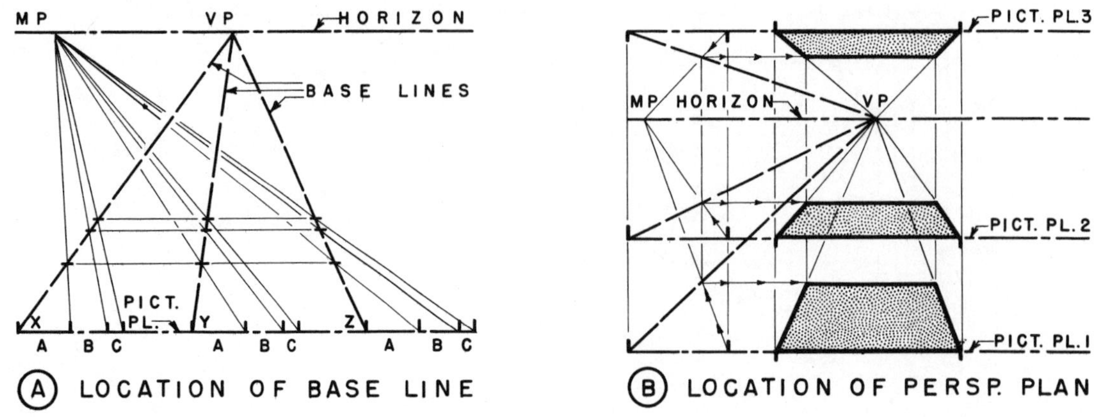

FIG-87 DETAILS OF PERSPECTIVE PLAN METHOD

Figure 87A shows graphically that any line from the vanishing point can be used as a base line to make the perspective plan, and that the resulting perspective depths will be the same regardless of which line is used. With a given horizon, picture plane line in perspective plan, vanishing point VP, and measuring point MP, three base lines are drawn from VP to the picture plane. From the intersections of these base lines and the picture plane at points X, Y, and Z, the same measurements, A, B, and C, have been laid out in order to the right. The construction lines from each of these identical sets of depth measurements to the measuring point give exactly the same perspective depths. This is true because the measuring point is the vanishing point of a set of parallel lines, which transfers equal measurements in perspective from the picture plane to lines perpendicular to the picture plane. Since all lines drawn to the vanishing point in one-point perspective represent lines perpendicular to the picture plane and likewise all lines drawn to the measuring point are lines of the set transferring the equal measurements, any line to the VP can be used as a base line.

Figure 87B shows that with a given horizon, vanishing point, measuring point, and horizontal location of width measurements, the distance between the horizon line and perspective plan position of the picture plane has no effect on the resulting perspective. All three positions of the picture plane give the same horizontal spacing of vertical lines. The perspective plan can be drawn either above or below the perspective. When the perspective plan is drawn very near the horizon, it becomes inaccurate because it is so thin that the intersection of lines (which are almost parallel) cannot be accurately determined. The floor in Fig. 86 could be used for the perspective plan.

The width and depth measurements of Figs. 85 and 86 have been kept entirely separate in order to make the construction more easily understood. In actual practice some line of the perspective plan is selected as a base line and the width, and depth measurements overlap. This procedure has been followed in Figs. 88 and 89. In all cases the base line must be drawn through the depth measurement for the picture plane.

The construction of heights in Fig. 88 is similar to those in Fig. 85, except that many of the heights are traced around hidden corners. These hidden construction lines are dotted.

In Fig. 89 the heights of the windows and wainscoting are traced around wall surfaces. The top of the fireplace opening is projected to the vanishing point from its scale-height in the picture plane. The height of the triangular prism is carried around two imaginary corners; one at the intersection of the wall and picture plane, one on the wall surface on the right side.

The measuring point can be used on either side of the vanishing point. In Figs. 85 and 86 it has been used on the left, and in Figs. 88 and 89 on the right. Two measuring points, one on each side, can be used if desired.

The elevation and section views are not necessary as a part of the perspective drawing. They have been drawn in the examples to make the construction of heights visually evident.

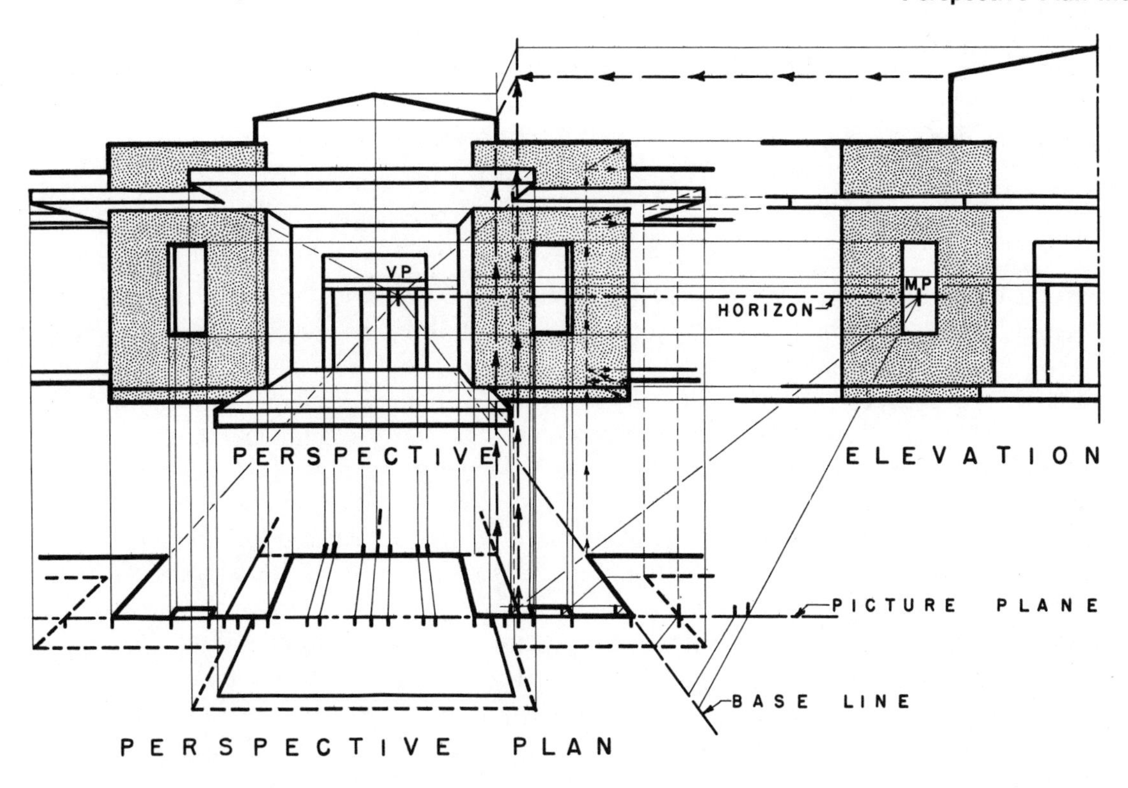

FIG-88 ONE-POINT EXTERIOR-PERSPECTIVE PLAN METHOD

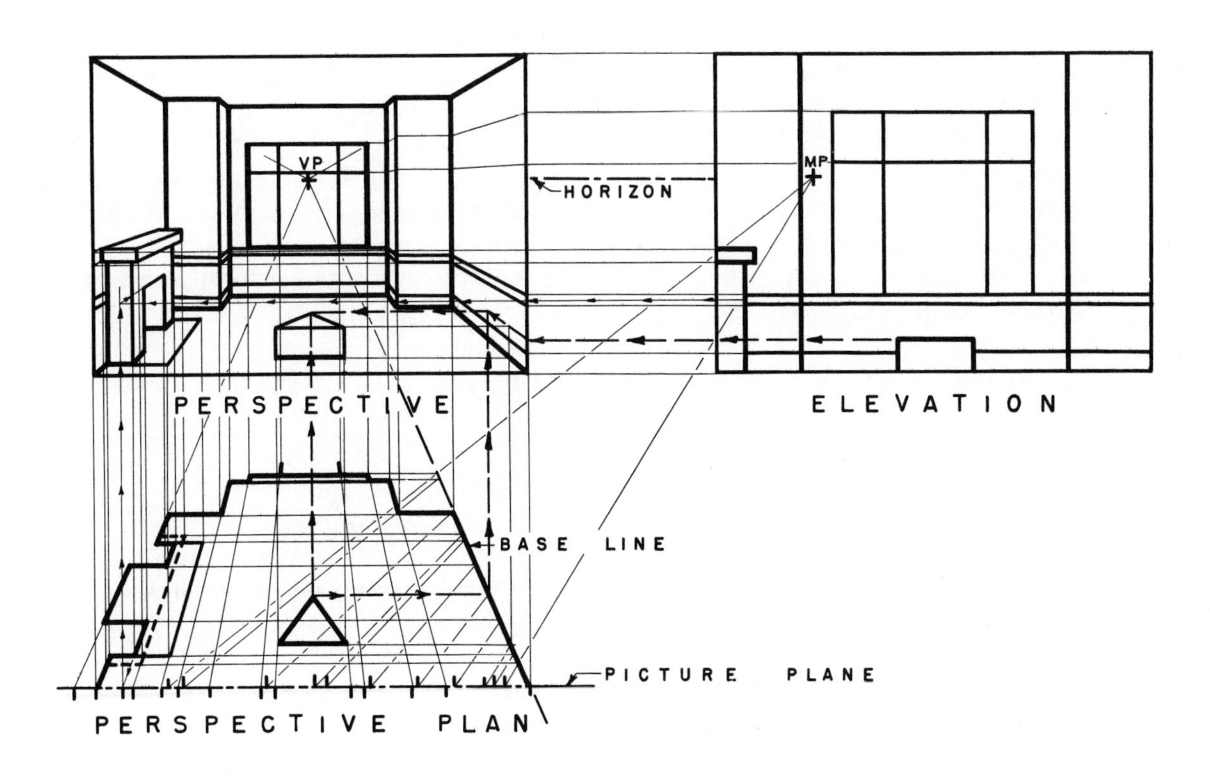

FIG-89 ONE-POINT INTERIOR-PERSPECTIVE PLAN METHOD

CHAPTER 12
Three-Point Perspective

Three-point perspective is not often used in architectural drawing. However, there are occasions when it should be used either to show an object as it would ordinarily be seen or to show it from a position which gives a striking effect.

Whenever the observer looks up or down obliquely upon an object, the resulting view is a three-point perspective. Therefore, when the observer looks up at a tall building from the street or down obliquely on a low piece of furniture, he is viewing the object as it would be drawn in three-point perspective.

In three-point perspective either the picture plane or the object is tilted so that all three sets of typical lines of the object are inclined to the picture plane. Each of the three sets of lines will then converge to its vanishing point.

The direct projection method of three-point perspective is illustrated in Figs. 90, 91, and 92.

In Fig. 90 the drawing of the perspective was divided into parts (A), (B), (C), (D), and (E), which are explained in the following paragraphs, marked to agree with the drawings.

(A) Shows the multi-view drawings of the object, which is a simple rectangular prism.

(B) The plan in this illustration shows the chosen relation between the plan of the object and a horizontal line in the inclined picture plane, which is called the ground line, or GL. This plan is turned with the ground line horizontal. From this plan and the heights of the elevation in (A), an elevation is drawn looking parallel to GL and consequently parallel to the picture plane. The position of the station point is selected and the line of the center of vision drawn through SP toward the approximate center of the elevation. The picture plane line is drawn perpendicular to the line of the center of vision through the elevation of the GL.

(C) The elevation parallel to the picture plane including the object, picture plane, and station point has been turned to make the picture plane vertical. From this elevation and the plan of (B), a plan parallel to the picture plane is drawn as shown. This plan parallel to the picture plane is an axonometric drawing of the object, picture plane, and station point. Note that the corners of the top and bottom of this special plan are not right angles. The station point must be on the vertical center line of the plan or the object will lean to one side in the perspective.

(D) Shows the use of the plan parallel to the picture plane, and the elevation parallel to the picture plane to work out the perspective by the direct projection method, without the aid of vanishing points.

(E) Shows the method of locating the three vanishing points and their use in drawing the perspective.

The vertical vanishing point is located by drawing a line from the elevation of the SP parallel to the vertical lines of the elevation of the object to meet the picture plane at X. Then from SP in plan, a line is drawn parallel to the vertical lines of plan to meet a horizontal line from X in the required vanishing point VV of vertical lines.

The horizon is located by drawing a line from SP of the elevation parallel to the horizonal lines of elevation to meet the picture plane at H. The horizon is the horizontal line drawn through H.

The vanishing points of the two sets of horizontal lines are located by drawing lines from SP in plan parallel to the horizontal lines of plan to meet the picture plane in points Y and Z. From these points, vertical lines are drawn to the horizon to locate VL and VR. The perspective is then worked out using the direct projection method and vanishing points.

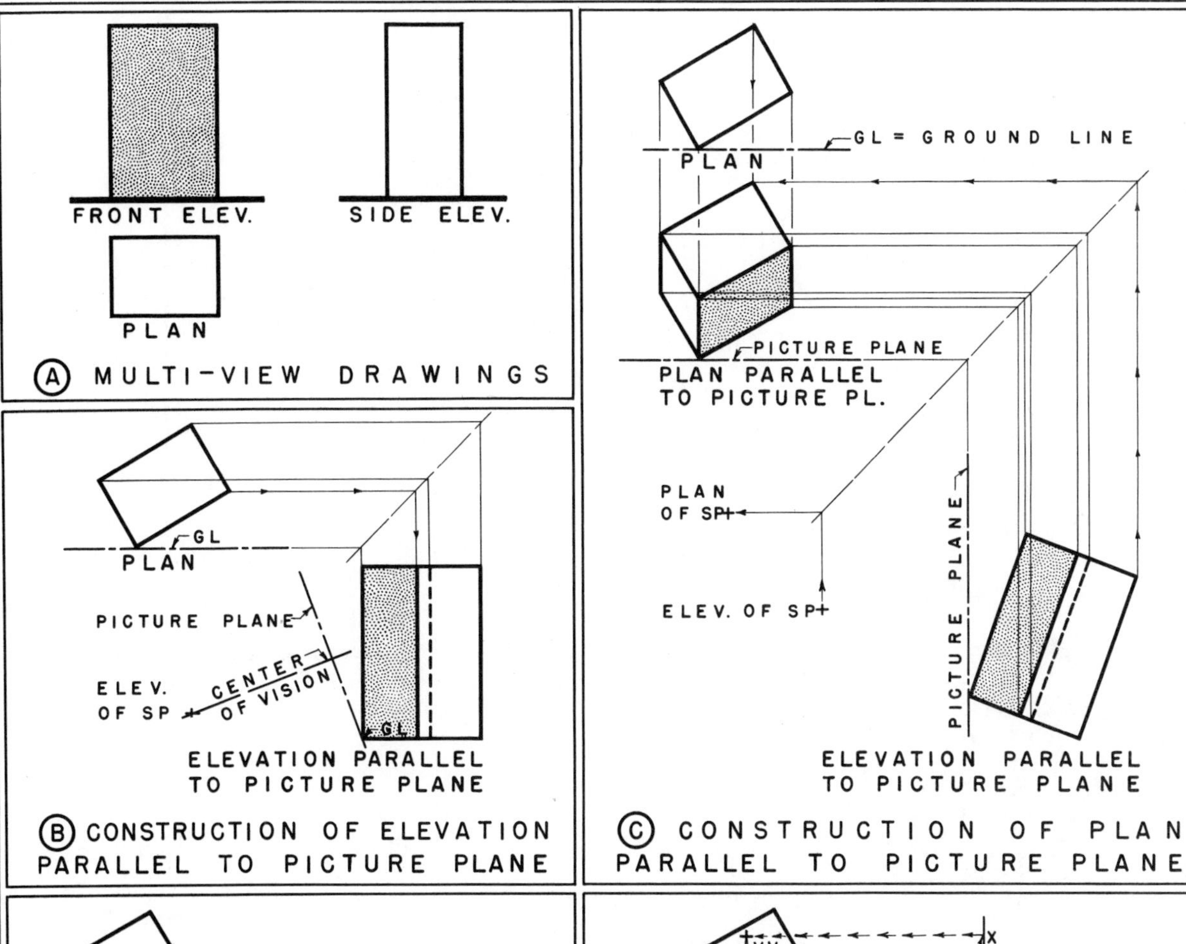

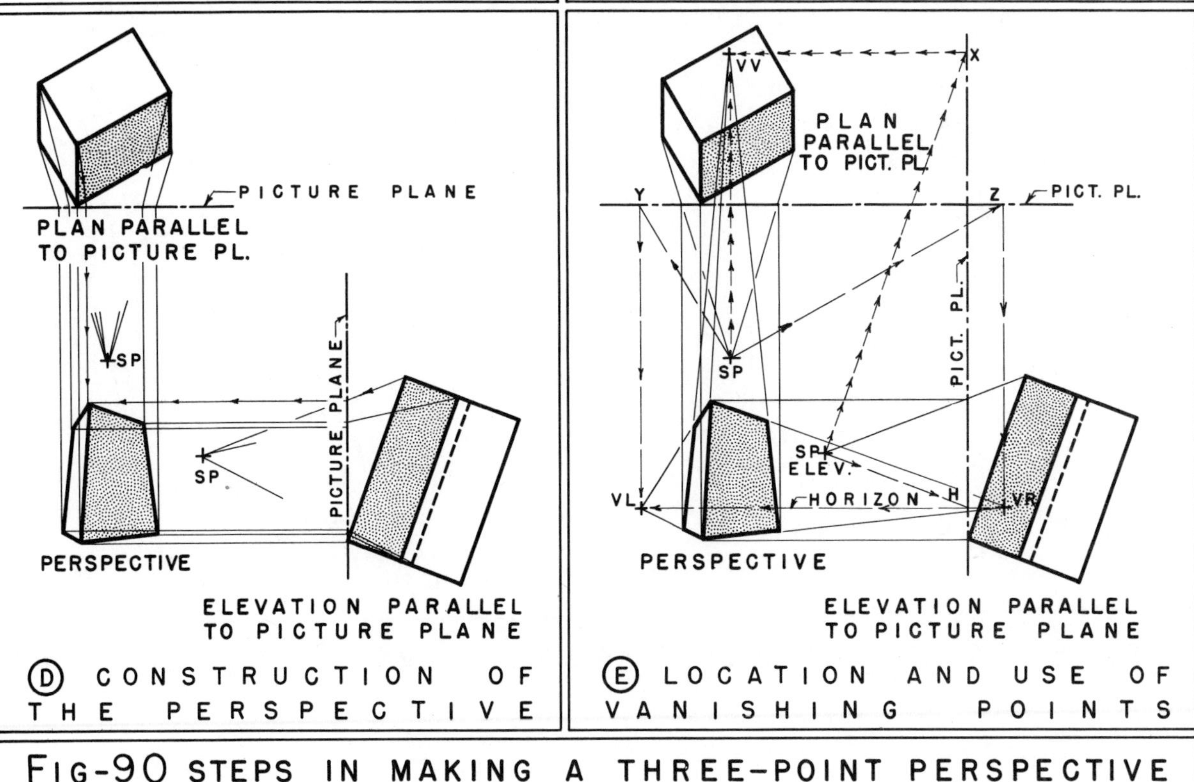

FIG-90 STEPS IN MAKING A THREE-POINT PERSPECTIVE

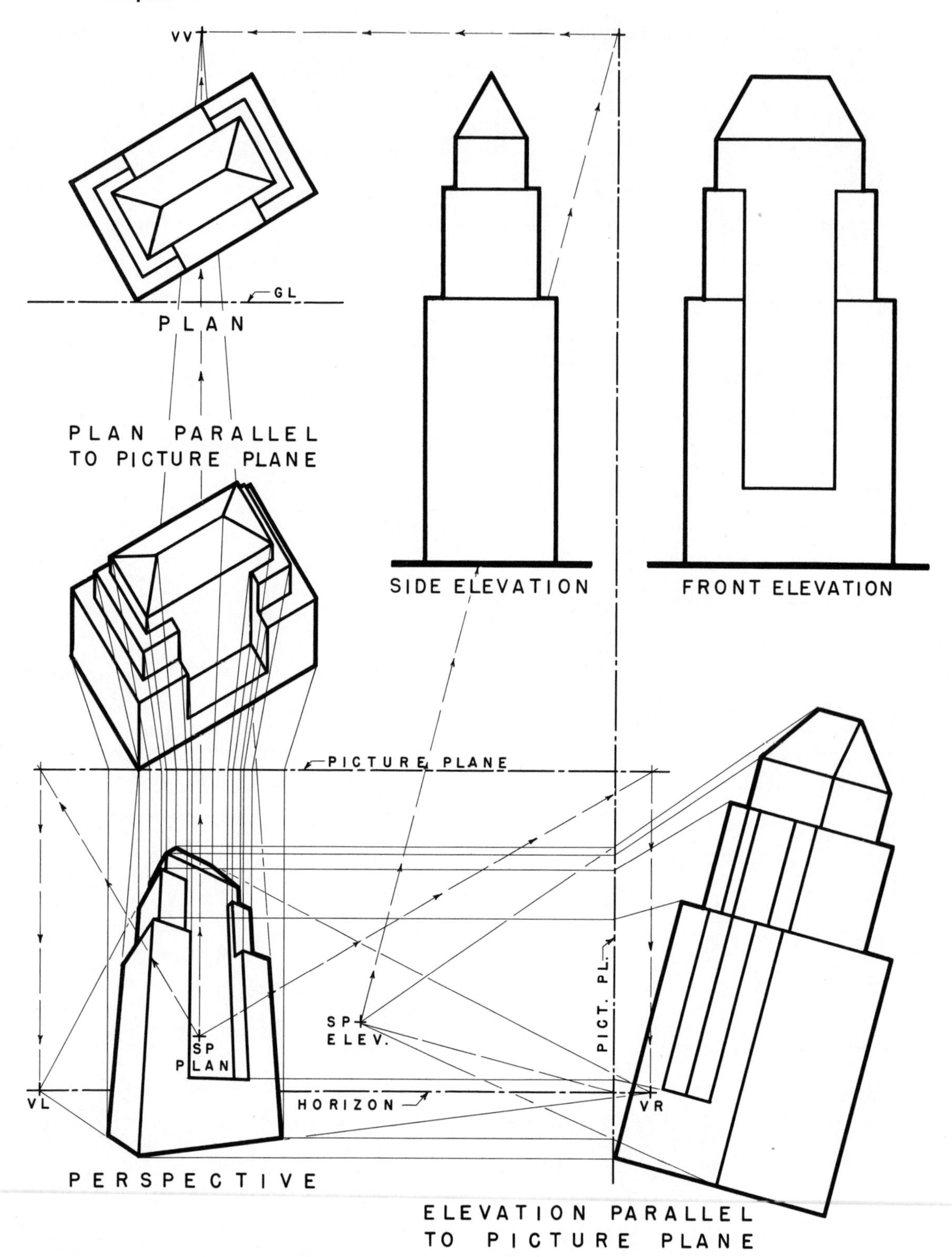

FIG-91 THREE-POINT PERSPECTIVE OF A BUILDING

In Figs. 91 and 92 the construction of the plan parallel to the picture plane, and elevation parallel to the picture plane are omitted. These drawings were made like those in Fig. 90.

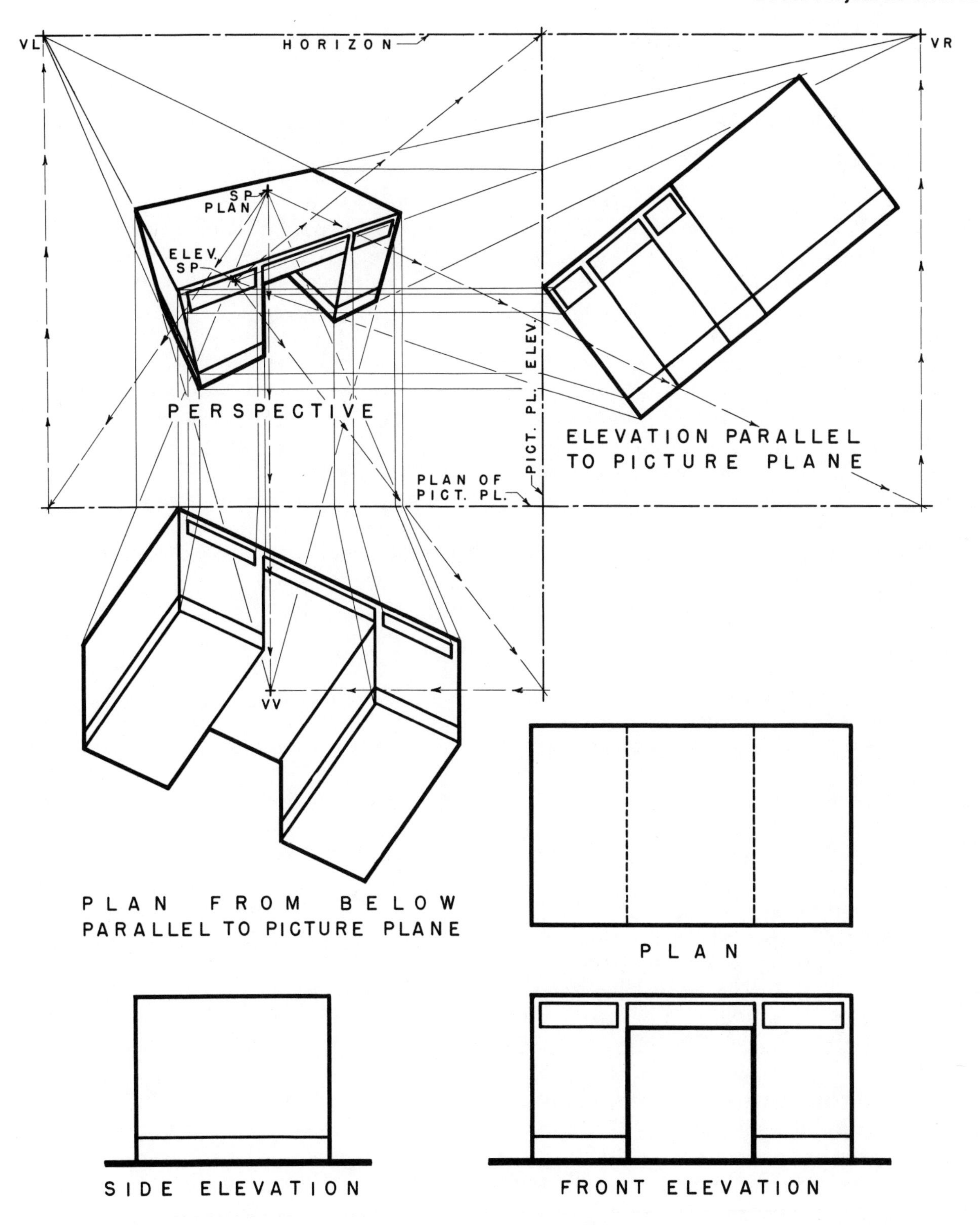

FIG-92 THREE–POINT PERSPECTIVE OF A DESK

In Fig. 92 the plan parallel to the picture plane is made looking up from below because it requires a smaller number of concealed lines for the construction of the perspective drawing.

The perspective plan method of three-point perspective does not require the construction of any auxiliary drawings except the perspective plan, and even this may be drawn to partly coincide with the lines of the perspective itself. In the illustrations for the following discussion an orthographic plan and a special elevation have been shown as a part of the construction for the diagram. Although it is necessary to consider the sizes and shapes of these drawings, they can be made in block outline only or entirely omitted. However, they are an aid in selecting a satisfactory station point. The measurements for the perspective plan and for the heights are laid out to scale on measuring lines in the picture plane. These measurements are brought into perspective position by drawing toward the measuring points to meet base lines and then toward the vanishing points.

The construction of the diagram and a simple three-point perspective has been divided into a number of steps in the illustrations of Fig. 93.

I–Shows the plan view of the object, station point (SP), line of center of vision (CV), and ground line (GL). The station point is placed at any desired location. The line of center of vision is then drawn from the station point through the center of the plan. The ground line is drawn perpendicular to the line of center of vision and through the corner of the plan which is nearest the SP.

II–The plan of Step I is turned with the ground line in a vertical position for this step.

III–The elevation of the object and ground line is drawn looking parallel to the ground line. The station point is located at any desired height at the horizontal distance from the object shown in plan. The elevation view of the line of center of vision is drawn from the station point through the approximate center of the object. The picture plane is then drawn through the ground line and perpendicular to the line of center of vision. The horizontal line from the station point is parallel to the horizontal lines of the object, and intersects the picture plane at the horizon line. The vanishing points of all horizontal lines are located on the horizon. The vertical line from the station point is parallel to vertical lines of the object, and intersects the picture plane in the vanishing point (VV) of all vertical lines.

IV–Shows the view perpendicular to the picture plane of the horizon, ground line, and horizontal line on which VV the vertical vanishing point is located, at its intersection with the center line. The center line is drawn at any desired position. The horizontal distance from the horizon line to the station point from Step III is here laid out on the center line below the horizon line. From SP lines are drawn at angles L and R (the angles of the plan with the GL shown in Step I) to intersect the horizon line in VL and VR, the vanishing points of the two typical sets of horizontal lines of the object. The two measuring points for horizontal dimensions MR and ML are then located as in two-point perspective by making VL to MR = VL to SP and VR to ML = VR to SP. The measuring point MVR is located on the line VV–VR at the distance VV–SP taken from Step III and measured from VV in Step IV. This completes the diagram of the three vanishing points and three measuring points needed for the construction of a three-point perspective by this method.

In explanation of Step IV it may be stated that the triangle SP–VL–VR is a plan view which is superimposed on the horizon of the diagram. The angles L and R and the horizontal line through SP are a part of this plan, which is used to locate the measuring points MR and ML on the horizon.

V–Shows the method of constructing the perspective of the object. From the intersection of the center line and the ground line, lay out on the ground line the distance A taken from the plan of Step I to locate the position of the corner of the perspective plan. The plan dimensions are then laid out on the ground line, and the perspective plan constructed in exactly the same way as in two-point perspective. The vertical lines of the perspective are drawn from VV through the points of the perspective plan.

The heights of this perspective are determined in the following manner: From the corner B on the GL a line is drawn parallel to VV–VR and the scale heights are laid out on this line from B. A second line is drawn from VV through B (in this case to coincide with the near corner of the walls) and lines are drawn from MVR through the measurements on the first line to intersect the second line and determine the heights of points on the object, as shown in Fig. 93, Step V.

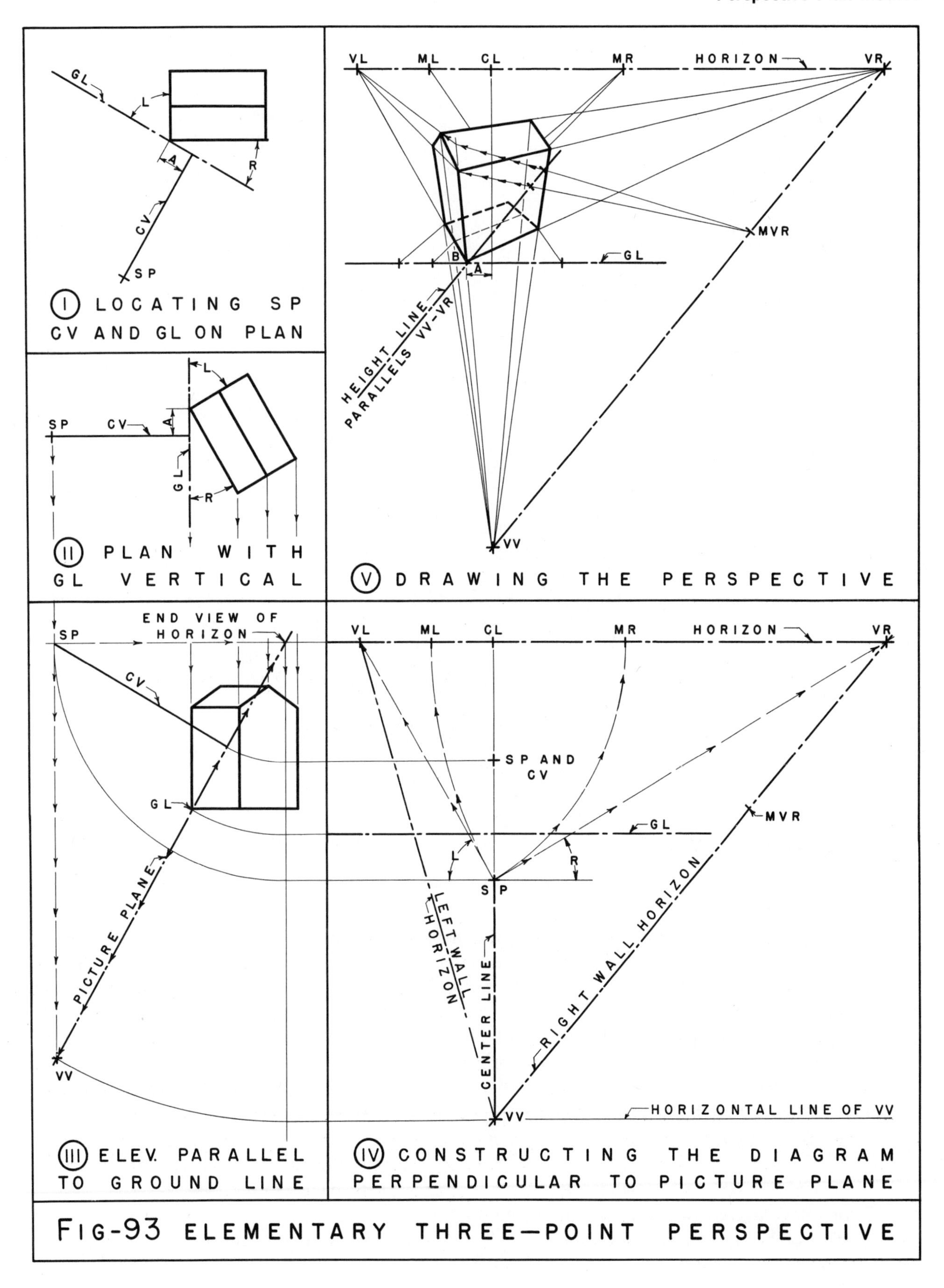

FIG-93 ELEMENTARY THREE-POINT PERSPECTIVE

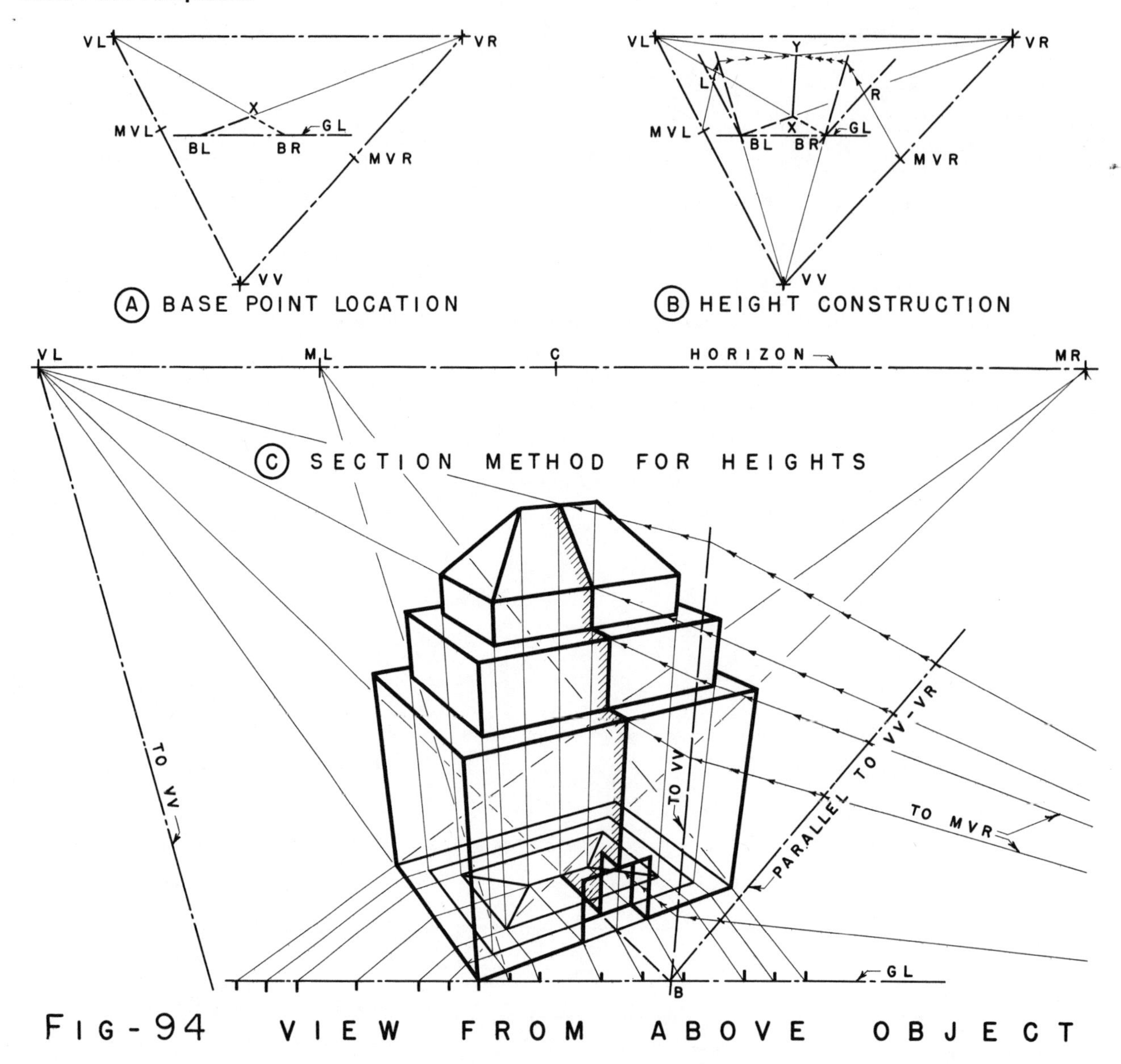

FIG-94 VIEW FROM ABOVE OBJECT

A line can be drawn anywhere through the perspective plan from either VL or VR and its intersection with the ground line used as a base point for height construction, as point B was used in the illustration of Fig. 93 V. MVR is the vanishing point of lines which transfer heights from any line which parallels VV–VR to a vertical line (from VV) drawn through the intersection of the line of scale heights and the ground line. The heights can then be traced from the vertical line to the correct vanishing point and into perspective position. There are two vertical measuring points, one on VV–VR and one at the same distance from VV on line VV–VL. In using the second measuring point of vertical lines, MVL, the line of scale heights is drawn parallel to VV–VL.

Figure 94A illustrates the procedure of extending a line from VL through the perspective plan point X of a line of which the height is to be found to locate the base point BR. This line is shown with short dots. A similar line from VR with long dots locates base point BL for point X.

Figure 94B shows the complete construction for the same height X–Y from each of the two measuring points of vertical lines. Since both measuring points give the same result, either can be used for height construction. The two scale-heights are BL–L and BR–R.

In Fig. 94C the line drawn from VL to locate the point B touches the plan of each line of

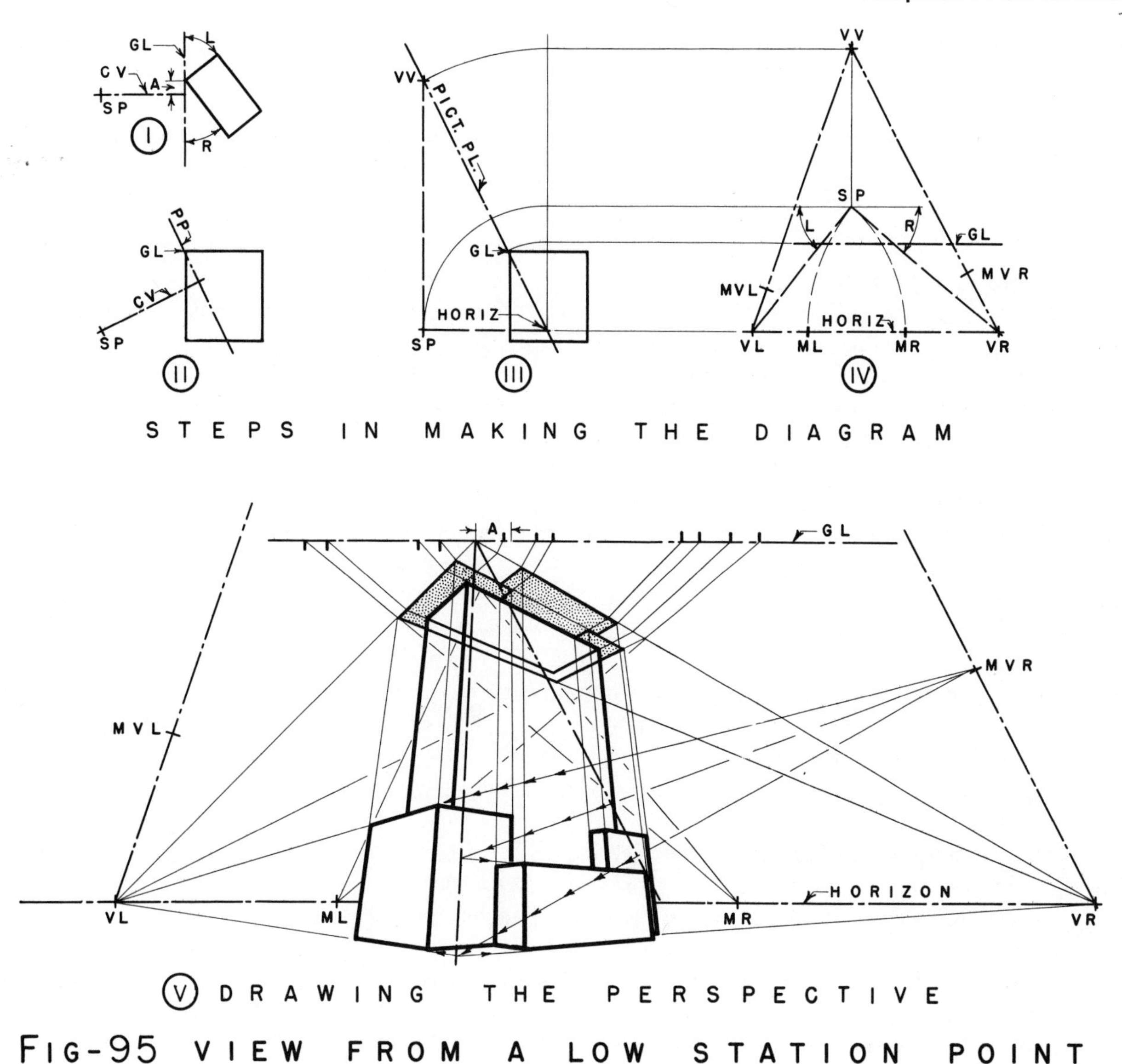

FIG-95 VIEW FROM A LOW STATION POINT

which the height is to be determined, and all the height constructions are made from the height measurements on the line from VV through point B. These lines of the height construction outline a section through the perspective of the building. This section has been cross-hatched to make it clearly visible in the drawing.

In Fig. 95 small-scale drawings of the development of the diagram for a three-point perspective when the line of center of vision slopes up are shown in I, II, III, and IV. The ground line has been placed through the nearest top corner of the rectangular box enclosing the building. This corner touches the picture plane so that the GL lies in the picture plane, Fig. 95 II. The plan part of the diagram has been inverted with SP above the horizon instead of below it. This position saves space in constructing the diagram and obtains exactly the same result, Fig. 95 IV.

Since the GL has been located at the plane of the top of the building, the perspective plan is drawn in this plane instead of in the bottom plane of the building, as in Fig. 94. In views looking up, the base plane of the building is often too nearly on the horizon to give an accurate perspective plan. However, the ground line and plane of the perspective plan can be located at any convenient height either above or below the horizon.

CHAPTER 13
Perspective Theory and Practice

The preceding chapters have described the one-, two-, and three-point systems of perspective, and explained for each of the three systems the most commonly used methods of making perspective drawings. The previous explanation has, in most cases, given only the information necessary for an understanding of the simple mechanical drafting processes. It is the purpose of this chapter to provide additional information which will give the reader a better understanding of some of the theory of perspective drawing, and a knowledge of some of the manipulations and short cuts used in practice.

THE LOCATION OF VANISHING POINTS AND LINES. The construction procedure for locating the vanishing points of the sets of typical lines which are not parallel to the picture plane has been explained in discussions of the methods of making perspective drawings. The constructions for locating the necessary measuring points for the perspective plan method have also been explained. These are the only vanishing points which are essential to the construction of a perspective drawing. Lines which do not belong to one of the three typical sets of lines of the object can be located in perspective by working out the positions of the end points of the lines and connecting them. This method has been used in the hip, valley, and gable lines of roofs in the examples. Whenever there are a considerable number of parallel lines which do not belong to one of the typical sets, it is more convenient and more accurate to locate and use the vanishing point for those lines.

The vanishing point of any set of parallel lines is located where the line of the set which passes through the station point intersects the picture plane. The vanishing line of any set of parallel planes is located where the plane of the set which passes through the station point intersects the picture plane.

The vanishing points of all lines parallel to a plane are located on the vanishing line (horizon) of the plane. Thus the horizon line of a perspective drawing is the vanishing line of all horizontal planes, and the vanishing points of all horizontal lines are located on the horizon. Furthermore, the two sets of typical vertical planes or wall planes have vanishing lines or wall horizons on which the vanishing points for all lines in those planes are located. The use of vanishing points on the wall horizons is illustrated in Fig. 96D, E, and F.

In one-point perspective there is only one wall horizon. It is the vanishing line of all vertical planes perpendicular to the picture plane and the locus of the vanishing points of all lines in those planes, Fig. 96A. This wall horizon is a vertical line, since it is the intersection of two vertical planes. It passes through V, the vanishing point of lines perpendicular to the picture plane. The second set of wall planes is parallel to the picture plane and has no wall horizon.

In two-point perspective there are two wall horizons, since both sets of typical wall planes are oblique to the picture plane, Fig. 96B. These wall horizons are vertical lines because they are the intersections of vertical planes with the vertical picture plane. They are drawn through VL and VR, the vanishing points of horizontal lines in the planes.

In three-point perspective the wall horizons are the lines of intersection of vertical wall planes with an inclined picture plane and are therefore inclined lines, Fig. 96C. The vanishing point of horizontal lines in the left wall planes is VL while VR is the vanishing point of horizontal lines in the right wall planes, and VV is the vanishing point of vertical lines which lie in both sets of wall planes. The line VL–VV passes through the vanishing points of two sets of lines in the left wall planes and is therefore the left wall horizon. Likewise VR–VV is the right wall horizon.

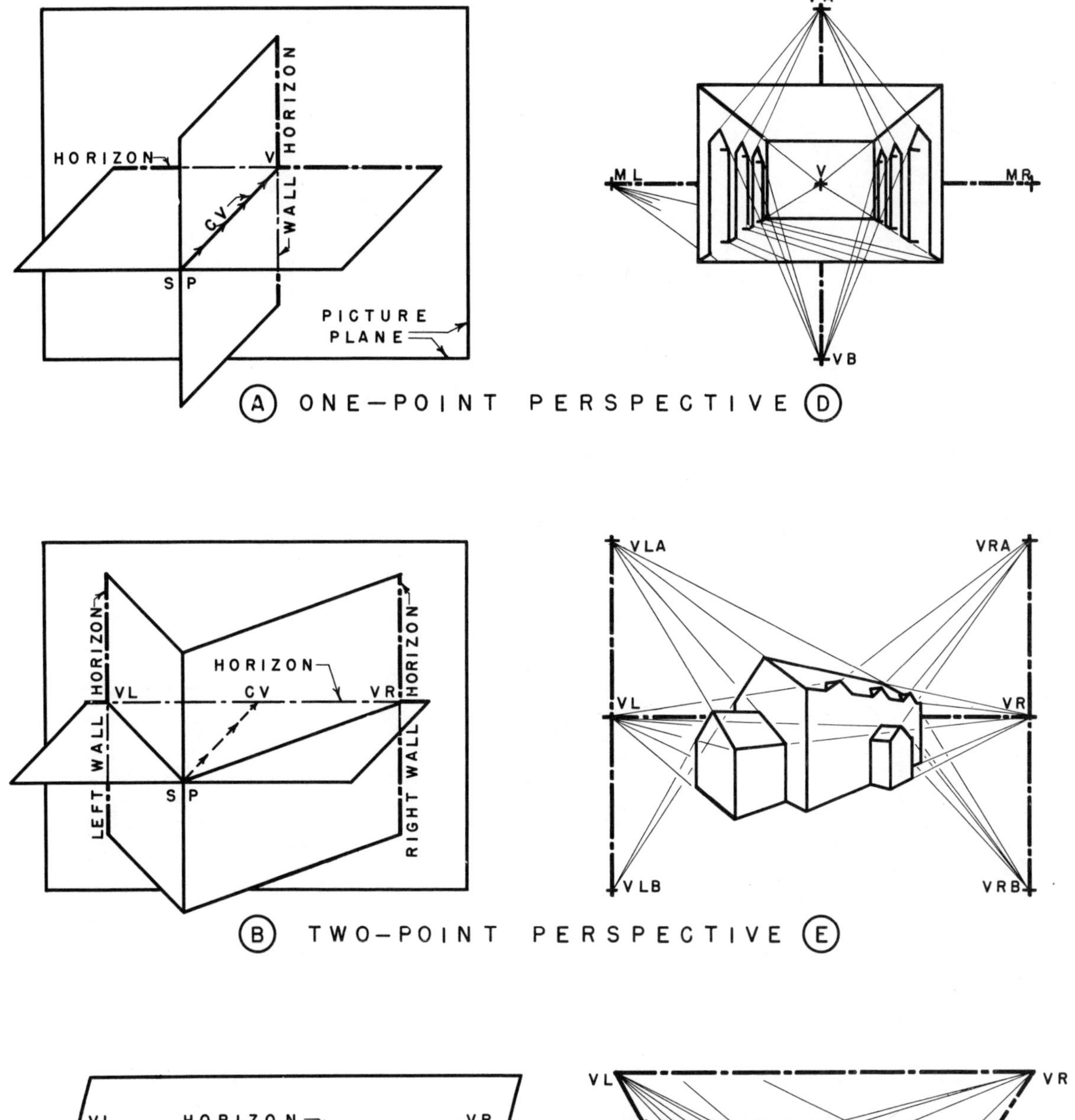

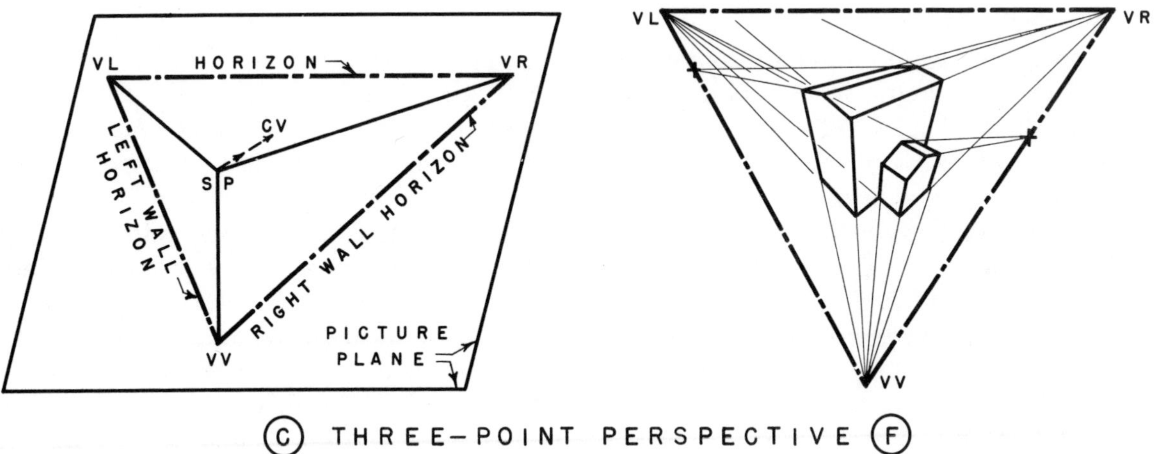

FIG-96 VANISHING LINES OR HORIZONS

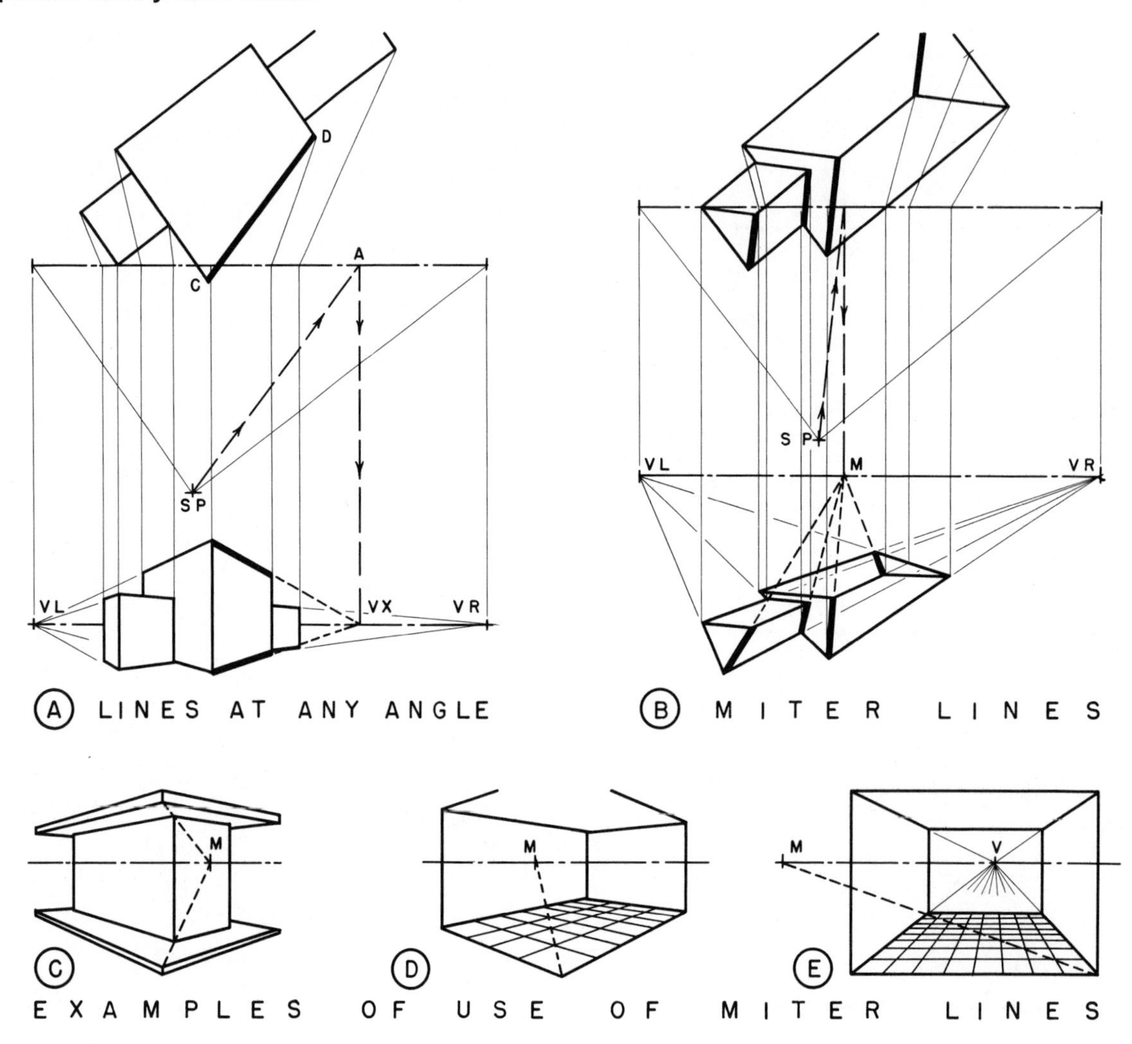

FIG-97 VANISHING POINTS OF HORIZONTAL LINES

The vanishing point of any horizontal line, C–D, and of all lines parallel to C–D, is found by drawing a line through the station point in plan, Fig. 97A, parallel to the given line C–D to intersect the picture plane. This intersection A is the plan position of the required vanishing point. The perspective position VX of the vanishing point will be on the horizon at the intersection with a vertical line from the plan position.

The miter point is the vanishing point of a set of horizontal lines at 45° with typical sets of horizontal lines of the object. The position of a miter point is located by the method of finding the vanishing point of any horizontal line. There are two miter points. Usually one is accessible in two-point perspective, but the other is too far away to be used conveniently. When the plan is turned at 45° with the picture plane in two-point perspective, one set of miter lines parallels the picture plane and is horizontal. The measuring points of one-point perspective, as used in the perspective plan method, are also the miter points. They can be located by laying out the distance from the station point to the picture plane on each side of V on the horizon. Figure 97B shows the use of a miter point in two-point perspective for drawing the hip and valley lines in a perspective plan. In Fig. 97C, D, and E three examples are given of the use of miter points in making perspective drawings. Miter points in wall planes are discussed in chapter 14.

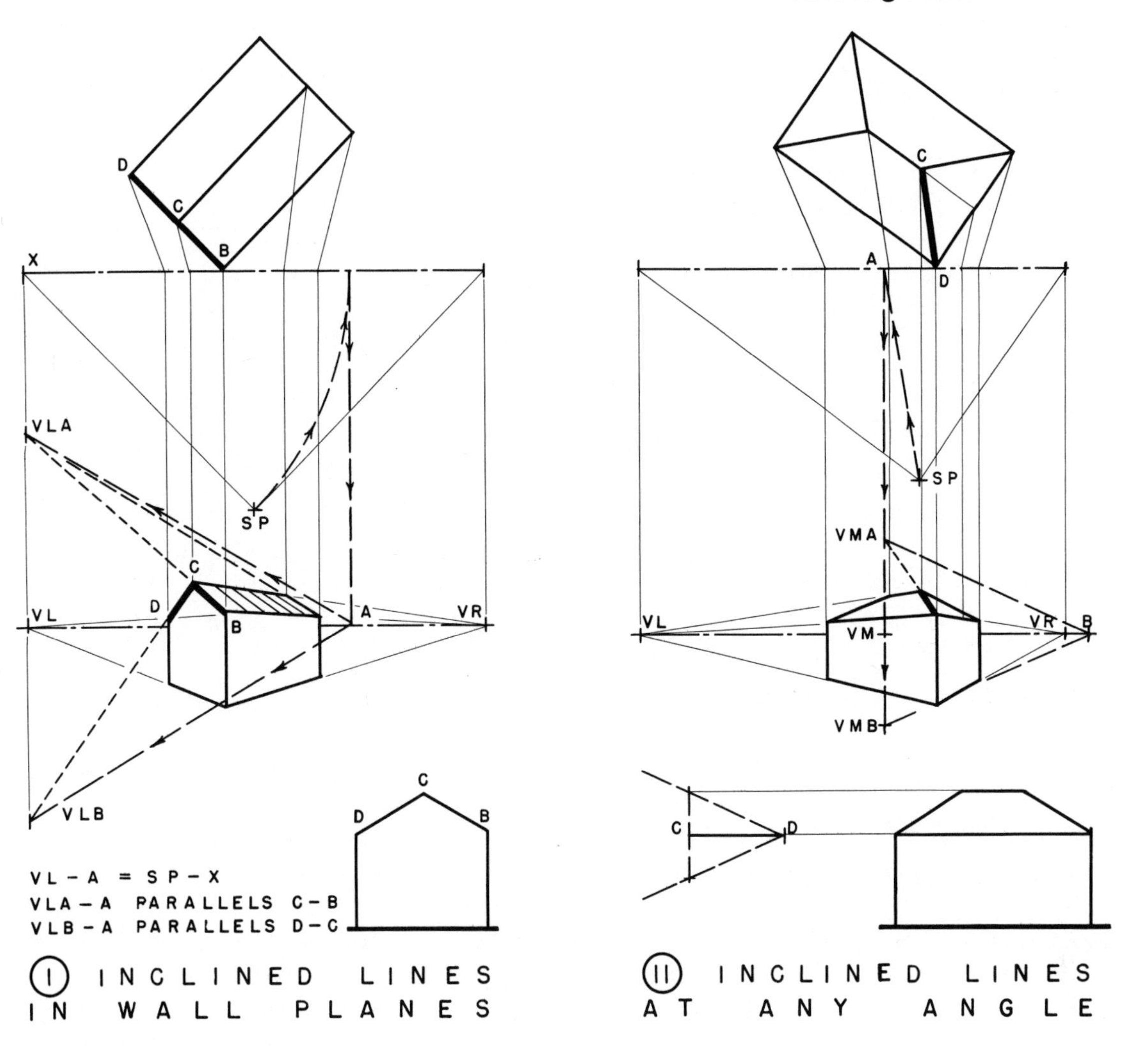

FIG-98 VANISHING POINTS OF INCLINED LINES

The location of the vanishing points of inclined lines which lie in the wall planes is illustrated in Fig. 98 I. The lines through the station point parallel to the lines C–B and D–C of the gable pierce the picture plane in VLA and VLB, the vanishing points of the lines C–B and D–C respectively. These vanishing points are located by laying off from VL on the horizon a distance VL–A which is equal to SP–X, then drawing lines parallel to the elevation view of lines C–B and D–C from A to meet the left wall horizon in points VLA and VLB, the required vanishing points.

When the inclined line is not in the wall plane, a line is drawn from the station point in plan parallel to the plan direction of the inclined line to meet the picture plane, Fig. 98 II. From this intersection A, a vertical line is drawn to the perspective drawing. This vertical line is the line of intersection of a vertical plane through SP–A with the picture plane. It is then the horizon of all vertical planes parallel to SP–A and the locus of all vanishing points of lines in those planes. From the intersection VM of the horizon and the vertical horizon, lay out a distance VM–B on the horizon equal to SP–A. From B inclined lines are drawn at the angle of the inclined lines of the object to locate VMA and VMB, the required vanishing points. The end elevation does not show the true direction of these inclined lines. Their true direction is found by laying out the horizontal distance C–D from plan and the height from side elevation as shown.

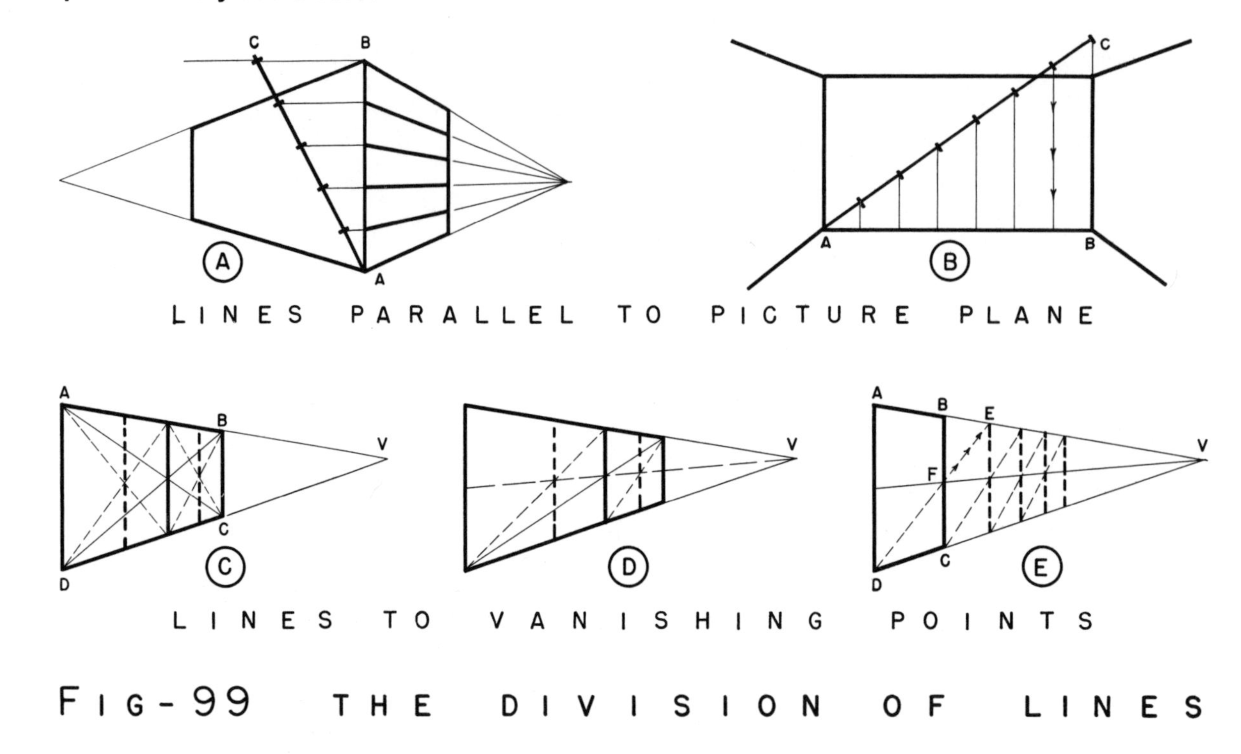

FIG-99 THE DIVISION OF LINES

THE DIVISION OF LINES. Lines may be divided in perspective by working out each point by methods already explained. However, these methods sometimes become laborious, and the draftsman welcomes any short cut which will allow him to work out perspective divisions more directly.

Lines parallel to the picture plane, such as vertical lines in one- and two-point perspective and the set of horizontal lines parallel to the picture plane in one-point perspective, are divided in the same proportion in perspective as in the actual lines. Proportional divisions can therefore be laid out in perspective on any line parallel to the picture plane by any method for making proportional divisions. In Fig. 99A the vertical line A–B is divided by the common drafting method. From B a horizontal line is drawn of indefinite length. When the divisions are to be of equal size, choose a scale on which the required number of divisions is somewhat larger than the line to be divided. Then place the zero point of the scale at A and pivot until the required division is on line B–C when the zero point is at A. Mark divisions on A–C and draw horizontal lines to divide A–B. A similar construction is shown for the division of a horizontal line in Fig. 99B. When the measurements are of unequal size, it may be more convenient to mark them on the edge of a strip of paper which is then used instead of the scale. The subdivision of lines not parallel to the picture plane is more difficult, since the more distant divisions are progressively smaller.

The method of diagonals applies to parallelograms in perspective. The center of a parallelogram is located at the intersection of its diagonals, Fig. 99C. A line through the center parallel to two sides of the parallelogram divides the other two sides and the parallelogram into two equal divisions. This method can be repeated with each half or fourth of the original parallelogram and continued indefinitely. The given parallelogram or any of its lines can thus be divided into 2, 4, 8, 16, etc., equal parts. Instead of drawing both diagonals for each new division, a center line and one diagonal may be used, as in Fig. 99D. The reverse of the above procedures may be used, and instead of dividing a given parallelogram, equal parallelograms may be added to it, Fig. 99E. By drawing a line from one corner, D, of the parallelogram A–B–C–D through the midpoint F of an opposite side to meet a side extended, the corner E of a second adjoining parallelogram of equal size is located. This construction can be repeated with each new parallelogram to obtain any desired number of repetitions of size of the original parallelogram.

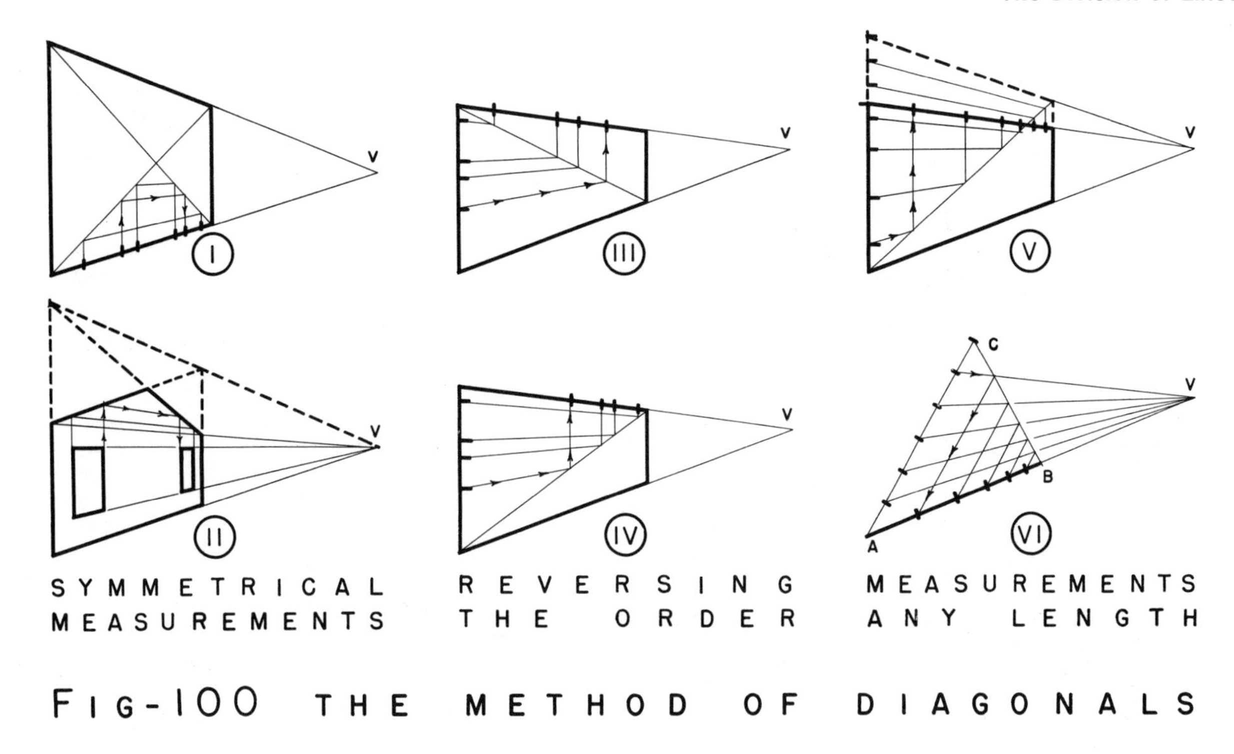

FIG-100 THE METHOD OF DIAGONALS

When divisions are given in one half of a parallelogram, equal divisions may be laid out in the other half by means of the two diagonals and lines parallel to the sides of the parallelogram, Fig. 100 I. The base of any isosceles triangle may be divided in this way since the other two sides are the half diagonals of a parallelogram, Fig. 100 II.

Divisions on any side of a parallelogram can be transferred to an adjacent side in the same proportion by the use of a diagonal and lines parallel to the sides of the parallelogram, Fig. 100 III and IV. One diagonal reverses the order of spacing given by the other diagonal. This method is useful when one line of the parallelogram is a vertical line or other line which is parallel to the picture plane, so divisions may first be laid out on the line parallel to the picture plane and then transferred to the adjacent side. When the diagonal is the diagonal of the perspective of a square, the divisions will represent equal spaces on the two lines. When the diagonal does not represent a line at 45° with the adjacent sides used, the divisions are proportional but not equal.

If the line on which the measurements are first laid out is of indefinite length, Fig. 100 V, then any convenient scale can be used for the measurements.

Any given line A–B, Fig. 100 VI which is drawn to a vanishing point in perspective can be divided by using any line A–C—of indefinite length which touches the end of the line to be divided—as a measuring line on which the measurements are laid out to any convenient scale. Connect the last measurement C with the end B of the line to be divided. Draw lines from the measurements on A–C parallel to A–B (that is, to its vanishing point) to intersect C–B. From these points of intersection draw lines actually parallel to A–C to make the required divisions on A–B. It should be noted that the measurements from A on A–B reverse the order on A–C, so that unsymmetrical measurements must be laid out in reverse order on A–C to be in correct sequence on A–B. A–C may be any existing line touching the end of A–B, or it may be any line drawn at random from the end of A–B. When a new line is drawn as a measuring line, it is assumed to be a line parallel to the picture plane so that lines parallel to it will actually be parallel in perspective. When an existing line of the perspective is used, it is assumed that the measurements are laid out on a line parallel to the picture plane which has exactly the same perspective position as the line used, and that therefore all lines parallel to the measuring line are parallel in perspective.

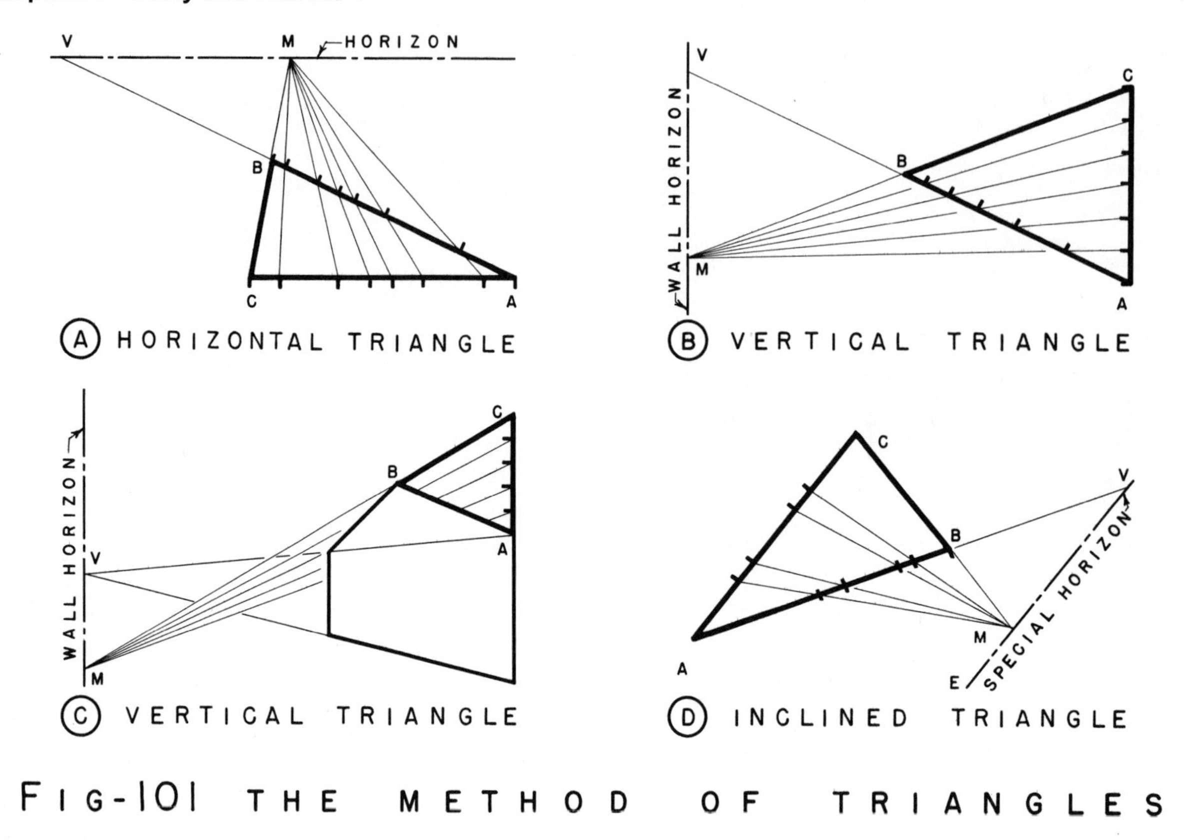

FIG-101 THE METHOD OF TRIANGLES

The method of triangles is a variation of the method of diagonals. If the vanishing point for line C–B, Fig. 101A, can be located, then measurements can be transferred directly from line C–A to A–B by drawing lines from the measurements on C–A to the vanishing point of C–B and finding their intersections with A–B. When the measuring line and the line to be divided are horizontal lines, the triangle is in a horizontal plane and the vanishing point of the horizontal connecting line C–B is on the horizon at M where C–B extended intersects it.

When the line to be divided and the measuring line are in a vertical plane, the vanishing point of the closing line, C–B, of the triangle will be found on a vertical line through the vanishing point for horizontal lines in the given vertical plane, Fig. 101B. When a vertical measuring line is used, the measuring line and line to be divided are in a vertical plane and are divided by this method, as shown in Fig. 101B and C. Either a horizontal line, Fig. 101B, or an inclined line, Fig. 101C, can be divided by this method. Any scale may be used on the chosen measuring line, but it is more convenient to select a scale which will bring the vanishing point within easy reach. When the same line can be divided by using either a vertical or horizontal triangle, the most convenient and accurate construction should be used.

Any line, in any direction, which touches the end of the line to be divided may be used as a measuring line if the vanishing point M for the measurements is located on a line drawn parallel to the measuring line through the vanishing point of the line to be divided, Fig. 101D. Given: A–V and V–E, any two lines drawn to the same vanishing point V. Required: To divide A–B, a part of A–V, into any required divisions. From A, draw a line of measures parallel to V–E. The vanishing point M is located on V–E by drawing a line from the last measurement, C, through B. In this case V–E is assumed to be the line of intersection with the picture plane of a plane through A–V. A–C is assumed to be in the same plane, and since it is parallel to V–E, it is therefore parallel to the picture plane and measurements on it can be laid out to scale. Figures 102 and 103 illustrate the divisions of lines on perspective drawings. Note that vertical divisions are laid out where any scale fits vertically between the two converging lines to give the required divisions, Fig. 102.

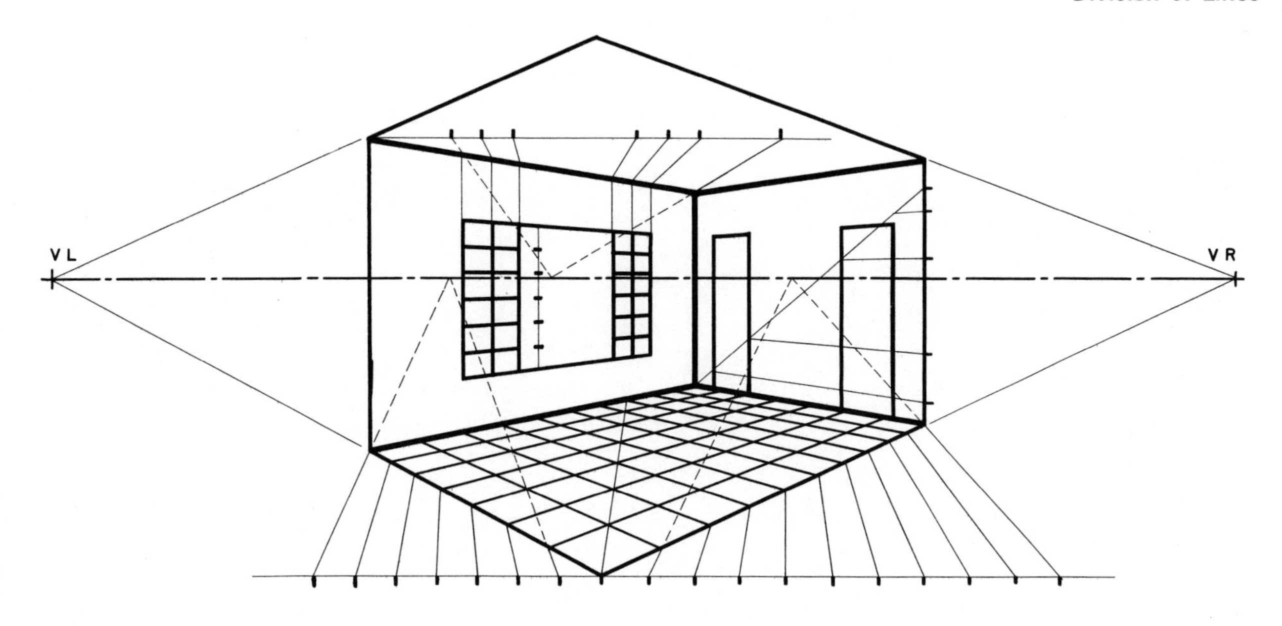

FIG-102 INTERIOR EXAMPLE OF LINE DIVISION

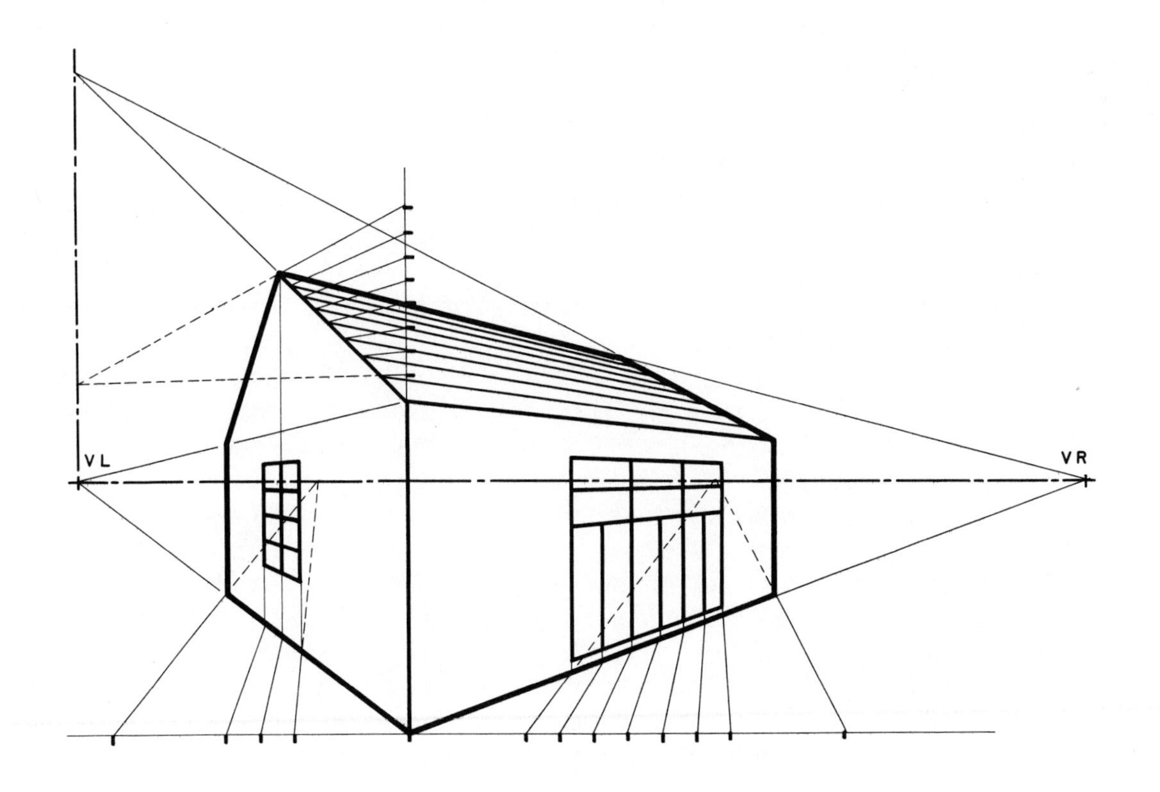

FIG-103 EXTERIOR EXAMPLE OF LINE DIVISION

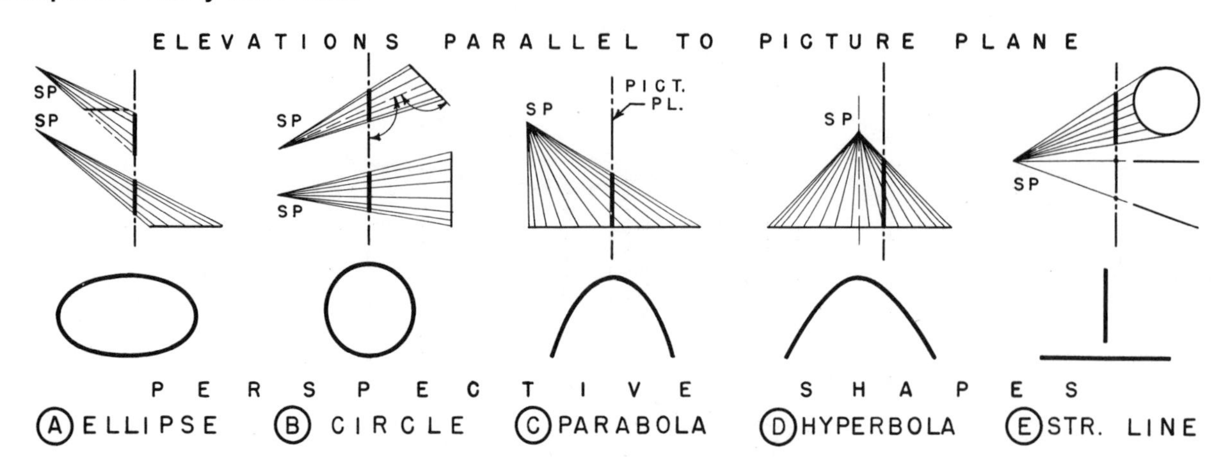

FIG-104 POSSIBLE SHAPES OF CIRCLES IN PERSPECTIVE

THE CIRCLE IN PERSPECTIVE. The perspective of a circle is the intersection of the cone of rays from the station point to the circumference of the circle with the picture plane. The resulting shape of the perspective of the circle can be any of the conic sections, which consist of the ellipse, circle, parabola, and hyperbola, Fig. 104A, B, C, and D. The type of conic section depends on the angle the picture plane makes with the cone of rays, whether the cone be a right or an oblique cone.

The ellipse is the most common form of the perspective of a circle. When the circle is behind the picture plane, the cone of rays from the station point to the circle is cut through by the picture plane. When the circle is in front of the picture plane, the rays are considered to extend beyond the base of the cone to meet the picture plane, Fig. 104A. The perspective of a circle is an ellipse except when, due to special conditions, it becomes one of the geometric shapes shown in Fig. 104B, C, D, and E. In practice it will be found that the perspectives of circles are almost always ellipses.

The circle is the perspective of a circle under two conditions: (1) when the circle is parallel to the picture plane; (2) when the axis of the cone of rays makes equal and opposite angles with the plane of the circle and the picture plane, Fig. 104B.

The parabola is the perspective of the visible part of a circle when the picture plane is parallel to one edge of the cone of rays, Fig. 104C.

The hyperbola is the perspective of the visible part of a circle when the picture plane is parallel to the axis of the cone of projectors, Fig. 104D.

The straight line is the perspective of a circle whenever the projectors from the station point are parallel to the plane of the circle, Fig. 104E. This condition most frequently exists when a horizontal circle is at the horizon. It may occur with circles in wall planes or in an oblique position.

In one-point perspective, circles in one set of wall planes are parallel to the picture plane and their perspectives are circles. It is then only necessary to locate the perspectives of the center and radius of such a circle and use the compass to draw it, Fig. 105 I.

The simplest methods of working out the perspectives of circles which are not parallel to the picture plane are the point method and the method of circumscribing polygons. While these methods are sometimes tedious to use, they are simple in theory and easily understood.

THE POINT METHOD. Any point on a circle can be located in perspective from its plan and elevation positions, Fig. 105 II, when the circle is in a vertical plane; and from its plan position and height, Fig. 105 III, when the circle is in a horizontal plane. Any number of points can be located in the same way and the perspective of the circle drawn through the points so located. Points may be taken at random in using this method, or a system of lines may be used, as illustrated in Fig. 105 II, so that one measurement serves for two points.

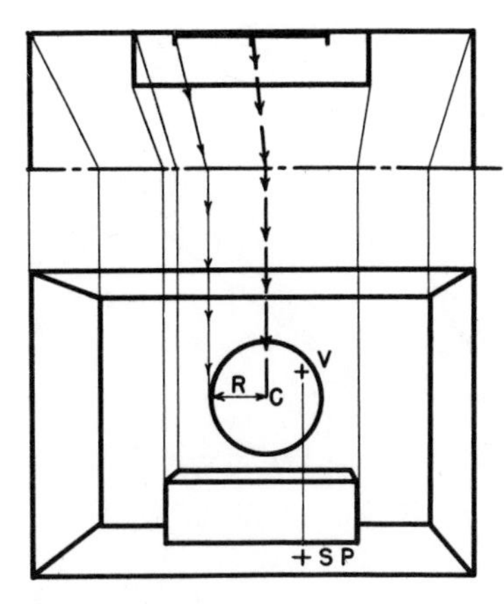

(I) VERTICAL CIRCLE PARALLEL TO PICT. PL.

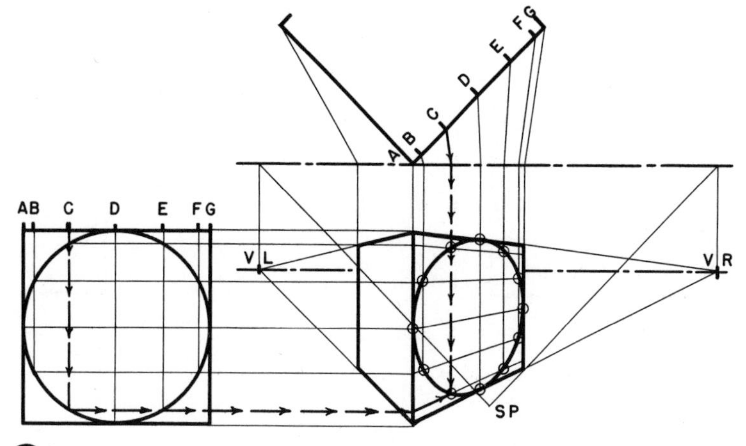

(II) VERTICAL CIRCLE TURNED OBLIQUELY TO PICTURE PLANE

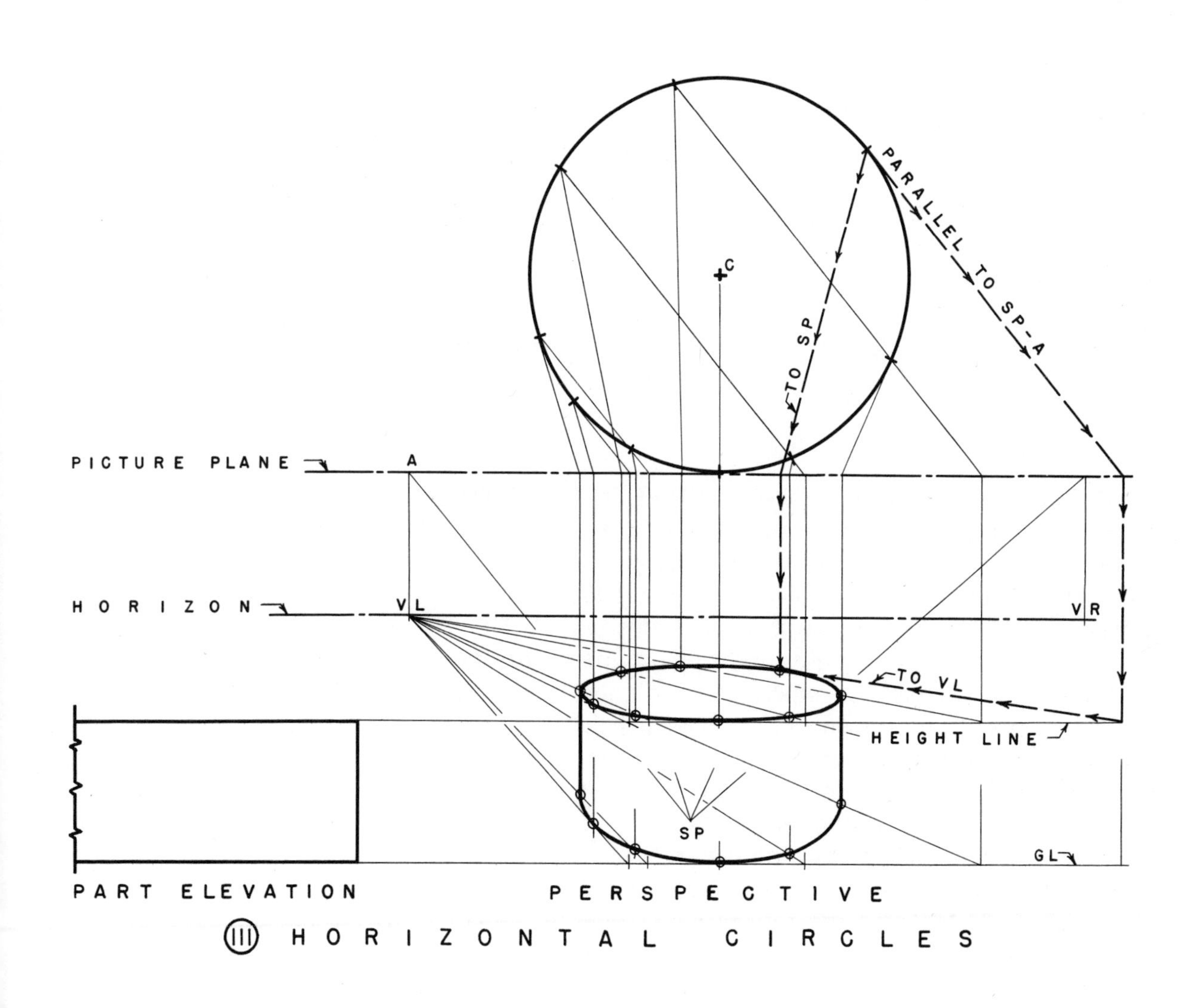

(III) HORIZONTAL CIRCLES

FIG-105 POINT METHOD OF PERSPECTIVE OF CIRCLES

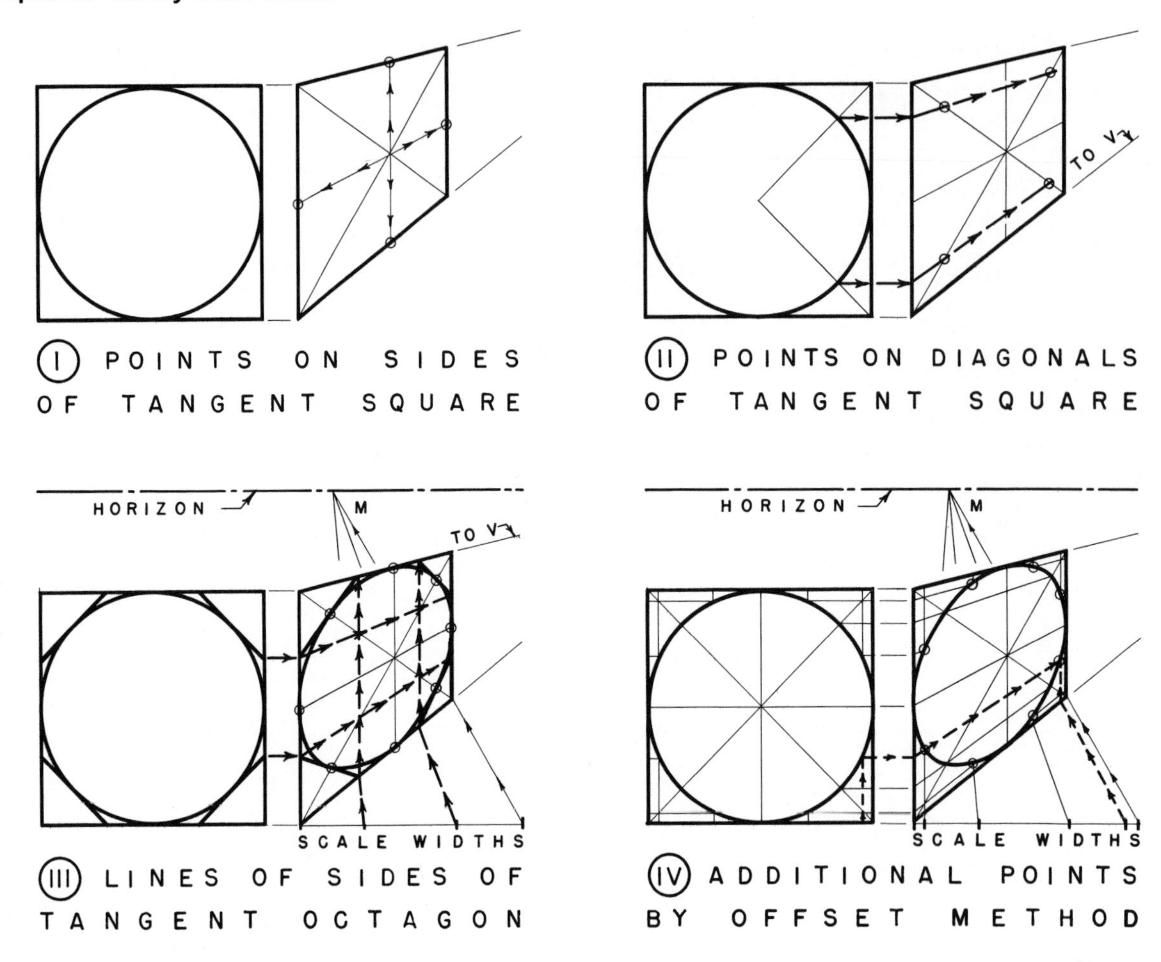

FIG-106 TANGENT POLYGON METHOD FOR CIRCLES

METHOD OF CIRCUMSCRIBING SQUARE AND DIAGONALS. When the tangent square has been worked out in perspective, the points of tangency of the midpoints of the four sides and the circle can be located by drawing the diagonals of the square, then drawing its center lines through the intersection of the diagonals, Fig. 106 I. The points of intersection of the circle and the diagonals of the square can be located as shown in Fig. 106 II, giving a total of eight points on the ellipse. The circle in elevation or plan is necessary to obtain the points on the diagonals. The four sides of the octagon which cut off corners of the square are drawn in Fig. 106 III. They locate the points of tangency with the circle at their intersections with the diagonals of the square. These sides of the octagon are very useful in determining the shape of the perspective ellipse. When additional points are desired, they can be located by the offset method, as shown in Fig. 106 IV. The perspective widths for Fig. 106 III and IV can be worked out either from plan or by the line division method used in the illustrations.

When the perspective of a circle is very small, the tangent square may be a sufficient guide in drawing the ellipse, Fig. 107C, top corners. When this minimum construction is used for a larger horizontal circle, the lines of tangency from SP which locate the extreme width of the ellipse, Fig. 107B, are useful. The near side of the octagon is also included here. The complete tangent octagon gives sufficient data for the experienced draftsman on large ellipses. The miter point is useful in drawing one diagonal of the square and two sides of the octagon, Fig. 107A.

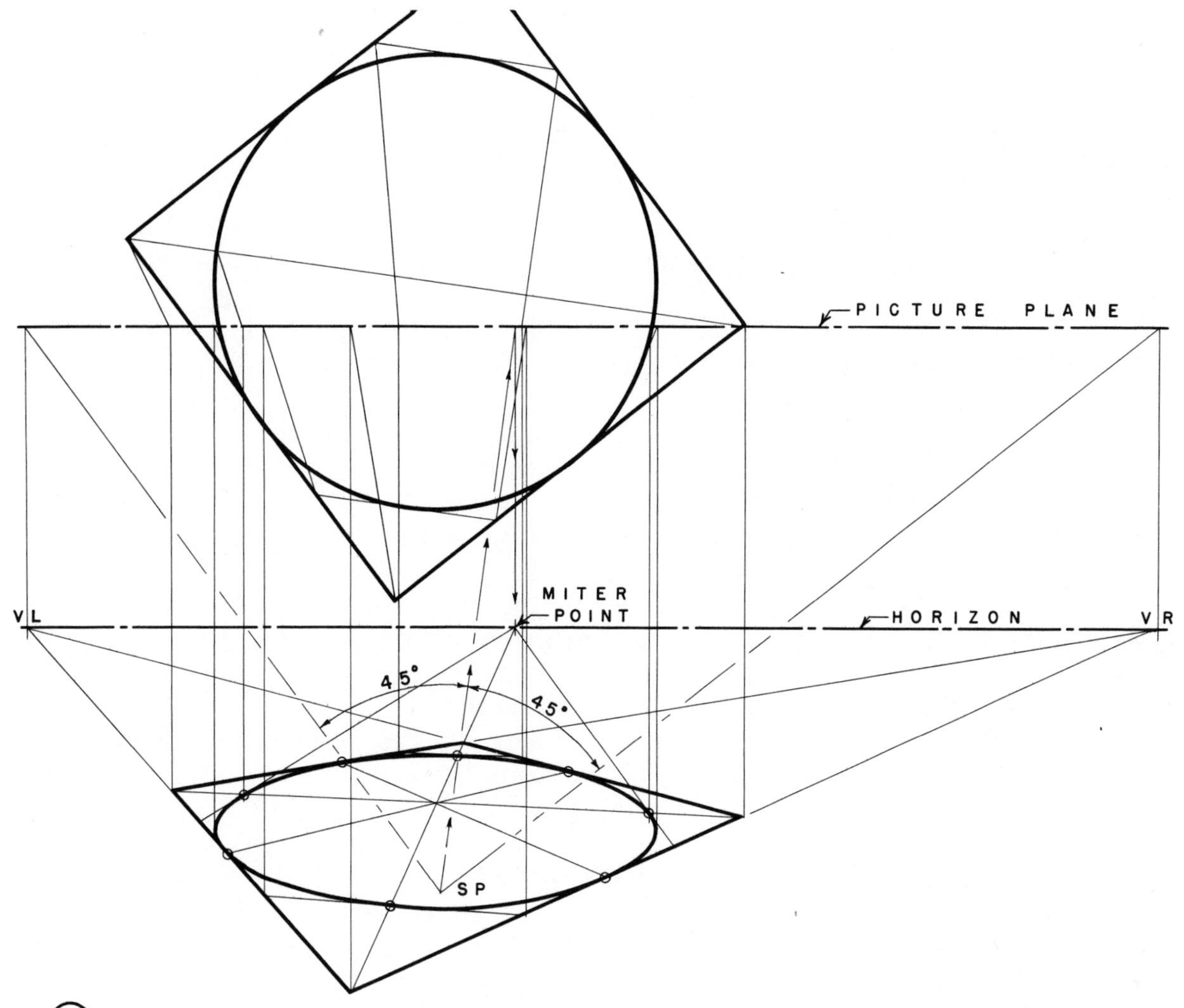

(A) HORIZONTAL CIRCLE BY TANGENT POLYGON METHOD

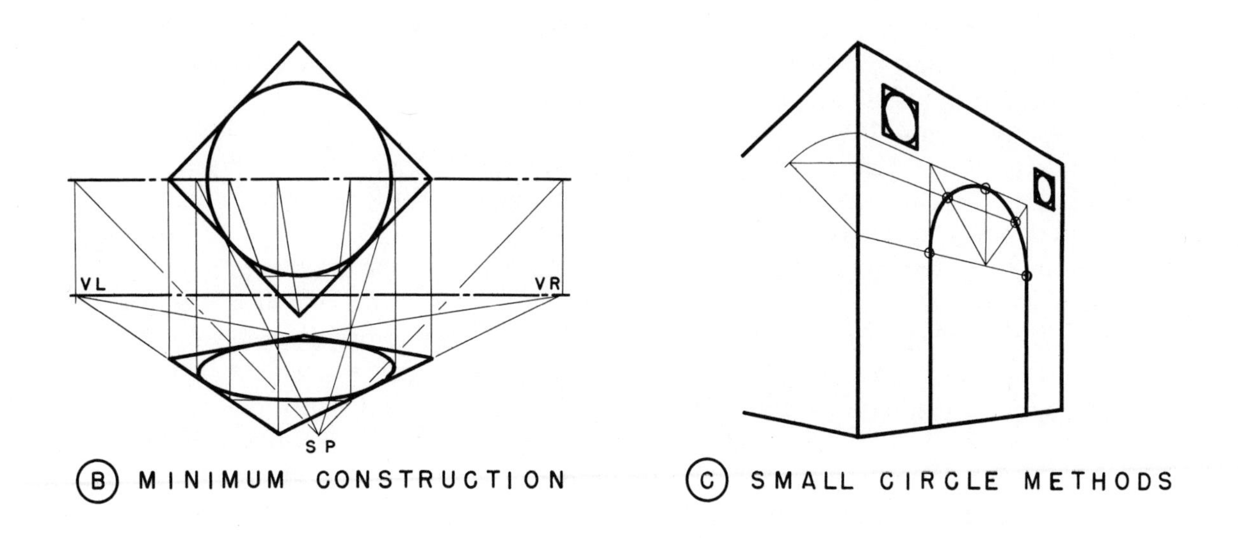

(B) MINIMUM CONSTRUCTION

(C) SMALL CIRCLE METHODS

FIG-107 AMOUNT OF CONSTRUCTION REQUIRED

METHODS USING AXES OR CONJUGATE DIAMETERS. The methods of constructing ellipses from their axes or diameters permit the location of any number of points on an ellipse and require only a few construction lines. The construction used depends on the position of the ellipse.

The direction of the ellipse which is the perspective of a circle varies with the position of the circle and the angle from which it is seen, Fig. 108A. When a vertical circle centers on the horizon, the major axis of its perspective ellipse is a vertical line and the minor axis is a horizontal line located on the horizon. When a horizontal circle centers on the vertical center line of the perspective, the major axis of the ellipse will be horizontal and the vertical minor axis will be located on the center line. The major and the minor axes of the perspective ellipses can be located easily for circles in these positions, and the ellipses can be constructed from their axes.

Figure 108B shows the location of the axes for a vertical circle which centers on the horizon. First locate A–B. Then bisect A–B and project back to plan to locate point C. Draw a semicircle centering on plan line of circle as a diameter. Draw C–D perpendicular to plan line of circle. Lay out distance C–D above and below horizon on vertical measuring line. Project from measurements to vanishing point to locate ends of vertical axis.

To find the perspective position of the horizontal circle centering on the center line in Fig. 108C, draw tangents to plan of circle through station point and locate points of tangency as shown. Line A–B, connecting the points of tangency, will be the horizontal axis and line D–E, the vertical line through the center of the circle, will be the vertical axis of the ellipse. Find perspective positions of axes.

After the axes are located, any number of points on the ellipse can be found by the trammel method, Fig. 108E. To use the trammel method, lay out on the edge of a strip of paper the distances O–L equal to one-half the major axis and O–M equal to one-half the minor axis. When L is on the minor axis and M is on the major axis at any position, O is a point on the ellipse. The ellipse can be drawn freehand through points so located, or a french curve can be used.

When a circle does not center on either the horizon or center line, its axes will be oblique lines and they cannot be located readily. However, it is a fairly simple matter to locate conjugate diameters for the inclined ellipses and construct them from this information. Two diameters of an ellipse are conjugate when each is parallel to the tangents at the end of the other. Any straight line through the center of an ellipse which terminates at the edges is a diameter.

When a vertical circle does not center on the horizon, the conjugate diameters are located by the same method used for finding the axes in Fig. 108B. The center of the height measurement will not fall on the horizon, but the construction is similar in other respects.

Typical construction for location of the conjugate diameters of the perspective ellipse of a horizontal circle which does not center on the center line is shown in Fig. 108D. The tangent points A and B of projectors from the station point to the circle are located in plan. The perspective C–D of the line A–B connecting these points will be one diameter of the ellipse. From the midpoint E of C–D, draw a vertical line to meet the picture plane at F; then, through this point F, draw a projector from SP through the circle to locate line G–H. The perspective of G–H is the diameter I–J of the ellipse which is conjugate to C–D.

The construction of an ellipse from its conjugate diameters is shown in Fig. 108F. Draw a line through the end I of either diameter perpendicular to the other diameter of the ellipse. From I on this line, lay off a distance I–K equal to one-half the length of the diameter to which I–K is perpendicular. Draw a line of indefinite length from K through E, the intersection of the diameters. This line L–K and the diameter C–D extended are the trammel axes. Lay out the distances X–Y–Z on the trammel equal to R–I–K. When Z is on trammel axis K–L, and X is on trammel axis C–D, Y will locate a point on the ellipse. An infinite number of points can be located in this manner.

It may be observed from the drawings of Fig. 108B, C, and D that the perspective of the center of the circle will not be the center of the ellipse, nor will a diameter of the circle be the major axis of the ellipse, since the major axis passes through the center of the ellipse and all diameters must go through the center of the circle.

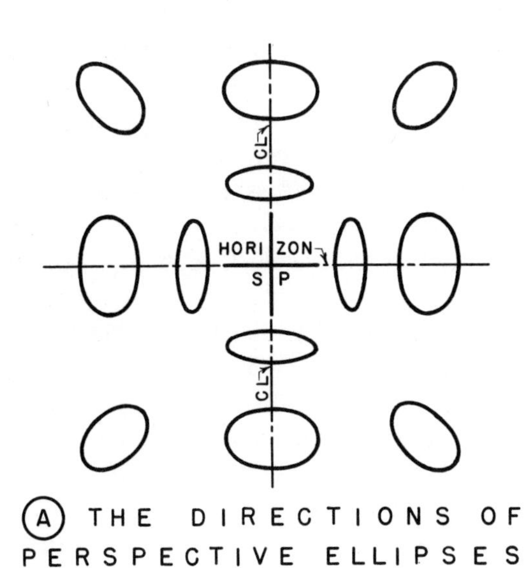

(A) THE DIRECTIONS OF PERSPECTIVE ELLIPSES

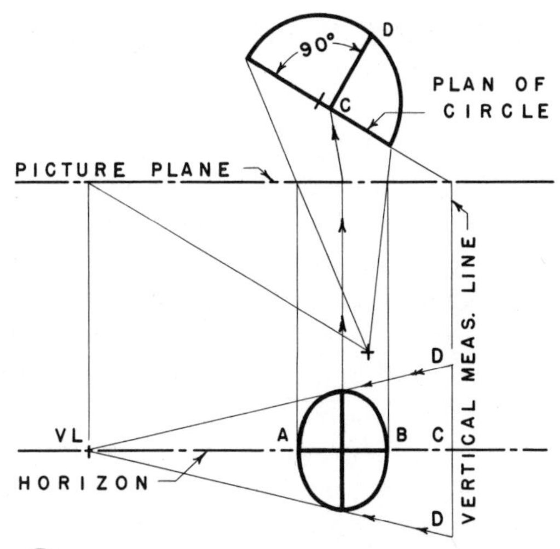

(B) VERTICAL CIRCLE CENTERING ON HORIZON

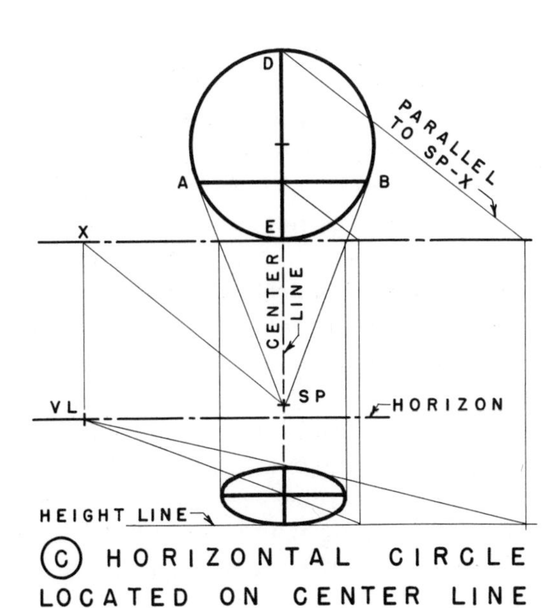

(C) HORIZONTAL CIRCLE LOCATED ON CENTER LINE

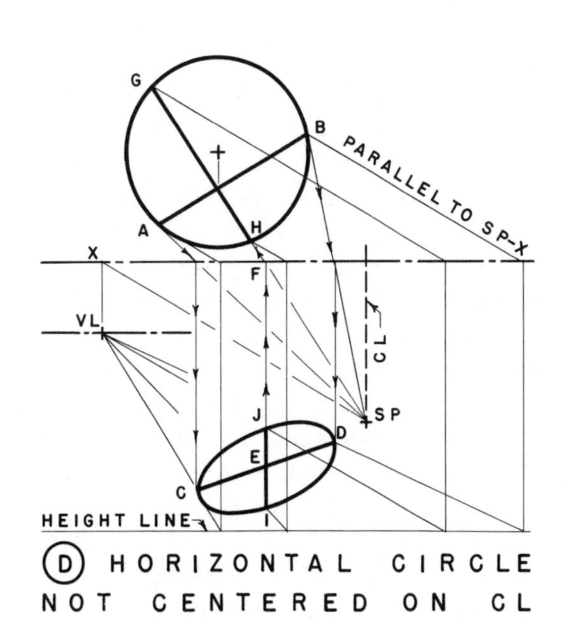

(D) HORIZONTAL CIRCLE NOT CENTERED ON CL

(E) ELLIPSE CONSTRUCTED FROM THE TWO AXES

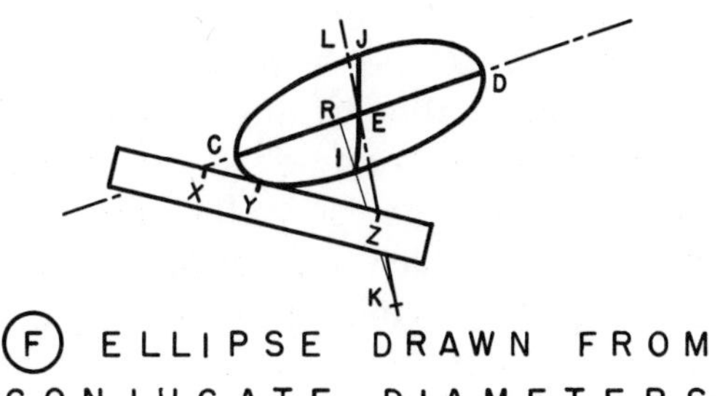

(F) ELLIPSE DRAWN FROM CONJUGATE DIAMETERS

FIG-108 CONSTRUCTION OF PERSPECTIVE ELLIPSES

REFLECTIONS IN ARCHITECTURAL PERSPECTIVES. Reflections occur most frequently on the horizontal surfaces of reflecting pools or other bodies of water. Reflections are also sometimes shown in a rendering or photograph on surfaces of pavements or walks as they may appear in rainy weather or at night. Interior perspectives often include reflections in mirrors parallel to the walls and from polished surfaces of floors. Correctly represented, reflections add to the interesting and natural effect of a rendering. It is therefore important for the delineator to be familiar with the common characteristics of reflections so he can represent them accurately in his drawings.

The section view of Fig. 109A shows the station point, the edge view A–B of the horizontal reflecting surface, and a line C–X extending vertically above the reflecting plane. The projectors from SP to A and B will be reflected from the mirror at the angle at which they strike it. These reflections, A–D and B–E, cut off the segment D–E of line C–X. The reflection of D–E as seen from the station point appears to be below the reflecting surface at DR–ER, located by extending the projectors from SP. When the line D–E is perpendicular to the reflecting surface, the line DR–ER will be a continuation of line D–E. It can be proved by similar triangles that D–E and DR–ER are equal and that they are equidistant from the plane of the reflecting surface.

Since the reflection DR of any point D is on the perpendicular from D through the reflecting plane which bisects the line D–DR, the reflection represents a duplication in reverse of the object.

If the reflecting surface were removed and a hole left in its place, the view of the inverted object DR–ER seen through the opening would exactly duplicate the reflection of the object D–E on the reflecting surface. This method of considering the mirror to be a hole through which the reverse of the object is drawn as a continuation of the perspective simplifies the problem. Figure 109B, C, and D shows three different arrangements of mirrors in plans for perspective drawings and suggests the reversal of the designs beyond the mirror. When the mirror is in a vertical position as in these three cases, the reflection is the reverse of the object from side to side, B and D, or from front to back, C. When the mirror is in a horizontal position the reflection is turned upside down, Fig. 109A and F. The reversing always takes place on the plane of the mirror surface.

Any plane reflecting surface parallel to one of the three sets of typical planes continues the perspective system of the object, and the three sets of typical lines appear in the perspective of the reflection as they do in the perspective of the object. That is, they remain parallel or converge to the same vanishing points as the lines of the object.

A reflection represents the reverse of the object; however, it cannot be an exact duplicate of the object in reverse, for it must be seen from a different angle. If it were possible to see a reflection with the station point in the plane of the reflecting surface, then the reflection would be an exact duplication of the object. The intersection of the object and reflecting plane would be a straight line in perspective and the reflection would give an exact repetition on one side of the intersection line of the distances of the object on the other side. The sequence of drawings of Fig. 109E demonstrates that the nearer the intersection of the reflecting surface and object to the horizon, the greater the similarity between object and reflection.

Oblique lines in any direction which parallel the reflecting plane are parallel to their reflections. Therefore the object and reflected lines will either be parallel or will vanish to the same vanishing points in a continuation of the same perspective system.

Horizontal lines in any direction are parallel to a horizontal reflecting surface, and the lines and their reflections vanish to the same vanishing points, which are located on the horizon.

Oblique lines which are not parallel to the mirror will slant in the opposite direction in the reflection, Fig. 109F. When the oblique lines of the object slant in two directions at the same slope as in a gabled roof, and have the same plan direction, the reflection of a line will be drawn to one of the two vanishing points VLA or VLB and the same line of the object to the other. When there is only one set of oblique lines, the vanishing point for the reflection of these lines will be on the opposite side of the horizon from the vanishing point for the object lines, and will be an equal distance from the horizon on the vertical line through the vanishing point. In other words, it will duplicate the VLA, VL, VLB arrangement of vanishing points.

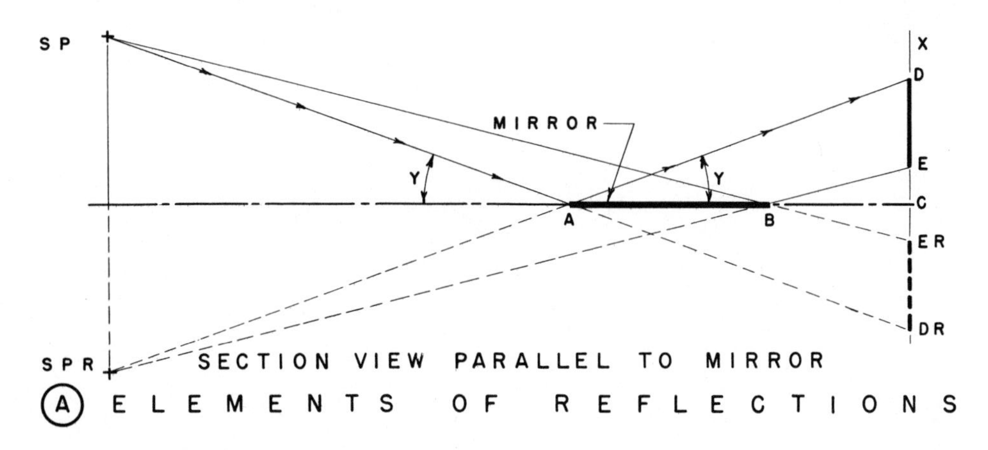

Ⓐ ELEMENTS OF REFLECTIONS

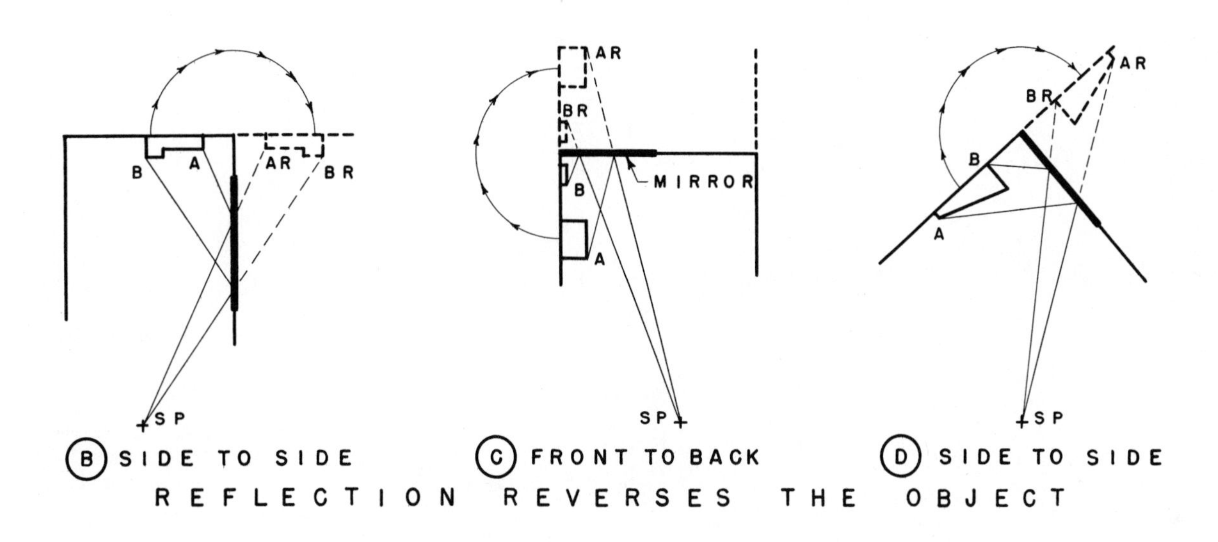

Ⓑ SIDE TO SIDE Ⓒ FRONT TO BACK Ⓓ SIDE TO SIDE

REFLECTION REVERSES THE OBJECT

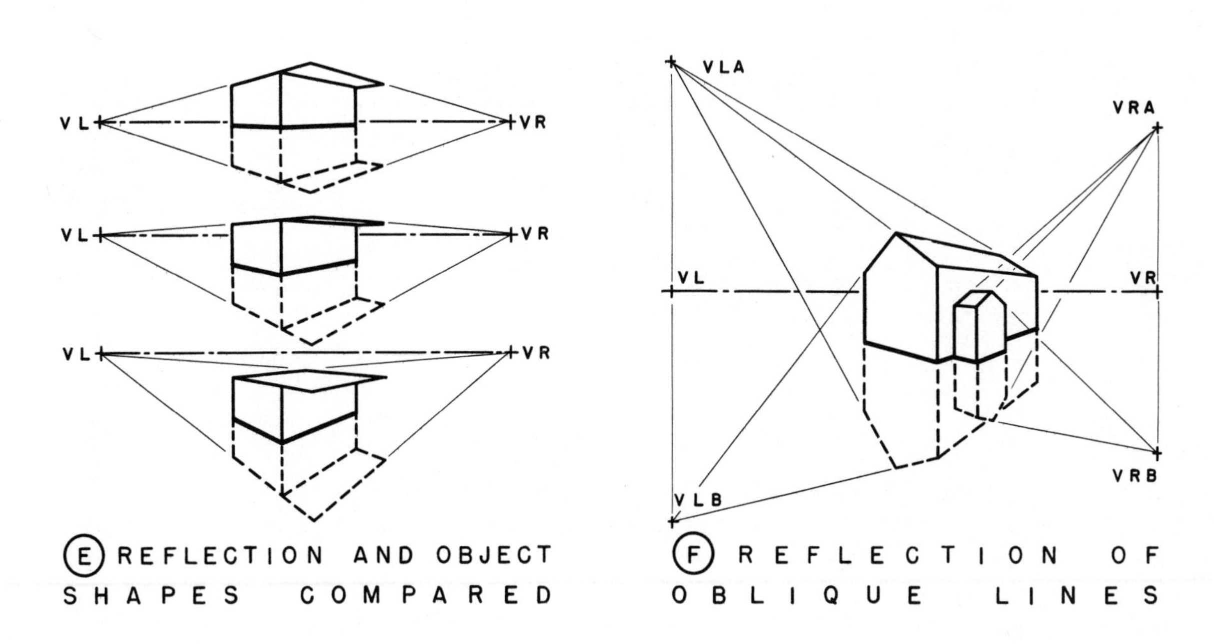

Ⓔ REFLECTION AND OBJECT SHAPES COMPARED

Ⓕ REFLECTION OF OBLIQUE LINES

FIG-109 PRINCIPLES OF REFLECTIONS

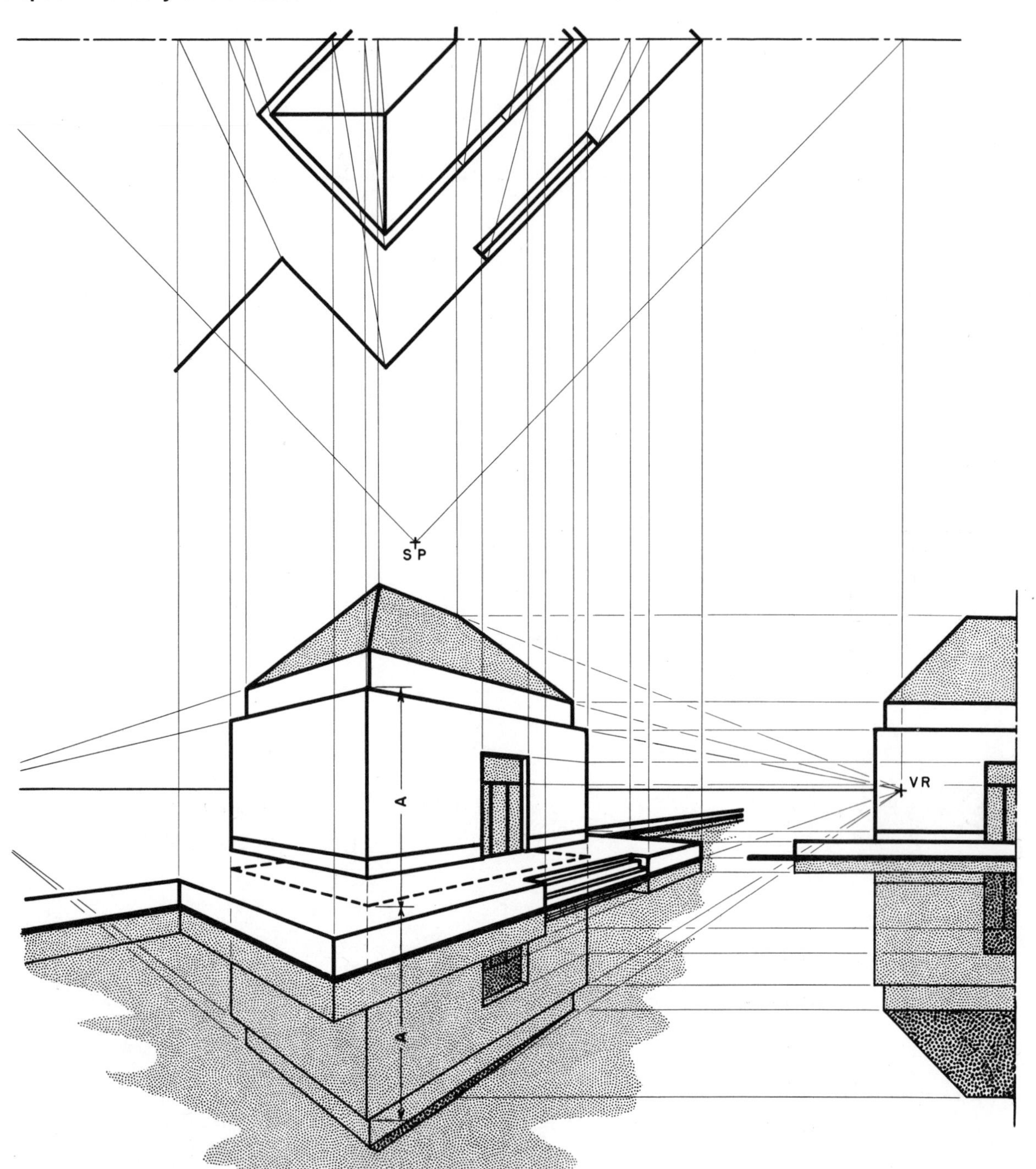

FIG-110 REFLECTIONS ON AN EXTERIOR PERSPECTIVE

In the simple examples of reflections previously used, the objects were drawn touching the horizontal reflecting planes. In architecture it is unusual for a building to be entirely surrounded by water which comes up to the walls. In almost all cases steps and paved areas on the ground with landscape materials form a foreground for buildings. When, as in the illustration of Fig. 110, the building does not touch the reflecting surface, it may be expedient to draw the imaginary intersection. This intersection will take the form of a perspective plan vertically below the object on the plane of the mirror showing the parts of the object which are to be reflected. Then, the reflection of any point on the object will be as far below its position on the perspective plan

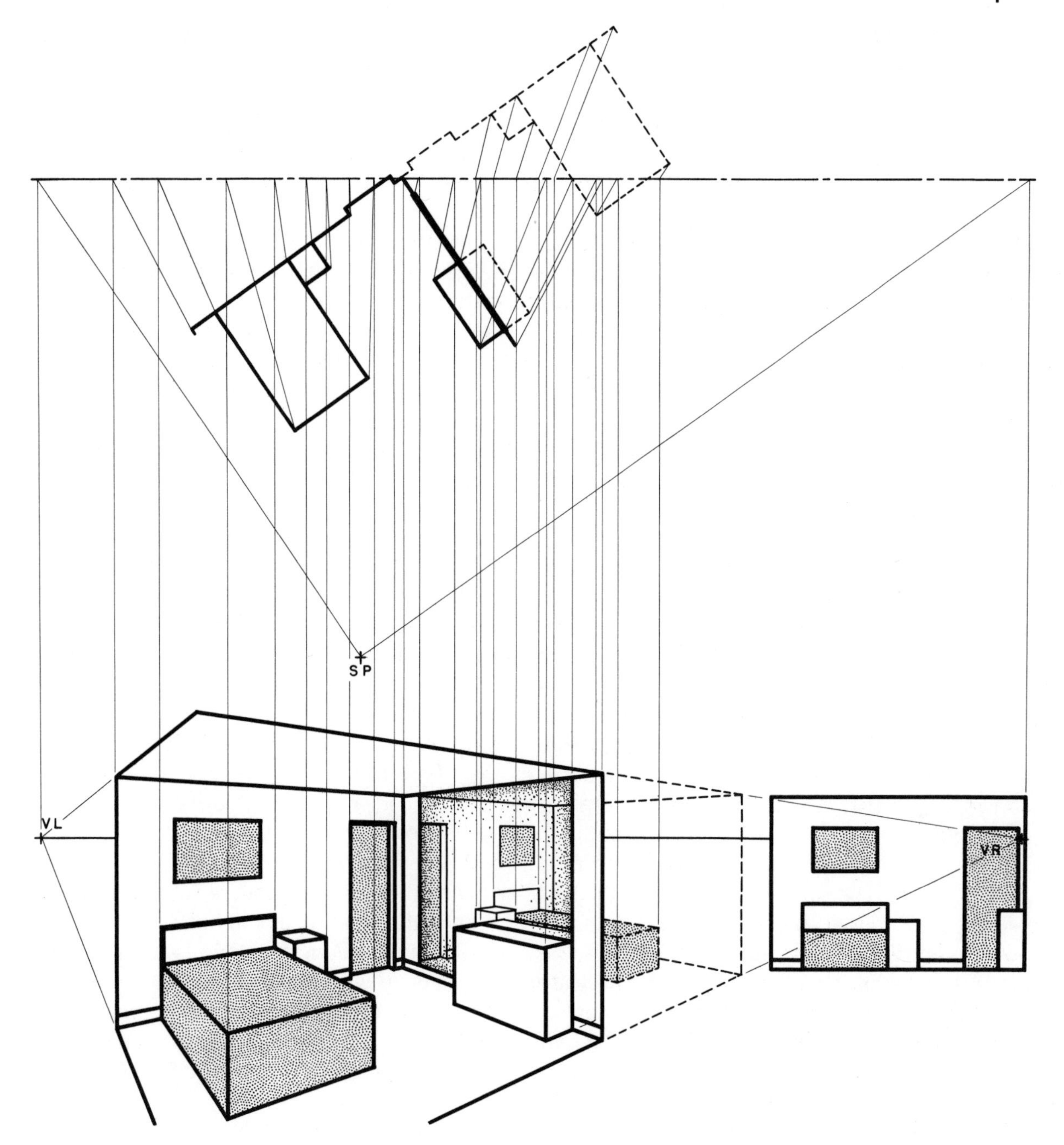

FIG-111 REFLECTIONS ON AN INTERIOR PERSPECTIVE

intersection as the point on the object is above. It is possible to lay out a great deal of a reflection by measurement of equal distances from the real or imaginary intersection with the reflecting surface. A part of the imaginary intersection of the extensions of the main wall planes and the reflecting surface is shown with dotted lines in Fig. 110.

In the two-point perspective of an interior shown in Fig. 111 the reverse from left to right of the entire wall is shown with solid lines where the reflection falls onto the mirror and with dotted lines where it extends beyond the wall on which the mirror is attached. The reflection is much farther from the station point than the object and consequently appears much smaller.

DISTANT VANISHING POINTS. Sometimes the chosen station point will give vanishing points which are located beyond the area of the board on which the perspective is being made.

Extending of the board surface to provide a steady support for the distant vanishing point is the simplest solution of this difficulty. This can be done by fastening two boards together with a strip of heavy paper, three or four inches in width, which is securely attached to both boards with thumb tacks, as shown in Fig. 112A. The surface can also be extended with cardboard and blocking.

When the T-square is too short to reach the distant vanishing point, a straight, thin strip of wood of the required length can be used instead of the T-square. It is also possible to use a string fastened to a pin at the vanishing point and stretched straight. Points can be marked along the string at a distance which can be reached by the T-square and the lines drawn along the T-square.

Railroad curves are thin strips of wood cut to circular arcs of various radii. They are sometimes used with a special T-square to draw lines radiating from a center, Fig. 112B. These curves can be obtained from drafting instrument stores, or the student can make them himself from thin wood. The special T-square has one edge of the blade equidistant from the corners of the working edge of the head. The head should be made to extend from both flat surfaces of the blade so it can be used on either side of the drawing.

When such a T-square is placed with the head against the concave edge of a circular arc strip, the working edge of the blade is the perpendicular bisector of a chord of the arc. Therefore, the line of the edge of the blade extended passes through the center of the arc. The correct position of the curve can be found by measuring the length of the radius of the curve from the vanishing point along the horizon; then, with the curve touching this point and the T-square held in position against the curve, move the T-square and the curve until the blade of the T-square is in line with the horizon. The curve should then be fastened to the board with small brads.

An ordinary T-square can be used with the railroad curves if two brads are driven into the head at equal distances from the working edge of the blade and on a line perpendicular to it, as shown in the sketch. These extending brads are then placed against the curve.

Straight strips of thin wood which are cut to exactly the same length as the head of the T-square can be used as a guide for a standard T-square in order to draw lines from a distant vanishing point, Fig. 112C. The strips are fastened to the board with their corners touching. The first strip should be held against the head of the T-square and even with the ends of the head. The T-square is moved until the working edge of the blade lines up with the horizon. The strip is then fastened to the board. Strips on each side of the first strip are lined up with a string from the vanishing point. This arrangement is approximately correct. With the special T-square it is accurate.

The linead shown in Fig. 112D is a mechanical device for drawing lines which radiate from a distant center. It is made up of a blade and two adjustable arms which slide on pins or small brads which are driven into the board.

Two scales placed perpendicular to the horizon can be used to draw lines to a distant vanishing point, Fig. 112E. In the illustration one scale is twice the size of the other. The smaller scale is located exactly midway between the vanishing point and the larger scale. Any convenient ratio of the two scales can be used if they are correctly located. The scales can be marked on the drawing paper or on straight strips of heavy paper which are attached to the drawing board. When the scale divisions are kept relatively small, this is a very satisfactory method.

Proportional measurements and proportional vanishing points can be used to determine the directions of lines to a distant vanishing point, as shown in Fig. 112F. The method is practical when only a few lines are to be drawn to this vanishing point or when a number of lines all pass through the same vertical line on which the proportional measurements can be laid out. Required: to draw from point A on vertical line A–B a line to distant vanishing point VR. From B lay out to the right on the horizon any fraction of the distance to VR from B. From B on the vertical line B–A lay out the same fraction of the distance from the horizon to A. The line from A to VR will parallel the line through the two fractional measurements.

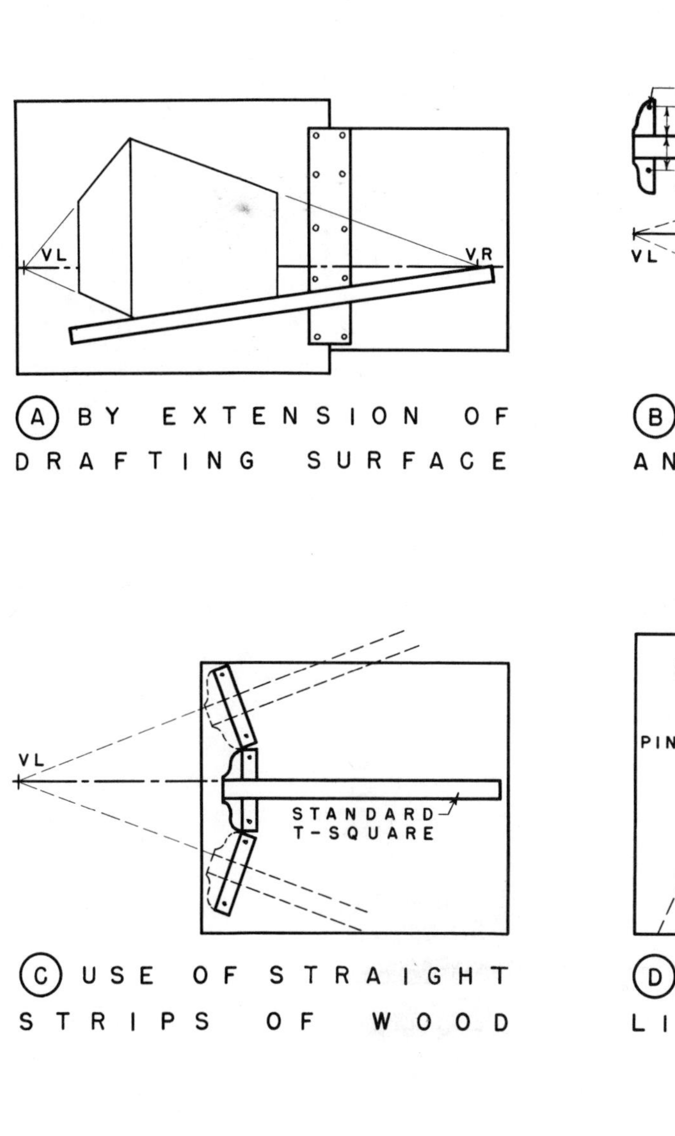

Ⓐ BY EXTENSION OF DRAFTING SURFACE

Ⓒ USE OF STRAIGHT STRIPS OF WOOD

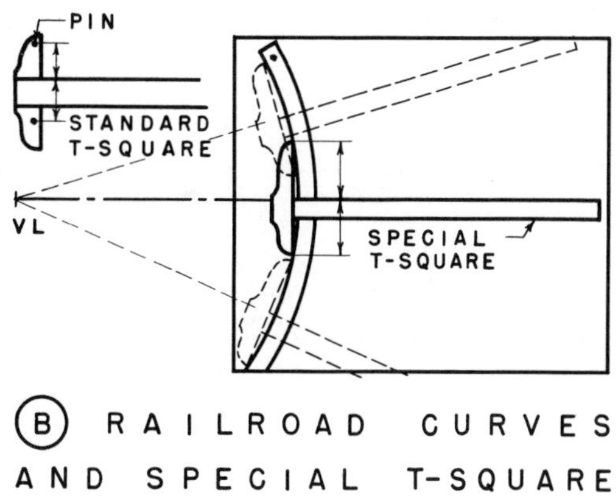

Ⓑ RAILROAD CURVES AND SPECIAL T-SQUARE

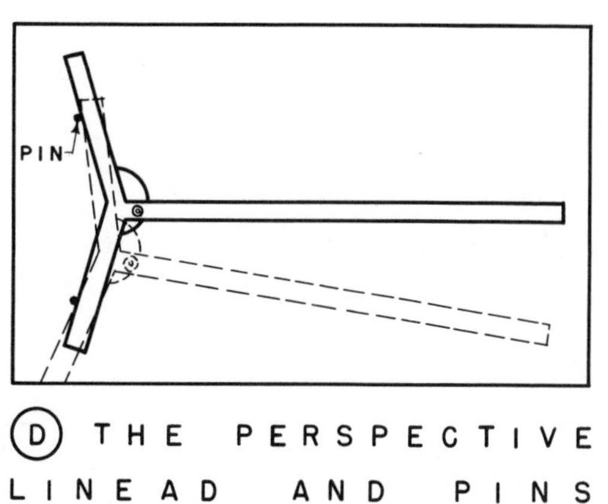

Ⓓ THE PERSPECTIVE LINEAD AND PINS

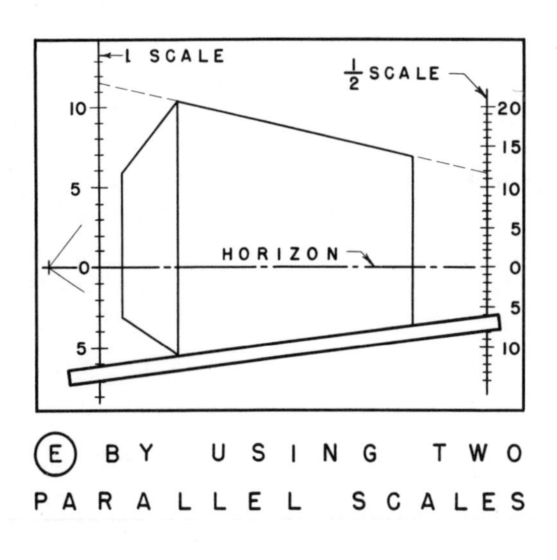

Ⓔ BY USING TWO PARALLEL SCALES

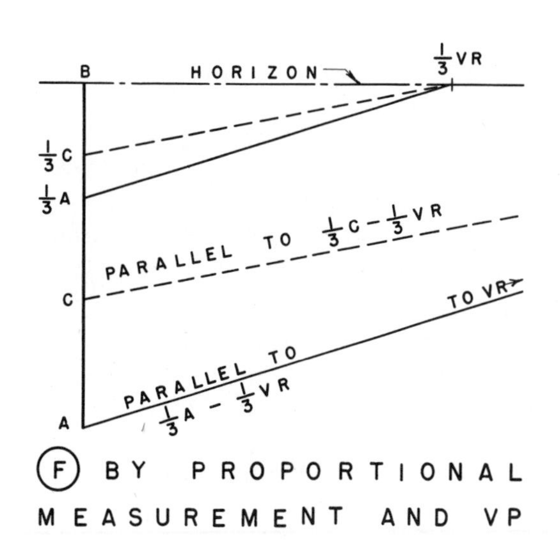

Ⓕ BY PROPORTIONAL MEASUREMENT AND VP

FIG-112 DRAWING TO DISTANT VANISHING POINTS

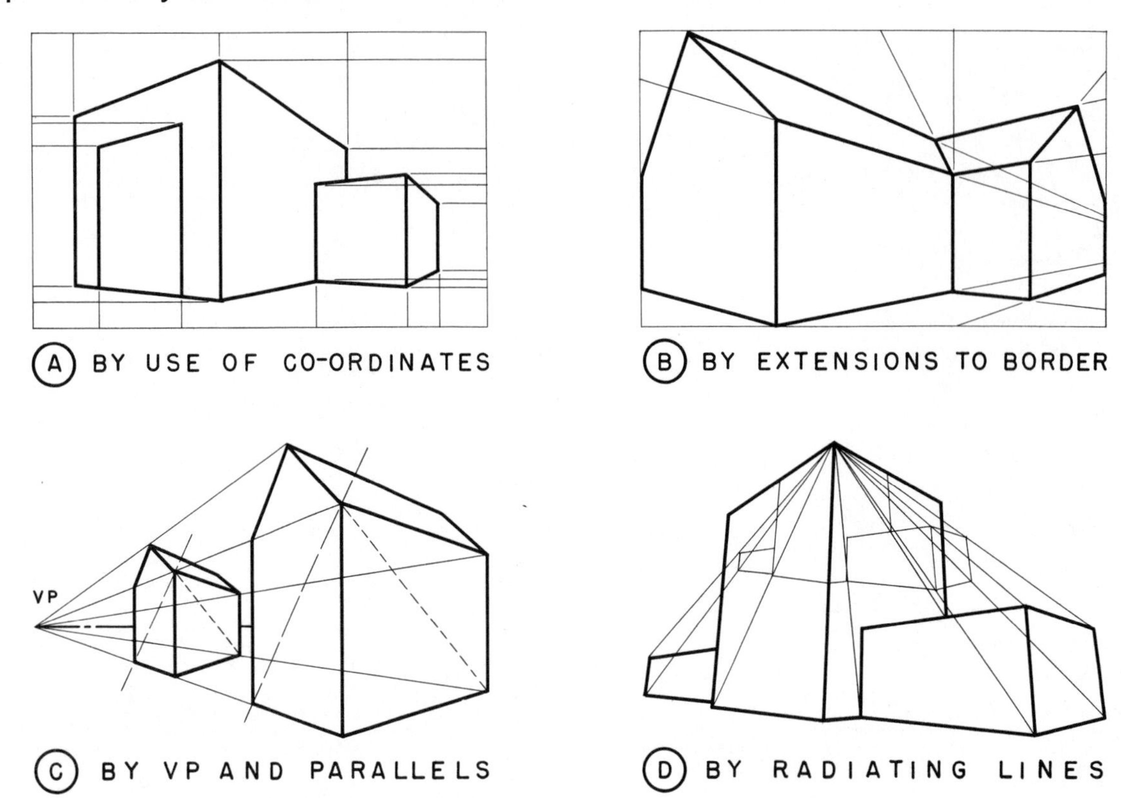

FIG-113 ENLARGING PERSPECTIVE DRAWINGS

THE ENLARGING OF PERSPECTIVE DRAWINGS. It is sometimes difficult or impractical to make the perspective directly at the size required. Several methods by means of which a small perspective drawing can be enlarged to any desired size are shown in Fig. 113. After the main shapes of the perspective are enlarged, minor divisions for doors, windows, wall treatments, etc., can be worked out directly on the large perspective by methods of divisions of lines, or transferred from the small perspective.

Border measurements are used in Fig. 113A and B. In Fig. 113A vertical and horizontal measurements are used along an enclosing rectangular border to locate points on the enlarged perspective from similar border and measurements on the small perspective. When the larger drawing is some simple multiple of the size of the smaller drawing, the measurements from the smaller drawing can be repeated the required number of times on the larger one. Thus, when the size is to be doubled, each small measurement would be used twice. When there is no simple size ratio, proportional dividers may be used, or one of the drafting methods of enlarging a series of measurements can be used. Figure 113B is similar to Fig. 113A, but the lines of the perspective drawing are extended to the border to locate the points of measurement. In many cases it is simpler to locate only important lines of the perspective drawing from the border measurements then to lay out other measurements directly on these important lines.

Parallel and radiating lines are used in Fig. 113C and D for enlarging the perspectives. This method makes use of the fact that when one line of the small drawing is parallel to the same line of the large drawing, then all the lines of one drawing will be parallel to the same lines of the other drawing. Parallel lines are drawn to locate points where lines of the perspective drawing begin or end. In Fig. 113D one point of the two drawings is made to coincide. A line drawn from this point through any point on the small perspective will pass through the same point on the larger perspective. This method requires only the space necessary for the larger drawing.

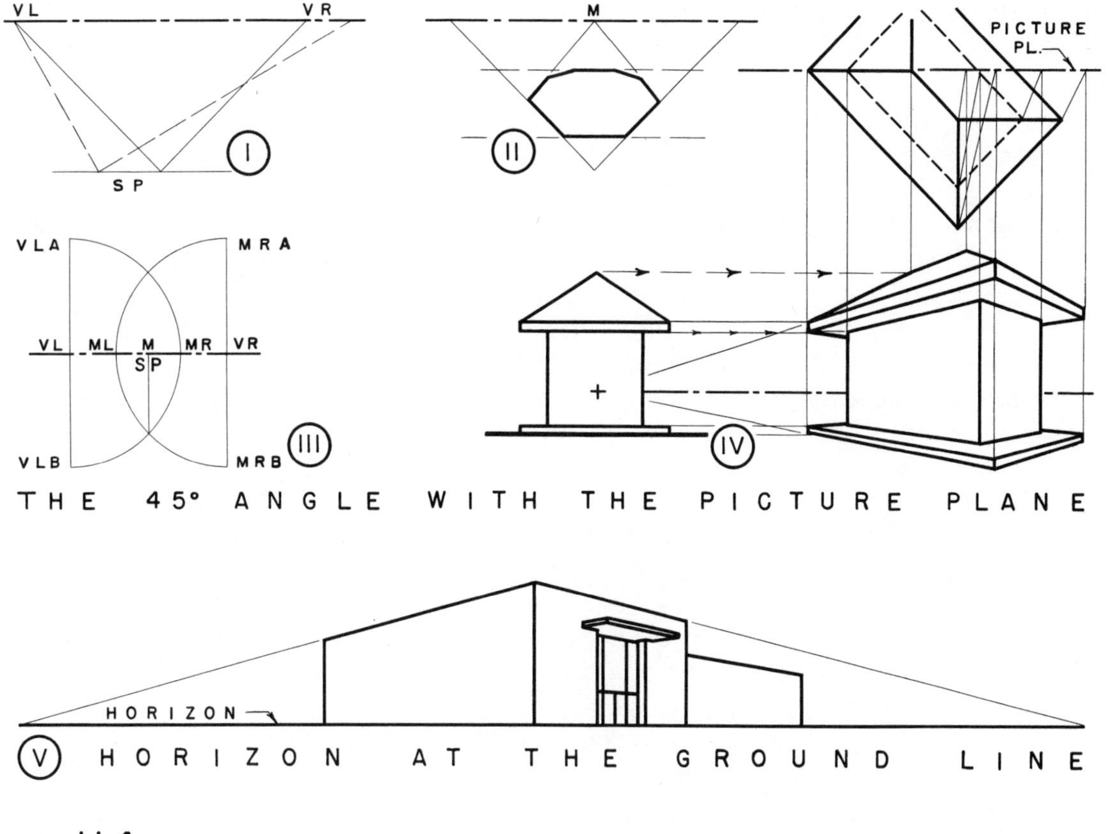

FIG-114 SPECIAL POSITIONS OF THE OBJECT

ADVANTAGES OF THE 45° ANGLE OF THE OBJECT WITH THE PICTURE PLANE. With a given distance of the station point from the object, the minimum distance between vanishing points is obtained, Fig. 114 I. This position of the object simplifies construction of shadows with light parallel to the picture plane.

When the object is turned at 45°, one set of 45° lines in horizontal planes will remain horizontal in perspective since they are parallel to the picture plane, and the other set will vanish in an easily accessible miter point, Fig. 114 II. In other two-point perspective positions of the object, one of the miter points is too far away to be used conveniently.

The vanishing and measuring points are symmetrical about the center, or perspective position of the station point, which is also a miter point. The complete diagram of the vanishing points of the two typical sets of horizontal lines and the measuring and miter points on the horizon and wall horizons requires the use of only two measurements, Fig. 114 III. The distance from the station point to the picture plane is laid out on each side of the center along the horizon to locate the vanishing points. The distance from the vanishing points to the station point is laid out from each vanishing point on the horizon and wall horizons to locate the measuring points.

The determination of heights is simplified because the picture plane can be placed through all the equal projections at one corner of the plan, Fig. 114 IV.

HORIZON ON THE GROUND LINE. The position of the horizon coinciding with the ground line, Fig. 114 V, has the following advantages in perspective: (1) It simplifies the problems of shadow-casting and presentation because there need be no perspective of ground and walks in the horizontal plane of the base of the building. (2) It gives the maximum variation in silhouette at the top of the building, except for station points below the ground line. (3) It gives a good view below horizontal surfaces which are at any appreciable distance above the ground line.

DISTORTION IN PERSPECTIVE DRAWINGS. Any perspective drawing is a true picture of the object when it is seen from the position of the station point. However, a perspective is rarely seen from the exact position of the station point. The observer takes a position from which he can see the drawing in a comfortable and satisfactory manner. This position is usually opposite the center of the perspective drawing and at a greater distance from it than the station point. Figure 115A shows in the top sketch a common relation between the position of the station point used in making the drawing and a natural position for the eye of a person looking at the same drawing. The sketch at the bottom of Fig. 115A shows that spaces at the edge of the perspective appear smaller from the station point than they do from a more distant point of observation. As the lines of sight from the station point approach the center and become more nearly perpendicular to the picture plane, this difference decreases and the pictorial effects from the two distances more nearly coincide.

Parts seen at an acute angle from the station point in a perspective drawing vary from similar parts near the center of vision in both size and shape. Figure 115B is the perspective of a number of spheres from a very close station point. The sphere at the center appears as a circle in the drawing, while those around the edges are ellipses which would be seen as circles from the station point. The directions of the ellipses are different. They are all turned with their major axes radiating from the center of vision or perspective position of the station point. These ellipses are the shapes on a flat surface which would look like spheres from the angle at which they would be seen from the station point. A satisfactory perspective drawing must give approximately the same pictorial effect from a natural viewing position that it does from the position of the station point from which the drawing was made. In order to avoid excessive distortion in perspective drawings of spheres and circles, the station point should be at a sufficient distance so that a 30° cone of vision will include all the spheres and circles shown. This angle of vision is so small that the difference in shapes seen from the SP of the drawing and eye position in looking at the drawing will be negligible. Figure 115C shows an objectionable amount of distortion in a perspective drawing. The distortion is caused by the station point being too near the object with too great a difference between the effect from the station point and a natural view of the drawing. In this drawing the chair has a square seat as shown in plan, but the perspective of the chair is long and thin. In Fig. 115D the SP has been moved farther away with improved perspective effect.

Some rule for the minimum distance from the object is usually followed in order to avoid such extremes as shown in C. When the station point is at a sufficient distance from the object so that everything shown in the perspective drawing is included in a 45° cone with the station point at the apex, the results are usually satisfactory. Perspectives of interiors show the largest sized parts of the drawings in the corners, where distortion is greatest and, because of the increased size, becomes most offensive. For this reason the corners of interior perspectives are sometimes cut off either to a circular outline or to an irregular unfinished edge. When an interior perspective is completed in a rectangular outline, the corners should come within the 45° cone of vision to avoid objectionable distortion. While it seems helpful to give rules for minimum distance from station point to object by a limiting angle of vision, such rules should not be regarded as inflexible. They are reasonably safe, conservative devices which will serve as a guide for the person who does not have much experience. They may produce dull, uninteresting perspectives. The experienced person will choose his station point to suit the design and to obtain the desired effect.

Placing the station point far to one side of the object is a common mistake in laying out a perspective drawing, Fig. 115E and F. The perspective drawing obtained from this station point can give a true picture of the object only when seen out of the corner of the eye, with the observer looking straight ahead from the position of the station point. Actually the object would not be seen from the station point from which it is drawn, but would be seen with the center of vision toward the center of the object as shown in Fig. 115F, in which the plan has been revolved until the dotted picture plane line of Fig. 115E is horizontal. The object would actually never appear as it is drawn in Fig. 115E unless it is a part of a group and near the right edge of the group with the center of interest at the center of vision.

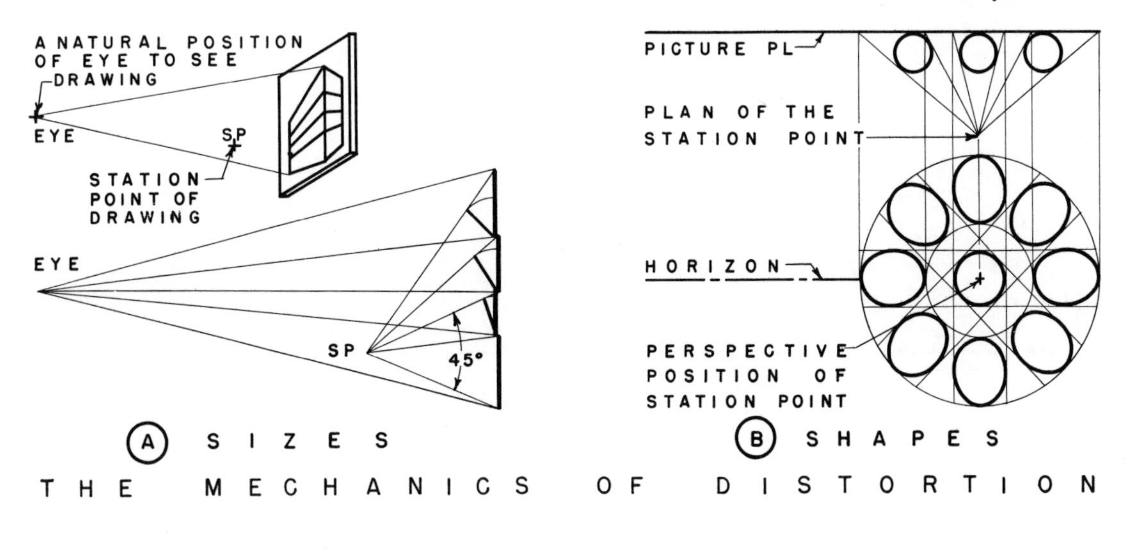

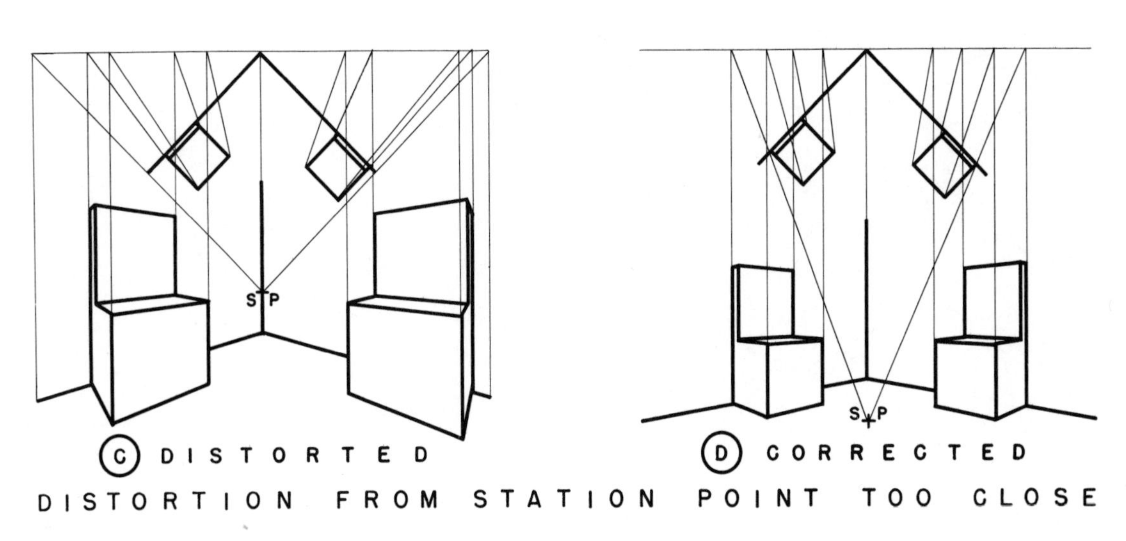

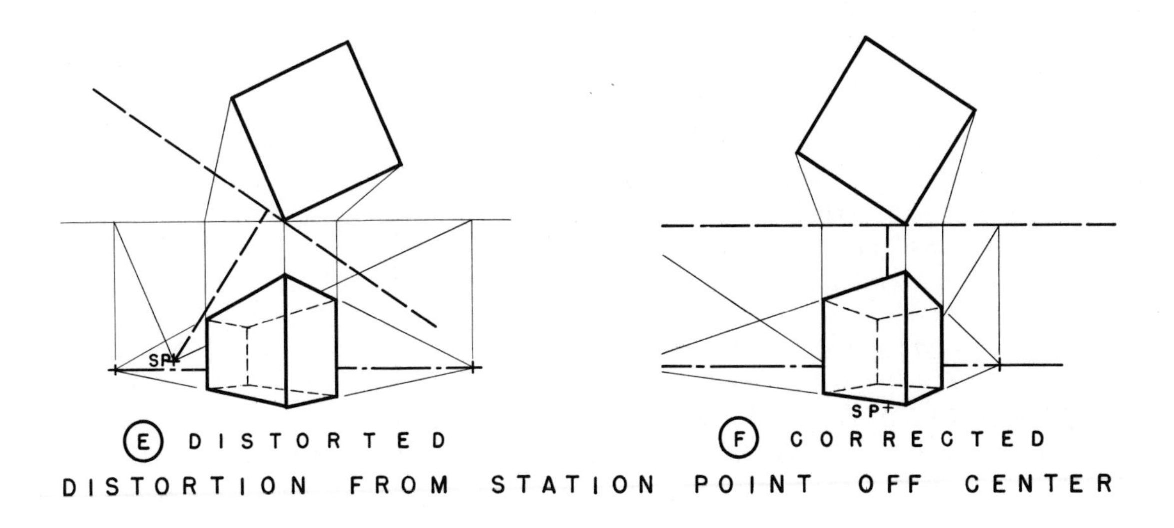

FIG-115 DISTORTION IN PERSPECTIVE DRAWINGS

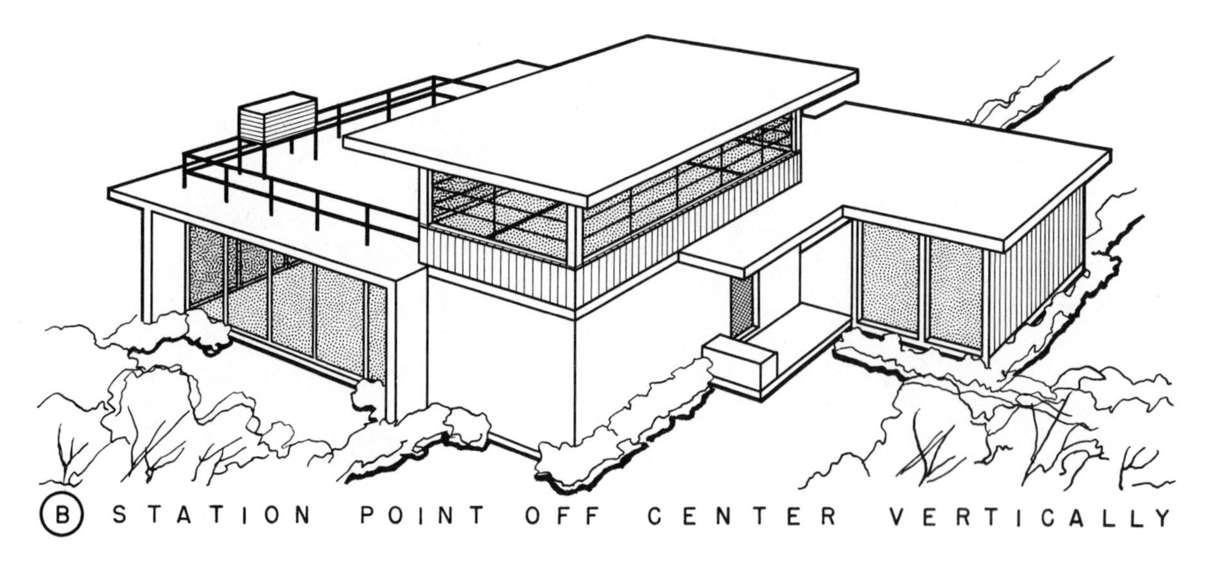

FIG-116 SPECIAL CASES OF SP OFF CENTER

DISTORTION IN PERSPECTIVE. When a plan is drawn for the direct projection or common method and the draftsman discovers that one side of the building does not occupy as much perspective width as desired, there is a great temptation to take the easy way out. The station point can readily be moved to one side to get a different view of the building. However, this places the center of vision to one side of the perspective and causes distortion. *The masses of the building will not represent in perspective the shapes and proportions shown in plan.* The correct procedure is to turn the plan until the desired perspective widths are obtained when the SP is located on center, as shown in Fig. 115F, not with distorted proportions as shown in Fig. 115E.

When the center of interest of the perspective drawing does not coincide with its center of width, the SP may be placed in line with the center of interest. This is the point on which the observer would naturally focus his attention in looking at the drawing. Figure 116A illustrates this condition.

ACCEPTABLE DISTORTION. Theoretically an aerial view, Fig. 116B, or a worm's-eye view with the station point off center vertically, should appear offensively distorted. However, there are compensating factors. The position of the SP is obvious. The vertical lines of the object remain vertical, thus retaining their true direction in the perspective. We are accustomed to photographs, taken with a camera having a rising front, which have these same characteristics. In fact, the more correct three-point perspective often gives the observer a jolt by appearing less natural than the aerial view.

FIG-117 DRAMATIC EFFECT FROM DISTORTION

DESIRABLE DISTORTION. A very close station point is not always an evil thing. It is often possible to obtain a dramatic effect from a very close station point and still avoid offensive distortion, Fig. 117. When we look at a building from a very close position or from inside the structure we see clearly through only a small angle of vision. However, we are conscious of other surrounding forms which are seen less clearly but nevertheless add to our impression. These near objects help to set the stage and to influence our feelings. A perspective made to show near lines, areas, and masses from a close SP may often appear more interesting and dramatic than one made according to rules.

DRAWING IN VERSUS WORKING OUT. Often the draftsman is tempted to draw on the perspective without actually constructing the positions of the lines from measurements. Lines should never be drawn in because of ignorance of perspective construction. They may properly be drawn in to the correct vanishing points without measurements when the draftsman understands their positions and can locate them as accurately by eye as by measurements. Lines of window reveals, window divisions, small moldings, small projections, and details of various kinds can often be drawn on a perspective without being constructed. In many cases the result is more correct than the laborious construction of the same details by an equally expert draftsman who does not have the ability and training to visualize their forms and positions. The draftsman should be sure that he has represented the building correctly and has not deceived his client concerning the shapes of the building.

CHAPTER 14
The Measuring-Point Method

MEASURING POINTS. The only measuring points used in previous examples of one- and two-point perspective were those located on the horizon, Fig. 118A and B. These measuring points were used to transfer horizontal dimensions from the horizontal measuring line to the perspective of a horizontal line of the object. In the perspective plan method of three-point perspective a measuring point was used to transfer height measurements also. In practically all of the examples of construction of perspective drawings previously given, one or more auxiliary drawings were used as a necessary part of the construction. By a more extensive use of measuring points it is possible to eliminate auxiliary drawings entirely from the perspective construction.

When the perspective of any line A–V, Fig. 118C, is given by its intersection A with the picture plane and its vanishing point V, the distance V–SP can be laid out in any direction from V to locate a measuring point M. If a plane be passed through the three points V, M, and A, the line V–M is the horizon of the plane, and a line through A parallel to V–M is the intersection of the plane with the picture plane. This line through A, which lies in the picture plane, is then the line on which measurements are laid out and from which they are transferred to A–V by using M as a measuring point. Since the only requirement for M is that it must be a distance SP–V from V on the picture plane, it can be located at any point on a circle which has V as a center and a radius SP–V. However, the measuring points situated on the horizon and wall horizons are usually conveniently located, easy to use, and sufficient for all construction purposes. Figure 118D, E, and F shows typical diagrams of horizons, vanishing points, and circles on which the measuring points are located for the three systems of perspective drawing with the lettering employed in the following examples for the most commonly used measuring points.

In one-point perspective the measuring points on the horizon and on the wall horizon are all miter points. The measuring points ML and MR on the horizon are the vanishing points of 45° lines in the floor, ceiling, and all other horizontal planes. These measuring points transfer measurements from horizontal lines in the picture plane to the perspectives of horizontal lines which are perpendicular to the picture plane. The measuring points MA and MB are the vanishing points of the two sets of 45° lines in wall planes perpendicular to the picture plane. They transfer measurements from vertical lines in the picture plane to the perspectives of horizontal lines perpendicular to the picture plane. The diagram, Fig. 118G, shows the perspective of the inside of a cube and the diagonals drawn on the four interior faces of the cube by lines to the various measuring points.

In two-point perspective the measuring points MLA and MLB are the vanishing points of 45° lines in the left wall planes, and MRA and MRB are the vanishing points of 45° lines in the right wall planes. They are therefore miter points. These measuring points transfer measurements from a vertical measuring line to a horizontal measurement correction line or base line. Figure 118H shows the two-point perspective of the outside of a cube and shows how the measuring points are used to draw the diagonals of the wall faces of the cube. Since they do not transfer measurements across a right angle, ML and MR are not miter points. They transfer measurements across the acute angles made by the horizontal measuring line and horizontal lines in the wall planes. The miter point M is the vanishing point of one set of 45° lines in floor planes, the other is usually too far away to be used. None of the measuring points lettered on the diagram for three-point perspective, Fig. 118F, is a miter point. The use of these measuring points has been explained under the perspective plan method of three-point perspective.

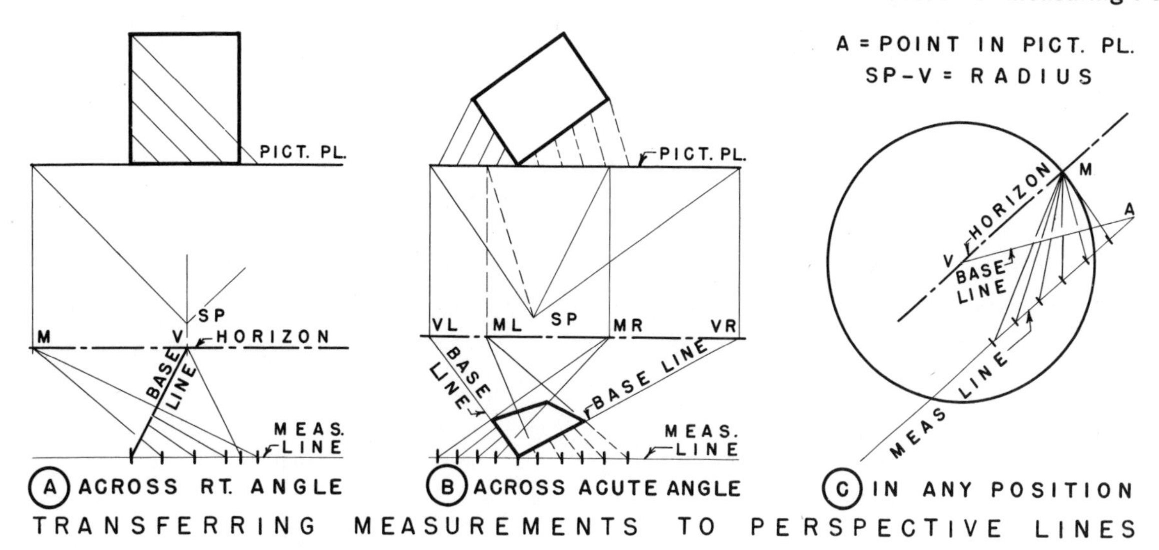

TRANSFERRING MEASUREMENTS TO PERSPECTIVE LINES

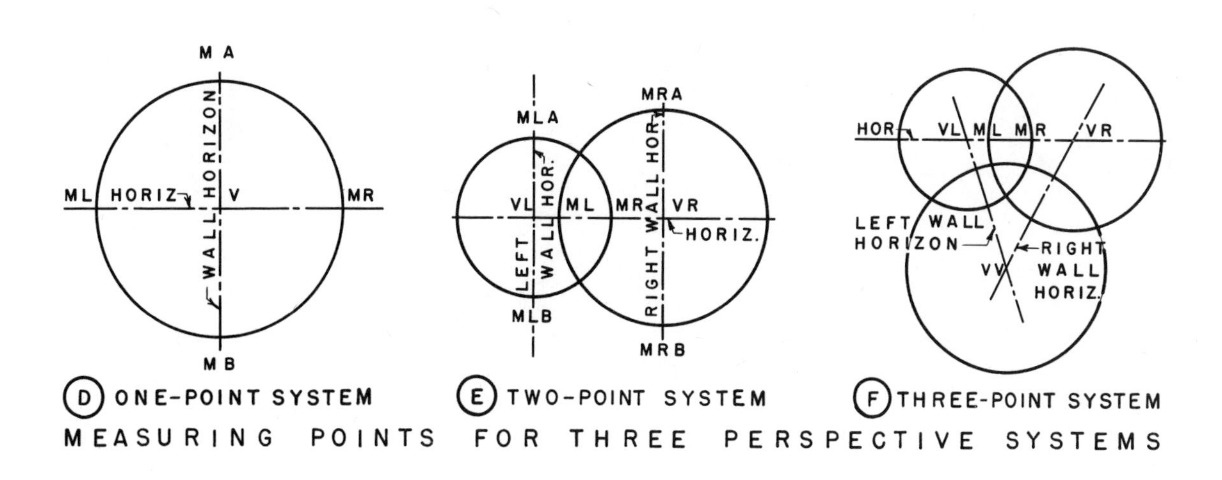

MEASURING POINTS FOR THREE PERSPECTIVE SYSTEMS

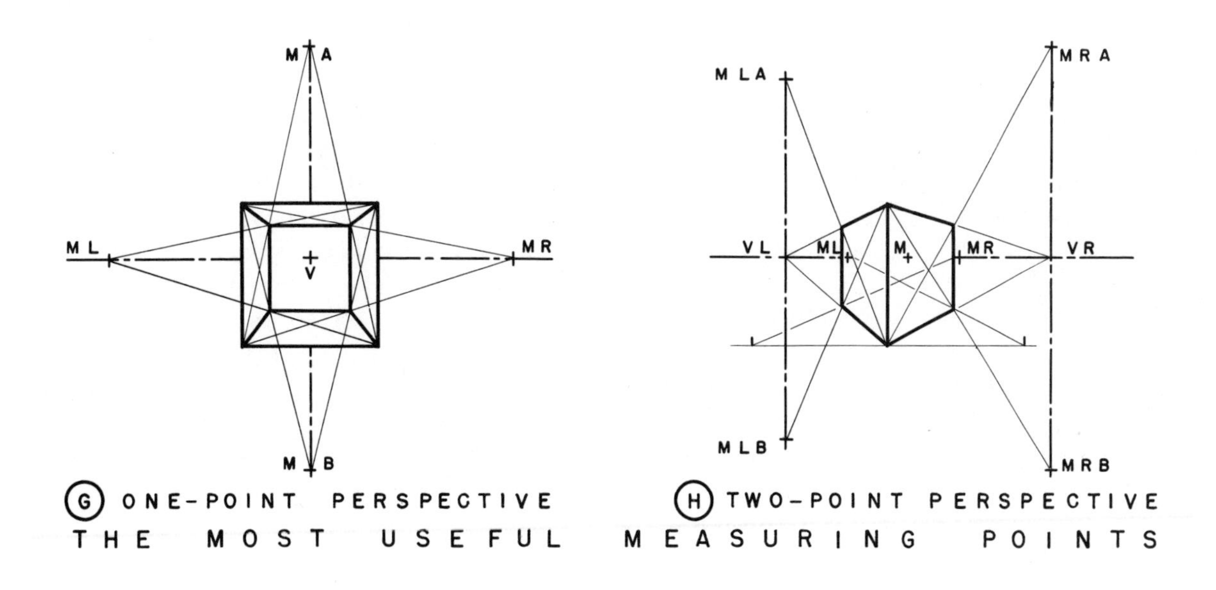

THE MOST USEFUL MEASURING POINTS

FIG-118 THE LOCATION OF MEASURING POINTS

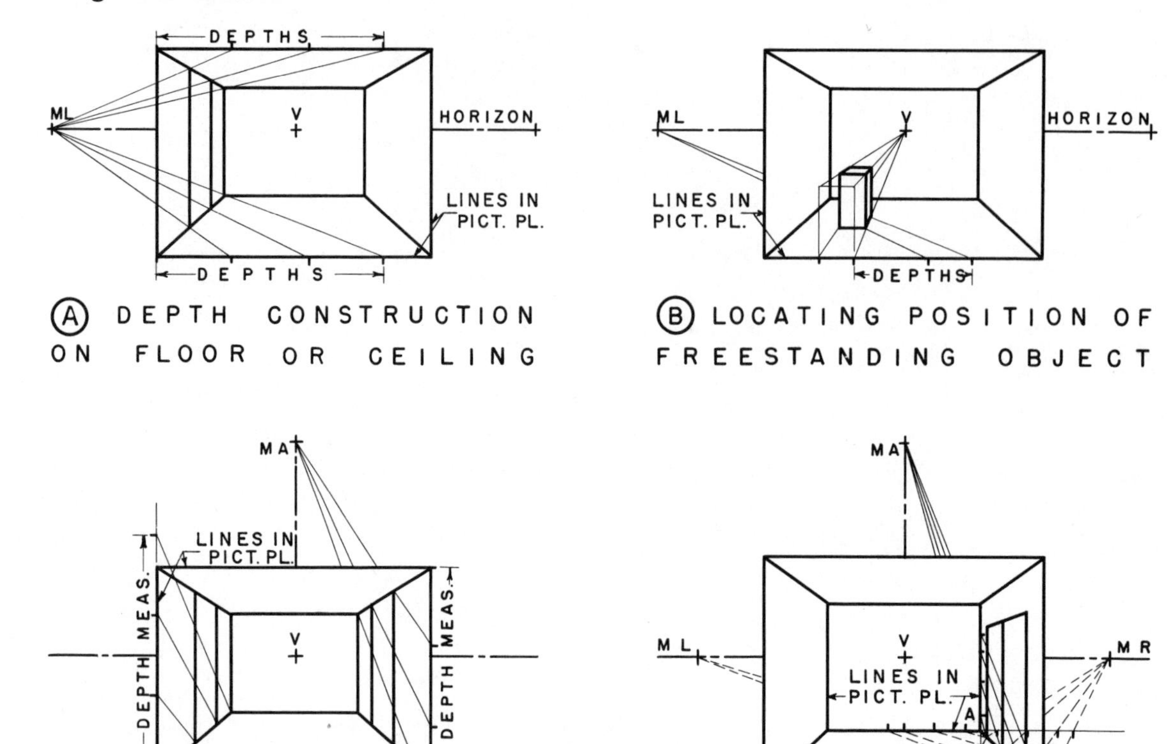

FIG-119 USES OF MEASURING POINTS IN ONE—POINT PERSPECTIVE

In the construction of a one-point perspective any convenient one (or more than one) of the measuring points can be used. When using ML or MR, the construction for distances from the picture plane can be made on either the floor or ceiling, as shown in Fig. 118A. When the horizon is very low, the floor area becomes so thin that the construction there becomes inaccurate or even impossible, and the same condition exists on the ceiling plane when the horizon is high. In such cases the construction can be laid out on the larger horizontal area or on the wall areas. Depth construction in the wall planes is illustrated in Fig. 118C, where MA and MB are used as measuring points to secure the same results as were obtained in Fig. 118A by using ML.

Construction for a freestanding object is shown in Fig. 119B. The width and depth measurements are laid out on the edge of the floor where it intersects the picture plane. The width measurements are traced toward V along the floor, and the depth measurements are laid out from the measurement of one of the lines to V and traced to ML to determine the depths, at their intersections with the line to V from which the depth measurements began.

In Fig. 119A, B, and C the measurements were laid out on the intersection lines of the walls, floor, and ceiling with the picture plane. Any horizontal line in the picture plane which touches the end of the line to V, which is used as a measurement correction line, can be used for the measuring line with ML or MR as the measuring point. Likewise, any vertical line in the picture

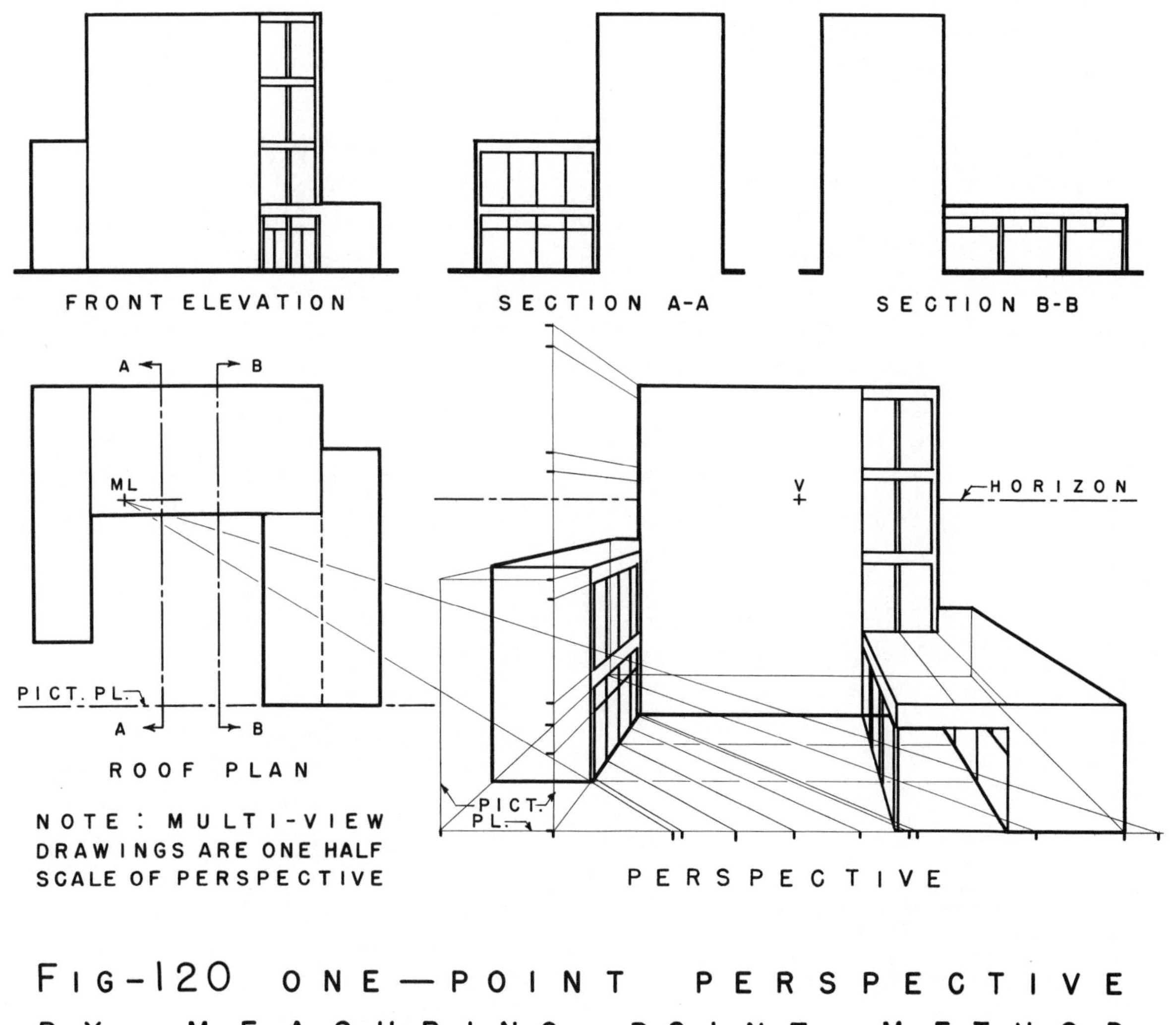

FIG-120 ONE—POINT PERSPECTIVE BY MEASURING POINT METHOD

plane which touches the end of the line to V, which is used as the measurement correction line, can be used for the measuring line with MA or MB as the measuring point.

In Fig. 119D the end wall of the room is assumed to be in the picture plane and the measuring lines on the drawing are the sides, top, and bottom of the end wall. Since the room extends in front of the picture plane, the construction lines extend from V and the M points. There are usually a number of ways in which the construction can be worked out for the same points. As an example, the construction for the doorway on the right wall has been made from all four measuring points. The four sets of measurements for this construction all begin at point A. Two are laid out on the vertical line through A and the other two on the horizontal line through A. All four constructions give the same result. It cannot be emphasized too strongly that there are usually many possible variations of the construction of any part of a perspective drawing. Learn what each measuring and vanishing point will do, then choose the most convenient and most accurate construction for each part of a given perspective problem.

Figure 120 gives a more detailed example of construction of a one-point perspective by use of measuring and vanishing points. In this example only one measuring point has been used in order to keep the required space small. The small-scale multi-view drawings are included to explain the design. They are not used as auxiliary drawings for working out the construction of the perspective.

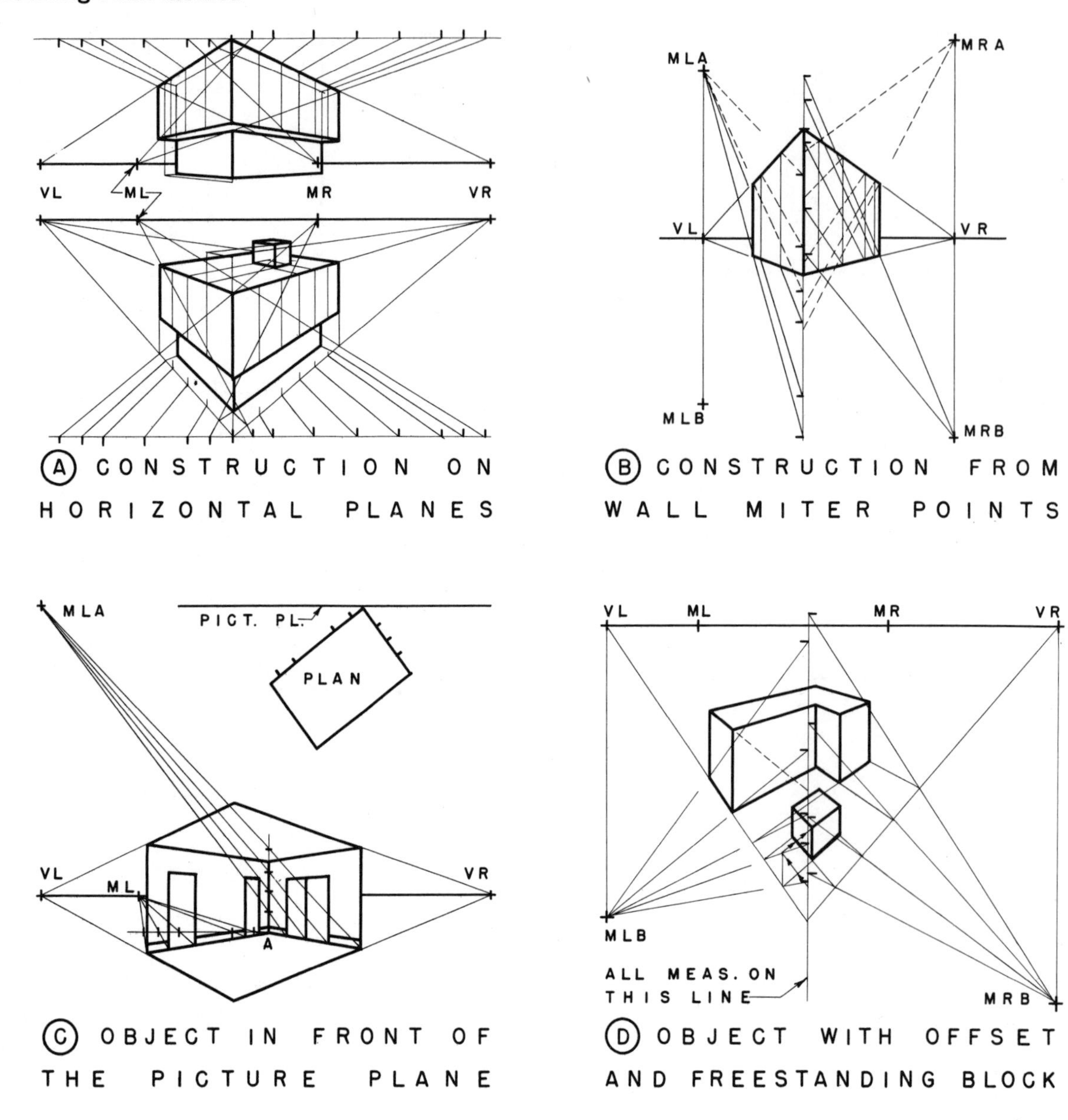

FIG-121 CONSTRUCTION BY MEASURING POINT METHOD

The construction of two-point perspectives by use of measuring points is illustrated in Figs. 121 and 122. In Fig. 121A the lower drawing has the horizontal distances along the walls worked out in the ground plane by the perspective plan method. The construction is made on the perspective itself without the use of a separate perspective plan. When the horizon is low on the building, as in the top example of Fig. 121A, the construction can be drawn more accurately in the plane of the top of the building than in the ground plane. In the lower drawing, the position of the top block has been worked out in the plane of the roof. Part of the construction can be done in one plane, part in another. In Fig. 121B the entire construction has been made with the measuring points on the wall horizons. One measuring point for each wall is sufficient, but all four may be used. When the measurements extend beyond the limits of the paper, it is sometimes possible to use a higher or lower measurement reference line in order to keep all the scale measurements in reach. In Fig. 121B the ground line of the left wall has been used as the measurement correction line. By using the top corner of the wall as the correction line, the measurements and construction would be raised and a great deal of space saved, as shown by the dotted construction lines to MLA.

The object in Fig. 121C is in front of the picture plane in the position shown by the small-scale plan. Typical constructions are shown from two of the measuring points. When the object is in this position, the construction lines are drawn away from the measuring point to increase the measured size. In Fig. 121A and B, where the object is behind the picture plane, the construction lines were drawn toward the measuring points to decrease the measured size.

In Fig. 121D construction is shown for a simple block object with offsets and for a smaller freestanding block in front of it.

Figure 122 shows a more detailed example of this method of perspective drawing. In this example the necessary part of the perspective plan has been constructed on the ground plane. Most of the vertical lines of the perspective have been drawn up from this plan. The heights have been laid out to scale on the vertical measuring line. Any scale which will give the correct number of vertical divisions can be used in a vertical position to divide the space between two lines to a VP. This method has been demonstrated to the left of the main block shape. The method of line division by use of a triangle was used to divide the main right wall into vertical bands.

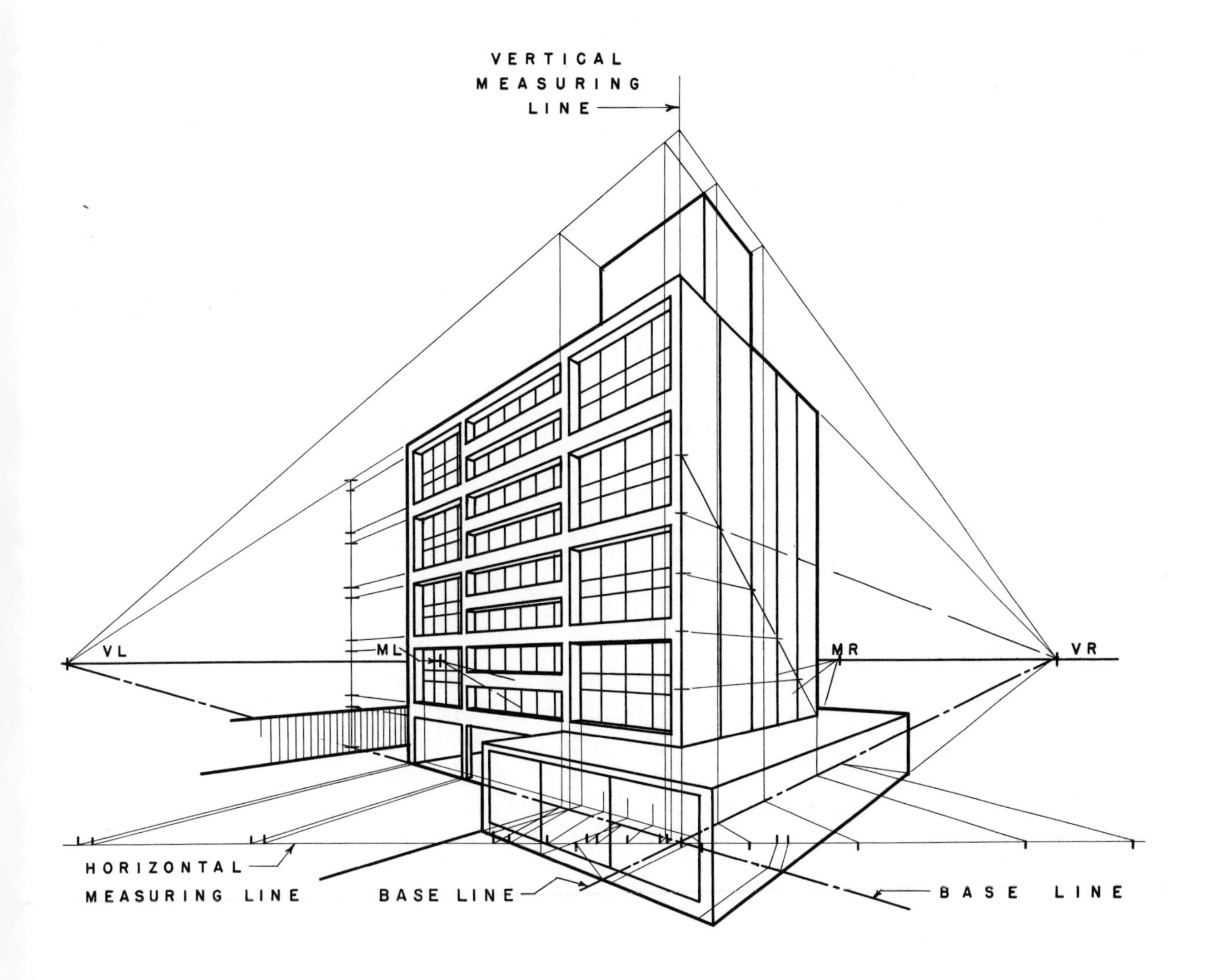

FIG-122 EXAMPLE OF MEASURING POINT METHOD

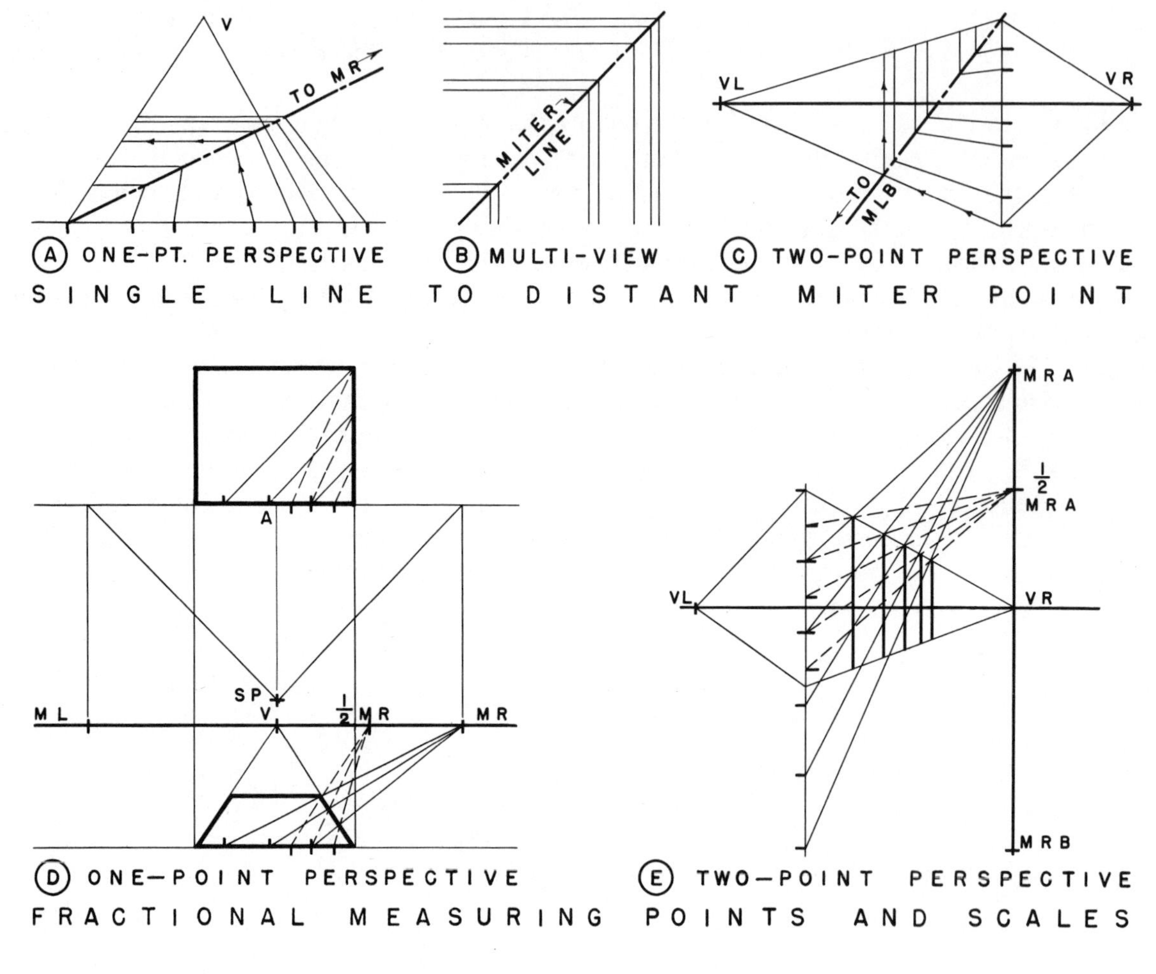

FIG-123 SPACE SAVING DEVICES

When the measuring point is at a distance, it is sometimes inconvenient to draw a number of lines to the one point. The same results can be secured in one-point perspective by using a single line to the measuring point. All depth measurements are then carried toward the vanishing point to meet the line to the measuring point, which is a miter line and, in this case, serves as a measurement reference or correction line. The example, Fig. 123A, shows this construction on a horizontal plane of a one-point perspective. It can be applied to a wall plane also, when a line to a measuring point on the wall horizon is used as the correction line and a vertical line is used for the measurements.

Figure 123C shows the same construction applied to a wall surface in two-point perspective. It should be noted that the measuring points on the wall horizons are miter points and that these constructions of Fig. 123A and C are an application of the turning of measurements around a 90° angle by use of a 45° intersection line. The equivalent in multi-view orthographic drawing is often used at corners of openings and panels by the draftsman, Fig. 123B.

This construction cannot be as conveniently used in two-point or three-point perspective.

The construction may spread out too far because the scale measurements extend beyond convenient limits in spite of the use of the single line to the measuring point. It is possible to restrict the area required for measuring points and measurements by using fractional measuring points and fractional scales. It has previously been explained that equal measurements can be transferred from the measuring line to a measurement correction line by drawing to a measuring point. The measuring point is then the vanishing point of the set of parallel lines which transfers

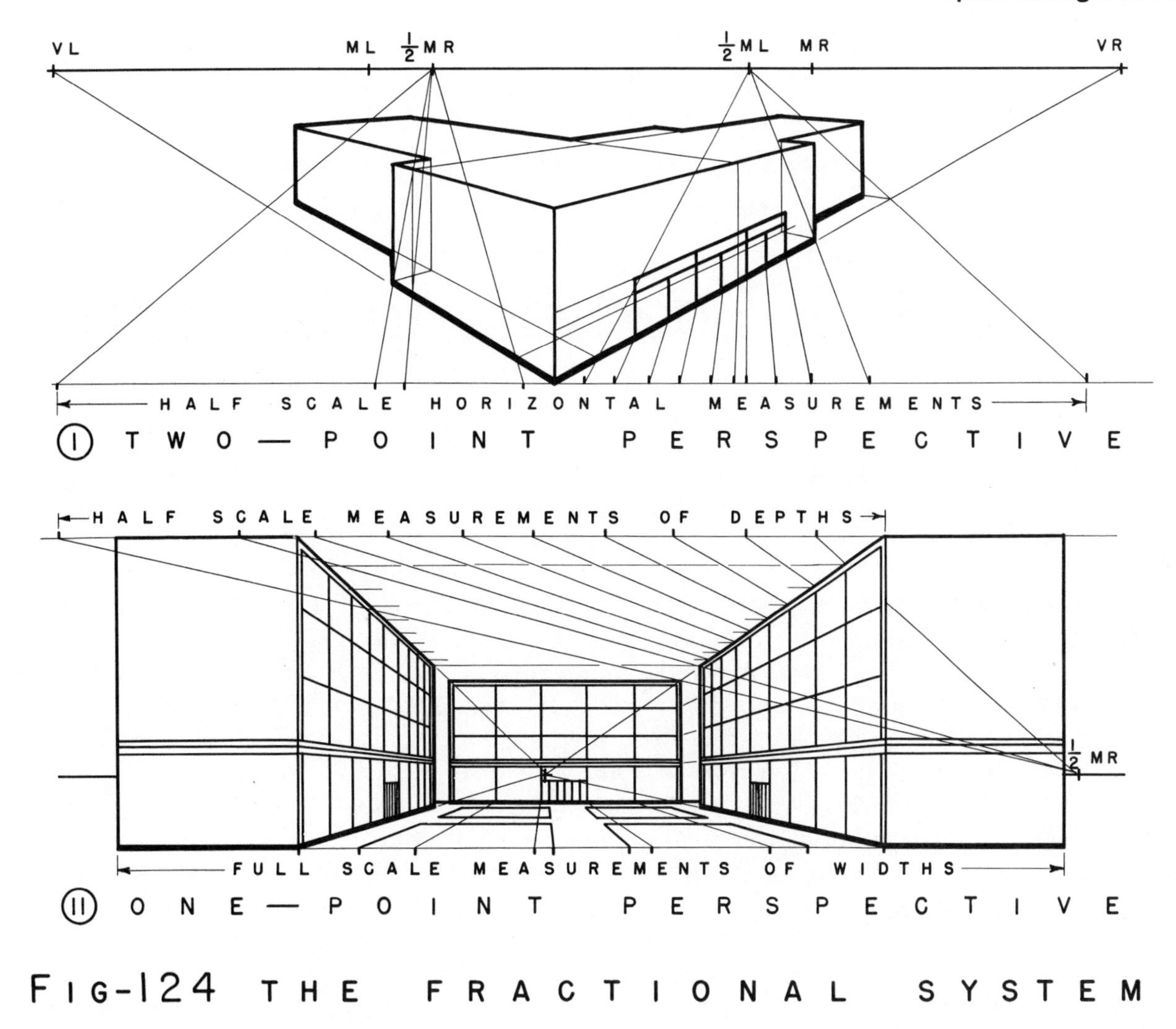

FIG-124 THE FRACTIONAL SYSTEM

equal measurements from one line to another. It is possible to transfer unequal measurements by the same procedure.

The plan of Fig. 123D shows, with the solid parallel lines, how equal measurements can be transferred across an angle. The dotted lines are drawn in the direction to transfer measurements made at half-scale on the measuring line to full-scale on the line to which the measurements are transferred. The perspective equivalent of this comparison is shown in the lower part of Fig. 123D. The distance V–MR is made the usual measuring point distance, that is, equal to V–SP. The measuring point for half-scale measurements $\frac{1}{2}$MR is located one-half the distance V–SP from V. Therefore, $\frac{1}{2}$MR is the midpoint of the distance V–MR. Any desired fractional scale can be used if the correct fraction of the distance V–MR is laid out from V to locate the fractional measuring point.

The amount of space saved by use of fractional measuring points is often very advantageous in one-point perspective. In two-point perspective the measuring points on the horizon are between the vanishing points and are usually conveniently located. There is, however, the advantage of shortening the space required for measurements when they extend too far. When the measuring points on the wall horizons are used for two-point perspective, they extend far above and below the remainder of the construction. Fractional measuring points can then be used on the wall horizons of two-point perspective to good advantage, as shown in Fig. 123E. Examples of the use of fractional measuring points to reduce the amount of space required for measurements and measuring points are given in Fig. 124 I for two-point and in Fig. 124 II for one-point perspective.

PART FOUR
Shades and Shadows

CHAPTER 15
Principles of Shades and Shadows

Everyone likes the sunlight. People are more cheerful when the sun shines. Almost everyone is conscious of sunlight; very few persons are equally conscious of shadows as an essential accompaniment of sunshine. Wherever there are buildings, animals, ships, clouds, trees, shrubs, rocks, or other objects extending above the surface of land or water, there are shadows when the sun shines. These shadows form an essential part of the pattern of a landscape, a piece of pottery, or a building. Since shadows are inevitably a part of any object which is to be placed in the light, their forms and masses must be considered in studying a design if that design is to be completely successful. A knowledge of shadow shapes and of the methods by which they are correctly and accurately constructed on various types of drawings is an essential part of the training of any draftsman or designer of three-dimensional objects.

THE USE OF SHADOWS. Shadows are especially useful in architectural drawing and design because they make the drawings more easily understood. The shades and shadows express the shapes of surfaces, showing whether they are curved or flat, slanting or vertical. In multi-view drawings shadows are especially valuable because they bring out the third dimension; the distance back, in what would otherwise be a two-dimension drawing. The lines and masses of shadows form an important part of an architectural design and should be a part of the studies made in the development of the design. When the correctly drawn shadows are unpleasant or disturbing, there is something wrong with the design and it should be revised to produce a more harmonious effect.

Shadows are almost indispensable on rendered presentation drawings. They add to the picture effect of drawings, making them much more easily understood by the client. The rendered shadows give even the designer a clearer understanding of the appearance of the projected building and aid him in perfecting its design. Shadows on most objects in bright sunshine are very positive dark areas. They are never pale and anemic. Shadows from artificial lighting vary widely in their darkness with the distance from the light source and the strength of the light.

Figure 125A shows a picture of a model of buildings. The picture was made on a cloudy day. The tones of different planes vary appreciably and give a certain amount of interest to the buildings. There is also some shading from the building forms onto the ground plane, which is caused from the sky as a source of light. In Fig. 125B the same buildings are shown in sunshine with shadows which bring out details, distances, and forms of the design more clearly than they were shown in the first photograph.

There is an even greater difference between a drawing and rendering of the same building. A drawing gives an especially flat appearance because there is no variation of shading to suggest texture and materials. The shadows of a rendering are a most important element in its pictorial effect. A knowledge of shades and shadows should be considered not as an end in itself but as a means to an end—the production of more natural and expressive presentation drawings. This knowledge is a useful tool for the draftsman and designer just as a knowledge of the manipulations of drafting and the principles of design are tools leading to better drawings and designs.

Ⓐ PHOTOGRAPH OF MODEL ON A CLOUDY DAY

Ⓑ PHOTOGRAPH OF SAME MODEL IN SUNSHINE
STUDENT MODEL BY MICHAEL E. WERNER

FIG-125 THE EFFECT OF SHADOWS ON BUILDINGS

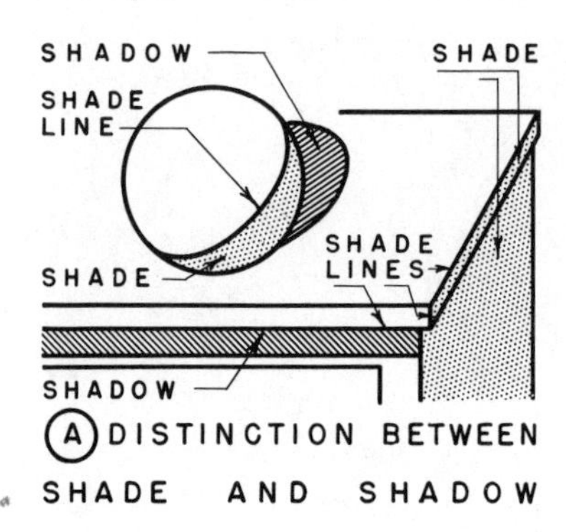

(A) DISTINCTION BETWEEN SHADE AND SHADOW

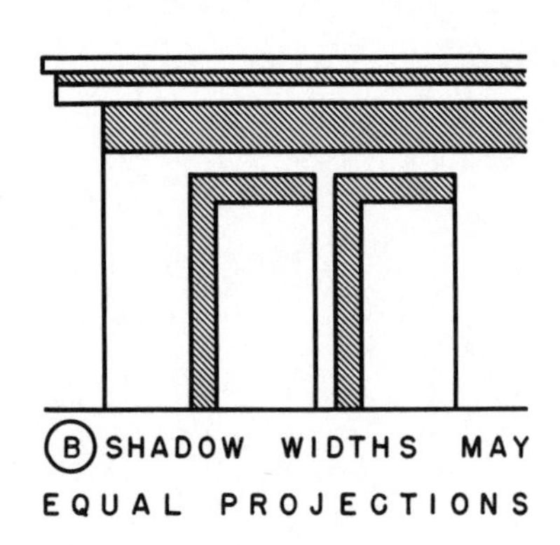
(B) SHADOW WIDTHS MAY EQUAL PROJECTIONS

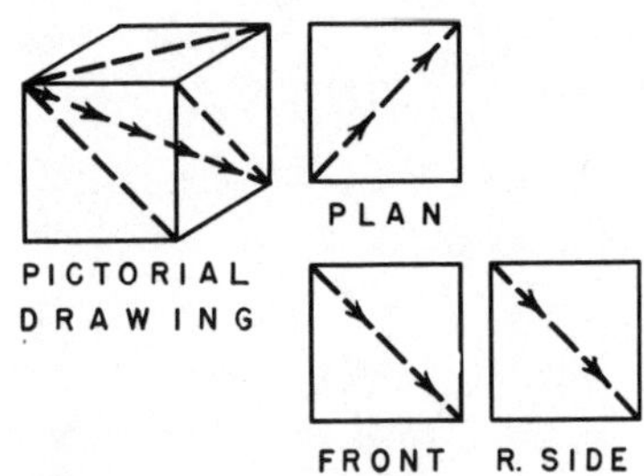

(C) THE CONVENTIONAL DIRECTION OF LIGHT

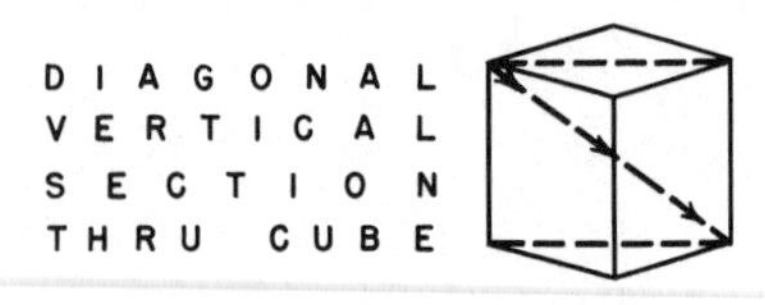

(D) TRUE DIRECTION OF A CONVENTIONAL RAY

FIG-126 DEFINITION OF SHADOW TERMS

SHADES AND SHADOWS. A shade occurs when the shape of the object excludes the light rays from part of its surface, Fig. 126A. The lines between the areas of light and shade are called shade lines. On a curving surface, such as that of a sphere, the shade line is the line of tangency of light rays to the curving surface. On objects made up of plane surfaces, a shade line is the edge where a surface in light meets a surface in shade. A shadow travels through the air from one object to another, or from one part of an object to another part of the same object.

THE CONVENTIONAL DIRECTION OF LIGHT. In casting shadows it is necessary to assume a source and direction of light. The source of light is usually assumed to be the sun, and the rays of light are considered to be parallel. The direction of light used in practically all shadow-casting gives shadow widths which are equal to the projections from wall surfaces of vertical and horizontal shade lines which are parallel to the picture plane and the wall. Characteristic examples of shadows which are equal to the projections making them are shown in Fig. 126B.

If a cube is placed so that its sides are parallel to the three coordinate planes of elevation, plan, and side elevation, then its diagonal from the top left front corner to the lower right rear corner gives the conventional direction of light and the three views of the cube give the apparent directions of light in the three typical drawings, Fig. 126C. The conventional direction of light is used in all the following discussions and illustrations of shades and shadows on multi-view drawings, except some examples in Chapter 19.

THE 45° DIRECTION. Since the direction of light in front elevation, plan, and side elevation views is the diagonal of a square, it is a 45° line in all three drawings. Therefore, shadows may be traced by using the 45° triangle on these drawings. A ray of light travels equally in three directions, (1) to the right, (2) down, and (3) back, as shown by edges of the cube. The 45° triangle should be regarded as a tool for measuring equal distances in two directions, in front elevation down and to the right, in side elevation down and back, and in plan back and to the right. It is usually the most convenient way to measure shadow widths, but any means of measuring equal distances such as dividers, scale, or paper strips may be used if more convenient.

THE TRUE DIRECTION OF LIGHT. Since the light rays are at an angle to all the planes of projection, the true direction of light is not seen in any of the multi-view drawings. In order to see the true direction of the conventional ray of light, it is necessary to use an auxiliary plane perpendicular to plan and parallel to the direction of light. The true direction of a ray of light is represented by the diagonal of a cube, which is the diagonal of a rectangle of which the short sides are edges of the cube and the long sides the diagonals of the top and bottom of the cube. The true direction of light may readily be constructed as shown in the bottom drawing of Fig. 126D, and will be found useful in constructing some shadows.

SHADOWS OF SOLIDS. Architecture is made up of volumes and masses which are usually the shapes of the simple geometric solids used either singly or in combinations. Shadows on architectural drawings are the shadows of solids or of hollow masses. The shadow of any solid is bounded by the shadows of the shade lines of the object, Fig. 127 I. Only those lines which mark the divisions between light and shade on an object can cast shadows. Therefore, if the shade lines on the drawings of an object can be located by inspection, the shadows of these shade lines can then be determined to give the outline of the shadow of the object.

PLANES OF SHADOW. The straight shade lines of an object make planes of shadow. Therefore the shadows of these straight lines are the intersections of their planes of shadow with the surfaces on which the shadows fall. (1) The position of the shade line, (2) the location of the eye of the observer, (3) the direction of light, and (4) the shape of the surface on which the plane of shadow ends are the factors which determine the shape of the shadow as shown on the drawing.

THE STUDY OF REAL SHADOWS. Observation of the shadows on buildings, parts of buildings, and on other objects will help the student to understand relations of objects and shadows and to visualize the various shadow shapes on drawings. The observation of actual shadows out of doors will be more valuable if a time is chosen when the sunlight is most nearly in the direction used in casting shadows on drawings. In the northern hemisphere in the latitude of the United States the direction of sunlight is approximately correct in the middle of the morning on the east side of a building and in midafternoon on the south side of a building. The direction of sunlight varies greatly with the season as well as with the latitude, so the observer should choose the best time of day and view of buildings to observe in his locality for the time of the year.

An important thing to keep in mind when observing actual shadows is that the shadows appear on the real object as they would on a multi-view drawing only where the observer looks perpendicular to the wall plane of the side observed. Figure 127 II shows a pictorial view and Fig. 127 III three multi-view drawings of shadows on the same object. The pictorial view often helps the observer to understand the shadow shapes and the solutions of shadows on the multi-view drawings.

USE OF MODELS IN STUDYING SHADOWS. In studying shadows in general or in solving specific shadow problems, models will be found of great help in analyzing problems, in locating shade lines, and in visualizing the solutions. Either sunlight or an artificial light may be used. If an artificial light is used, it should not be too close to the model, or the diverging rays will enlarge the shadow so much that the study will lose its value. Models for specific problems may be made of blocks, boxes, cans, modeling clay, folded paper, or any other material which can be quickly obtained and easily used. In the use of models the light should be in the conventional direction.

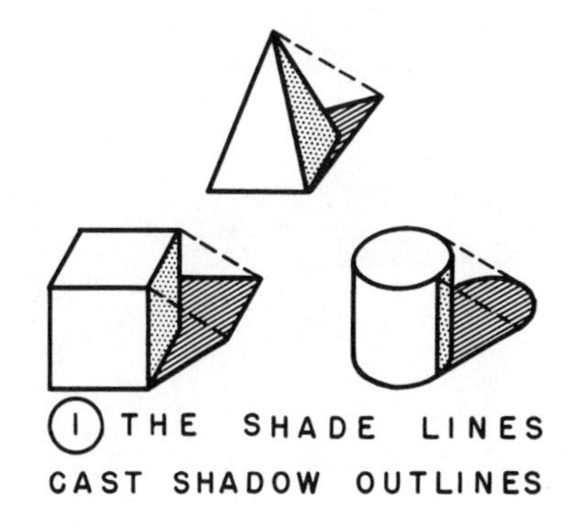

(I) THE SHADE LINES CAST SHADOW OUTLINES

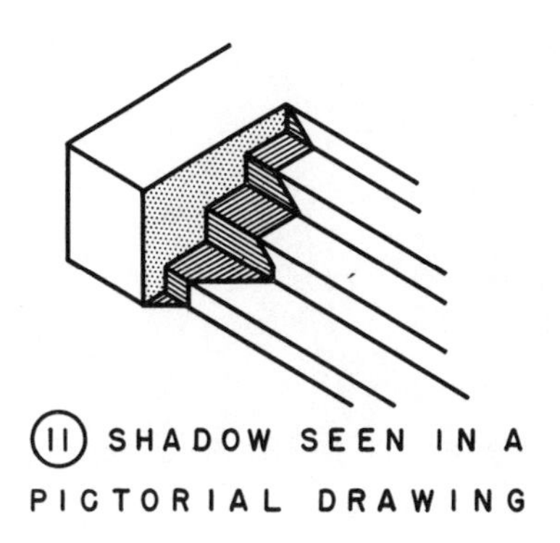

(II) SHADOW SEEN IN A PICTORIAL DRAWING

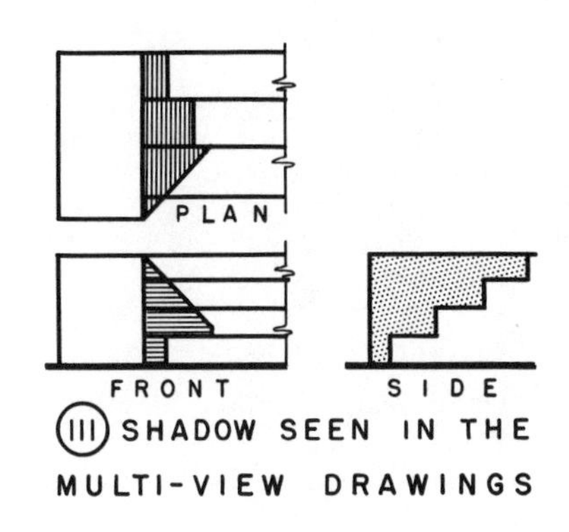

(III) SHADOW SEEN IN THE MULTI-VIEW DRAWINGS

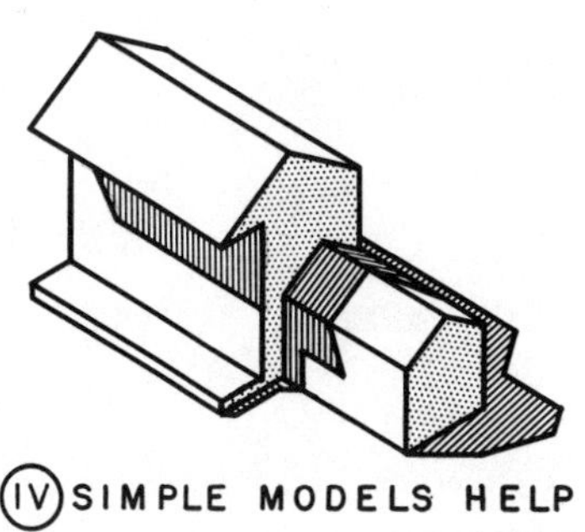

(IV) SIMPLE MODELS HELP TO EXPLAIN SHADOWS

FIG-127 THE STUDY OF SHADOW SHAPES

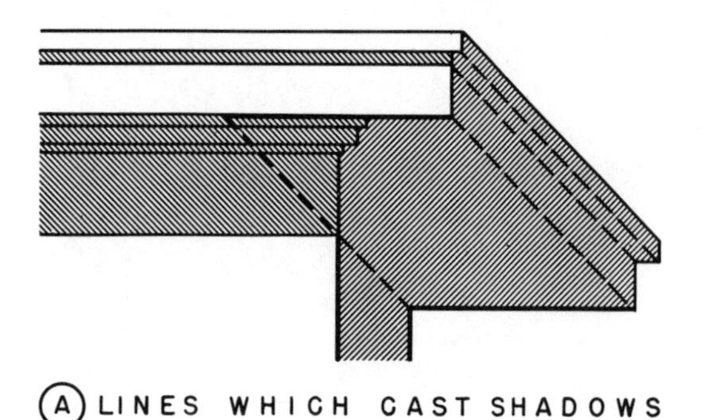

(A) LINES WHICH CAST SHADOWS

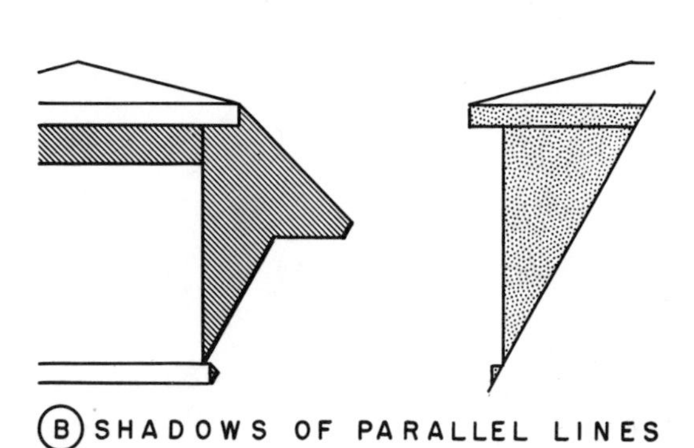

(B) SHADOWS OF PARALLEL LINES

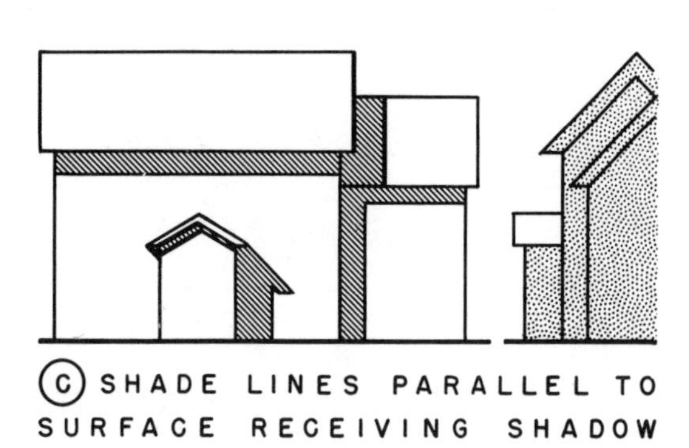

(C) SHADE LINES PARALLEL TO SURFACE RECEIVING SHADOW

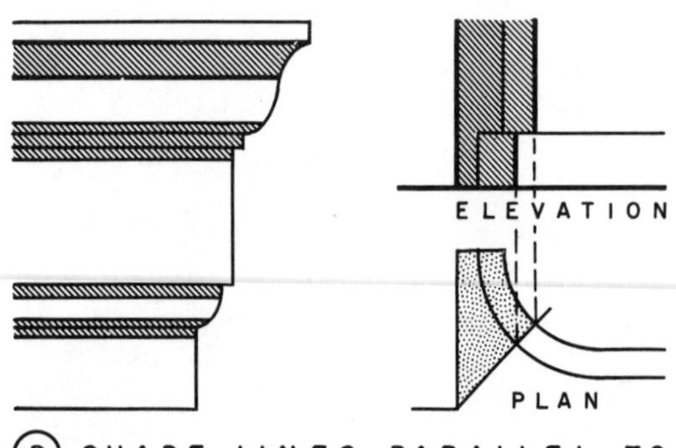

(D) SHADE LINES PARALLEL TO LINES IN SHADOW SURFACE

FIG-128 PRINCIPLES OF SHADES AND SHADOWS

Before attempting to work out the shadows on drawings it is necessary for the draftsman to understand the drawings themselves, the object which they represent, and the direction of light to be used for the shadows. It is assumed that the reader has this necessary training and information.

PRINCIPLES OF SHADOW-CASTING. A knowledge of some of the simple geometric and self-evident principles used in casting shadows will make the problems of working out shadows more easily understood. Several of these helpful principles are described and illustrated in the numbered paragraphs on this and the following page. The use of a light and a simple model will help the reader to verify and understand these principles.

1–A line in shade or shadow cannot cast a shadow because light does not strike it. The lines of the moldings underneath the cornice in Fig. 128A are entirely in shadow and do not cast shadows. When part of a line is a shade line in light and part of the line is in shadow, then only the part of the line which is in light will cast a shadow. The vertical corner of the wall in Fig. 128A is an example of a line which is partly in light and partly in shadow. By first determining which parts of the object are in shadow, it is possible to locate the shadow of the object without finding shadows of lines which do not make part of the shadow outlines.

2–Shadows of parallel lines are parallel when they fall on the same plane or on parallel planes, Fig. 128B. This is true regardless of the relation of the parallel lines to the plane receiving the shadow and of the direction of the plane receiving the shadow. This principle can often be applied to problems to simplify the working out of shadows of parallel lines and to secure greater accuracy. In the case of slanting shadow lines such as those from the dormer onto the roof the direction can be determined most accurately from the longest shadow; then the others can be drawn parallel to it. When the direction of a shadow line is known, the construction of the shadow is simplified.

3–The shadow is parallel to the line making the shadow when (1) the line is parallel to the plane receiving the shadow, or (2) the line is parallel to the straight lines in the surface receiving the shadow. The shadows on the house of Fig. 128C illustrate the first condition. The shadow of the cornice onto the wall below, the shadow of the vertical corner of the main wall onto the smaller wall surface, and the shadow of the right edge of the main roof onto the parallel lower roof surface are all illustrations of this principle. The second condition is illustrated by the horizontal molding and the two vertical cylindrical corners in Fig. 128D.

4–The shadow of any plane figure on a parallel plane is identical in shape, size, and direction with the figure. This relation is true regardless of the angle at which the area and the parallel plane are turned, Fig. 129 I. When part of the shadow is behind the plane figure making the shadow, as in the center example, the visible part of the shadow is identical with the part of the figure which makes the shadow. When the plane figure is part of a solid, as in the case of the example of the block on the right of Fig. 129 I, then the part of the shadow made by the end of the block follows this rule.

5–A shadow is visible only where it falls on a visible surface which is in light. The triangular shadow below the left edge of the dormer roof in Fig. 129 II is visible because it falls on the main roof. There is no similar visible shadow at the left edge of the main roof because there is no visible surface receiving the shadow. The block at the left of Fig. 129 II is set out from the wall so far that none of its shadow is visible in elevation. All of the shadow falls on the floor plane. The relation of the second block to wall and floor planes makes part of the shadow visible in elevation and part in plan.

6–Any line on a plane surface appears to be a straight line when the observer looks parallel to the plane surface, Fig. 129 III. Since the entire plane surface will be seen as a line when the observer looks parallel to the plane, then any line in the plane will appear to be straight. It is often puzzling to the student of shades and shadows that a shadow line which he knows is curved, or irregular, is supposed to be drawn as a straight line on a drawing. Objects, areas, and lines are shown in drawings as they would appear from a certain viewpoint. This viewpoint for multi-view drawings often gives an unnatural appearance to some details.

7–When the observer looks at the end of any straight line, so that the line is seen as a point, then the shadow of the line will appear to be straight regardless of the shape of the surface receiving the shadow. The line makes a plane of shadow. Since the observer is looking parallel to the line, he is also looking parallel to the plane of shadow made by the line and any line in the plane of shadow appears to be straight. The shadow line lies in the plane of shadow and therefore appears to be a straight line when seen parallel to the plane, as illustrated in the front elevation of Fig. 129 IV. Any line seen in end view in elevation, plan, perspective, or any other drawing will cast a straight-line shadow in that view where it is seen as a point. A simple model made of boxes and cans with either sunlight or a single artificial light will help the reader understand this type of shadow.

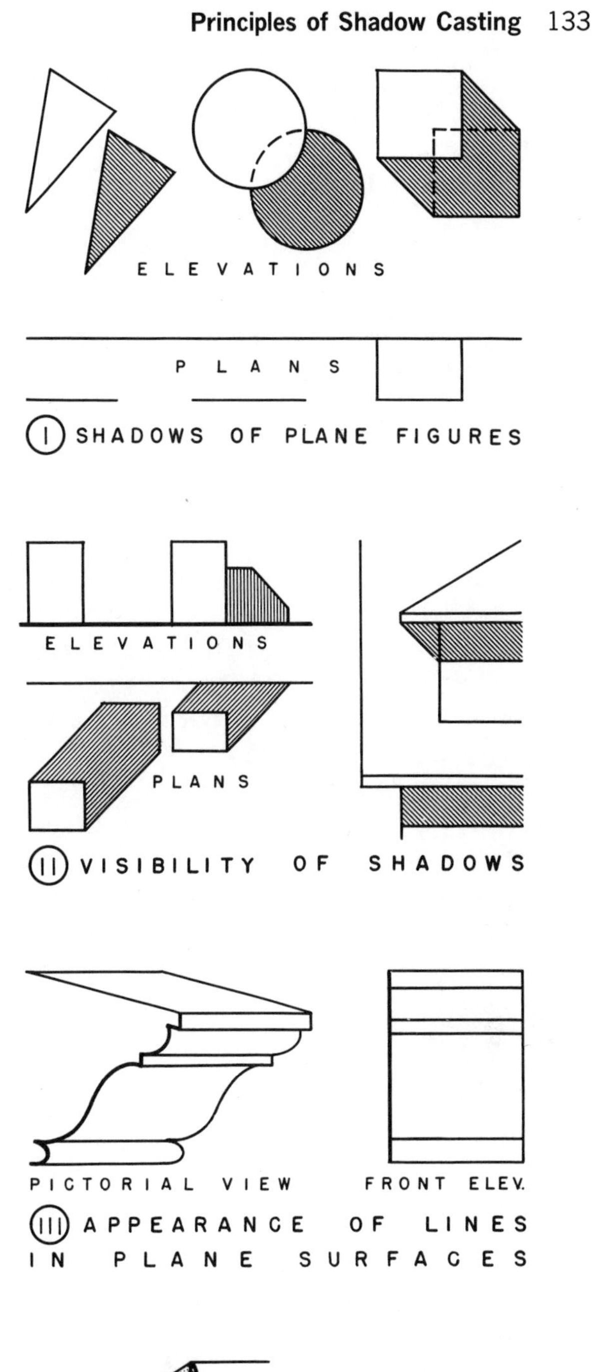

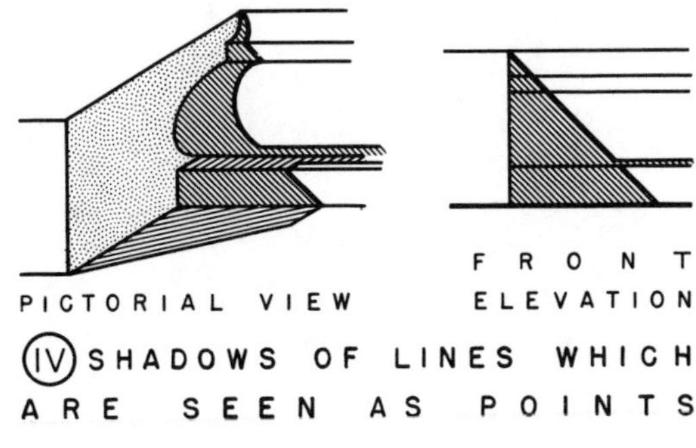

FIG-129 PRINCIPLES OF SHADES AND SHADOWS

CHAPTER 16

Shadows of Lines and Circles

SHADOWS OF TYPICAL LINES. The three sets of typical straight lines mentioned in preceding chapters are common to practically all architectural motives. These lines, which occur more frequently than any others in architecture, are (A) the horizontal lines perpendicular to front view, (B) vertical lines, and (C) horizontal lines parallel to front view, Fig. 130A, B, C. The draftsman who can find the shadows of these three sets of typical lines under varying conditions will be able to work out a large proportion of the shadows on architectural drawings.

Figure 130A, B, and C shows the planes of shadows cast by the three typical lines. The pictorial drawings show in solid cross-hatching the shadow planes cast within the shapes of the transparent cubes by each of the three lines. These planes are extended to the boundaries of the cubes with dotted cross-hatching to make the directions of the planes of shadow more apparent. In the front elevation the plane of shadow from the line perpendicular to the front view appears as a line, while the slanting 45° surfaces of the shadow planes of the two lines parallel to the front elevation plane are seen as areas in the front view.

In addition to the three sets of typical lines there are other lines that are widely used in architecture. The most common of these lines are slanting lines parallel to the front view, horizontal lines at an angle to the front view, slanting lines at an angle with all views, circles parallel to the three projection planes, and irregular curves.

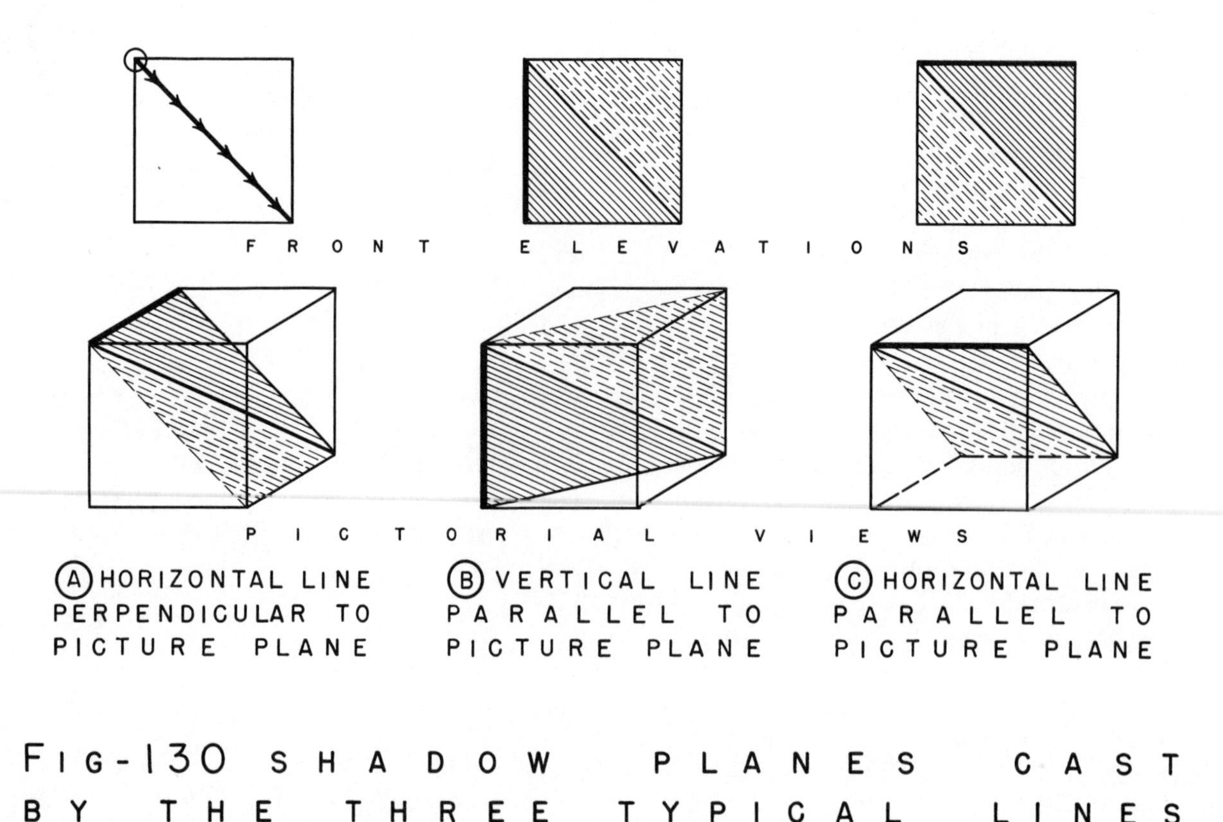

FIG-130 SHADOW PLANES CAST BY THE THREE TYPICAL LINES

These two groups of common lines are shadow-casting shade lines of practically all walls, openings, cornices, belt courses, steps, columns, chimneys, dormers, roofs, and arches. Their shadows make up the shadows of most architecture. The shadows of these lines can be located by 45° projection or other methods of measuring equal distances whenever the surface receiving the shadow can be represented by a line in any one of the three typical views. Whenever the surface on which the shadow falls cannot be represented by a line, as in the case of a sphere or cone, then some other method must be used to determine the shadow. Some of the most useful of the special methods of casting shadows of this type are (1) the slicing method which uses a series of vertical sections parallel to light rays, (2) the method of tangent surfaces, and (3) the method of auxiliary shadows. These additional methods of casting shadows will be explained on page 173.

A horizontal shade line perpendicular to front elevation appears as a point in the front view. Therefore the observer is looking parallel to the line and to its plane of shadow, Fig. 130A. The intersection of the plane of shadow with any surface will coincide with the front view of the plane which is a straight line down and to the right at 45°, Fig. 131, front elevations.

A second method of considering the shadow of this line is that in the front elevation view every point on the line is represented by one point. Therefore, any point on the line will cast its shadow down and to the right at 45° from this point, which is the front elevation of every point on the line. Since all points on the line have their shadows at 45° from the same point, they form a straight 45° line down and to the right as seen in the front elevation in Fig. 131 I and II.

When the shadow outline is seen from other positions, it will not appear to be a continuous straight line unless the surface receiving the shadow is one continuous plane surface. The pictorial drawing of the base course in Fig. 131 I shows how the actual shape of the shadow outline conforms to the shape of the surface on which the shadow falls.

When the straight-line shadow cast by a straight line which is seen in end view is interrupted by other shadows, the different parts of the shadow cast by the line seen in end view will be parts of a continuous straight line, Fig. 131 II.

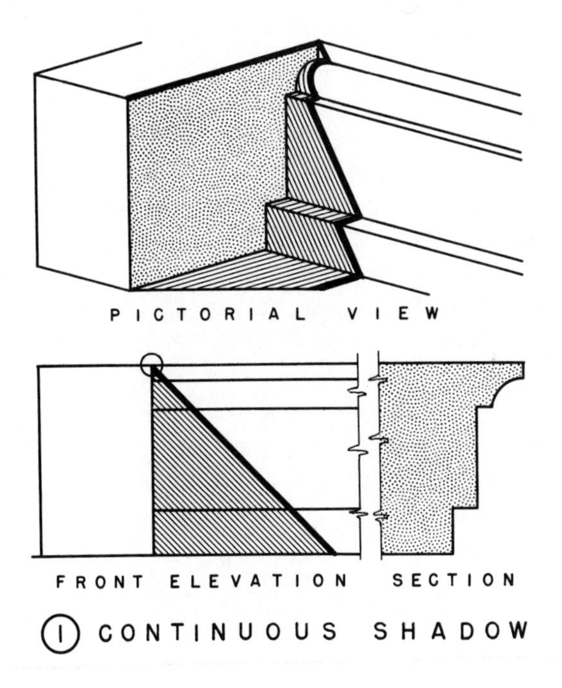

(I) CONTINUOUS SHADOW

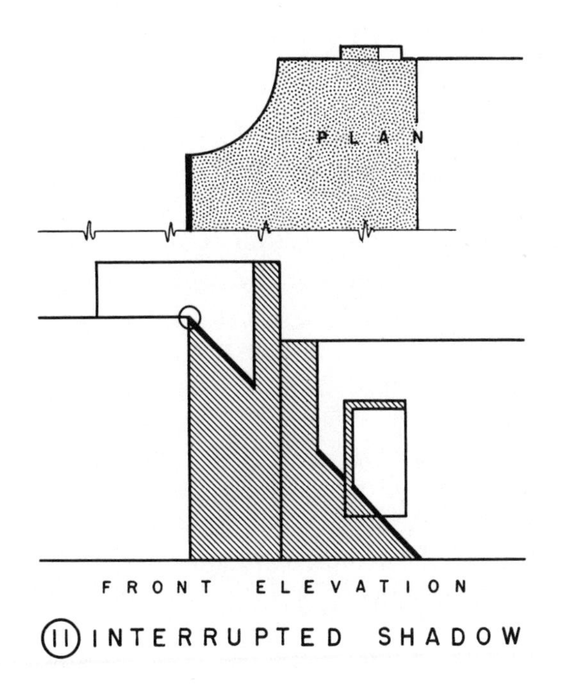

(II) INTERRUPTED SHADOW

FIG-131 SHADOWS OF HORIZONTAL LINES PERPENDICULAR TO PICTURE PLANE

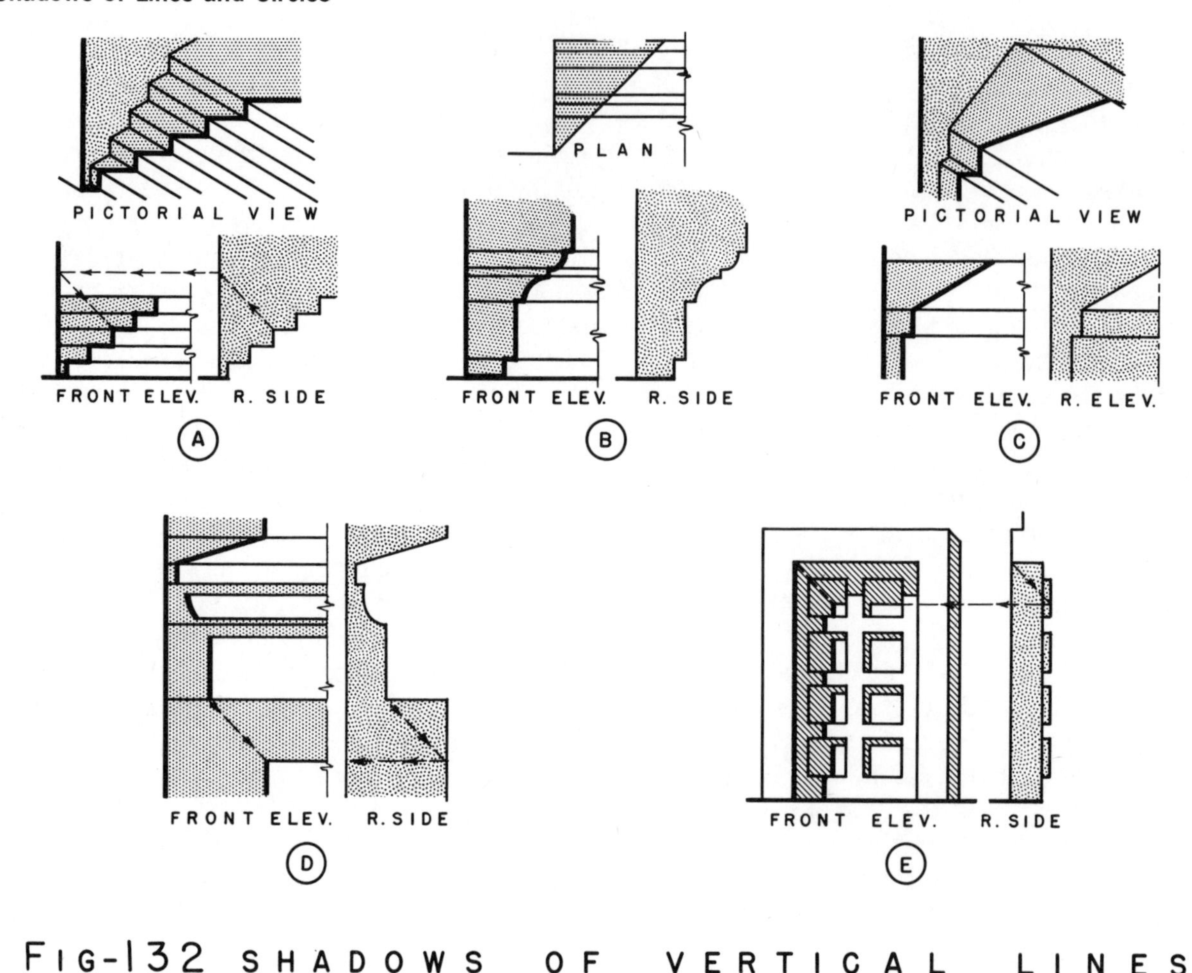

FIG-132 SHADOWS OF VERTICAL LINES PARALLEL TO THE PICTURE PLANE

Vertical shade lines form the shadow-casting lines at the corners of walls, sides of windows, doors, dormers, chimneys, posts, cylindrical columns, pedestals for balustrades, buttresses at the sides of steps, and other architectural features. It is a rare thing indeed to find an architectural structure in which there are no vertical shadow-casting shade lines.

A vertical line casts a plane of shadow back away from the observer and to the right at 45° in the front elevation view. The shadow of a vertical line is the intersection of its shadow plane with the surface on which the shadow falls. If the surface receiving the shadow is a vertical plane or a curved vertical surface, the shadow is parallel to the line, as shown in the drawings on the right side of Fig. 128C and D. Its distance to the right from the elevation of the line is equal to the distance back in plan. If the plane of shadow strikes any surface in which all horizontal lines are parallel to front elevation, in the front view its intersection with these surfaces will give the same shape as the right side view of the surfaces and the same distances from the line, as shown in Fig. 132A, B, and C. Horizontal belt courses, cornices, base courses, opening treatments, steps, roofs, and washes follow this rule. This is true because the shadow plane extends to the right and back equally at all points. The side elevation shows the distance back; the front elevation shows the distance to the right from the vertical line which causes the shadow edge.

The shadows of vertical lines often run into the shadows of other lines, as shown in Fig. 132D and E. However, the parts of the shadows made by the vertical lines always follow the theory outlined above. It should be noted that the term R. SIDE is used on several of the multi-view drawings of Fig. 132. These drawings could be elevations or sections. They are sections here.

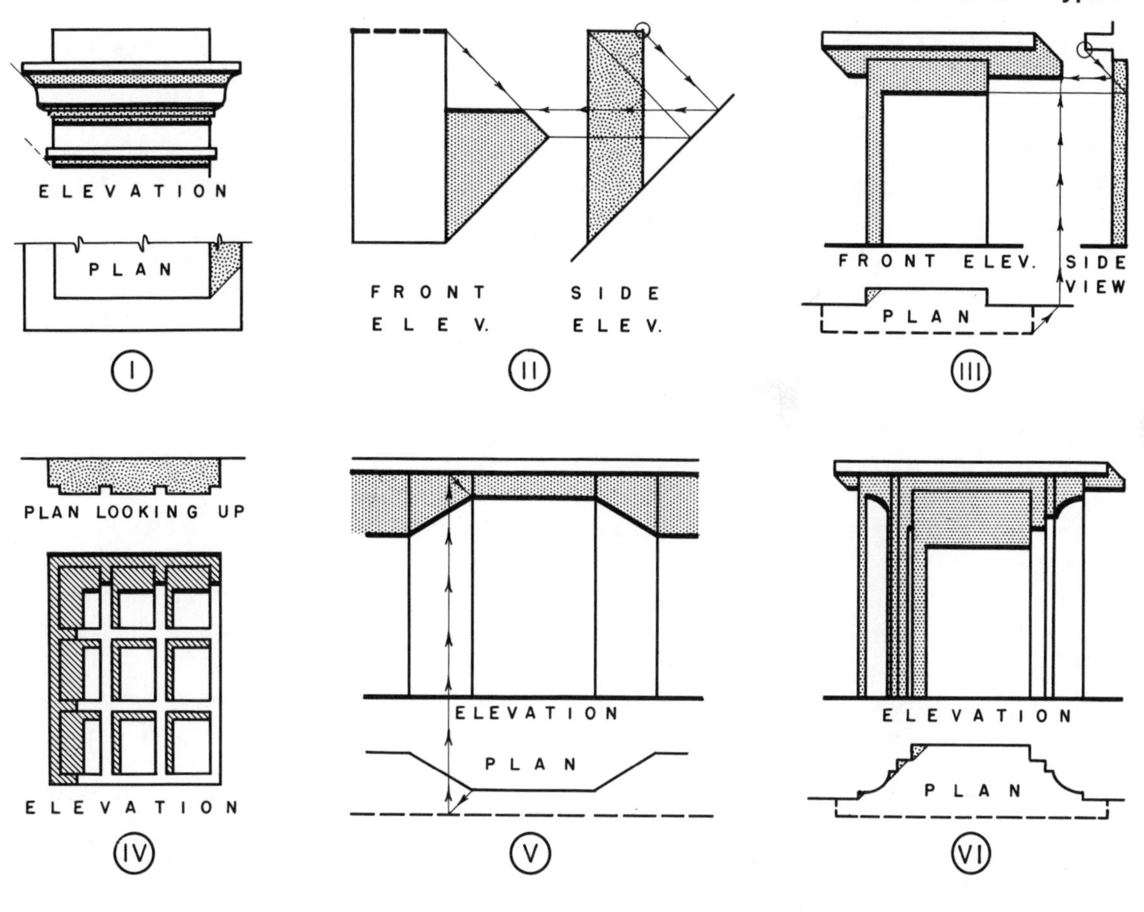

FIG-133 SHADOWS OF HORIZONTAL LINES PARALLEL TO THE PICTURE PLANE

Horizontal shade lines parallel to the front elevation plane and picture plane cast planes of shadow which extend back away from the observer and down at an angle of 45° with the elevation plane. The shade lines of cornices, architraves of colonnades, marquees, cantilever slabs, sills, and tops of openings, balconies, and chimneys contain examples of this type of line. Whenever the shadow plane intersects a plane surface which is parallel to the line or a curving surface in which horizontal lines are parallel to the line, the shadow is parallel to the shade line, Fig. 133 I.

The vertical distance from the shade line to its shadow in elevation is equal to the horizontal distance perpendicular to the elevation plane in plan or side view, since the shadow plane goes down and back equally. The distances can be measured easily in plan or side elevation and transferred to the front elevation as shown in Fig. 133 III, when the surface receiving the shadow is vertical. If the surface receiving the shadow is curved or slanting with horizontal lines in the surface parallel to front view, the shadow depth can be more easily determined by using the 45° triangle in side view, as in Fig. 133 II, for the shadow on the roof. When there are identical horizontal moldings or projections around a right-angled corner as shown in Fig. 133 I, the 45° lines from the ends of the shade lines intersect the corner profile at the correct depth for the shadow.

When the shadow of a horizontal line parallel to front elevation falls on a vertical surface having vertical offsets or vertical moldings, the elevation view of the shadow is the same shape as the plan looking up; the reverse of the ordinary plan, Fig. 133 IV, V, and VI. Moreover, the shadow will be the same distance from the shade line in elevation as the distance from the shade line to the surface receiving the shadow in plan view.

CIRCLES. Circles are commonly found in columns, arches, circular buildings, towers, windows, doors, fountains, pedestals, and other elements of architecture. Most of these circles in architectural motifs are parallel to the plan, elevation, or section view. That is, they are parallel to one of the three coordinate planes as shown in Fig. 134A. In this illustration elevation, plan, and side elevation views are shown of the same circles. The circles parallel to the elevation plane are numbered 1 in all views. Circles parallel to the side elevation are numbered 2, and circles parallel to plan are numbered 3. As shown in these three views, circles appear as circles when they are parallel to the view and as straight lines when they are perpendicular to the view.

A flat circular disk, such as a pan lid, may be used for a model to cast shadows with light in the proper direction and will be of great help to the student in visualizing the various shadows of circles.

When the circle appears as a circle in any view and is parallel to the plane on which the shadow falls, its shadow will be a circle of the same size as the circle casting the shadow. The position of the shadow may be found by locating the shadow of the center of the circle. The radius used in drawing the shadow must in all cases be the radius of the circle casting the shadow, Fig. 134B. Care must be used to see that the correct center points are used for the construction to locate the shadow of the center of the circle, and that the 45° construction is carried to the plane which receives the shadow. This method of constructing the shadow applies to any arc of a circle as well as to complete circles, and is further illustrated in Fig. 135 I, II, IV, and V.

If the distance A from the circle to the plane receiving the shadow is known, it is not necessary to have two views to find the shadow of the center of the circle, Fig. 135 III and VI. The distance A may be laid out vertically below the center of the circle in the front view, Fig. 135 III, and a line drawn from this point horizontally across to the right to meet a 45° line from the center of the circle, thus locating the shadow of the center of the circle. This construction measures a distance down and a distance to the right equal to the distance back. In plan the distance would be measured back and to the right, as shown in Fig. 135 VI.

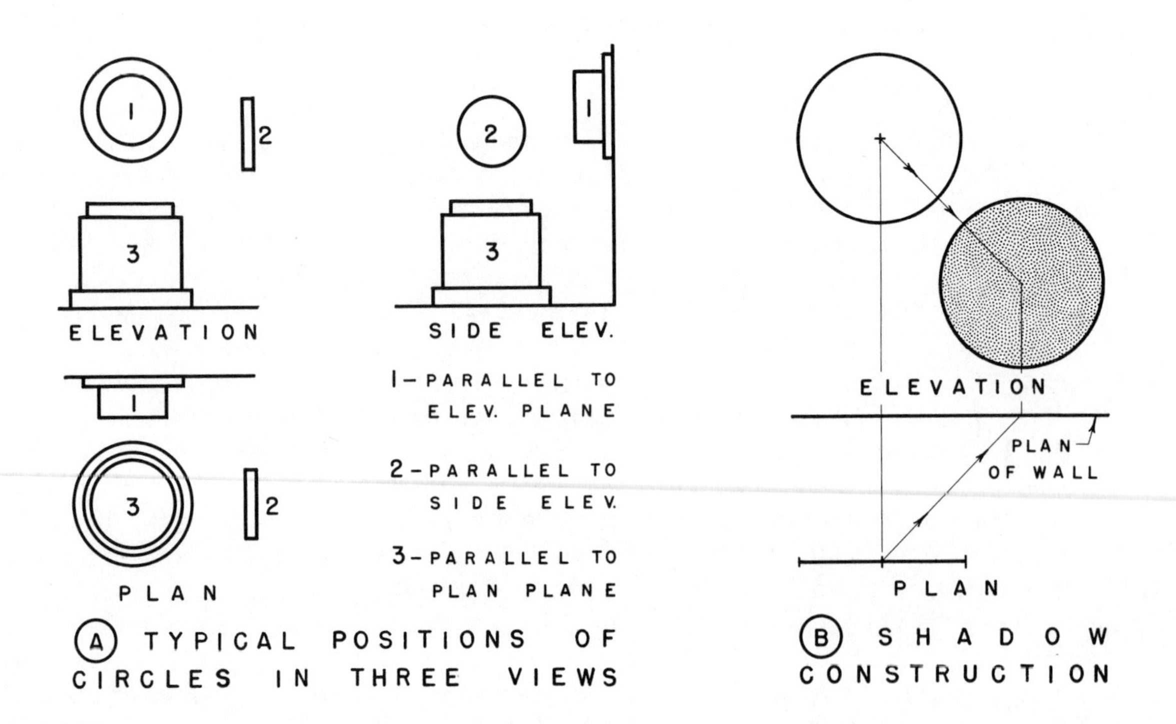

FIG-134 CIRCLES PARALLEL TO PICTURE PLANE

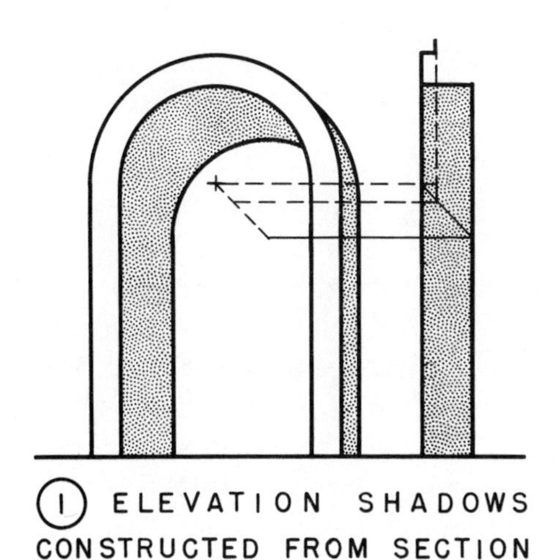

(I) ELEVATION SHADOWS CONSTRUCTED FROM SECTION

(IV) PLAN SHADOWS CONSTRUCTED FROM ELEV.

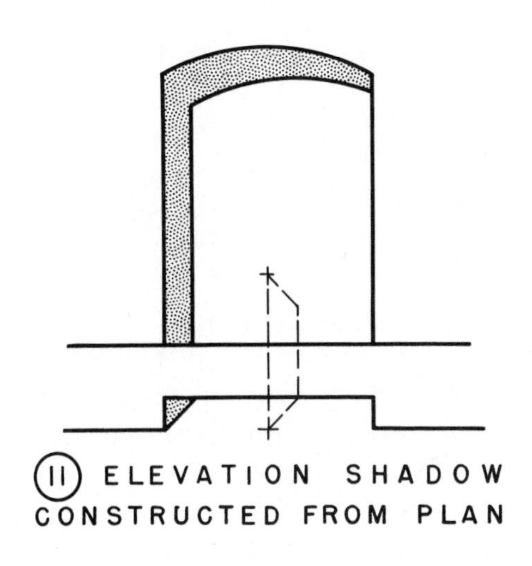

(II) ELEVATION SHADOW CONSTRUCTED FROM PLAN

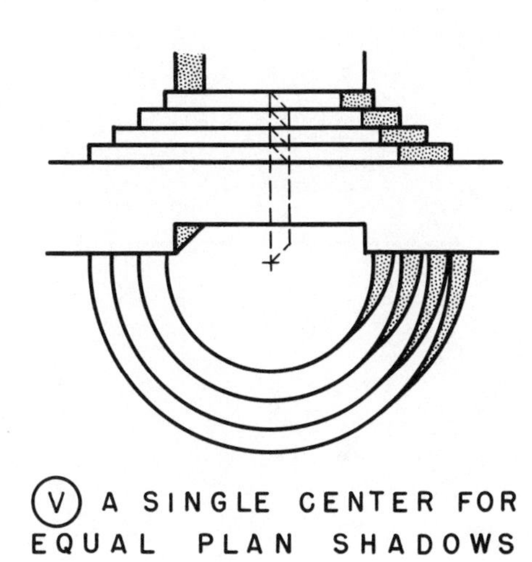

(V) A SINGLE CENTER FOR EQUAL PLAN SHADOWS

(III) ELEVATION SHADOW WITHOUT AUXILIARY VIEW

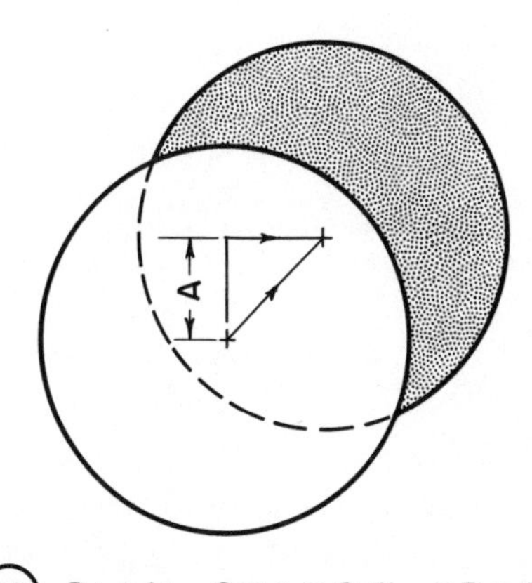

(VI) PLAN SHADOW DRAWN WITHOUT AUXILIARY VIEW

FIG-135 SHADOWS OF CIRCLES PARALLEL TO PICTURE PLANE

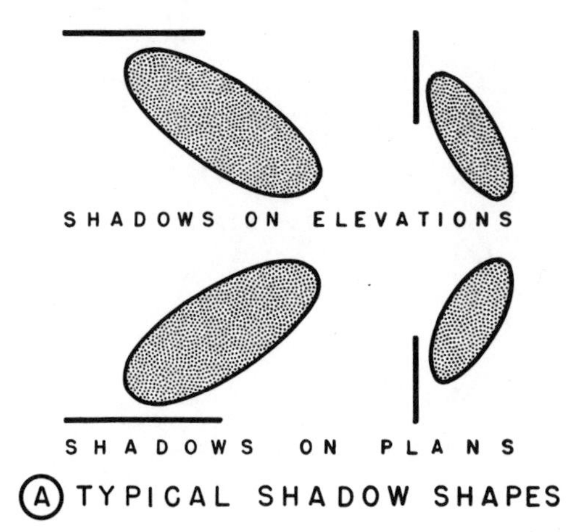

(A) TYPICAL SHADOW SHAPES

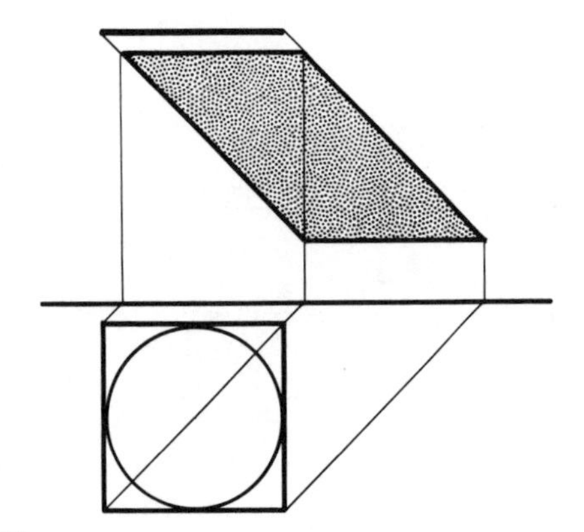

(B) SHADOW OF TANGENT SQUARE

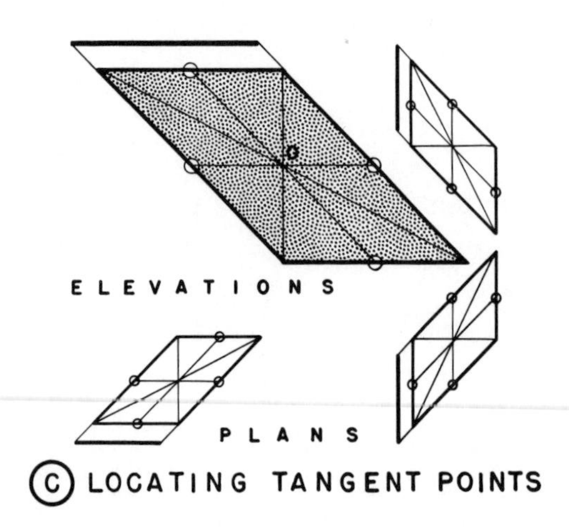

(C) LOCATING TANGENT POINTS

FIG-136 SHADOWS OF CIRCLES PERPENDICULAR TO THE PICTURE PLANE

When the circle appears as a line in any view and the shadow falls on a plane parallel to the coordinate plane of that view, the shadow is an ellipse. (If the circle should be turned parallel to the light rays its shadow would be a line.) However, this position is rare. The most common positions of such circles and the shapes of their shadows are shown in Fig. 136A. One circle is parallel to plan the other parallel to side view.

The shadow of the tangent square is used in finding the shadow of a circle in one of these positions. It locates the points of tangency of the square and circle. Then the ellipse can be drawn inside the shadow of the square. The square should be placed with two sides parallel and two perpendicular to the plane receiving the shadow, as shown in Fig. 136B. The two sides parallel to the picture plane will have their shadows parallel to the line view of the circle, and the two perpendicular to the picture plane will have 45° line shadows parallel to the direction of light in the drawing. In elevations the 45° shadows will go down and to the right, in plan back and to the right, Fig. 136C. After the shadow of the square has been found, its diagonals can be drawn to locate its center, which is the shadow of the center of the square and circle. Lines parallel to the shadows of the sides of the square drawn through this center point, O, locate the centers of the sides of the shadow. They are the points of tangency of the square and circle. The ellipse can be drawn through these four points with the curve tangent to the shadow of the square at each of the four points.

The shadow of the circumscribing octagon determines the shape of the shadow ellipse much more accurately. It provides four additional points of tangency and four additional lines which are tangent to the shadow ellipse. The shadow of the octagon can be found by 45° projection as shown in Fig. 137 I, or it may be constructed directly on the shadow of the square as shown in Fig. 137 II. With the center, O, of the shadow as a center and a radius to the nearest corners of the shadow of the square, draw arcs from those corners to meet the nearest center line. Through these two intersections, X and Y, draw lines parallel to the nearest sides of the shadow of the square and intersecting with its diagonals. These four points on the diagonals of the shadow of the square are points of tangency of the circle and the four sides of the octagon which do not coincide with sides of the square. These four sides of the octagon can be drawn parallel to the diagonals of the shadow of the square through the four points just located. The sides through the two points on each diagonal are drawn parallel to the other diagonal.

If the distance, A, of the circle from the plane receiving the shadow is known, the entire construction of the shadow of the octagon and shadow of the ellipse may be made without reference to any view except the one in which the shadow is found. The position of the shadow of the side of the square nearest the plane on which the shadow falls may be found by measuring the distance A perpendicular to the line representing the circle in the direction in which the shadow will go, Fig. 137 II. The shadows of the two sides of the square which are perpendicular to the picture plane will be drawn from the extremities C, D of the circle in the 45° direction of light in the view. A line drawn perpendicular to the circle C–D from the corner B is a diagonal of the shadow of the square and meets the 45° line from C in the corner E of the shadow of the square. A line drawn from E parallel to C–D to meet the 45° line from D locates the fourth corner F and completes the shadow of the tangent square. The construction can now be completed. The method of constructing the shadow of a circle by using the tangent octagon is usually sufficiently accurate.

If it is necessary to determine a greater number of points, the shadow ellipse can be constructed by the method of conjugate diameters explained on page 106. The diagonals of the shadow of the square are conjugate diameters of the ellipse, and the tangent octagon points located on them give their lengths. A greater number of points can also be located by the point method explained for perspectives of circles, or by the parallelogram method of constructing an ellipse. The shadow of the tangent square would be used as the parallelogram for the construction.

When parts of the shadow of the same circle fall on parallel planes, one method is to work out the complete shadow on all of the planes and then use only the parts of the shadow which fall on each plane. A second method is to construct the complete shadow on one plane and transfer parts of it to the proper positions on the other planes by making a tracing and moving it to the correct location in each case, Fig. 137 III. Guide lines should be made on the tracing so that it can be lined up properly when shifted. The 45° lines of the sides of the shadow of the square may be very conveniently used as guides for alignment, since the tracing should be shifted parallel to them. The shadows of the center of the circle on the two planes were used for the distance to shift the tracing.

When the shadow falls on more complex surfaces, the point method may be the most convenient means of determining the shadow.

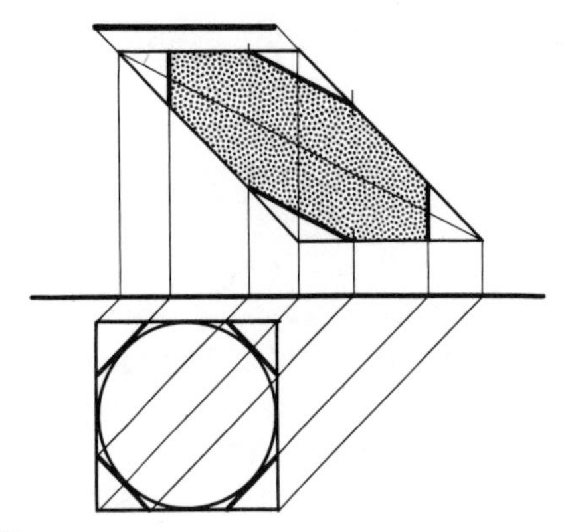

(I) DRAWING TANGENT OCTAGON

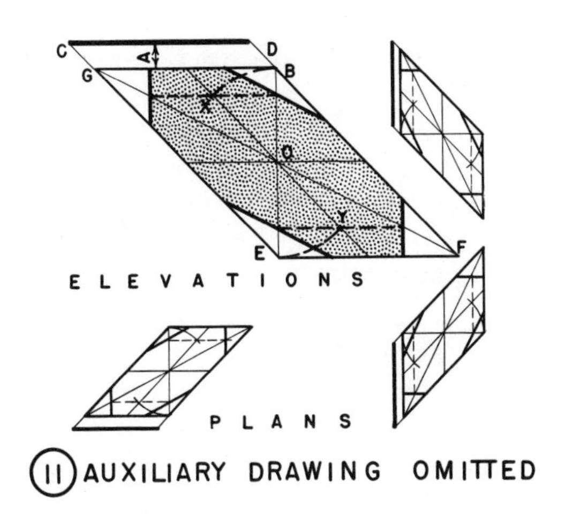

(II) AUXILIARY DRAWING OMITTED

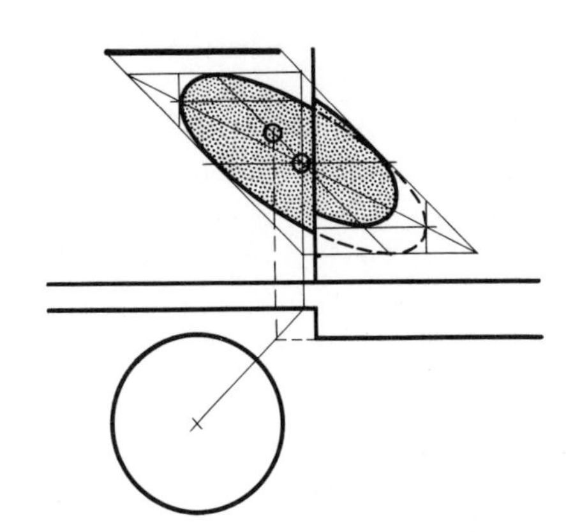

(III) SHADOW OVER AN OFFSET

FIG-137 SHADOWS OF CIRCLES PERPENDICULAR TO THE PICTURE PLANE

SLANTING LINES PARALLEL TO FRONT ELEVATION. These lines occur in pediments, roofs, railings, octagonal windows, buttresses, and other details. When the surface receiving the shadow is parallel to front elevation, the shadow is parallel to the line making the shadow. Since the shadow of any point on the line extends back, to the right, and down equally, its location can be determined by measurement or by 45° projection when the distance back is known.

In Fig. 138A the shadow B of a point on the slanting shade line is located by construction from plan which gives the distance to the right. The construction for point C is made by transferring the distance down of the shadow from the section. The point A on the shadow line is located without the use of either plan or section. Two vertical lines, which are spaced horizontally to equal the distance back, are drawn across the slanting line. From the intersection of the vertical line on the left and the shade line, a 45° line is drawn down and to the right to meet the second vertical line and locate a point A on the shadow. It will be noted that the three methods give the same result, a point on the shadow line, which is then drawn parallel to the shade line.

The width of the shadow on the right side of the pediment can be located by using one of the construction methods used on the left, or by drawing a 45° line from the intersection of the two slanting shade lines at the top of the pediment to meet the shadow line on the left and locate the corner of the shadow. The shadow on the right is drawn parallel to lines on that side.

When the slanting lines are at 45°, as in Fig. 138B, those which extend down and to the right at 45° will cause planes of shadow which are perpendicular to front view and directly behind their shade lines. Therefore, their shadows will not be visible in front elevation. When the slanting lines that extend down and to the right are at a steeper angle than 45°, there will be no visible shadows under the lines, but there will be a shadow above them and to the right as shown in Fig. 138C.

SLICING METHOD. When the form in which the slanting lines parallel to the elevation plane occur is complicated by moldings, the simplest method of finding the shadows and shade lines is to draw on the slanting members an intersection of a plane perpendicular to the plan and back and to the right at 45° from the front elevation. This is a vertical plane parallel to the direction of light. The measurements for drawing this intersection can be taken from the elevation of the corner, as shown in Fig. 138D, when the projections at the side and in front are equal. When the projections are not equal around the corner, then the projections for the front can be obtained from a section view. When the reflected plan is available, the intersection points can readily be determined by drawing a 45° line in plan to represent the intersecting 45° vertical plane. It is usually sufficiently accurate to use measurements for the plane surfaces only and draw the entire molding shapes freehand. However, additional points can be located on molding profiles, as shown by the dotted construction line in Fig. 138D, when necessary.

Any shade point on the intersection line of this 45° plane and the slanting surfaces will have its shadow on the intersection line, since the plane is parallel to the rays of light and all points in the plane have their shadows in the plane. Therefore, by drawing 45° lines from projecting corners of the intersection line to meet the intersection line at a lower level, and by determining the tangent points of light on moldings, a point on each shadow and shade line can be located. Through these points the shadow and shade lines can be drawn parallel to the slanting lines. This method of shadow construction is called the slicing method.

The octagonal and hexagonal windows, and the buttress of Fig. 138E and F are parallel to the planes on which the shadows fall. The shadows are therefore exact duplications of the shapes of the objects, and are moved down and to the right at 45° to their correct positions.

HORIZONTAL LINES OBLIQUE TO ELEVATION. These lines occur in objects which have plans containing oblique elements or octagonal, hexagonal, or other polygonal shapes. The slicing method can be used to find the shades and shadows on the oblique parts of the object. The slicing section can be worked out from plan as shown in Fig. 138G and H.

When the oblique parts of the object are at 45° with the elevation plane, the true direction of light can be used at the octagonal corner on the left to determine shade and shadow line positions. This will give the same result as the slicing method.

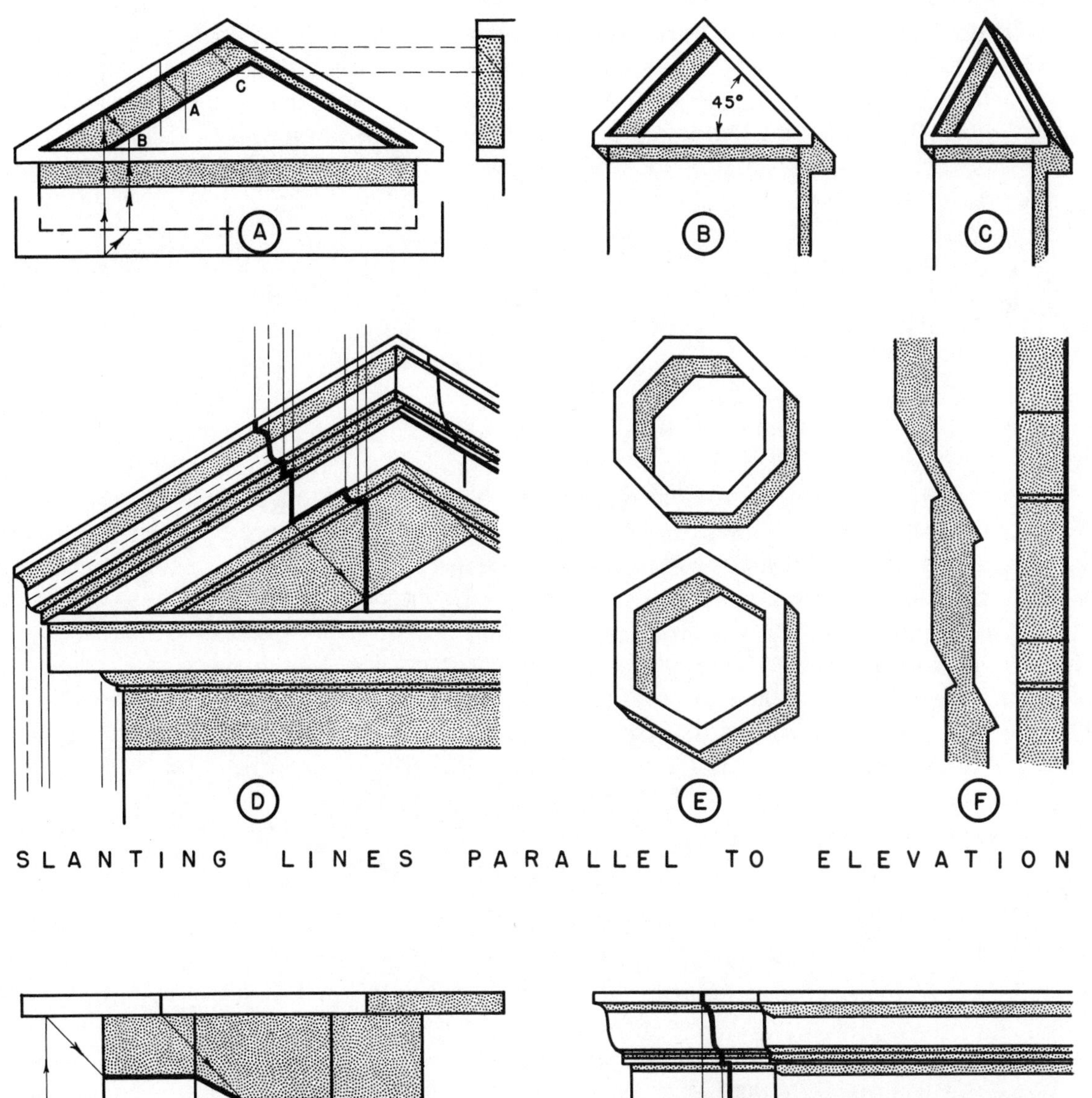

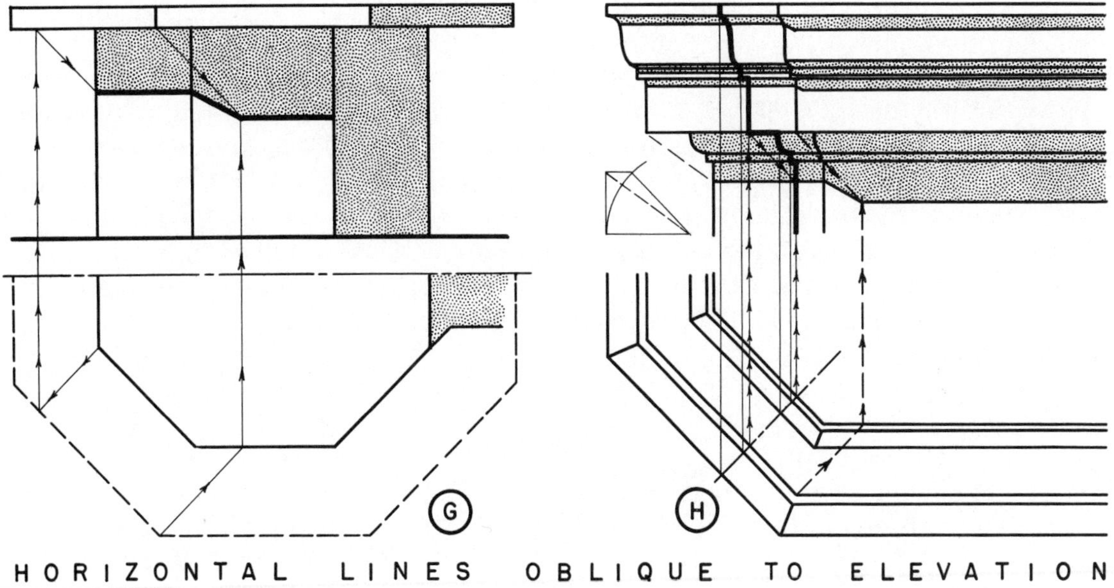

FIG-138 SHADOWS OF SLANTING AND OBLIQUE LINES

THE SHADOW OF ANY STRAIGHT LINE. When the shadow falls on a plane surface, it can be located by finding the shadows of the ends of the line and connecting them with a straight-line shadow. Any two points may be used, but the farther apart the points are taken the more accurate the result. Figure 139A shows the shadow of a straight line which is at an angle to all the coordinate planes. In this case the entire shadow falls on the elevation plane. In Fig. 139B the line is near the intersection of the floor and wall, so that part of the shadow falls in elevation and part in plan. The simplest method of finding the lower end of the shadow line in elevation is shown in the construction from the section with arrows indicating the order in which the lines were drawn. The 45° line drawn from the lowest point on the wall in section locates the point A on the section view of the line which casts its shadow on the bottom line of the wall. The horizontal line to the left locates the elevation of the point and the 45° line from elevation locates its shadow at B. The vertical line locates the shadow of the point in plan at C.

When the shadow of a straight line at any angle falls upon a broken surface made up of parallel planes, the direction of the entire shadow should be found on one plane and this direction used in all parts of the shadow. This procedure is desirable because slight inaccuracies in construction sometimes cause shadow lines which should be parallel to be drawn at an angle with each other. This is especially true of short lines. When the shadow of the inclined line crosses other shadow areas, the lower end of one segment of the shadow of the line will be on a 45° line with the top of the segment below it as shown at the top and bottom of the window in Fig. 139C.

Shadows of curved lines. When the shadow of a curved line falls on a plane surface, the shadow of a series of points taken at random on the curve may be found by 45° projections as illustrated in Fig. 139D for two points. These shadow points can then be connected to form a smooth curve for the shadow. In using this method the draftsman should be sure to use the same point in both views. Vertical lines may be used to locate front and plan views of the same points when the drawings line up vertically. When front and side views are used and they line up horizontally, a horizontal line from a point on a given line in one view will locate the same point in the other view, Fig. 139E.

It is sometimes advantageous to choose a line on which it is desired to find the shadow, then locate the point casting the shadow at this chosen point and determine the shadow of the point. This method of procedure is illustrated in Fig. 139B and is also used in Fig. 139E to locate the shadow of the curved line at the edges of the broken surfaces. To find the location of a shadow on the line A–A in the front view of Fig. 139E, a ray of light is traced backward from corner A in side view (which is the side view of A–A) to find the point X which casts its shadow on line A–A. A line is then drawn across horizontally from the side view of X to find the elevation of X. The shadow of X is located by drawing a 45° line from X in elevation to intersect with line A–A at B. This intersection is the required shadow point. The entire shadow may be found by finding the shadows of a number of selected points and drawing the shadow outline through them. Note that another point can be found from the above construction by continuing the line from X in front view to intersect with the horizontal shadow line below A–A at C.

Reflected shadows. Reflected light is often assumed in rendering to cast reflected shadows and reflected lights in the shadow areas of the plate. These reflected shadows, which are darker, and reflected lights, which are lighter than the general shadow tone, bring out details in shadow areas. They are especially helpful in large shadows which may otherwise seem lacking in detail.

The most commonly used direction for reflected light is that shown in the pictorial diagram of Fig. 139F and illustrated in the shadows of Fig. 139G. This conventional direction of reflected light is up, back, and to the left and appears as a 45° line in the plan, front elevation, and side elevation or section views. This direction is then the diagonal of a cube from the lower, right, front corner to the top, left, rear corner. This direction of reflected light makes a darker shadow above and to the left of a projection. It is the usual practice to show reflected shadows from small projections only. Reflected lights are shown on slanting and molded surfaces which are nearly perpendicular to the rays of reflected light, and on corners which face the reflected light.

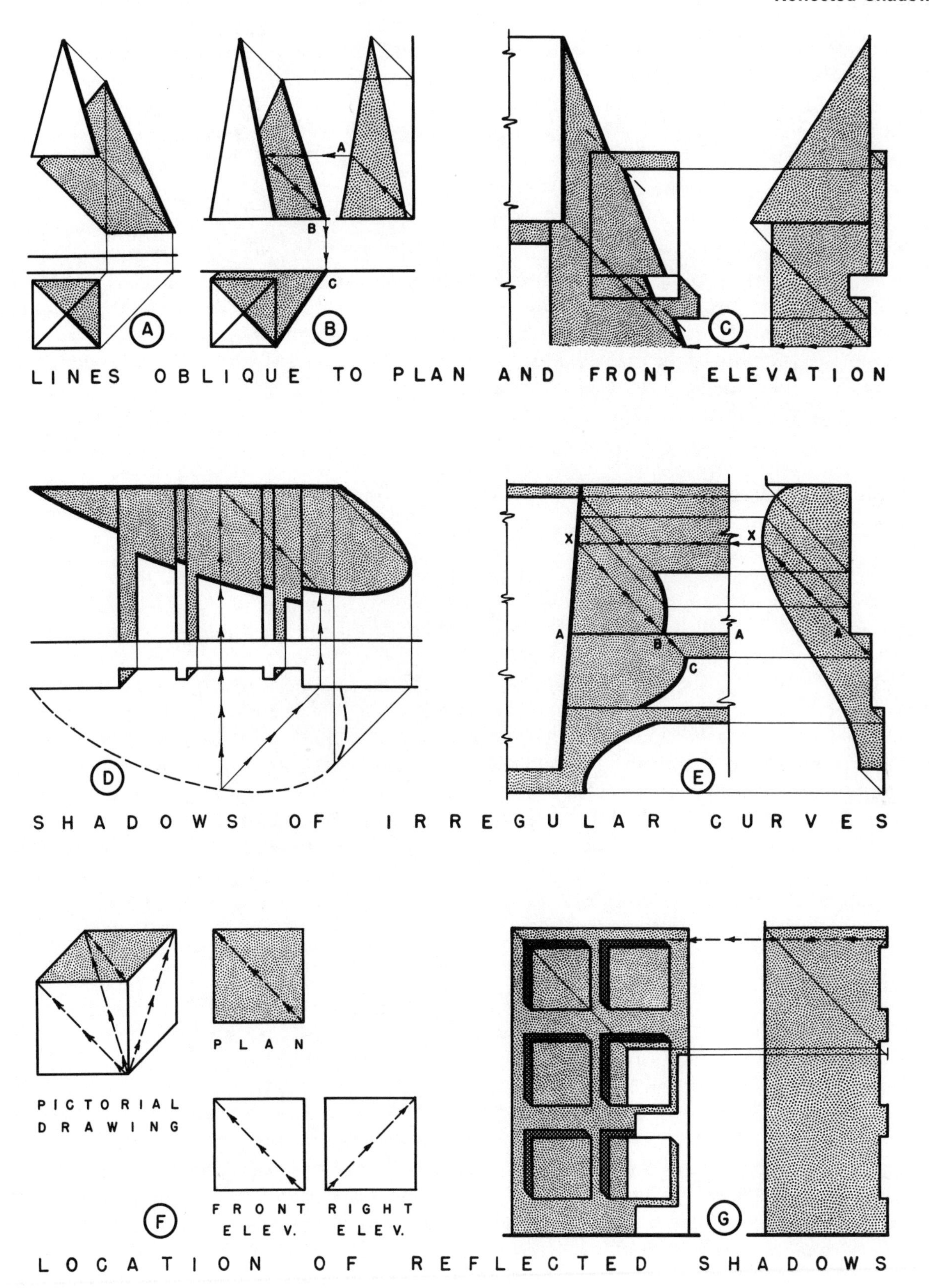

FIG-139 DIRECT AND REFLECTED SHADOWS

CHAPTER 17
Shadows of Architectural Elements

The shadows on a building are made up of the shadows of the various architectural elements of which the building is composed. These elements—such as steps, openings, and horizontal bands—offer separate problems in shadow-casting, which often have little or no relation to each other. It is therefore practical to study the shadows of the various parts of buildings separately, more completely, and at larger scale than would be possible on drawings of complete buildings.

An orderly and systematic approach to the problem of constructing the shadows of any object will help to prevent confusion and wasted time and effort. It will also prevent unnecessary drawing, erasing, and consequent damage to the drawing paper. Spend some time studying the drawing, then work out the shadow which is nearest first, next closest second, and so on in order to the most distant last. This order of working out the shadows is advantageous because it is much easier to find the shadow of an object after determining which parts of the object are in shadow and which are in light, so that the length of the shadow-casting shade lines are known.

STEPS. Most step treatments have at their sides shadow-casting walls, abutments, balustrades, or railings which are either horizontal and parallel to the shape of a single step, slanting and parallel to the slope of the flight of steps, or which slant with the steps and curve out at the bottom where the steps are wider. Figure 140 illustrates the shadows on a few commonly used step treatments. In Fig. 140A the step abutment is made up of a block which has all its surfaces parallel to the three coordinate planes. Its shade lines, which cast shadows on the steps, are the vertical line A–B and the horizontal line A–C perpendicular to the front view. The corners of the steps on the left side of the front view and the lower edge of the shadow from the block form the same profile as the section view of the steps and have the same relation to the line A–B. Line A–C makes a 45° straight-line shadow in elevation. The plan and side view are not necessary for the construction of the shadow in elevation. They are shown here to make the shadows more easily understood.

Sometimes a series of step blocks is used in a long flight of steps to avoid the undesirable height of a single block, Fig. 140B. In this case, as in the example of Fig. 140A, there is no necessity for a side or plan view if the tread size and the distance back from the face of each block to the first riser behind it is known.

In Fig. 140C the tops of the straight walls or balustrades at the sides of the steps slant up, so that their height above the steps is constant. In this case a side view is necessary to find the shadow of the slanting shade line. By the method of selecting points (previously used in Fig. 139B and E) the inclined shadow can be found on one step-riser. All the other riser shadows, which are shadows of this same line, will be parallel to the one which was constructed and will have the same distance from the shade line since its distance above the steps is constant.

Often the steps are wider at the bottom and a curving block or wall is used to form the transition to the uniform width above, as shown in Fig. 140D. Under such conditions the curved shade line casting shadows on the risers is constantly changing in direction and the shadows on the risers from this line will all be at different angles. The shadows can be found by use of the side view. Usually it is sufficient to find a shadow point at the top and bottom of each riser, but, if necessary, additional points can be determined on horizontal lines drawn on the risers.

Figure 140E shows a typical L-shaped arrangement of a stairway and the characteristic shadows in elevation and plan. If the railing is elaborate and the motif repeats, the tracing and transfer method may be used to advantage after the shadow of one motif has been constructed.

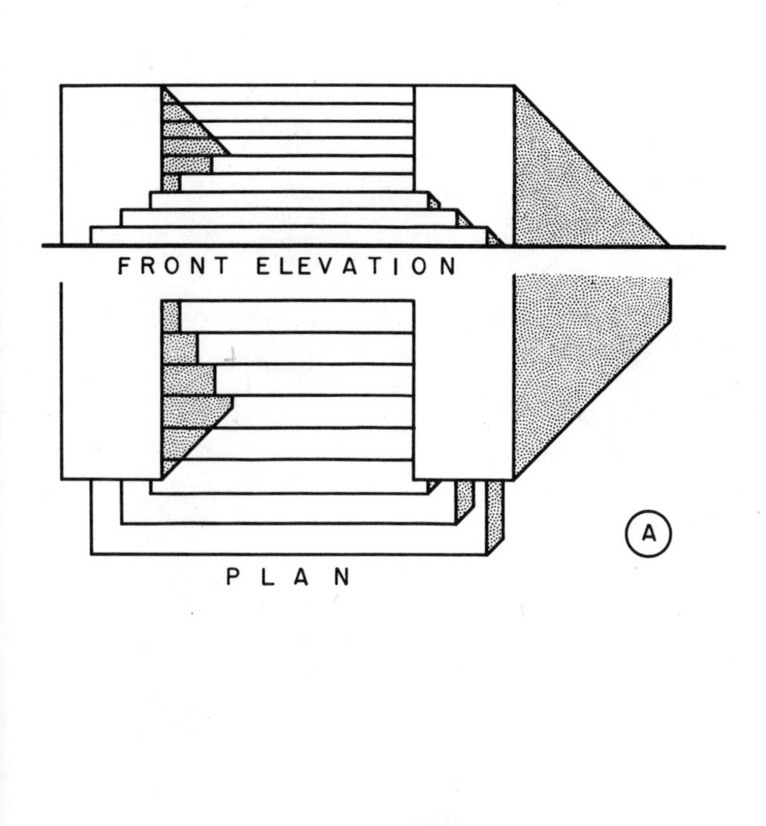

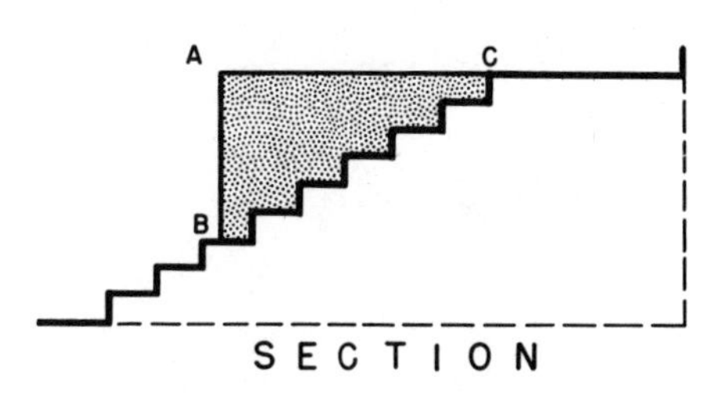

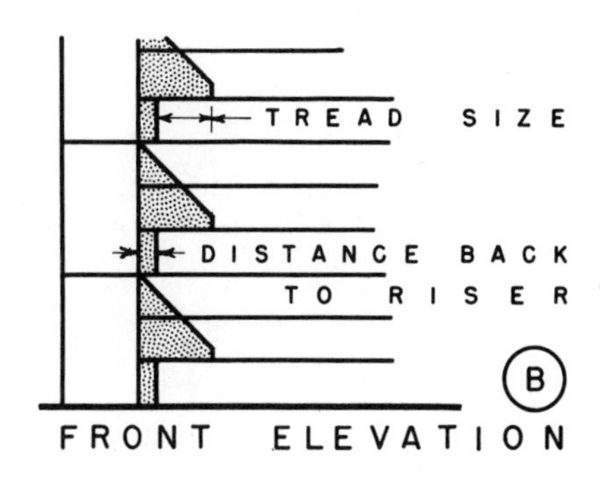

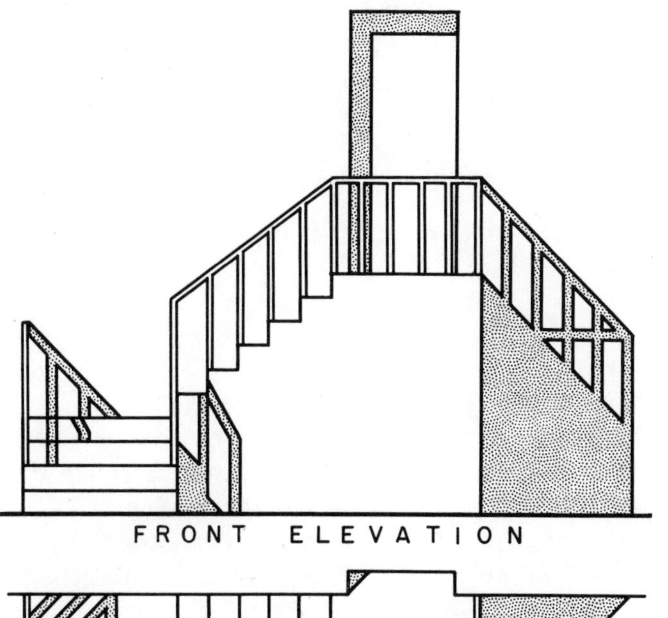

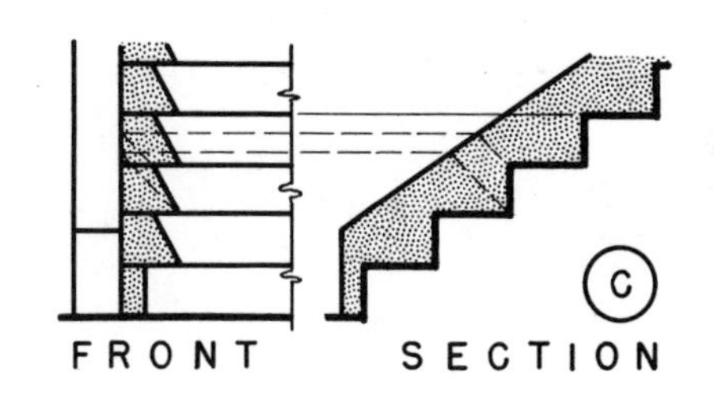

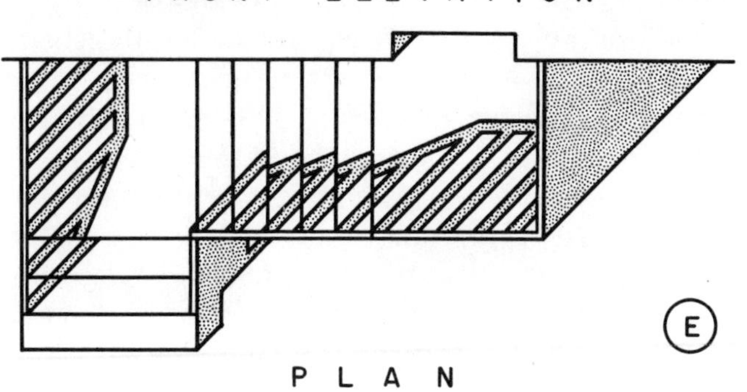

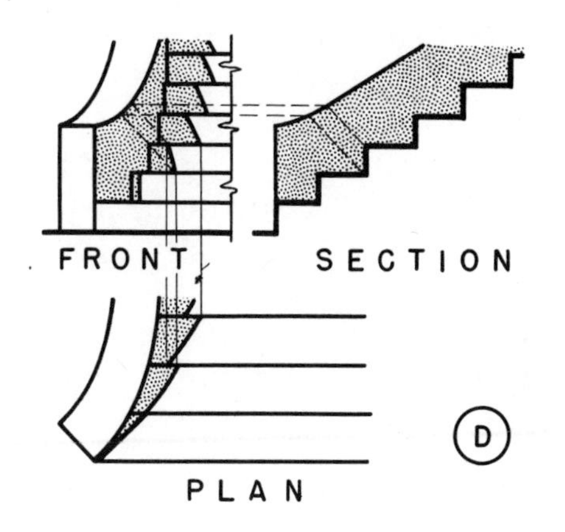

FIG-140 THE SHADOWS OF STEPS

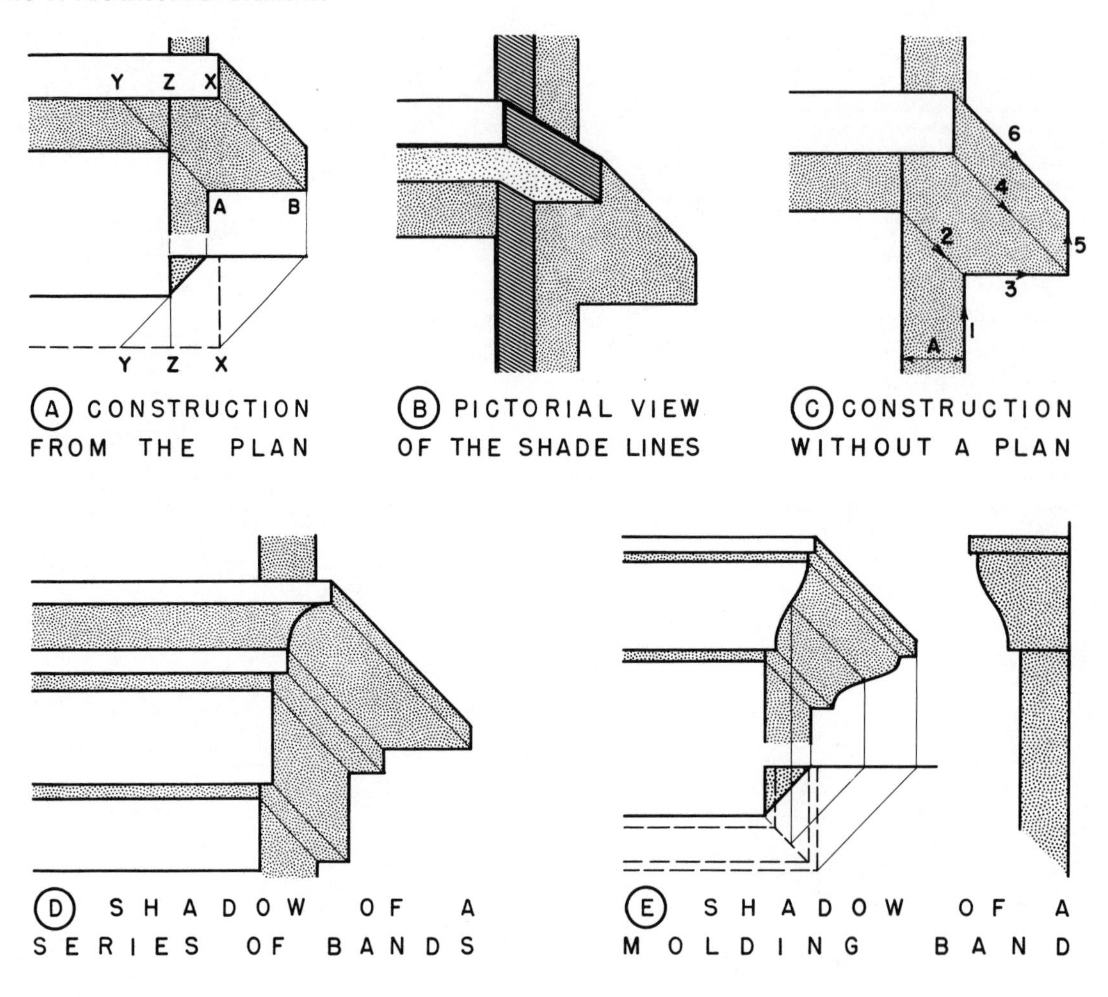

FIG-141 SHADOWS OF HORIZONTAL BANDS

PROJECTING HORIZONTAL BANDS. Belt courses, pilaster capitals, overhangs, and cornices often have projecting horizontal bands which cast shadows from their corners onto wall surfaces behind them. The shadows of the corners of these horizontal bands are puzzling because the shadow shapes are different from the shapes of the corners making the shadows. Figure 141A, B, and C provides illustrations of the simplest type of projecting band. It extends the same distance on the side and in front. A study of the pictorial view of Fig. 141B will help in locating the shade lines on the band. These shade lines belong to the three typical sets of lines, and their shadows have been discussed in detail in the preceding chapter. The horizontal part A–B of the shadow outline is longer than the projection Z–X to the right in elevation which makes a part of the shadow. If a ray of light is traced back over the wall corner in plan or in elevation, it will be found that a part of the horizontal shade line to the left of the corner of the wall casts its shadow over the corner. The length Y–Z of this part of the line is equal to the length which projects beyond the corner to the right in elevation. Therefore, the length of the horizontal shade line casting its shadow over the corner of the wall is twice the length of the projection, and consequently, the length of the horizontal part of the shadow is twice that of the projection.

If the distance back in plan is known from the nearer wall surface to the farther one, there is no need of either a plan or side view in drawing the shadow. The amount of the distance back is laid out to the right of the corner, as shown at A in Fig. 141C, to find the position of the vertical

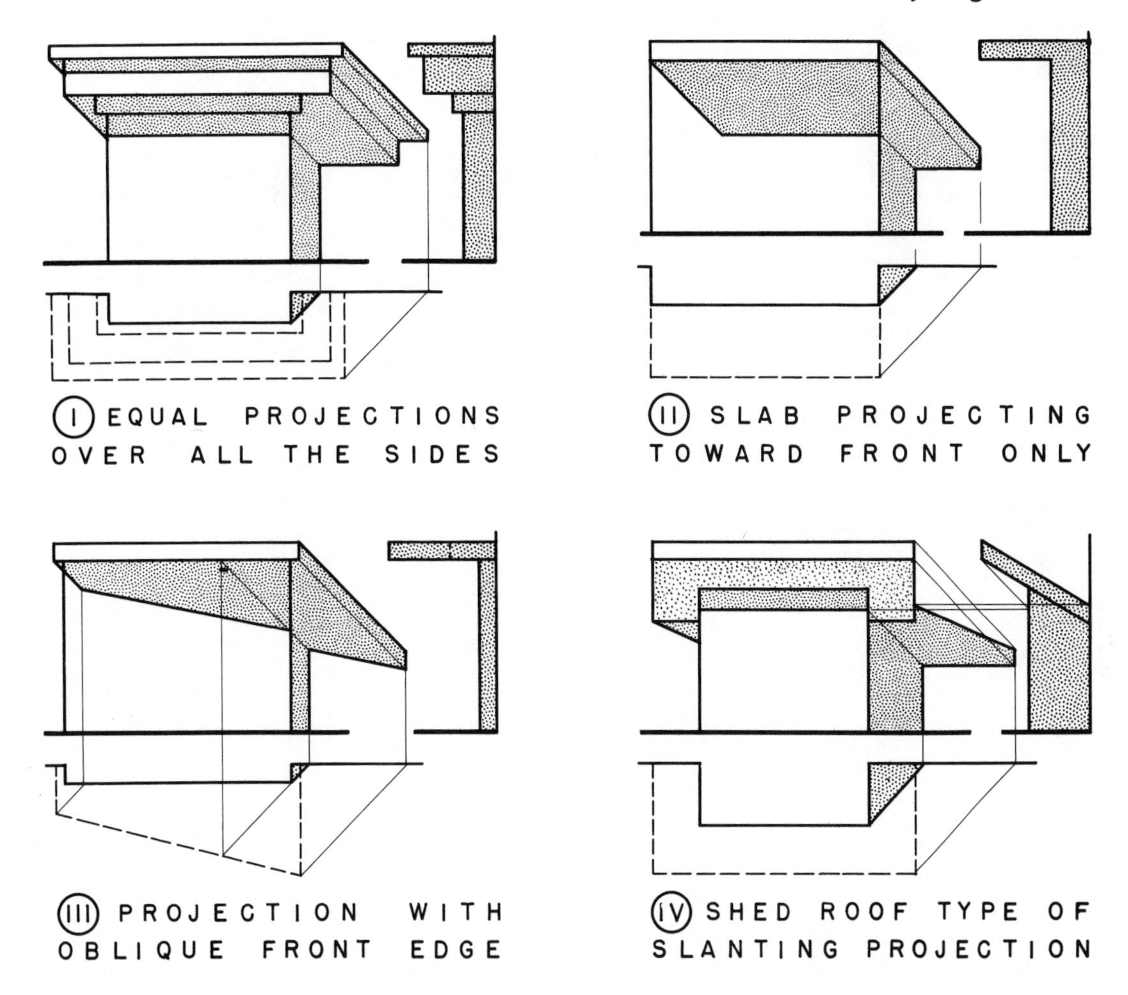

FIG-142 SHADOWS OF BASIC OVERHANG SHAPES

shadow of this corner. The other construction and shadow lines are drawn in the order given by the numbers on the lines and in the directions shown by the arrows. This construction method can be used on more complicated problems, such as that of Fig. 141D,

Moldings in a design make the problem of locating the shadows appear to be much more difficult. However, it should be kept in mind that no lines in shadow cast shadows. When a molding or a part of a molding is in light, the right corner intersection of the molding which is a 45° straight line in plan, is a shadow-casting shade line. The shadow of this curved shade line may be found by the point method, using the plan with the elevation view as illustrated in Fig. 141E. The side view could be used instead of the plan for this construction.

The basic overhang shapes shown in Fig. 142 are used in shelters over openings, on extending wings of buildings, and as extensions of roof surfaces. They are here represented as terminating against wall surfaces. Figure 142 I represents an equal overhang of a cornice on all sides. Figure 148 II has the overhang on the front only. This type may be used for a sunshade or shelter over a doorway, window, or side of a building. The near edge of the overhang in III is oblique to the wall plane. The two slanting shadow lines from the front edge of the overhang are parallel, since they are shadows of the same line on parallel surfaces. The shed roof form shown in IV occurs in complete roofs and as part of inverted gable roof structures. The two slanting shadow lines are parallel, since they are shadows of parallel lines on the same plane surface.

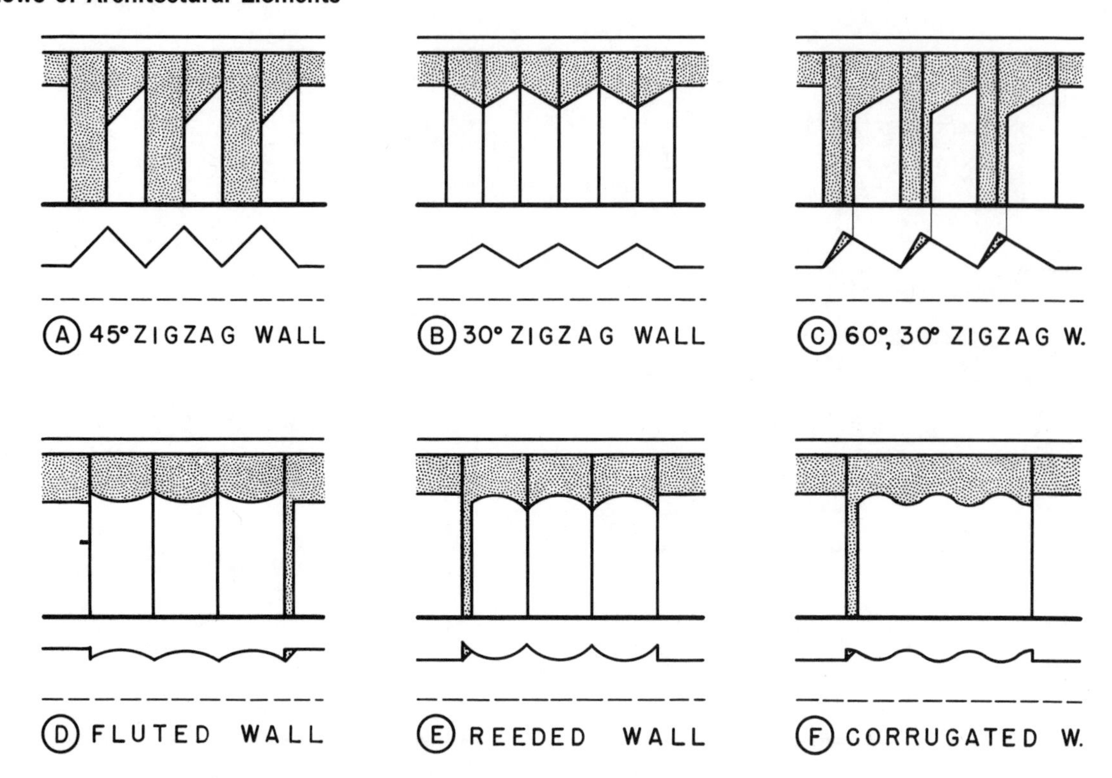

FIG-143 SHADOWS ON VERTICAL WALL TREATMENTS

Several vertical treatments of wall surfaces are illustrated in Fig. 143, where each example is terminated with a plain overhang at the top. Treatments of this nature occur in surface details at small scale and in larger-scale schemes for window or wall areas.

The equal bevels of zigzags are seldom at a greater angle than 45° with the general wall plane. At this angle one set of inclined surfaces is in shade and the other in light, as shown in A. With an angle of less than 45° all the inclined areas are in light, B. In C one set of inclined planes is at 30° and the other 60°. In this case the projecting corner casts a shadow over the 60° surfaces and onto the 30° planes. When the plan shapes are reversed, there will be no vertical shade or shadow with the conventional direction of light from the left. The light can then be assumed to come from the right for the more interesting shadow effect. Fluting, reeding, and corrugations are seldom deep enough to cause vertical shade or shadow bands. In all these vertical treatments the shadow outline below the overhang reverses the plan shape.

Overhangs with openings or perforations reduce the amount of light below them and also produce interesting play of light and shadow. Two types of such overhangs and their shadows are illustrated in Fig. 144 I and II. In I the beams which make up the structure of the skeleton overhang are all of the same size in cross section. Observation of some of the characteristics of the shadow will help the student to construct such shadows more easily and to avoid errors. Three points should be noted: (1) The horizontal shadow of the beam at the front edge will have a height A + B, the sum of its height and width. (2) The horizontal widths of the 45° shadows of the beams perpendicular to the wall are equal to A + B. (3) When the front and left edge beams are of the same size, the two corners C and D of the shadow will be on the same vertical line.

The first two of the above numbered points apply to the eggcrate type overhang of Fig. 144 II. The shadows of the square perforations have the characteristics of shadows of horizontal squares perpendicular to the wall. Two corners of each light area are on the same vertical line.

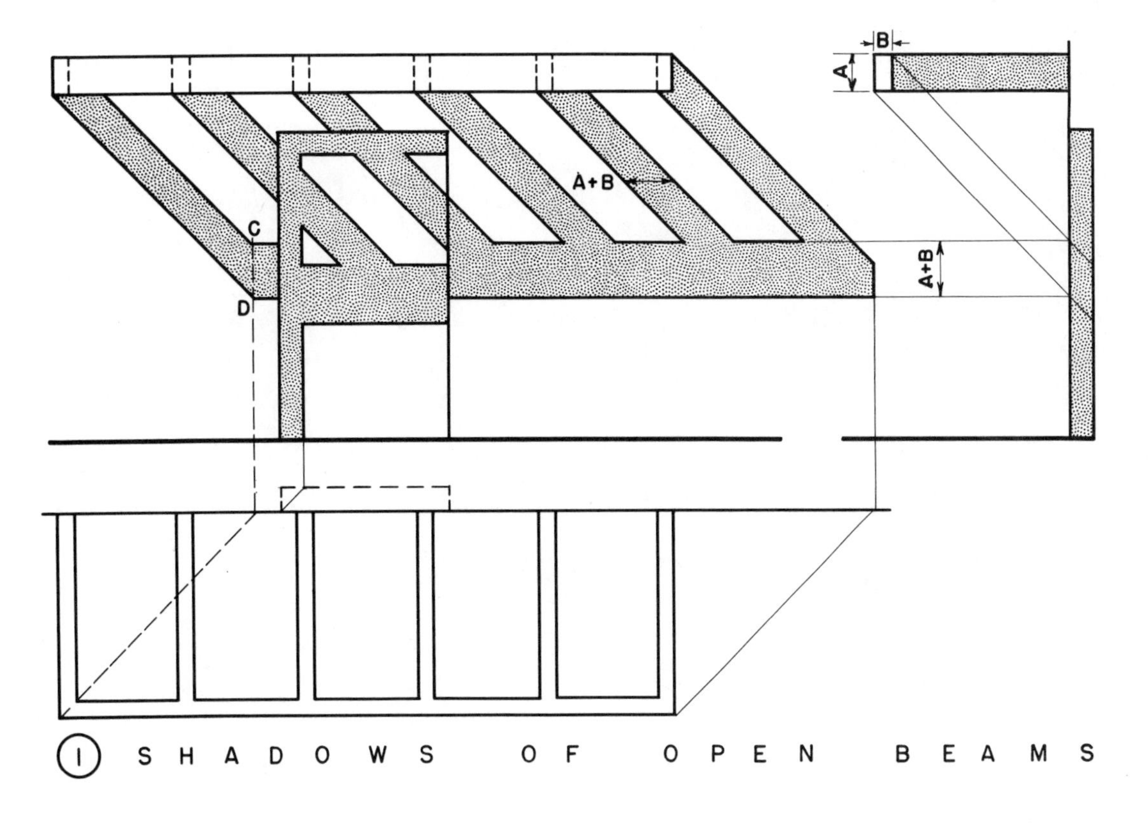

(I) SHADOWS OF OPEN BEAMS

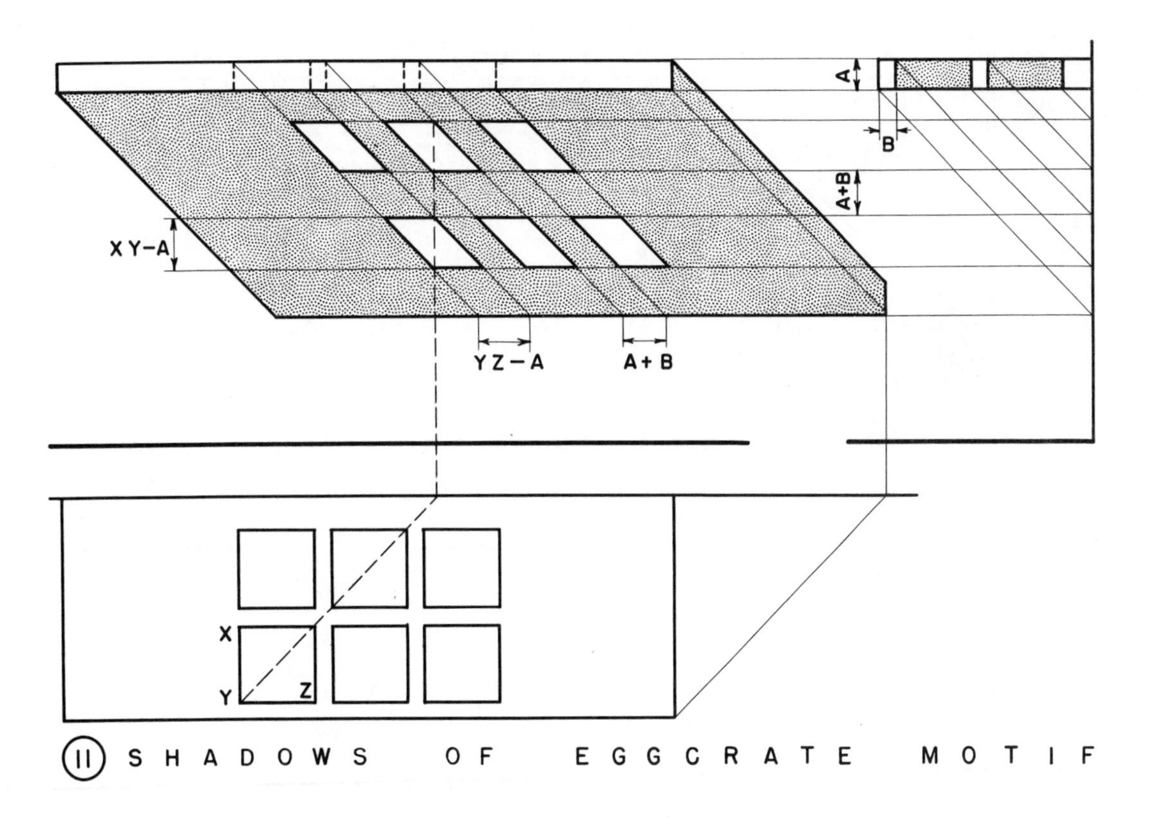

(II) SHADOWS OF EGGCRATE MOTIF

FIG-144 SHADOWS OF PERFORATED OVERHANGS

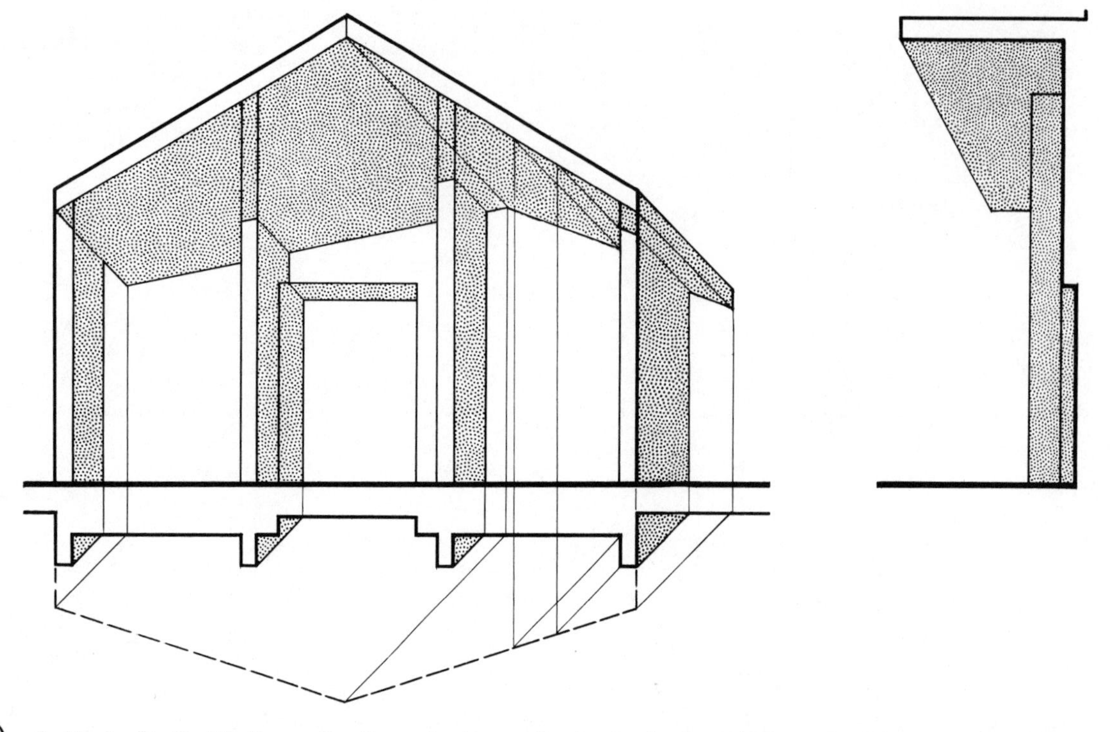

(A) SHADOWS OF AN OBLIQUE GABLE ROOF

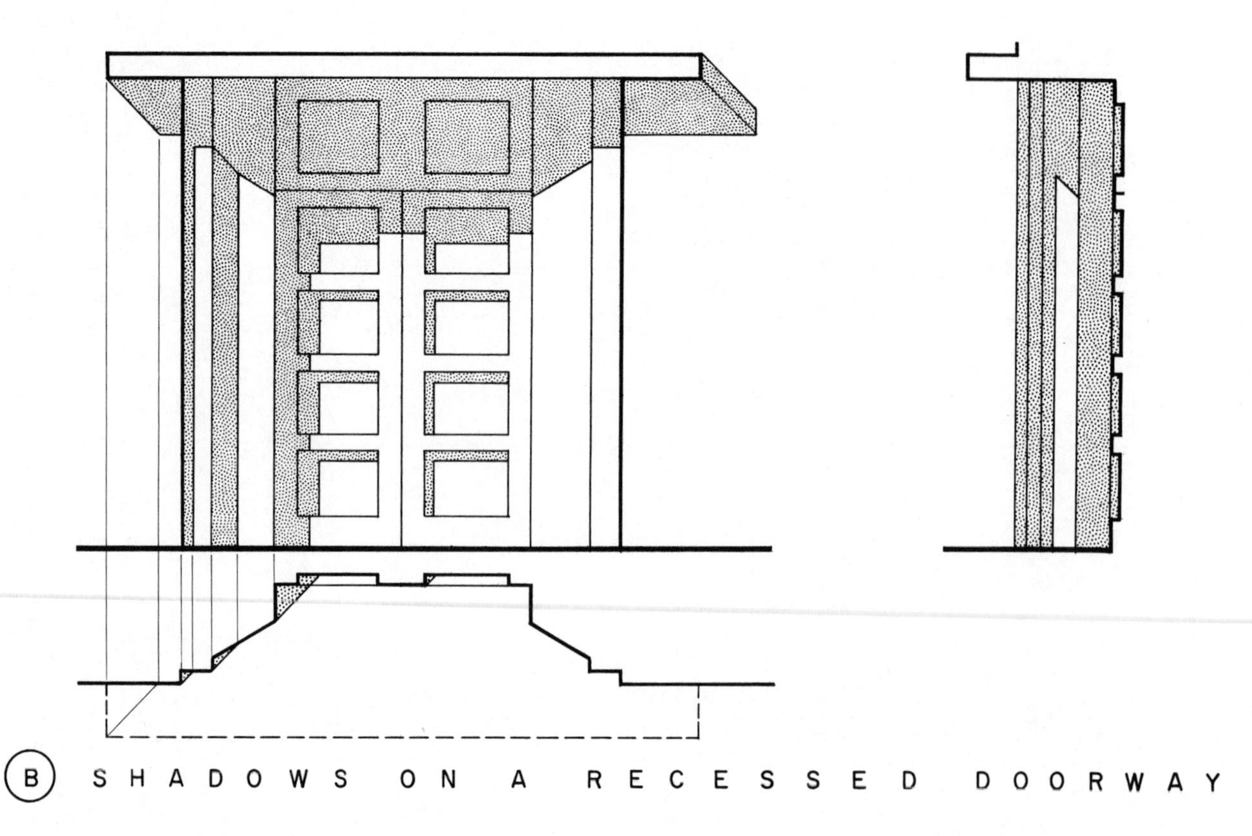

(B) SHADOWS ON A RECESSED DOORWAY

FIG-145 SHADOWS OF EXTENDING ROOFS

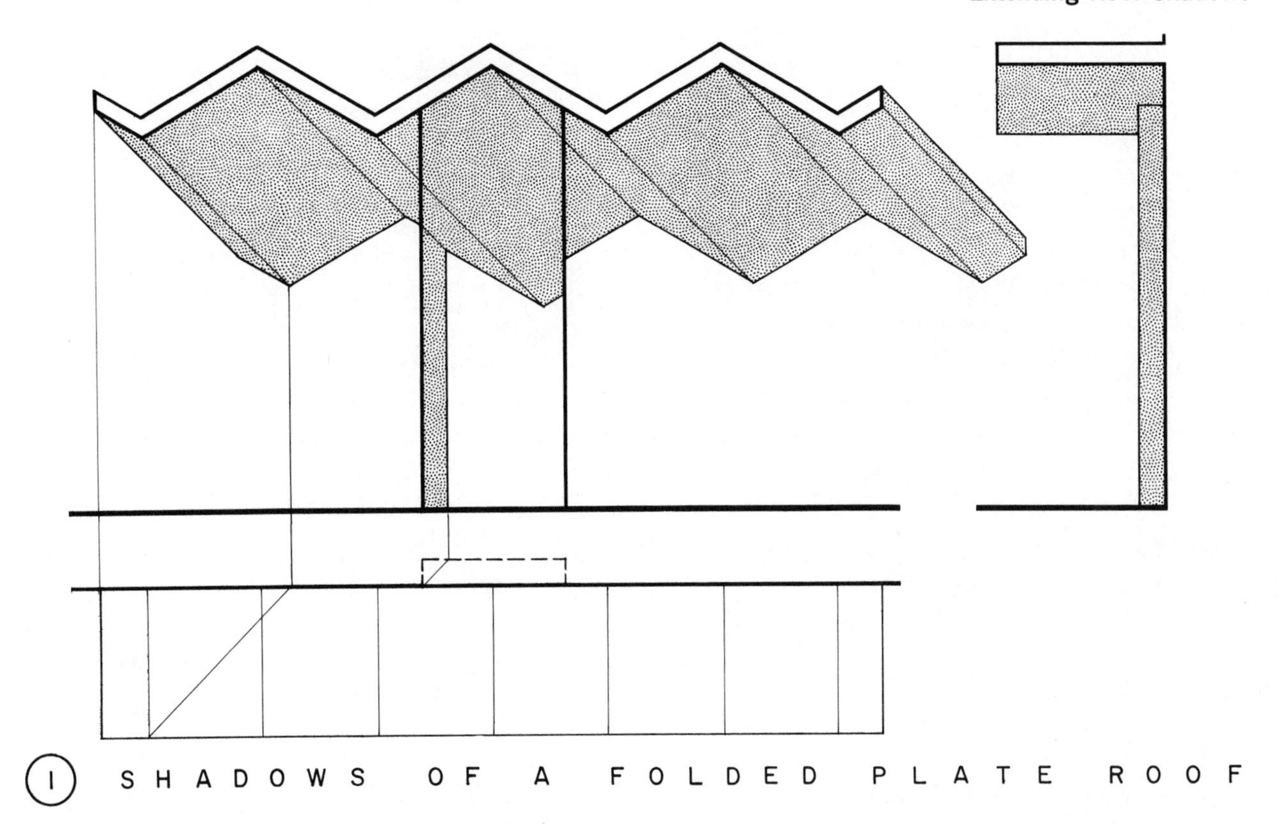

(I) SHADOWS OF A FOLDED PLATE ROOF

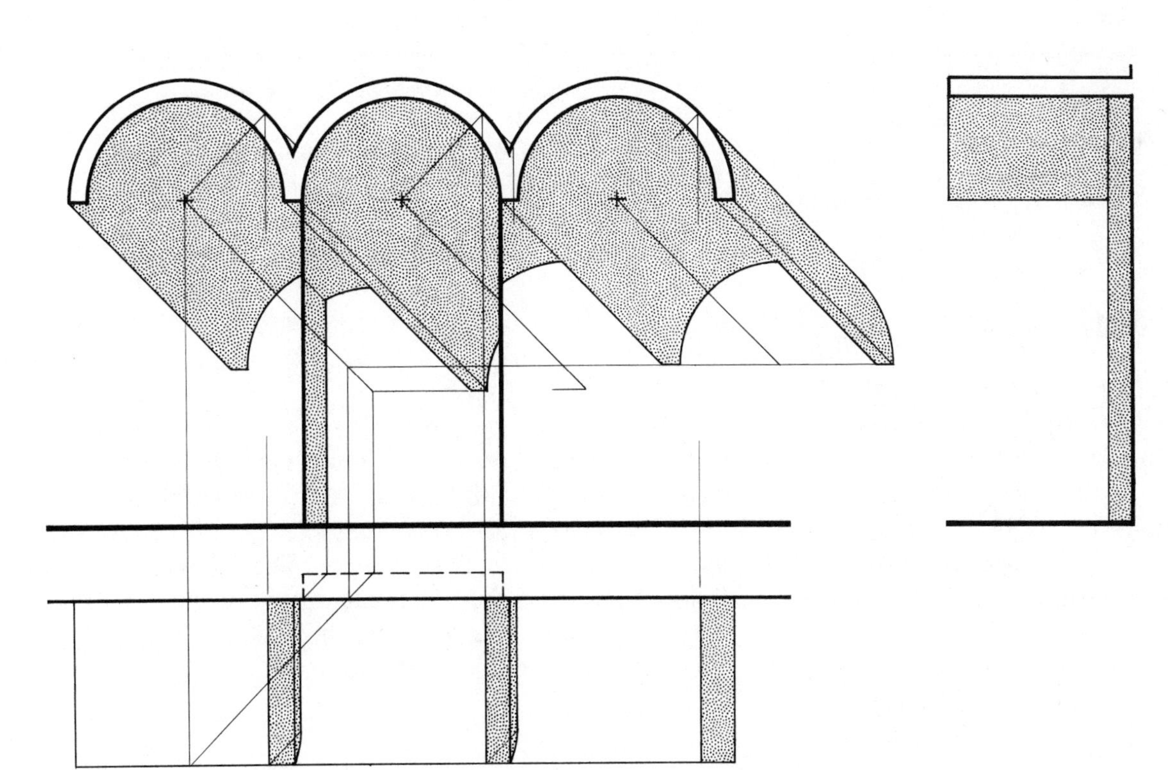

(II) SHADOWS OF A VAULTED ROOF

FIG-146 SHADOWS OF EXTENDING ROOFS

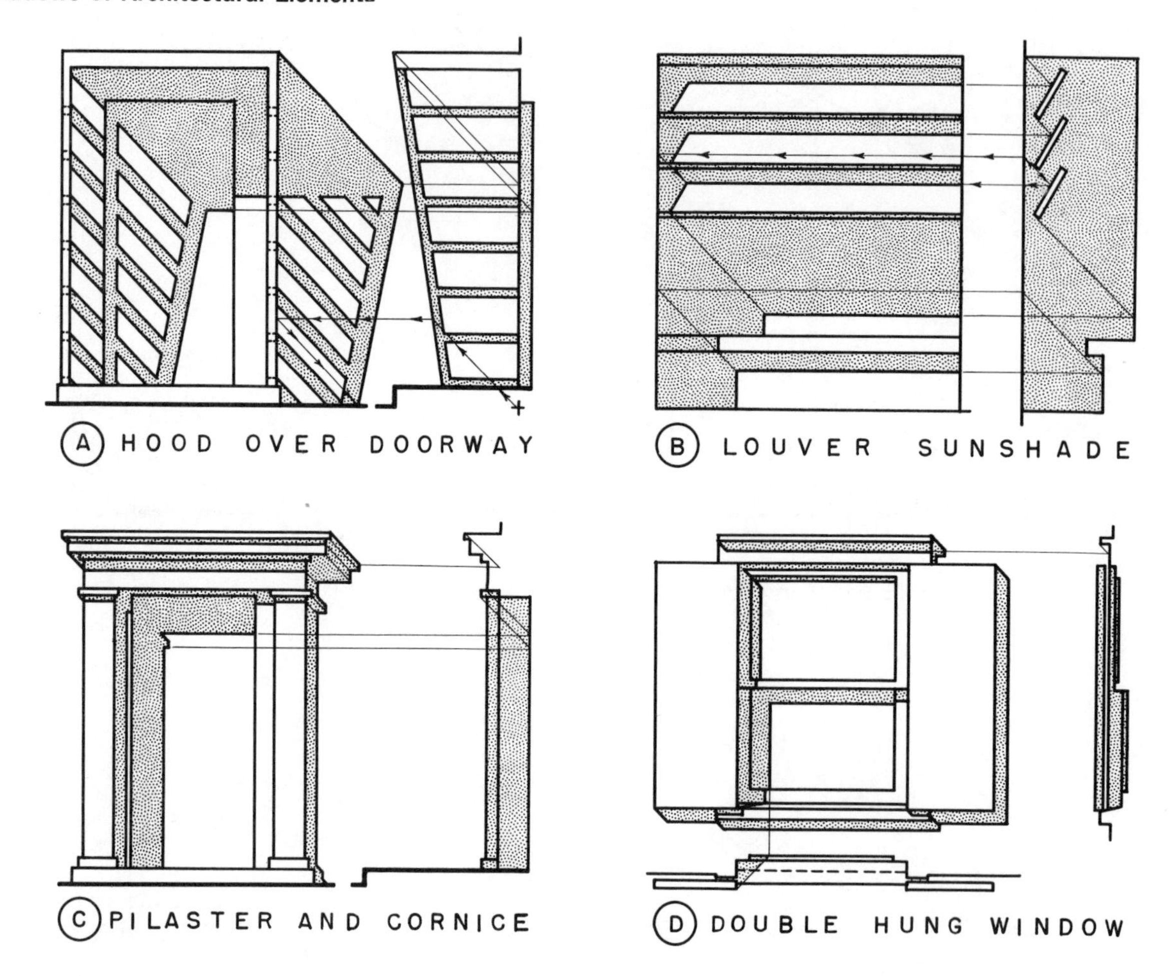

FIG-147 SHADOWS OF RECTANGULAR OPENINGS

OPENINGS. The shadows of openings are made up to a great extent of the shadows of the three sets of typical lines, shadows of other commonly used lines, and of the shadows of projecting bands. The shadows of these lines and projecting bands have been explained in detail in the preceding pages. In example A of Fig. 147 the shadows of the inclined posts are parallel. After the direction of the right edge of the right post was established, the other post shadow lines were drawn parallel to it. The end positions of the horizontal side members were used in elevation in determining the locations of the 45° lines of their shadows. These small squares would not be visible on the object and would not normally be shown on the drawing. The louvered sunshade of B gives an example of repeating shadows of a vertical line on the slanting surfaces. The angle of the slanting shadow lines duplicates the angle of the louvers in section view.

The two examples of Fig. 147C and D give shadows of projecting horizontal bands in simplified door and window treatments.

The circular window and arched opening of Fig. 148 I and II require the application of the method of finding the shadow of a circle on a surface parallel to the circle. When only a semicircle, or a small segment of a circle, casts the shadow, the construction is the same as for finding the shadow of a complete circle. It is necessary to keep in mind that when the circle is parallel to the surface receiving the shadow: (1) the radius of the circle making the shadow is always used to draw the shadow; (2) the shadow of the center of the circle making the shadow must be located on the plane receiving the shadow; (3) the shadow of the center of the circle must be located on

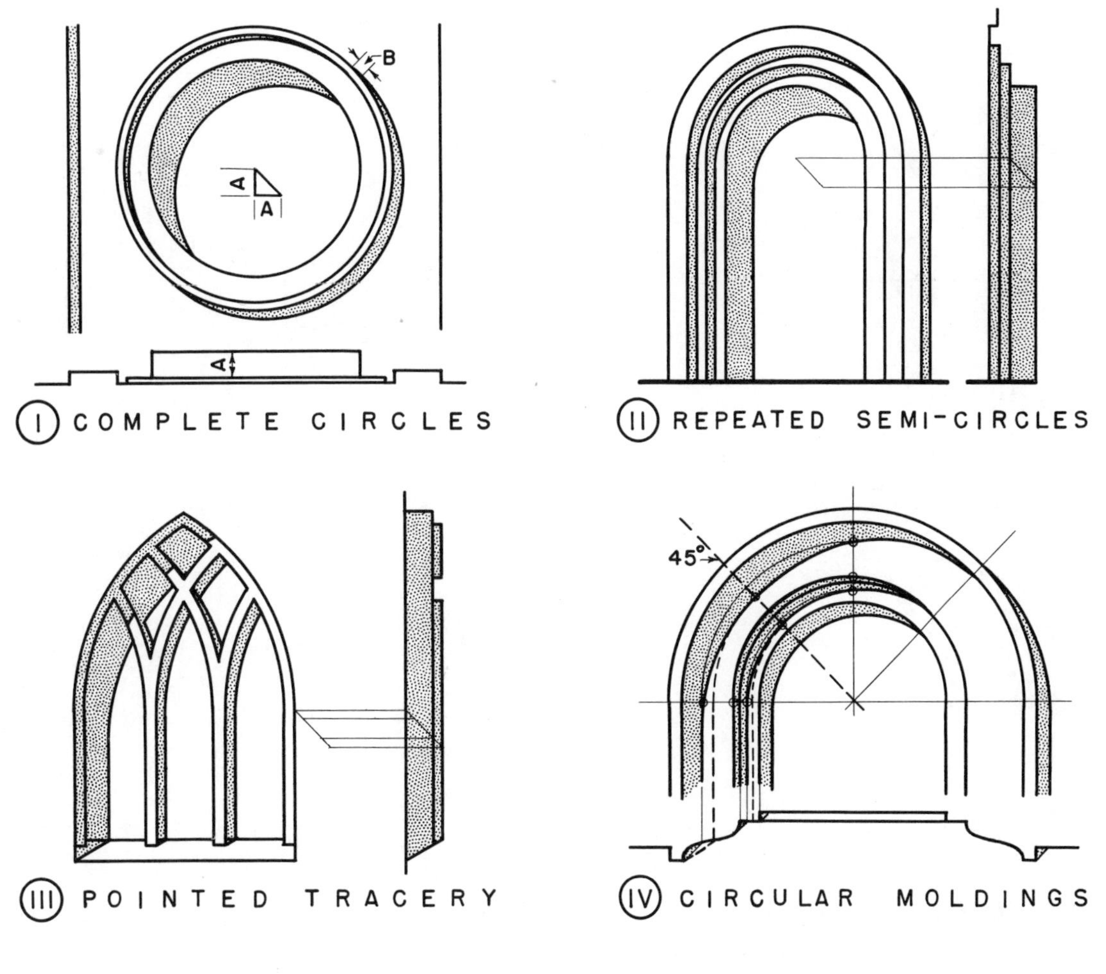

FIG-148 SHADOWS OF CIRCULAR OPENINGS

a 45° line which is drawn down and to the right from the elevation of the center of the circle; (4) the distance from the center to its shadow on this 45° line is the diagonal of a square of which a side is the distance A back from the center of the circle making the shadow to the plane receiving the shadow, as shown in Fig. 148 I. The circular part of the shadow which is cast on the outside, below, and to the right in Fig. 148 I is an exact semicircle. It is connected to the window by a straight line, B, which is the shadow of the shade line on the cylindrical surface which extends from the circle to the wall. Often the projection is so slight that the straight line is negligible.

When an arched opening, such as that of Fig. 148 III, is drawn at small scale, it is often sufficiently accurate to disregard moldings and find the shadow as though the same shade line cast all of each shadow. The simplified shadow can then be drawn from centers, or the shape can be traced and transferred.

When any kind of arched opening, circular window, or curved pediment is made up of moldings or irregular shapes, the light areas may vary in width around the curve and the shade lines may change in position at different points. The shadow widths where the moldings are vertical and horizontal will be the same and can be determined either from plan or section, Fig. 148 IV. The shadow widths on the 45° line through the center of the semicircles on the left side can be determined by using the true direction of light on plan or section and transferring the distances thus obtained. When this construction does not give a sufficient number of points, the slicing method of pages 142 and 173 can be used at different places around the curve to locate additional points.

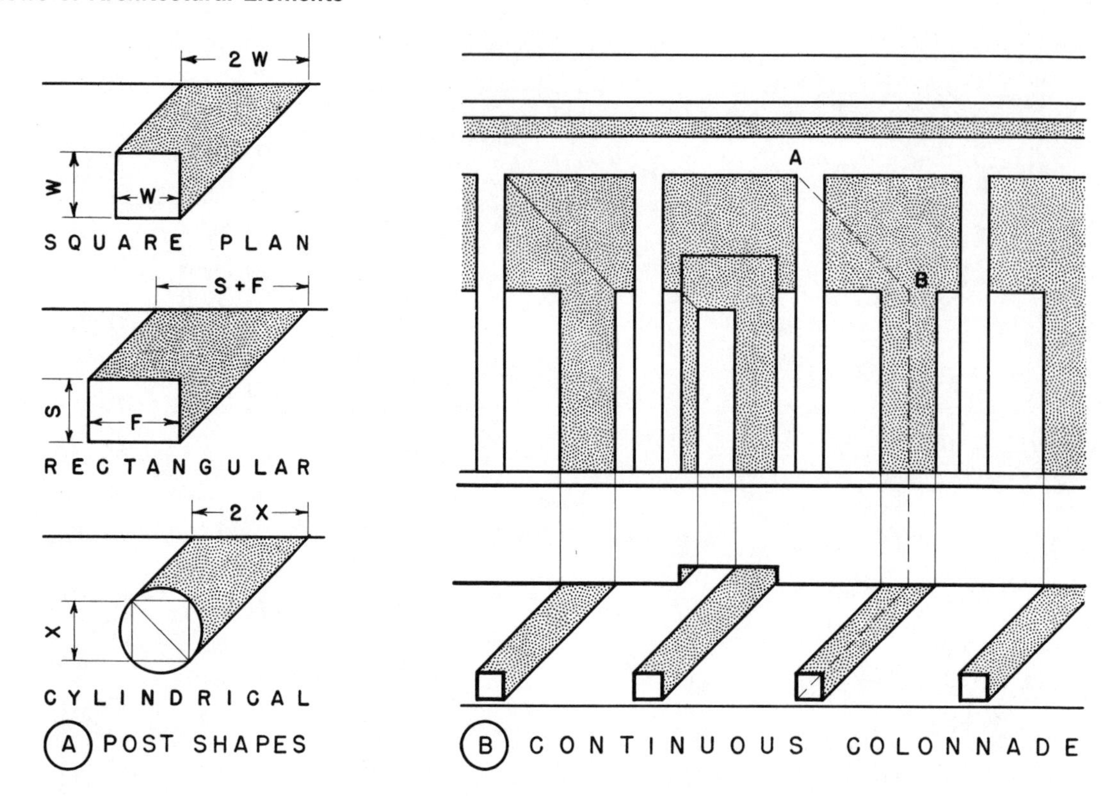

FIG-149 SHADOWS OF COLONNADES

COLONNADES AND PORTICOS. The shadow of a column on a surface parallel to front view is wider than the front view of the column. Therefore it is impossible to hide the shadow of a column behind another column of the same size as the one making the shadow. The width of the shadow of a square post is twice the elevation width of the post, Fig. 149A. When the post is rectangular the width of the shadow is the sum of the front and side dimensions of the post. The width of the shadow of a cylindrical column is twice the width of the inscribed square.

It is possible to work out the shadows of a colonnade without reference to the plan if the distance back and the relation of the lintel and column are known. The depth of the shadow below the architrave is equal to the distance back from its shade line to the wall. When the face of the column shaft or square post is in the same vertical plane with the shade line of the architrave, a 45° line drawn from point A, Fig. 149B, will locate the center line of a vertical shadow of the post or column at its intersection with the shadow of the architrave. The vertical shadow can then be drawn in at the correct width centering on this line.

The portico in Fig. 150 I has the same shade lines as the colonnade of Fig. 149B. It has, however, in addition the shadows from two long shade lines perpendicular to elevation at points C and D and the shade lines at the right vertical corner D–E of the entablature and parapet. The shadow of the left corner of the architrave coincides with the shadow of the center line of the corner column.

The oblique lines on the right side of the octagon in Fig. 150 II cast vertical shadow lines on the wall, since they are in the same vertical planes as light rays.

The shadow of the architrave of the semicircular portico of Fig. 150 III can be found by any of the methods of finding shadows of circles in this position. The shadows on the tops of the columns can be found by the point method.

The shadow of the curved shade line in Fig. 150 IV is the same shape as the elevation of the curve since the shade line is parallel to the wall.

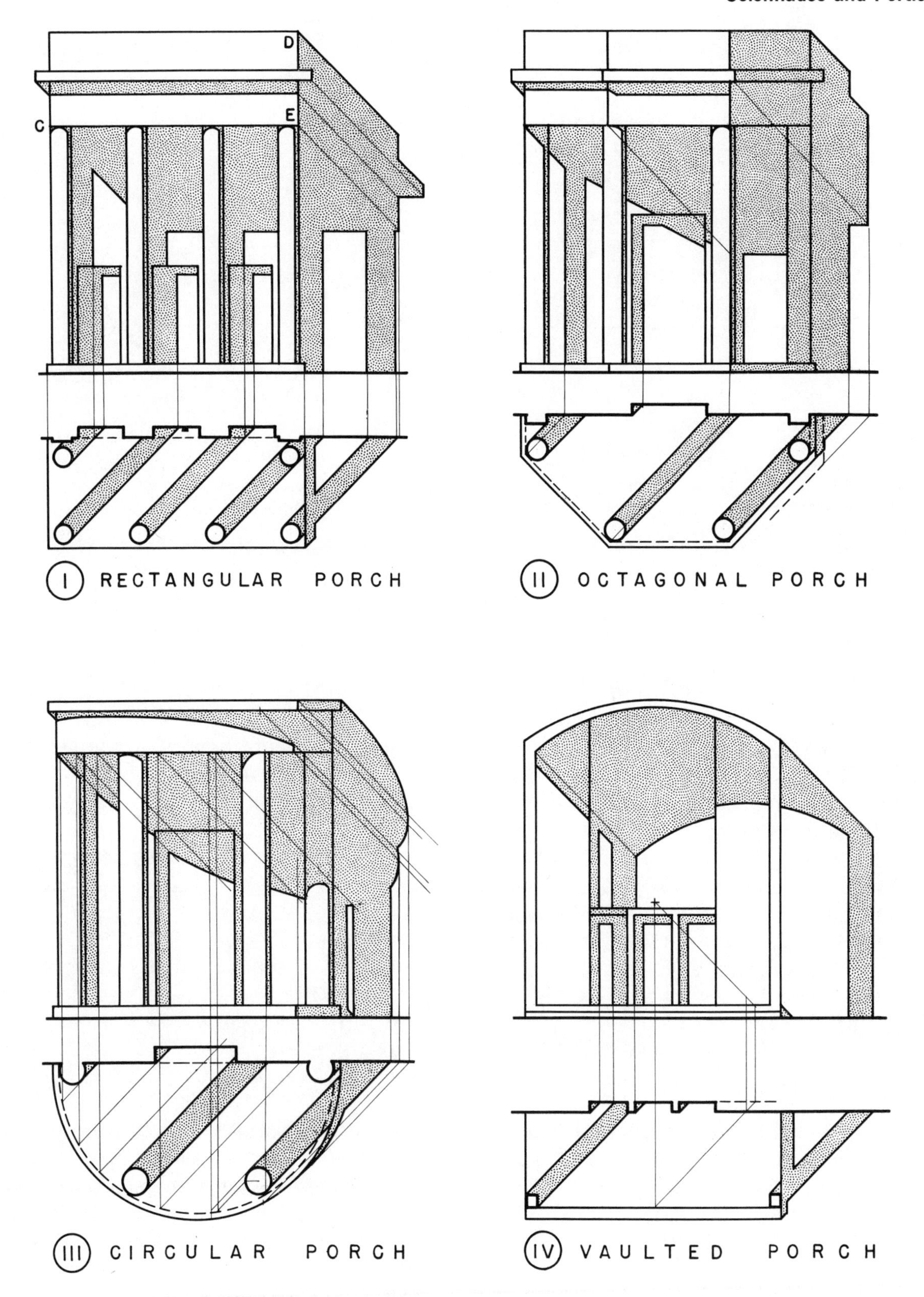

FIG-150 SHADOWS OF SIMPLE PORCH SHAPES

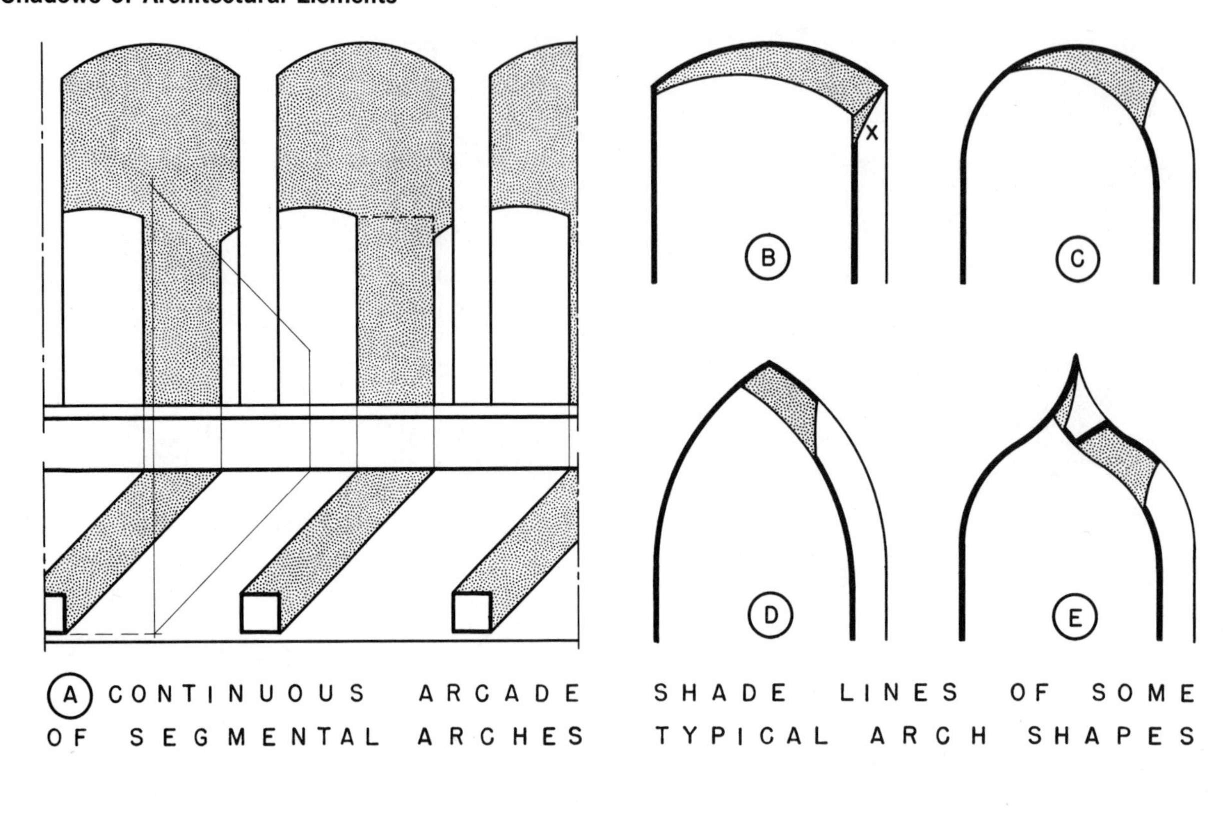

(A) CONTINUOUS ARCADE OF SEGMENTAL ARCHES

SHADE LINES OF SOME TYPICAL ARCH SHAPES

FIG-151 SHADOWS OF ARCHES

ARCADES. The simplest kind of arcade shadow is that of segmental or other flat curved arches in which the curve does not go beyond a 45° tangent at the steepest place, Fig. 151A. Such an arcade replaces the horizontal shade line of the architrave of a colonnade with the curving lowest outside line of the arch. It is similar in other respects. Part of the shadow of the right side of the shade line of the arch falls on the left side of the pier as shown at X in the oblique drawing, Fig. 151B. The left end of the shadow of the arch is complete on the wall to the shadow of the pier and consequently is lower than the right end.

When the curve of an arch goes beyond the 45° line, light strikes the soffit of the arch from the 45° point on down, as shown in Fig. 151C, D, and E. Then, instead of having a continuous shade line, as in the segmental arch, the shade line is on the front edge part of the way around and on the back edge for the remainder of the distance. In finding the shadows of most arcades it is therefore necessary to locate the shadows of both the inside and outside curves of the arches and then use the parts which outline the largest possible shadow area, as shown in Fig. 152 I and II.

The shadows of arch shapes which cannot be drawn with a compass can be found by either the point method or the tracing and transfer method. The tracing method can be used only when the shade line of the arch is parallel to the wall on which the shadow falls. In using this method the shadows of the vertical center line of the arch and its highest point may be used as guides in locating the tracing. This construction must be repeated for inside and outside edges, Fig. 152 II.

When a part of the arcade is perpendicular to the elevation, the shadows of those arches which are perpendicular to the elevation are parts of ellipses when the arches are parts of circles, Fig. 152 III and IV. The shadows may be found by any of the methods of finding shadows of circles in this position. The shadows of arches having more than one center may be found by the methods used above, but it may be easier to use the point method of finding the shadow of the curved line.

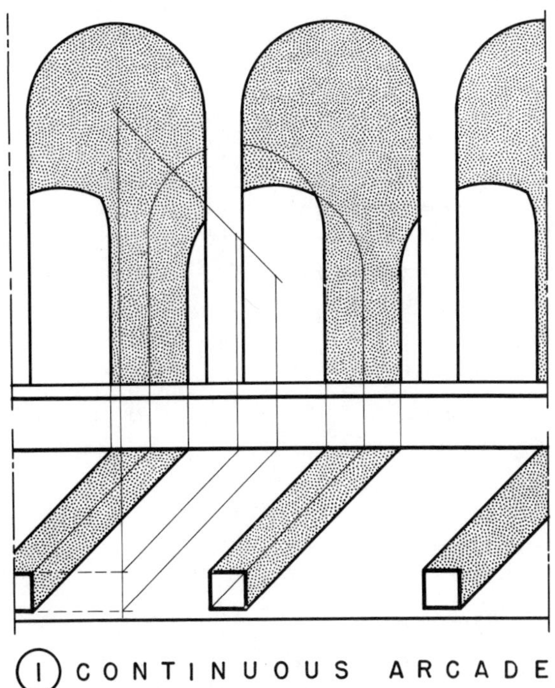

(I) CONTINUOUS ARCADE SEMI-CIRCULR ARCHES

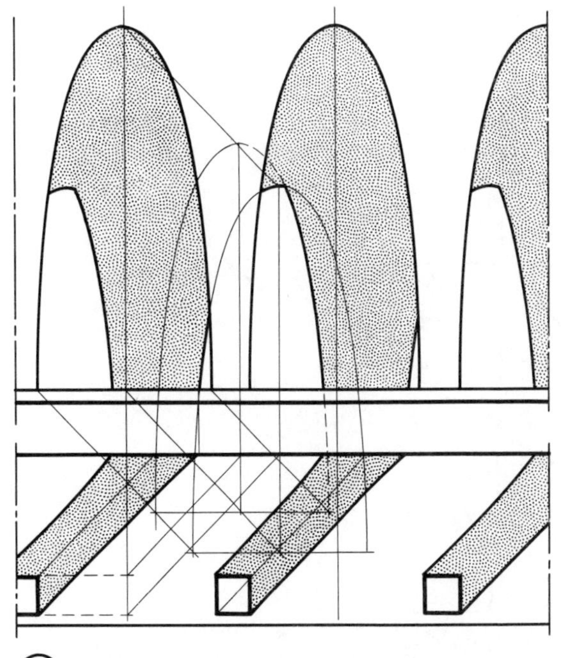

(II) CONTINUOUS ARCADE OF ELLIPTICAL ARCHES

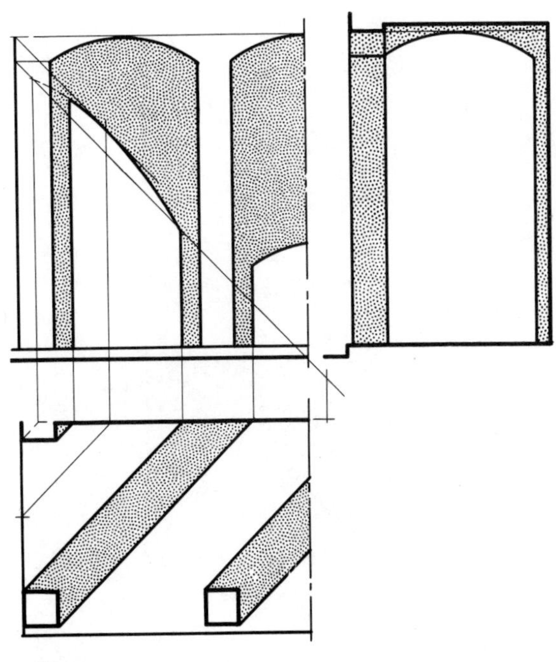

(III) CORNER OF ARCADE OF SEGMENTAL ARCHES

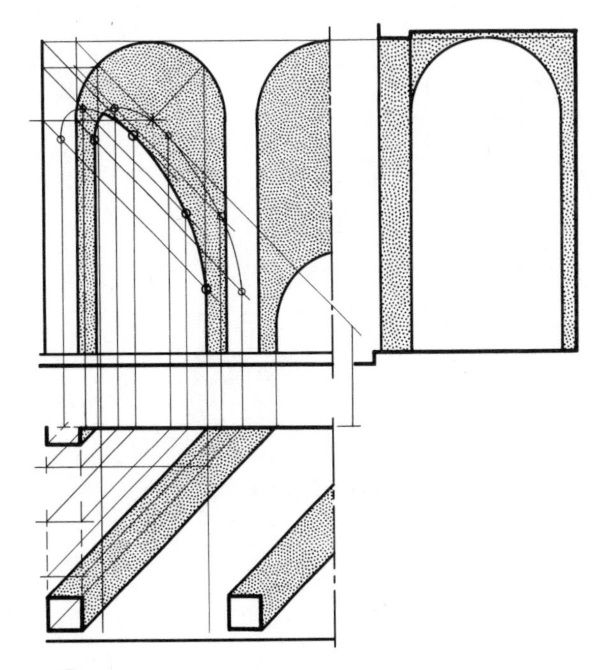

(IV) CORNER OF ARCADE OF SEMI-CIRCULAR ARCHES

FIG-152 SHADOWS OF ARCADES

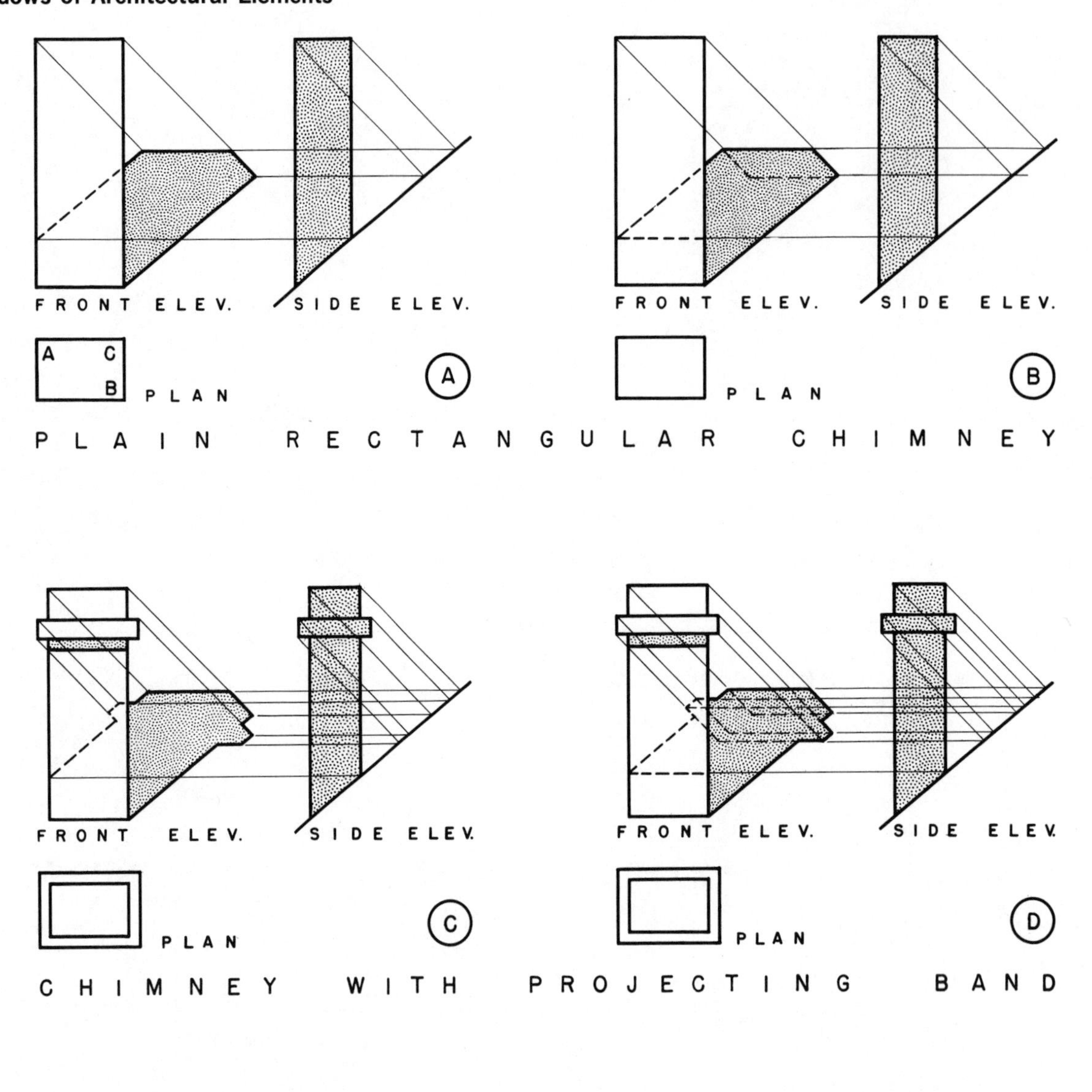

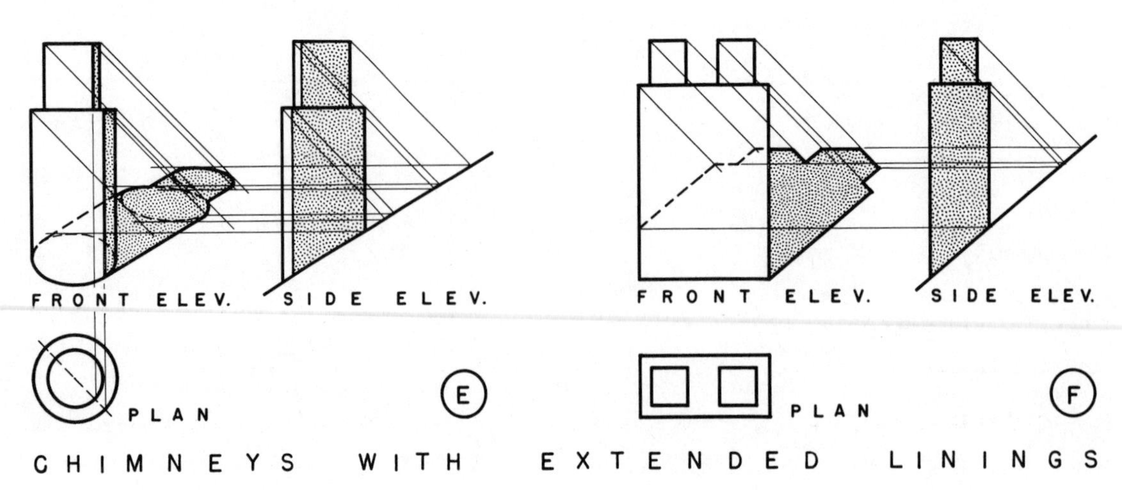

FIG-153 SHADOWS OF SIMPLE CHIMNEY FORMS

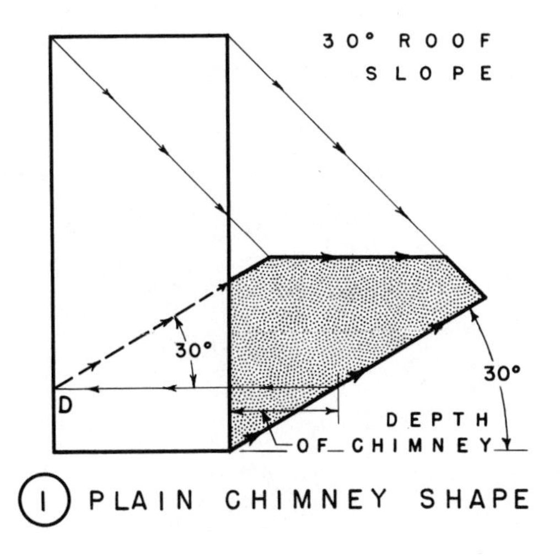

(I) PLAIN CHIMNEY SHAPE

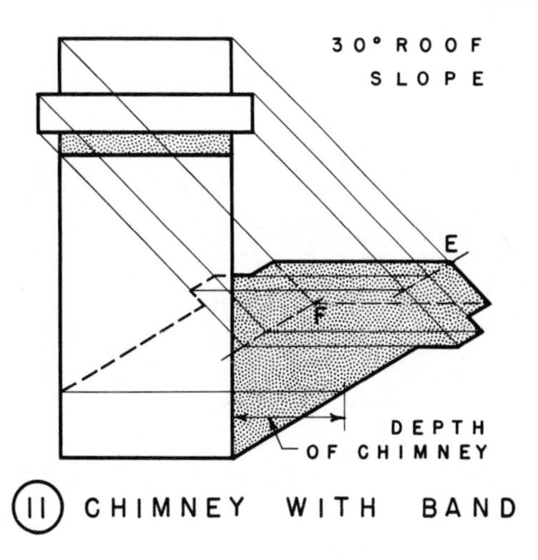

(II) CHIMNEY WITH BAND

FIG-154 SHADOWS WITHOUT AUXILIARY DRAWINGS

CHIMNEYS. The common basic chimney shape in which the top is a horizontal rectangle with two sides parallel and two perpendicular to the elevation plane has the three principal line types as its shade lines, Fig. 153A. They are (1) vertical lines at corners A and B in plan, (2) horizontal line A–C parallel to the elevation plane, and (3) line C–B which is perpendicular to elevation. The shadows of these line types have been discussed in pages 134–137. Their shadows may be found directly, Fig. 153A, or the entire shadow of the rectangle of the top may be found and its outside corners connected to the outside corners of the intersection of the roof and chimney as shown in B.

In C the shadows of the shade lines are found directly by using the side elevation. In D the complete shadows of the three rectangles of the top of the chimney and the top and bottom of the projecting band are found. The outside corners of the shadow of the top are connected to the outside corners of the intersection of chimney and roof. The outside corners of the shadows of top and bottom of the band are connected. The shadow is then the outside line of the figure thus formed. This method shown in D requires less accurate analysis of shadow-casting shade lines than the direct method of C. Furthermore, the shadow is more easily visualized from the pattern of the construction lines.

The cylindrical chimney of E has an elliptical intersection line with the roof in front elevation. When the roof is a 45° slope, the intersection will be a circle. These ellipses of the roof intersection and top of the chimney are small enough to be drawn from the shadow of the tangent square.

When the slope of the roof and the depth of the chimney are known, the shadow of the chimney on the roof can be found without a side elevation. The shadows of the vertical lines are at the same angle as the slope of the roof on which the shadow falls. The height of point D can be worked out from the depth of the chimney and slope of the roof, Fig. 154 I.

In Fig. 154 II the shadow of the main mass of the chimney is found as in Fig. 154 I. Lines are drawn through points E and F parallel to the shadows of the vertical shade line corners of the chimney. These lines are the imaginary shadows of the two vertical corners of the chimney which do not cast actual shadows; namely, the left front and right rear corners. These lines are the roof intersections of vertical miter planes through these corners parallel to the direction of light. The shadows of the projecting left front and right rear corners of the band will fall on these two lines. From the shadows of these points the shadow outline can be completed, as shown.

In drawing the shadows of chimneys the principle that shadows of parallel lines are parallel should be applied whenever possible.

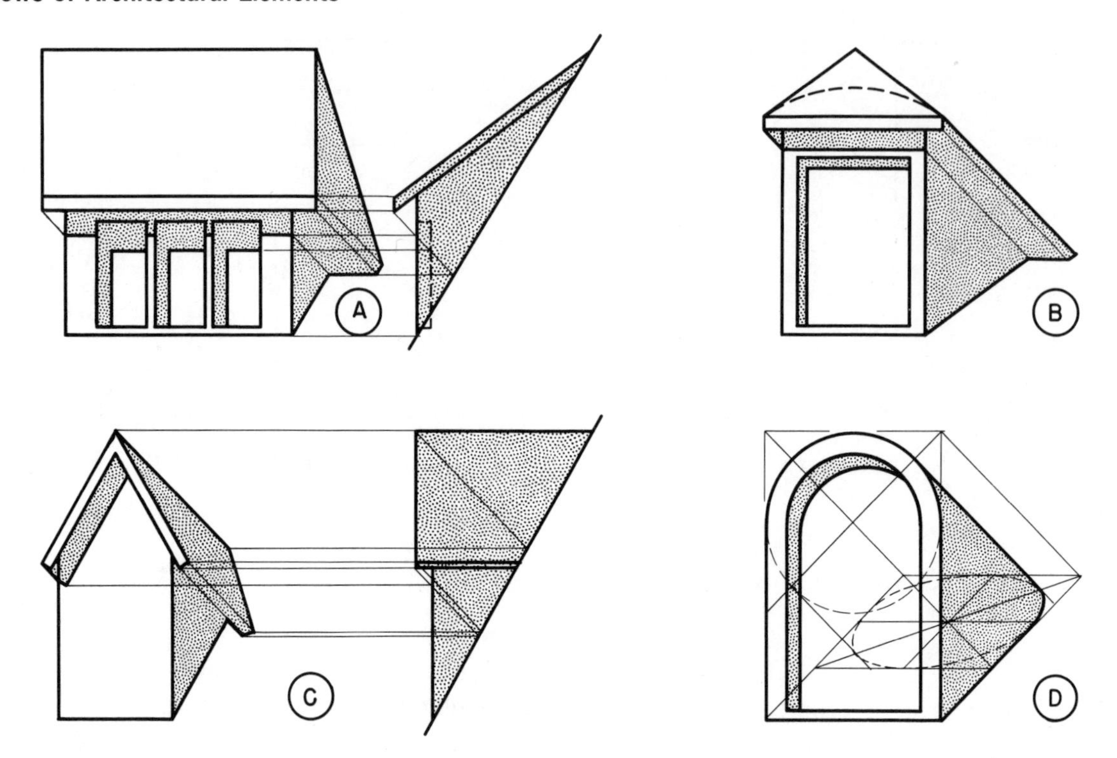

FIG-155 SHADOWS OF SIMPLE DORMER SHAPES

DORMERS. In finding the shadows of dormers the side view, Fig. 155A, is helpful in determining the shade lines and understanding the problem, but it is often unnecessary in casting the shadow. The entire shadow of this example can be constructed by use of front elevation alone. The shadow of the right vertical shade line is first drawn from its intersection with the roof at the slope of the roof on which the shadow falls. The remainder of the shadow is then constructed by 45° projection as shown. There is no visible shadow on the roof under the left edge of the cornice. Since the cornice slopes up on the sides of the dormer, the dormer roof conceals this shadow.

When the hip, curved, or gable roof of a dormer is not steeper than 45°, it will not cast a shadow, and in most cases the shadow of the part below the roof can be cast without use of side view, Fig. 155B. When the slope is steeper than 45° the shadow can be found by use of side elevation as in Fig. 155C. When the dormer has a hip roof at more than 45° and the main roof on which the shadow falls is at the same slope as the dormer roof, the shadow can be found without use of side view. The shadow of the hip of the dormer will parallel the front elevation view of the hip line because the hip is parallel to the main roof.

In constructing the shadow of the dormer with a semicircular-shaped roof which has its front edge in the same plane as the front corner of the dormer, Fig. 155D, no side elevation is necessary. In the example shown, the shadow of the tangent quadrilateral around the entire circle was found on the roof. Two sides of this quadrilateral are vertical lines and two are at the angle of the slope of the roof. The diagonals were drawn and the four shadow points located on them by projection as shown. The elliptical shape was then drawn inside the shadow of the quadrilateral.

In constructing dormer shadows the following facts should be used: (1) the shadow of a vertical line onto a roof will be at the slope of the roof receiving the shadow; (2) the shadows of parallel lines will remain parallel when they fall on the same plane; (3) it is often worth while to find the direction of the shadow of a short line by using a longer line in the same direction for greater accuracy.

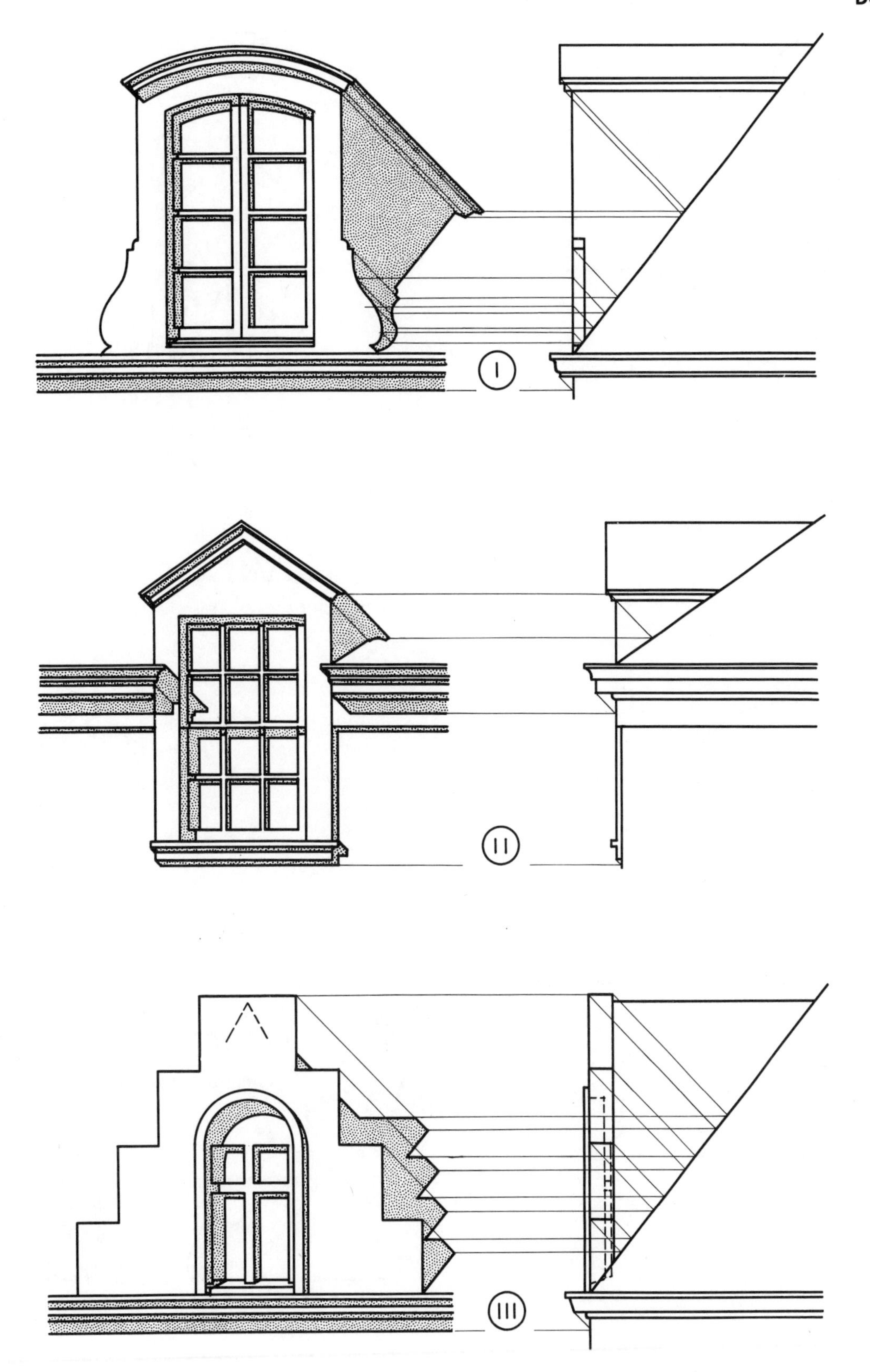

FIG-156 EXAMPLES OF DORMER SHADOWS

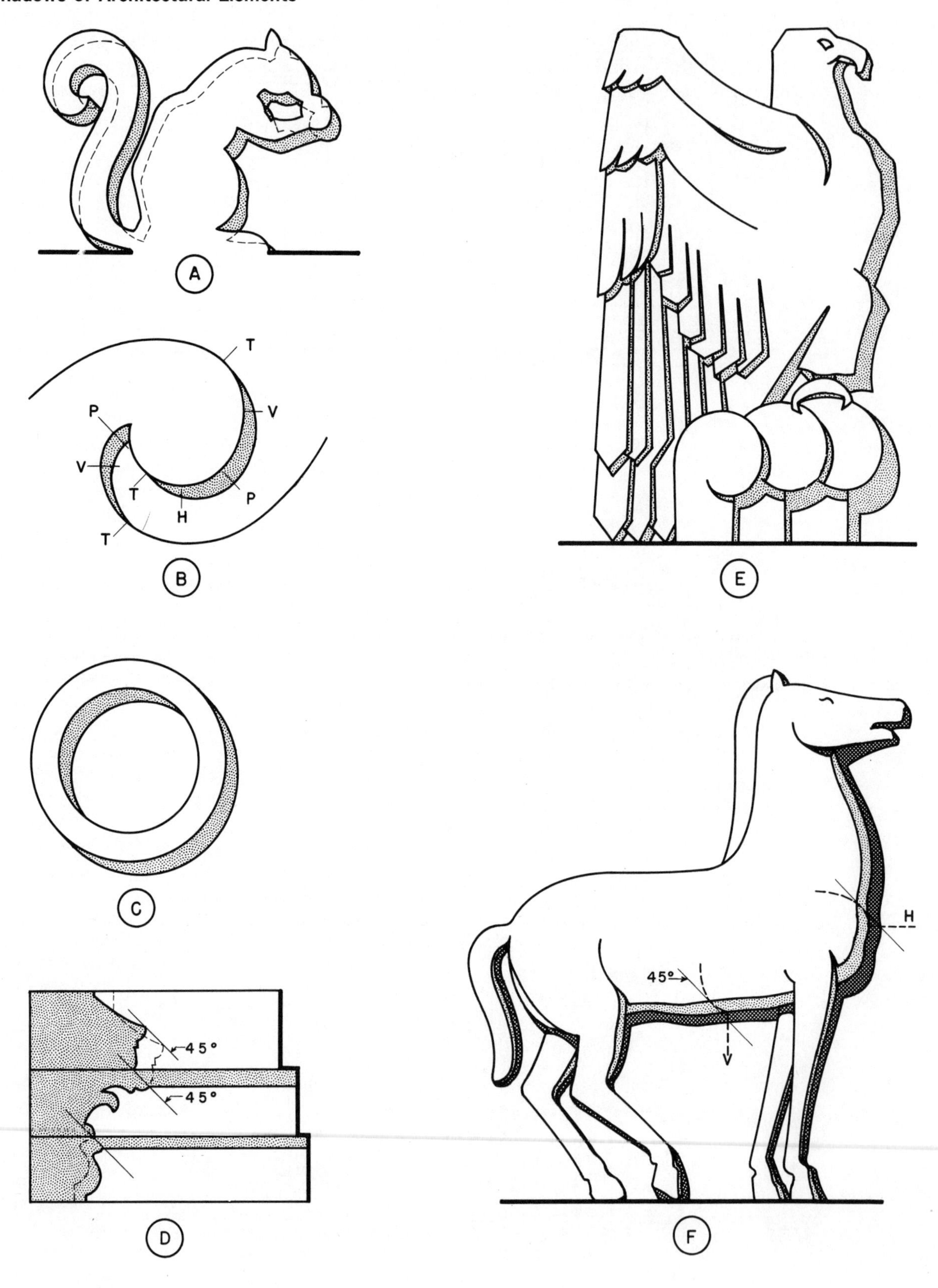

FIG-157 SHADOWS OF ORNAMENT AND SCULPTURE

SCULPTURE AND ORNAMENT. The effectiveness of sculpture and ornament depends to a very great extent on shadows. Shadow masses and shapes form a striking and important part of their design. An understanding of these shadows and the ability to give a sympathetic interpretation of them will be useful in the work of the designer and the draftsman.

When the projection of the sculpture is constant, the shadow may be determined by tracing the part of the outline which casts a shadow, moving this outline to the correct shadow position, and transferring it as in Fig. 157A. It should be noted that in shadows of this type: (1) Where the profile is tangent to the horizontal and vertical, the shadow is equal to the projection as at H and V in Fig. 157B. (2) Where the profile is perpendicular to the direction of light in the drawing, as at P, the shadow is widest. This greatest width is equal to the diagonal of a square of which a side is the amount of projection. (3) Where the profile is tangent to the direction of light, as at T, the shadow disappears in a sharp point. It is usually a simple matter for a good draftsman to draw in these shadows directly without measuring, if he will keep in mind the important points enumerated and described above.

An inspection of the varying shadow widths of the circular ring in Fig. 157C will help the student to proportion his shadows correctly at different points on the profile of ornament with a constant projection. The drawing of such a ring and its accompanying shadows with the correct shadow width for his drawing will be even more helpful, since the shadow width on the ring will exactly equal that of the ornament where the lines making the shadows are in the same direction. In Fig. 157A, B, and C the short 45° lines connecting the edges of the shadow and object have not been shown, since they are rather inconsequential. With a larger projection it would be necessary to show these straight-line tangents which are explained for Fig. 148 I.

When the amount of projection of the shade lines of sculpture varies, shadow-casting problems become more involved. Unless the student clearly understands the design and its variations in projection, it may be necessary for him to draw several profiles through the object. In Fig. 157E the projection varies but the surfaces remain flat, so that the shade lines are in all cases the edges of areas.

When there are shades on the object so that the outlines of areas are not the shadow-casting shade lines, it is helpful to first work out the shade lines and then their shadows. Shade and shadow points can be located by drawing vertical and horizontal profiles at V and H in Fig. 157F.

IRREGULAR SHADOWS OVER BROKEN SURFACES. When an irregular shadow falls on a broken or molded surface, as in the case of the shadow of a column capital on a treatment around a window or doorway, Fig. 157D, it is often easier to draw the entire shadow on one of the planes and then move the different parts to suit the differences in projection. In this example the complete shadow was drawn on the center plane. Where the surface receiving the shadow is nearer than the plane on which the shadow was found, the shadow moves up and to the left to compensate for the difference in projection. Where the surface receiving the shadow is farther away than the surface on which the shadow was found, the shadow moves down and to the right to make up for the difference in projection. When the surface is made up of a series of parallel planes, the tracing method may be used for transferring parts of the shadow to the correct locations.

SHADOWS WHICH IT IS IMPRACTICAL TO WORK OUT. There are motives used in architecture which are so complex in form as to make the working out of their shadows impractical, especially when they are drawn at small scale. The shadows of complex column capitals, gargoyles, lamp posts, sculpture, and other ornamental forms are examples. Under such conditions some parts of the shadow can usually be worked out or approximated by the methods already described and the remainder drawn in from imagination. There are good examples available with shadows cast and rendered for many of the examples of historic ornament. These can be followed whenever they are at hand. When such drawings are not available for the design, the best solution for complex forms is to actually make a model of the ornament and with the light in the correct direction sketch the shadow forms from the model.

CHAPTER 18
Shadows of Circular Solids

SURFACES OF REVOLUTION. Geometrically a surface of revolution is formed by revolving an outline form about a straight line as an axis. A cylinder is formed by revolving a rectangle about one side, a cone by revolving a right-angled triangle about one side of the right angle, and a sphere by revolving a semicircle on its diameter. All the architectural forms which are, or could be, formed by turning on a lathe are surfaces of revolution. It is a characteristic of a surface of revolution that any plane perpendicular to the axis will have a circle as its line of intersection with the surface.

In architecture, columns, circular towers, circular buildings, conical roofs, domes, niches, balusters, vases, urns, and fountains are examples of surfaces of revolution. They add a great deal of interest to architectural forms.

CYLINDERS. The shadow-casting lines of a cylinder are its two vertical shade lines and the semicircles connecting them on the top and bottom, as shown in the pictorial view of Fig. 158A.

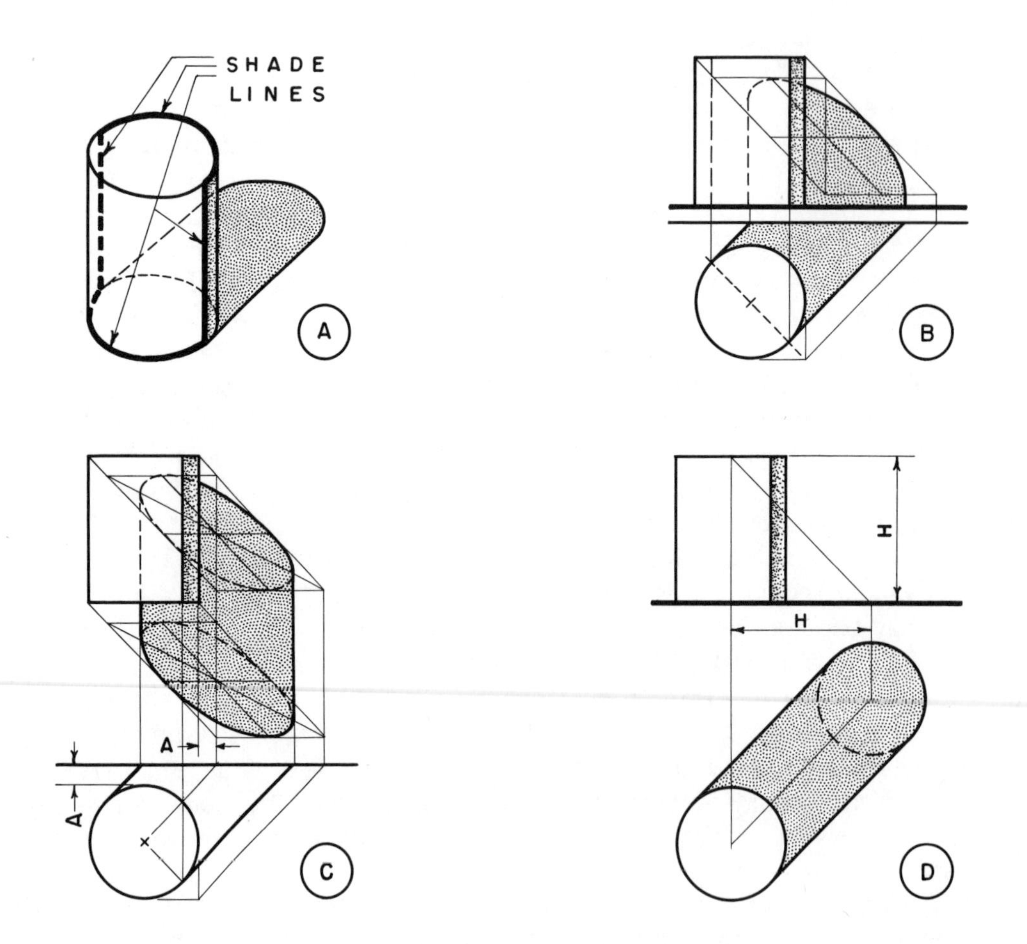

FIG-158 SHADES AND SHADOWS OF CYLINDERS

The shadow is here represented as falling on a plan plane. In Fig. 158B the vertical shade lines in the elevation are found by finding the tangent points of light on the plan. The most accurate method of determining the points of tangency is to draw the perpendicular to the tangents. The shadows of the vertical shade lines may then be determined by 45° projection and the shadow from the top by any of the methods used for shadows of circles.

When the entire shadow of the cylinder falls on the same plane, the complete shadows of the circles of the top and bottom can be found and then connected by tangent lines, Fig. 158C elevation, and D plan. The shadows can be constructed directly on the elevation by using measurement A and on plan by using H as shown.

The shadow in a hollow semicylinder is shown in Fig. 159 I. The shadow begins at the shade point A. The curving part of the shadow outline made by the shade line on the top edge of the cylinder is found by the point method. The curved shadow in Fig. 159 II is the reverse of the plan shape and is drawn with a compass.

The shadow of a square block or abacus on a cylinder is the shadow of its two shade lines on the lower edge. These shade lines are shown in plan of Fig. 159 III as A–B, which is perpendicular to elevation, and B–C, which is parallel to front elevation and casts a circular shadow on the cylinder. This circular shadow is the reverse of the plan shape of the front of the abacus and cylinder. The shadow of a projecting circular band onto a cylinder can best be found by the point method by taking points either at random or at the important positions shown in plan in Fig. 159 IV.

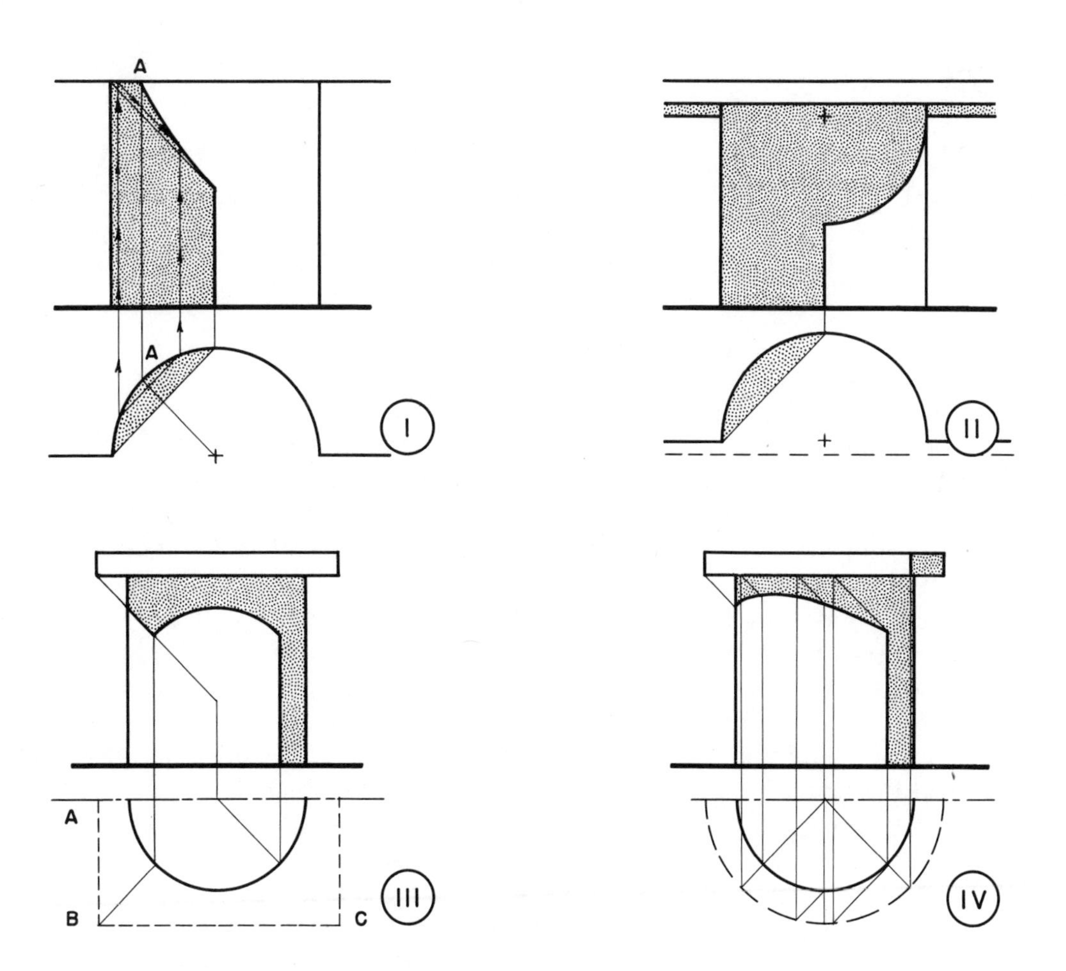

FIG-159 SHADOWS ON CYLINDRICAL SURFACES

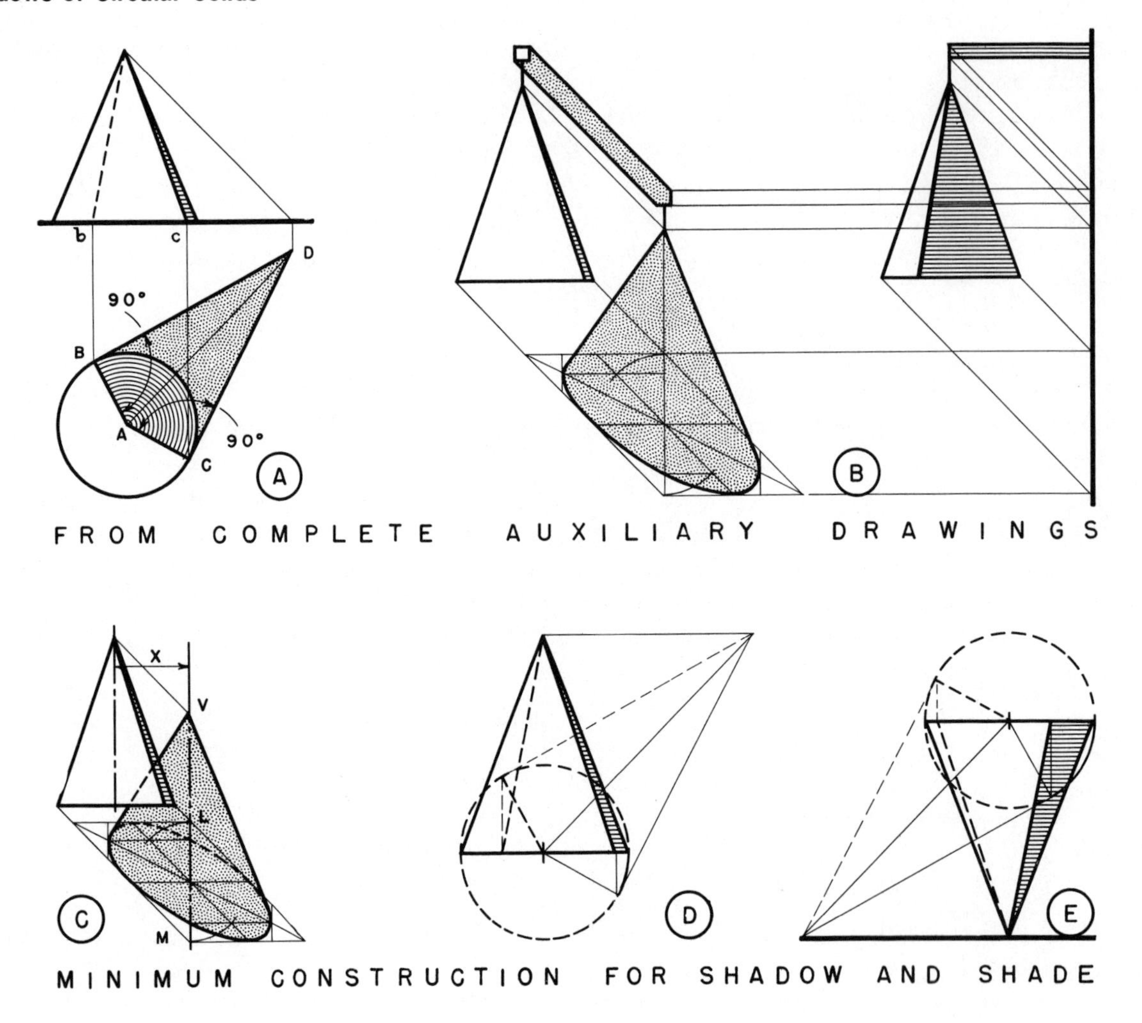

FIG-160 SHADES AND SHADOWS OF CONES

CONES. The shadow of a cone in either plan or elevation is found by connecting the shadow of the apex to the shadow of the base by tangent lines, Fig. 160A plan, and B elevation. In Fig. 160A the entire shadow of the cone falls in plan. The plan and the shadow of the base coincide. Point D, the shadow of the apex, is located by 45° projection from the elevation and plan of the apex. From point D lines D–B and D–C are drawn tangent to the circular base of the cone. The points of tangency B and C are located accurately by drawing lines A–B and A–C from A perpendicular to D–B and D–C respectively. A–B and B–C are the shade lines of the cone in plan view. The shade lines in elevation are located by finding the elevation positions b and c of plan points B and C and then connecting them to the elevation of the apex.

The method of determining the shade lines on a cone is, then, to locate the shadow of the cone in plan; find the points of tangency of the shadows of the shade lines and base of the cone in plan; locate these points of tangency in elevation and connect them to the apex of the cone.

In Fig. 160B the cone is suspended and its entire shadow falls on a wall plane. A complete side view is used to make the construction clear. In C the shadow of a similar cone is located without use of an auxiliary drawing. The distance X from the axis of the cone to the wall is laid out to the right of the axis in the elevation to locate a vertical line VM. The shadows of the apex and two corners of the tangent square around the base of the cone fall on this line. The construction for the shadow of the base can be completed as shown here and described on page 141.

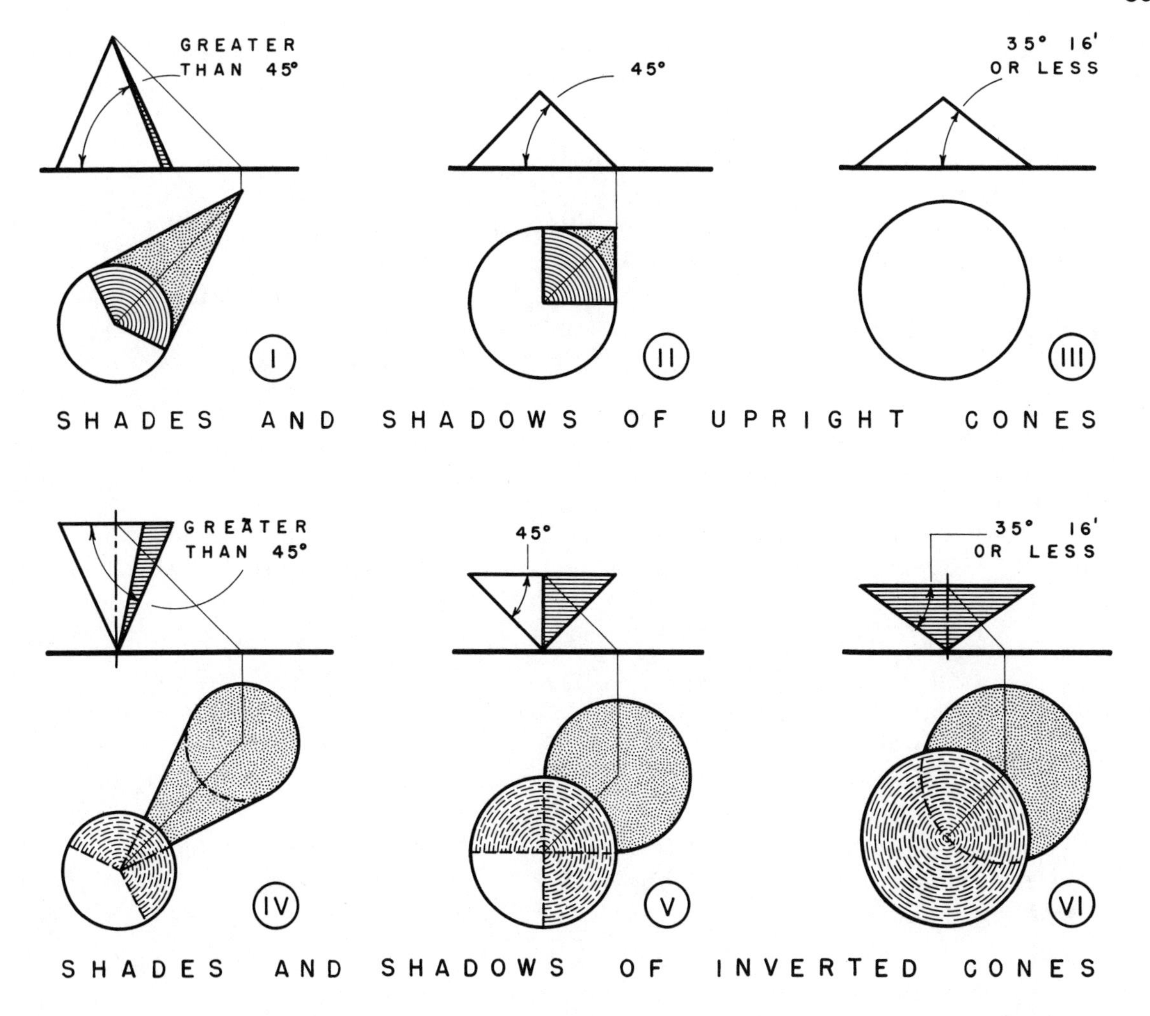

FIG-161 INFLUENCE OF CONE SHAPES ON SHADOWS

In Fig. 160D and E the necessary parts of the plans are drawn in on the elevations of the cones to find the shade lines. This method saves space and uses the minimum construction.

Figure 161 illustrates the variation of shade in elevation and plan, and of shadow in plan, for different shapes in upright and inverted right cones. An upright cone has a visible shade in elevation when its slope is steeper than 45°, Fig. 161 I. When its slope is 45°, its shadow on the plane of the base and its shade form a square in plan, Fig. 161 II. There is no visible shade in elevation. The inverted 45° cone has the right half of the elevation in shade and the left half in light. Three-fourths of the plan has a concealed shade as seen from above. When the slope of a cone is equal to or flatter than the angle of the true direction of light, its entire slant surface is in light, Fig. 161 III, when it is in an upright position; and the entire slant surface is in shade when the cone is inverted, Fig. 161 VI. The elevation shadows are not shown in Fig. 161. However, the complete elevation shadows of the different cones can be pretty accurately visualized from Fig. 160C, where the shadow will serve also for Fig. 161 I since the two cones are in the same position and have similar proportions. For the shadow in Fig. 161 IV the shadow of the apex is placed below the shadow of the base, but in other respects the shadow is similar to Fig. 160C. For 45° cones the point L of Fig. 160C will be the apex of the shadow of the upright cone and M of the inverted cone. The elevation shadows for Fig. 161 III and VI are shadows of the base circles only and are identical ellipses.

SPHERES. The sphere is used in architecture in buildings, domes, niches, light globes, and decorative and other forms. The shade line on a sphere is a great circle which has its plane perpendicular to the direction of light. In front view the complete shade line is an ellipse which has its major axis on the diameter perpendicular to the front view direction of light and its minor axis on the diameter parallel to the direction of light, Fig. 162A. The major axis is a diameter of the elevation of the sphere. The length of the minor axis can be determined by drawing lines at 30° with the major axis, through either of its extremities, to intersect with the line of the minor axis. Both axes being determined, the ellipse can be drawn in by trammel-point method, described on page 106, or by other methods.

As an alternate construction, several points on the shade line of a sphere can be determined by the following methods and the shade line drawn through these points. The Roman numerals of the following explanation refer to illustrations of Fig. 162B: (I) Find the two extremities A and B of the major axis by finding the tangent points of light at the top right and lower left. (II) Find the ends of the minor axis by drawing lines, at 30° to A–B from either point A or B to locate points C and D on the perpendicular bisector of A–B. (III) Find points on the horizontal and vertical center lines by drawing horizontal and vertical lines from points A and B. (IV) The tangent point of the true direction of light on the front view of the sphere gives the height of the lowest point of the shade line. The distance of the lowest point from the edge of the sphere can be determined by drawing the plan of the intersection with the sphere of a horizontal plane through this point and locating the shade point on this circle of intersection. Because of the symmetry of the shade line, the highest, extreme right, and extreme left points of the shade ellipse can be located by similar constructions or by measurements from the position of the lowest point. In (V) all twelve of these points have been located and the curve drawn through them.

As shown in Fig. 162C, the vertical center G–H of front view is the major axis g–h of side view of the shade-line ellipse, and the tangent points of light in the side view of the sphere are on the same horizontal level as those in front view. Furthermore, the horizontal center line E–F of front view is the major axis e–f of plan, and the tangent points of light in the plan view of the sphere are on the same vertical lines as the tangent points of light in its front view.

The shadow of a sphere can be found by the point method from the shade line of elevation and side elevation as shown in Fig. 162D or from elevation and plan.

The shadow can also be located by finding the shadows of a number of circles on the surface of the sphere and drawing the tangent line around them, Fig. 162E. In using this method the circles should be parallel to the surface on which the shadow falls, so their shadows will be circles.

The shadow in a semicircular niche with a half-dome (fourth of a hollow sphere) at the top is the shadow of the vertical left edge and the connecting top edge which is the part of the semicircle to the point of tangency of light on the upper right at A, Fig. 162F. The shadow of the vertical shade line falls on the cylindrical shape and can be found by 45° projection from plan. Any number of points on the shadow of the part of the curving shade line at the top of the niche which casts its shadow on the cylindrical shape can be found by the point method. The curving shadow begins at the shade point A on the top right tangent to the curve of the top of the niche and ends tangent to the vertical shadow line at point C. It is usually sufficiently accurate to find points A, B, and C, Fig. 162F, and draw in the shadow tangent to a 45° line at A and to a vertical line at C.

The method of 45° projection cannot be used to obtain points on the spherical surface of the niche because this surface cannot be represented by a line in plan or side view. A shadow point can be located on the spherical surface by the following procedure. (1) Draw a line D–E of Fig. 162G through the niche in plan parallel to the face of the wall around the niche. This line is the plan view of a vertical plane parallel to elevation plane and cutting through the niche. (2) Draw the intersection of the plane and niche in elevation. This is the arch shape projected up from points D and E. (3) Find the shadow of the semicircular edge of the niche on plane D–E. (4) The intersection F of this line with the line of intersection of the plane and niche gives a point on the shadow line. Any number of points can be located by repeating the above procedure with different planes.

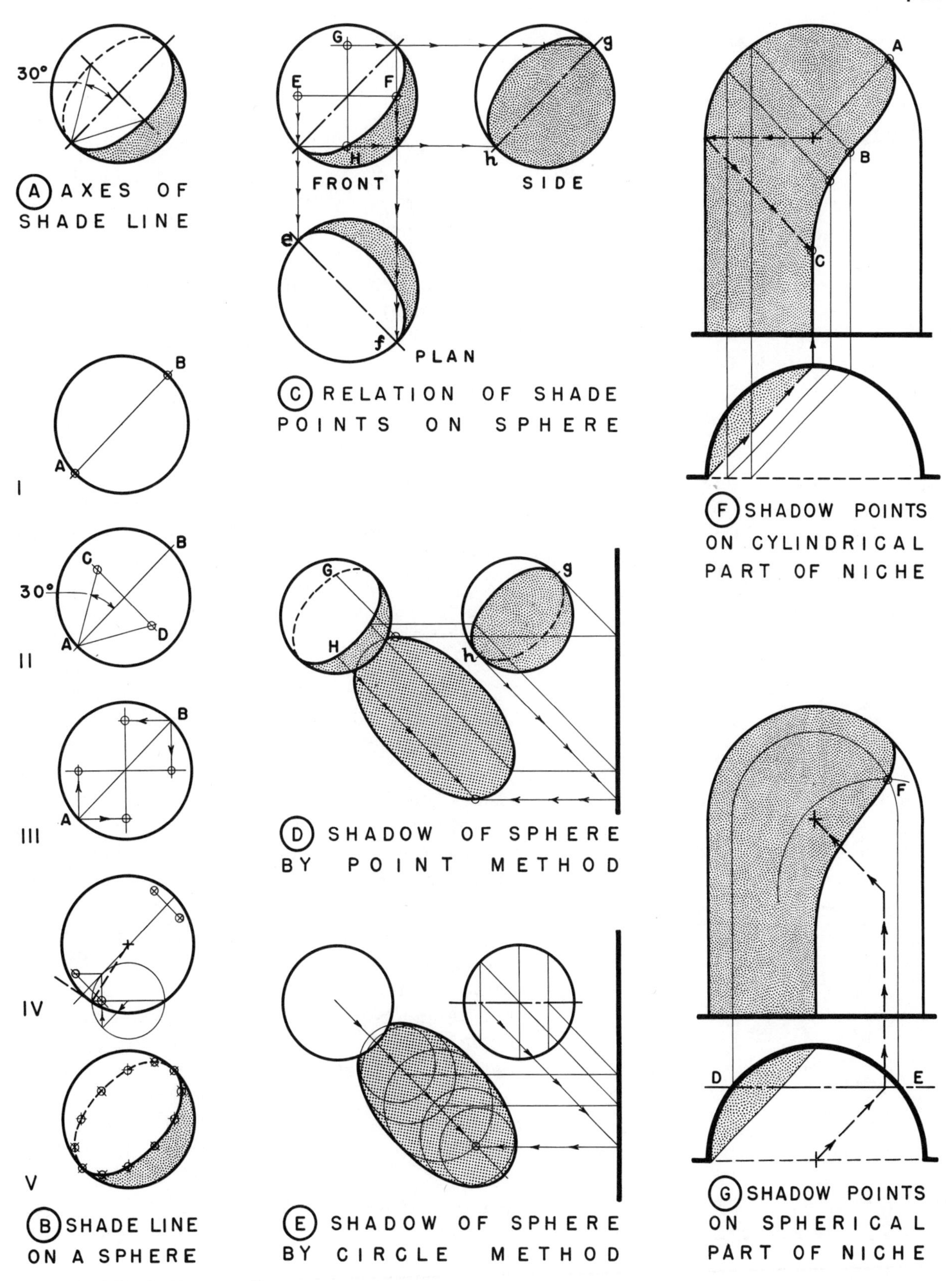

FIG-162 SHADES AND SHADOWS OF SPHERICAL SHAPES

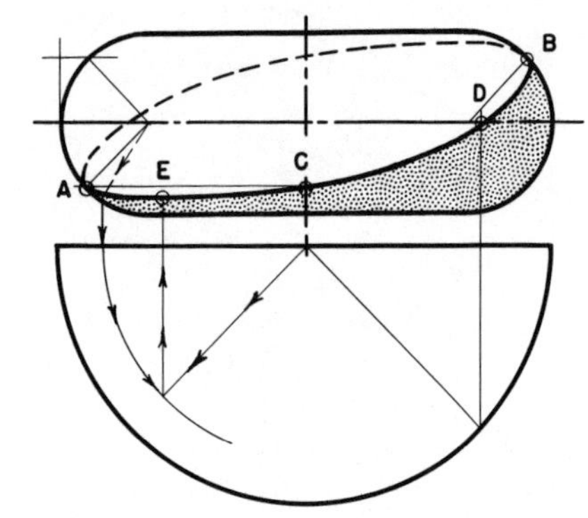

Ⓐ THE SHADE LINE ON A CONVEX MOLDING

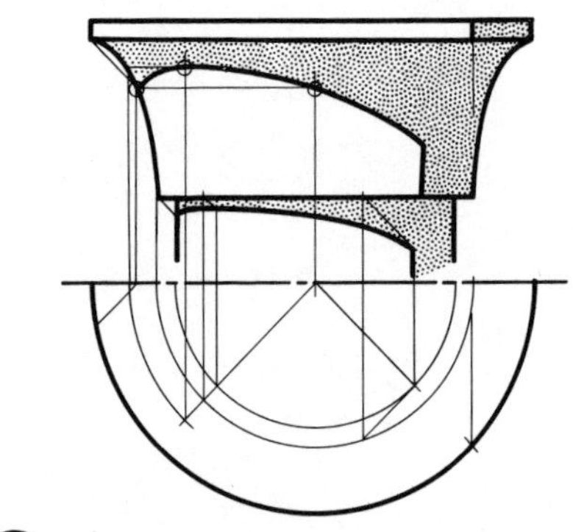

Ⓑ THE SHADOW OF A SMALL PROJECTION

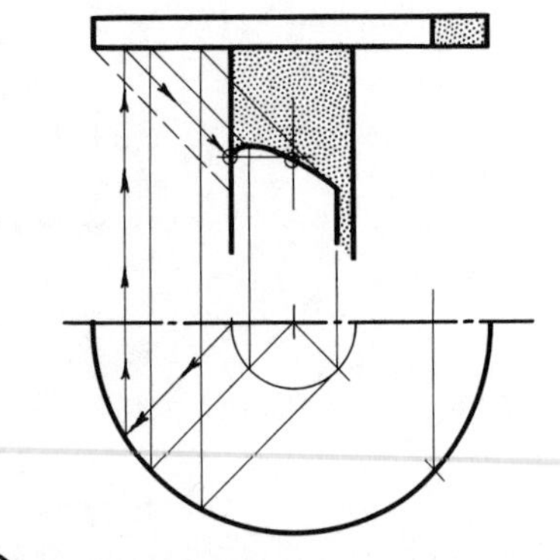

Ⓒ THE SHADOW OF A LARGE PROJECTION

FIG-163 THE METHOD OF IMPORTANT POINTS

SHADOW-CASTING METHODS. The method of 45° projection has been used for practically all the preceding examples. It is the simplest and most useful of all shadow-casting methods. However, there are some problems which cannot be solved by this method. The draftsman should become familiar with all the following methods of finding shadows on surfaces of revolution and use the one which is best suited to each part of a problem.

The method of important points is an application of the method of 45° projection to locate the position of the shade or shadow line on a form at critical points. On a surface of revolution the points on the two edges, the center, and the highest, and lowest points are usually sufficient to allow the shade or shadow line to be drawn with reasonable accuracy. In Fig. 163A these five points have been located on a torus molding. The visible shade line on the elevation of the torus starts and ends at the 45° tangent points A and B at the lower left and top right edges of the molding. The shade line is on the same horizontal level at the center and left edge. Therefore the center point C can be located by drawing a horizontal line from point A to meet the vertical center line. The shade line of the torus coincides with the shade line of a tangent cylinder at the horizontal center line where the surface of the torus is tangent to the vertical cylinder. Therefore the point D can be located by finding the 45° tangent point on the plan of the greatest diameter of the torus which is its horizontal center line. The height of the low point E of the shade line can be found by using the true direction of light to determine the point of tangency on the left edge, as for a sphere. The horizontal position of the low point is then determined from the plan of the horizontal circle on which it occurs. It should be noted that the ends of the shade line are tangent to the profile of the torus at A and B and that they do not meet the profile at an angle. This method of important points may be used for other convex surfaces of revolution shapes as well as for the torus.

When the projection is slight, this method may also be used with reasonable accuracy to find points on the shadows of projecting shade lines of circular forms as shown in Fig. 163B. Only three points, the left edge, center, and high points, can be determined under projecting edges by this method when the profile of the surface receiving the shadow is curved or slanting, as at the top of this example. When the profile of the surface receiving the shadow is cylindrical, as in the case of the lower shadow band, any number of points can be determined by 45° projection. If the projection of the shade line is large in comparison with the diameter of the part of the object receiving the shadow, the method is too inaccurate, for it assumes that the extreme left edge of the shade line casts its shadow on the left profile of the object. The amount of error on an example and the correct construction for the left edge and center are illustrated in Fig. 163C. There is no error at the 45° point from using the true direction of light on the profile.

The method of auxiliary shadows can be used when the shade line is a circle or an arc. In Fig. 164 I the circular shadow of shade line A–B can easily be found on any parallel plane. The intersection of this shadow and the line of intersection of the plane and object gives a point on the shadow. Any number of points can be found by this method by using planes at different levels through the object. In the example a point Z is located on plane X–Y.

The miter plane or slicing method uses vertical miter planes parallel to light which intersect with the object. This method is especially useful where the form is complex and it is difficult to determine the location of the shadow-casting shade lines. The theory of this method has been explained in Fig. 138D and H. Its application to surfaces of revolution is shown in Fig. 164 II. The 45° triangle is used on the lines of intersection of the miter planes and object to determine shade and shadow points. The miter plane through the center of the object locates the narrowest parts of shadow areas and the widest parts of light areas. A single miter plane and its intersection are illustrated here. Several such constructions would be used in most cases.

The method of tangent surfaces is useful in locating points on the shade lines of vases, balusters, and other motifs which vary from the simple geometric solids in form. The location of one point on the shade line of an urn is shown in Fig. 164C. The point is found by drawing a cone tangent to the profile of the urn at the level where it is desired to find the point. The shade line of the tangent cone is then found. On the horizontal line C–D, representing the elevation of the circle of tangency of the cone and urn, the shade line of the cone and urn will coincide at point E. If, as in this example, the circle of tangency is used as the base of the cone the shade line of the cone need not be drawn in. A separate tangent cone construction must be used for each point located by this method.

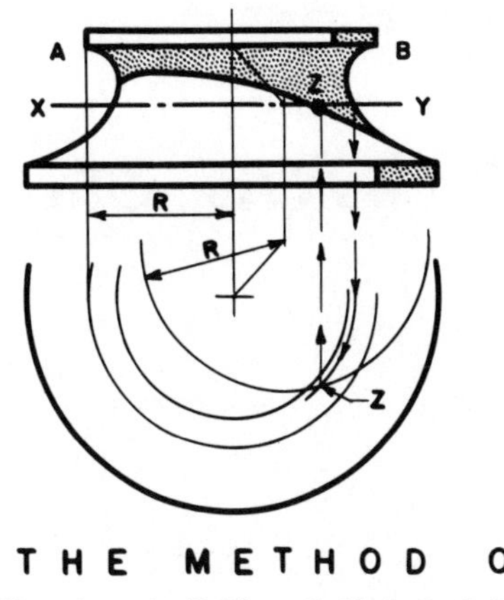

(I) THE METHOD OF AUXILIARY SHADOWS

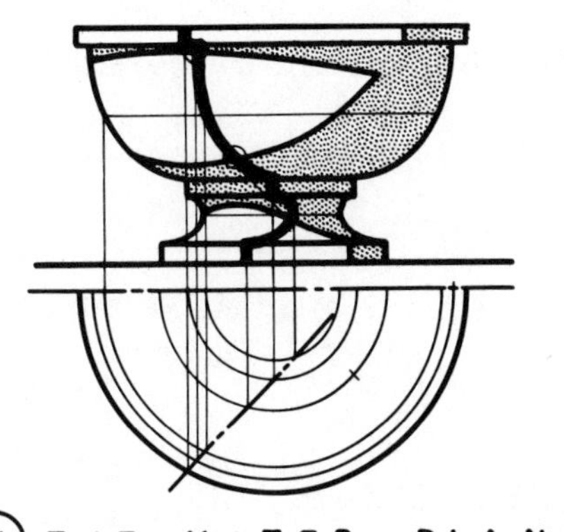

(II) THE MITER PLANE OR SLICING METHOD

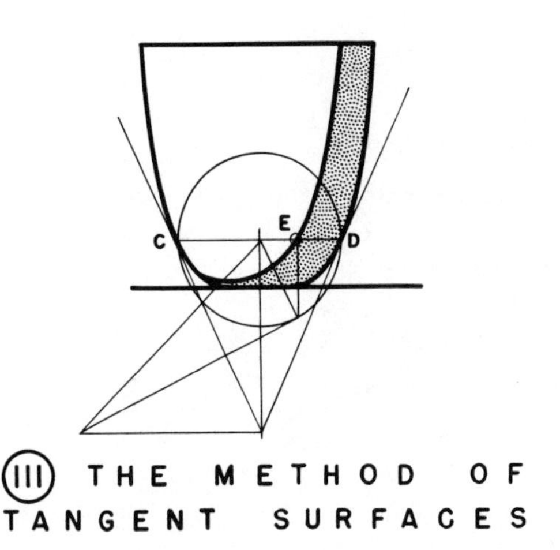

(III) THE METHOD OF TANGENT SURFACES

FIG-164 OTHER SHADOW-CASTING METHODS

CHAPTER 19
Shadows on Buildings

The shadows on buildings are made up of the shadows of their separate elements and of the shadows of the lines of the buildings themselves. The shadows of elements and lines have been treated in detail in preceding chapters. It is the purpose of this chapter to discuss some of the problems which are encountered in casting shadows on entire buildings and to provide several simplified illustrations of shadows on buildings. Although the problems of shadow-casting can most effectively be treated at large scale, as the problems of finding shadows of separate elements and even individual lines, the actual practice of shadow-casting frequently deals with complete buildings. The shapes of the masses of buildings are not always presented in the most effective way by using the conventional direction of light.

REVERSING THE DIRECTION OF LIGHT. A source of light from the right side of the elevation instead of from the left will often give more interesting shadows where the plan shapes extend forward on the right. In the example of Fig. 165A the conventional direction of light from the left gives a monotonous horizontal shadow from the roof onto the wall, and does not bring out the different projections of the mass shapes of the building. When the direction of light is changed to come from the right, there are additional shadows which express the projections of the walls, and the cornice shadow is broken up, Fig. 165B. Such a change in the direction of light is justified whenever it produces shadows which are more interesting or which make the design more readily understood. It may be done to produce the effect of late afternoon or early morning in a rendering.

THE ANGLE OF LIGHT. Sometimes a shadow falls in a position where its outline does not effectively explain the design. Figure 165C shows the shadow of the cornice falling exactly on the line of the top of the window opening. The shadow of the edge of the porch roof comes at the bottom of the window, and most of the top members of the cornice are in shadow. When an angle of less than 45° with the horizontal is used, all of these shadows are materially improved. In this case, Fig. 165D, a 35° angle was used in elevation and side elevation and the 45° direction used in plan. This variation of the direction of light does not appreciably complicate the construction of the shadow. The angle of light can be changed whenever awkward positions of shadows occur with the conventional direction of light, or whenever the delineator wishes to secure a different pictorial effect than can be secured by using the conventional direction.

REPEATING SHAPES. Identical features of the architecture must produce identical shadows. In working out such shadows the draftsman often works out each of the shadows with scrupulous care and fails to see that he has allowed disturbing variations because of inaccuracies of construction. The best procedure is to work out one example of the repeating shadow as carefully as possible, then duplicate this shape for all the repetitions, Fig. 165E and F. This principle applies to the simple shadows of windows, cornices, and pilasters, as well as to more complex shapes.

SHADOWS ACROSS CURVING AND OFFSET SHAPES OF A BUILDING. These shadows are often disturbing to the delineator because they do not seem to be logical. Figure 165G shows a shadow which is often puzzling to the draftsman. The extending wall on the left casts a 45° straight-line shadow over the cylindrical wall shape and the adjoining wall. Since the line casting this shadow is seen as a point in this view the shadow will appear to be straight for any direction of light which produces a shadow on the curving surface. The only way in which this shadow can be shown curved is by looking at the object from a different angle. This can be accomplished by using a pictorial drawing, as at H, in which the line casting the shadow is seen as a line, not as a point as in G.

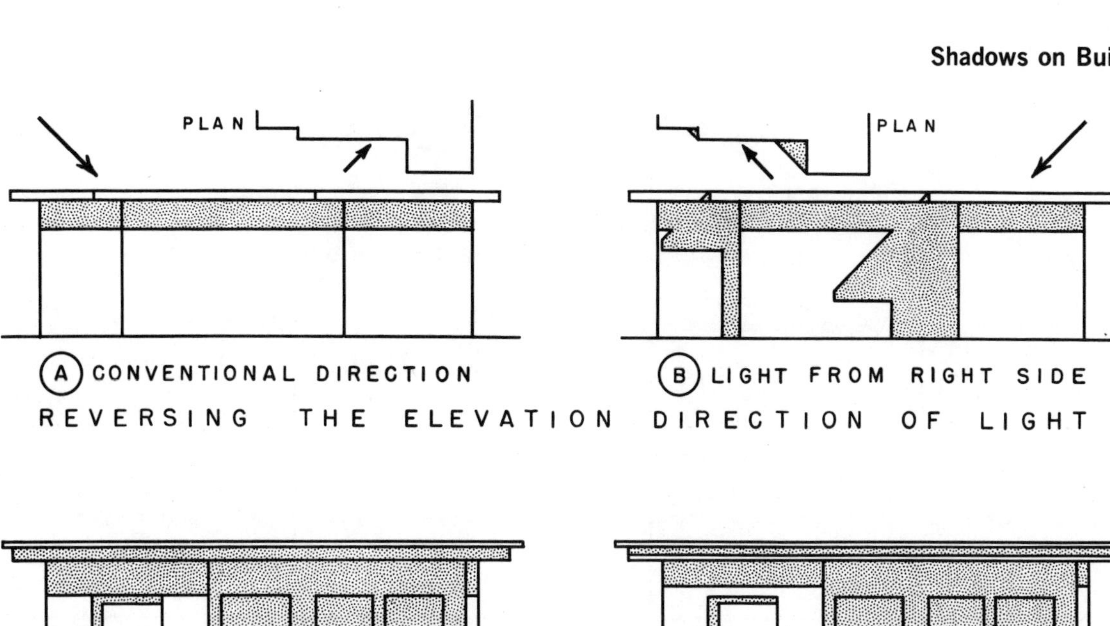

REVERSING THE ELEVATION DIRECTION OF LIGHT

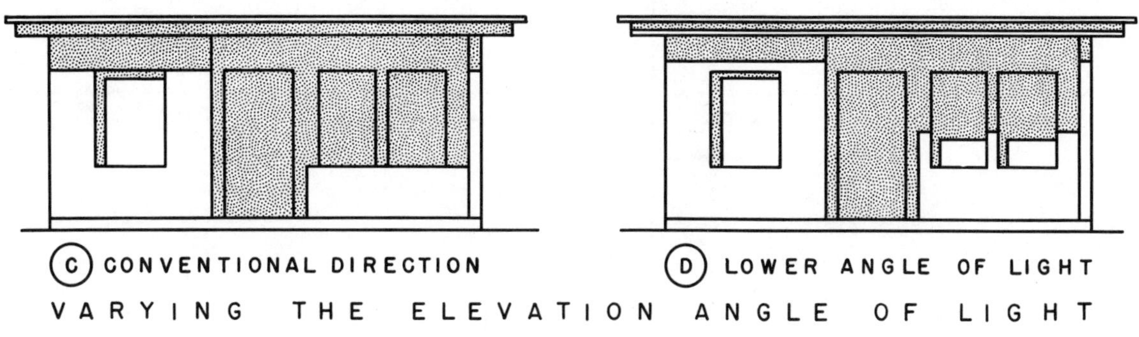

VARYING THE ELEVATION ANGLE OF LIGHT

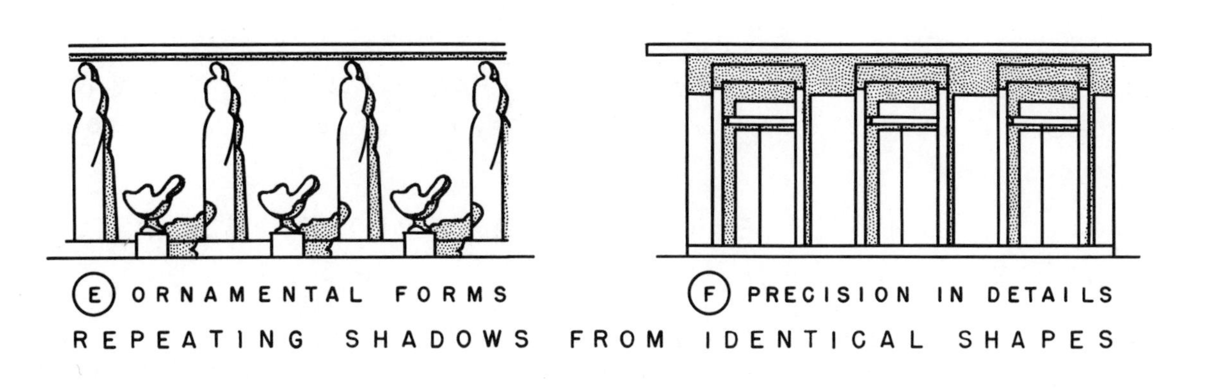

REPEATING SHADOWS FROM IDENTICAL SHAPES

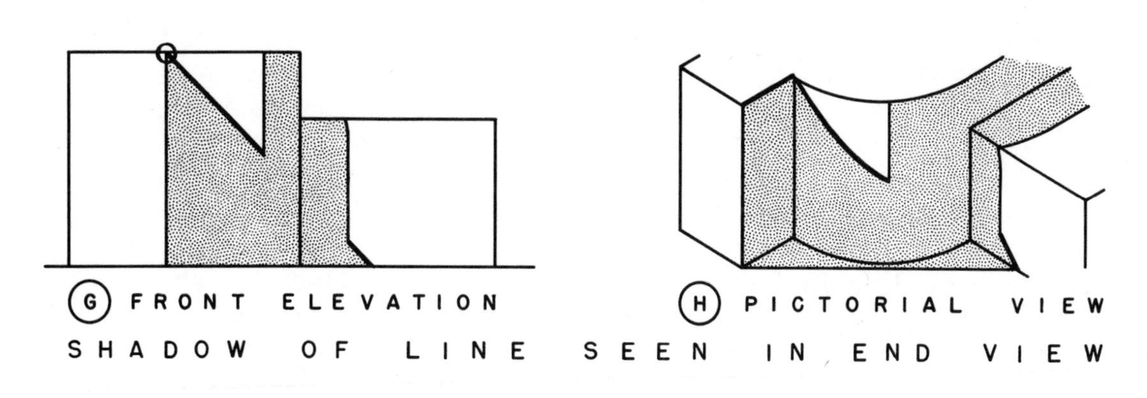

SHADOW OF LINE SEEN IN END VIEW

FIG-165 SHADOWS ON BUILDINGS

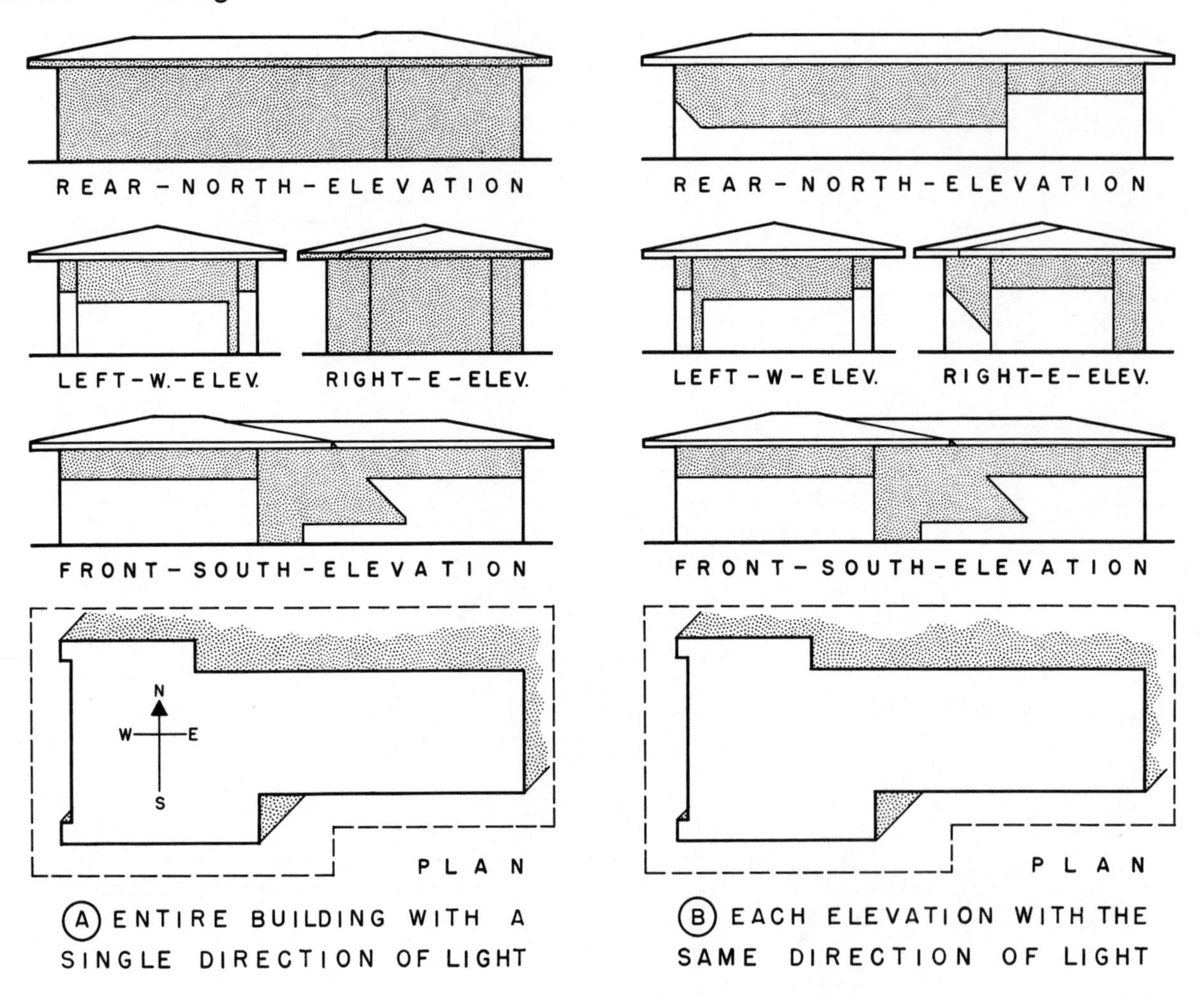

FIG-166 LIGHT DIRECTION FOR A SET OF ELEVATIONS

Quite frequently the person who is casting shadows on elevations of a building for the first time works out shadows on the principal elevation and then is puzzled about treatment of the other three views. Two general procedures can be followed.

1–The direction of light for the entire building can be assumed to be that used for the principal elevation. Then the left elevation will have a 45° direction of light from the right (with front 45° from the left) and the rear and right side views will be completely in shadow, Fig. 166A. While this is a consistent method of treating the shadow-casting problem for a set of elevations, there are some objections to it. Only two of the elevations will have shadows cast on them, and those two use different directions of light. The two which are completely in shadow will be dark and blank.

2–The direction of light can be assumed to be the same on each of the four elevations with the direction for plan shadows conforming with the front elevation direction, Fig. 166B. While in theory this may be illogical, in practice it is sometimes more satisfactory than the first method. It makes the elevations easier to understand and gives greater uniformity of dark and light.

If we assume that the primary purpose of shadows on drawings is to explain the design shapes of the object, then the second method is far superior. Drawings which are in complete shadow are no easier to understand than drawings without shadows. However, if the purpose is to show lighting conditions on the building at a specific time, the first method must be used.

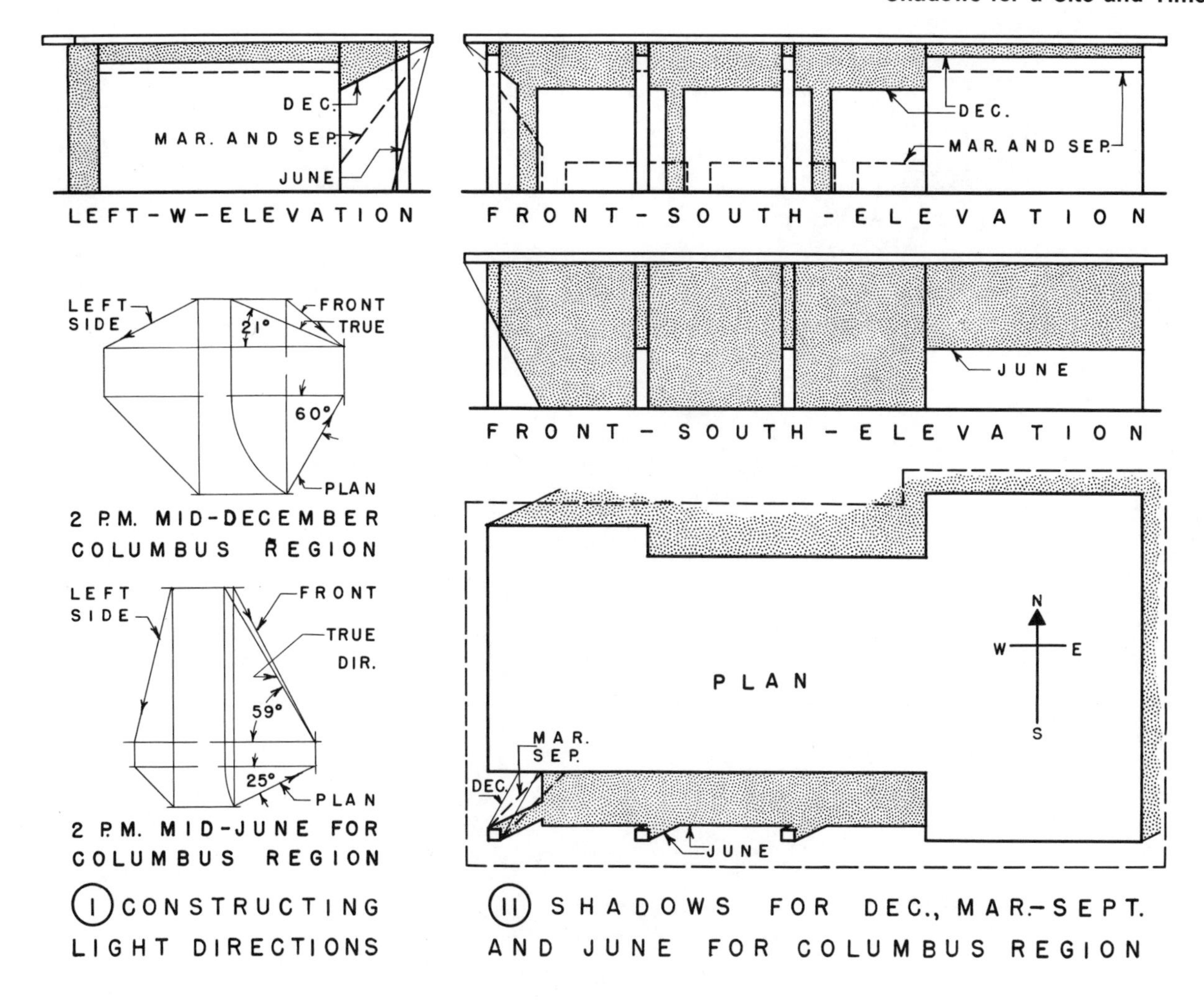

FIG-167 SHADOW CONSTRUCTION FOR A SITE AND TIME

When the plan direction of light is not 45°, the front and side elevation directions cannot be the same angle. It is therefore necessary to construct the angle of one elevation direction when the other is assumed. The shadows are then worked out using these three directions.

Whenever exactness of shadows for a particular location and time are desired, it is possible to obtain the information necessary for their construction from climatic data. One source of such information is the "House Beautiful Climate Control Guide" published in bulletins of the American Institute of Architects for regions of the United States. This guide gives approximate data on (1) the hourly compass direction of the sun in a horizontal plane for each midmonth and (2) the midmonth sun height at hourly intervals throughout the day. The first of these items is then the plan direction of light and the second the true direction of light. It is possible to construct the two elevation directions of light and work out shadows for a definite site and time from these data, Fig. 167 I.

In the example given in Fig. 167 II the shadows have been worked out for a site in the Columbus, Ohio region on the two elevations in sunlight at 2:00 p.m. for December 15th and June 15th. These times pretty well contrast the two extremes of sun height throughout the year. The average direction is most nearly given by the March and September data. This average for a building facing south is almost exactly 45° in plan and about 52° in elevation. The shadows from these average directions are shown by dotted lines in the elevations at the top of the sheet.

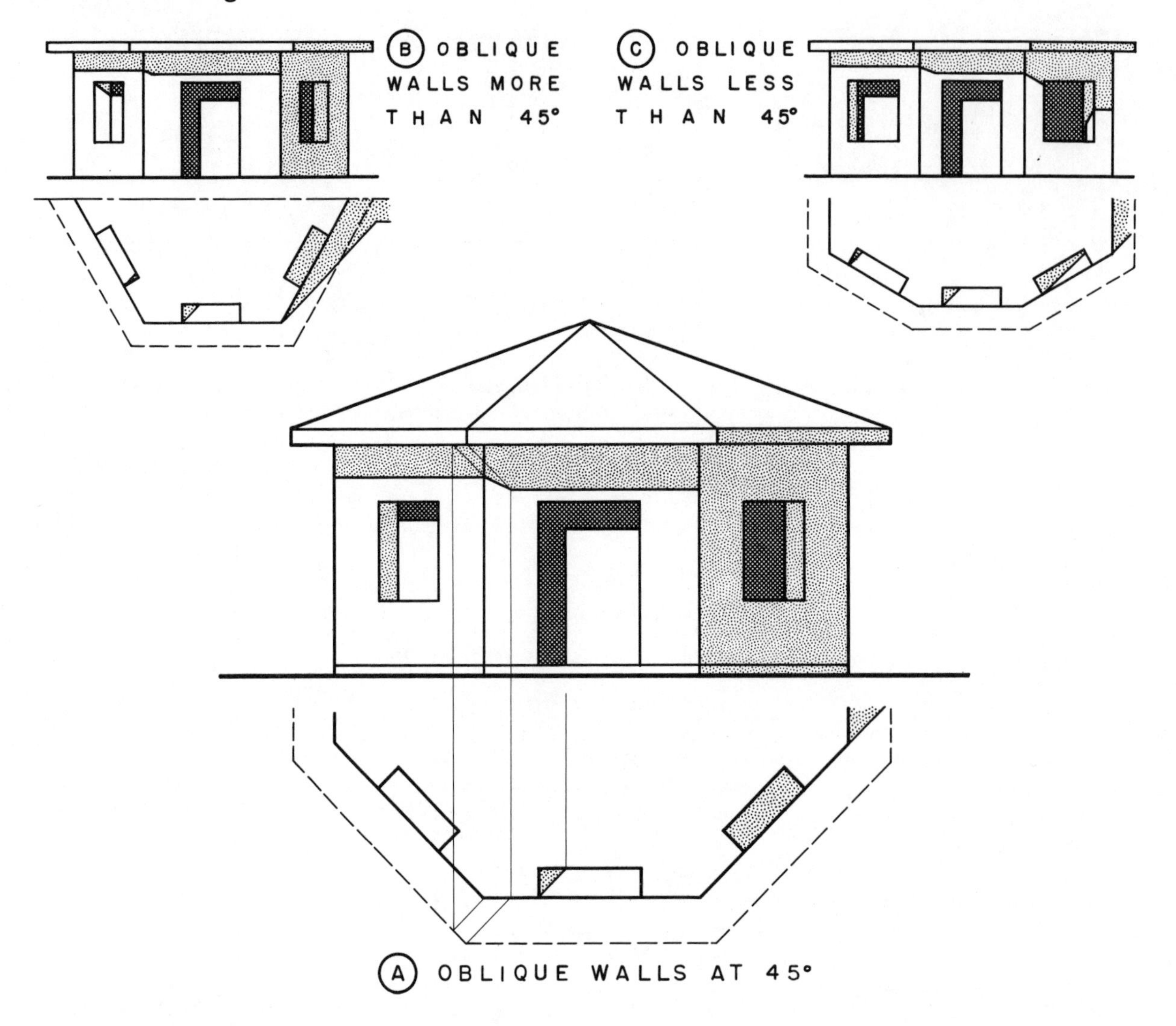

FIG-168 SHADOWS ON BUILDINGS WITH OBLIQUE WALLS

Buildings with oblique walls may be symmetrical on both horizontal axes with polygonal plans, symmetrical on one horizontal axis, or entirely unsymmetrical. The examples used here are all of the polygon type with an oblique wall on each side of the elevations. This type gives the maximum shadow variation, and the theory applies to unsymmetrical buildings as well as to symmetrical.

The shadows on a simple octagonal building with 45° oblique walls are shown in Fig. 168A. The right face of the octagon is entirely in shade. The wall on the left is turned toward the light and has a smaller shadow under the cornice than has the center wall. Part of the cornice shade line of the left side casts its shadow on the front wall. Although the door and windows have the same depth into the wall, the window on the left has a smaller shadow than the door at the top because of the direction in which it is turned. There is no shadow on the left edge of the window, but the vertical surface perpendicular to the wall is in shade. When the oblique wall is at more than 45°, as in the case of a hexagonal building, the edge of the left window opening is in light, Fig. 168B. When the oblique walls are at an angle of less than 45° with the front, the right wall is partly in light. There is a vertical shadow in the left window, Fig. 168C. The left and center walls have the maximum difference in shadow heights under the cornices when the side walls are at 45°.

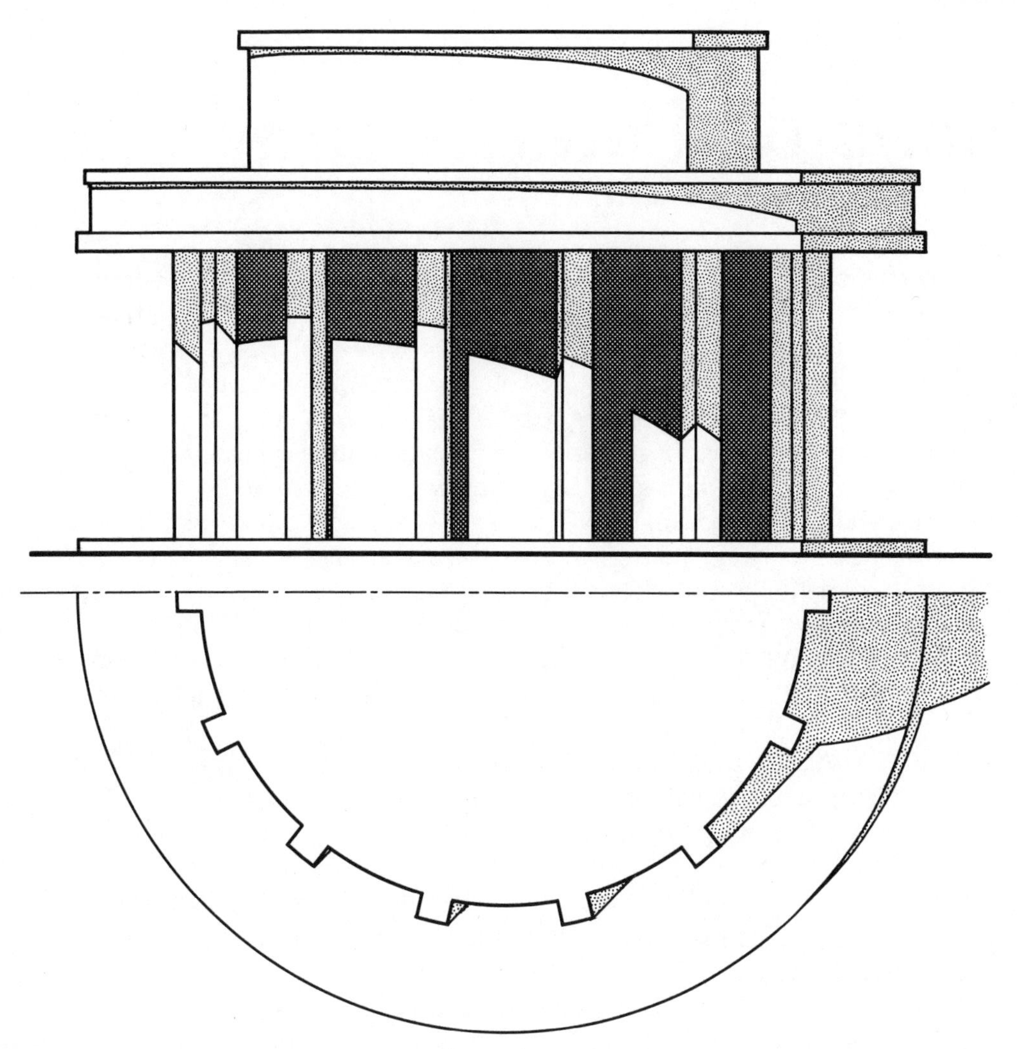

FIG-169 SHADOWS ON A CIRCULAR BUILDING

The circular building with piers, columns, or windows repeating around the curved part presents a continually changing view of the surfaces and changing shadow conditions and shapes, Fig. 169. On the parts of a curving wall most nearly perpendicular to light, the reveals will make small shadows or none at all. Where outside surfaces approach a direction parallel to light, shadow widths and depths increase greatly. When the shadow shapes are drawn correctly, they are interesting and expressive. When they are incorrectly drawn, surfaces may appear warped and details crude.

A reasonable attitude should be adopted toward shadow-casting. The objective is to obtain a precise representation of the shadows. The easiest and quickest method of obtaining this result is the best. There are frequently shadows on details, sculpture, or ornamental forms which are very difficult to work out. The person who is able to visualize their shapes can often draw these shadows satisfactorily without constructing them.

Shadows should never be faked; that is, they should never be drawn in without knowing that their basic sizes and shapes are correct. However, there are many people who can draw in shadows on ornamental forms and architectural details as expressively and faithfully as they can be worked out by the more mechanically minded person.

CHAPTER 20
Shadows on Paraline Drawings

A pictorial drawing offers a more complex problem in shadow-casting than a multi-view drawing because it shows more of the object. In each multi-view drawing only one of the three sets of typical planes is visible. Pictorial drawings show all three sets of typical planes. In a multi-view drawing, therefore, shadows are visible on only one of the sets of typical planes, while in a pictorial drawing shadows are visible on all three typical planes. Figure 170A gives a comparison between the shadows of a simple object as shown in an elevation and a pictorial drawing. Although they are more complex, shadows on pictorial drawings are often easier to understand.

There are two general methods of approach to the working out of shadows on a pictorial drawing: (1) the shadows may be worked out on the necessary multi-view drawings and then transferred by measurements to the pictorial drawing; (2) the shadows may be located directly on the pictorial drawing either by measurements or by using the direction of light and the directions of shadows of typical lines on the typical planes. The first method uses less theory and requires more work. The second method is more difficult to understand but is shorter and less tedious to use.

SHADOWS ON PARALINE DRAWINGS. The shadows on different types of paraline drawings present similar problems and are solved by the same methods in most cases. Since the same principles and theory apply to shadows on all of these types of pictorial drawings, the following explanation is given for all of them.

A–The shadow is parallel to the line making the shadow when the line is parallel to the surface on which the shadow falls. This principle is illustrated by the shadows of the front edge of the roof on the wall and ground in Fig. 170A.

B–The shadows of parallel lines are parallel when they fall on the same plane or on parallel planes. The shadows of the square posts in Fig. 170B are parallel when they fall on the wall surfaces. Likewise, the shadows of the posts on the horizontal planes of the floor and ground are parallel to each other. The lines made with long dots connect the top right front corner of each post with its shadow. They are therefore lines of rays of light connecting points on the object and the shadows of those points. Since the rays of light are considered to be parallel in shadow-casting, these lines are parallel in any kind of axonometric or oblique drawing.

C–The shadow of any plane figure on a surface parallel to the plane of the figure is identical in shape, size, and direction with the figure. This principle is illustrated in the shadows of the horizontal rectangle, vertical circle, and horizontal octagon of Fig. 170C.

Figure 170D illustrates the method of constructing the direction of light on an axonometric or oblique drawing by measurements. In this example the height of the vertical corner A–B is laid out in the direction of each of the other two axes to locate point D, the shadow of A. When using the conventional direction of light A–B, B–C, and C–D represent equal distances which are laid out below, back of, and to the right of A at the correct scale. Since point D is the shadow of point A, the line A–D is the direction of light for the drawing and furthermore line B–D is the shadow of the vertical line A–B on the horizontal plane. All the rays of light and all the shadows of vertical lines on horizontal surfaces in a drawing using these directions will be parallel to A–D and B–D respectively.

When using the 45° plan direction of light in isometric drawing, in symmetrical dimetric drawing, and in 45° plan oblique drawing, the line B–D will be a T-square line when one side of the object is in shadow. That is, it will actually be a horizontal line on the drawing. In all other oblique drawings and unsymmetrical dimetric, the line B–D will be an oblique line, Fig. 170E.

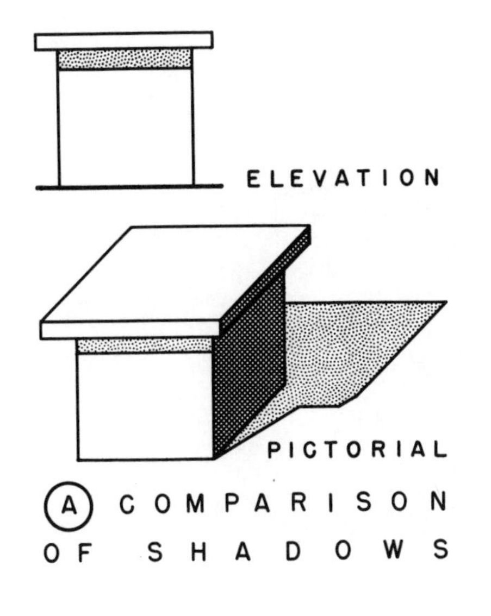

(A) COMPARISON OF SHADOWS

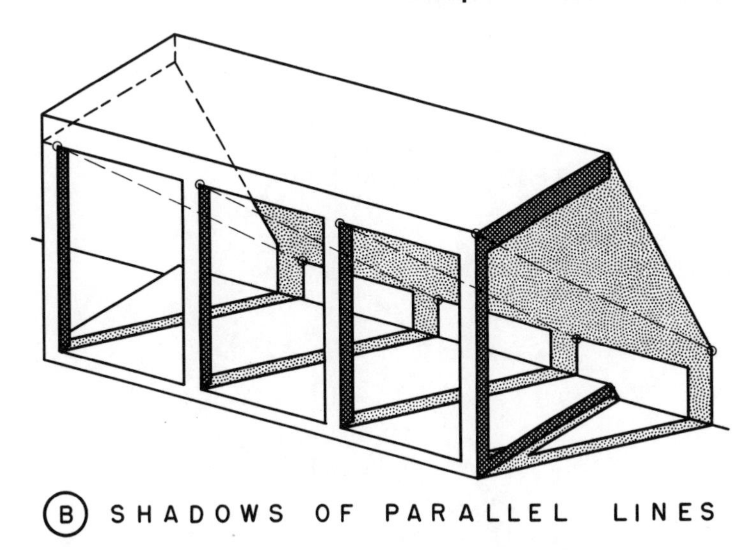

(B) SHADOWS OF PARALLEL LINES

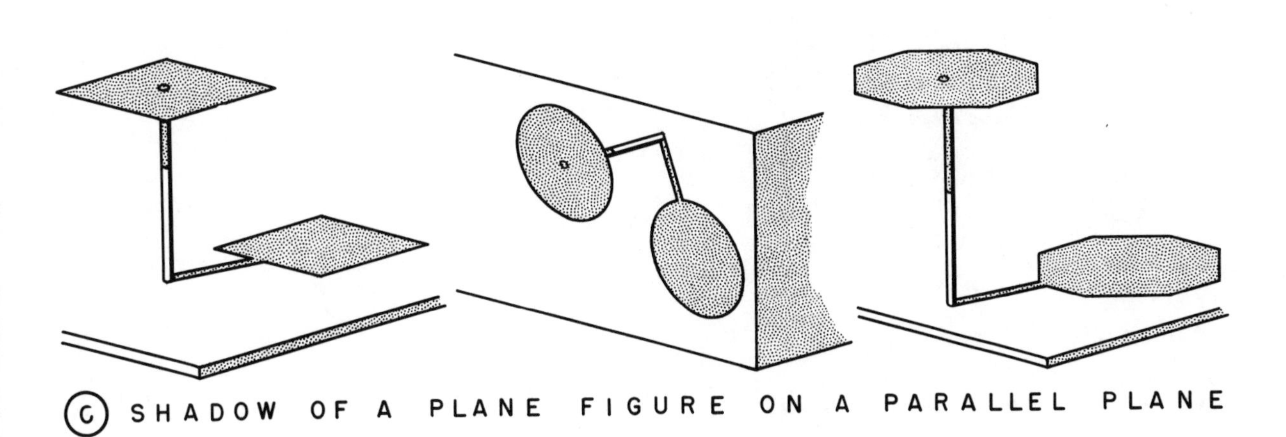

(C) SHADOW OF A PLANE FIGURE ON A PARALLEL PLANE

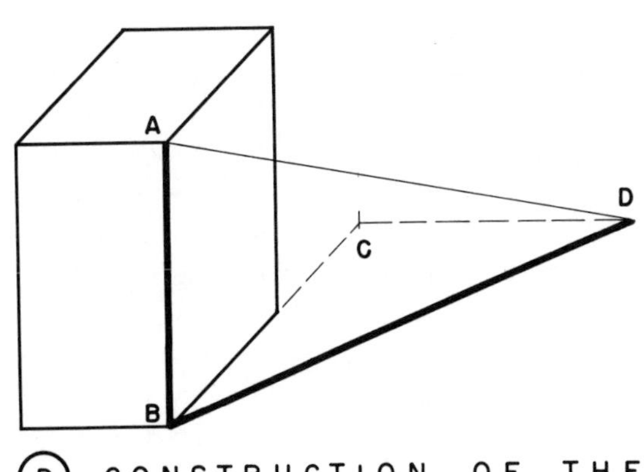

(D) CONSTRUCTION OF THE DIRECTION OF LIGHT

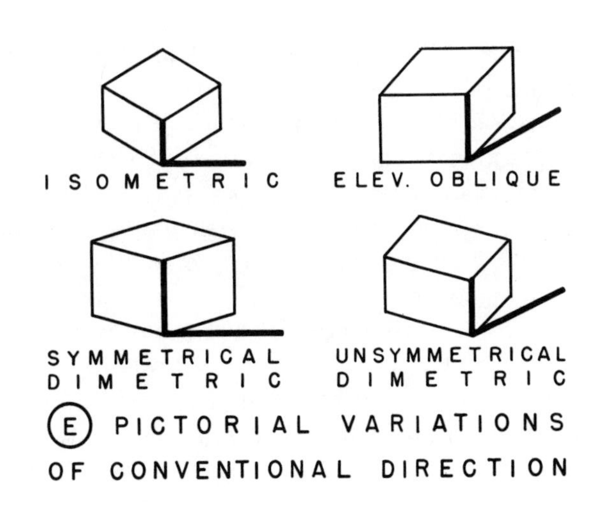

(E) PICTORIAL VARIATIONS OF CONVENTIONAL DIRECTION

FIG-170 PRINCIPLES OF SHADOWS ON PARALINE DRAWINGS

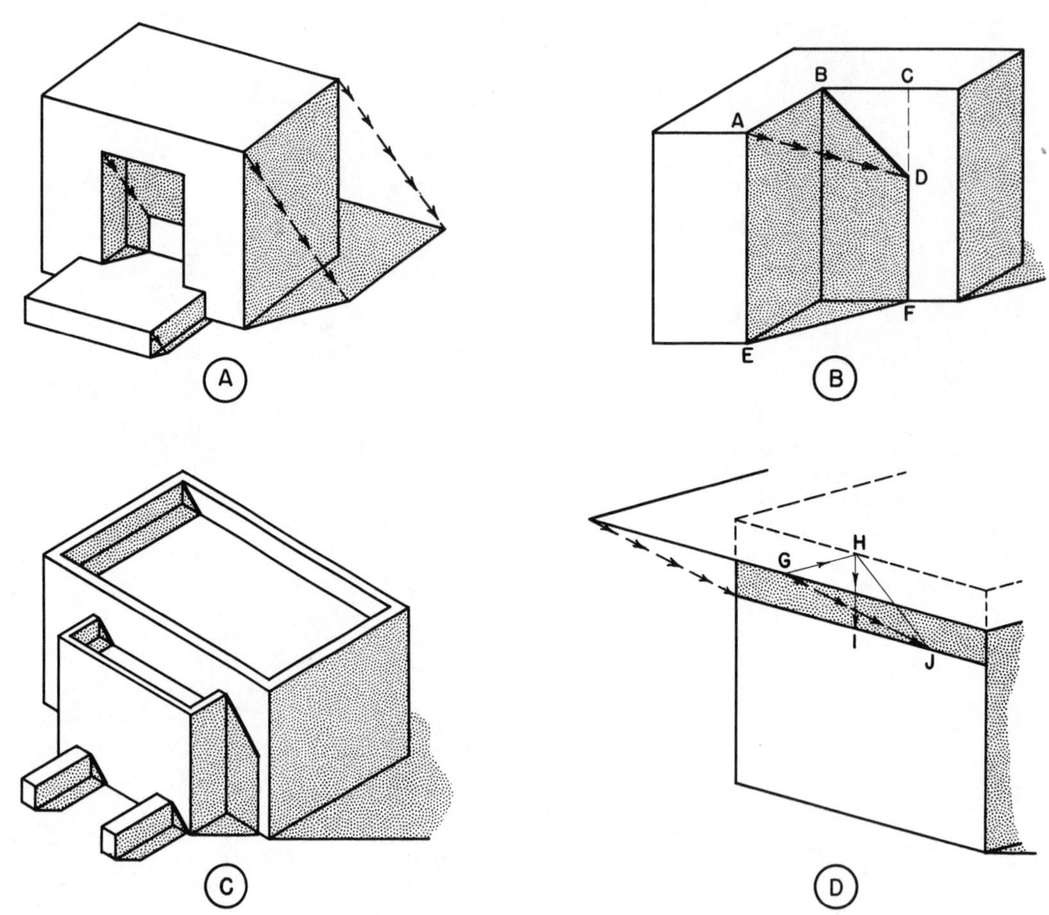

FIG-171 PARALINE SHADOW CONSTRUCTION

Figure 171A illustrates the use of the principles of parallel lines, the direction of light, and the direction of the shadows of vertical lines on horizontal surfaces to construct shadows. In this illustration all of the shadow lines are either parallel to the lines making the shadows or they are the shadows of vertical lines on horizontal surfaces. In Fig. 171B the line A–B introduces another type of shadow in the problem. This horizontal line is parallel to one of the axes of the drawing and is perpendicular to the wall plane on which the shadow falls. Its shadow B–D is therefore a 45° line on the wall surface when the conventional direction of light is used. The direction of B–D can be determined by the same construction used in Fig. 171A. From point E, a line E–F is drawn in the direction of shadows of vertical lines on horizontal surfaces. Where this line strikes the wall at F, a vertical line is drawn to meet a light direction line from A to point D. Then B is connected to D to complete the shadow outline. Point D can also be located by measuring equal distances to the right and down from B in the wall plane on which the shadow falls. Lines B–C and C–D represent such measurements. As shown in Fig. 171C, all lines perpendicular to a set of typical planes cast parallel shadows on those planes.

The depth of a shadow under a projecting band can be determined by using the direction of light at the corner when the equal projection carries around the corner, Fig. 171D. This construction is correct only when the plan direction of light is 45° so that the corner of the overhang casts its shadow on the corner of the wall. The depth of the shadow can also be determined by tracing a horizontal line G–H perpendicular to the wall from the shade line of the projection to its inter-

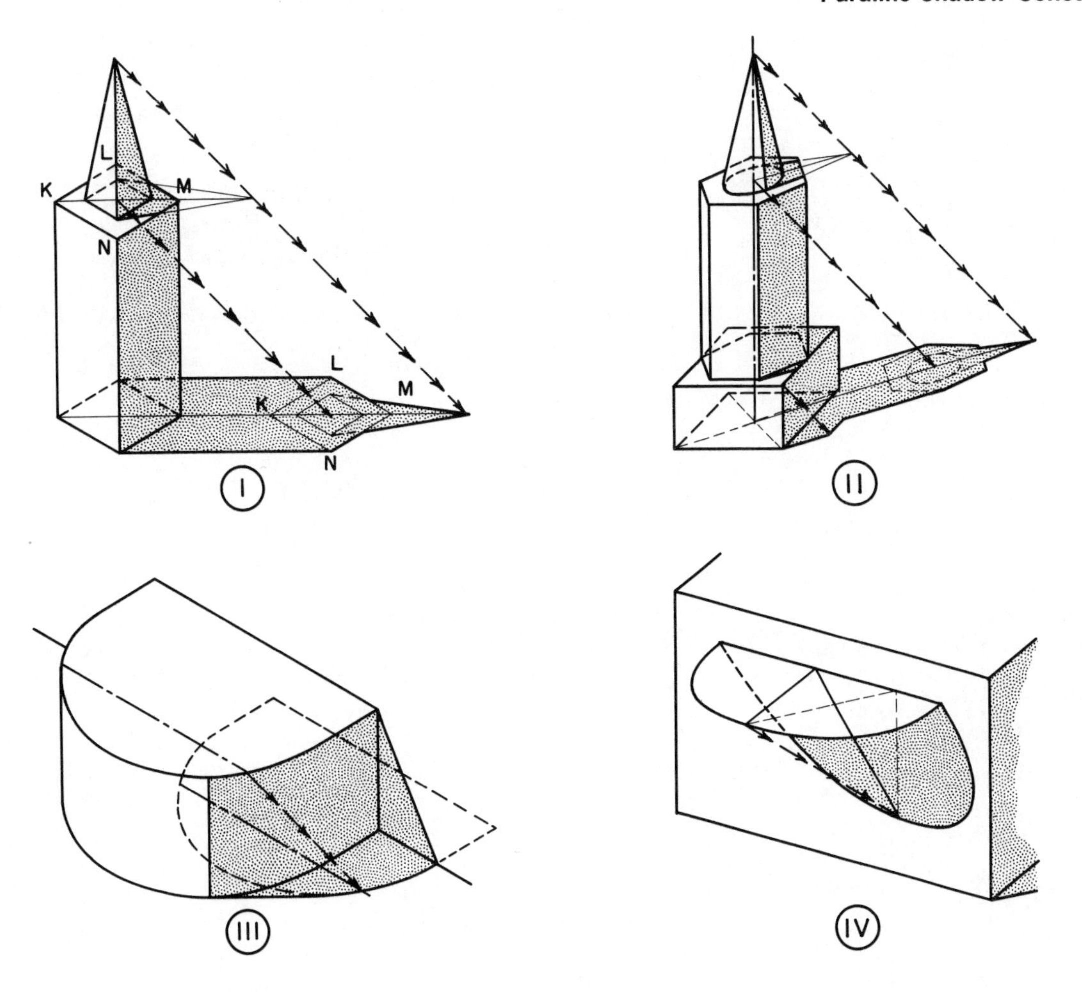

FIG-172 PARALINE SHADOW CONSTRUCTION

section with the wall surface, then measuring the same distance down from H to locate I, a point on the shadow line. The end of the imaginary shadow of G–H at J will give the same result.

Almost all the shadows on paraline drawings can be located by applying the principles of parallel lines and using the simple constructions previously explained. Figure 172 shows some additional examples of such problems. The construction of the shadow of the tower in Fig. 172 I on the horizontal plane at its base looks difficult but is actually quite simple. The shadow of any horizontal section such as K–L–M–N of the tower is exactly the same in shape, size, and direction as the section making the shadow. The shadow of the vertical center line of the tower can be located by using the direction of the shadow of a vertical line on a horizontal surface and the direction of light. The shadow section can then be located on the shadow of the center line and drawn to duplicate and parallel the section on the object. Lines drawn connecting the shadow sections complete the shadow outline. Figure 172 II shows the same tower in oblique drawing.

Another application of the principle of the shadow of a plane figure on a parallel plane is found in circular or irregular curves. Figure 172 III shows how such a shadow can be found by locating the shadow of one point then transferring the shape to the shadow position.

Figure 172 IV shows how the shadow of a projecting curved horizontal area can be located on the wall below it. This is done by finding the shadows of lines drawn from the shade line perpendicular to the wall to locate points on the shadow outline. The thin dotted lines show a second method of locating the same point.

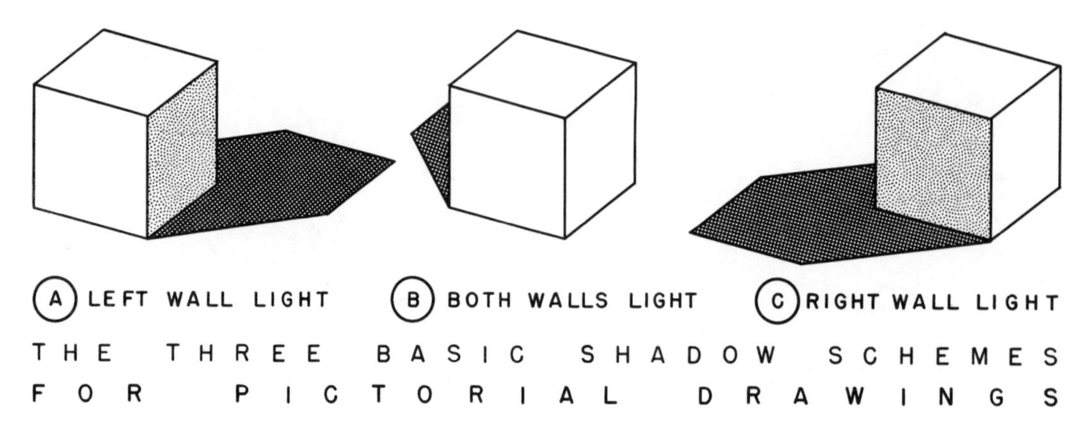

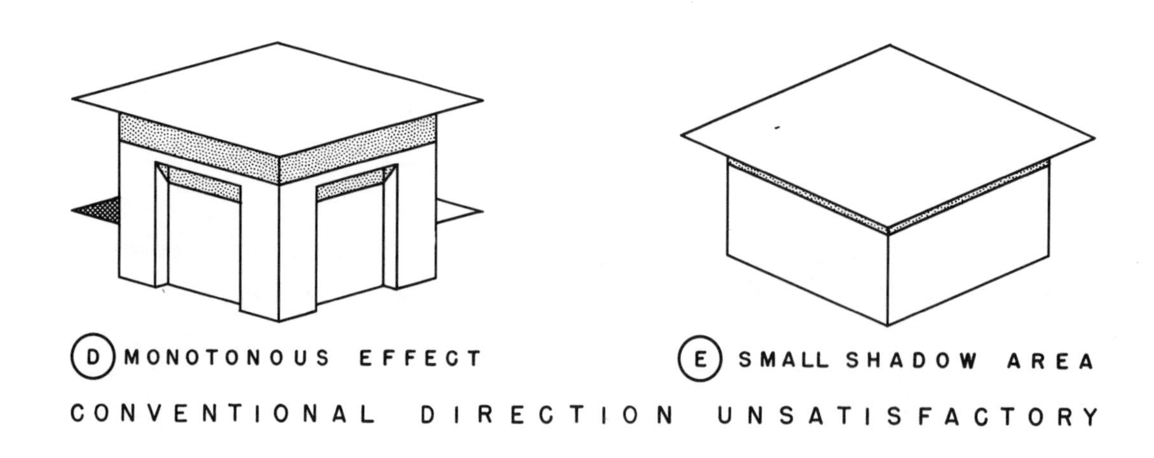

FIG-173 THE CONVENTIONAL DIRECTION OF LIGHT ON PARALINE DRAWINGS

There are three basic schemes for the direction of light for casting shadows on pictorial drawings, as shown in the illustrations of Fig. 173A, B, and C: (A) light from the left side with the light striking left wall planes and leaving all right wall planes completely in shadow; (B) light direction from the front so that light strikes both sets of wall planes; (C) light from the right side with light striking right wall planes and leaving all left wall planes completely in shadow.

When the conventional direction of light traveling equally in the three coordinate directions of the drawing is used, there is no variation possible in the shadow effect on a given drawing beyond that of the three basic schemes. However, with other relations of the direction of light to the planes and lines of the object, variation in shadow effect is possible in each of the basic schemes.

The conventional 45° direction of light may be unsatisfactory for some pictorial drawings. This direction of light may be unsatisfactory in either one or both of the following two ways on a pictorial drawing: (1) The plan direction of light may be so related to the object that the two visible sets of wall surfaces of the drawing are monotonously alike in shadow treatment and the shadows of vertical lines are concealed, as shown in Fig. 173D. (2) The conventional direction of light may be unsatisfactory on a pictorial drawing because: (a) the shadows of projecting horizontal edges may be entirely concealed; (b) such a small portion of them may be visible as to give a poor effect, Fig. 173E; (c) they may be too large; (d) the edges of shadows may come at an awkward place

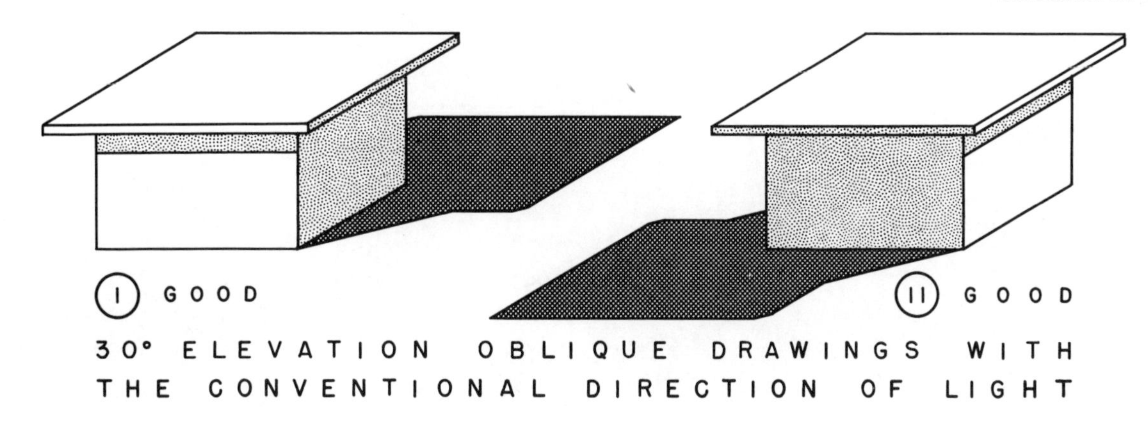

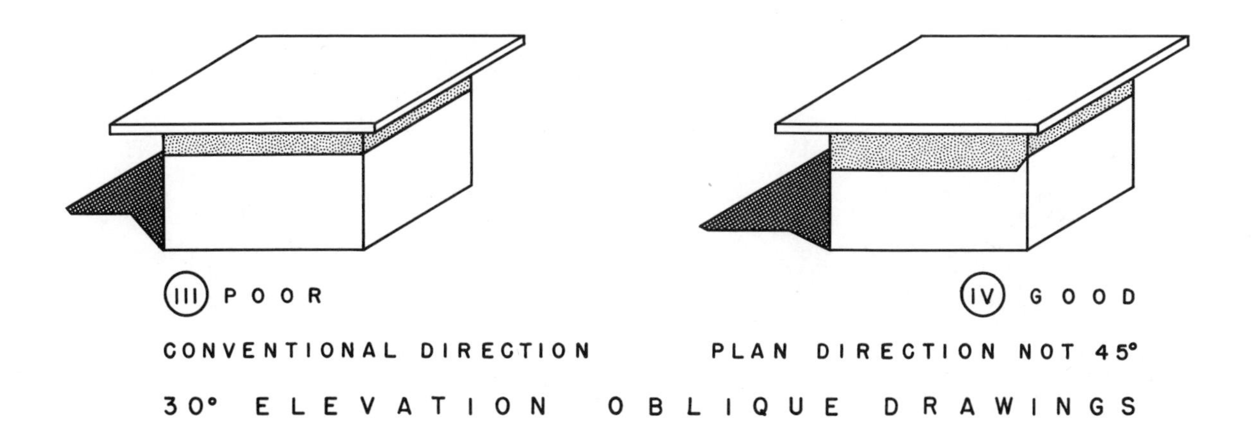

FIG-174 VARIOUS DIRECTIONS OF LIGHT FOR SHADOWS ON OBLIQUE DRAWINGS

in the design. The conventional direction of light from the side gives very large shadows on the ground plane. However, it is not always necessary to show the entire shadow.

It is impossible to use a single direction of light and secure the best possible shadow effect on every pictorial drawing. The 45° directions of light have the advantage of simplicity of construction, since the shadows travel down, back, and to the side equally and can be located by equal measurements at the scale or scales of the drawing along the three axes. When the shadows of projecting bands are concealed or are too small to be effective, the distance down of the shadow can be made greater than the distances back and to the side in any ratio which gives satisfactory shadows. Furthermore, when the two visible wall planes of the object are both in light, the plan direction of light can be changed to provide variety in shadows on the two wall surfaces, Fig. 174 IV.

Elevation oblique drawings with the oblique lines at 30° or less give reasonably good shadow effects with the conventional direction of light from the side, Fig. 174 I and II. When a greater angle than 30° is used for the drawing, it may be necessary to use a steeper angle for light in order to obtain satisfactory shadows under overhangs.

When both walls are in light, the corner of an equal overhang always casts its shadow on the corner of the wall below with 45° plan direction of light, Fig. 174 III. This is true in any kind of drawing. It produces an unnatural effect which would usually be unsatisfactory.

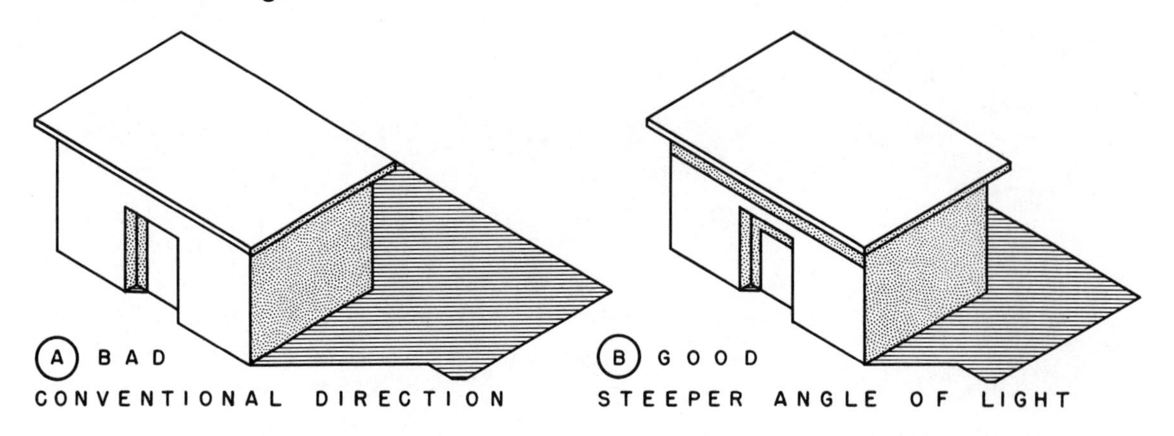

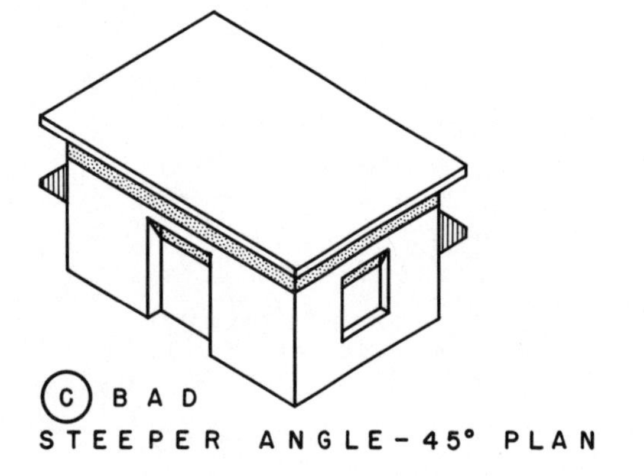

FIG-175 THE DIRECTION OF LIGHT FOR SHADOWS ON ISOMETRIC DRAWINGS

Isometric drawings never give a satisfactory shadow effect with the conventional direction of light looking down from above the object. When one set of visible wall surfaces is in light and the other in shadow, the vertical shadows in openings are visible on the walls in light. However, the horizontal shadows are exactly covered by the projecting edges, and the edge of the roof at the back of the object aligns exactly with its shadow on the background, Fig. 175A. If the distance down of the shadows is increased, the shadows of horizontal lines become visible, the shadow on the ground is smaller, and relation between the object and its shadow is improved, Fig. 175B. A simple method of securing this result is to use the scale of the drawing on the two horizontal axes and use a somewhat larger scale to measure the shadow depths on the vertical axis. For example, when the isometric drawing is made at a scale of $\frac{1}{8}''$ the shadow measurements on horizontal axes can be made at that scale and shadow measurements on vertical lines made at $\frac{3}{16}''$.

There are no visible shadows on an isometric drawing with the conventional direction of light when both sets of visible wall surfaces of the object are in light. The shade lines of the object exactly coincide with their shadows. When a steeper angle of light is used, the shadows will appear as shown in Fig. 175C. However, the shadows of most vertical lines will still be hidden, and it is necessary to change the plan direction of light also, as shown in Fig. 175D, in order to secure satisfactory shadows. Three different scales can be used to work out the direction of light and the directions of the shadows of the three axis lines on planes perpendicular to them. These

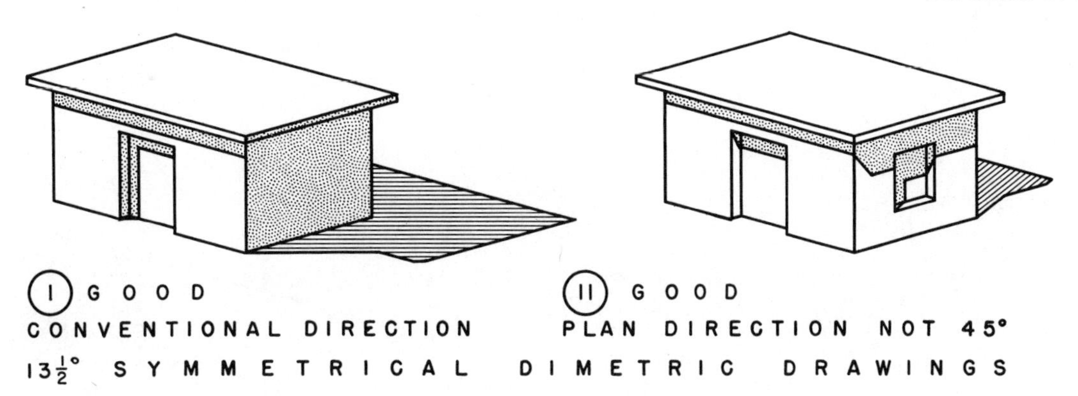

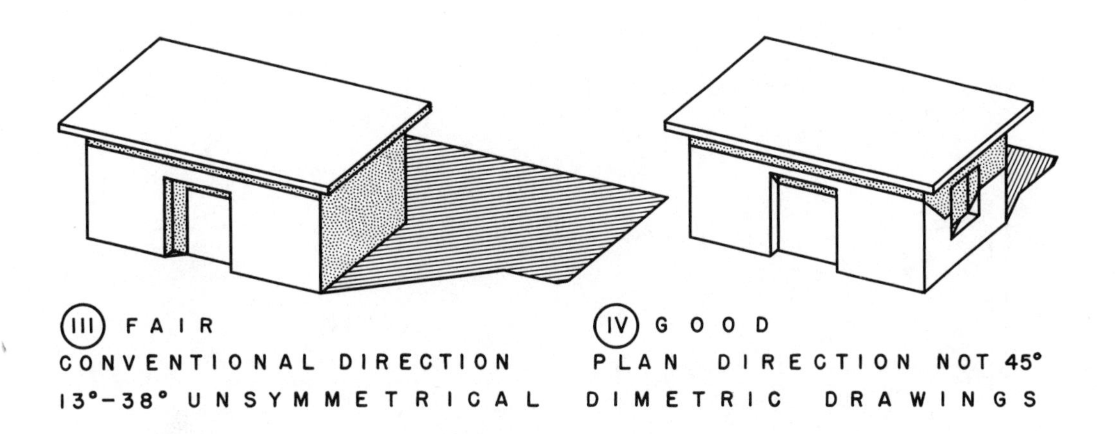

FIG-176 THE DIRECTION OF LIGHT FOR SHADOWS ON DIMETRIC DRAWINGS

directions of shadows and the direction of light can be used to simplify the shadow construction. In the example of Fig. 175D the scales used for shadow measurements were $\frac{3}{8}$″ for verticals, $\frac{3}{16}$″ for horizontals to the right, and $\frac{1}{8}$″ for horizontals to the left.

Symmetrical dimetric drawing is most useful when drawn at an angle of $13\frac{1}{2}$°. The conventional direction of light from the side, leaving one set of wall planes in light, is satisfactory for this type of drawing, as shown in Fig. 176 I. With both walls in light, the shadow effect with the conventional direction of light is about the same as that obtained with the steeper angle for the isometric drawing of Fig. 175C. When the plan angle of light is changed from 45° the shadows are more satisfactory, as shown in Fig. 176 II. In this drawing one horizontal scale is reduced to one-half the scale of the lines of the drawing for shadow construction.

Unsymmetrical dimetric drawings in which the vertical scale of the drawing is the same as the larger of the scales for horizontal lines gives satisfactory shadows with the conventional direction of light from the large-scale side, Fig. 176 III. However, the conventional direction from the small-scale side is unsatisfactory because shadows of overhangs will coincide with their shade lines. A steeper angle of light must be used to give shadows under overhangs. With both walls in light, shadows of overhangs will be concealed on the small-scale side. A change of plan direction to give shadows of horizontals on the small-scale side improves the shadow effect, Fig. 176 IV. When the verticals of the drawing are at the small scale, the conventional direction of light is unsatisfactory.

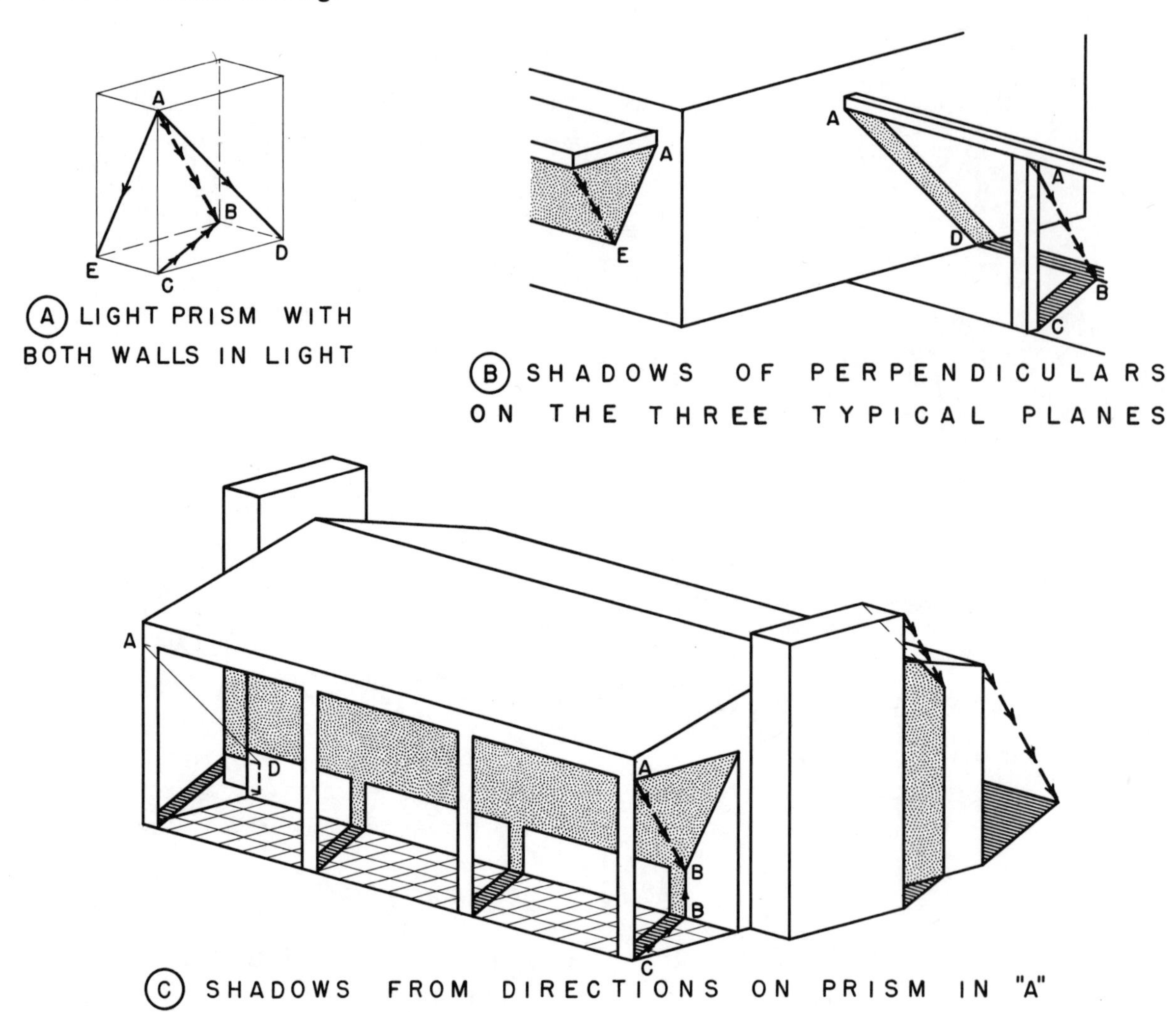

(A) LIGHT PRISM WITH BOTH WALLS IN LIGHT

(B) SHADOWS OF PERPENDICULARS ON THE THREE TYPICAL PLANES

(C) SHADOWS FROM DIRECTIONS ON PRISM IN "A"

FIG-177 THE LIGHT DIRECTION METHOD FOR SHADOWS

It is possible to cast shadows on parallel-line pictorial drawings without using any measurements for the shadow constructions. A direction of light A–B and a direction for the shadow C–B of a vertical line on a horizontal plane are assumed, Fig. 177A. The directions of the shadows of the other two axis lines on the planes to which they are perpendicular are then worked out graphically. It is possible to work out the shadows on a drawing from these four directions. In fact, the first two are often sufficient.

A prism of light direction can be drawn to give these four directions as shown in Fig. 177A. A vertical line A–C is first drawn as a corner of the prism. From the top point A the direction of light A–B is drawn to meet C–B, the shadow of A–C on a horizontal plane. The diagonal of the prism is A–B, and C–B is the diagonal of the bottom of the prism. The remainder of the prism is drawn around these three lines, using lines parallel to the three sets of lines of the drawing on which shadows are to be constructed. The direction of the shadow of a perpendicular to the right wall plane is A–D, and the direction of a shadow of a perpendicular on a left wall is A–E.

Figure 177B is a drawing of a part of a building showing the three typical planes with lines perpendicular to each of them. This illustration explains the use of the light directions of the prism in Fig. 177A. The same letter symbols are used on some of the lines of these two drawings to

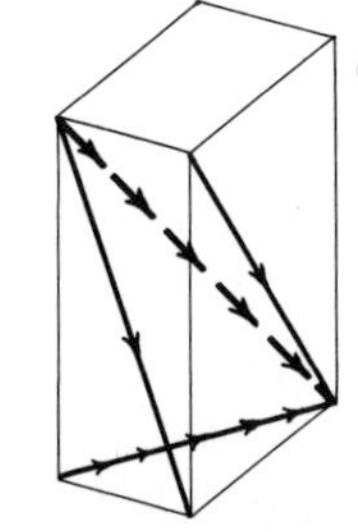

I LIGHT PRISM WITH ONE WALL IN LIGHT

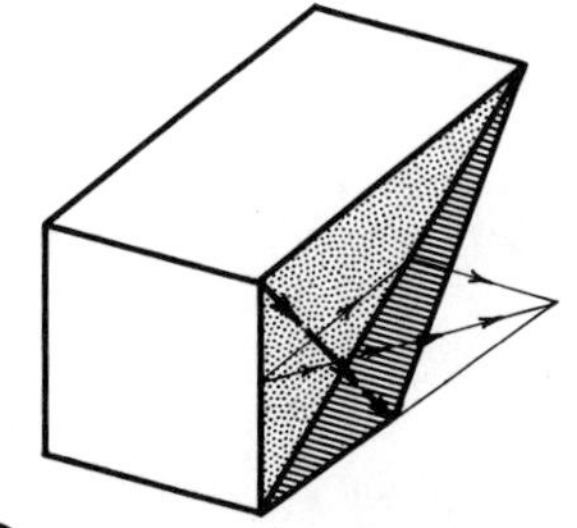

II CONSTRUCTION WITH PLAN LIGHT DIRECTION

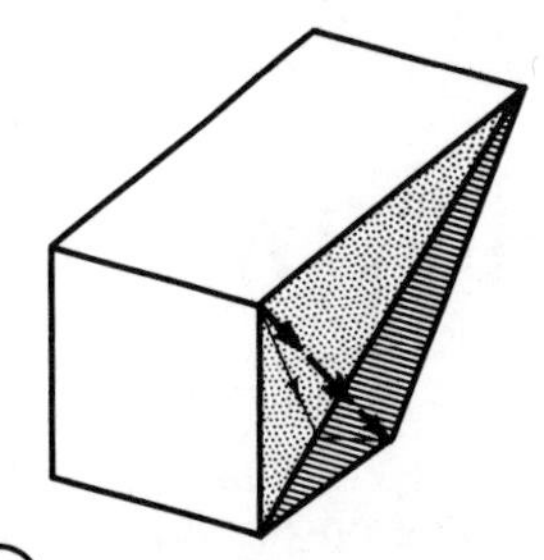

III CONSTRUCTION WITH R. WALL LIGHT DIRECTION

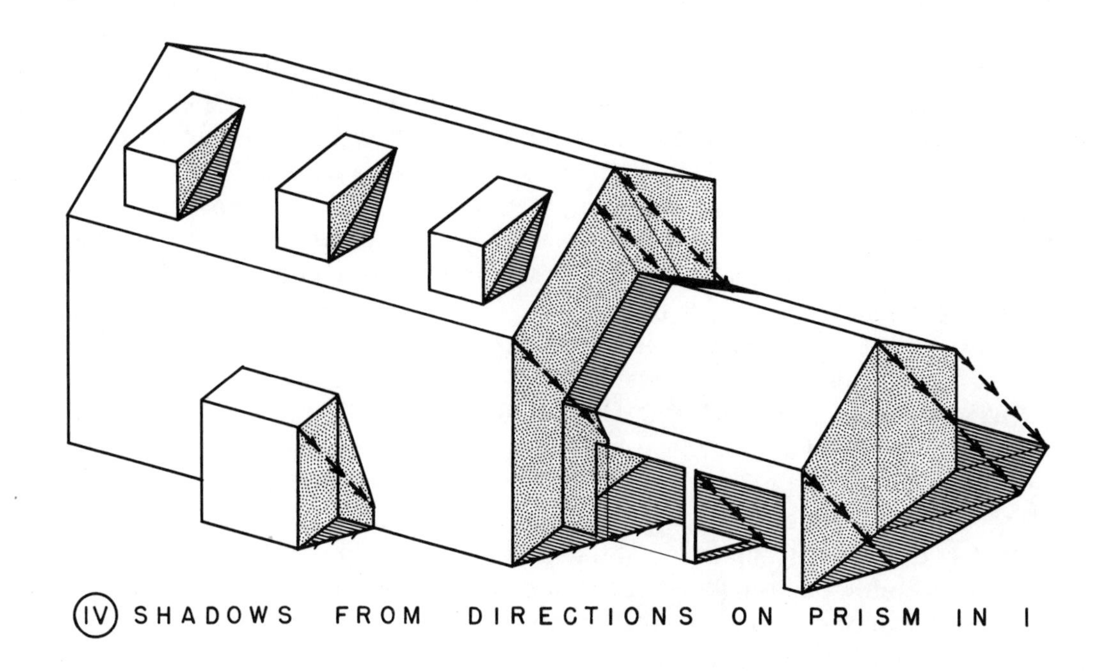

IV SHADOWS FROM DIRECTIONS ON PRISM IN I

FIG-178 SHADOWS BY LIGHT DIRECTION METHOD

show that they are parallel to each other. The shadows on the simple block building shape of Fig. 177C are worked out by using the directions given in the light prism of Fig. 177A and lines parallel to the three sets of typical lines of the drawing.

This light-direction method of casting shadows is easy to use. It permits the use of any possible light direction and is not restricted by scale ratios. When using this system it is possible to derive the light direction from a chosen position for an important shadow. In Fig. 177C point B can be the chosen location of the shadow of point A. This position gives a pleasing proportion for the shadow depth under the porch and interesting angles for the shadows of perpendiculars to walls and floor. Line A–B is then the chosen direction of light rays and C–B is the shadow of a vertical on the floor plane. From the directions of these two lines the light prism can be constructed. The A–B and C–B directions may be adequate for shadow construction.

In Fig. 178 the light-direction prism and shadows from the directions established by the prism are shown with one set of wall planes in shadow. The prism must always parallel the lines of the drawing on which it is to be used. If the drawing is an isometric, then the prism must be in isometric also. Often a shadow can be worked out in different ways. The two enlarged drawings of the dormer in Fig. 178 II and III show two methods of constructing this shadow.

CHAPTER 21
Shadows on Perspective Drawings

Shadows on perspective drawings follow the same general principles as do those in multi-view and parallel-line pictorial drawings. Many of the shadow lines of a perspective drawing are parallel to the lines casting the shadows and are therefore a part of the same system of lines. These shadow lines either vanish to the same points as the lines of the object or remain parallel in perspective, as do other lines of the set.

Shadow areas can be worked out on the multi-view drawings and then transferred to the perspective drawing just as the outlines of other areas would be drawn in perspective. This method is sometimes preferred by the draftsman, for it requires no new theory either of shadows or of perspective. It requires the construction of shadows on the elevation or elevations which appear in light in the perspective drawing and on the plan, then the construction of the perspective shadows from these. Even to the person who is proficient in perspective drawing, this roundabout method may seem tedious. Furthermore, the construction becomes more complex when any direction of light other than the conventional one is used.

There are two general divisions of shadow-casting directly on perspective drawings: (1) when light rays are parallel to the picture plane; (2) when light rays are oblique to the picture plane.

LIGHT RAYS PARALLEL TO THE PICTURE PLANE. Light rays in this position will remain parallel in perspective. The shadows of vertical lines on horizontal planes are parallel horizontal lines and are drawn with the T-square, since they are parallel to the picture plane. This system of parallel light rays and parallel horizontal shadows of vertical lines can be used only in two-point perspectives with one set of wall planes in light, the other in shadow. It cannot be used in two-point perspective to place both walls in light. It is not satisfactory for one-point perspectives, since the light rays are parallel to one set of wall planes, thus producing a poor shadow effect. Although its shadow effects are limited, it is a simple and often satisfactory system for shadows in two-point perspective drawings.

The shadow effect in a given two-point perspective drawing can be varied in two ways only. (1) Light rays can come from either side, so that either one of the two sets of wall planes can be in light, Fig. 179A and D. (2) The angle of light can be varied to produce various sizes of shadows on the wall in light, Fig. 179A, B, and C. When the angle of light is changed, the amount and shape of the shadow area on the ground plane is varied also. The widths of vertical shadows, such as those in the doors of Fig. 179A, B, and C, remain the same regardless of the angle of light. This width is determined by the plan direction of light and the amount of projection, both of which are constants.

When the plan of the object is turned at 45° to the picture plane, the rays of light in the perspective drawing can be in the direction of the diagonal of a cube, thus giving the conventional direction of light. This direction can be easily constructed, as shown in Fig. 179E.

The direction of light and the direction of shadows of vertical lines on horizontal surfaces are often sufficient information for working out all the shadows of a perspective drawing directly on the perspective itself, since the directions of many of the shadow lines are known. The shadows of the perspective drawing of Fig. 179F were worked out from this information. It should be observed that the plan direction of light can be used for actual shadows of vertical lines and also on horizontal planes in shadow, either top or bottom surfaces, to trace shadow construction. Imaginary extensions of surfaces are used to locate points A, B, C, and D to give directions of lines A–B, C–E, and D–F of Fig. 179F. Line G–K is an imaginary shadow of a continuation of vertical corner G–H above the building. Point K gives the direction for shadow line L–M.

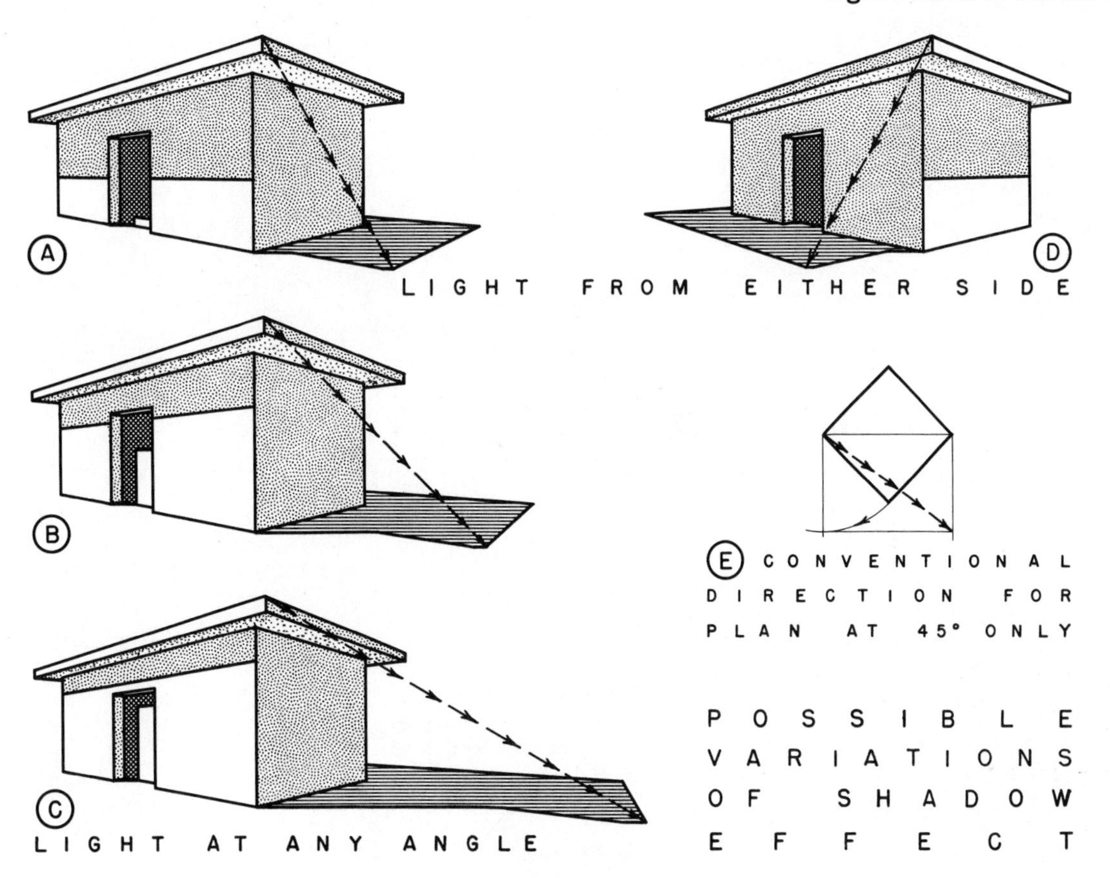

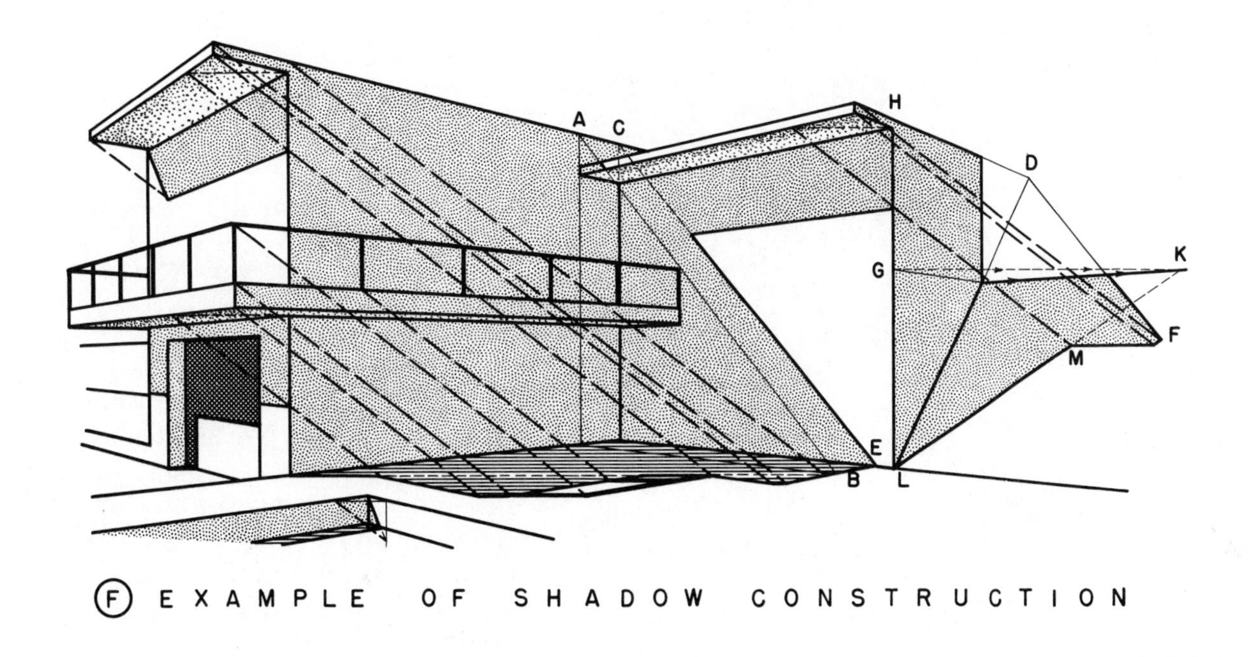

F EXAMPLE OF SHADOW CONSTRUCTION

FIG-179 SHADOWS WITH THE LIGHT RAYS PARALLEL TO THE PICTURE PLANE

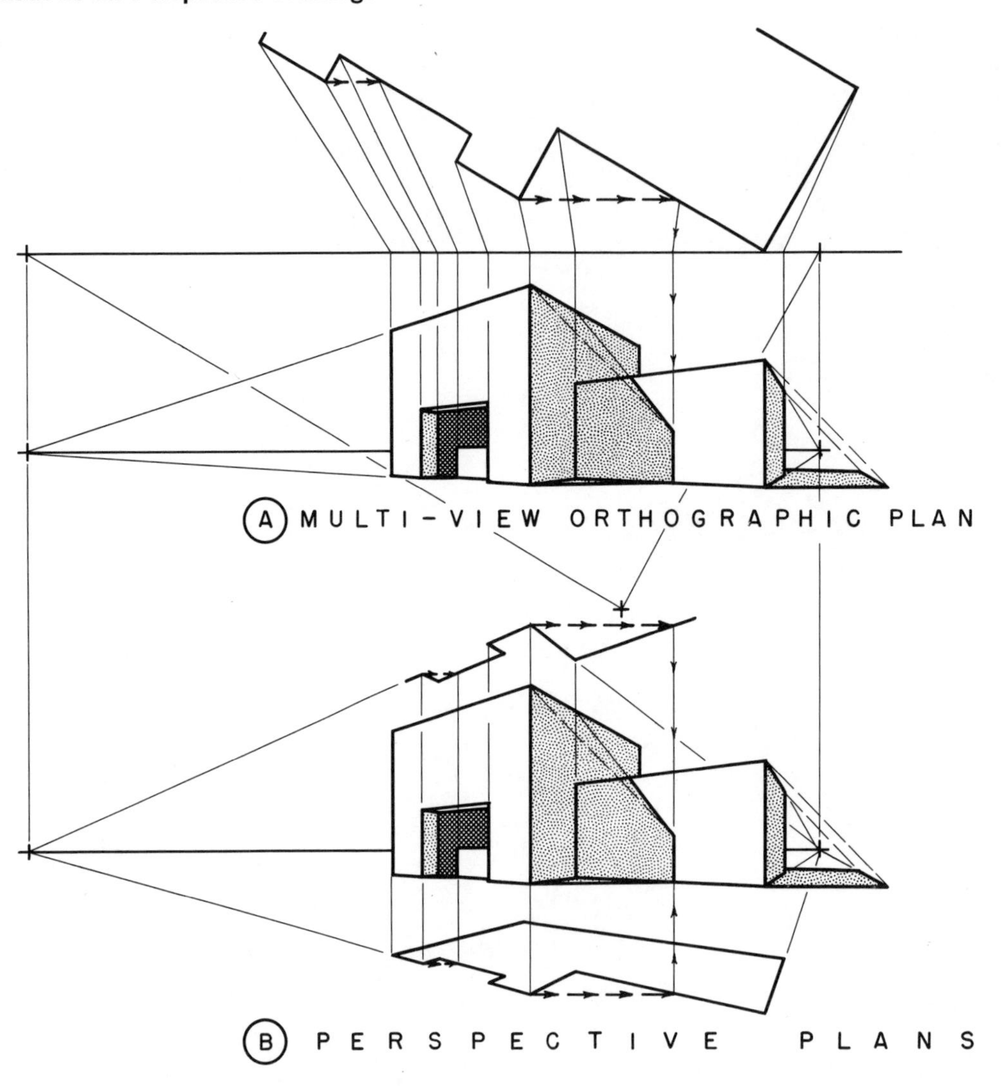

FIG-180 CONSTRUCTION FROM AUXILIARY PLANS

Whenever the horizontal planes of the perspective drawing become so thin that it is difficult and inaccurate to work out shadow constructions on them, there are two alternatives. Greater accuracy can be secured by: (1) drawing the positions of horizontal shadows on the auxiliary plan, either orthographic or perspective, which was used for construction, then projecting them to the perspective drawing, Fig. 180A and B; (2) constructing the minimum necessary part plan in perspective vertically either above or below the perspective drawing to secure a larger area and locate the shadow position, as shown both above and below the building in Fig. 180B. The construction from existing auxiliary drawings can be made very easily. It is also very easy to make the part plan for the necessary construction. Existing verticals on the perspective of the building are extended to locate corners for the part plan. The lines of the part plan go to the vanishing points of the perspective. Usually only a few lines are needed for the shadow construction, and they can be removed as soon as the shadows are located.

On many perspective drawings this auxiliary construction from plans is unnecessary. On others it may be needed for only a small proportion of the shadow constructions. It is rather rare to find such a flat perspective drawing that a great deal of construction is needed from auxiliary plans.

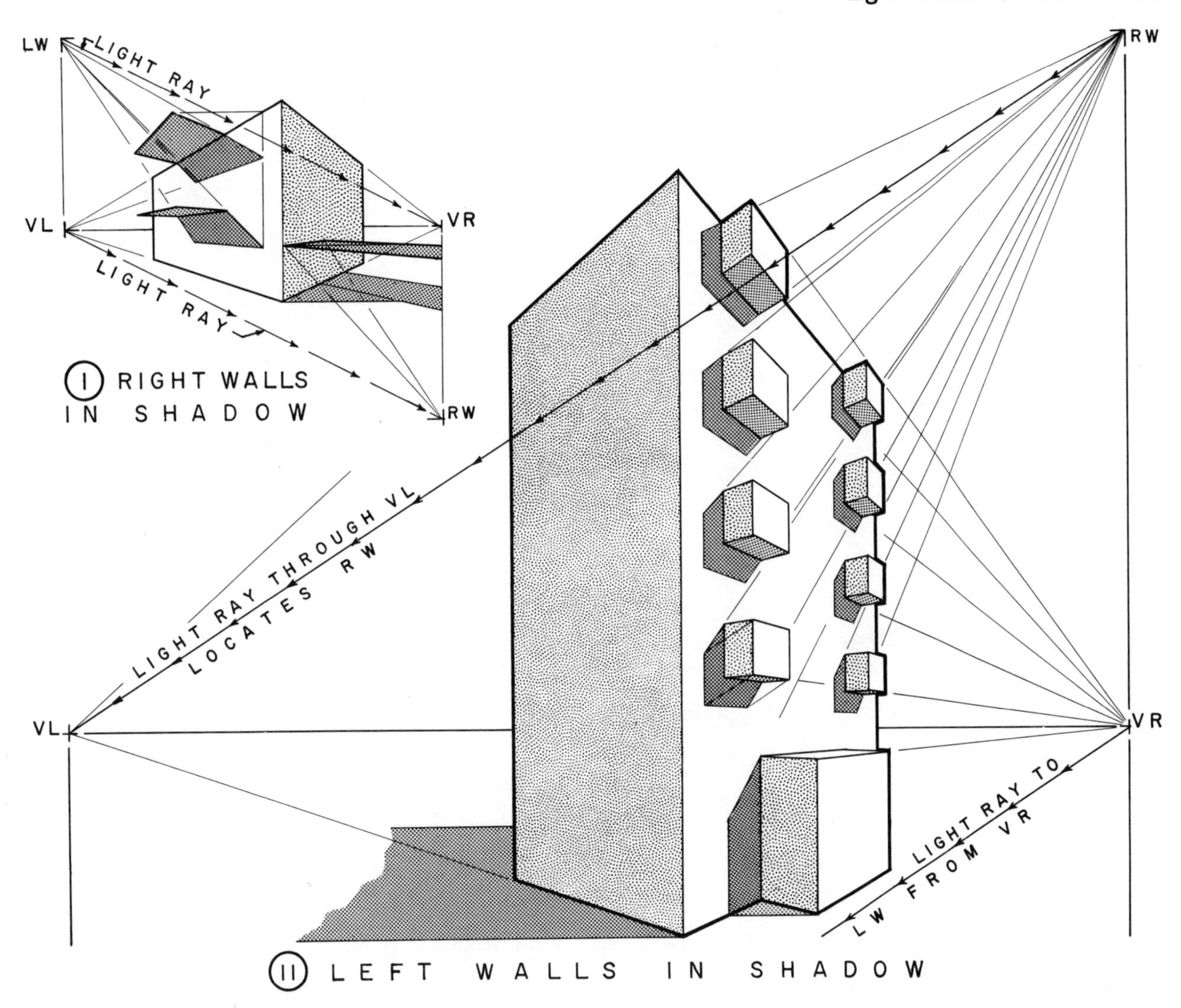

FIG-181 LOCATION AND USE OF WALL SHADOW VPS

Shadows of perpendiculars to wall planes on the planes to which they are perpendicular are lines oblique to the picture plane in two-point perspective. Therefore these shadow lines vanish to vanishing points. The vanishing point LW for shadows of perpendiculars on left wall planes is located on the vertical through VL, Fig. 181 I. This vertical is the horizon of all left wall planes. It is therefore the locus of vanishing points of all lines in left wall planes. The vanishing point RW of shadows of perpendiculars on right wall planes is located on the vertical line through VR.

The positions of LW and RW on the verticals through VL and VR respectively can be located in different ways with light parallel to the picture plane. A very easy and accurate method uses the direction of light rays to locate LW and RW. The light ray through VR meets the vertical through VL in point LW, Fig. 181 I. The light ray through VL meets the vertical through VR in point RW, Fig. 181 I and II.

These vanishing points of perpendiculars on the two wall planes may provide an easier and more accurate method of obtaining some shadows, especially repeating ones, which vanish to one of these points. These LW and RW points are sometimes inconveniently far away from the perspective. The point for the shadows of lines on the wall planes in light is the more useful one.

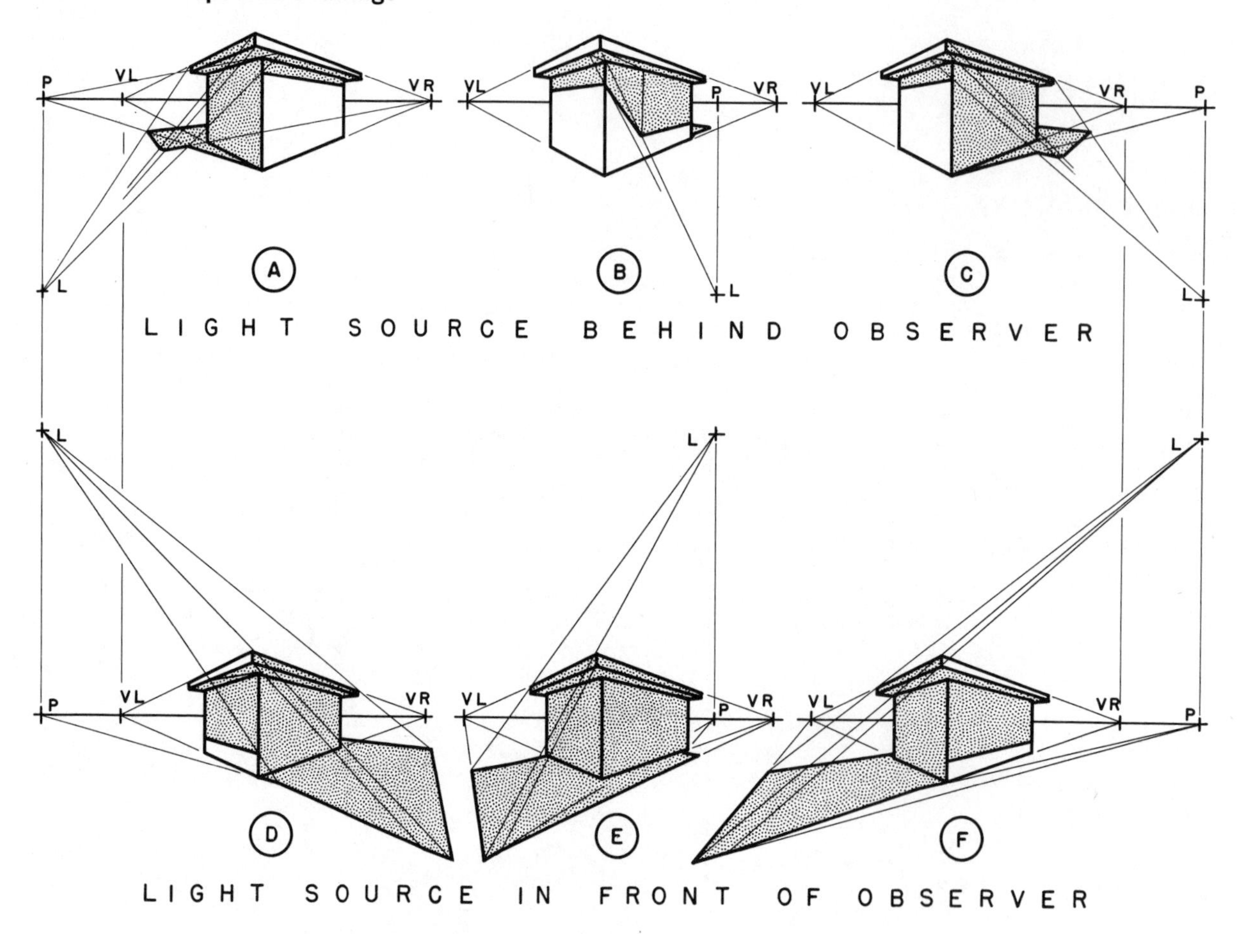

FIG-182 BASIC SHADOW SCHEMES WITH LIGHT RAYS OBLIQUE TO PICTURE PLANE

LIGHT RAYS OBLIQUE TO PICTURE PLANE. When the rays of light are not parallel to the picture plane, shadows can be worked out directly on a perspective drawing by the same construction methods used in the preceding chapter on axonometric and oblique drawings. The sets of parallel lines which are used for the shadow construction on perspective drawings usually converge to vanishing points, instead of being actually parallel as they are for the parallel-line pictorial drawings. The vanishing point of light rays, L, and the vanishing point of shadows of vertical lines on horizontal planes, P, will often be found sufficient for all shadow construction on an entire drawing.

Point L below the horizon represents the light source behind the observer and gives the three basic shadow schemes which are most commonly used, Fig. 182A, B, and C. They are: (A) When the shadow vanishing points L and P are located to the left of VL, the left wall planes are in shadow. (B) When points L and P are located between the vanishing points of the perspective, both walls are in light. (C) When L and P are located to the right of VR, the right wall planes are in shadow. The shadow effects will be better when the shadow vanishing point P is far from VL and VR.

When point L is above the horizon, as shown in Fig. 182D, E, and F, the light source is in front of the observer and the shadow areas are large on the object and ground. When points P and L are between the vanishing points, both wall surfaces are in shadow. While lighting with L above the horizon is not often used, it may be employed to produce dramatic shadow forms. This is especially true of open objects to give light areas and break up the shadow. See Fig. 184.

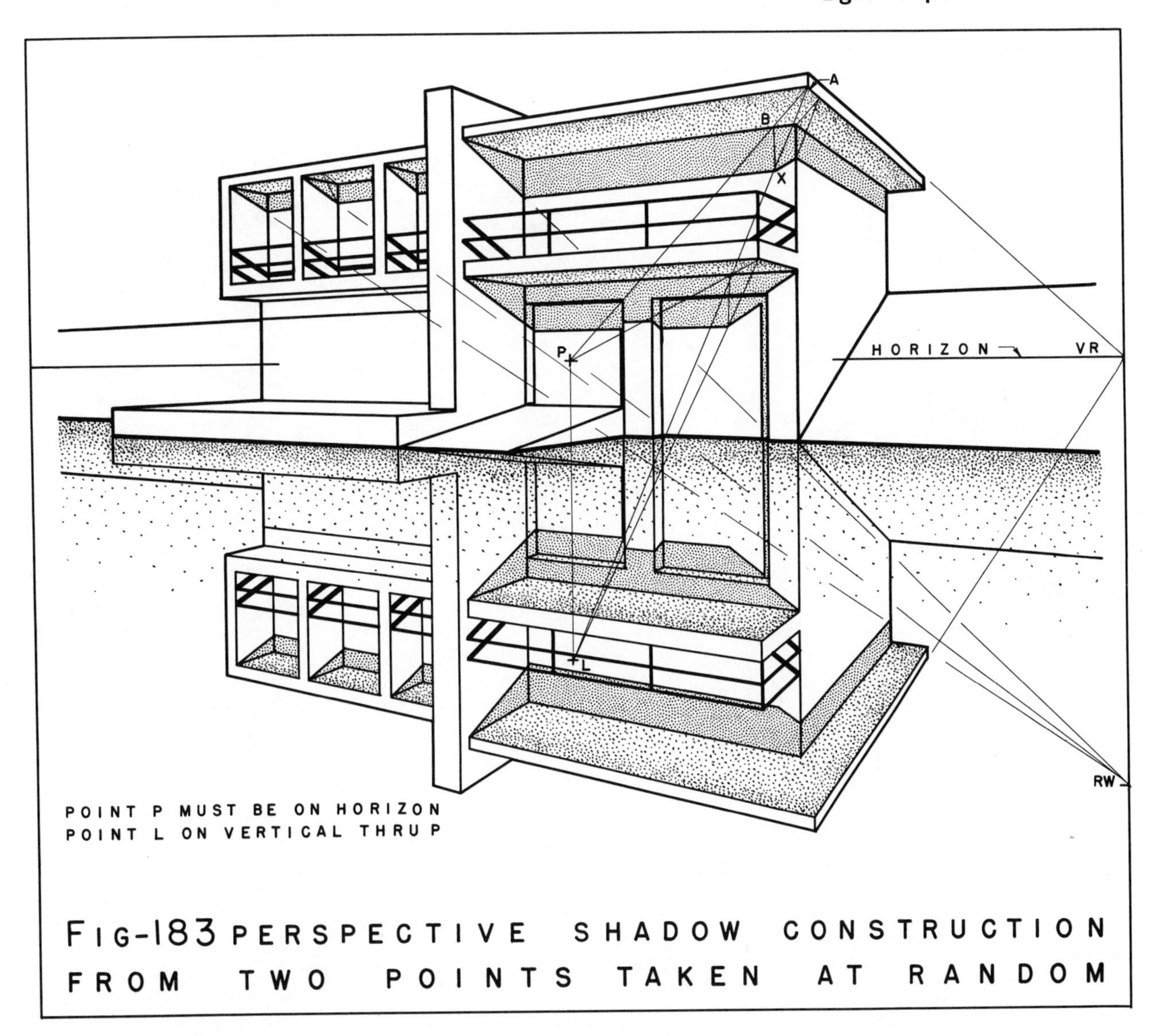

FIG-183 PERSPECTIVE SHADOW CONSTRUCTION FROM TWO POINTS TAKEN AT RANDOM

The positions of L and P may be taken at random on any vertical line which meets the horizon and gives good shadow effects. Point P must be on the horizon and L on the vertical line through P. It is assumed that the draftsman will consider the effect to be obtained and choose positions which he thinks will give good shadows for the perspective. One method of selecting these two points is illustrated in Fig. 183. Point X is selected as the shadow of point A. A vertical from X locates B on the edge of the horizontal surface through A, and A–B extended intersects the horizon in P, the vanishing point of the plan direction of light. A vertical from P intersects A–X extended in L, the vanishing point of light rays. Points L and P are used for the remainder of the shadow construction.

P and L are the only shadow vanishing points actually needed for this drawing, although RW, the vanishing point of shadows of perpendiculars on right wall planes (the right wall direction of light), is shown. This point is easily accessible and useful, since several lines vanish to it. The lines which vanish to RW in the perspective of the building will vanish to a similar point in the reflection. This point is located on the vertical through RW and is the same distance above the horizon that RW is below it. The construction for locating RW and LW is shown in Fig. 186.

It should be observed that the four symbols for shadow vanishing points, L, P, LW, and RW, are the initial letters of the words Light, Plan, Left Wall, and Right Wall, which suggest the light ray and shadow lines to which the letters refer.

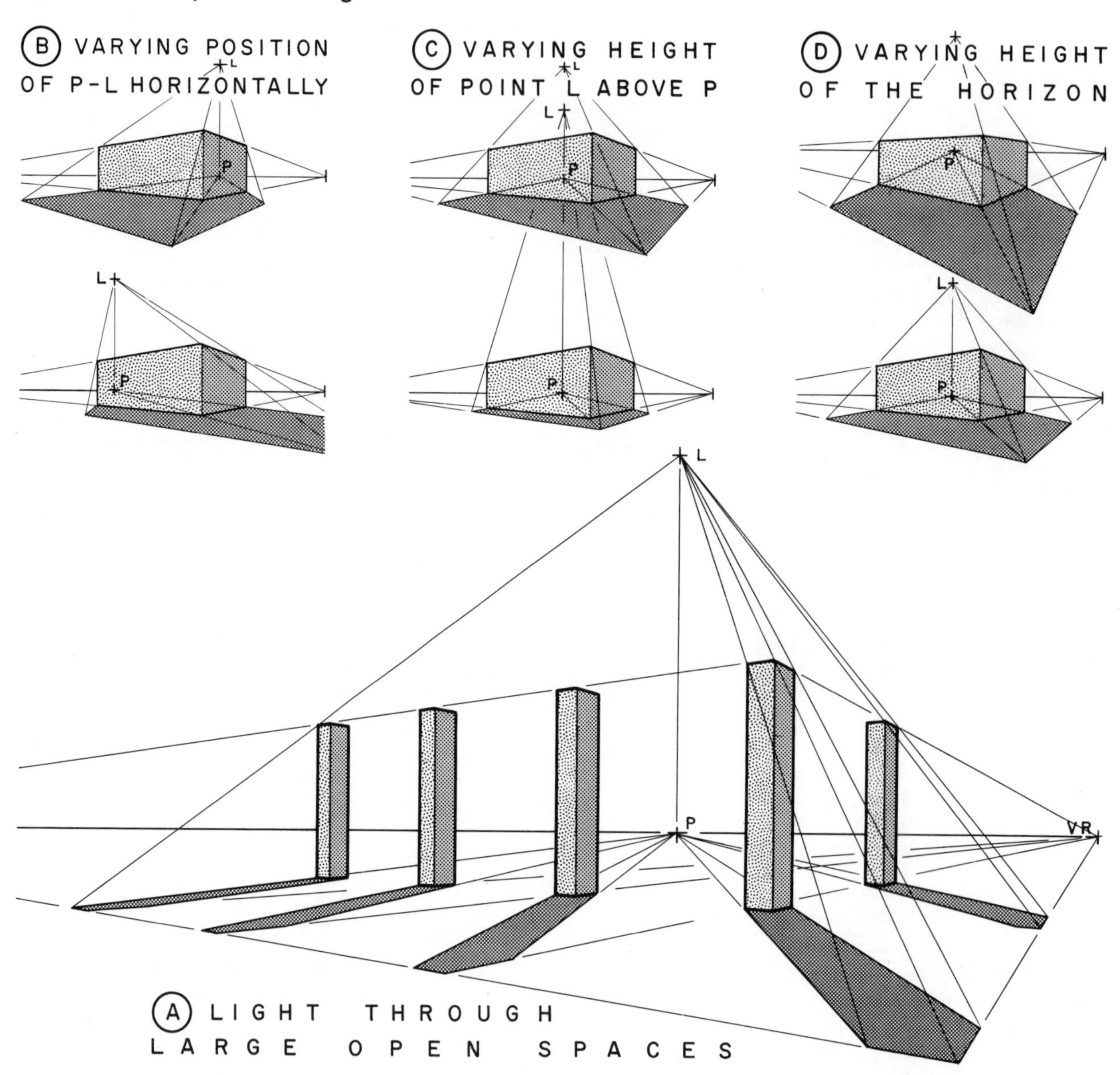

FIG-184 TWO-POINT EXTERIORS WITH L ABOVE P

L above P for two-point exterior perspective shadows may sometimes be found very useful. Two of the effective uses for this shadow arrangement are (1) to give the appearance that the actual site would give on a proposed building, (2) for shadows of an open structure. An open structure such as that of Fig. 184A will often look more dramatic with the spreading and enlarged shadows which come toward the observer. The open object and a single small object or series of small objects can be given greater interest and importance by this type of shadow effect.

Three variables which control the shadow effect are illustrated in Fig. 184B, C, and D. (B) The horizontal position of P and L determines whether the shadows go to the right, to the left, or are balanced about the center of the perspective. When they are outside the space between the two VPs, there will be light on one wall area, Fig. 182. (C) The height of L above P controls the lengths of shadows. The higher L is located, the shorter the shadows, and the lower L is located, the longer the shadows. (D) The higher the horizon, the longer the shadows.

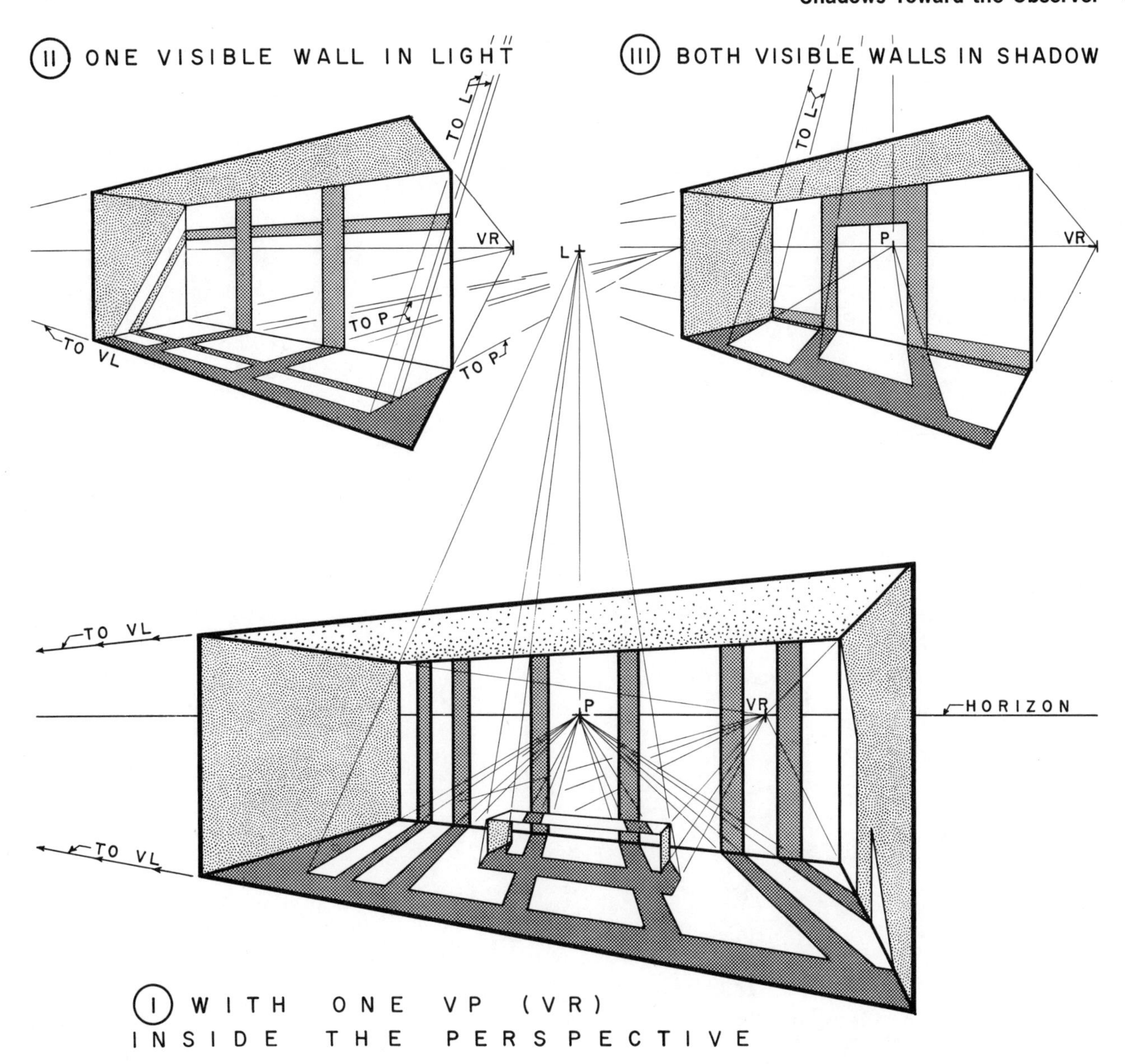

FIG-185 TWO-POINT INTERIORS WITH L ABOVE P

L above P for interior shadows through large open wall areas from the sun as a source of light are very effective. The light areas spread out toward the observer. The distance that they extend into the interior is controlled by the height of L above P. In Fig. 185 I the light areas extend almost the full width of the room. A lower position for L could have them going part way up the wall, which is not shown here. This wall and its light and shadow areas could be shown in a "ghost" effect. A higher position of L would make the near edge of the light area closer to the openings, thus reducing the area in light.

The perspective layout used in Fig. 185 I allows three walls of an interior to be shown in a two-point perspective with light on one side wall. The standard two-point perspective layout will have light on one wall when point P is outside the space between the two VPs and openings are located to allow light to enter through the other wall, Fig. 185 II. When point P is between the two VPs, both of the visible wall surfaces will be in shadow, Fig. 185 III.

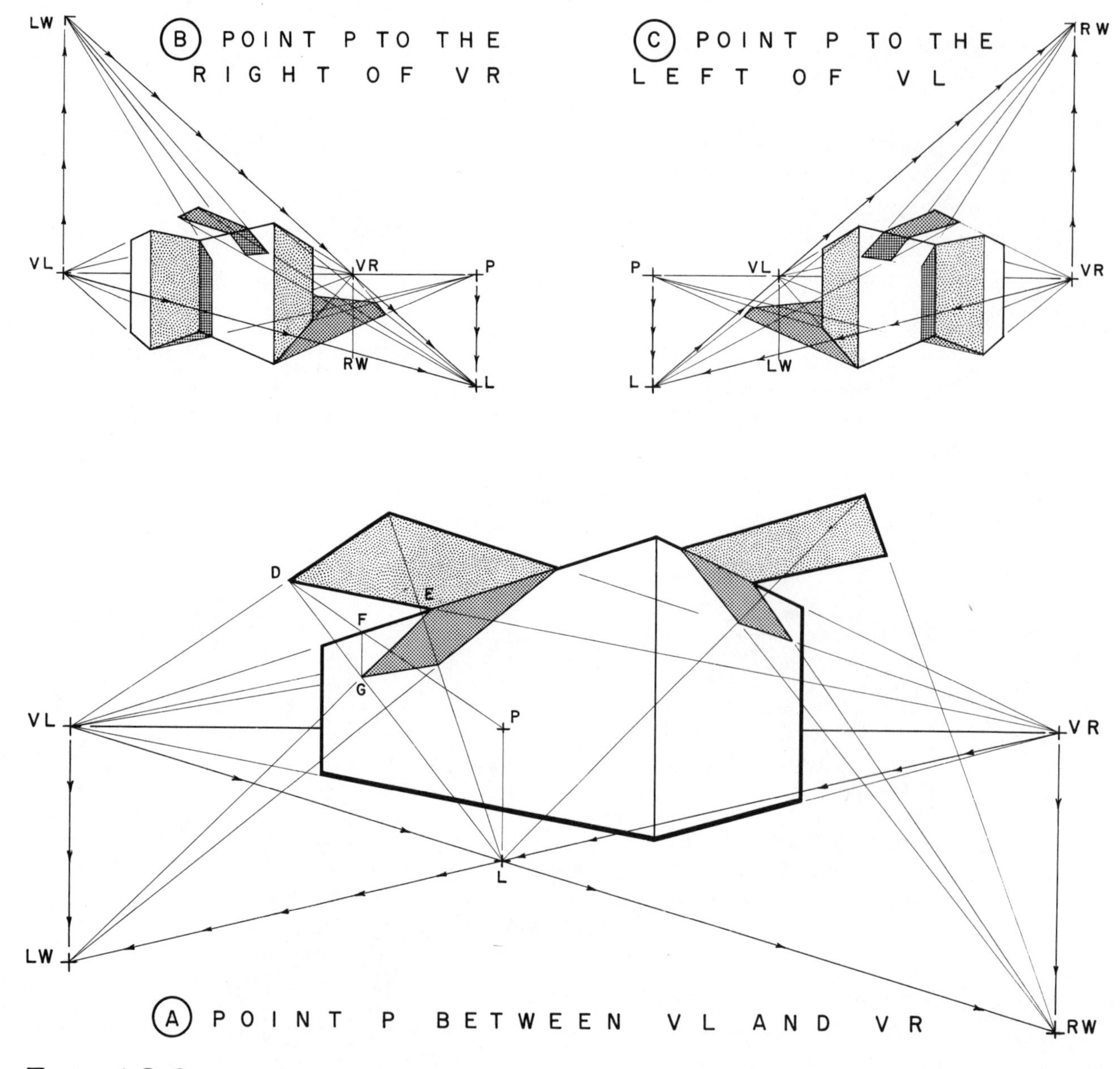

FIG. 186 LOCATION OF WALL SHADOW VANISHING POINTS

Wall shadow vanishing points give the directions of shadows of perpendiculars to wall planes on the planes to which they are perpendicular. These shadows can be constructed by using lines to P and L without the use of the wall shadow VP. An example of this construction is given in Fig. 186A for the shadow of the perpendicular D–E on the left wall. D–F is drawn toward P, D–G is drawn toward L to meet the vertical from F in point G, E–G is the shadow of D–E.

LW can be located by extending E–G to meet the vertical through VL. This construction for LW is usually sufficiently accurate from a long shadow. It may be inaccurate from a small wall shadow line. When LW is located, all shadows of all perpendiculars to left wall planes will go toward this point. When there are several shadows like E–G, the wall shadow VP will save time and give greater accuracy, especially for small lines, than the construction to P and L.

A more accurate method is to extend a line from VR through L to meet the vertical through VL in point LW. Line VR–L–LW is the intersection of plane of D–E–G and the picture plane.

Shadows can be worked out for a definite site with reasonable accuracy. Data giving the plan direction (H) and true direction (T) of sunlight for different regions of the United States for specific times of day and days of the year are available. These data can be obtained from climate analyses, such as those published in the AIA Bulletins in collaboration with House Beautiful for specific regions, times of day, and month.

Plan direction of light for an assumed site is given in Fig. 187 I. This direction is given in its relation to the north arrow as it would be on a site plan. When this direction is used on the multi-view plan for the construction of the perspective in Fig. 187 III, it is turned for correct relation to the north arrow on the plan. This direction on the plan is used from SP to locate X on the picture plane. The vertical from X locates point P on the horizon and goes through point L.

The true direction of light (true angle with a horizontal plane) is needed to locate the position of L on the vertical through P. The distance SP–X is laid out on the picture plane line to locate point Y, as shown in the plan of Fig. 187 III. The vertical from Y locates point Z on the horizon. The true direction of light given in Fig. 187 II is drawn from Z to meet the vertical through P and locate L. With VL, L, and VR located, the wall shadow points can be located by the method described for Fig. 186, which is used on 187 III.

The general pattern of the construction lines for Fig. 187 III would be similar for all shadow schemes which have point P between VL and VR. When one set of wall planes is in shadow, the locations of LW and RW would vary as shown in Fig. 186 B and C. The line on which P and L are located is outside the space between the two VPs when one set of wall planes is in shadow.

(I) PLAN DIRECTION OF LIGHT FROM TIME + SITE DATA

N

H

(II) TRUE DIRECTION OF LIGHT FROM TIME + SITE DATA

T

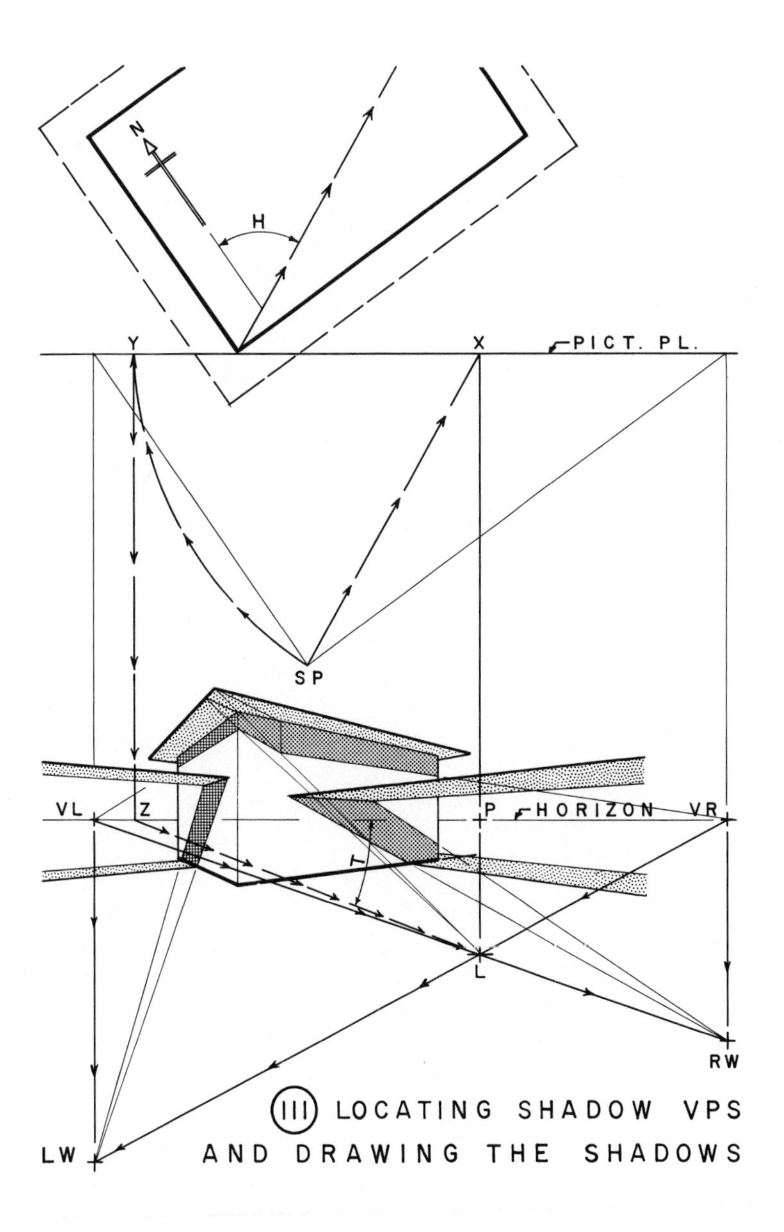

FIG-187 SHADOWS CONSTRUCTED FROM TIME AND SITE DATA

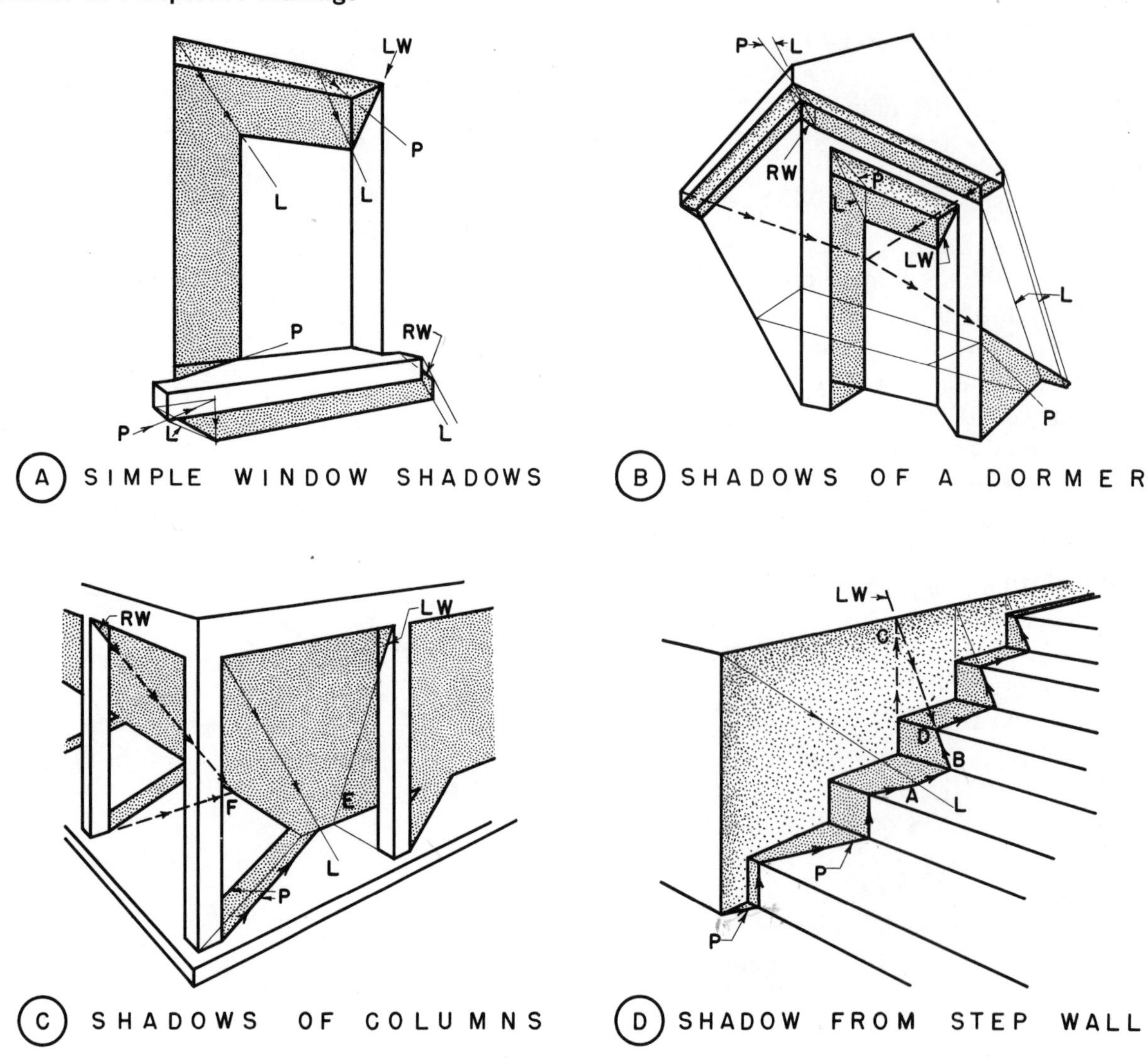

FIG-188 USE OF SHADOW VANISHING POINTS

The illustrations of Fig. 188 show the use of shadow vanishing points on commonly used architectural details. The letters on some of the construction lines refer to the vanishing points shown on the two preceding pages. The lines so marked are drawn to the vanishing points to which the letters refer. In all these examples the construction was made with the two points P and L. However, lines which vanish to points LW and RW are so labeled.

(A) The shadow in the window can be worked out from either the lower left corner or top right corner, since both show the horizontal surface clearly. The concealed surface of the sill is used to trace a line to P to locate the shadow of the lower left corner of the sill on the wall.

(B) The dormer cornice shadow is constructed by using the lower horizontal surface for lines to point P. A horizontal section is traced through the right edge of the side wall of the dormer and the adjoining roof. A line is traced to point P in this section to locate a point on the sloping shadow cast onto the roof from the right vertical corner of the wall. This point and the lower end of the right corner determine the direction of the sloping shadow from the corner of the dormer.

(C) The shadow of the columns on the floor is constructed with lines to points P and L. The

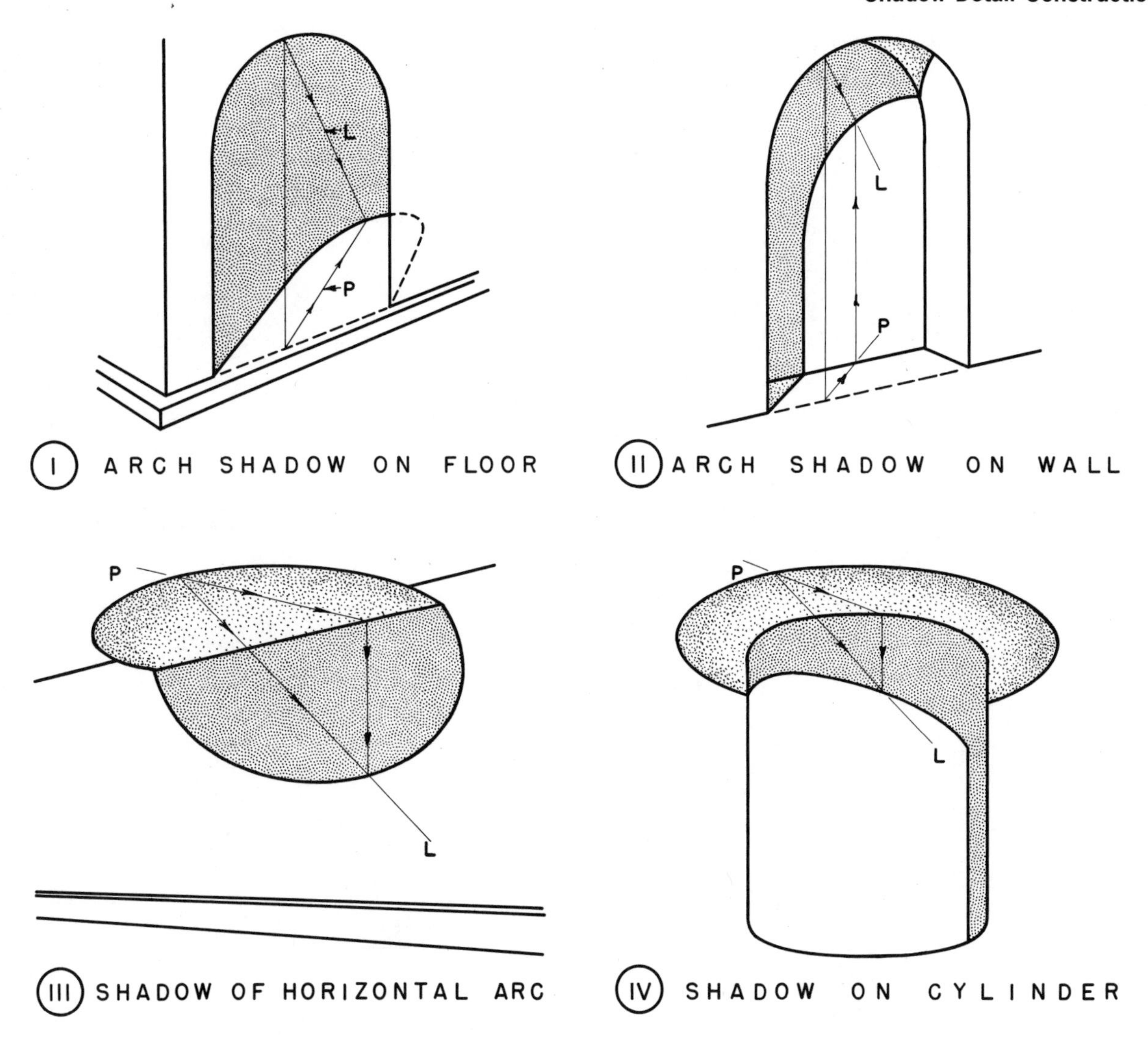

FIG-189 CURVED SHADOWS IN PERSPECTIVE

shadow on the side of the left column goes to RW and the right one to LW. Each can be drawn by finding the intersection of the plane of the side of the column extended to the shadow of the beam on the floor, then connecting these points, E and F, to the tops of the columns.

(D) The construction of the shadow outline across the steps begins at the bottom. It consists of lines to P on horizontal surfaces and vertical lines on the risers as far as point A, the shadow of the end of the vertical shade line. The remainder of the shadow profile goes to VR on the treads and to LW on the risers. Instead of using point LW, the vertical corner of the third riser was extended to the horizontal shade line at point C. This point was then connected to point B where the shadow on the tread touches the bottom of the riser to give line B–D on the riser. The same operation was repeated for each riser with this type of shadow.

In each of the four examples of shadows of curved lines in Fig. 189, the construction for a single one of the points required for the shadow outline is made from the shadow vanishing points P and L. The reader may observe that each construction triangle to locate one point on the shadow outline is a part of a vertical plane parallel to light rays which intersects the object.

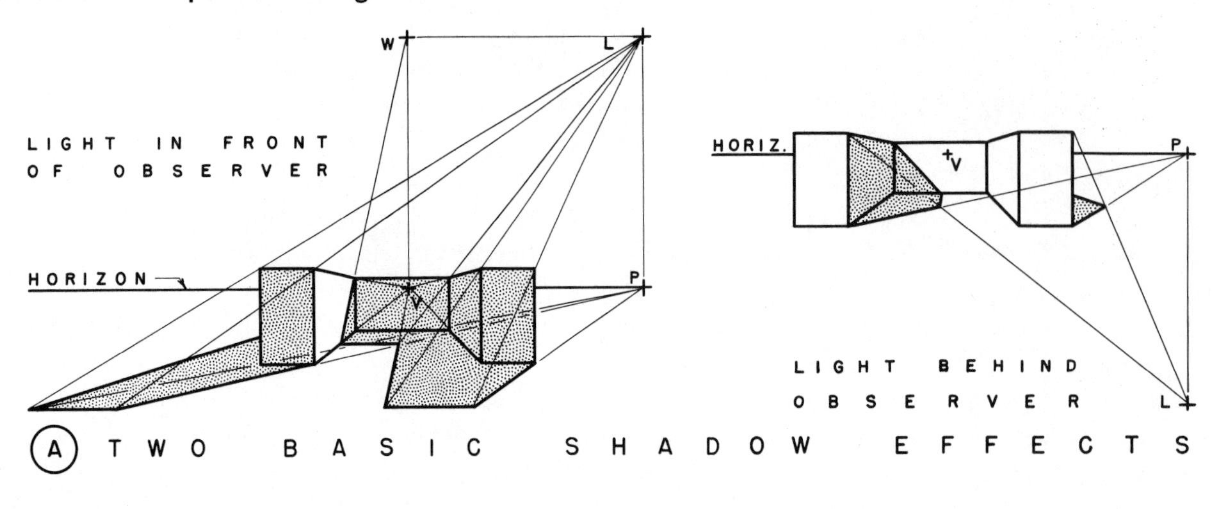

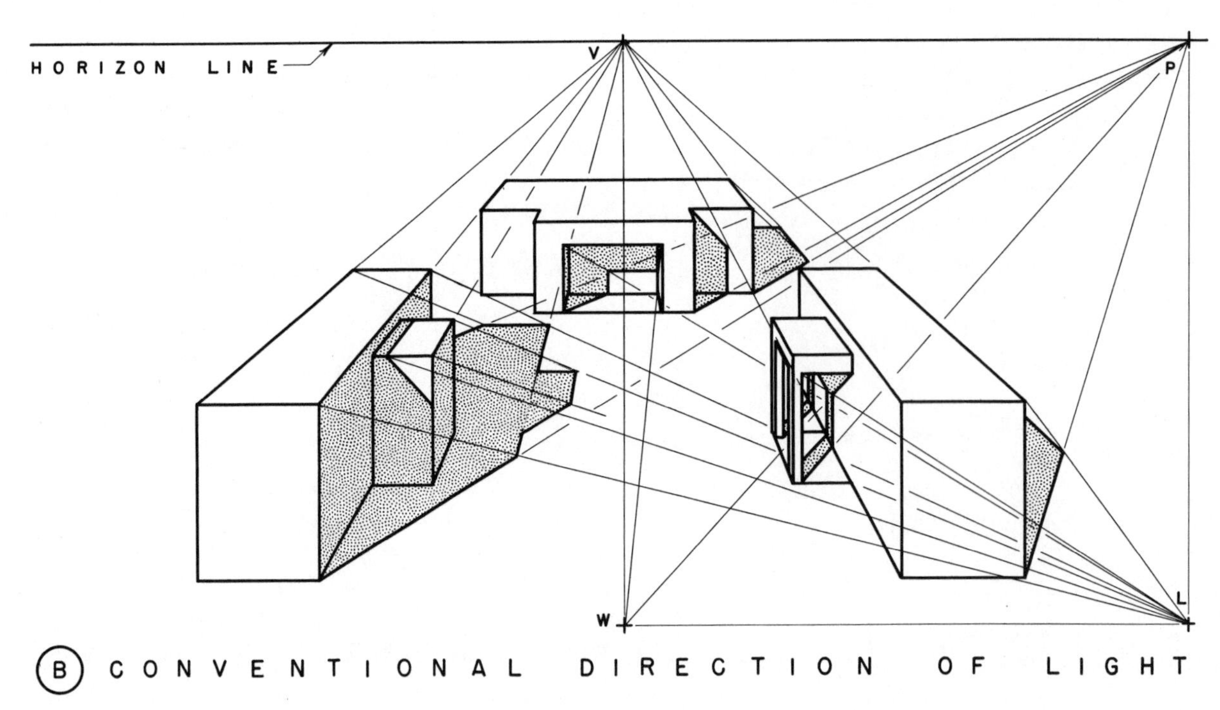

FIG–190 SHADOWS IN ONE–POINT PERSPECTIVE

In one-point exterior perspective the shadow effect can be varied (1) by having the light source either in front of or behind the observer, Fig. 190A; (2) by having the light from either left or right side; and (3) by using different angles of light in the four basic shadow schemes obtained in items one and two above. The angle of light is varied by shifting the P–L line horizontally and (or) by varying the distance from P to L. As in two-point perspective, point L is above the horizon when the light source is in front of the observer and below the horizon when the light rays come from behind the observer. Point L is always located where the ray of light through the SP strikes the picture plane. Therefore, when the light comes from behind and above the SP, the ray through SP goes down to meet the picture plane below the horizon and locate L.

The conventional direction of light often gives satisfactory shadows in one-point perspective; figure 190B is an example of its use. The locations of P, the plan direction of light and the vanishing

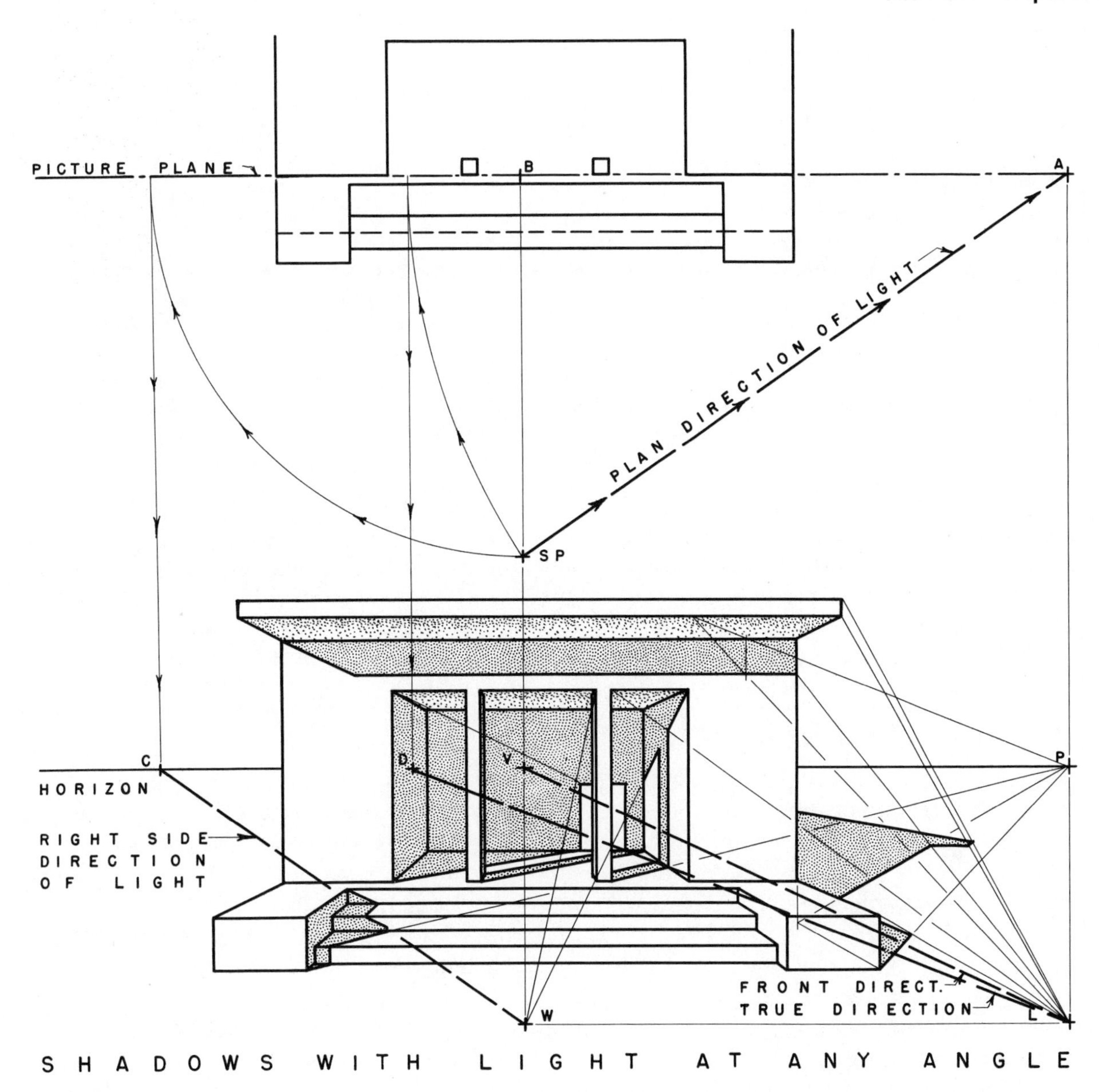

FIG-191 SHADOWS FROM P AND L TAKEN AT RANDOM

point of shadows of vertical lines on horizontal surfaces; L, the vanishing point of light rays; and W, the vanishing point of shadows cast by perpendiculars to the wall planes which are perpendicular to the picture plane, are easily found. The four vanishing points, V, P, L, and W, form the four corners of a square of which the distance SP to the picture plane is a side.

Points P and L can be taken at random in one-point perspective, as in two-point perspective. Point P can be taken anywhere on the horizon and point L anywhere on a vertical through P. Figure 191 gives an example of shadow construction when points P and L are located for a desired shadow effect. With points V, P, and L given, point W is on the vertical through V and on the horizontal through L. V–P–L–W is a rectangle. The line V–L is the front-view direction of light and D–L is the true direction of light. Although the multi-view directions are of little use, they are constructed here from points P and L for the person who wishes to use them.

PART FIVE
Study and Presentation Graphics

CHAPTER 22
Variations of Light and Shadow

Architectural shadows has been limited in preceding chapters to the construction of the shapes of the shadow areas. Variations of darkness of shadows and of intensity of light are considered to be a part of rendering. It is the purpose of this chapter to explain some of the basic variations of light and shadow which are useful devices in the conversion of a drawing into a rendering.

Lines are essential elements of drawing. The emphasis of lines, as outlines of areas of a design, in a rendering may cause a stiff, artificial, and unreal appearance. When these rigid outlines are omitted entirely or subordinated and the shapes brought out by shading, there is usually a better representation of the object. Compare Fig. 166 south elevation and Fig. 192.

Tone is the light and dark relation of areas. It is the basic foundation of all rendering. It is as important in color rendering as in monochrome and black-and-white renderings. The tones may be produced by smooth shading or by uneven textures which may represent materials of the design.

Simple, flat, smooth tones have been used on the areas of the elevation of Fig. 192. Each area has a flat treatment and is therefore the same tone (darkness) throughout. This type of shading produces a very simplified rendering. The tones provide very clear separations of shadow and light areas, roof and wall areas, and the two planes of shrubs. A less emphatic difference of tone is used to separate the two roof areas. The near wall is made lighter in light and darker in shadow than the more distant wall to make the near wall seem closer. This treatment is often used in rendering for two purposes, (1) to make the near and distant parts of the object appear in their proper locations by making greater contrasts of dark and light on the near surfaces, and (2) to focus interest on an area with bright contrasts of light and dark and make other areas duller and less interesting.

FIG-192 SIMPLE BASIC TONES OF RENDERING

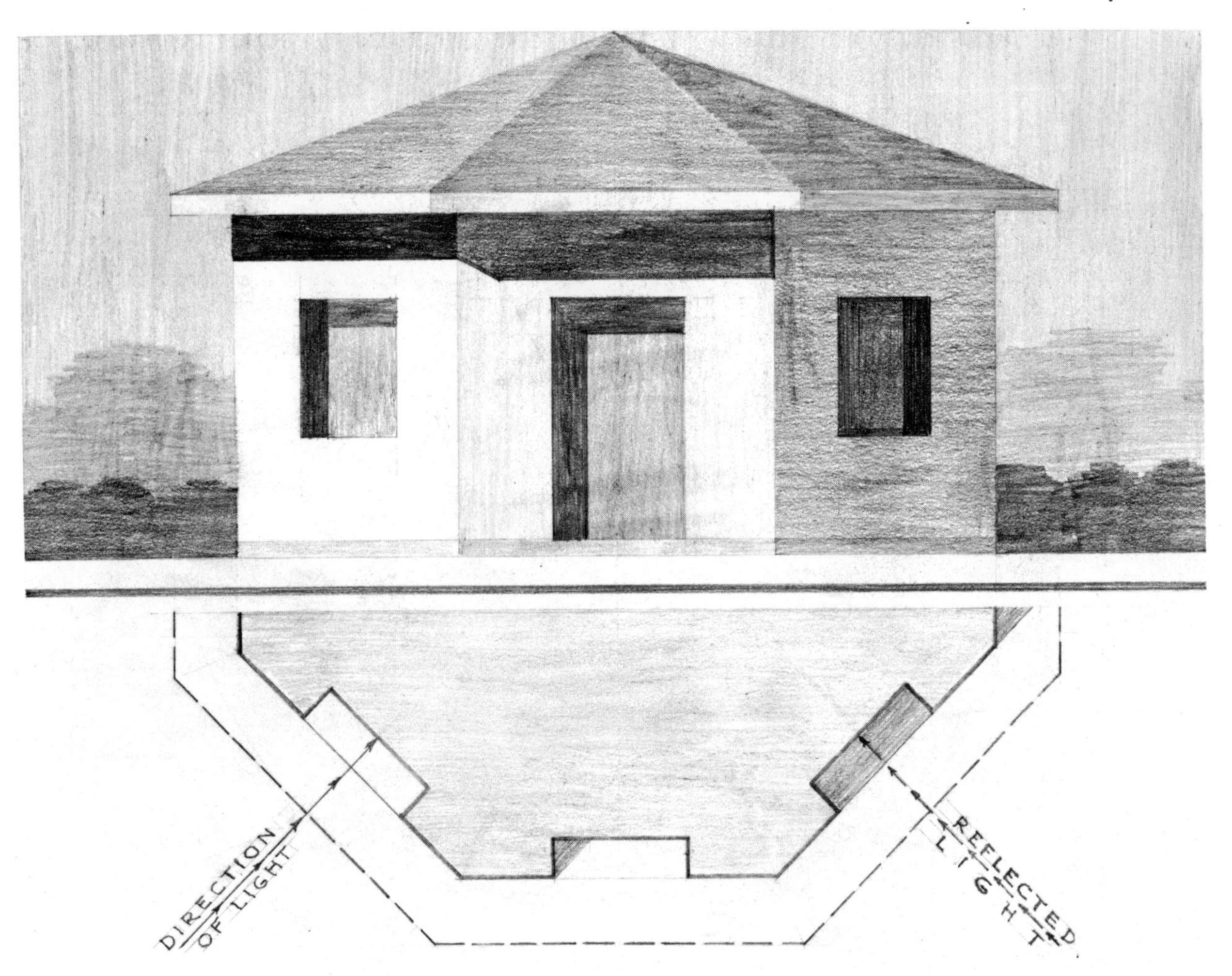

FIG-193 TONE VARIATIONS ON OBLIQUE AREAS

An object with oblique planes requires variations of tones in light areas and in shadow areas to express the forms of the design. The illustration of Fig. 193 is an enlargement of Fig. 168A. The two illustrations should be compared with each other and also with the more complete effects of finished renderings in Chapter 23.

The three roof planes of Fig. 193 are each turned at a different direction to the conventional rays of light for multi-view drawings. Each roof plane is made a different tone appropriate to its relation to the light rays. The left area has light most nearly perpendicular to it, receives the most light, and is lightest. The center area is more oblique to light and is a medium tone. The right area is most nearly tangent to light, receives the least light, and is darkest.

The wall plane areas of Fig. 193 are varied in tone in both light and shadow. The left wall in light is perpendicular to light rays in plan and is the lightest. The center wall area in light is oblique to light rays in plan and is slightly darker than the left area. The right wall area is completely in shade or shadow.

The shadows under the overhang on the three wall surfaces are affected by reflected light. The plan direction of reflected light is shown by the dotted arrows of Fig. 193. This direction of reflected light makes the left overhang shadow darkest, the center a little lighter, and the right one lightest. It separates shadow areas on walls and brings out detail forms in shadow.

Flat tones sometimes produce an interesting simple rendering. Only a small number of flat tones can be used on a rendering and provide clear separation of areas. It is difficult and sometimes impractical or impossible to express curving forms with flat tones.

Graded shading often appears on real objects. The use of gradations of tones in several ways is useful in shading for renderings. Graded shading helps to separate areas, express form and distance, and produce a clearer, more realistic, and natural appearance, Figs. 194 and 195. Some of the ways in which graded shading can be used effectively in rendering are enumerated below. Some of these can be clearly seen in nature or on buildings or other objects. Others can be seen by a careful observer, who is sensitive to variations of light and dark, but are not obvious to a casual observer.

1–A succession of more distant forms of groups of trees, hills, mountains, or other masses can be made dark at the top of each rank and faded to the bottom. Each succeeding more distant group would usually be made less emphatic to express distance. This sort of gradation can be seen more clearly in nature on days when there is low fog or haze. It is used in painting and Japanese prints as well as rendering.

2–The edge of a light area adjoining a shadow appears lighter than the general tone of the light area and the edge of the shadow area appears darker where it touches the light area. This phenomenon often appears quite clearly both in sunlight and artificial light. The casual observer may never notice it. The darker edge of the shadow is often used in rendering.

3–Long vertical shadows may appear lighter at the bottom because of reflected light from horizontal surfaces. Grading long shadows in this way may add life to a rendering.

4–Shadows on exterior walls under large overhangs may shade gradually from dark at the top to light at the bottom because of more light from the sky on the bottom. The lower edge of the shadow would be darker and grade up quickly.

5–Grading on oblique roof or wall surfaces expresses the receding areas.

6–A very slight grading is useful to separate two areas in light or shadow from each other.

FIG-194 SIMPLE SHADING WITH GRADATIONS

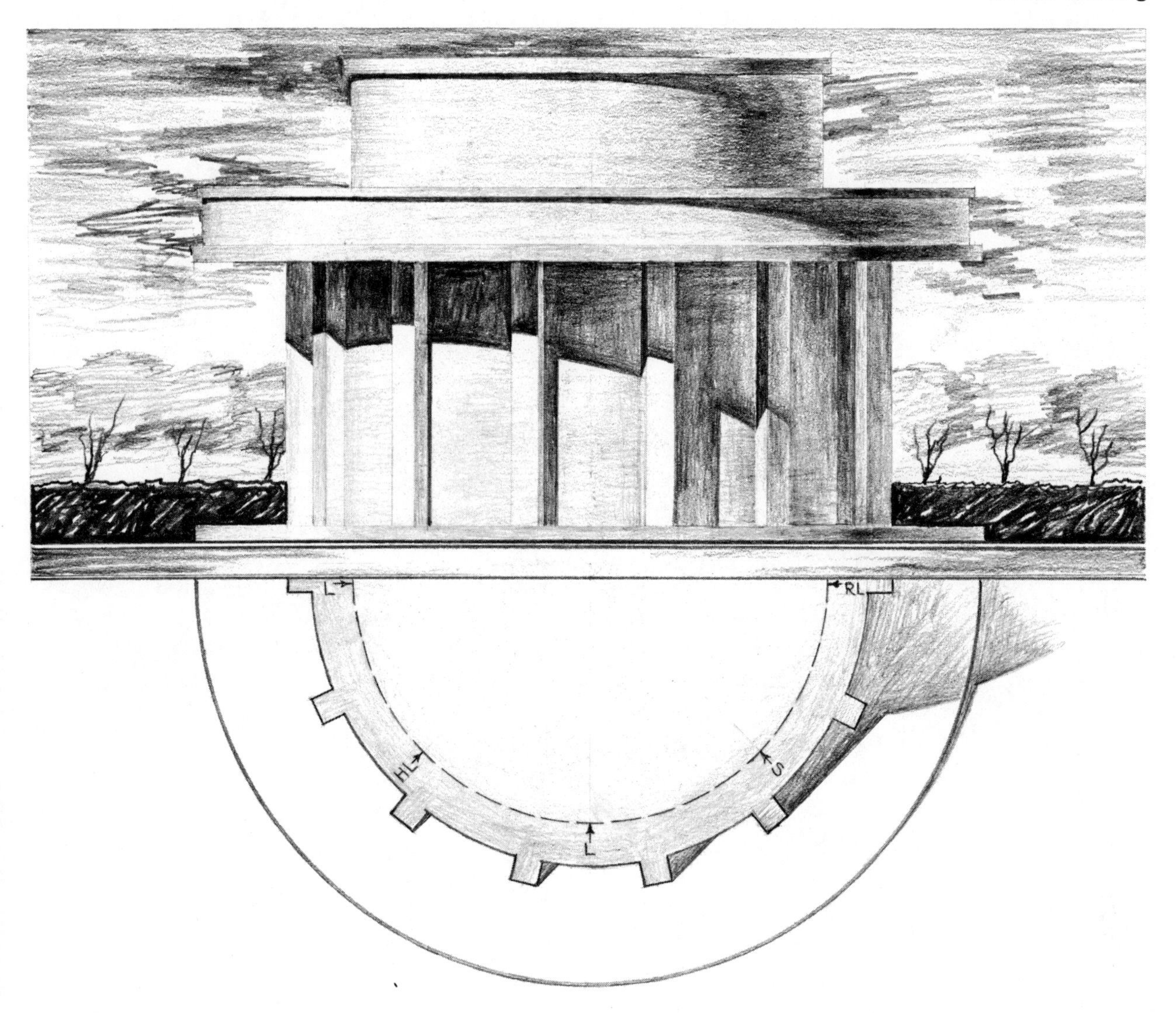

FIG-195 SHADING ON A CIRCULAR BUILDING

Shading of a vertical cylindrical form in light is most clearly illustrated in Fig. 195 (see Fig. 169 and compare) by the highest band above the columns. There should be a gradual change of tone throughout the entire width of the cylinder. The lightest part of the cylinder is on the vertical above point HL where light is perpendicular to the dotted plan of the cylinder. The darkest area centers on the vertical above the point S of tangency of light in plan. The left edge and center of the cylinder are at the same angle (45°) to light and should be the same darkness, points L. The right edge RL should be lighter than the shade line area to express the cylindrical shape. However, all the area from the shade line to the right edge should be a definitely dark shadow.

Shadows under extending bands should follow the same general system as the overhang shadow of Fig. 193. These shadows are darkest on the left and lightest on the right. Small shadows in general should appear darker than large shadows like the one under the large overhang of Fig. 195.

A large shadow area such as that under the largest overhang should be rendered according to the direction of reflected light. It should have variations of tone to bring out the shapes of the different areas and express their forms. Shadows which are too light are insipid and uninteresting.

(A) RIGHT WALLS IN SHADOW

(B) BOTH WALLS IN SUNLIGHT

(C) LEFT WALLS IN SHADOW

(D) BASIC TONES ON EXTERIOR PERSPECTIVES

FIG-196 SHADING EXTERIOR PERSPECTIVES

A perspective drawing shows more areas of an object and its surroundings than an elevation. An elevation of the block shown in the perspective of Fig. 196A, B, C would give one area only. A perspective drawing shows two wall planes and the ground. An aerial view would also show the top of the block, making a total of four basic areas in the perspective to one in the elevation. The shading of a perspective drawing to separate areas becomes much more involved than the shading of one or a number of multi-view drawings.

Separation of areas in rendering is an essential part of clear expression of the forms of the object represented. In Fig. 196A and C there are three general tones, one wall in light, one wall in shadow, and the shadow on the ground plane. Shading on the ground area is often varied to help adjoining areas, express distance, and to focus interest in a more complete rendering. In Fig. 196B both walls are in light. Since light strikes the left wall more directly, it has been made slightly lighter than the right wall to bring out the corner more clearly. It should be observed from real objects and from renderings that separation of areas can be very emphatic or very slight. An observation of exteriors and interiors of buildings and of any objects with plane surfaces will be helpful to the student. It should convince him that planes which are oblique or perpendicular to each other are almost always different in darkness where they meet. Interested and acute observation of light, shadows, planes, and textures of buildings and renderings are of great help in learning to do good rendering.

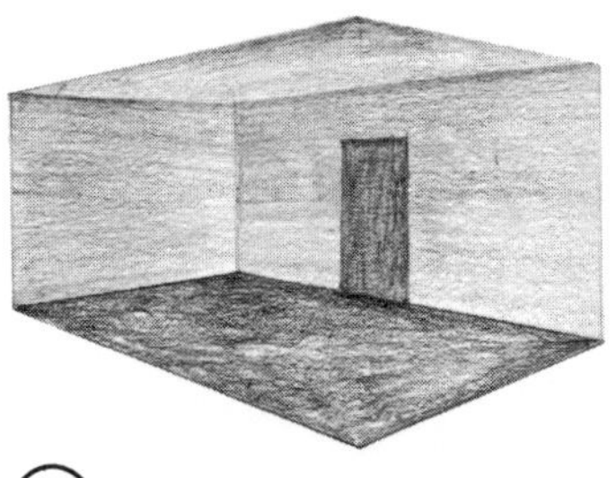

(I) GENERAL UNIFORM LIGHT

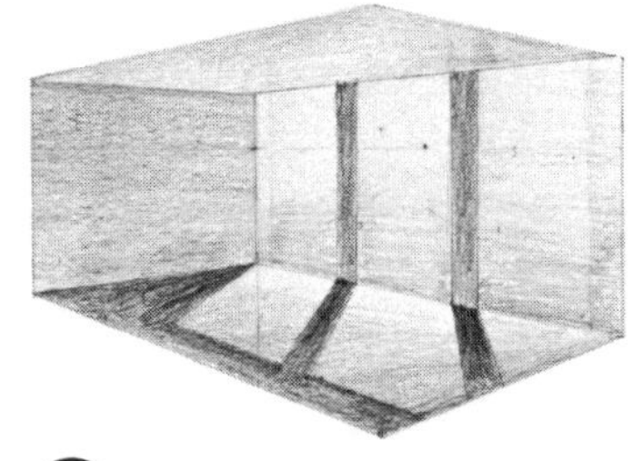

(II) SUNLIGHT AND SHADOW

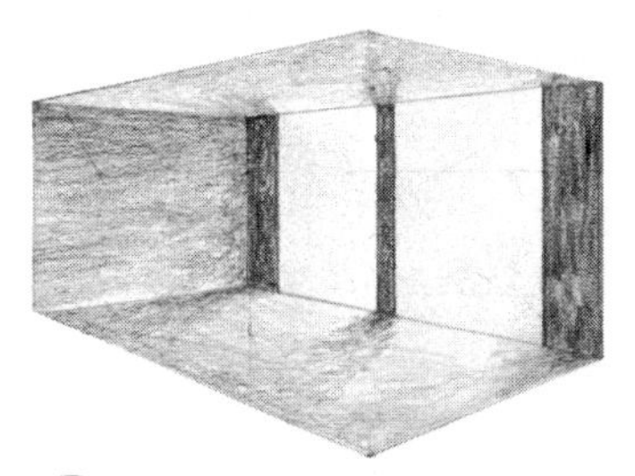

(III) LIGHTING FROM THE SKY

(IV) INTERIOR WITH SUNLIGHT

FIG-197 TONES ON INTERIOR PERSPECTIVES

Interiors may have greater variations of lighting than exteriors. Three general types of interior lighting and shading are suggested in Fig. 197 I, II, and III. (I) There may be a general overall lighting of the interior from several sources with no source emphasized. (II) There may be sunlight through large openings lighting the interior with definite sunlight and shadow areas. (III) The sky may furnish the light for the room with no clearly defined separation of light and dark areas. Figs. 196D and 197 IV show that all wall planes in the same direction should appear to have the same general dark and light tones for shadow and light areas. This system will help to produce a feeling of unity and simplicity in the rendering.

There are variations of lighting on both exteriors and interiors which influence the resulting tones and gradations. Reflections of light and color may add life and variety to a design.

When the design of an interior provides obvious sources of light, the shading should explain these sources. When the sources of the lighting are concealed, the design will be explained by rendering the lighting effect from these sources.

Only a few basic considerations have been discussed in this brief introduction to rendering. It is hoped that the discussion of shading in rendering and the examples of student and professional rendering will be useful to the student. Entire books have been written on rendering. Some are on one type of rendering only. The student who wishes to become an expert delineator should read and study some of the more complete treatises on this subject.

CHAPTER 23
Architectural Rendering

Most of the illustrations of this chapter are reproduced from the renderings for projects designed in architects' and other designers' offices. They are typical of the most artistic and precise finished pictorial work which is done by expert delineators. They are excellent examples of the professional use of perspective drawing and shadows. Renderings of this type are often made to explain to a client the proposed design for his project. They are also frequently used for publicity and promotion purposes. These and less elaborate study renderings are helpful to the architect in designing buildings. The original renderings probably averaged about 22 × 28 inches in size. They were much larger than their reproductions in this book.

The pen-and-ink renderings of Figs. 198 and 199 show considerable variation in technique. Fig. 198 was made almost entirely with rather fine freehand pens. The materials of the building and the planting have been given texture by using many fine lines. Ink spray has been used on the paving. Fig. 199 I has a great many ruled ink lines, a considerable number of freehand ink lines, and dots used in masonry and background. Fig. 199 II has excellent expression with long-line freehand pen technique. All three of these ink renderings have excellent shadow tones.

RENDERING BY VOLKER KLOTZ

FIG-198 EXAMPLE OF PEN AND INK RENDERING

(I) RENDERING BY PAUL RUDOLPH
TWITCHELL AND RUDOLPH – ARCHITECTS

(II) DESIGN AND RENDERING BY G. C. RUDOLPH

FIG-199 EXAMPLES OF PEN AND INK RENDERING

(A) RENDERING BY RALPH A. ANDERSON, JR
WILSON, MORRIS & CRAIN-ARCHTS.

Pencil rendering can be used to produce flat tones, graded tones, modeling of curved surfaces, and representation of textures and materials. It is a very flexible medium. Figs. 200A and 201 I are simple pencil renderings with good contrast of tone and expression of form. Figs. 200B and 201 II have interesting representations of trees, grass, walks, roofs, buildings, and shadows. Their representations of people add interest and suggest the scale of the buildings. The reflections on the pavement in Fig. 200B add interest to the foreground area. In Fig. 201 II the light and dark contrasts and dark areas of the foreground help to focus interest on walks and entrances.

Some characteristics of renderings which are not commonly found in drawings are (1) shadows, (2) tones to separate areas and masses, (3) expression of distance away of different parts of the object, (4) the focus of interest by means of shading and variation of light and dark or color contrasts, (5) surroundings provided by the site, landscape treatment, automobiles, people, etc.

(B) RENDERING BY J. HENDERSON BARR
EERO SAARINEN AND ASSOCIATES-ARCHITECTS

FIG-200 EXAMPLES OF PENCIL RENDERING

Techniques of rendering are rather numerous and varied. A single medium such as pencil, colored pencils, freehand pen and ink, ruling pen and ink, air brush, pastels, water color, or tempera may be used for an entire rendering. Often more than one medium, a mixed technique, may be used on a single rendering, since some media are particularly good for one type of work but not as easily used for another purpose. As an illustration, pastels are good for larger areas but are not as good as pencil, water color, or tempera for small bright or dark areas. Water color is particularly good for graded washes, modeling of curved forms, and gradual change of color.

When learning to render, better results may be obtained by using a single medium on a rendering until some considerable facility is gained in using several individual media. After learning how to handle each of several different media, the use of more than one medium for a rendering may be employed more confidently and with better results.

(I) RENDERING BY GERALD M. MCNERTNEY
G. MEREDITH MUSICK - ARCHITECT

(II) RENDERING BY GEORGE COOPER RUDOLPH
SKIDMORE OWINGS AND MERRILL - ARCHITECTS

FIG - 201 EXAMPLES OF PENCIL RENDERING

Water color requires more technical skill and training than most of the media used for architectural renderings. When used in light and medium dark washes it does not obliterate lines and detail washes over which it is run. When very dark it is practically opaque and can be applied in small areas to cover lighter washes satisfactorily. It is an extremely flexible and expressive medium. It can be used for tints, flat tones, graded washes, modeling of curved forms, and fade-outs.

Variations can be expected in the technique employed by different delineators and by any delineator on different projects. The illustrations of Figs. 202 and 203 show a great deal of variation in style of rendering. This may be due to the subject of the rendering or to the wishes of the delineator. Fig. 203 II is a bold and contrasty rendering with graded washes and a wet-paper technique sky characteristic of water color. Fig. 203 I has much of the large area rendering done with wide brush strokes. Fig. 202 is a polished presentation using pencil and water color.

RENDERING BY ADAM JIMINEZ
EGGERS AND HIGGENS—ARCHITECTS

FIG-202 WATER COLOR AND PENCIL RENDERING

(I) INTERIOR DESIGN BY JAY SETLOW
SUGAR LOAF LODGE, SUGAR LOAF, FLORIDA

(II) RENDERING BY MAC JOHNSON
WELTON BECKET AND ASSOCIATES—ARCHITECTS

FIG-203 EXAMPLES OF WATER COLOR RENDERING

Tempera is one of the rendering media which is most widely used by professional delineators. It produces a solid effect. It does not normally have any of the paper-like quality sometimes obtained with other rendering media. One tempera color can often be painted over another to effectively hide the color beneath. It does not require the skillful handling which is necessary to avoid streaks with water color and other transparent wash media. Water color is much the same wet or dry. Tempera is frequently different in darkness and color when it dries. Samples must be allowed to dry to determine their appearance on the rendering.

Opaque ruling-pen washes can be made on water color renderings for thin window divisions, thin shadows, and other small straight spaces which do not exceed the width limits of the ruling-pen lines. Tempera will usually take ruling pen washes also but may require greater care.

Examples of tempera renderings are shown in Figs. 204, 205, 206, and 207. The aerial view of Fig. 204 subdues the surroundings and focuses on the building. The distant scenery is very effectively faded back in both Figs. 204 and 205. Fig. 206 is a very good typical tempera rendering of clouds, building, landscape, and foreground. Fig. 207 I provides a light and airy effect. Fig. 207 II gives a clear representation of ground pattern and building.

RENDERING BY ART ASSOCIATES
FRANKFORT, SHORT, EMERY & MCKINLEY-ARCHITECTS

FIG-204 EXAMPLE OF TEMPERA RENDERING

RENDERING BY ART ASSOCIATES
DEMONSTRATION RENDERING PROJECT

FIG-205 EXAMPLE OF TEMPERA RENDERING

RENDERING BY VINCENT FURNO
KAHN AND JACOBS—ARCHITECTS

FIG-206 EXAMPLE OF TEMPERA RENDERING

(I) RENDERING BY RUDOLPH, RUSSELL & FLEURY
SKIDMORE, OWINGS & MERRILL—ARCHITECTS, ENGINEERS

(II) RENDERING BY RUDOLPH, RUSSELL & FLEURY
HOUSE DISPLAY, NEW YORK WORLD'S FAIR

FIG-207 EXAMPLES OF TEMPERA RENDERING

(A) RENDERING BY GILBERT H. HALL
HOLABIRD & ROOT & BURGEE—ARCHITECTS

(B) RENDERING BY FOSTER H. HYATT
CLEMMONS & GINGLES—ARCHITECTS & ENGINEERS

FIG-208 EXAMPLES OF RENDERING

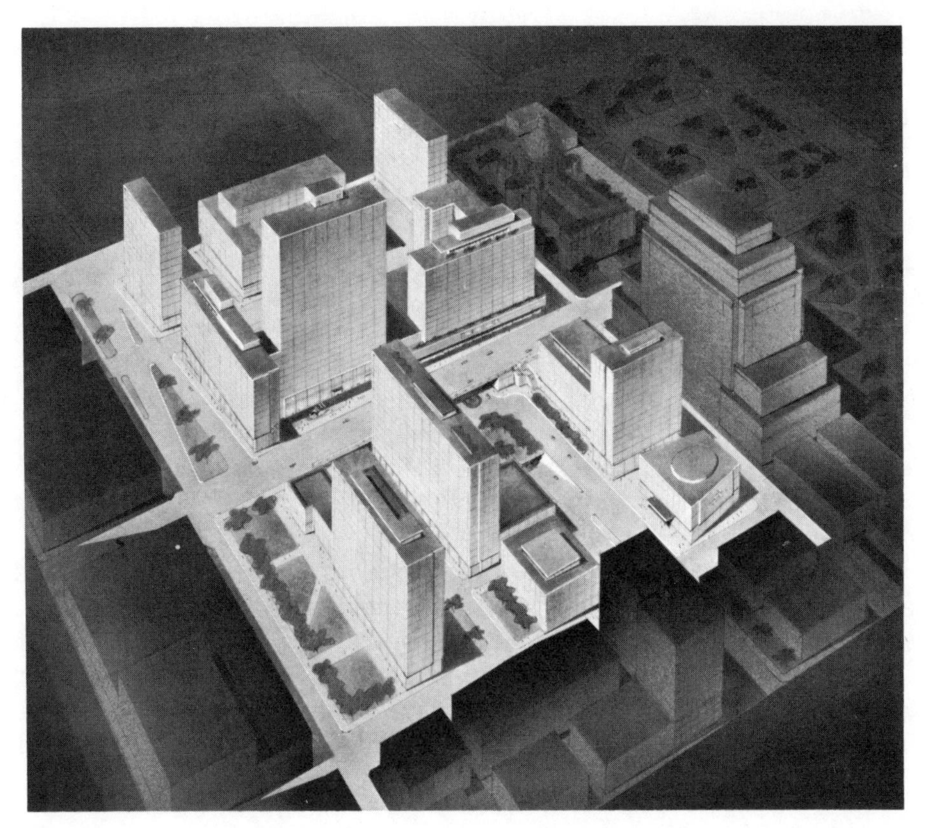

(I) OFFICE OF THE CHIEF ARCHITECT
CANADIAN NATIONAL RAILWAYS

(II) RENDERING BY E. CHARLES BASSETT
EERO SAARINEN AND ASSOCIATES–ARCHITECTS

FIG-209 EXAMPLES OF RENDERING

CHAPTER 24
Architectural Models

Architectural models are usually miniature three-dimensional representations of the design. They can be made to include the shapes of the surrounding site and the masses or detailed representation of surrounding buildings. Streets, walks, trees, shrubs, grass, lakes, and other features of the surroundings can also be represented. The finished models vary a great deal in their completeness of representation of the design. Models are often made to study one or more features of a design such as masses, circulation, relation of elements, or interior volumes. A model may be made to give a clear, colorful, and attractive representation of the complete project for presentation, display, promotion, or other purposes.

The models shown in Figs. 210 and 211 vary in several respects. The residence models in Fig. 210 are very simply made of gray cardboard (chipboard) and dowel rods. They are primarily studies of masses and fenestration. Fig. 211 I is a mass study of surroundings and buildings. The contours of the site are made with layers of foamed styrene. The masses of the buildings are made of several layers of styrene. The trees are the dried flowers of a yarrow weed. Fig. 211 II is a modeling clay mass study of a group of buildings and surrounding areas and streets.

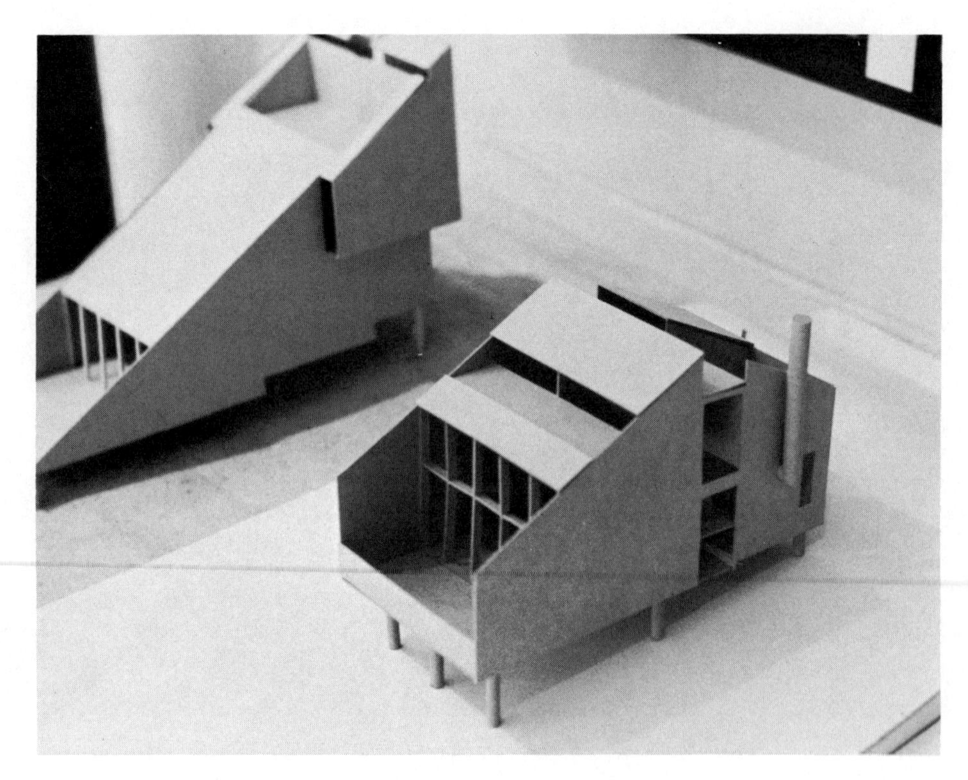

BY GARY L. GREENWELL, LEFT – JOHN C. SENHAUSER, RIGHT

FIG-210 ARCHITECTURAL STUDENT STUDY MODELS

(I) STUDENT MODEL BY JANET M. JOHNSON

(II) STUDENT MODEL BY JOHN M. KURAK, JR.

FIG-211 EXAMPLES OF BLOCK STUDY MODELS

Architectural models have several advantages over drawings. One of their principal advantages is that the design can be seen from different distances, different positions around the project, and from different heights. It can be viewed from every possible position. A second important advantage of models is that with the use of contour layers it is much easier to work out a design on a sloping site. Fig. 213 I shows four small photographs of a model which were taken from different directions. Fig. 213 II is an enlargement of one of the photographs shown in I. This is a well-finished model which was made for presentation and display use. Fig. 212 is a photograph of a cardboard model. It is a study of building masses, exterior circulation, parking, and the surrounding site.

Models illustrated in Figs. 214 and 215 were made to present solutions for different phases of design. In Fig. 214A the white structure is an old building which is to be preserved. The arrangement and masses of the surrounding buildings and the treatment of pavement, planting, and interesting related minor features are the design problem in this model. Fig. 214B shows the motor hotel, restaurant, surrounding planting, and some of the pedestrian and automobile circulation of this project. Fig. 215 I is a photograph of a presentation model of a building and its surroundings. Fig. 215 II is a structural detail of the main building shown in Fig. 215 I.

One disadvantage of architectural models is the amount of space required for constructing and keeping them. It is practical to store many drawings and renderings. A great deal more space is required to store even a few fragile models. It is usually possible for a school of architecture or an architect's office to keep some of their best and most useful models. It is rather general practice to take photographs of models and then usually dispose of the models.

A drawing or rendering is very good for representing the appearance of an architectural project from one point of view. A model is much better for showing the design from all angles. Renderings are excellent for representation of colors, materials, textures, details, and surroundings.

STUDENT MODEL BY JAMES BRUCE THOMAS

FIG-212 MODEL FOR STUDY AND PRESENTATION

(I) PHOTOGRAPHS FROM DIFFERENT DIRECTIONS

(II) STUDENT MODEL BY ERIC G. TWICKLER

FIG-213 EXAMPLE OF PRESENTATION MODEL

(A) STUDENT MODEL BY J. P. WODOSLAWSKY, JR.

(B) STUDENT MODEL BY SYLVANUS DOUGHTY

FIG-214 EXAMPLES OF ARCHITECTURAL MODELS

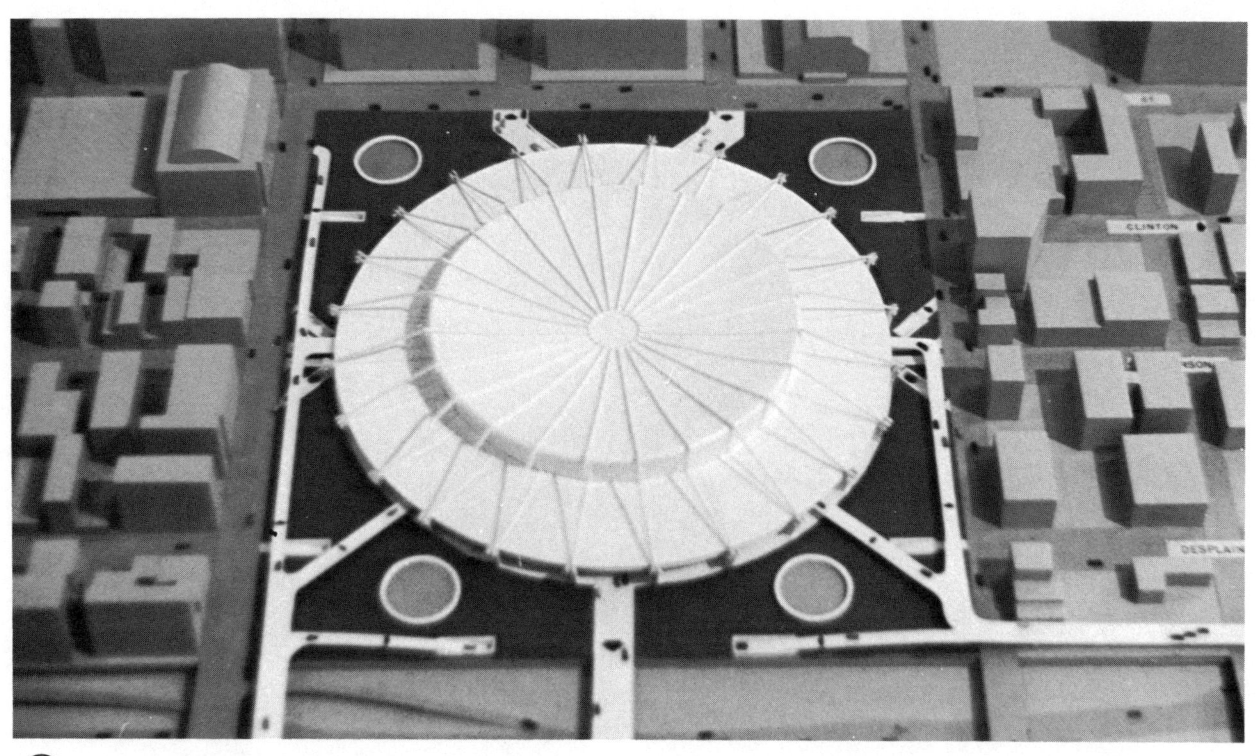

(I) STUDENT SITE MODEL BY THOMAS V. SCESNIAK

(II) STUDENT DETAIL MODEL BY THOMAS V. SCESNIAK

FIG-215 EXAMPLES OF ARCHITECTURAL MODELS

Ⓐ MODEL BY OSMENT ARCHITECTURAL MODELS
FRITZEL, KROEGER, GRIFFIN & BERG – ARCHITECTS

Ⓑ MODEL BY WILLIAM TAZELAAR AND DAVID WELLS
HARRY WEESE & ASSOCIATES-ARCHITECTS & ENGINEERS

FIG-216 PROFESSIONAL ARCHITECTURAL MODELS

A great many architectural models are constructed by architectural students as an important part of their study of design. Some architectural offices make part or all of the models which are built for their design projects. Other architectural offices have a part, at least of the more elaborate presentation models, made by professional model builders.

Figure 216B is a photograph of an architectural study model which was constructed in the architect's office by office personnel. It was made from gray chipboard and photographed by the office staff. The texture was produced by using a grain screen.

Figures 216A and 217 are photographs of presentation models made by a professional architectural model studio. Fig. 217 is rather complete in details and seems photographically real. Fig. 216A gives a clear representation of locations, shapes, and arrangement of buildings on the site without any attempt at realism in details of buildings and surroundings.

MODEL BY OSMENT ARCHITECTURAL MODELS
JAVA, DANIELS, BUSBY-ARCHITECTS

FIG-217 PROFESSIONAL PRESENTATION MODEL

PRESENTATION MODEL BY DAVID WELLS
HARRY WEESE & ASSOCIATES–ARCHITECTS & ENGINEERS

FIG-218 EXAMPLE OF PRESENTATION MODEL

PROFESSIONALLY MADE PRESENTATION MODEL
HARRY WEESE & ASSOCIATES-ARCHITECTS & ENGINEERS

FIG-219 EXAMPLE OF PRESENTATION MODEL

Figure 218 shows two photographic views of a presentation model. The model was constructed in the architects' office by a member of their staff. The model was made of colored cardboard with ruled lines for wall texture and details. Metallic tape was used for the windows and polyurethane sponge for the trees. Light reflections from the metallic tape can be seen on the pavement in the top photograph.

The model shown in the photograph of Fig. 219 was made and photographed by a professional architectural model studio. A cloud backdrop was used for the photograph.

Ingenuity and inventiveness are very essential qualities in a person who builds fine architectural models. The person who likes to work out the best methods of producing, finishing, and putting together the parts of a model will usually excel at model building. The model builder needs the abilities of an inventor, a designer, and an artist to produce excellent finished models. Some models are made of very simple block shapes and plain areas which are easy to make. A good contrast of tone and color will make a model much more attractive and easily read.

MODEL BY OSMENT ARCHITECTURAL MODELS
KIVETT AND MYERS—ARCHITECTS, PLANNERS

FIG-220 MODEL FOR SITE AND TRAFFIC FLOW ANALYSIS

MODEL CONSTRUCTED IN ARCHITECTS' OFFICE
KIVETT AND MYERS—ARCHITECTS, PLANNERS

FIG-221 MODEL OF TYPICAL UNIT OF BUILDINGS

The site model of Fig. 220 and the more detailed model of Fig. 221 were made for the same design. The master plan of Fig. 220 was made for the land and traffic-flow analysis and bond promotion. The contour layers express the variations of levels in the site and help to explain the relation of the circulation to the site. This model was made at a scale of 1″ = 300′.

The more detailed model of Fig. 221 shows the design of one of the typical terminal buildings. It was made at a scale of 1″ = 40′. Since it is $7\frac{1}{2}$ times the scale of the site model, it shows more of the details of the group of buildings and its immediate surroundings. This larger-scale model was constructed of chip board in the architects' office.

The variations which occur in architectural model building are partially expressed by the illustrations of this chapter. These variations are limited only by the imagination of the designer and the inventiveness of the model builder. The materials available for use are almost always adequate to represent clearly the creations of the designers.

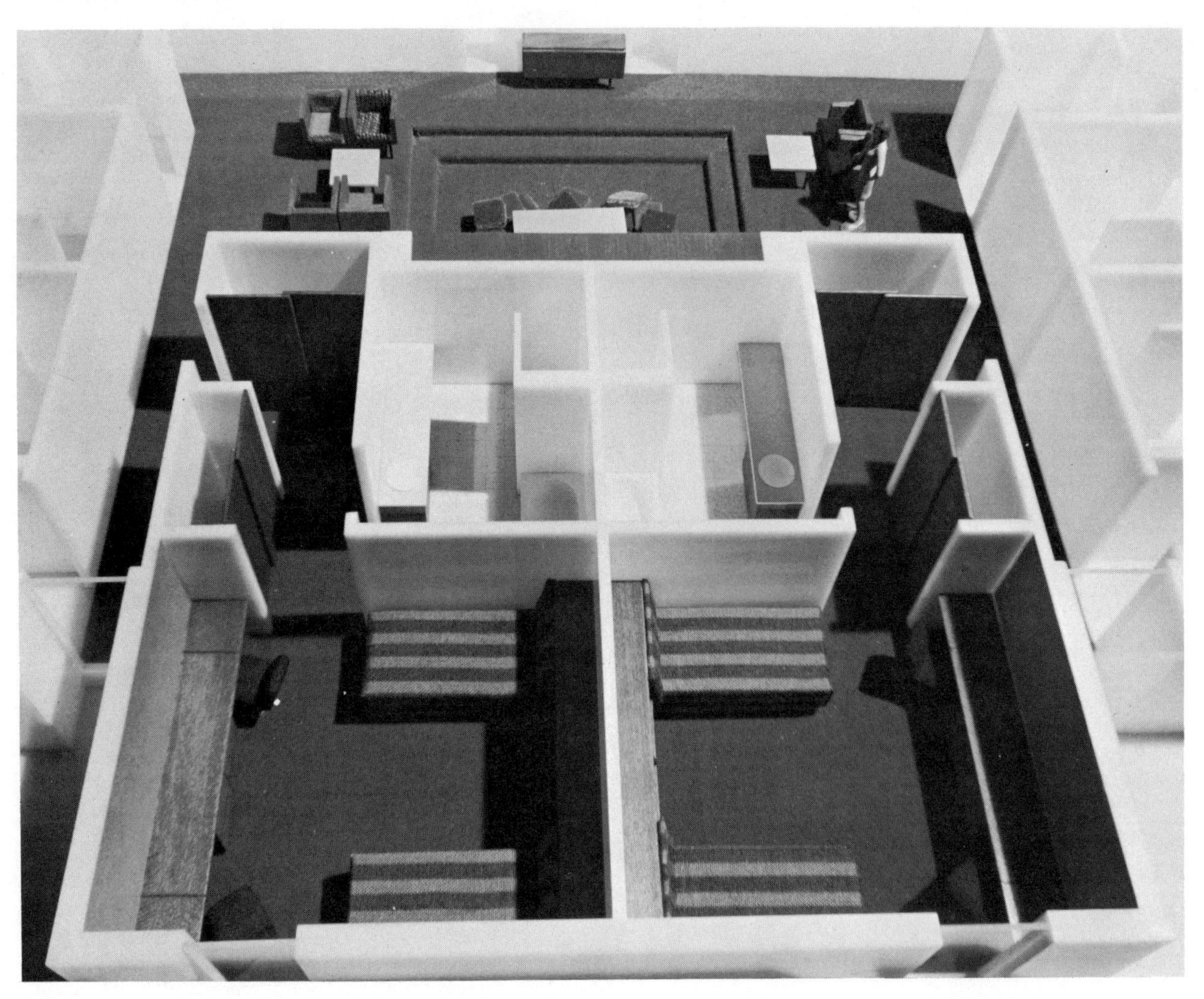

MODEL BY OSMENT ARCHITECTURAL MODELS
FOLGER AND PEARSON—ARCHITECTS

FIG-222 MODEL SHOWING AN INTERIOR ARRANGEMENT

Wall materials vary a great deal and so do their treatments to represent walls. Block models which are made of solid wood or clay for building shapes are perhaps the simplest of all. The block shapes may be painted with tempera or other paints. Sheets of balsa wood, gray chip board, illustration board, colored or white mat board, and clear or colored acrylic plastic are some of the common wall materials for architectural models. The various cardboard materials can be painted and have lines ruled on them. Tempera or water colors can be used to make realistic representations of stone or other materials on cardboards and on balsa wood. Sometimes it is better to do all the art work before cutting out the pieces. Adhesives should be quick drying and permanent. Interior bracing is often required to hold sheet material in place.

The interior model of Fig. 222 shows a two-room unit of a dormitory in an academy for training airline stewardesses. The walls are apparently made of a foamed plastic such as styrene. Care must be used in the choice of an adhesive for this material. Some cements will dissolve the plastic. The model has an attractive realistic representation of furnishings.

M O D E L   C O N S T R U C T I O N
B Y   S Y L V A N U S   D O U G H T Y

Index